Beginning OS X
Apps Development

Michael Privat
Robert Warner

Apress®

Beginning OS X Lion Apps Development

ISBN-13 (pbk): 978-1-4302-3720-4

ISBN-13 (electronic): 978-1-4302-3721-1

President and Publisher: Paul Manning
Lead Editors: Steve Anglin and Michelle Lowman
Development Editors: Douglas Pundick and James Markham
Technical Reviewer: James Bucanek
Editorial Board: Steve Anglin, Mark Beckner, Ewan Buckingham, Gary Cornell, Morgan Ertel, Jonathan Gennick, Jonathan Hassell, Robert Hutchinson, Michelle Lowman, James Markham, Matthew Moodie, Jeff Olson, Jeffrey Pepper, Douglas Pundick, Ben Renow-Clarke, Dominic Shakeshaft, Gwenan Spearing, Matt Wade, Tom Welsh
Coordinating Editor: Jennifer L. Blackwell
Copy Editor: Kim Wimpsett
Compositor: MacPS, LLC
Indexer: SPi Global
Artist: SPi Global
Cover Designer: Anna Ishchenko

Distributed to the book trade worldwide by Springer Science+Business Media, LLC., 233 Spring Street, 6th Floor, New York, NY 10013. Phone 1-800-SPRINGER, fax (201) 348-4505, e-mail orders-ny@springer-sbm.com, or visit www.springeronline.com.

For information on translations, please e-mail rights@apress.com, or visit www.apress.com.

Apress and friends of ED books may be purchased in bulk for academic, corporate, or promotional use. eBook versions and licenses are also available for most titles. For more information, reference our Special Bulk Sales–eBook Licensing web page at www.apress.com/bulk-sales.

Any source code or other supplementary materials referenced by the author in this text is available to readers at www.apress.com. For detailed information about how to locate your book's source code, go to http://www.apress.com/source-code/.

To my loving wife, Kelly, and our children, Matthieu and Chloé.

—Michael Privat

To my beautiful wife, Sherry, and our wonderful children,
Tyson, Jacob, Mallory, Camie, and Leila.

—Rob Warner

Contents at a Glance

Contents

About the Authors

 **Michael Privat is** the president and CEO of Majorspot, Inc., developer of several iPhone and iPad apps:

- Ghostwriter Notes
- My Spending
- iBudget
- Chess Puzzle Challenge

He is also an expert developer and technical lead for Availity, LLC, based in Jacksonville, Florida. He earned his master's degree in computer science from the University of Nice in Nice, France. He moved to the United States to develop software in artificial intelligence at the Massachusetts Institute of Technology. Coauthor of *Pro Core Data for iOS* (Apress, 2011), he now lives in Jacksonville, Florida, with his wife, Kelly, and their two children.

Rob Warner is a senior technical staff member for Availity, LLC, based in Jacksonville, Florida, where he works with various teams and technologies to deliver solutions in the health-care sector. He coauthored *Pro Core Data for iOS* (Apress, 2011) and *The Definitive Guide to SWT and JFace* (Apress, 2004), and he blogs at www.grailbox.com. He earned his bachelor's degree in English from Brigham Young University in Provo, Utah. He lives in Jacksonville, Florida, with his wife, Sherry, and their five children.

About the Technical Reviewer

 **James Bucanek** has spent the past 30 years programming and developing microcomputer systems. He has experience with a broad range of technologies, from embedded consumer products to industrial robotics. James is currently focused on Macintosh and iPhone software development. When not programming, James indulges in his love of the arts. He earned an associate's degree from the Royal Academy of Dance in classical ballet and occasionally teaches at Adams Ballet Academy.

Acknowledgments

When I was first presented with the opportunity to coauthor this book with Rob Warner, I was both excited and nervous. I was excited because our previous book on Core Data has been a success and Rob is a great partner to work with. But I was nervous because of the time investment we would both have to pour into this. In the end, we pulled and pushed each other to the finish line to produce this new book, and, once again, it was all worth it.

My wife, Kelly, and my children, Matthieu and Chloé, have thankfully been very supportive throughout the project and helped me with words of motivation and a constant flow of coffee. Matthieu and Chloé think it's cool that their dad wrote a book, and I'm all about impressing my kids while I still can.

As always, the folks at Availity with whom I spend my daylight time have all been encouraging to Rob and me in this effort. Availity is a company that promotes continuous professional self-improvement, and this is yet another example. Among plenty of other folks, Trent Gavazzi, Ben Van Maanen, and Steve Vaughn have all stopped by with words of encouragements that went a long way when I felt overwhelmed between work and writing.

Lastly, it's only fair to acknowledge the Apress team for their constant support and for providing resources to help with the completion of the project. The technical reviewer they hired to work with us, James Bucanek, was a wealth and knowledge. James, I apologize for that time I made you spit your coffee all over your monitor with my writing....

Michael Privat

Although writing can be easy, writing well never is, at least for me. I agonize over word choices, sentence constructs, and flow. Never does writing become more difficult, however, than in this section, as we try to thank those who helped create this book, whether directly or indirectly. The danger of omitting someone who merits thanks lurks behind every paragraph, and the peril of sounding trite or rote looms in every sentence. If you've been overlooked or unfairly treated, I blame the editors!

Actually, working with the people at Apress has been another great adventure. From the beginning ideas for this book to its conclusion, we've been supported and challenged to greatness. Steve Anglin always has great ideas and doesn't settle for almost. Jennifer Blackwell was both patient and pleasant as we worked through issues. Going through my e-mail reminds me of more key folks who provided direction or assisted: Michelle Lowman, Debra Kelly, Douglas Pundick, James Markham, and Kim Wimpsett. Our technical reviewer, James Bucanek, was both fastidious and amazing, keeping us on our toes, steering us right, and helping us solve some technical challenges. Thanks, James!

Thank you, Sherry, for letting me chase my dreams.

Juggling two book projects while holding down a full-time job and raising a family can cut into one's sleep schedule. Tyson has now dubbed me "Sleepyhead Codesauce," and my other children roll their eyes at my "nerd books" and "nerd meetings." Thanks, Tyson, Jacob, Mallory, Camie, and Leila for letting me have my fun and for putting up with my crankiness.

Conning Michael Privat into writing yet another book with me was somewhat devious—I've learned he can't back down from a challenge. Thanks, Michael, for climbing on board one more time. This book was another great ride, and I'd have been stuck without you. Betcha can't write one on Dart.

Working my day job at Availity provides me opportunities to learn and grow from some amazing people. Once again, I thank all of them for their support and interest, particularly Trent Gavazzi, Jon McBride, and the rest of the senior team. As more and more Availity people get Macs, I expect to see Graphique on a lot of desktops soon.

Finally, I thank my parents and my siblings for the love of learning and writing that we share. Thanks for your support and your interest.

Rob Warner

Introduction

Mac OS X offers an amazing development environment for scores of technologies. It seems that developers from numerous camps are migrating to Mac en masse. Scan the room at any Ruby or Rails conference, for example, and you'll see programmers coding on Macs almost exclusively. As developers move to Mac, almost inevitably they eventually discover the itch to write native tools on the Mac platform. We've written this book to help those of you who hear the siren call of Xcode and just need a little guidance through the rocky waters of Objective-C and Cocoa to be able to develop your own apps.

The Premise

We based this book on a simple premise: the best way to learn to program in a new language or environment is to build something real, something finished, something that's actually useful. Too many books on programming leave out things like error handling or help files or other programming topics that might be considered on the periphery of teaching programming principles or language topics so they can focus on the core of what they're trying to teach. While this focus can be useful, it leaves a gap between building an almost-product and building a finished product, leaving readers to seek information elsewhere for crossing that chasm. Our pledge is to bridge that gap in this book. By taking you from project creation through adding features to finishing the project to publishing it in the Mac App Store, we hope to give you the information you need to finish projects, not just start them.

It's been an interesting premise. It's brought challenges and discussions about what to include, what to leave out, and how best to illustrate certain aspects of Mac OS X development. As we've developed this application, assumptions we made early about topics that would be essential proved trivial, and topics we deemed unimportant reared up as integral to the product. We've had to adjust as we went, including as many topics as made sense in the context of the app, a graphing calculator called Graphique.

Developing a complete application as part of a beginning book presented its own challenges as well. Getting a real application to "done" often involves some deeper topics or code that doesn't seem strictly a beginner's domain. We've tried to balance completeness, correctness, and simplicity in the code base for the application we develop and hope we've succeeded.

We believe the final app, available in the Mac App Store, is useful. We also believe that its source code and the text of this book can help you learn to develop complete apps fit for publishing.

The Audience

You have a Mac, and you want to develop apps for it. That's our audience. We target more specifically folks who want to publish those apps in the Mac App Store and devote a detailed chapter to doing so. You can ignore that chapter if you don't want to publish through the Mac App Store.

This is a beginner's book, but we don't teach the basics of programming here, so if you don't know what a `for` loop is or shy from a command prompt, you might struggle. We do teach the basics of programming in Objective-C and Cocoa for Mac OS X, so if you understand programming basics, even if you know nothing about programming for the Mac, you'll do fine in this book. Advanced programmers moving from other languages or platforms will find this book useful, as will iOS developers looking to leverage their Cocoa skills to the Mac OS X platform.

How This Book Is Organized

This book begins with preparing your computer to build OS X Lion apps by walking you through the installation of Xcode, the development tool for building OS X apps. You then create the project for Graphique, the graphing calculator you build throughout this book. By the time you finish the first chapter, you'll be able to build and run the fledgling Graphique.

Each subsequent chapter adds more functionality to Graphique, building on the project from the previous chapter. The downloadable source code captures the state of the project at the end of each chapter, so if you insist on skipping a chapter, you can. To get the most from the book, though, work through it from the first page to the last, typing in the code, building the project, and running it as you go. After your initial read, keep this book handy for reference, so you can jump to specific topics as you build your own applications.

The final chapter walks you through the sometimes-confusing process of submitting your app to the Mac App Store. Though you won't submit your copy of Graphique, since we already submitted the app and it's already available, you'll follow the same steps when you submit your own applications.

Source Code and Errata

The complete source code for Graphique, divided into chapters, can be downloaded from the Apress web site at `www.apress.com`. Download it, learn from it, and use it in your own applications. As we uncover bugs or typos in the book or code, we'll update the errata section on the Apress web site.

How to Contact Us

We'd love to hear from you, whether it's questions, concerns, better ways of doing things, or triumphant announcements of your apps landing on the Mac App Store. You can find us here:

Michael Privat:

E-mail: `mprivat@mac.com`

Twitter: `@michaelprivat`

Blog: `http://michaelprivat.com`

Rob Warner:

E-mail: `rwarner@grailbox.com`

Twitter: `@hoop33`

Blog: `http://grailbox.com`

Chapter 1

Starting to Build a Graphing Calculator

When Apple announced Mac OS X 10.7, also known as Lion, it did so under the banner "Back to the Mac." Mac OS X Lion incorporates lessons Apple has learned from the wildly successful iOS platform, available on iPhones, iPads, and iPod touch devices, and the excitement it has garnered presents lucrative opportunities for you, as a software developer, to create and distribute applications for this platform. Mac users consistently demonstrate passion for their computing platform, a willingness to pay for software, and a demand for quality and innovation. If your motivations don't issue from financial fountains, developing Mac software provides you with a way to return the passion for computing, quality, and innovation to the Mac user community. This book gives you all the information you need to develop and distribute apps that tap into that passion.

In this book, we develop a graphing calculator called Graphique. The project develops as we go through the book, and each chapter adds more functionality to the application. At the conclusion of the book, the Graphique app is complete, and we show you how to submit to the Mac App Store. The feature set for Graphique has been selected not just to make sure Graphique graphs calculations in a superior way but also to demonstrate Mac application principles that you can learn from and apply to your own applications. This book works best when you read it in front of your Mac, typing in the code, running the application along the way, and making sure you understand each principle as you go. This book also works well as a reference, allowing you to jump to a specific topic to understand how to implement it in your own projects.

To submit apps you develop to the Mac App Store, you must enroll in the Mac Dev Center program, which costs $99 a year. In addition to App Store submission privileges, your membership in the Mac Dev Center grants you the following:

- Access to prerelease versions of operating systems
- Access to prerelease versions of developer tools
- Technical support from Apple engineers

- ▨ Access to Apple developer forums
- ▨ Access to developer videos

To enroll in the Mac Dev Center, point your browser to http://developer.apple.com, click the link that says Mac Dev Center, and follow the instructions both to register as an Apple Developer, if you haven't already, and then to enroll in the Mac Dev Center. Apple will send you an e-mail when you are successfully enrolled, and you can then log in to the Mac Dev Center.

Using the Xcode Development Tools

The next section explains how to obtain and install Xcode, the tool Apple provides for developing Mac applications. If you've already installed Xcode or feel like you need no help obtaining and installing it, you can skip ahead to the section "Creating a Project."

Obtaining Xcode

Apple released Xcode 4 in March 2011 with a changed pricing structure. Joining the Mac Dev Center program (https://developer.apple.com/devcenter/mac/index.action) still costs $99 a year, but the Xcode software had always been free for anyone to download, install, and use to develop, compile, and distribute applications. In the new pricing structure, Xcode 4 became available as a free web download only to paying members of the Mac Dev Center and the iOS Dev Center. Apple directed all others to its App Store to buy Xcode 4 for $4.99. The web community reacted as if pricing had shot up to Visual Studio levels, demonstrating that the emotional gap between free and $5 far exceeds that between, say, $20 and $25. When Xcode 4.1 appeared in conjunction with the release of Lion, however, Apple dropped the price back to free, quelling any lingering resentment.

To download Xcode 4 as a Mac Dev Center member, point your browser to the Mac Dev Center (https://developer.apple.com/devcenter/mac/index.action) and follow the link featured prominently on the Mac Dev Center home page to download the Xcode 4 disk image. Be prepared to wait a while, because the disk image is large, and Apple doesn't do patches (meaning that upgrading to future versions will entail downloading the entire new version, not just the changed bits). If you don't want to join the Mac Dev Center or you just like using the App Store, you can search the App Store for *Xcode* and click the link to download it.

However you obtain Xcode 4, you must install it. Proceed to the next section for step-by-step instructions on how to do so.

Installing Xcode

The steps for installing Xcode differ slightly depending on whether you downloaded it from the Web or through the App Store. We cover instructions for installing the web download first.

Installing from the Web Download

Xcode downloads from the Web as a disk image (.dmg) file. Depending on your browser and its settings, the disk image file may automatically open, or you may have to double-click it to open it. Either way, the disk image file mounts as a virtual drive and opens in a Finder window, as shown in Figure 1–1.

Figure 1–1. *The mounted Xcode disk image*

You can read notes about Xcode and installation instructions by opening the About Xcode file. To begin the installation, double-click the Xcode icon, denoted by an open brown box. The installer launches and tells you that it will determine whether Xcode can be installed on your system, as shown in Figure 1–2. Click Continue.

After your system passes the checks, you get another window telling you that the installer is going to guide you through the installation, as shown in Figure 1–3. Apple takes you slowly and interactively through the installation process, and you'll click a number of buttons before the installation completes. In this window, click Continue.

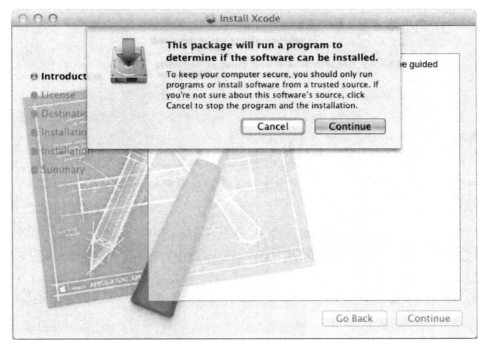

Figure 1–2. *Xcode determining whether it can install*

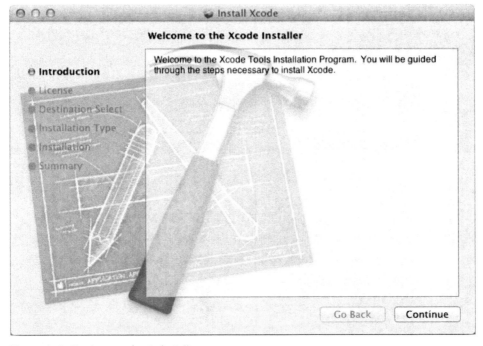

Figure 1–3. *Xcode preparing to install*

Anytime you install software, you must agree to things that you never read and, even if you did read them, you wouldn't understand. Our lawyers tell us to tell you to read all agreements carefully and consult with your lawyers before ever dreaming of clicking Continue. However you handle the next screen, shown in Figure 1–4, start to dismiss it by clicking Continue.

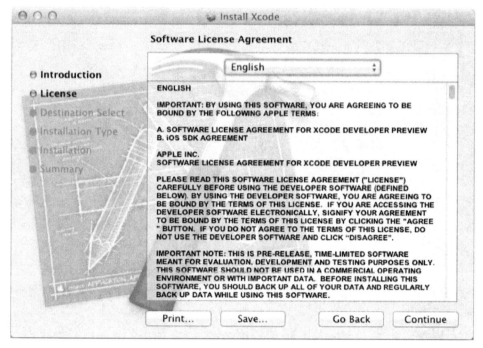

Figure 1–4. *The Xcode license agreement*

As soon as you click Continue, Apple asks you whether you actually agree to the terms you haven't read. Dismiss this message, shown in Figure 1–5, by studiously weighing all your options, by which we mean move your mouse pointer as fast as you can to the Agree button and click it.

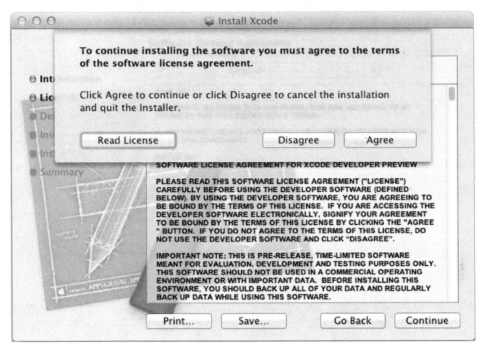

Figure 1–5. *Responding to the Xcode license agreement*

In the next dialog, shown in Figure 1–6, you have some choices. You can, for example, change the installation location from the default, which is /Developer (the `Developer` directory in the root of your boot drive). You probably should leave this at the default unless you have some reason to change it, such as that you want to run more than one version of Xcode on the same computer. The next option is whether to install the System Tools, which provide support for such tools as Instruments, the profiling tool, and Git, the version-control tool. You should install these. You should also install the UNIX Development tools, because many developer tools (such as various Ruby gems) you'll use over time will require that the UNIX Development tools be present so they can compile and install. Lastly, you can select to install or skip the documentation. We say to install it, because you'll count on it fiercely as you develop software, but it's your hard drive and your choice. If you don't install it, you'll need an active Internet connection any time you view documentation. After making your installation choices, click Continue.

Next, Apple offers you a Change Install Location button, as shown in Figure 1–7, to let you change the drive on which Xcode will install. If you feel compelled to relocate, do so, but then click the Install button to set the installation in motion. You'll be asked to type your password, as shown in Figure 1–8, so that the installer can write to privileged locations on disk. Type your password and click Install Software.

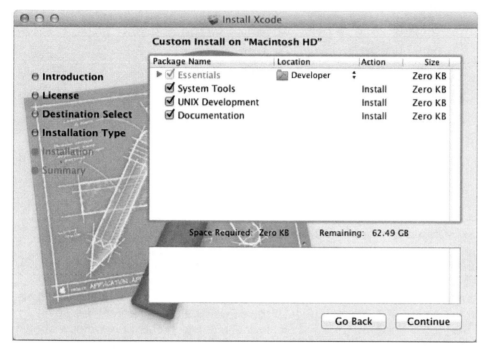

Figure 1–6. *Selecting Xcode installation options*

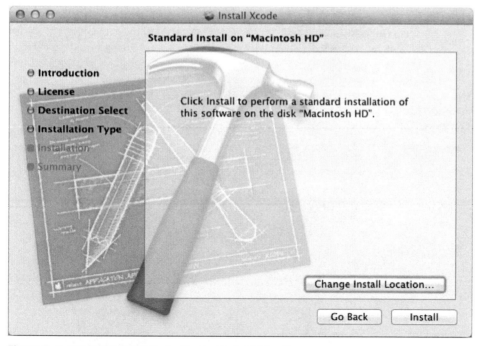

Figure 1–7. *The installer letting you change the install location*

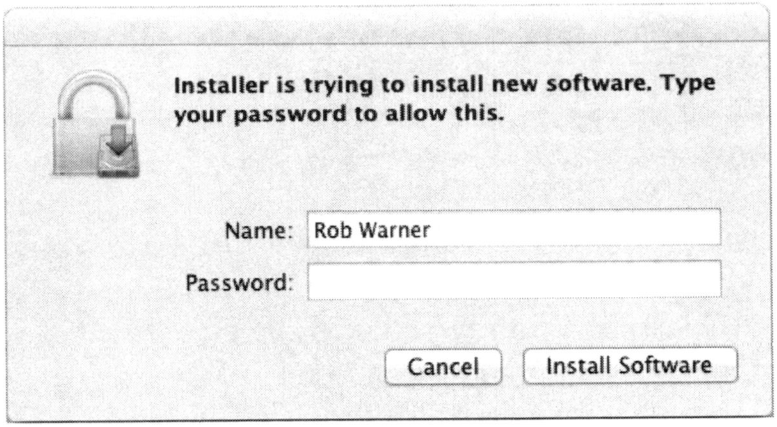

Installer is trying to install new software. Type your password to allow this.

Name: Rob Warner

Password:

Cancel   Install Software

Figure 1–8. *The installer prompting you for your password*

The next screen (shown in Figure 1–9) starts motoring through installation tasks, but it's going to take a while before Xcode is installed and ready to use. You'll be asked no more questions until the installation completes, though, so now you can step away for a bathroom break, to prepare your taxes, or to solve Fermat's Last Theorem in a novel way. When the installation finishes, it will gleefully chime and present the window shown in Figure 1–10. Click Close to dismiss it. Congratulations—you've installed Xcode and are ready to proceed to the section "Understanding Xcode."

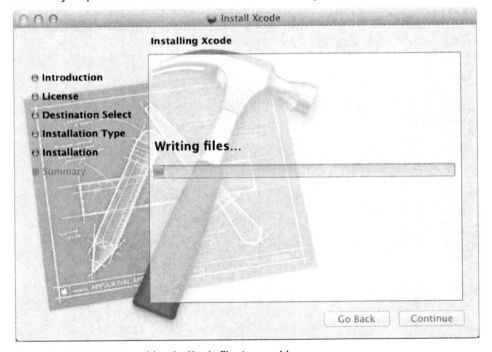

Figure 1–9. *The installer writing the Xcode files to your drive*

Figure 1–10. *The completion of a successful installation*

Installing from the App Store

If you want to install Xcode from the App Store, launch the App Store application and either go to the Developer Tools section or search for *Xcode*. Install as you would with any other app from the App Store: click the Free button to turn it into an Install App button, and then click the Install App button. Enter your Apple ID and password in the dialog that appears, and click Sign In. The Launchpad opens and displays the Xcode icon in muted gray tones, with a progress bar and the word "Downloading...," as shown in Figure 1–11. Depending on your connection speed, this download will take either a long time or a really long time. Go find something else to do while the download finishes.

Figure 1–11. *Xcode downloading in your Launchpad*

The App Store, unlike with other apps you install, doesn't install the Xcode app directly. Instead, when the download completes, the App Store installs an app into your /Applications directory called Install Xcode that, as the name suggests, is an installer for Xcode. It looks like Figure 1–12 in your Launchpad. Launch this app to begin installing Xcode.

Figure 1–12. *The Install Xcode app installed from the App Store*

The App Store version of Xcode offers a somewhat more streamlined installation process than the web-download version, using fewer screens that look a little different. When you launch the Install Xcode app, you see the splash screen shown in Figure 1–13. Yours may look a little different, depending on whether you already have a version on Xcode installed on your machine. Click Install to start the installation process.

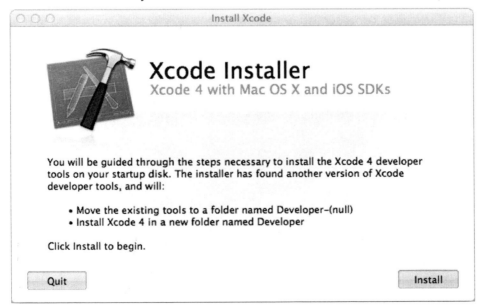

Figure 1–13. *The Xcode Installer splash screen*

The installer then shows the Xcode and the iOS SDK agreements, as shown in Figure 1–14. Click Agree to accept the agreements and proceed. You'll be prompted for your password so that the Xcode installer can install Xcode files to privileged areas on your drive, as shown in Figure 1–15. Type your password, click OK, and the installer starts copying files to your drive, as shown in Figure 1–16. When the installation completes, Xcode automatically launches.

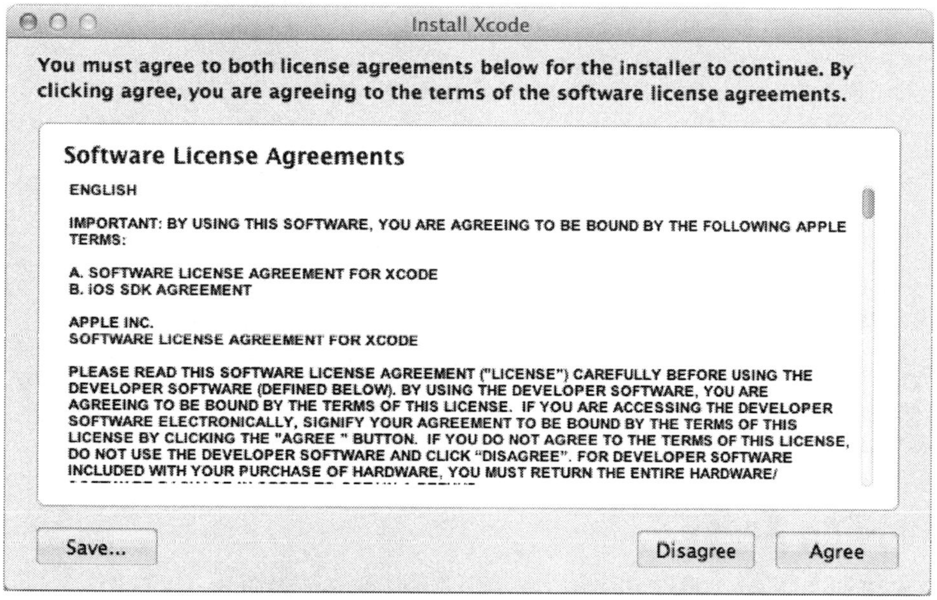

Figure 1–14. *The agreements for Xcode and the iOS SDK*

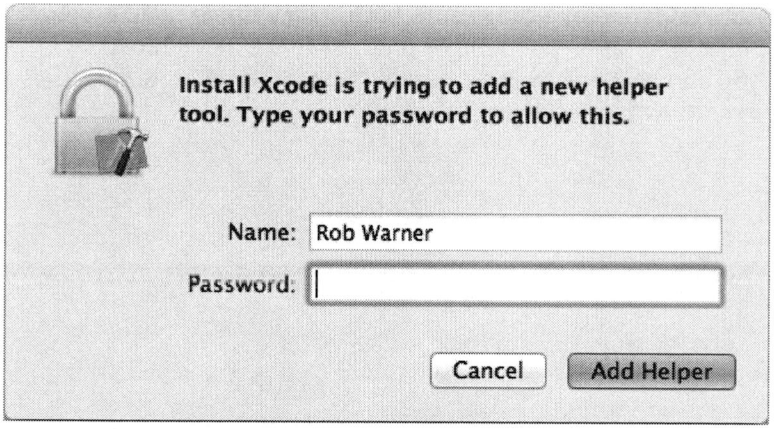

Figure 1–15. *Entering your password so the installer can proceed*

Figure 1–16. *The installer writing the Xcode files to your drive*

After you install Xcode from the App Store, you can reclaim about 3GB of disk space by backing up the Install Xcode app from /Applications, in case you ever want to reinstall without downloading, and deleting it from your drive.

Understanding Xcode

With Xcode safely installed, you're ready to launch it using your favorite launching method. When you launch Xcode, you see a splash screen, shown in Figure 1–17, that offers you the option to create a new Xcode project, connect to a source code repository, learn more about Xcode, open a browser to http://developer.apple.com, open one of your recent projects, or open some other project. This screen is usually helpful, but if you prefer, you can uncheck the box beside "Show this window when Xcode launches" to banish it from reappearing.

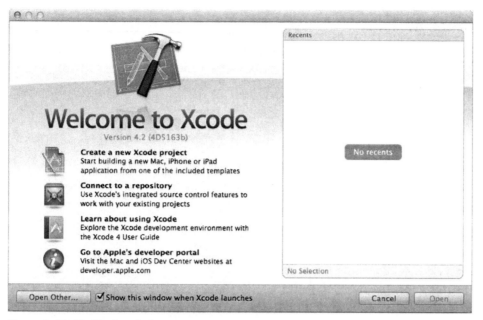

Figure 1–17. *The Xcode splash screen*

To acquaint yourself with the major sections of Xcode, proceed by clicking the "Create a new Xcode project" option. Xcode asks you to choose the template for your new project, so select Application under Mac OS X on the left and Command Line Tool on the right, as shown in Figure 1–18, and click Next. Xcode asks you for a product name and a type. For Product Name, type **HelloWorld**, for Company Identifier, type **book.macdev**, and for Type, select Foundation, as Figure 1–19 shows. Click Next. Xcode asks you where to create your project folder and offers you to create a local Git repository for the project. Select the parent directory for your project (something like Projects or Development in your home folder—wherever you normally store your coding projects), uncheck the box for creating a local Git repository for this project, and click Create. The Xcode integrated development environment (IDE) launches and opens your project, as shown in Figure 1–20.

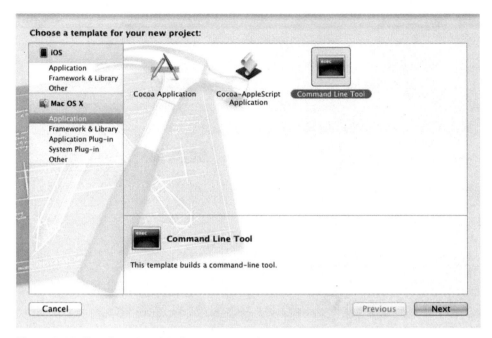

Figure 1–18. *Choosing a template for your new project*

Figure 1–19. *Naming your project and selecting its type*

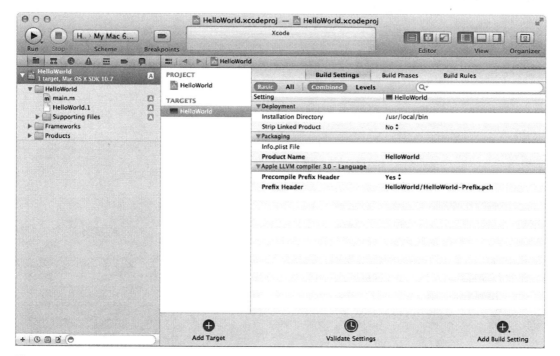

Figure 1–20. *The Xcode window with the HelloWorld project*

Expand all the folders on the left side of the screen and click the file main.m to view the generated source for this project. Also, click all three buttons above View in the toolbar across the top of the Xcode window. Refer to Figure 1–21 to understand the components of the Xcode window.

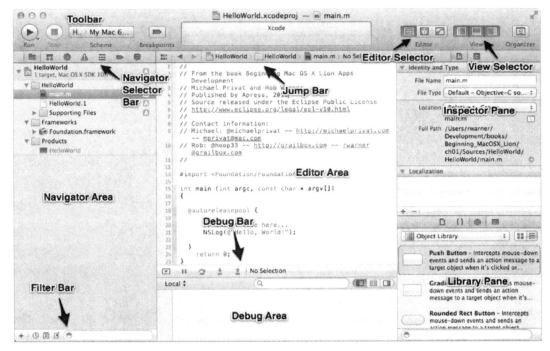

Figure 1–21. *The components of the Xcode window*

The busyness of the Xcode window can overwhelm developers, so we don't cover every aspect of every button, ribbon, or setting. Understanding the major areas of the Xcode window, however, can orient you sufficiently to give you an exploration context. Don't be afraid to click around and try things in Xcode to reveal more functionality than you realized was there. You can also hover over any of the various buttons in the Xcode window to display a tooltip that names and sometimes describes the control you're hovering over. The next few sections describe the major pieces of Xcode and prepare you for developing the Graphique project.

The Editor Area and the Jump Bar

The Editor Area sits in the middle of the Xcode window and usually dominates the focus of your interactions with Xcode. In the Editor Area, you edit the various files in your Xcode projects. This area changes the editor it uses to reflect the type of file you're editing. When you're editing a source code file, for example, it displays a modern source code editor with syntax highlighting, code completion, and the other features you'd expect from a programmer's text editor. If you're editing an Interface Builder file, the Interface Builder editor displays here. If you're editing a Core Data model, the Core Data Modeling tool takes over this area, and so on; the editor appropriate to the file you're editing displays.

The Jump Bar works with the Editor Area to allow you to jump to specific places in what you edit. You can, for example, jump to a specific file in your project and display it in the

Editor Area by clicking in the Jump Bar and selecting the file. You can also jump to a specific method in a file.

The Navigator Area and the Navigator Selector Bar

You navigate through your project in the Navigator Area. You use the Navigator Selector Bar to change which aspect of your project you want to navigate. When navigating through your project's files, for example, you select the Project navigator (the button on the upper left of the Navigator Selector Bar) to display the hierarchy of all the files related to your project. Clicking them opens them in the Editor Area.

You change the navigator that the Navigator Area displays by clicking the appropriate button in the Navigator Selector Bar. The navigators in Xcode are as follows:

- The Project navigator for navigating the files in your project

- The Symbol navigator for viewing your project's symbols such as classes and their methods

- The Search navigator for searching for specific text through all of your project's files

- The Issue navigator for displaying and jumping to the issues in your project (for example, compilation warnings or errors)

- The Debug navigator for displaying thread and other debug information when debugging your project

- The Breakpoint navigator for viewing all the breakpoints you've set in your project

- The Log navigator for viewing project logs, such as output from builds

The Filter Bar

Type text in the search field in the Filter Bar to dynamically filter what's displayed in the Navigation Area. If you're viewing the Project navigator, for example, for the HelloWorld project and you type **ma** in the search field, the Navigator Area hides everything that doesn't match the text *ma*, so only main.m displays.

The Filter Bar changes what it displays according to which navigator you've selected. When the Project navigator displays, for example, the Filter Bar shows a + button for adding a new file to the project.

The Debug Area and the Debug Bar

All Console output from your running code goes to the Debug Area. When debugging your project, you view the variables in your current debug context in the Variables View. The Variables View and the Console share the Debug Area, and you control what displays using the three buttons to the far right of the Debug Bar: one shows the

Variables View only, one shows both the Variables View and the Console, and one shows the Console only. The Debug Bar also gives you controls to use to step through your project when debugging.

The Inspector Pane, the Inspector Selector Bar, and the Library Pane

Together, the Inspector Pane and the Library Pane constitute the Utility Area. The Inspector Pane allows you to view and edit information specific to some item you've selected in the Editor Area. If you're editing a Core Data model, for example, you can view and edit information about the selected entity here. The Inspector Pane changes the buttons it displays across its top, depending on what kind of thing you're inspecting, so that you can switch among the various inspectors. This is an area where curious experimentation usually pays off.

The Library Pane shows libraries that you can interact with as you work on your projects. You can view libraries of code snippets, objects (useful when editing Interface Builder files), and others.

The View Selector

The View Selector allows you to show and hide the Navigator Area, Utility Area (the Inspector Pane and the Library Pane), and the Debug Area.

The Editor Selector

The Editor Selector has three buttons: one for showing the standard editor (for example, the source code editor for editing the currently selected file), the assistant editor (used to edit a file related to the one you're editing in the standard editor), and the version editor (used to compare different versions of your files as they change over time). Although you'll use the standard editor the most, you'll grow to rely on both the assistant and version editors for editing related files or understanding what has changed in files. Using the assistant editor, for example, you can display both an implementation file and its header file side by side.

The Toolbar

The Toolbar gives you something to click and drag to move your Xcode window around. It lets you choose what scheme you're currently using (for example, Debug vs. Release builds), lets you turn breakpoints on or off globally, shows you output about things like builds and issues, and gives you buttons to run, test, profile, analyze, and stop your application. Stop has its own button, while the other four operations share a button (click and hold the Run button to display a menu of the four buttons).

That covers the major areas of the Xcode interface. Click the Run button now to see your HelloWorld project build and run. You should see the text "Hello, World!" in the Console in the Debug Area, as shown in Figure 1–22.

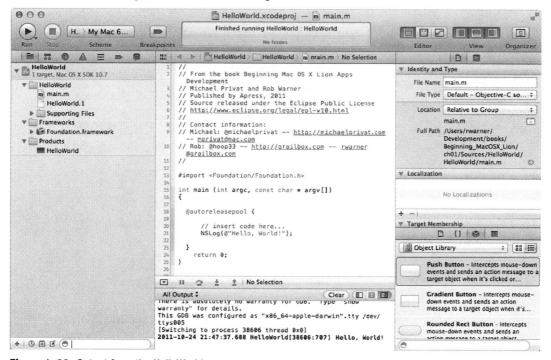

Figure 1–22. *Output from the HelloWorld app*

Creating a Project

Regardless of language and platform, creating the first piece of code of an application is often an exciting moment. It marks the point in time when the application morphs from concept to reality. In this section, we take this first step and create the first running shell of the Graphique application. In the vast majority of situations, the first few lines of code are the same regardless of the application. This isn't unique to Objective-C and Mac OS X. Every Java application, for instance, must have a `public static void main(String[] args)` method. Any Microsoft Windows application contains a fairly substantial amount of boilerplate code. Generally speaking, applications that run in a graphical environment require a larger amount of common initialization code. Thankfully, Xcode, like any respectable integrated development tool, generates all the setup for you. It does take away from the pleasure of typing the very first line of code, but as you create more and more applications, you will undoubtedly learn to appreciate the trade-off. Once Xcode is done generating the setup code, you will have a runnable application that will display a simple window. We then take you for a tour of what was created, why it was created, and where to go next.

To begin, launch Xcode and create a new project by selecting **File ➤ New ➤ New Project** from the menu. Note that you can also create a new project by pressing ⇧+⌘+N. From the list of application templates, select the Application item under Mac OS X on the left, as depicted in Figure 1–23, and pick Cocoa Application on the right.

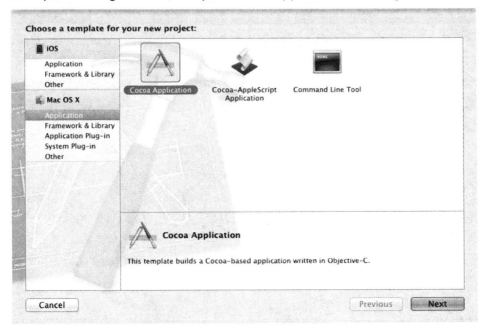

Figure 1–23. *Creating a new Cocoa application*

Click the Next button. The next screen presents you with options for configuring the code generator. For the Graphique app we build in this book, enter the following values:

- Product Name: Graphique
- Company Identifier: book.macdev
- Class Prefix: Graphique
- App Store Category: Utilities
- Create Document-Based Application: Unchecked (Document-based applications manage multiple documents and multiple windows, displaying a different document in each window. This is typically the case for applications such as word processors. Graphique, in contrast, is a single-document, single-window application.)
- Document Extension: Leave blank
- Use Core Data: Unchecked
- Use Automatic Reference Counting: Checked
- Include Unit Tests: Checked
- Include Spotlight Importer: Unchecked

Your screen should match Figure 1–24.

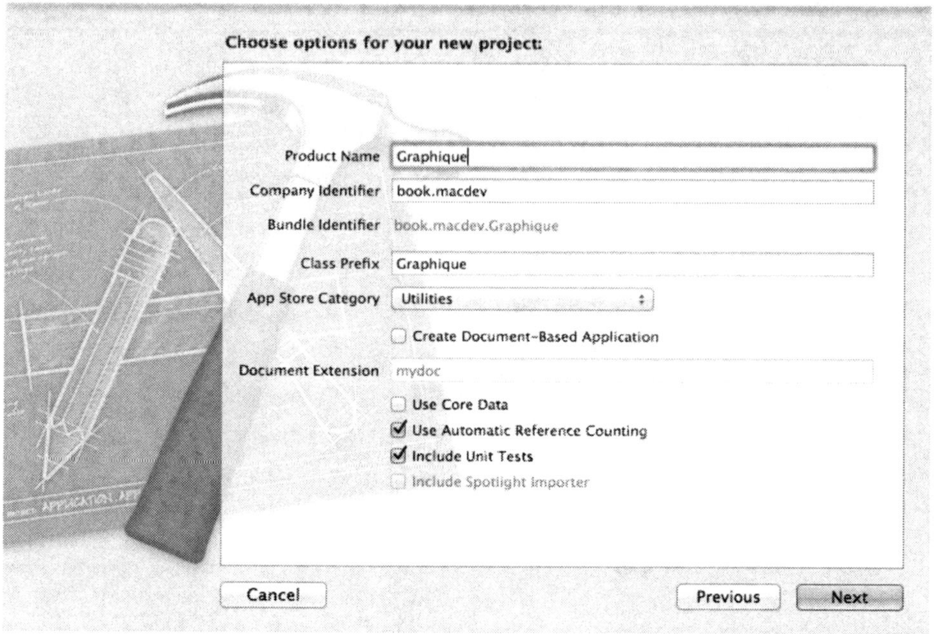

Figure 1–24. *The application options*

Clicking Next once the information is filled out pops up a save dialog asking for a location for where to put your project. Pick a folder and hit Save.

NOTE: The save dialog has a check mark that, if checked, will create a local Git repository. Although this is optional, we strongly recommend that you utilize a source-control repository when working on code. Not only will it help you keep your sanity when you try to track the change history of a file, but remote repositories also serve as excellent backups for when your workstation or laptop decides it has had enough with life.

Figure 1–25 shows the new project outfitted with all the necessary files to get started. In the next section, we explore the project and discuss what the artifacts generated are used for.

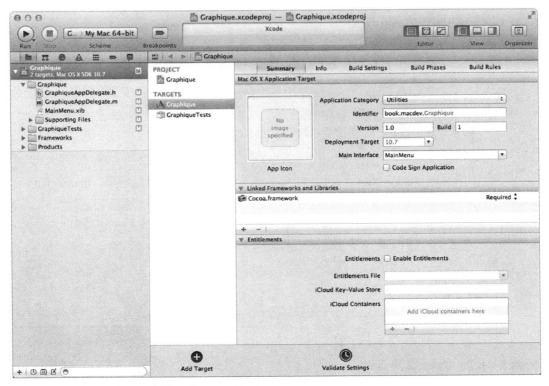

Figure 1–25. *The newly created Graphique application*

Before we start looking under the hood, however, let's indulge ourselves and see what the fruit of a few mouse clicks and key presses looks like. In Xcode, click the Run button to launch Graphique. The application launches, switches the menu bar to show the Graphique menu, and displays a blank window, as shown in Figure 1–26.

Figure 1–26. *The generated application running*

Although the application doesn't yet do anything useful, it offers some points of interest. The most obvious of these interesting points is that a window has opened so that the application is materialized on the screen. Another important detail is the existence of a menu in the system-wide menu bar. The menu has several default items; most of them are disabled, but some of them are active. If you select Graphique ➤ About Graphique, you see the about box with some text in it. Also worth mentioning is that the Graphique ➤ Quit Graphique menu item is working, including its keyboard shortcut (⌘Q).

It's time to quit drooling and to get to work. Use that Graphique ➤ Quit Graphique option and return to Xcode.

Understanding the Major Components

Now that you've had a chance to run the application and see what you got from the Xcode application template, it's time to raise the hood and put our hands in the grease. Xcode generates a few files, and it can be overwhelming at first glance. The first thought that crosses the Xcode novice's mind is typically "Where do I go from here?" or "What's all that stuff?" In this section, we take a methodical approach to enumerating all the pieces so that we can get started making this application our own. Figure 1–27 shows what the Xcode artifacts should look like in the Graphique project.

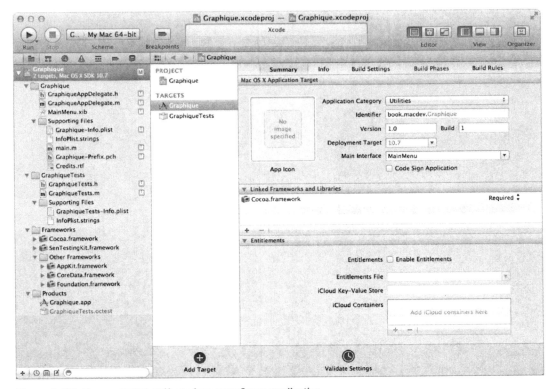

Figure 1–27. *The generated artifacts for a new Cocoa application*

The Project and Targets

In Xcode, artifacts are arranged in a tree structure. The top-level item—Graphique—represents the project. As you expect, every artifact belonging to the project is a subelement of Graphique in the tree structure, visually representing that the Graphique project contains all the other artifacts. A project defines two important sets of information:

- The set of files (source code and resources) available to the application build process

- The set of targets available to build the project into products

Targets define how to build your source files and resources into a packaged, runnable product. The runnable product can be the application itself but can also be a unit test suite. For now, we will set unit test suites aside and focus on the application product. This is the product that is built when you hit the Run button in Xcode.

Select Graphique in the Project navigator (in other words, the top level of the tree structure). In the editor window, you should see two targets listed: Graphique and GraphiqueTests. Select the Graphique target, as shown in Figure 1–27. The editor then shows more details about the selected target using several tabs. The default tab is the

Summary tab. It displays basic information about the product that will result from building this target. For the most part, it contains the information we entered in the project generation wizard in the previous section. The application icon is currently blank (which is materialized by a plain white icon at runtime). We won't worry about the icon for now and revisit it later in the book as we work through preparing the application for the Mac App Store.

Select the Build Phases tab. Build phases represent the steps in the build process. The default build phases are created for you, and in many cases, you won't need to add any new phase. The default phases list the source code files, frameworks, and resources that will be included in this build, as depicted in Figure 1–28.

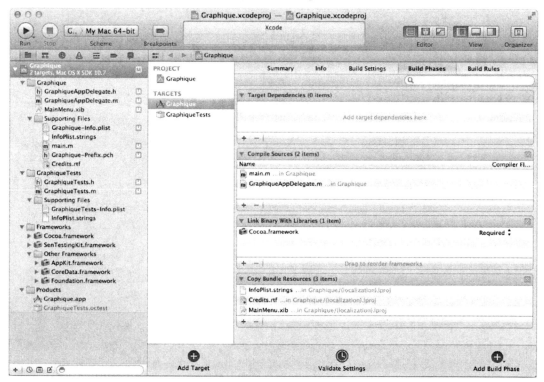

Figure 1–28. *The Graphique target build phases*

If you now select the GraphiqueTests phase and go to the Build Phases tab, you will notice, as shown in Figure 1–29, that the steps are slightly different. The first major difference is that the unit test target depends on the application target. This is to be expected since unit tests are all about testing the main application and therefore depend on the application building correctly. The last phase in this build target is called Run Script, which, as you might expect, runs an Xcode script that executes the unit tests.

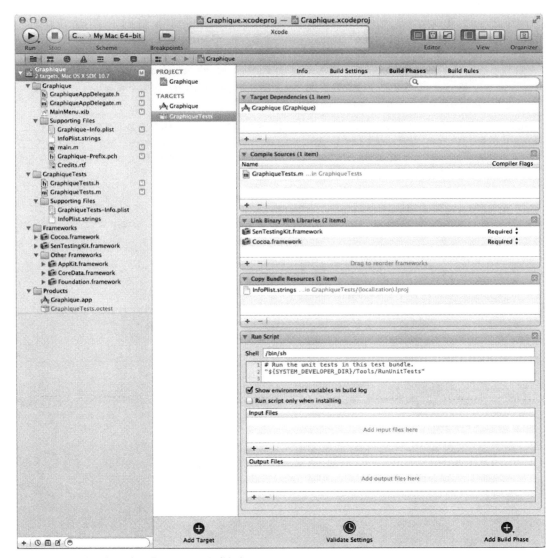

Figure 1-29. *The GraphiqueTests target build phases*

When the targets run, they produce the product, which then appears under the Products group in the Project navigator. The Graphique target generates a product called Graphique.app, which is the runnable application, while the GraphiqueTests target produces a product called GraphiqueTests.octest, which is the unit test suite.

The Application Architecture

In the remainder of this chapter, we will set the unit test target aside and focus on the application. Cocoa applications all have the same basic architecture. It is important to be familiar with it before getting started. Figure 1–30 illustrates this simple yet important structure.

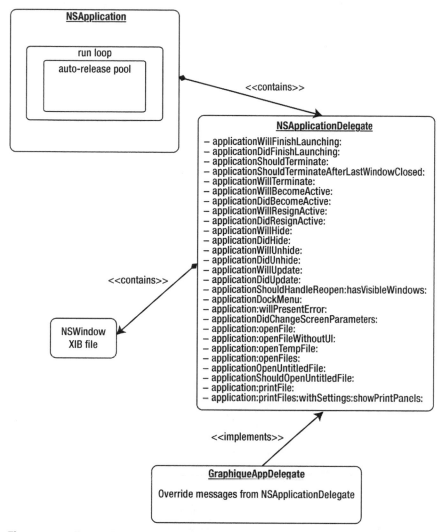

Figure 1–30. *The basic application architecture*

As a developer, you rarely find yourself having to extend the NSApplication class. Instead, you implement the NSApplicationDelegate protocol and let the NSApplication class manage the run loop and the rest of the application environment, such as the autorelease pool that handles garbage collection. As the application goes through its life cycle (start, stop, minimize, hide, and so on), the NSApplicationDelegate is notified, and your code can react to these notifications.

The application delegate also declares the window attribute, which is set through the graphical interface builder and defines the NSWindow instance to use to materialize the window. We explore the user interface objects in depth in the next chapters. For now, just remember that the application delegate defines the window for the application.

The Source Code and Resources

All the source code and resources used in the application are organized under the Graphique group, as shown in Figure 1–31.

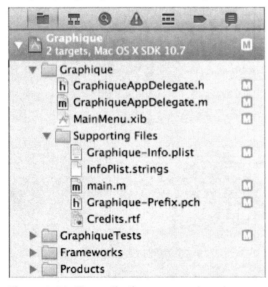

Figure 1–31. *The application source code and resources*

Working your way through the artifacts and understanding how they all fit together can be a maze. But just like Theseus walked out of the Labyrinth by following the string he had attached to the entrance and unwound as he advanced, we start from the place we are now and follow the linkages and dependencies.

Select the Graphique project in the navigator and go to the Summary tab of the Graphique target. There it shows, in the Main Interface drop-down, that an artifact called MainMenu drives the main interface. This is the starting point of our exploration. Go back to the Project navigator, find MainMenu.xib, and select it.

NOTE: XIB files, often called *nibs* because they are an evolution of the NIB files that had a `.nib` extension, contain the user interface layout information. Prior to Xcode 4, XIB files were opened in a separate application called Interface Builder (IB). As of Xcode 4, IB has been integrated into Xcode.

Although you can also lay out user interfaces programmatically, Interface Builder is a convenient point-and-click way to build your user interfaces. In the next chapter, we explain how to use Interface Builder. Figure 1–32 illustrates what you should see when you select `MainMenu.xib`. Make sure you select the Utilities button at the top-right corner of the Xcode IDE to see the right sidebar (in other words, the Utilities panel).

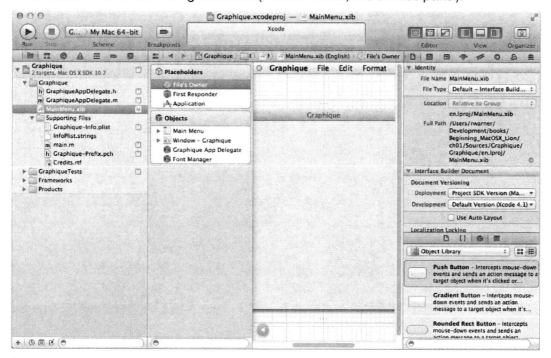

Figure 1–32. *The* `MainMenu.xib` *file in Interface Builder*

Interface Builder offers two types of entities:

■ Placeholders represent objects that exist within the runtime environment.

■ Objects represent objects that will be created when the XIB file is run.

If you select the File's Owner placeholder and select the Identity inspector tab in the Utilities panel, you will notice that the Interface Builder file is owned by an object of type `NSApplication`, which, as you may expect, is the root class for all applications. A Mac OS X application does not extend `NSApplication` directly. Instead, it is driven by setting the delegate property of `NSApplication` to a class that implements the

NSApplicationDelegate protocol. The NSApplication class makes the appropriate calls to its delegate throughout its life cycle (startup, shutdown, and so on). This is where the application-specific code begins. With the File's Owner (the NSApplication instance) still selected, go to the Connections inspector to see what the delegate is linked to. Figure 1–33 shows the Connections inspector tab selected.

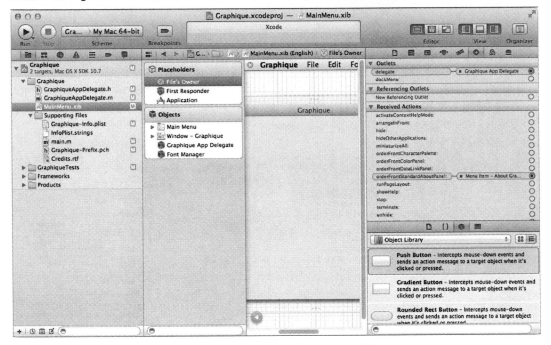

Figure 1–33. *The Connections inspector showing the application delegate link*

The connection shows the delegate set to the object named Graphique App Delegate. Select this object in the Objects section and go to the Identity inspector, as shown in Figure 1–34. Notice that this object is materialized in the application as a GraphiqueAppDelegate class.

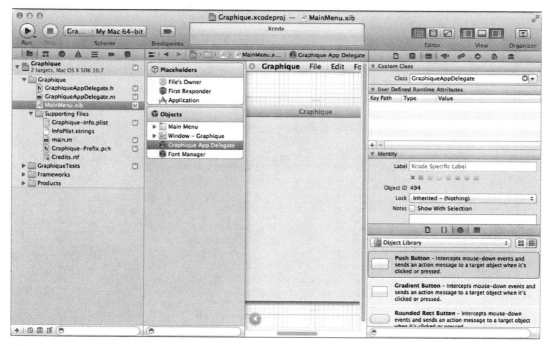

Figure 1–34. *Identifying the class used for an IB object*

We're almost at the beginning of the thread we're following. Open
GraphiqueAppDelegate.m and find the applicationDidFinishLaunching: method. Xcode
has conveniently inserted a comment stating "Insert code here to initialize your
application." This is where the thread we're following starts. Go ahead and add a log
statement to validate that we found the right method. Since no technical book is
complete without a couple of references to the enduring "Hello World!" statement, edit
the applicationDidFinishLaunching: method to look like this:

```
- (void)applicationDidFinishLaunching:(NSNotification *)aNotification
{
    NSLog(@"Hello World!");
}
```

Launch the application. The console automatically appears because you logged
something to it, and it displays a log message similar to the one shown here:

```
2011-08-26 06:26:33.685 Graphique[2960:407] Hello World!
```

Take a closer look at the NSApplicationDelegate protocol. It contains other methods
called at different points in the application's life cycle. NSApplicationDelegate methods
are called by the default notification center as the application interacts with the Mac OS
X environment.

> **NOTE:** You can always access the documentation quickly from the source code editor by using the Option+click shortcut. Open `GraphiqueDelegate.h` and Option+click the `NSApplicationDelegate` protocol to open the quick help view, as depicted in Figure 1–35. To get more in-depth documentation, click the book icon on the top right of the quick help window.

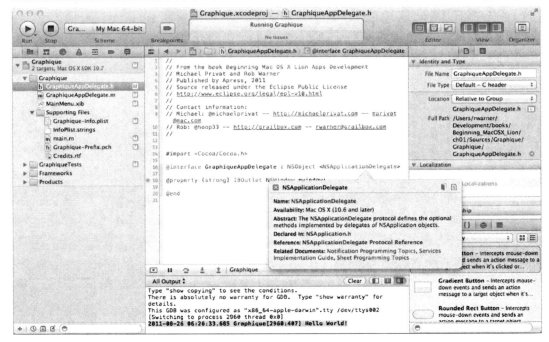

Figure 1–35. *Accessing the quick documentation from the source code editor*

You can be notified when your application becomes active, when it is about to quit, and so on. Override these methods in `GraphiqueAppDelegate.m` to have Graphique's underlying `NSApplication` instance invoke your code. Table 1–1 shows the available life cycle messages that your delegate can receive.

Table 1–1. *The NSApplicationDelegate Protocol Messages Dealing with the Application Life Cycle*

Method	Description
- (void)applicationWillFinishLaunching: (NSNotification*)aNotification	This is sent immediately before the application object is initialized.
- (void)applicationDidFinishLaunching: (NSNotification*)aNotification	This is sent immediately after the application object is initialized. This is the method you typically override to place your own initialization code.

Method	Description
- (NSApplicationTerminateReply) applicationShouldTerminate: (NSApplication*)sender	This is sent to the application when the operating system wants to close it or because the terminate: method has been invoked. You typically return NSTerminateNow to let the application close or NSTerminateCancel if you want to delay the closing, for example if you have cleanup work to do.
- (BOOL) applicationShouldTerminateAfterLastWindowClosed: (NSApplication *)theApplication	This method is called when the last window of the application has been closed. If you want your application to terminate, override this method in your delegate class and return YES, else return NO. By default, it returns NO.
- (void)applicationWillTerminate: (NSNotification*)aNotification	Called just before terminating the application. At this point, you no longer have a say on whether the application will terminate, but you still have an opportunity to do some work.
- (void)applicationWillBecomeActive: (NSNotification*)aNotification	Sent immediately before the application becomes active. An application becomes active when it is brought in front of all other running applications.
- (void)applicationDidBecomeActive: (NSNotification*)aNotification	Sent immediately after the application becomes active.
- (void)applicationWillResignActive: (NSNotification*)aNotification	Sent immediately before the application loses its active status.
- (void)applicationDidResignActive: (NSNotification*)aNotification	Sent immediately after the application loses its active status.

Plenty of other delegate methods are available. Although we touch on a few of them later in this book, we encourage you to look at the NSApplicationDelegate documentation to see them all.

Let's play around a little bit more and intercept one of these messages to clearly illustrate how this works. Open GraphiqueAppDelegate.m and add the methods shown in Listing 1–1.

Listing 1–1. *NSApplicationDelegate method implementations*

```
- (void)applicationDidBecomeActive:(NSNotification *)aNotification {
    NSLog(@"Application is active");
}

- (void)applicationDidResignActive:(NSNotification *)aNotification      {
    NSLog(@"Application is no longer active");
}
```

In effect, this is telling the Mac OS X environment that you want to intercept these messages. Start the Graphique application. As the window appears, you get the following log:

```
2011-08-26 06:34:14.479 Graphique[3077:407] Hello World!
2011-08-26 06:34:14.647 Graphique[3077:407] Application is active
```

Now switch to another application, and the following line is appended to the log:

```
2011-08-26 06:34:16.938 Graphique[3077:407] Application is no longer active
```

The About Dialog

One last piece of magic provided by the Xcode generator is the about dialog. While Graphique is running, select **Graphique ➤ About Graphique** in the menu to see the about dialog. This is the default implementation provided by the `orderFrontStandardAboutPanel:` method in the NSApplication class. To track down how the About Graphique menu item is linked to that method, open `MainMenu.xib` in Interface Builder. Remember that the File's Owner placeholder is actually the NSApplication instance. Expand the Main Menu object to see Menu Item - About Graphique, as shown in Figure 1–36. In the Connections inspector, you can see that this menu item is sending a message to the File's Owner (NSApplication) `orderFrontStandardAboutPanel:` method.

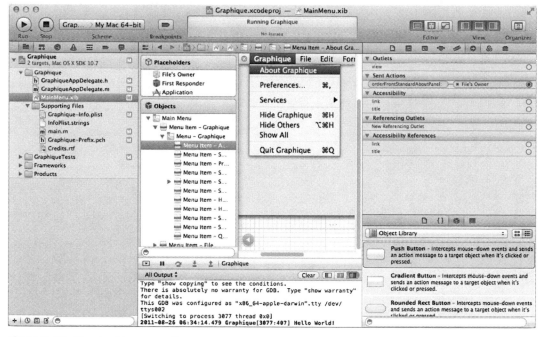

Figure 1–36. *The about box menu item*

The implementation of orderFrontStandardAboutPanel: creates a simple dialog box and uses the content of the Credits.rtf file that is present in the project. Find that file, open it, and see that it matches the content of the about dialog.

Summary

In this chapter, you got your hands on Xcode 4, installed it, and learned how to use it. You learned about the major components of the Xcode interface, navigated through them, and saw how to build and launch an application. You also started building the Graphique app and learned about some of the libraries, including Cocoa, that you'll use when building Mac OS X applications.

Although your Graphique application builds and runs, you've done precious little software development. Instead, you've been able to rely on Xcode's code generation and templates to get a working application. In the next chapter, however, you'll dive in to using Xcode's editors, including Interface Builder, to lay out the Graphique user interface and bind the user interface to code.

Chapter 2

Laying Out the User Interface

The appearance of an application often conveys an indelible first impression on users' minds, whether positive or negative, that strongly influences whether the application becomes a hit or simply moves to the virtual trash. Providing an attractive and usable interface remains one of the hallmarks of top applications.

Mac OS X offers an array of user interface widgets that, when intelligently stitched together, fuse to provide stunning and useful interfaces. In this chapter, we explore some of these widgets and how to incorporate them into the Graphique application. The widgets we explore include the following:

- Labels, which display static text
- Text fields, which allow users to enter text
- Buttons, used to let users initiate some action
- Toolbars, which display a strip of buttons with images
- Split views, which divide a view into two separate views
- Sliders, which allow users to select a value by dragging a "thumb" across a range of values
- Tables, which display tabular data

This chapter focuses only on using Mac OS X's widgets to create the user interface, not on responding to user input or reacting to events. Chapter 3 will tackle those topics.

Through this chapter, you build an interface that displays three different views, separated by split views:

- A view to enter equations
- A table of x, y values for an equation
- A tree that shows recently used equations

At the end of the chapter, the Graphique application will look like Figure 2–1.

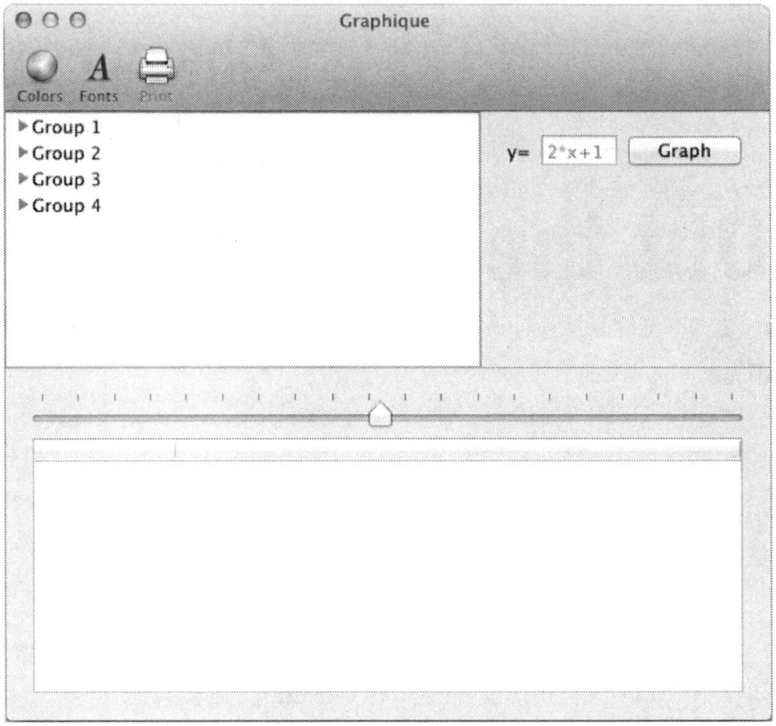

Figure 2–1. *The Graphique application when the layout is complete*

Creating the Split View

In the Graphique application, we want to give users a place to enter an equation. We also want to show users the graph that an equation generates. Finally, we want to show users a list of the equations they've already entered so that they can quickly retrieve equations and their resulting graphs. The user interface has one window, but we've outlined three different views that we want that window to display. Cocoa offers a class called NSSplitView that allows you to show two different views in the same window, with a movable separator between them. The separator can run horizontally or vertically, and you can also nest them to create multiple views in a window, all with movable separators between. We'll use the NSSplitView class to address the user interface needs of Graphique.

We refer to the three views that we want to display in the Graphique application like this:

- *Equation Entry View*: The place users can enter an equation

- *Recent Equations View*: The list of equations users have already entered

- *Graph View*: The graph represented by the equation in the Equation Entry View

We arrange these three views as shown in Figure 2–2, with a vertical separator, or splitter, between the Equation Entry View and the Recent Equations View, and a horizontal separator (splitter) between the top two views and the Graph View.

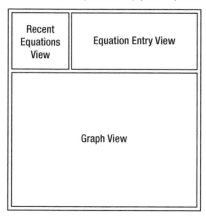

Figure 2–2. *The layout of the Graphique user interface*

Creating the Horizontal NSSplitView

To begin creating the desired view layout for Graphique, we first divide the window horizontally, with a view above and a view below and a movable separator between. Open MainMenu.xib in Xcode and select the Window – Graphique object from the Object hierarchy. You may need to click the button to show the Document Outline, as shown in Figure 2–3, to get your view to match ours. The Document Outline helps you understand the relationships among the various views.

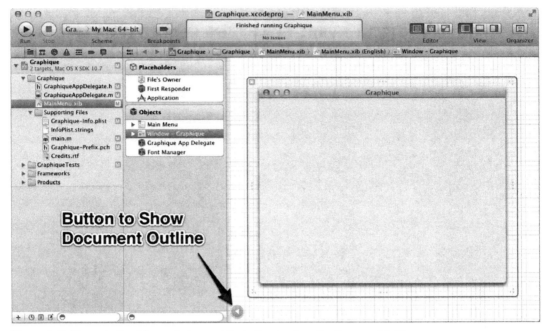

Figure 2–3. *The main Graphique window and the button to show the Document Outline*

Expand the Window object in the Object hierarchy to see the View object it contains, and then select the View object, as shown in Figure 2–4.

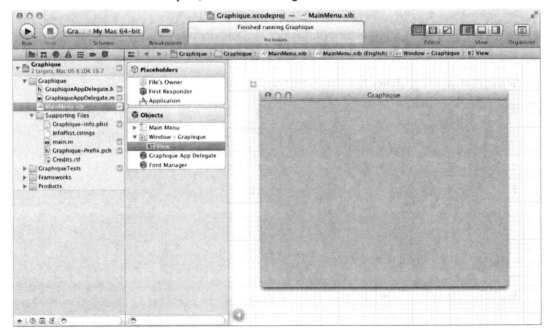

Figure 2–4. *The main Graphique window with the view selected*

Show the Utilities panel (on the right side of Xcode), show the Object Library in that panel, and type **horizontal** in the search field to show the Horizontal Split View object in the library, as Figure 2–5 shows. Drag a Horizontal Split View object onto the Graphique window and drop it. It should appear both in the Graphique window and in the Object view, below the view that's below the Graphique window, as shown in Figure 2–6. You should also see the two custom views that the split view contains.

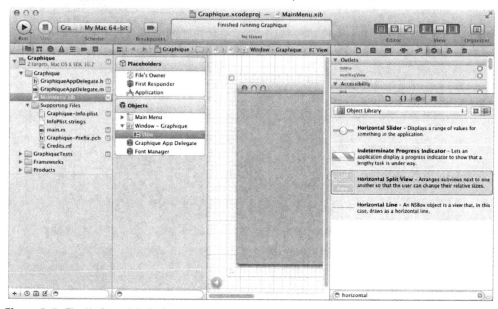

Figure 2–5. *The Horizontal Split View object in the Object Library*

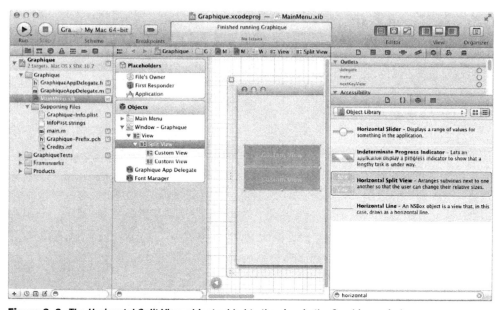

Figure 2–6. *The Horizontal Split View object added to the view in the Graphique window*

Now, resize the Horizontal Split View object to completely fill the window. We also want to make sure it continues to fill the window, even if the user resizes the window, so show the Size inspector and select all the springs and all the struts in the Autosizing view. In other words, click the two double-headed arrows inside the square and the four bars outside the square so they're all solid, as shown in Figure 2–7.

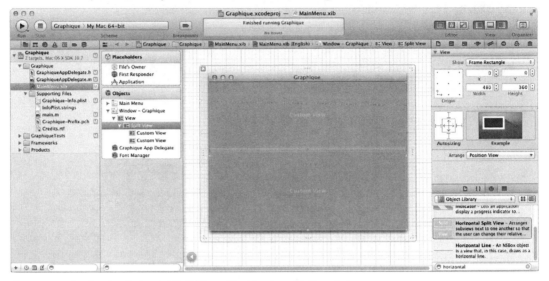

Figure 2–7. *Setting the Horizontal Split View object to size with the window*

Run the application. You should see a window split in half horizontally, as shown in Figure 2–8. Resize the window and make sure the split view continues to fill the view.

Figure 2–8. *The Graphique application with a Horizontal Split View object*

Creating the Vertical NSSplitView

The next step is to split the upper half of the Graphique window with a vertical split view. Go back to Xcode and drag a Vertical Split View object from the Object Library onto the upper half of the horizontal split view you just created. Drag and size it to fill the entire upper half of the horizontal split view, and select all its springs and struts in the Autosizing box so that it all looks like Figure 2–9.

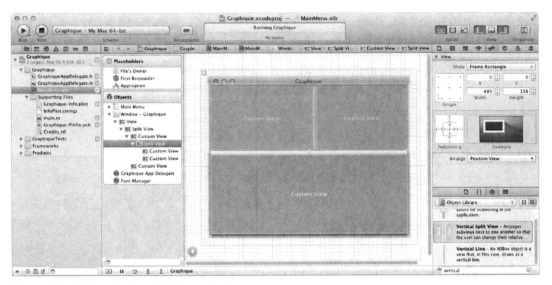

Figure 2–9. *Adding a Vertical Split View object*

Again, build and run the application. You should see a window that looks like Figure 2–10. Resize the window to make sure the split views continue to fill the window, and move the splitters around to confirm that they move.

Figure 2–10. *The Graphique application with both Horizontal and Vertical Split View objects*

We want to take one more step before moving on. Those splitters seem so thick and heavy, and the trend in Mac OS X applications points to using thin splitters. Go back to Xcode and select the Horizontal Split View object in the object hierarchy, go to the Attributes inspector, and change the style from Pane splitter to Thin divider. Then, do the same for your Vertical Split View object. When you build and run the application, it should resemble Figure 2–11.

Figure 2–11. *The Graphique application with thin dividers*

You've created the structure of the Graphique application layout. Next, you must create the actual views that the splitters will divide and swap them for the placeholder views. Read on to the next section to understand how to do that.

Creating the Equation Entry Panel

So far, you've learned how to do some basic layout. The real power of Xcode comes from the ability to break down the user interface into components. In this section, we build our first version of the equation entry component. The purpose of this component is to allow the user to specify an equation to graph. There are two important reasons for creating a component instead of just adding more individual widgets to the MainMenu.xib file:

■ *Code reuse*: Creating a clearly separated component allows you to reuse it in various contexts in your application. Think about the Cover Flow user interface component on your Mac. It is used in iTunes, but the same component is also used in Finder.

■ *Code isolation*: All the code pertaining to your component's internal function is kept within the component and not in some generic controller class. This allows you to improve the component in the future without impacting the rest of the application. In Chapter 4, we put this in practice by enhancing the equation entry component.

For this first version, we keep the component trivial. We'll have a label with the text "y=" and a simple text entry field where the user will type the equation as a function of x.

Using NSViewController

If you come from an iOS development background, you are already familiar with the all-important UIViewController class. The NSViewController class was introduced with Mac OS 10.5 (Leopard). Although it sounds like a parallel with iOS's UIViewController, it is not nearly as central. It is meant to manage custom views but not necessarily receive events from them, as is customary in the iOS world. The primary function of the NSViewController class is to materialize custom views from XIB files so that you can use them in your code. The NSViewController controller has a view attribute that it populates from the XIB file automatically.

Creating a new custom user interface component consists of creating a new NSViewController subclass and laying out its view in Interface Builder.

To keep things organized, create a group to store all the custom components by going to Xcode and doing the following:

1. Highlight the Graphique folder, and select **File ➤ New ➤ New Group** from the menu.

2. Call the new group **Views**.

3. Select the new group and create a new class by selecting **File ➤ New ➤ New File...** from the menu.

4. From the Mac OS X/Cocoa section, select Objective-C class, as illustrated in Figure 2–12, and click Next.

5. On the following screen, enter EquationEntryViewController for Class and select or type NSViewController as the superclass so it matches Figure 2–13. Click Next.

6. Make sure the Views group and the Graphique target are selected, and click Create.

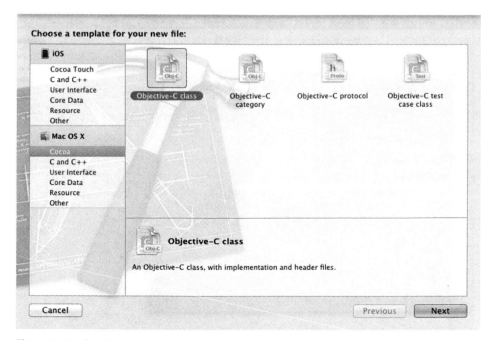

Figure 2-12. *Creating a new Objective-C class for the Equation Entry View controller*

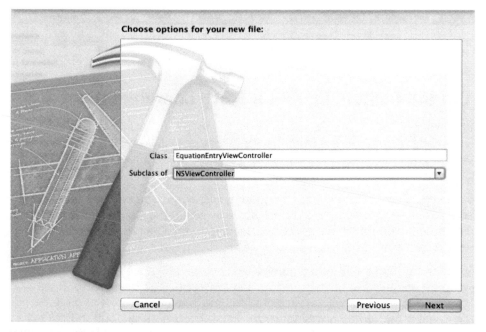

Figure 2-13. *Making the new view a subclass of* NSViewController

This process should have generated three files: EquationEntryViewController.h, EquationEntryViewController.m, and EquationEntryViewController.xib, as illustrated in Figure 2–14.

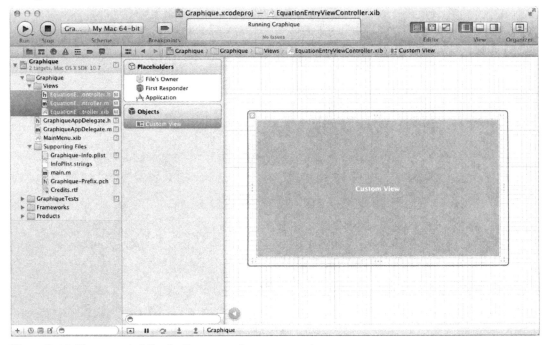

Figure 2–14. *The generated files for the new custom component*

Laying Out the Custom Equation Entry Component

Select EquationEntryViewController.xib to begin laying out its view. You can start dragging user interface components from the library onto it just like you did in the previous section. The only difference here is that you have isolated your custom component so you need to worry only about it and nothing else. This is code isolation.

If you select the File's Owner and look in the Identity inspector, you can see that the owner is the EquationEntryViewController class. Now select the Connections inspector tab and notice how the controller's view outlet is linked to the Custom View object. This is how the controller knows how to display its view.

Now let's finish laying things out. Add a label, a text field, and a push button. Change the label text to **y=** and the title on the push button to **Graph**. Size the view to fit, as shown in Figure 2–15. The user will be expected to type in a function of x and hit the Graph button in order for it to do anything useful. Handling events like button presses will be the focus of the next chapter. For now, we're simply planning and laying out our user interface.

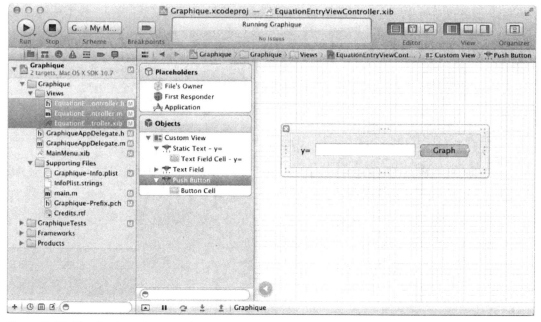

Figure 2–15. *The simple custom equation entry component*

A Primer on Automatic Reference Counting

Before moving on, you should understand what Automatic Reference Counting (ARC) is and what it means to Graphique. Introduced in Xcode 4.2, ARC eases some of the programming burden around memory management. Before the appearance of ARC, programmers dealt with a flood of program crashes and other issues related to how they handled allocating, retaining, releasing, and deallocating objects. Objective-C uses a retention count mechanism for determining whether to deallocate the memory for a given object, so the typical usage pattern for an object is as follows:

1. Allocate the object in memory.

2. Increment its retention count by sending it a `retain` message.

3. When done using the object, decrement its retention count by sending it a `release` message.

4. If the retention count reaches zero, deallocate the object.

Though the pattern is straightforward, its execution often isn't. Several parts of the code in an application, including framework code not visible to the programmer, can retain objects. Programmers can neglect to send proper `retain` and `release` messages or can incorrectly assume that objects are being retained when they aren't, or vice versa. Also, objects can create cyclical retention graphs, preventing proper releases from occurring.

When an object doesn't receive enough `release` messages to decrement its retention count to zero, it's never deallocated, and memory leaks. When an object is used after its retention count reaches zero, the object has been deallocated and no longer owns that memory, causing the application to crash.

ARC wrests the burden of memory management from programmers and gives it instead to the compiler. At compile time, ARC determines the proper places to insert `retain` and `release` messages so that memory for all objects is properly managed. If you, as a programmer, try to sneak your own `retain` or `release` calls into your code, ARC refuses to compile your code until you remove those calls.

One other aspect of memory management you should understand: the difference between strong pointers and weak pointers. Strong pointers are retained, whereas weak pointers aren't. You'll see in the Graphique code throughout the book both types of pointers. Use weak pointers when you don't need to retain an object, usually because the object's lifetime exceeds the lifetime of the object using it, and when retaining it could cause a cyclical retention graph.

For more information on ARC, see its documentation at `http://clang.llvm.org/docs/AutomaticReferenceCounting.html`.

Using IBOutlet

Of course, we've now created a custom component, but we haven't used it anywhere, so it would never show if we ran the application. To use it, we simply need to add it to the right split view. The problem is that our application code currently has no knowledge of the split views because they were only defined in Interface Builder. We need a way to let Interface Builder feed this information into our code. Enter IBOutlet!

IBOutlet is a marker that has no runtime behavior, but it gives a way for Xcode to link user interface components to objects. We illustrate how to do this by linking the two split views we created in the previous section to objects in the code. This is a two-step process:

1. Define the attribute that will hold a pointer to the user interface component.

2. Link the widget to the attribute.

Open `GraphiqueAppDelegate.h`. Declare two new attributes of type `NSSplitView` and define them as properties just like you would do with any other non-UI property. Only this time, we add the `IBOutlet` attribute to the `@property` directive, as shown in Listing 2–1, to let Xcode know that they are meant for Interface Builder to see them.

Listing 2–1. *GraphiqueAppDelegate.h*

```
#import <Cocoa/Cocoa.h>

@interface GraphiqueAppDelegate : NSObject <NSApplicationDelegate>

@property (strong) IBOutlet NSWindow *window;
@property (weak) IBOutlet NSSplitView *horizontalSplitView;
@property (weak) IBOutlet NSSplitView *verticalSplitView;

@end
```

Now open GraphiqueApplicationDelegate.m to automatically generate the property accessors for the two new properties with the @synthesize directive:

```
@synthesize horizontalSplitView;
@synthesize verticalSplitView;
```

Now you are ready for the second step. Open MainMenu.xib and expand the Window - Graphique tree in the Document Outline to be able to see both split views. Select the Graphique App Delegate object and Ctrl+drag to the horizontal split view (the highest in the hierarchy). Let go of the mouse button and select horizontalSplitView. Do the same for the verticalSplitView instance, connecting it to the other split view. This step links the split views to the appropriate attributes in the GraphiqueAppDelegate class. Any time you access these attributes in your code, you will indeed be referring to the UI component you laid out in Interface Builder.

Hooking Up the New Component to the Application

Now that our code knows how to refer to the split views, you can add your custom equation entry component to the main window. Open GraphiqueAppDelegate.h and add a property for the equation entry component, as shown in Listing 2–2.

Listing 2–2. *Adding an Equation Entry Component Property*

```
#import <Cocoa/Cocoa.h>

@class EquationEntryViewController;

@interface GraphiqueAppDelegate : NSObject <NSApplicationDelegate>

@property (strong) IBOutlet NSWindow *window;
@property (weak) IBOutlet NSSplitView *horizontalSplitView;
@property (weak) IBOutlet NSSplitView *verticalSplitView;
@property (strong) EquationEntryViewController *equationEntryViewController;

@end
```

Open GraphiqueAppDelegate.m and add an import for EquationEntryViewController.h:

```
#import "EquationEntryViewController.h"
```

Remove the three NSLog calls that you added in Chapter 1, leaving the methods that contained them. Add a @synthesize directive for the equationEntryViewController property. Now, go to the applicationDidFinishLaunching: method, allocate the instance of the custom view controller, and indicate that you want it to be initialized from the XIB file using the initWithNibName:bundle: method:

```
self.equationEntryViewController = [[EquationEntryViewController alloc]
initWithNibName:@"EquationEntryViewController" bundle:nil];
```

> **NOTE:** Remember that XIB files and NIB files are two different file formats to represent the same thing. NIBs were here first, and therefore you will notice that method names always refer to NIBs. Whenever they do, it's usually OK to specify a XIB file.

Now that we have an initialized controller, we can add it to the second spot in the vertical split view:

```
[self.verticalSplitView replaceSubview:[[self.verticalSplitView subviews]
objectAtIndex:1] with:equationEntryViewController.view];
```

> **NOTE:** The subviews of each split view are organized in left-to-right order for vertical split views and top-to-bottom order for the horizontal split views. The first subview is at index zero.

The complete method should look like Listing 2–3.

Listing 2–3. *Adding the Equation Entry View to the Application*

```
- (void)applicationDidFinishLaunching:(NSNotification *)aNotification
{
    self.equationEntryViewController = [[EquationEntryViewController alloc]
initWithNibName:@"EquationEntryViewController" bundle:nil];
    [self.verticalSplitView replaceSubview:[[self.verticalSplitView subviews]
objectAtIndex:1] with:equationEntryViewController.view]];
}
```

Launch the application, and you should see something like Figure 2–16.

Figure 2–16. *The Graphique application with a custom equation entry component*

Resizing the Views Automatically

Split views can be resized by dragging the separator. Resize the vertical split pane, and notice how the equation editor just slides to follow the separator. This is a reasonable behavior, but it is not optimum because we are wasting space. When resizing a split pane, users usually expect one side to contract and the other side to expand to fill the available space if possible. Select `EquationEntryViewController.xib`, select the Text Field, and open the Size inspector, as illustrated in Figure 2–17.

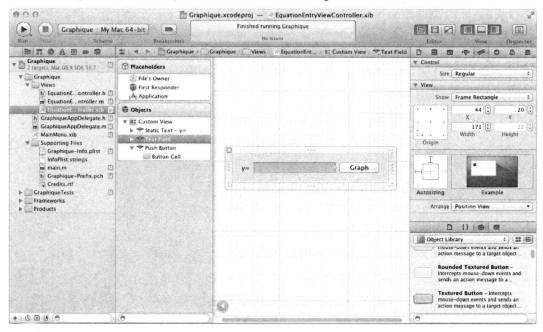

Figure 2–17. *The text field default size settings*

The Size inspector has two sections—Control and View—that allow you to specify the size of the component. In the Control section, you can pick a smaller size for each control. You have the choice among Regular, Small, or Mini. This is particularly useful if you have limited room on your user interface. The View section is of particular importance to manage automatic component resizing.

The autosizing schema shows how the component behaves as its parent component changes size. The schema shows two nested rectangles. The inner rectangle represents the selected component, the Text Field component in this case. The outer rectangle represents the parent component. Inside the inner component are two two-headed arrows, one running vertically and one running horizontally. If an arrow is enabled, this component resizes in that direction to expand or contract when the parent component changes size. The links between the outer rectangle and the inner rectangle are anchors. In this case, the Text Field component is anchored to the top-left corner of the parent component and is not set to resize. This means it will simply slide to follow the top-left corner of its parent component.

The inner-rectangle arrows are often referred to as *springs*, and earlier versions of Interface Builder depicted them as springs. The outer-rectangle anchors are often called *struts*. We use the terms *springs* and *struts* in this book.

The desired behavior is to have the label follow the left side of the parent, make the Graph button follow the right side of the parent, and have the Text Field component fill the available space in between. Since it makes no sense to expand vertically, we anchor all the components to the top boundary of the parent container.

Select the Label component, and set the autosizing schema to anchor to the top left with no resizing, as shown in Figure 2–18. It may already be set this way, so you may not have to make any changes.

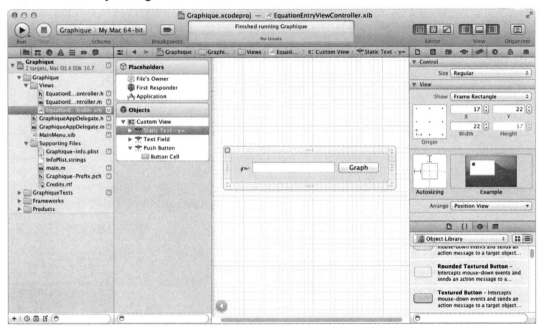

Figure 2–18. *Anchoring a component to the top-left corner*

Next, select the Graph button and anchor it to the top-right of its parent, as illustrated in Figure 2–19.

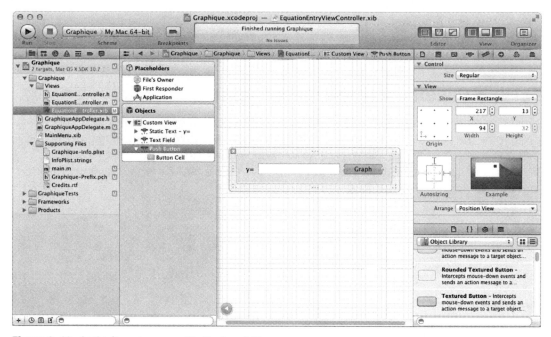

Figure 2–19. *Anchoring a component to the top-right corner*

Finally, select the Text Field component, and set its resizing strategy to expand horizontally to match Figure 2–20.

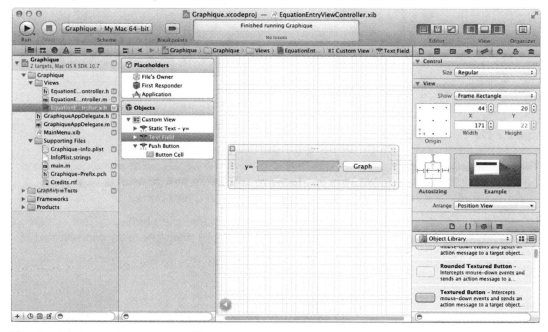

Figure 2–20. *Automatically resizing to fill the available horizontal space*

Launch the app and play around with the split pane separator. Notice how the equation editor resizes nicely to occupy the available space. If you size it too small, the display goes somewhat awry, but we'll fix that in Chapter 3.

Further Customizing the Components

Most Cocoa components can be customized via the Attributes inspector tab. To customize the text field in our custom view, select it and go to the Attributes inspector. In the Placeholder String field, type **2*x+1**, as shown in Figure 2–21, to have the text field display a sample equation to users so they'll have a hint for what they should type in that field.

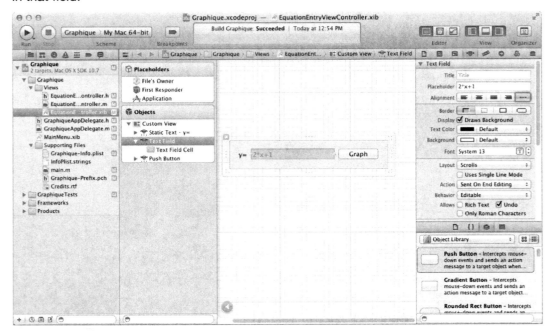

Figure 2–21. *Specifying placeholder text*

The placeholder string of a text field is text shown with a lighter color when nothing has been typed in the text field yet. It is used to give the user a hint of what is expected. Here, we want to show that the user is expected to type a function of x.

Launch the application again and see how the placeholder string behaves. It is shown before anything is typed, as illustrated in Figure 2–22, but disappears as soon as text is entered.

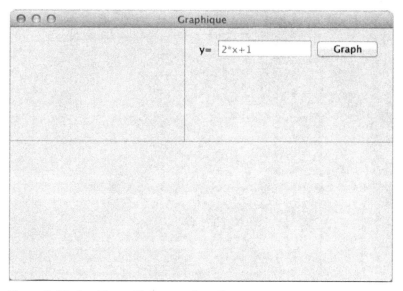

Figure 2–22. *Graphique with the equation editor*

Now you have a place for users to enter equations. Read the next section to add a place to display the results of an equation.

Creating the Graph Panel

We're stretching the truth a little when we call this next view a "graph" panel, because we're not yet ready to draw graphs in Graphique. Instead, we're going to create a view for displaying the equation's data as a table, with the domain in one column and the range in another. We also add a slider to allow people to adjust the domain interval that the table view displays. Once again, we're going to create a custom view but this time with two controls: the table view and the slider.

To begin, create a new class in the Views group, as you did in the previous section, called GraphTableViewController. As with the EquationEntryViewController class, make it an Objective-C class and a subclass of NSViewController. Xcode generates the three files you need: the header file, the implementation file, and the XIB or NIB file. Select GraphTableViewController.xib to open it in Interface Builder. You should see a view that says Custom View but is otherwise empty, as shown in Figure 2–23.

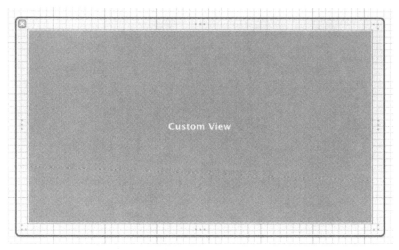

Figure 2–23. *The empty Graph View*

Adding the Horizontal Slider

That empty canvas begs for you to splash some art onto it, which you'll next do by dragging a Horizontal Slider object from the Object Library to the empty custom view. Drop it near the top of the view, using the helpful blue guides to position it, and make it span the width of the view. It should look like Figure 2–24.

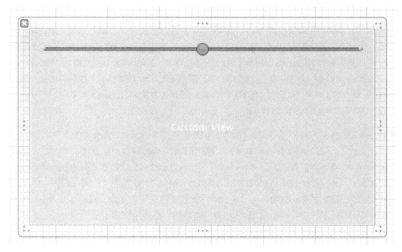

Figure 2–24. *The view with a Horizontal Slider object added*

We need to make some adjustments to the slider. First, we'll make the slider resize itself to span this view any time the view resizes, which happens when the user resizes the application window. With the horizontal slider selected, show the Size inspector. In the View section, find the Autosizing control and select the left, top, and right struts to anchor the slider to the left, top, and right of the view. Also, click the horizontal arrow inside the box (the *spring*) to make the slider stretch to fill the view. The Autosizing control should look like Figure 2–25.

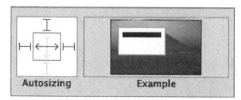

Figure 2–25. *The autosizing configured for the horizontal slider*

You also want to constrain the range of the horizontal slider to numbers that make sense for a domain interval. With the slider still selected, show the Attributes inspector, and in the Slider section, change the number of tick marks to 20. Set the minimum value to 0.10 and the maximum to 5.00, with the current set to 2.50. The Slider section should match Figure 2–26, and your view should look like Figure 2–27.

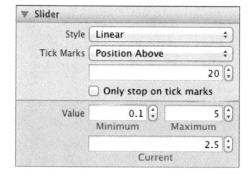

Figure 2–26. *Constraining the horizontal slider*

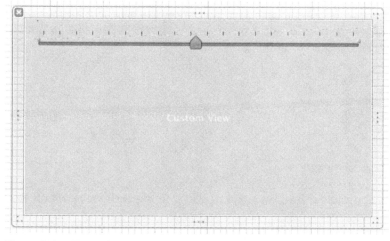

Figure 2–27. *The horizontal slider after applying the constraints*

With the slider in place and configured, we're halfway done creating the Graph View. In the next section, we add the table to complete the view.

Adding the Table View

Adding a table view to our custom view begins by dragging a Table View instance from the Object Library and dropping it on the view. Again, use the helpful blue lines to position and size it below the horizontal slider and to fill the rest of the view. Your view should look like Figure 2–28 when you're done.

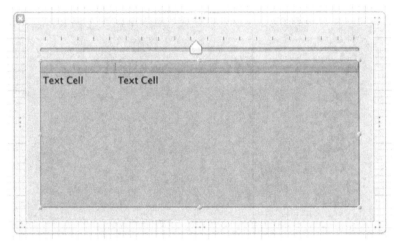

Figure 2–28. *The view after adding a table view*

The table looks perfectly positioned and sized now, but if the user were to resize the view by resizing the application window, the table would stay the same size and would no longer fill the part of the view allotted to it. To fix that, show the Size inspector, go to the Autosizing widget, and select the rop, left, bottom, and right struts, as well as both springs. The Autosizing widget should match Figure 2–29.

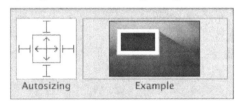

Figure 2–29. *The Autosizing settings for the table view*

Our custom view layout is complete. Next, we need to add it to the split view, which we do in the next section.

Adding the Graph Panel to the Application

To add the graph panel to the application, follow the pattern you used with the equation entry panel. This time, we want to swap it for the bottom view of the horizontal split view. Open GraphiqueAppDelegate.h and add a property for a GraphTableViewController instance, as shown in Listing 2–4.

Listing 2–4. *Adding a GraphTableViewController Instance*

```
#import <Cocoa/Cocoa.h>

@class EquationEntryViewController;
@class GraphTableViewController;

@interface GraphiqueAppDelegate : NSObject <NSApplicationDelegate>

@property (strong) IBOutlet NSWindow *window;
@property (weak) IBOutlet NSSplitView *horizontalSplitView;
@property (weak) IBOutlet NSSplitView *verticalSplitView;
@property (strong) EquationEntryViewController *equationEntryViewController;
@property (strong) GraphTableViewController *graphTableViewController;

@end
```

Go to GraphiqueAppDelegate.m, add an import statement for GraphTableViewController.h, and add a @synthesize directive for the graphTableViewController property. Edit the applicationDidFinishLaunching: method to create a GraphTableViewController instance and swap it for the horizontal split view's bottom view. The method should look like Listing 2–5.

Listing 2–5. *Adding the Graph Table View to the Application*

```
- (void)applicationDidFinishLaunching:(NSNotification *)aNotification
{
  self.equationEntryViewController = [[EquationEntryViewController alloc]
initWithNibName:@"EquationEntryViewController" bundle:nil];
  [self.verticalSplitView replaceSubview:[[self.verticalSplitView subviews]
objectAtIndex:1] with:equationEntryViewController.view];

  self.graphTableViewController = [[GraphTableViewController alloc]
initWithNibName:@"GraphTableViewController" bundle:nil];
  [self.horizontalSplitView replaceSubview:[[self.horizontalSplitView subviews]
objectAtIndex:1] with:graphTableViewController.view];
}
```

Build and run Graphique. You should see a window that looks like Figure 2–30. If you resize it, you should see the content in the custom views resize to fill their allotted spaces, as in Figure 2–31.

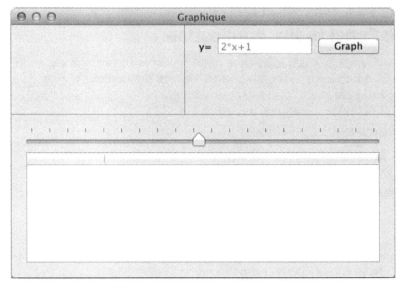

Figure 2–30. *Graphique with the graph panel added*

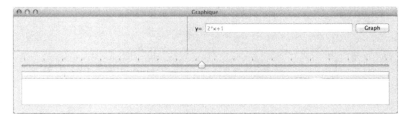

Figure 2–31. *Graphique after resizing the window*

The layout of the Graphique application is progressing. In the next section, we add the final panel, which shows the equations the user has already entered, to the split views.

Creating the Table of Recently Used Equations

The last major component of the application is the recently used equations. It provides a way for the user to get back to the equations that have been used in the past. We use this component to detail how to use the outline view, the Mac OS X implementation of a hierarchical tree view.

Just like we did for the other custom components, we create a new `NSViewController` subclass called `RecentlyUsedEquationsViewController`. This process creates the three new files you've come to expect. Figure 2–32 shows what you should see in Xcode.

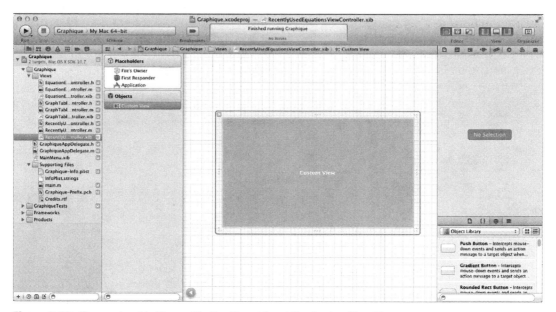

Figure 2–32. *The newly added* `RecentlyUsedEquationsViewController` *files*

Open `RecentlyUsedEquationsViewController.xib` and add an Outline View component from the standard component library. Since we don't want to see the header, highlight the Outline View object, and deselect the Headers check box on the Attributes inspector. We also want to see only one column—the hierarchy—so change the number of Columns to one, as shown in Figure 2–33.

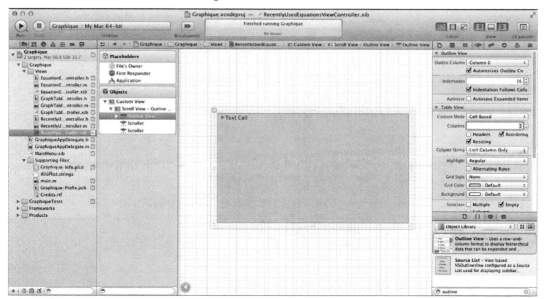

Figure 2–33. `RecentlyUsedEquationsViewController` *with an* `NSOutlineView` *added*

Select the Outline View component's parent, the Scroll View component right above it in the Document Outline. Open the Size inspector and select all the springs and struts so that the outline view fills the view, even after resizing, as you did with the graph table view, as shown in Figure 2–34.

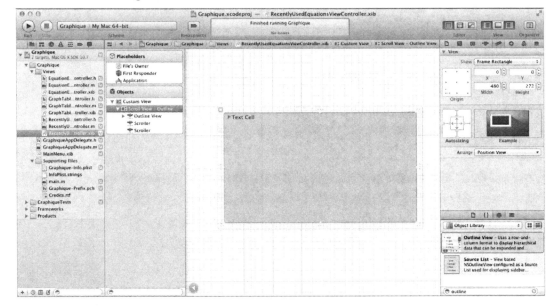

Figure 2–34. *The Outline View component set to fill its parent view*

As you did for the other two views you added, open GraphiqueAppDelegate.h and add a property for the recently used equations component, as shown in Listing 2–6.

Listing 2–6. *Adding a Recently Used Equations Property*

```
#import <Cocoa/Cocoa.h>

@class EquationEntryViewController;
@class GraphTableViewController;
@class RecentlyUsedEquationsViewController;

@interface GraphiqueAppDelegate : NSObject <NSApplicationDelegate>

@property (strong) IBOutlet NSWindow *window;
@property (weak) IBOutlet NSSplitView *horizontalSplitView;
@property (weak) IBOutlet NSSplitView *verticalSplitView;
@property (strong) EquationEntryViewController *equationEntryViewController;
@property (strong) GraphTableViewController *graphTableViewController;
@property (strong) RecentlyUsedEquationsViewController
*recentlyUsedEquationsViewController;

@end
```

Complete the task by opening GraphiqueAppDelegate.m to attach the new component to the user interface. Import RecentlyUsedEquationsViewController.h, add the

@synthesize directive for recentlyUsedEquationsViewController, and edit the applicationDidFinishLaunching: method to look like Listing 2–7.

Listing 2–7. *Adding the Recently Used Equations View to the Application*

```
- (void)applicationDidFinishLaunching:(NSNotification *)aNotification
{
  self.equationEntryViewController = [[EquationEntryViewController alloc]
initWithNibName:@"EquationEntryViewController" bundle:nil];
  [self.verticalSplitView replaceSubview:[[self.verticalSplitView subviews]
objectAtIndex:1] with:equationEntryViewController.view];

  self.graphTableViewController = [[GraphTableViewController alloc]
initWithNibName:@"GraphTableViewController" bundle:nil];
  [self.horizontalSplitView replaceSubview:[[self.horizontalSplitView subviews]
objectAtIndex:1] with:graphTableViewController.view];

  self.recentlyUsedEquationsViewController = [[RecentlyUsedEquationsViewController
alloc] initWithNibName:@"RecentlyUsedEquationsViewController" bundle:nil];
  [self.verticalSplitView replaceSubview:[[self.verticalSplitView subviews]
objectAtIndex:0] with:recentlyUsedEquationsViewController.view];
}
```

Outline views, just like table views, rely on a data source to provide data to display. Data sources for outline views have to comply with the NSOutlineViewDataSource protocol, which provides methods for describing the data to display. In this chapter, we want to show only how to display sample data, and we do not concern ourselves with how to retrieve it dynamically.

Our implementation will rely on two types of objects to represent the hierarchy. An equation node will represent one of the recently used equations, and a group node will be a node containing other nodes (think of it as a folder). We aren't yet defining the grouping criteria; this will come later when we put real data into the component.

Create a new class called EquationItem, a subclass of NSObject, with a method to return its text representation, as shown in Listing 2–8 and Listing 2–9.

Listing 2–8. *EquationItem.h*

```
#import <Foundation/Foundation.h>

@interface EquationItem : NSObject

- (NSString *)text;

@end
```

Listing 2–9. *EquationItem.m*

```
#import "EquationItem.h"

@implementation EquationItem

- (NSString *)text
{
    return @"2*x+4";
}
```

```
- (NSInteger)numberOfChildren
{
    return 0;
}
```

@end

For now, the equation is hard-coded, and an equation has no children. It is a leaf node in our hierarchy.

Now, create the GroupItem class to represent a group node, as shown in Listing 2–10 and Listing 2–11.

Listing 2–10. *GroupItem.h*

```
#import <Foundation/Foundation.h>

@interface GroupItem : NSObject
{
@private
  NSString *name;
  NSMutableArray *children;
}

@property (nonatomic, retain) NSString *name;

- (NSInteger)numberOfChildren;
- (id)childAtIndex:(NSUInteger)n;
- (NSString *)text;

- (void)addChild:(id)childNode;

@end
```

Listing 2–11. *GroupItem.m*

```
#import "GroupItem.h"

@implementation GroupItem

@synthesize name;

- (id)init
{
  self = [super init];
  if (self)
  {
    children = [[NSMutableArray alloc] init];
  }
  return self;
}

- (void)addChild:(id)childNode
{
  [children addObject:childNode];
}
```

```
- (NSInteger)numberOfChildren
{
  return children.count;
}

- (id)childAtIndex:(NSUInteger)n
{
  return [children objectAtIndex:n];
}

- (NSString *)text
{
  return name;
}

@end
```

Let's take a minute to go over the group item implementation. Just like the equation item, the group item has a method called numberOfChildren, but in this instance it relies on the array of children to evaluate its result. The array of children defined in the header file contains a list of subitems in the hierarchy. We build our hierarchy by creating a root node and adding items to it.

Creating the Data Source

Now that we have a data structure to hold our hierarchy, we define the data source to hook up to the outline view. Open RecentlyUsedEquationsViewController.h and make it implement the NSOutlineViewDataSource protocol, as shown in Listing 2–12. We also add a group item that represents the root node, which is going to be an invisible node holding the hierarchy together.

Listing 2–12. *RecentlyUsedEquationsViewController.h Implementing the NSOutlineViewDataSource Protocol*

```
#import <Cocoa/Cocoa.h>

@class GroupItem;

@interface RecentlyUsedEquationsViewController : NSViewController
<NSOutlineViewDataSource>
{
@private
  GroupItem *rootItem;
}

@end
```

For the data source to work, four methods must be implemented. For each of these methods, a nil item value serves to represent the root of the hierarchy, which we will interpret as the root item.

The first method returns the number of children the specified method has. It has the following signature:

```
- (NSInteger)outlineView:(NSOutlineView *)outlineView numberOfChildrenOfItem:(id)item
```

The second method returns whether a given item can be expanded. Typically, this means the item has children. Its signature looks like this:

```
- (BOOL)outlineView:(NSOutlineView *)outlineView isItemExpandable:(id)item
```

The third method is responsible for returning the child of the given item at the specified index. It has this signature:

```
- (id)outlineView:(NSOutlineView *)outlineView child:(NSInteger)index ofItem:(id)item
```

Finally, the fourth method returns the text to display for the given item, in the specified column. In our case for the moment, we use only one column. It uses this signature:

```
- (id)outlineView:(NSOutlineView *)outlineView objectValueForTableColumn:(NSTableColumn *)tableColumn byItem:(id)item
```

Open RecentlyUsedEquationsViewController.m and edit it to match Listing 2–13.

Listing 2–13. *RecentlyUsedEquationsViewController.m Implementing the Data Source*

```objc
#import "RecentlyUsedEquationsViewController.h"
#import "GroupItem.h"
#import "EquationItem.h"

@implementation RecentlyUsedEquationsViewController

- (id)initWithNibName:(NSString *)nibNameOrNil bundle:(NSBundle *)nibBundleOrNil
{
  self = [super initWithNibName:nibNameOrNil bundle:nibBundleOrNil];
  if (self)
  {
    rootItem = [[GroupItem alloc] init];

    for (int i = 0; i < 4; i++)
    {
      GroupItem *temp = [[GroupItem alloc] init];
      temp.name = [NSString stringWithFormat:@"Group %d", i + 1];

      for (int j = 0; j < 5; j++)
      {
        EquationItem *item = [[EquationItem alloc] init];
        [temp addChild:item];
      }
      [rootItem addChild:temp];
    }
  }
  return self;
}

- (NSInteger)outlineView:(NSOutlineView *)outlineView numberOfChildrenOfItem:(id)item
{
  return (item == nil) ? [rootItem numberOfChildren] : [item numberOfChildren];
}

- (BOOL)outlineView:(NSOutlineView *)outlineView isItemExpandable:(id)item
{
```

```
  return (item == nil) ? ([rootItem numberOfChildren] > 0) : ([item numberOfChildren] >
0);
}

- (id)outlineView:(NSOutlineView *)outlineView child:(NSInteger)index ofItem:(id)item
{
  if (item == nil)
  {
    return [rootItem childAtIndex:index];
  }
  else
  {
    return [(GroupItem *)item childAtIndex:index];
  }
}

- (id)outlineView:(NSOutlineView *)outlineView objectValueForTableColumn:(NSTableColumn
*)tableColumn byItem:(id)item
{
  return (item == nil) ? @"" : [item text];
}

@end
```

In the initWithNibName:bundle: method, we initialize our data source by hard-coding all the data. The code creates the root item and creates four groups in it named Group1, Group2, Group3, and Group4. Inside each group, we create five equations. Note that in each data source method, we use rootItem everywhere the item is nil. This concludes the implementation of our data source.

Displaying the Data

The last step in getting the recently used equations view to work is to tell the outline view which data source it is supposed to use. To set this up, open RecentlyUsedEquationsViewController.xib, select the Outline View object, and go to the Connections inspector. Ctrl+drag the dataSource connection to the File's Owner placeholder, as illustrated in Figure 2–35.

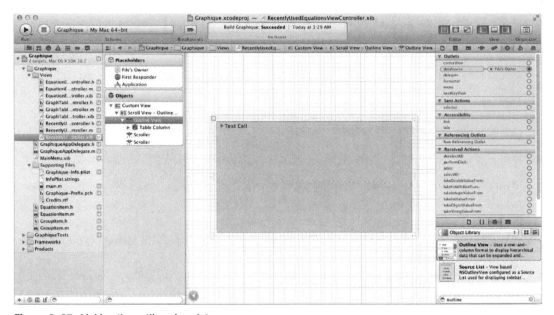

Figure 2–35. *Linking the outline view data source*

By default, the File's Owner of a `.XIB` file is the corresponding `.m` file. You've just linked the Outline View object's data source to the controller instance. Launch the application to make sure it all looks right. Figure 2–36 shows what you should expect.

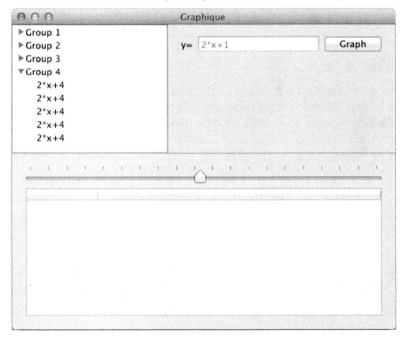

Figure 2–36. *The running outline view with sample data*

The split views are all filled with custom views. Many Mac OS X applications, however, offer a toolbar across the tops of their windows to provide quick access to frequently used operations. In the next section, we add a toolbar to Graphique.

Adding a Toolbar

Many applications offer a variety of tools across the top of the window, right below the title bar, represented by icons. These tools typically offer frequently used functions within the application, and providing them in the toolbar gives users quick access. Sometimes they duplicate functions that the menu provides but not always. In this section, we add a toolbar to Graphique. We don't change the stock toolbar icons yet, but we'll make changes during the course of the book as we unroll functionality for Graphique.

To add a toolbar to Graphique, select MainMenu.xib in Xcode to open it in the integrated Interface Builder, and then drag a Toolbar instance from the Object Library to the Graphique window. Drop it anywhere in the window, and it will magically jump to the top of the window and attach itself just below the title bar. Your window should look like Figure 2–37.

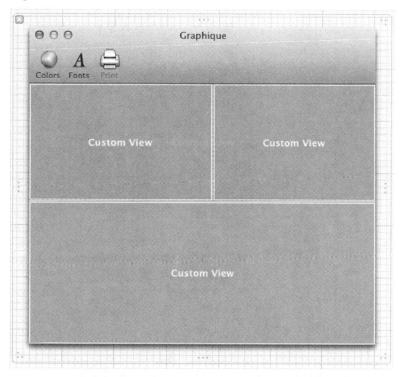

Figure 2–37. *The Graphique window in Interface Builder after adding a toolbar*

The stock toolbar comes with three tools: Colors, Fonts, and Print. If you build and run the application, you can see that clicking Colors brings up the standard color picker dialog, clicking Fonts brings up the standard font selection dialog, and clicking Print does nothing, because it's disabled. At this point, we're happy with the results. As we work through the book, we'll make the toolbar actually useful.

Summary

As you worked through this chapter, you used standard Mac OS X widgets and combined them to create an attractive, resizable, and functional user interface for the Graphique application. You saw how to combine standard widgets into custom views and how to display multiple custom views in a single window using split views. You learned about table views, outline views, struts and springs, placeholder text, and other Interface Builder topics. You built a great user interface.

Looks only go so far, however. At this point, Graphique looks good and resizes properly, and you can tell it to graph equations by entering them and clicking the Graph button. Like too many teenagers, however, Graphique ignores your requests and just slumps there on your screen, doing nothing. It's time to teach Graphique some manners and have it respond to user input—that's the subject of the next chapter.

Chapter **3**

Handling User Input

In the movie *The Sound of Music*, the governess Maria (played by Julie Andrews) teaches the Von Trapp children how to sing. In one scene, as she's introducing notes to the children, she teaches them a melody with note names that, while sounding good, has lyrics composed only of the names of notes: "Sol Do La Fa Mi Do Re...." One of the children, Brigitta, responds, "But it doesn't mean anything." Maria responds, "So we put in words." Right now, Graphique doesn't mean anything. It's just a user interface. In this chapter, we put in words. We put in the functionality that makes Graphique mean something. By the end of this chapter, Graphique will look like Figure 3–1. It will allow users to enter equations and graph them textually. It will be a functional application.

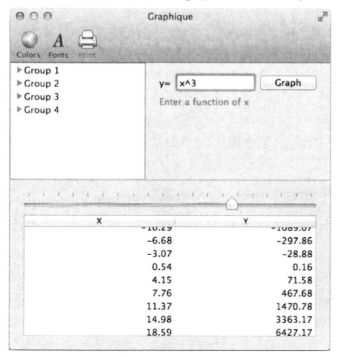

Figure 3–1. *The Graphique application at the end of this chapter*

Resizing the Views

Some people like their windows big, and some like them small. Some users have 30"
cinema displays, and some work from 11" notebook screens. Sometimes people will
want to see only the graph and hide the recent equations and the equation editor.
Sometimes people will want to drag the split views around and resize the entire
Graphique window. Maybe some people will want Graphique to take over their entire
desktops. You can control and customize the resizing behavior of Graphique's window
and views to improve how the user interacts with the application. In this section, you
learn how to do that.

Resizing the Window

Open MainMenu.xib in Xcode and select the Graphique window. Show the Attributes
inspector to see ways you can control the Graphique window's appearance and sizing
capability. The Attributes inspector should match Figure 3–2.

You can see a slew of options, but the ones we focus on here are the Resize check box
and the Full Screen drop-down, so locate those in the Attributes inspector. The Resize
check box is currently checked. Uncheck that and run Graphique. The Graphique
window looks as it did before, but as you move the mouse to the window sides or
corners, you see that the mouse pointer no longer turns into a resizing arrow, and you
can't resize the window. We obviously don't want to constrain our users to a single
window size, so quit Graphique and recheck the Resize check box.

The other option we want to look at, Full Screen, is currently set to Unsupported. Full
Screen support is new with Lion, but applications must explicitly specify this option to
gain support for it. When you run Graphique, you see no Full Screen control in the
upper-right corner of the window. Change this setting to Primary Window and run
Graphique. You see that now the Graphique window has the Full Screen control in its
upper right, which looks like two opposing arrows pointing northeast and southwest, as
shown in Figure 3–3. Click this button to make Graphique fill your screen. We'll leave
this setting so users can do the same when they run Graphique.

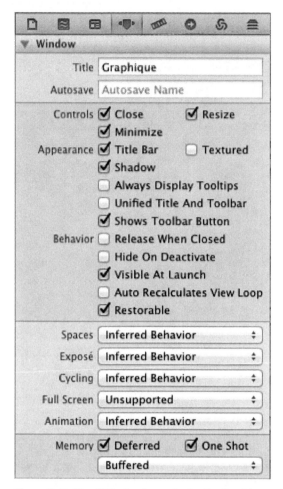

Figure 3–2. *The Attributes inspector for the Graphique window*

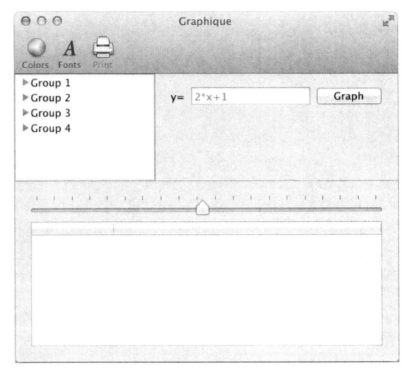

Figure 3–3. *The Graphique window with Full Screen support*

Constraining the Split View Sizes

As the Graphique application currently stands, users can resize the split views to dimensions that don't make sense. They can, for example, size the Equation Entry View so small that the text field and button no longer fit. Using the NSSplitViewDelegate protocol, you can control the minimum size of your split views and also whether double-clicking the splitter will collapse the view.

Constraining the Minimum Size

NSSplitViewDelegate has two methods for controlling the size of its views: splitView:constrainMinCoordinate:ofSubviewAt: and splitView:constrainMaxCoordinate:ofSubviewAt:. These methods receive the index of the view to the left of the divider, in the case of a vertical split view, or the index of the view above the divider, in the case of a horizontal split view. In your implementation of these methods, you return a float value that represents the minimum or maximum proposed value for the width or height of the view, as appropriate. For vertical split views, you return a width, and for horizontal split views, you return a height. For splitView:constrainMinCoordinate:ofSubviewAt:, you return a minimum, and for splitView:constrainMaxCoordinate:ofSubviewAt:, you return a maximum. To constrain the minimum width of a view to 100 pixels, for example, you'd add this method:

```
- (CGFloat)splitView:(NSSplitView *)splitView
constrainMinCoordinate:(CGFloat)proposedMinimumPosition
ofSubviewAt:(NSInteger)dividerIndex
{
  return 100.0;
}
```

To properly display the Equation Entry View, we must allow it to shrink only to 175 pixels. That allows 82 pixels for the Graph button, 30 pixels for the y= label, and 63 pixels for the text field and any padding.

Constraining the Maximum Size

Dragging a split view's divider prompts your delegate's method to be called to constrain its size. Because we want to set a minimum size for the right view (the Equation Entry View), we must prevent the divider from extending past a certain point. This means we must impose a maximum size constraint on the divider so that it does not go beyond its overall width minus the minimum width we want to impose on the Equation Entry View. To do this, make `RecentlyUsedEquationsViewController` the delegate for the vertical split view, and implement the `splitView:constrainMaxCoordinate:ofSubviewAt:` method to return a maximum size of the total width of the split view minus 175 pixels. Begin by declaring that `RecentlyUsedEquationsViewController` implements the `NSSplitViewDelegate` in `RecentlyUsedEquationsViewController.h`, as shown in Listing 3–1.

Listing 3–1. *RecentlyUsedEquationsViewController.h*

```
#import <Cocoa/Cocoa.h>

@class GroupItem.h;

@interface RecentlyUsedEquationsViewController : NSViewController
<NSOutlineViewDataSource, NSSplitViewDelegate>
{
@private
  GroupItem *rootItem;
}

@end
```

At the top of `RecentlyUsedEquationsViewController.m`, use #define to avoid using a magic number:

```
#define EQUATION_ENTRY_MIN_WIDTH 175.0
```

implement the `splitView:constrainMaxCoordinate:ofSubviewAt:` method to get the overall width of the split view, subtract 175 pixels, and return the result, as shown in Listing 3–2.

Listing 3–2. *Constraining the Maximum Width*

```
# pragma mark - NSSplitViewDelegate methods

- (CGFloat)splitView:(NSSplitView *)splitView
constrainMaxCoordinate:(CGFloat)proposedMinimumPosition
ofSubviewAt:(NSInteger)dividerIndex
{
  return splitView.frame.size.width - EQUATION_ENTRY_MIN_WIDTH;
}
```

Finally, go to GraphiqueAppDelegate.m, find where you create the RecentlyUsedEquationsViewController instance in the applicationDidFinishLaunching: method, and set the instance as the delegate for the vertical split view, as in Listing 3–3.

Listing 3–3. *Setting the RecentlyUsedEquationsViewController Instance as the Vertical Split View Delegate*

```
recentlyUsedEquationsViewController = [[RecentlyUsedEquationsViewController alloc]
initWithNibName:@"RecentlyUsedEquationsViewController" bundle:nil];
[self.verticalSplitView replaceSubview:[[self.verticalSplitView subviews]
objectAtIndex:0] with:[recentlyUsedEquationsViewController view]];
self.verticalSplitView.delegate = recentlyUsedEquationsViewController;
```

Run Graphique and drag the vertical divider left and right. You find that you can drag it only so far to the right before it stops, as shown in Figure 3–4, leaving enough room to render the Equation Entry View's label, text view, and button.

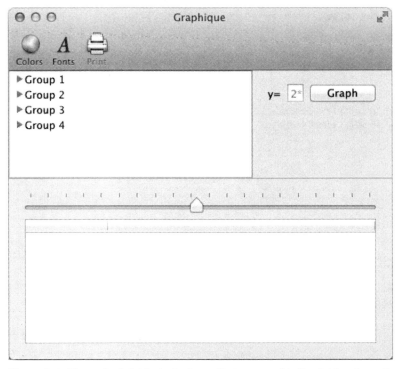

Figure 3–4. *The vertical divider in the top split view moved to the right as far as it will go*

Just as you're ready to check this item off your task list, however, you try resizing the window and discover that you can shrink the window smaller than 175 pixels wide, and the Equation Entry View gets crunched. The splitView:constrainMaxCoordinate:ofSubviewAt: method is called in response to moving the split view divider, not when resizing the window. What you must do is constrain the width of the window, which you learn how to do next.

Constraining the Window Size

To constrain the minimum overall window size and preserve the width of the Equation Entry View, you must do two things:

1. Constrain the window size.

2. Implement the splitView:resizeSubviewsWithOldSize: from NSSplitViewDelegate.

To address the first item, open MainMenu.xib, select Window – Graphique, and open the Size inspector. Check the box beside Minimum Size, and enter 175 for width and 200 for height, as shown in Figure 3–5.

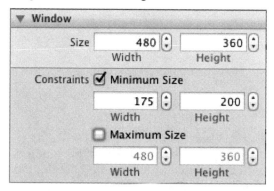

Figure 3–5. *Constraining the minimum size of the window*

This will set the minimum size of the window's content, ignoring any borders or other chrome, to 175 pixels wide and 200 pixels tall.

If you build and run Graphique now, however, you see that the minimum size of the window is constrained but that the split view resizes proportionally and the Equation Entry View becomes too narrow, as shown in Figure 3–6.

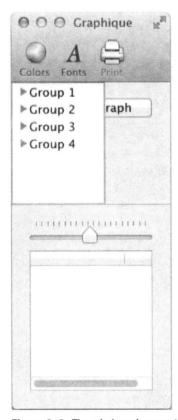

Figure 3–6. *The window size constrained but the Equation Entry View still too narrow*

When a split view resizes, it calls its delegate's `splitView:resizeSubviewsWithOldSize:` method, passing the size of the split view as it was before it was resized. In this method, you should adjust the sizes of the subviews inside the split view, taking into account the divider width. For our algorithm, we take the following approach:

- The Equation Entry View must be 175 pixels wide, less the divider width.

- As the window resizes, the Recent Equations View should stay the same size, and the Equation Entry View should grow or shrink.

- The Recent Equations View should shrink if it must to accommodate the Equation Entry View.

- We should try to make the Recent Equations View at least 100 pixels wide, as afforded by the window size and the Equation Entry View, unless it's been collapsed to zero width.

To accomplish this, add a #define for the preferred minimum width of the recently used equations view:

```
#define PREFERRED_RECENT_EQUATIONS_MIN_WIDTH 100.0
```

Next, add the code in Listing 3–4 to RecentlyUsedEquationsViewController.m.

Listing 3–4. *splitView:resizeSubviewsWithOldSize:*

```
- (void)splitView:(NSSplitView *)splitView resizeSubviewsWithOldSize:(NSSize)oldSize
{
  // Get the new frame of the split view
  NSSize size = splitView.bounds.size;

  // Get the divider width
  CGFloat dividerWidth = splitView.dividerThickness;

  // Get the frames of the recently used equations panel and the equation entry panel
  NSArray *views = splitView.subviews;
  NSRect recentlyUsed = [[views objectAtIndex:0] frame];
  NSRect equationEntry = [[views objectAtIndex:1] frame];

  // Set the widths
  // Sizing strategy:
  // 1) equation entry must be a minimum of 175 pixels minus the divider width
  // 2) recently used will stay at its current size, unless it's less than 100 pixels
wide
  // 3) If recently used is less than 100 pixels, grow it as much as possible until it
reaches 100
  float totalFrameWidth = size.width - dividerWidth;

  // Set recently used to the desired size (at least 100 pixels wide), or keep at zero
  // if it was collapsed
  recentlyUsed.size.width = recentlyUsed.size.width == 0 ? 0 :
MAX(PREFERRED_RECENT_EQUATIONS_MIN_WIDTH, recentlyUsed.size.width);

  // Calculate the size of the equation entry based on the recently used width
  equationEntry.size.width = MAX((EQUATION_ENTRY_MIN_WIDTH - dividerWidth),
(totalFrameWidth - recentlyUsed.size.width));

  // Now that the equation entry is set, recalculate the recently used
  recentlyUsed.size.width = totalFrameWidth - equationEntry.size.width;

  // Set the x location of the equation entry
  equationEntry.origin.x = recentlyUsed.size.width + dividerWidth;

  // Set the widths
  [[views objectAtIndex:0] setFrame:recentlyUsed];
  [[views objectAtIndex:1] setFrame:equationEntry];
}
```

Read through this method and its comments to understand what it's doing. This method gets the overall new size of the split view, calculates the sizes of the two views (the Equation Entry View and the Recent Equations View) according to the earlier rules, and sets the sizes into the views. Build and run Graphique and resize the window. You should see that you can stretch the window, which stretches the Equation Entry View, as shown in Figure 3–7. You can shrink the window, which should shrink the Equation Entry View and, eventually, the Recent Equations View, as shown in Figure 3–8. Finally, you should be able to stretch the window again and see that the Recent Equations View grows to 100 pixels (if it hasn't been collapsed to zero width) and then stops expanding, as shown in Figure 3–9.

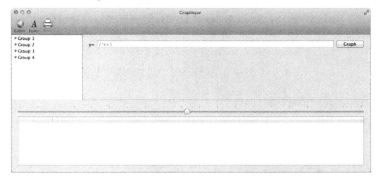

Figure 3–7. *Resizing Graphique stretches the Equation Entry View*

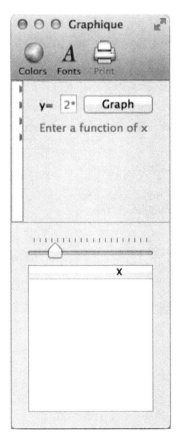

Figure 3–8. *Graphique with the Recent Equations View shrunk*

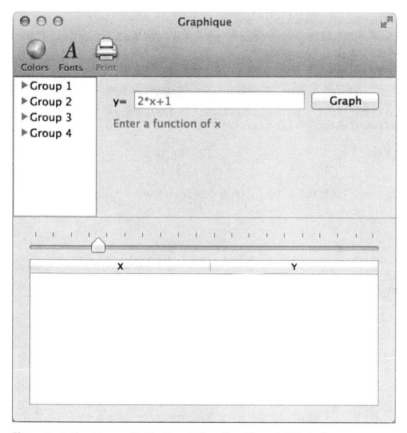

Figure 3–9. *Graphique with the Recent Equations View at 100 pixels*

Collapsing a Subview

Before we move on from handling user interaction with our split views, we want to add one more touch: if the user double-clicks the vertical divider between the Recent Equations View and the Equation Entry View, we hide (or collapse) the Recent Equations View. To do this, we implement two methods from NSSplitViewDelegate:

- splitView:canCollapseSubview: returns whether a particular split view can collapse

- splitView:shouldCollapseSubview:forDoubleClickOnDividerAtIndex: is called when the user double-clicks a divider

When the user double-clicks a divider, splitView:shouldCollapseSubview:forDoubleClickOnDividerAtIndex: is called twice, once for the first view and once for the second. You should either return NO for both or return YES for only one, because the result of returning YES for both is undefined. If you return YES for a view, and splitView:canCollapseSubview: also returns YES for that view, then the view will collapse and disappear.

In our implementation for these methods, which we place in
RecentlyUsedEquationsViewController.m, we return YES if the specified subview is the
Recent Equations View. Add the code from Listing 3–5 to
RecentlyUsedEquationsViewController.m.

Listing 3–5. *NSSplitViewDelegate Methods to Allow Collapsing the Recent Equations View*

```
- (BOOL)splitView:(NSSplitView *)splitView shouldCollapseSubview:(NSView *)subview
forDoubleClickOnDividerAtIndex:(NSInteger)dividerIndex
{
  return subview == self.view;
}

- (BOOL)splitView:(NSSplitView *)splitView canCollapseSubview:(NSView *)subview
{
  return subview == self.view;
}
```

Build and run Graphique, and double-click the vertical divider between the Recent
Equations View and the Equation Entry View, and the Recent Equations View should
disappear, as shown in Figure 3–10.

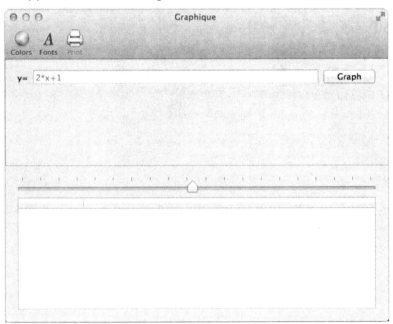

Figure 3–10. *Graphique with the Recent Equations View collapsed*

Handling window and split view resizing can be a chore to do properly, but if
implemented correctly, it can create a more friendly user experience.

Handling Button Presses

In the previous chapter, you learned how to use IBOutlet to attach Interface Builder UI components to variables in the code. In this section, we show you how to send events and call methods in your code from UI components.

The whole idea of the application is to graph an equation curve. So far, we've built the UI components that handle inputting the equation, but we haven't yet done anything with that equation. Let's change that. We want to be able to graph an equation when the user clicks the Graph button or when the user presses the Return key when the equation text field has the focus.

The Model-View-Controller Pattern

Apple, with the Cocoa framework, has done a great job staying consistent with the classic Model-View-Controller (MVC) design pattern. In essence, the MVC pattern states that responsibilities should be divided among three major components of the application. The model holds the data. The view displays the data. The controller makes decisions based on events. Events can be triggered by changes in the view (for example, the user clicks a button), but they could also be triggered by changes in the data or by other controllers in the application. Figure 3–11 shows how the components interact.

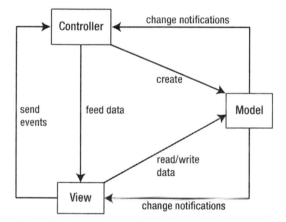

Figure 3–11. *The Model-View-Controller pattern*

Using IBAction

We are now ready to have our controller receive events. Methods that receive UI events all have a similar signature. Their return type must be IBAction, and they must have a single id argument. If you look closer at the documentation, you will notice that IBAction is actually defined as void. Similar to IBOutlet, IBAction is simply a marker that helps Interface Builder locate the method.

Since we want to receive an event from the Equation Entry View, the appropriate controller for receiving the event is EquationEntryViewController. Add a new method to that controller and call it equationEntered:. For now, we will make it print a statement in the Console when the event is activated. The method should like as shown here:

```
- (IBAction)equationEntered:(id)sender
{
  NSLog(@"Equation entered");
}
```

Don't forget to add - (IBAction)equationEntered:(id)sender; to EquationEntryViewController.h to make the method visible outside that class.

Next, open EquationEntryViewController.xib, select the Graph button, and open the Connections inspector. In the connections, you will notice the Sent Actions selector entry. Click the empty circle and drag to the File's Owner placeholder. A pop-up appears and shows your new method, as shown in Figure 3–12.

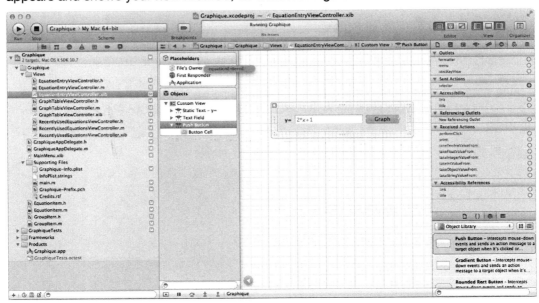

Figure 3–12. *Linking a button to its action*

Select the method and the link should be created, as illustrated in Figure 3–13.

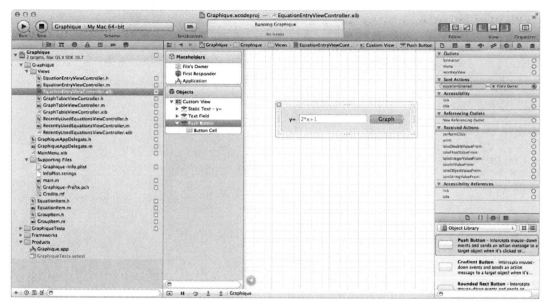

Figure 3–13. *The button linked to its action in the File's Owner*

Save and launch the app. Every time you click the Graph button, the equationEntered: method executes and prints a statement in the log console.

To wire the Return key to the same action, go back to EquationEntryViewController.xib in Xcode, select the text field and the Connections inspector, and link the text field's selector entry to the equationEntered: method so that pressing Return will fire the same notification.

> **NOTE:** Action methods require an argument typically named sender. The sender is, as its name implies, the component that has emitted the notification. In our case, sender is the button instance.

Creating the Model: Equation

When users enter equations, they do so in the form of strings of characters. To keep everything clean, it is usually best to create a data structure that will hold the data and also help access the data in a controlled manner. In our case, the data structure is an equation, so let's create a new subclass of NSObject called Equation with a convenience init: method that will accept a string in the form of an NSString. Create a new Objective-C class called Equation by selecting **File ➤ New ➤ New File...** from the menu. Be sure to make it a subclass of NSObject.

By creating a custom model class, we hide the fact that, for now at least, an equation is simply represented as a string. Find the code for the header file, Equation.h, in Listing 3–6, and the code for the implementation file, Equation.m, in Listing 3–7.

Listing 3–6. *Equation.h*

```
#import <Foundation/Foundation.h>

@interface Equation : NSObject
{
@private
  NSString *text;
}
@property (nonatomic, retain) NSString *text;

- (id)initWithString:(NSString*)string;

@end
```

Listing 3–7. *Equation.m* **with its Custom** *init* **Method**

```
#import "Equation.h"

@implementation Equation

@synthesize text;

- (id)initWithString:(NSString *)string
{
  self = [super init];
  if (self) {
    self.text = string;
  }
  return self;
}

- (NSString *)description
{
  return [NSString stringWithFormat:@"Equation [%@]", self.text];
}

@end
```

Our equation code would not be complete without a method to evaluate the equation for a given value. For simplicity, we assume that the variable is always named x in every equation. Edit Equation.h again to declare a new method:

```
- (float)evaluateForX:(float)x;
```

Implementing this method could be its own chapter. Between the use of grammars and semantic trees, there would be plenty to write. Here, we focus on implementing this method so that it is functional enough to help illustrate the rest of the examples in the book. Luckily for us, Mac OS X is based on the Unix operating system, which comes with the awk command. In this implementation, we leverage that command to do all the work. We don't dive into that code here; for further reading, review the NSTask documentation for launching programs from within your program.

Listing 3–8 shows Equation.h with the additional method, and Listing 3–9 shows Equation.m with the implementation of the method.

Listing 3–8. *Equation.h with the evaluateForX: Method*

```objc
#import <Foundation/Foundation.h>

@interface Equation : NSObject
{
@private
  NSString *text;
}
@property (nonatomic, retain) NSString *text;

- (id)initWithString:(NSString *)string;
- (float)evaluateForX:(float)x;

@end
```

Listing 3–9. *Equation.m with the evaluateForX: Method*

```objc
#import "Equation.h"

@implementation Equation

@synthesize text;

- (id)initWithString:(NSString*)string
{
  self = [super init];
  if (self) {
    self.text = string;
  }
  return self;
}

- (float)evaluateForX:(float)x
{
  NSTask *task = [[NSTask alloc] init];
  [task setLaunchPath: @"/usr/bin/awk"];

  NSArray *arguments = [NSArray arrayWithObjects: [NSString stringWithFormat:@"BEGIN {
x=%f ; print %@ ; }", x, self.text], nil];
  [task setArguments:arguments];

  NSPipe *pipe = [NSPipe pipe];
  [task setStandardOutput:pipe];

  NSFileHandle *file = [pipe fileHandleForReading];

  [task launch];

  NSData *data = [file readDataToEndOfFile];

  NSString *string = [[NSString alloc] initWithData:data encoding:
NSUTF8StringEncoding];
  float value = [string floatValue];
```

```
  return value;
}

- (NSString*)description
{
  return [NSString stringWithFormat:@"Equation [%@]", self.text];
}

@end
```

We pass the evaluateForX: method a float value for x, and it uses awk to calculate the value for y and return it as a float.

Communication Among Controllers

The Graphique application has three controllers at play: EquationEntryViewController, GraphTableViewController, and RecentlyUsedEquationsViewController. These three controllers must be able to exchange information to tie the application together. We tie them together through the application delegate. Because all three controllers are available as properties of the application delegate, any class that can get a hold of the application delegate can get a handle to any of the controllers. This setup is handy to facilitate the communication between controllers. It is the responsibility of GraphTableViewController to plot curves, for example, so once we have a new equation in our EquationEntryViewController instance, we want to tell our GraphTableViewController instance to draw it.

Add a new method called draw: to GraphTableViewController. For now, the method in GraphTableViewController.m should look this:

```
- (void)draw:(Equation *)equation
{
  NSLog(@"Draw equation: %@", equation);
  NSLog(@"value for x=4, y=%f", [equation evaluateForX:4.0]);
}
```

Later in this chapter, we'll substitute a real implementation. Make sure to also define this method in GraphTableViewController.h, as shown in Listing 3–10.

Listing 3–10. *GraphTableViewController.m Declaring the New Draw Method*

```
#import <Cocoa/Cocoa.h>
#import "Equation.h"

@interface GraphTableViewController : NSViewController

- (void)draw:(Equation *)equation;

@end
```

Declare a new IBOutlet property of type NSTextField in EquationEntryViewController.h. Call it textField and link it to the equation entry text field in Interface Builder as you learned how to do in the previous chapter. See Listing 3–11.

Listing 3–11. *Adding an outlet to* `EquationEntryViewController.h`

```
#import <Cocoa/Cocoa.h>

@interface EquationEntryViewController : NSViewController

@property (weak) IBOutlet NSTextField *textField;

- (IBAction)equationEntered:(id)sender;

@end
```

We want to call the `draw:` method from the equation entry controller, passing the `Equation` object created from the text in `textField`, when the Graph button is clicked. Edit the `equationEntered:` method in `EquationEntryViewController` to match Listing 3–12. Be sure to import `Equation.h`, `GraphiqueAppDelegate.h`, and `GraphTableViewController.h` for the names to resolve.

Listing 3–12. *The* `equationEntered:` *Method Communicating with* `GraphTableViewController`

```
- (IBAction)equationEntered:(id)sender
{
  GraphiqueAppDelegate *delegate = NSApplication.sharedApplication.delegate;

  Equation *equation = [[Equation alloc] initWithString:[self.textField stringValue]];
  [delegate.graphTableViewController draw:equation];
}
```

In this implementation, we simply get ahold of the application delegate and send the equation to the appropriate controller. The application delegate serves as a bridge between the controllers.

In Graphique, we now allow the user to enter an equation, and we tell the appropriate controller to draw the equation, but we don't know whether the equation we're going to draw is valid. In the next section, we validate the user input.

Validating Fields

Field validation is not necessary for your application to function, but your users will expect a polished user interface and will reward you for your efforts with App Store comments leading to extra sales. You can't have a nice slick user interface without implementing field validation. By validating the input, you limit the possibilities for things to go wrong, and therefore you improve your users' satisfaction. In this section, we show you two options for validating: after the user submits the data and while the user is entering the data.

Validating After Submitting

In this section, we implement validation of the equation entry field. The validation will be invoked as the user clicks the Graph button and will display an error message when things go wrong.

Writing a Validator

The first step of any validation process is to define the rules to validate. In our Graphique application, we use a small set of rules to keep things simple. Table 3–1 shows the possible errors and the codes we associate with them. Adding an error code with each error makes it easier for your users to report problems, especially if your application is translated into several languages.

Table 3–1. *The Graphique Error Codes*

Code	Description
100	Invalid character typed. Only x()+-*/^0123456789. are allowed.
101	Consecutive operators are not allowed.
102	Too many open parentheses.
103	Too many closed parentheses.

Since we've been diligent about creating a model to hold our data (in other words, the Equation class), we should put our validator code inside our model. After all, what object knows more about equations than the Equation class itself? Open Equation.h and declare the following method:

```
- (BOOL)validate:(NSError **)error;
```

We also must implement the validate: method in Equation.m. The validate: method must do three things:

1. Detect any errors

2. Assign an error code and error message to any detected errors

3. Produce an NSError object for a specified error code and error message

The third item, producing an NSError object for a specified error code and error message, represents a discrete piece of functionality and should be broken out to a separate method. We don't want code outside the Equation class to call this code, however, so we don't want to include this method in Equation's public interface. To achieve both these aims, putting this functionality into a method but hiding the method from outside the Equation class, we create a private category.

You can read more about categories in the Apple documentation at http://developer.apple.com/library/mac/#documentation/Cocoa/Conceptual/ObjectiveC/Chapters/ocCategories.html, but categories can be simply summed up as collections of methods that are added to a class at runtime. You could, for example, create a category that adds a method called romanNumeralValue: to NSNumber so that you can write code like this:

```
NSNumber *num = [NSNumber numberWithInt:2011];
NSLog(@"%@", [num romanNumeralValue]);
```

to get output like this:

```
2011-05-10 06:40:52.690 MMXI
```

In our case, we create a category containing a single method,
`produceError:withCode:andMessage:`, and we declare the category not in a separate
header file but at the top of `Equation.m` above this line:

`@implementation Equation`

This makes the method visible only for the `Equation` class, and we can call it just as if
we'd declared the method normally in `Equation.h`. Open `Equation.m` and add the code
shown in Listing 3–13. Note that we haven't shown the existing methods to save paper;
don't remove them!

Listing 3–13. *The Equation Validation Method and the Private Category*

```
@interface Equation ()
- (BOOL)produceError:(NSError**)error withCode:(NSInteger)code
andMessage:(NSString*)message;
@end

@implementation Equation

// The rest of the implementation code . . .

- (BOOL)validate:(NSError **)error
{
  // Validation rules
  // 1. Only digits, letters '.', 'x', '(', ')', '+' , '-' , '*', '/', '^', ' ' allowed
  // 2. There should be the same amount of closing and opening parentheses
  // 3. no two consecutive operators

  // Counters for '(' and ')'
  NSUInteger open = 0;
  NSUInteger close = 0;

  NSString *allowedCharacters = @"x()+-*/^0123456789. ";

  NSCharacterSet *cs = [NSCharacterSet
characterSetWithCharactersInString:allowedCharacters];
  NSCharacterSet *operators = [NSCharacterSet characterSetWithCharactersInString:@"+-
/*^"];

  unichar previous = 0;

  for(NSUInteger i=0; i<text.length; i++)
  {
    unichar c = [text characterAtIndex:i];
    if(![cs characterIsMember:c])
    {
      // Invalid character
```

```
        return [self produceError:error withCode:100 andMessage:[NSString
stringWithFormat:@"Invalid character typed. Only '%@' are allowed", allowedCharacters]];
    }
    else if(c == '(') open++;
    else if(c == ')') close++;

    if([operators characterIsMember:c] && [operators characterIsMember:previous])
    {
        // Two consecutive operators
        return [self produceError:error withCode:101 andMessage:@"Consecutive operators
are not allowed"];
    }

    if(c != ' ') previous = c;
  }

  if(open < close)
  {
    // Invalid character
    return [self produceError:error withCode:102 andMessage:@"Too many closed
parentheses"];
  }
  else if(open > close)
  {
    // Invalid character
    return [self produceError:error withCode:103 andMessage:@"Too many open
parentheses"];
  }

  return YES;
}

- (BOOL)produceError:(NSError**)error withCode:(NSInteger)code
andMessage:(NSString*)message
{
  if (error != NULL)
  {
    NSMutableDictionary *errorDetail = [NSMutableDictionary dictionary];
    [errorDetail setValue:message forKey:NSLocalizedDescriptionKey];
    *error = [NSError errorWithDomain:@"Graphique" code:code userInfo:errorDetail];
  }
  return NO;
}
```

The implementation checks for the four rules we defined earlier in this section and produces the appropriate error with the appropriate error code when necessary.

Unit Testing

Unit testing refers to the practice of writing nonproduction code that exercises a portion of the application in order to validate that it functions as expected in an isolated environment. Different developers adopt unit testing to various degrees. Some developers insist on subjecting every single line of code to unit testing. Others are stubbornly resistant to writing any kind of unit testing code. We leave it to you to find the ideal amount of unit testing for your projects. Typically, however, algorithms are ideal candidates for unit tests. This is certainly true for our validation method.

When we created the Graphique project, Xcode generated a `GraphiqueTests` class in the `GraphiqueTests` folder. This is the main unit test harness for the application. Open `GraphiqueTests.m` and add one method for each test you want to run. Since we have four validation rules, we need to have at least five methods (although we encourage you to write more to test more cases). Our five cases represent a successful case and one failure case for each validation rule. For those failure cases, we check that we actually got a failure and that the failure is reporting the proper error code.

Remember our validation rules from Table 3–1. It's always best to not look at the code you're testing when writing the unit tests. It keeps them independent and unbiased.

Listing 3–14 shows how the methods are implemented. For every case where something we expected didn't happen, we invoke the `STFail()` function to report the unit test failure.

Listing 3–14. `GraphiqueTests.m`: *Unit Tests for the Equation Validation Method*

```
#import "GraphiqueTests.h"
#import "Equation.h"

@implementation GraphiqueTests

- (void)setUp
{
  [super setUp];
}

- (void)tearDown
{
  [super tearDown];
}

- (void)testEquationValidation
{
  NSError *error = nil;
  Equation *equation = [[Equation alloc] initWithString:@"( 3+4*7 /(3+ 4))"];
  if(![equation validate:&error])
  {
    STFail(@"Equation should have been valid");
  }
}

- (void)testEquationValidationWithInvalidCharacters
{
  NSError *error = nil;
  Equation *equation = [[Equation alloc] initWithString:@"invalid characters"];
  if([equation validate:&error])
  {
    STFail(@"Equation should not have been valid");
```

```objc
  }

  if([error code] != 100)
  {
    STFail(@"Validation should have failed with code 100 instead of %d", [error code]);
  }
}

- (void)testEquationValidationWithConsecutiveOperators
{
  NSError *error = nil;
  Equation *equation = [[Equation alloc] initWithString:@"2++3"];
  if([equation validate:&error])
  {
    STFail(@"Equation should not have been valid");
  }

  if([error code] != 101)
  {
    STFail(@"Validation should have failed with code 101 instead of %d", [error code]);
  }
}

- (void)testEquationValidationWithTooManyOpenBrackets
{
  NSError *error = nil;
  Equation *equation = [[Equation alloc] initWithString:@"((4+3)"];
  if([equation validate:&error])
  {
    STFail(@"Equation should not have been valid");
  }

  if([error code] != 102)
  {
    STFail(@"Validation should have failed with code 102 instead of %d", [error code]);
  }
}

- (void)testEquationValidationWithTooManyCloseBrackets
{
  NSError *error = nil;
  Equation *equation = [[Equation alloc] initWithString:@"(4+3))"];
  if([equation validate:&error])
  {
    STFail(@"Equation should not have been valid");
  }

  if([error code] != 103)
  {
    STFail(@"Validation should have failed with code 103 instead of %d", [error code]);
  }
}

@end
```

> **NOTE:** The STFail() function is used to report unit test failures, which is different from
> reporting validation failures. In the case of testing validation failures, we call STFail() when the
> code did not return an error as expected.

To launch the unit tests, you can use the shortcut ⌘+U. Alternatively, you can click and
hold the Run button on the top-left corner of the Xcode window and select Build for
Testing (it may say "Test" instead, depending on the build status) from the drop-down to
start running the tests, as shown in Figure 3–14.

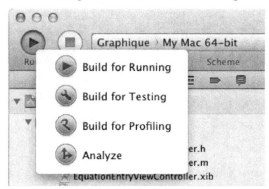

Figure 3–14. *The unit test launcher*

When you run the test, you will get some failures, as illustrated in Figure 3–15, indicating
something has gone wrong.

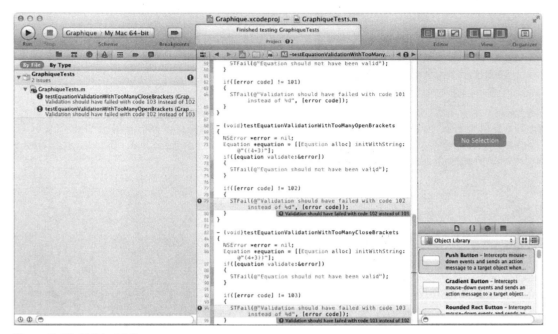

Figure 3–15. *Unit test failures*

The two errors are related to error codes 102 and 103 not being generated correctly. If you go back to `Equation.m`, you can find the logic for generating these two errors:

```
if(open < close)
{
  // Invalid character
  return [self produceError:error withCode:102 andMessage:@"Too many closed
parentheses"];
}
else if(open > close)
{
  // Invalid character
  return [self produceError:error withCode:103 andMessage:@"Too many open parentheses"];
}
```

Whoops, we've swapped error code 102 (too many open brackets) and error code 103 (too many closed brackets). We apologize to those readers who did notice the problems before running the unit tests and thought we had made a mistake. As a reward for continuing to read this chapter, we clear up this confusion for you. Change the logic to return the right code, as shown here:

```
if(open < close)
{
  // Invalid character
  return [self produceError:error withCode:103 andMessage:@"Too many closed
parentheses"];
}
else if(open > close)
{
  // Invalid character
```

```
    return [self produceError:error withCode:102 andMessage:@"Too many open parentheses"];
}
```

Now run the unit tests again. This time they should be successful, and the Console output should show something similar to the following example:

```
Executed 5 tests, with 0 failures (0 unexpected) in 0.000 (0.002) seconds
```

Displaying an Alert Window

So far, we've written our validation code and verified that it measures up to our expectations by using unit tests. It's now time to hook the validation code up to the user interface and display the error message when a problem occurs. Since we want validation performed when the user clicks the Graph button, we add our invocation to the validator in the `equationEntered:` method of the `EquationEntryViewController` class. When validation fails, we want to display a message box with the error code and message. Cocoa offers a convenient way to display message boxes using the `NSAlert` class.

Edit the `equationEntered:` method in `EquationEntryViewController.m`. For the alert delegate to work, you must add the `alertDidEnd:returnCode:contextInfo:` method. It is called when the user closes the `NSAlert` box. In our case, we don't want to do anything. It may be used to clear the input field. The code for both methods is shown in Listing 3–15.

Listing 3–15. *The Code for Displaying Alerts*

```objc
- (void)alertDidEnd:(NSAlert *)alert returnCode:(NSInteger)returnCode
        contextInfo:(void *)contextInfo
{

}

- (IBAction)equationEntered:(id)sender
{
  NSLog(@"Equation entered");
  GraphiqueAppDelegate *delegate = [NSApplication sharedApplication].delegate;

  Equation *equation = [[Equation alloc] initWithString: [self.textField stringValue]];

  NSError *error = nil;
  if(![equation validate:&error])
  {
    // Validation failed, display the error
    NSAlert *alert = [[NSAlert alloc] init];
    [alert addButtonWithTitle:@"OK"];
    [alert setMessageText:@"Something went wrong. "];
    [alert setInformativeText:[NSString stringWithFormat:@"Error %d: %@", [error
code],[error localizedDescription]]];
    [alert setAlertStyle:NSWarningAlertStyle];

    [alert beginSheetModalForWindow:delegate.window modalDelegate:self
didEndSelector:@selector(alertDidEnd:returnCode:contextInfo:) contextInfo:nil];
  }
```

```
    else
    {
      [delegate.graphTableViewController draw: equation];
    }
}
```

Launch the Graphique application, enter an invalid equation like **1++x**, and click the Graph button. The validation error should appear as shown in Figure 3–16.

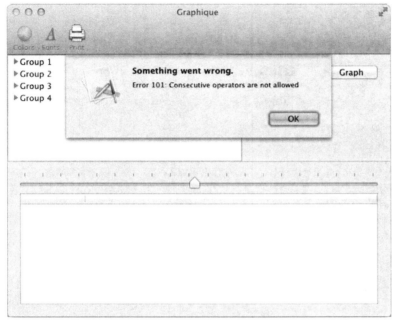

Figure 3–16. *Validation error shown in an NSAlert message box*

A Better Way: Real-Time Validation

Performing field validation is essential to providing good feedback to your users when they do something wrong, but your app will feel a lot more natural to the users if you can catch errors earlier and provide the feedback while they are doing something wrong. This section is dedicated to do just that.

Adding a Feedback Label

If we pop up an alert box every time the user types something wrong, this will undoubtedly generate a lot of frustration; users get scolded after they've done something wrong and have to then dismiss the alert. Instead, we can display the error message while they're typing in invalid equations by adding a label to the equation entry component that can hold the error message that we're currently displaying in an alert. This approach gives users real-time feedback on how they're misstepping in an unobtrusive way that doesn't require that they click an OK button. Open

EquationEntryViewController.h and declare a new NSTextField property called feedback, as Listing 3–16 shows.

Listing 3–16. *EquationEntryViewController.h with the New Feedback Text Field*

```
#import <Cocoa/Cocoa.h>
#import "Equation.h"

@interface EquationEntryViewController : NSViewController

@property (weak) IBOutlet NSTextField *textField;
@property (weak) IBOutlet NSTextField *feedback;

- (IBAction)equationEntered:(id)sender;

@end
```

Edit EquationEntryViewController.m to synthesize the new property as well.

Catching Text Change Notifications

The next step is to catch notifications sent when the equation is typed so we can validate the equation. NSTextField is a subclass of NSControl, which automatically fires a notification each time its text changes that its delegate can catch by implementing the controlTextDidChange: method.

In EquationEntryViewController.m, simply implement the method as shown in Listing 3–17. This code creates an Equation object from the text in the text field and calls its validate: method. If the validate: method returns an error, the code puts the error message in the label you created for this purpose (note that you've created it in code only at this point; we'll add it to the user interface shortly). Otherwise, it clears the label.

Listing 3–17. *The controlTextDidChange: Implementation*

```
- (void)controlTextDidChange:(NSNotification *)notification
{
  Equation *equation = [[Equation alloc] initWithString: [self.textField stringValue]];

  NSError *error = nil;
  if(![equation validate:&error])
  {
    // Validation failed, display the error
    [feedback setStringValue:[NSString stringWithFormat:@"Error %d: %@", [error
code],[error localizedDescription]]];
  }
  else
  {
    [feedback setStringValue:@""];
  }
}
```

Table 3–2 shows the methods you can implement to catch text-related notifications on any subclass of NSControl.

Table 3–2. *The Text-Related Notification Methods on* `NSControl`

Method	Description
`-(void)controlTextDidBeginEditing:(NSNotification *)obj;`	Called whenever the control is about to switch to edit mode
`-(void)controlTextDidEndEditing:(NSNotification *)obj;`	Called whenever the control is about to switch out of edit mode
`-(void)controlTextDidChange:(NSNotification *)obj;`	Called whenever the control's text has changed

Wiring It All Together in Interface Builder

So far, we've declared an attribute for our feedback panel and we've implemented the method needed to catch the change notifications, but we haven't tied the feedback panel to a component on the interface, and we have not set our controller as the entry field's delegate. Open `EquationEntryViewController.xib` to set this up.

First, resize the view to be tall enough to accommodate the feedback. Then, add a Wrapping Label object to the equation entry component, as shown in Figure 3–17. This will be our feedback label. Remove the title text and change the placeholder text to "Enter a function of x" or something helpful to the user. This placeholder text will appear whenever there is no title (that is, no validation error).

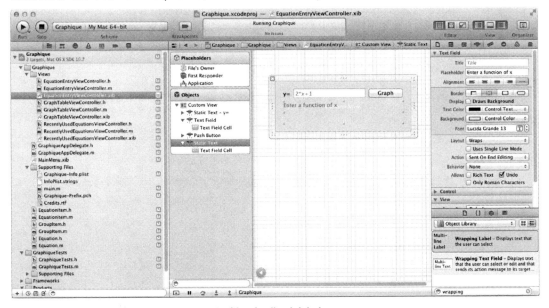

Figure 3–17. *The equation entry component with a feedback label*

Select the File's Owner (the controller in this case) and connect the `feedback` outlet to the newly added wrapping label, as illustrated in Figure 3–18.

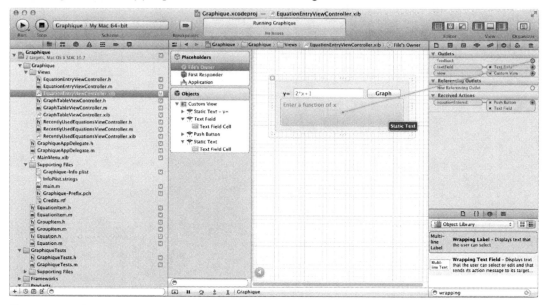

Figure 3–18. *Linking the feedback attribute to the UI component*

The last step is to set the controller as the delegate for the equation entry field. Select the equation entry text field and link its `delegate` property to the File's Owner so that it matches the illustration in Figure 3–19.

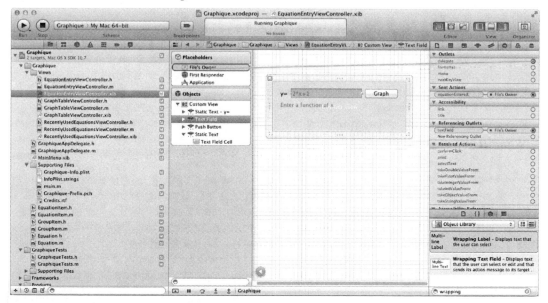

Figure 3–19. *Setting the text field delegate in Interface Builder*

Launch the application and type in an invalid equation to see the real-time validation in action, as shown in Figure 3–20.

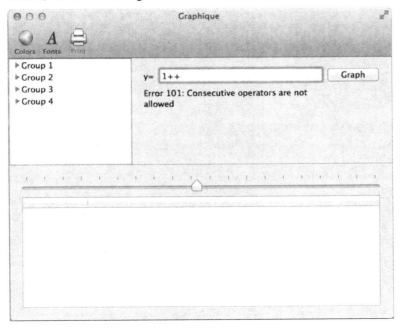

Figure 3–20. *Real-time validation error*

Graphing the Data

Everything we've done on the Graphique application to this point sets the stage for what we're going to do in this section: graph the data. Graphing data is Graphique's *raison d'etre*, and without this capability, all the beautiful layout and responsiveness to user input means naught. In this chapter, we graph the data textually in a table with two columns: the first column, labeled X, represents the domain, and the second column, labeled Y, shows the range. This means that for a given X value, you can see its corresponding Y value in the same row in the table. We show the graph with the domain -50 to 50, with a default interval between X values of one. Later in this chapter, we allow users to select the interval between X values.

We start by putting the labels on the graph table view and setting up the alignment of the columns. In Xcode, select `GraphTableViewController.xib` and expand the Objects view, drilling down until you see the two Table Column entries below the Table View, as shown in Figure 3–21. With the first Table Column entry selected and the Attributes inspector open, enter X in the Title field and click the Center alignment button. Drag the small blue dot between the X column and second column to the right to make both columns about the same size. Switch to the Identity inspector and enter X in the Identifier field.

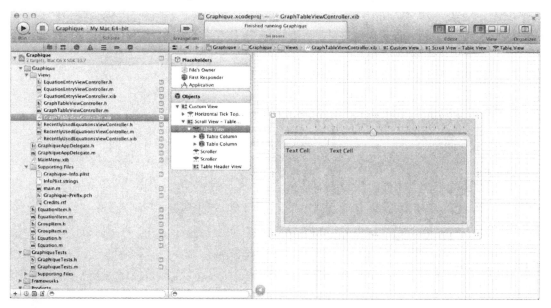

Figure 3–21. *Setting up the table columns in the Graph View*

Next, you want to set the data in the columns to be right-aligned, so click the triangle beside the table column you just adjusted to display the Text Field Cell item below it, and select that Text Field Cell item. In the Attributes inspector, click the Right alignment button to right-align the cell. At this point, the view should look as it does in Figure 3–22.

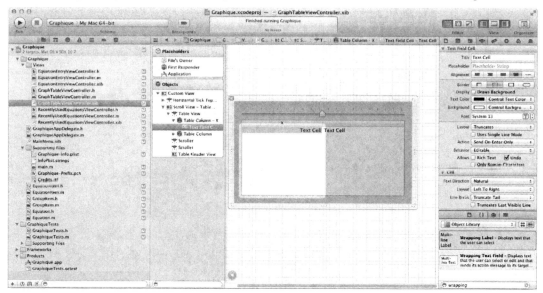

Figure 3–22. *The X column set up properly*

Move on to the second column and repeat the same steps, substituting Y for the label and the identifier for the column and making sure to set the alignment for the second column's Text Field Cell item as well. See Figure 3–23 for how the Graph View should now look.

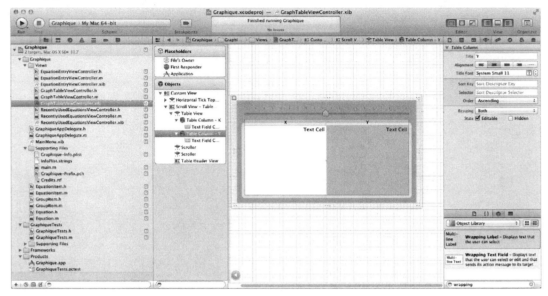

Figure 3–23. *The Graph View with the columns titled X and Y*

Calculating and Caching the Data

When the user clicks the Graph button, we could simply store the equation and then calculate the X and Y values for the table each time the table needs to display them (for example, as the user scrolls more rows of the table into view). This would save us the up-front time of calculating all the values for the table but might reduce the smoothness of scrolling the table if the equation is sufficiently complex.

We also could set up a cache for the data, calculating the data for a row the first time the table displays that row and caching the results so that the next time the table must display that row we can pull the information from the cache rather than recalculate it. This is often a best-of-both-worlds approach: we don't spend a lot of time up front calculating data, and the table scrolls reasonably smoothly as we fill the cache and then absolutely smoothly once we're just pulling cached values.

The third approach we could take, and in fact the one we use in Graphique, is to just calculate all the values for the table when the user clicks the Graph button and cache them. Then, as the table needs to display any of the values, we feed them directly from the cache. We take this approach for the following reasons:

- When the user clicks the Graph button, they expect something compute-intensive to happen. They can live with some amount of unresponsiveness from the application while it complies with the request to graph the data. When users scroll the table, they expect the table to just scroll and would become frustrated if the table jerked or lagged.

- We plan to graph a relatively small number of points. The domain, as we stated earlier, goes from -50 to 50, or 101 points. Later in this chapter we allow users to adjust the interval between domain points as low as 0.10, but even if they go that low, we'll be calculating a maximum of 1,010 values, not hundreds of thousands or even millions.

- In the next chapter, we display an actual graph of the equation along the same domain of -50 to 50, so we will need all the values computed so we can display the entire graph.

Most problems have many approaches, and your duty as a developer is to explore those options and arrive at a solution that best meets your users' expectations.

For Graphique, we compute all the values when the user clicks the Graph button and store each one as a CGPoint, which is a struct that has an x value and a y value, both floats, which is perfect for our needs. We store them in an NSMutableArray, taking advantage of NSValue's ability to transform a CGPoint into an object, because NSMutableArray can store only objects, not primitive values like CGPoint. Each time the user clicks the Graph button, we clear out the cache, recompute all the values, and store them in the cache. Since we haven't yet set up the ability to talk to the table from the code, we don't yet tell the table to reload itself; we'll set that up later in the chapter.

Begin by creating an instance of NSMutableArray to serve as the cache. Open GraphTableViewController.h and add an NSMutableArray instance called values, as shown in Listing 3–18.

Listing 3–18. *GraphTableViewController.h with the Cache Added*

```
#import <Cocoa/Cocoa.h>
#import "Equation.h"

@interface GraphTableViewController : NSViewController

@property (nonatomic, retain) NSMutableArray *values;

-(void)draw:(Equation*)equation;

@end
```

Now, open GraphTableViewController.m, add a @synthesize line for the values member and adjust the initWithNibName: method to create the values array. Update the draw: method to fill the cache with the appropriate values for the equation. Note that we currently log the points to the console, because we haven't yet set up the table to display the values. See Listing 3–19.

Listing 3–19. *The Updated* `GraphTableViewController.m`

```
#import "GraphTableViewController.h"

@implementation GraphTableViewController

@synthesize values;

- (id)initWithNibName:(NSString *)nibNameOrNil bundle:(NSBundle *)nibBundleOrNil {
  self = [super initWithNibName:nibNameOrNil bundle:nibBundleOrNil];
  if (self) {
    self.values = [NSMutableArray array];
  }
  return self;
}

- (void)draw:(Equation*)equation
{
  // Clear the cache
  [values removeAllObjects];

  // Calculate the values
  for (float x = -50.0; x <= 50.0; x++)
  {
    float y = [equation evaluateForX:x];
    NSLog(@"Adding point (%0.2f, %0.2f)", x, y);
    [values addObject:[NSValue valueWithPoint:CGPointMake(x, y)]];
  }
}
```

Build and run Graphique, and enter **3*x+7** in the equation entry field. Click the Graph button, and inspect the Console. You should see output for all 101 points that looks like the few lines of output listed here:

```
2011-08-30 06:26:17.597 Graphique[37034:407] Adding point (-3.00, -2.00)
2011-08-30 06:26:17.603 Graphique[37034:407] Adding point (-2.00, 1.00)
2011-08-30 06:26:17.608 Graphique[37034:407] Adding point (-1.00, 4.00)
2011-08-30 06:26:17.614 Graphique[37034:407] Adding point (0.00, 7.00)
2011-08-30 06:26:17.619 Graphique[37034:407] Adding point (1.00, 10.00)
2011-08-30 06:26:17.624 Graphique[37034:407] Adding point (2.00, 13.00)
2011-08-30 06:26:17.630 Graphique[37034:407] Adding point (3.00, 16.00)
```

We are successfully calculating and caching data, but the table remains blank. Read the next section to understand how to fill the table with data.

Talking to the Table: Outlets and Delegates

You saw outlets in Chapter 2 when we created outlets for the NSSplitView instances called horizontalSplitView and verticalSplitView. As you may recall, we marked these outlets with the tag IBOutlet in the code so that Interface Builder could recognize them, and we connected the outlets in the code with actual NSSplitView instances created in Interface Builder. We're going to do the same thing with the table view in GraphTableViewController.xib, connecting it to an NSTableView instance variable in the GraphTableViewController class called graphTableView.

The other thing we're going to do to the GraphTableViewController class is to make it the delegate for the table view in GraphTableViewController.xib. Delegates are a frequently used design pattern in Cocoa, and they represent classes that conform to a known protocol that other classes can delegate functionality to. Table views use delegates for two major pieces of their functionality:

- Providing the data for the table to show (the NSTableViewDataSource protocol)

- Interacting with the table or customizing its view (the NSTableViewDelegate protocol)

Since we're just going to display data in the table for now, without providing any means for users to interact with the table (other than to scroll it), we can safely ignore the NSTableViewDelegate protocol, but we must implement the NSTableViewDataSource protocol to provide data for our graphTableView to display. This protocol has two methods we're going to implement: one that returns the number of rows in the table and one that returns the value for a specific cell (row and column) in the table.

Edit GraphTableViewController.h, declare that it implements the NSTableViewDataSource protocol, and add a member called graphTableView. The code should look like Listing 3–20.

Listing 3–20. *GraphTableViewController.h*

```
#import <Cocoa/Cocoa.h>

#import "Equation.h"

@interface GraphTableViewController : NSViewController <NSTableViewDataSource>

@property (nonatomic, retain) NSMutableArray *values;
@property (weak) IBOutlet NSTableView *graphTableView;

-(void)draw:(Equation*)equation;

@end
```

In GraphTableViewController.m, add a @synthesize line for graphTableView, and then open GraphTableViewController.xib. We're going to connect the table view instance in Interface Builder to the graphTableView instance in the code. Ctrl+drag from File's Owner to the table view, and in the resulting pop-up select graphTableView. Now, when GraphTableViewController.xib loads, the table view will be connected to the graphTableView instance.

Go back to GraphTableViewController.m to implement the NSTableViewDataSource protocol. The first method to implement returns the number of rows in the table, which should match the number of values in the values cache. The method looks like Listing 3–21.

Listing 3–21. *Method to Return the Number of Rows in the Table*

```
- (NSInteger)numberOfRowsInTableView:(NSTableView *)tableView
{
  return values.count;
}
```

The second method returns the value for a specific cell. The method is passed an NSInteger for the row the table needs the value for and an NSTableColumn instance representing the column the table is requesting the value for. Remember when we set the identifiers for the table columns to X and Y? That's what we use to determine which table column to return the value for. First, we pull the CGPoint instance for the row out of the cache, and then we get the value for the X or Y column, depending on which table column we've been passed. Note that we must return an object, not a primitive float. We could use NSNumber's numberWithFloat: method to convert the float value to an NSNumber object and return that, but instead we return an NSString so we can control how the return value is formatted in the table—in this case, with two digits after the decimal point. The method implementation looks like Listing 3–22.

Listing 3–22. *Method for Returning a Cell's Value*

```
- (id)tableView:(NSTableView *)aTableView objectValueForTableColumn:(NSTableColumn
*)aTableColumn row:(NSInteger)rowIndex
{
  CGPoint point = [[values objectAtIndex:rowIndex] pointValue];
  float value = [[aTableColumn identifier] isEqualToString:@"X"] ? point.x : point.y;
  return [NSString stringWithFormat:@"%0.2f", value];
}
```

The last thing we must do to display data in the table is to update the draw: method to tell the table to reload after we've loaded the cache. We can also remove the log message that lists all the points, since we can now see the points in the table. The method now looks like Listing 3–23.

Listing 3–23. *The Updated* draw: *Method*

```
- (void)draw:(Equation*)equation
{
  // Clear the cache
  [values removeAllObjects];

  // Calculate the values
  for (float x = -50.0; x <= 50.0; x++)
  {
    float y = [equation evaluateForX:x];
    [values addObject:[NSValue valueWithPoint:CGPointMake(x, y)]];
  }
  [self.graphTableView reloadData];
}
```

At this point, you've updated the GraphiqueTableViewController class to be an adequate data source for graphTableView, but you haven't yet told graphTableView to use the GraphiqueTableViewController as its delegate. Open GraphTableViewController.xib, select the Table View, and open the Connections inspector. Drag from the circle to the right of dataSource to File's Owner to make that connection, as shown in Figure 3–24.

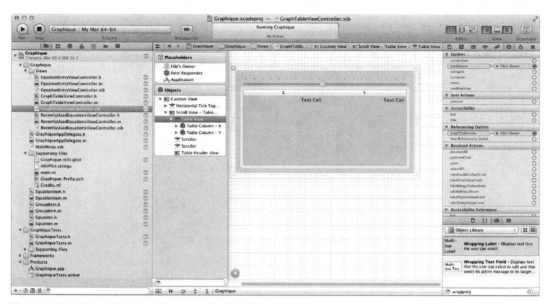

Figure 3–24. *Connecting the data source for the table view*

Build and run Graphique, enter **3*x+7** in the equation entry field, and click the Graph button. You should see your table fill with data, as shown in Figure 3–25. Enter various other equations in the equation entry field and click the Graph button after each one to see the table update with the new data.

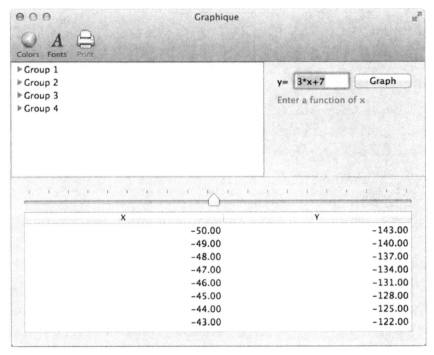

Figure 3–25. *The table with data*

Graphique now successfully graphs data by displaying values in a table. Before we close this chapter, however, we add one more ability to the application: the ability to change the interval between X values. This is the subject of the next section.

Changing the Interval in the Domain

When we laid out the Graph Table View panel, we included both a table, which we just finished filling with data, and a Slider control that we said would allow users to change the interval between X values. We now fulfill our promise to implement that feature.

When we configured that slider, we set its range in the Attributes inspector in Interface Builder from 0.10 to 5.00. As the user slides the handle left and right and clicks the Graph button, we should update the interval between X values in the table. This will mean clearing the cache and recalculating the values for the table to show. We already have a method for clearing the cache, recalculating the values, and reloading the table data called draw:. We must now make two changes to the Graphique application:

- Default the slider's initial position to 1
- Update the calculation loop in the draw: method to step by the selected interval instead of just the default of 1

To accomplish both these items, we take advantage of a Cocoa mechanism called key-value coding.

Using Key-Value Coding

Cocoa provides a mechanism called *key-value coding* (KVC) that allows you to set and get the value of a variable by its name, which we refer to as a *key*. Think of key-value coding as one entry in a map, hash, or dictionary. Suppose, for example, that you had a variable called foo. Its key is an NSString instance: @"foo", and we could set its value using code like this:

```
[self setValue:@"bar" forKey:@"foo"];
```

This would set the value of the variable foo to @"bar". We could get the value back out of foo by using this code:

```
[self valueForKey:@"foo"];
```

The value of this approach may not be immediately apparent, and we know all you compile-time safety advocates are squirming right now because compilers won't ensure that you spelled the name of the key correctly, but key-value coding can be a valuable approach to getting and setting values. You could, for example, use the same code to loop through a list of keys to set values on variables. The direct application for key-value coding for what we're doing, though, is what Cocoa calls binding. With binding, we can tie a graphical control—in our case, the slider—to a key, so that as we update the control, we update the value. Conversely, as we update the value, we update the control. Let's see how this works.

Open GraphTableViewController.h and add a CGFloat member called interval. Your file should match the code in Listing 3–24. Note that key-value coding works with objects, and CGFloat is just a primitive float, but Cocoa will take care of wrapping interval with the NSNumber object wrapper as necessary for getting and setting its value through key-value coding.

Listing 3–24. *GraphTableViewController.h*

```
#import <Cocoa/Cocoa.h>
#import "Equation.h"

@interface GraphTableViewController : NSViewController <NSTableViewDataSource>

@property (nonatomic, retain) NSMutableArray *values;
@property (weak) IBOutlet NSTableView *graphTableView;
@property (nonatomic, assign) CGFloat interval;

-(void)draw:(Equation*)equation;

@end
```

In GraphTableViewController.m, add an @synthesize line for interval, and in the initWithNibName: method, set its initial value to 1.0, as in Listing 3–25.

Listing 3–25. *The initWithNibName: Method Updated to Set interval to 1*

```
- (id)initWithNibName:(NSString *)nibNameOrNil bundle:(NSBundle *)nibBundleOrNil
{
  self = [super initWithNibName:nibNameOrNil bundle:nibBundleOrNil];
```

```
  if (self) {
    self.values = [NSMutableArray arrayWithCapacity:0];
    self.interval = 1.0;
  }
  return self;
}
```

Binding the Value to the Slider

This is where key-value coding gets fun. Open `GraphTableViewController.xib`, select the slider (make sure to select the Slider Cell object), and open the Bindings inspector. Expand the Value group (underneath the Value section), check the box by Bind to:, and select File's Owner from the drop-down, which binds the slider to the owning `GraphTableViewController` instance. Then, type **self.interval** in the Model Key Path field, as shown in Figure 3–26. The value of the slider is now bound to the instance variable interval through key-value coding, and changing one will change the other (and vice versa). To prove this, build and run the application. Before, the slider started right in the middle of its range at 2.5 (OK, not exactly the middle but awfully close). Now, it starts at 1.0, as shown in Figure 3–27.

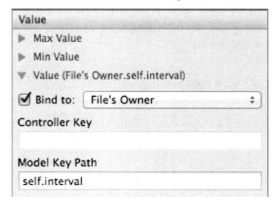

Figure 3–26. *Selecting the variable to bind the slider to*

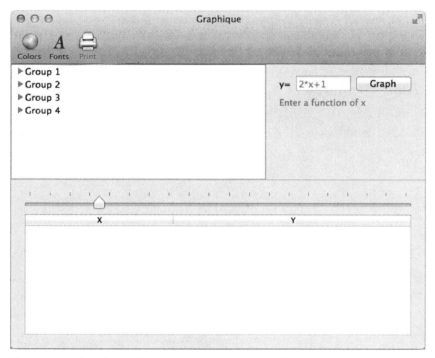

Figure 3-27. *Graphique with the slider bound to* `interval`, *set to 1.0*

You can prove this by changing the initial value you set interval to in `initWithNibName:`. Set it to 5, for example, and build and run Graphique to see that the slider starts to the far right of its range. Note that you can set interval to values beyond the slider's range without ill effects. The slider will do its best to show the value of interval by moving to its appropriate extreme, and the interval will retain the value you set. Moving the slider, however slightly, will bring interval back into its range.

The last thing we must do to incorporate the slider into the Graphique application is to step the calculation loop by the value of interval. Update the `draw:` method to match Listing 3-26.

Listing 3-26. *The* `draw:` *Method Incorporating the Interval*

```
- (void)draw:(Equation*)equation
{
  // Clear the cache
  [values removeAllObjects];

  // Calculate the values
  for (float x = -50.0; x <= 50.0; x += interval)
  {
    float y = [equation evaluateForX:x];
    [values addObject:[NSValue valueWithPoint:CGPointMake(x, y)]];
  }
  [self.graphTableView reloadData];
}
```

Build and run Graphique. Push the slider to the far right, enter **x^2-3** in the equation entry field, and click Graph. You should see an interval of 5 between X values, as shown in Figure 3–28. Now, push the slider to the far left and click Graph. The interval should now be 0.1, as shown in Figure 3–29.

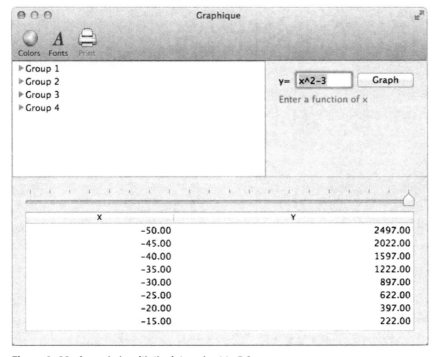

Figure 3–28. *A parabola with the interval set to 5.0*

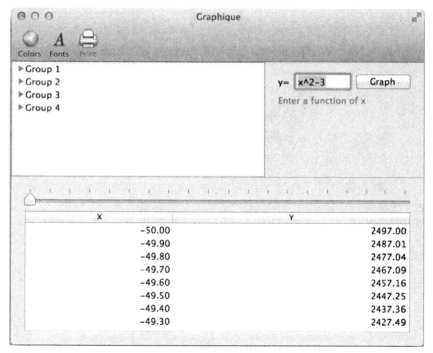

Figure 3–29. *The same parabola with the interval set to 0.1*

Binding the slider to the interval instance variable through key-value coding made the task of adjusting the interval simple.

Summary

If we were developing Graphique purely as an open source application, we'd call this version 0.1 and release it now. It's a working application that allows users to enter equations. It validates the equations. It displays appropriate error messages. It graphs the equations textually by showing the domain and corresponding range values. It even allows users to change the domain interval. It's ready to ship to the open source community to get feedback and invite other contributors.

The App Store community generally differs from the open source community, however. Whereas the open source community tends to be more technical and generally encourages early releases with limited functionality so that they can get involved in contributing code and shaping the direction of the application, the App Store community includes swaths of people who don't write code, don't want to mess with fledgling apps early in their development cycles, and want to use (and pay for) complete products. Graphique still lacks features important to a graphing calculator—say, for example, a graphical graph. In the next chapter, we add a graph and an improved equation entry field. Make no mistake, however: at this point, Graphique means something.

Chapter 4

Pimp My UI

At this point in its evolution, Graphique indeed means something. It does something. It's serviceable. It accepts an equation, evaluates it, and lists x, y values. It's also a little embarrassing: it's a graphing calculator that doesn't graph. That flaw is difficult to hide or gloss over. We can't really be proud of Graphique until it graphs equations.

The equation entry field is a little shameful, too, in a Notepad kind of way: monochromatic text, stiff syntax, and anemic validation. Before we can be proud of Graphique, we must provide a better equation editor.

In this chapter, we create graphs, and we improve the equation editor. By the time we're done, the UI for Graphique will look like Figure 4–1.

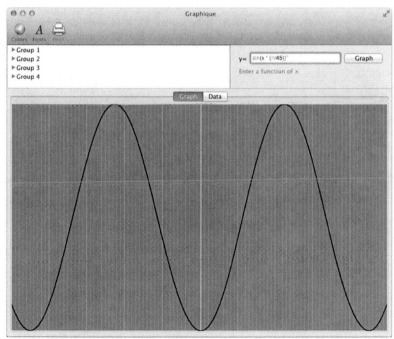

Figure 4–1. *The Graphique application at the end of this chapter*

Creating a Graph View

You've learned a lot about building user interfaces using Interface Builder (IB), but sometimes you should step off the beaten path and create user interface components that cannot be built by assembling the standard widgets that come with the platform. In this section, we go through the exercise of create a custom view that will trace our graph instead of just displaying a table of values as we've done thus far.

To create a custom view in Cocoa, you typically create a new class that subclasses the NSView class and implement the drawRect: method in order to paint your customized view on the screen.

Creating a Custom View

The first step is to create, inside the Views group, a new Cocoa Objective-C class called GraphView and make it a subclass of NSView. This will create the usual GraphView.h and GraphView.m files. Leave the implementation as is for now; we will get back to it shortly.

1. Open GraphTableViewController.xib and drag a new Custom View object to the Objects panel. The new custom view should be a top-level object, a sibling of the already existing Custom View object.

2. Select the new Custom View object and change the class to GraphView in the Identity inspector. Your setup should match Figure 4–2.

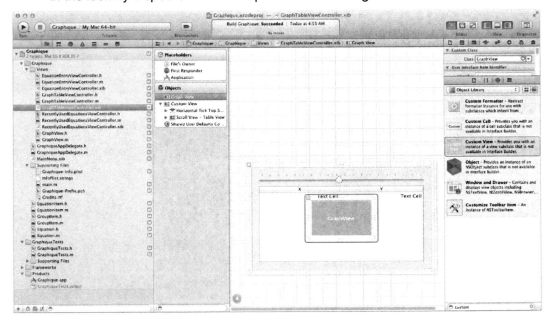

Figure 4–2. *The Graph View in Interface Builder*

Linking the New Custom View to the Controller

If you ran the application at this point, you would not notice anything different. This is because the GraphTableViewController's view is still set to the table view. For our purpose, we change the view to point to our new GraphView. This will activate GraphView and deactivate the table view. In the next section, we show you how to keep both views active, but for now we'll leave only GraphView active. Select the File's Owner and go to the Connections inspector. Change the view attribute to point to Graph View, as shown in Figure 4–3.

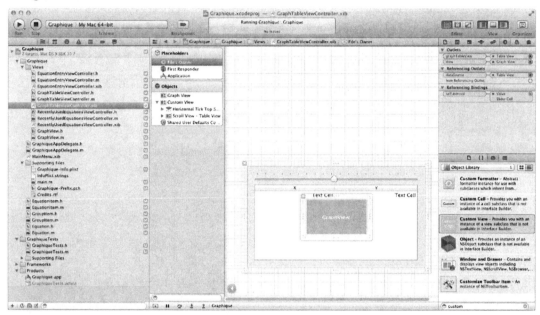

Figure 4–3. *The controller pointing to a different view*

You can try running the app again. This time nothing is displayed or graphed when you enter an equation. This is because you have linked the controller's view to the new GraphView, which doesn't yet have any code for painting anything. Before we get to the painting part, there is still a bit of wiring to do. First, we need to make sure the controller knows how to access the GraphView. Second, we need to make sure our GraphView knows how to get a hold of the data points it needs to plot.

Open GraphTableViewController.h and add a new IBOutlet property of type GraphView, as shown in Listing 4–1.

Listing 4–1. *GraphTableViewController.h with a Reference to GraphView*

```
#import <Cocoa/Cocoa.h>

#import "Equation.h"

@class GraphView;
```

```
@interface GraphTableViewController : NSViewController <NSTableViewDataSource>

@property (nonatomic, retain) NSMutableArray *values;
@property (weak) IBOutlet NSTableView *graphTableView;
@property (nonatomic, assign) CGFloat interval;
@property (weak) IBOutlet GraphView *graphView;

-(void)draw:(Equation*)equation;

@end
```

Be sure to synthesize the new graphView property in the GraphTableViewController.m
implementation file and add the appropriate import: #import "GraphView.h". Then go to
GraphTableViewController.xib and follow the usual procedure for linking properties:
select the File's Owner and open the Connections inspector. Link the graphView
property to the Graph View object.

We now turn our attention to GraphView. The controller is responsible for calculating the
points to plot. The view needs a way to get to where the points are stored. Open
GraphView.h and add a new IBOutlet property of type GraphTableViewController, as
shown in Listing 4–2.

Listing 4–2. *GraphView.h with a Handle to the Controller*

```
#import <Cocoa/Cocoa.h>

@class GraphTableViewController;

@interface GraphView : NSView

@property (assign) IBOutlet GraphTableViewController *controller;

@end
```

Now open GraphView.m, import the GraphTableViewController.h header file, and
synthesize the property, as shown in Listing 4–3.

Listing 4–3. *GraphView.m with the Synthesized Property*

```
#import "GraphView.h"
#import "GraphTableViewController.h"

@implementation GraphView

@synthesize controller;

- (id)initWithFrame:(NSRect)frame
{
    self = [super initWithFrame:frame];
    if (self)
    {
        // Initialization code here.
    }

    return self;
}
```

```
- (void)drawRect:(NSRect)dirtyRect
{
  // Drawing code here.
}

@end
```

Go back to GraphTableViewController.xib. This time, select the Graph View object and go to the Connections inspector. Link the controller property to the File's Owner.

In order to make sure everything is linked properly, select File's Owner and verify that the connections match Figure 4–4.

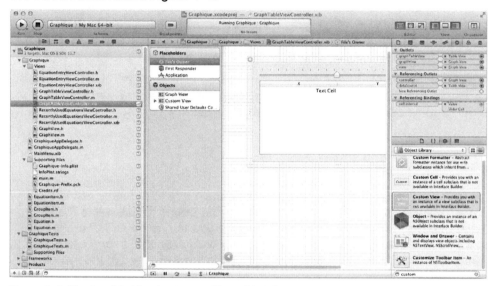

Figure 4–4. *The* GraphTableViewController *with all its connections*

The last step to add the custom Graph View is to tell the custom view to repaint itself whenever a new equation has been entered. For this, we add a call to NSView's setNeedsDisplay: method in the controller, as shown in Listing 4–4.

Listing 4–4. GraphTableViewController.m *with a Call to Refresh the Custom View*

```
-(void)draw:(Equation*)equation
{
  // Clear the cache
  [values removeAllObjects];

  // Calculate the values
  for (float x = -50.0; x <= 50.0; x += interval)
  {
    float y = [equation evaluateForX:x];
    [values addObject:[NSValue valueWithPoint:NSMakePoint(x, y)]];
  }
  [self.graphTableView reloadData];

  [self.graphView setNeedsDisplay:YES];
}
```

> **NOTE:** We've kept the call to reload the table data as well. This is because we intend to show both graph views (table and plot) later in this section, so we keep them both up-to-date.

Plotting the Graph

Now that everything is properly wired, it is time to implement the drawing function. Cocoa calls the NSView drawRect: method when a custom view needs to be painted. The method is given an area that it deems dirty and needs repainting. The first time the view is painted, that area is the size of the view. If the view is resized, then the drawRect: method is called again with the new size. We simply override this method in GraphView in order to take control of the painting of our custom view.

In Cocoa, most of the drawing functions are done via the NSBezierPath class. This class provides a way to create paths to draw from the single line to complex parametric curves. In our graphic calculator, we simply draw lines between the sampled points of the curve.

Finding the Boundaries

To allow the view to resize cleanly, we want to scale the curve to fit neatly inside the view. In order to achieve this, we must go through all the points to determine the minimum and maximum values of the curve. Once we find the range and domain extremes, we use the view's dimension, through its bounds property, in order to compute the scaling factors. The code to do all this, shown in Listing 4–5, goes at the top of GraphView's drawRect: method.

Listing 4–5. *Computing the Horizontal and Vertical Scaling Factors*

```
float minDomain = CGFLOAT_MAX;
float maxDomain = CGFLOAT_MIN;

float minRange = CGFLOAT_MAX;
float maxRange = CGFLOAT_MIN;

for (NSValue *value in controller.values)
{
  NSPoint point = [value pointValue];
  if(point.x < minDomain) minDomain = point.x;
  if(point.x > maxDomain) maxDomain = point.x;

  if(point.y < minRange) minRange = point.y;
  if(point.y > maxRange) maxRange = point.y;
}

float hScale = self.bounds.size.width / (maxDomain - minDomain);
float vScale = self.bounds.size.height / (maxRange - minRange);
```

Painting the Background

The next step consists in setting up the colors we want to use and painting the background. Colors are defined by the NSColor class, which offers several ways of defining a color. You have options to choose predefined colors like [NSColor whiteColor] or use component-based colors like RGBA (Red, Green, Blue, and Alpha transparency) using colorWithDeviceRed:green:blue:alpha:. In our case, we use RGBA colors. Painting the rectangular background is an easy task since the drawRect: method gives us the rectangular area to paint and Cocoa has the NSRectFill function already defined. Listing 4–6 shows how to set up the colors and paint the background. It sets up colors for the background, the axes, the grids, and the curve (or actual graph).

Listing 4–6. *Setting the Colors and Painting the Background*

```
NSColor *background  = [NSColor colorWithDeviceRed:0.30 green:0.58 blue:1.0 alpha:1.0];
NSColor *axisColor = [NSColor colorWithDeviceRed:1.0 green:1.0 blue:1.0 alpha:1.0];
NSColor *gridColorLight = [NSColor colorWithDeviceRed:1.0 green:1.0 blue:1.0 alpha:0.5];
NSColor *gridColorLighter = [NSColor colorWithDeviceRed:1.0 green:1.0 blue:1.0
alpha:0.25];
NSColor *curveColor = [NSColor colorWithDeviceRed:.0 green:0.0 blue:0 alpha:1.0];

[background set];
NSRectFill(dirtyRect);
```

Plotting the Graph

Now we're ready to start drawing the actual plot of our graph. In Cocoa, lines are defined using NSBezierPath just like any other paths. As you can probably imagine, a line (in the computer graphics sense of the term at least) is defined by a start and an end point. Mathematically oriented people would probably much rather call it a segment, but in Cocoa, it's a line. Let's take a look at what it takes to draw the domain axis.

First, we declare the new path:

```
NSBezierPath *domainAxis = [NSBezierPath bezierPath];
```

Next, we specific how thick we want the line to be. In our case, we're happy with a 1-pixel line:

```
[domainAxis setLineWidth:1];
```

Then it's just a matter of defining the beginning and the end of the line. Notice how we scale them using the scaling factors we defined earlier:

```
NSPoint startPoint = { 0, -minRange * vScale};
NSPoint endPoint   = { self.bounds.size.width, -minRange * vScale };
[domainAxis moveToPoint:startPoint];
[domainAxis lineToPoint:endPoint];
```

The last step is to define the color to use and then stroke the line:

```
[axisColor set];
[domainAxis stroke];
```

We repeat the same procedure for the range axis, adding a pretty background grid and even for the curve itself, where we draw lines between each point. Listing 4–7 shows the full drawRect: method .

Listing 4–7. *The* GraphView's drawRect: *Method to Plot the Graph*

```
- (void)drawRect:(NSRect)dirtyRect
{
  // Step 1. Find the boundaries

  float minDomain = CGFLOAT_MAX;
  float maxDomain = CGFLOAT_MIN;

  float minRange = CGFLOAT_MAX;
  float maxRange = CGFLOAT_MIN;

  for (NSValue *value in controller.values) {
    NSPoint point = [value pointValue];
    if(point.x < minDomain) minDomain = point.x;
    if(point.x > maxDomain) maxDomain = point.x;

    if(point.y < minRange) minRange = point.y;
    if(point.y > maxRange) maxRange = point.y;
  }

  float hScale = self.bounds.size.width / (maxDomain - minDomain);
  float vScale = self.bounds.size.height / (maxRange - minRange);

  // Step 2. Paint the background

  NSColor *background  = [NSColor colorWithDeviceRed:0.30 green:0.58 blue:1.0
alpha:1.0];
  NSColor *axisColor = [NSColor colorWithDeviceRed:1.0 green:1.0 blue:1.0 alpha:1.0];
  NSColor *gridColorLight = [NSColor colorWithDeviceRed:1.0 green:1.0 blue:1.0
alpha:0.5];
  NSColor *gridColorLighter = [NSColor colorWithDeviceRed:1.0 green:1.0 blue:1.0
alpha:0.25];
  NSColor *curveColor = [NSColor colorWithDeviceRed:.0 green:0.0 blue:0 alpha:1.0];

  [background set];
  NSRectFill(dirtyRect);

  // Step 3. Plot the graph

  if(controller.values.count == 0) return;

  // Paint the domain axis
  {
    NSBezierPath *domainAxis = [NSBezierPath bezierPath];
    [domainAxis setLineWidth: 1];
    NSPoint startPoint = { 0, -minRange * vScale};
    NSPoint endPoint   = { self.bounds.size.width, -minRange * vScale };
    [domainAxis moveToPoint:startPoint];
    [domainAxis lineToPoint:endPoint];
    [axisColor set];
    [domainAxis stroke];
```

```
}

// Paint the range axis
{
  NSBezierPath *rangeAxis = [NSBezierPath bezierPath];
  [rangeAxis setLineWidth: 1];
  NSPoint startPoint = { -minDomain * hScale, 0 };
  NSPoint endPoint   = { -minDomain * hScale, self.bounds.size.height };
  [rangeAxis moveToPoint:startPoint];
  [rangeAxis lineToPoint:endPoint];
  [axisColor set];
  [rangeAxis stroke];
}

// Paint the grid. Every 10 steps, we use a less transparent grid path for major lines
{
  NSBezierPath *grid = [NSBezierPath bezierPath];
  NSBezierPath *lighterGrid = [NSBezierPath bezierPath];

  for(int col=minDomain; col<maxDomain; col++)
  {
    NSPoint startPoint = { (col - minDomain) * hScale, 0};
    NSPoint endPoint = { (col - minDomain) * hScale, self.bounds.size.height };
    if(col % 10 == 0)
    {
      [grid moveToPoint:startPoint];
      [grid lineToPoint:endPoint];
    }
    else
    {
      [lighterGrid moveToPoint:startPoint];
      [lighterGrid lineToPoint:endPoint];
    }
  }

  int vStep = pow(10, log10(maxRange - minRange)-2);
  if(vStep == 0) vStep = 1;

  for(int row=-vStep; row>=minRange; row -= vStep)
  {
    NSPoint startPoint = { 0, (row - minRange) * vScale};
    NSPoint endPoint = { self.bounds.size.width * hScale, (row - minRange) * vScale };

    if(row % (vStep*10) == 0)
    {
      [grid moveToPoint:startPoint];
      [grid lineToPoint:endPoint];
    }
    else
    {
      [lighterGrid moveToPoint:startPoint];
      [lighterGrid lineToPoint:endPoint];
    }
  }
```

```
    for(int row=vStep; row<maxRange; row += vStep)
    {
      NSPoint startPoint = { 0, (row - minRange) * vScale};
      NSPoint endPoint = { self.bounds.size.width * hScale, (row - minRange) * vScale };

      if(row % (vStep*10) == 0)
      {
        [grid moveToPoint:startPoint];
        [grid lineToPoint:endPoint];
      }
      else
      {
        [lighterGrid moveToPoint:startPoint];
        [lighterGrid lineToPoint:endPoint];
      }
    }

    [gridColorLighter set];
    [lighterGrid stroke];
    [gridColorLight set];
    [grid stroke];
  }

  // Paint the curve
  {
    NSBezierPath *curve = nil;

    for(NSValue *value in controller.values)
    {
      NSPoint point = [value pointValue];
      NSPoint pointForView = { (point.x - minDomain) * hScale, (point.y - minRange) *
vScale };

      if(curve == nil)
      {
        curve = [NSBezierPath bezierPath];
        [curve setLineWidth:2.0];
        [curve moveToPoint:pointForView];
      }
      else
      {
        [curve lineToPoint:pointForView];
      }
    }

    [curveColor set];
    [curve stroke];
  }
}
```

Of course, paths don't all have to be lines. Notice in the previous listing how the curve path is defined. We put the entire path together by calling lineToPoint:, but the path is not actually drawn until we're out of the loop and call the stroke method. NSBezierPath instances are constructed using lines but also using other shapes like ellipses or rectangles.

Now that the custom view is implemented, you can start the app, enter an equation, and watch it be drawn, as illustrated in Figure 4–5.

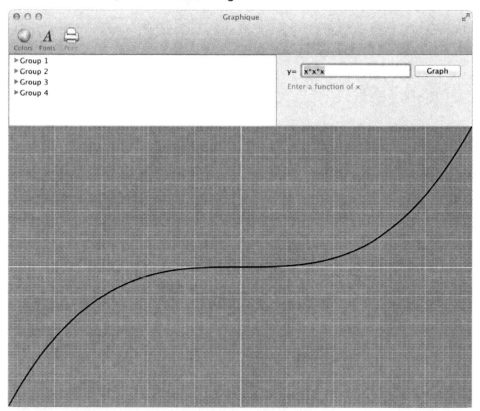

Figure 4–5. *Graphique with a plotted equation*

Toggling Between Text and Graph

So far we've created two representations of an equation. First we built a UI component that displays the equation data in a table. We also built another UI component that graphically plots the equation. But we haven't been able to have both of them attached to the application at the same time so we can toggle between them. In this section, we bridge this gap by adding a tab view. Tab views are a type of view that is already outfitted with tab controls so you can navigate through subviews you attach to each tab. In this section, we replace the view of the GraphTableViewController with a tab view and set up two tabs, one for each representation of an equation.

Adding the Tab View

Start by opening GraphTableViewController.xib. We're first going to focus on making sure the anchors and resizing masks are properly set on the two existing views. Each of them should be set to resize in all directions and be anchored to all edges. This step is taken to ensure that the graph views will occupy all the space they can within the tab views, as shown in Figure 4–6.

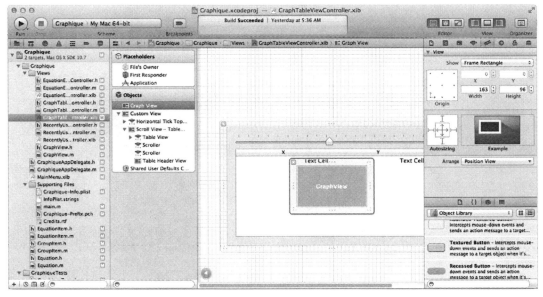

Figure 4–6. *The graph views set to maximize in all directions*

The next step is to actually add the tab view, which will eventually become the view associated with the GraphTableViewController controller.

Find Tab View in the Object Library and drag it to the Objects panel as a sibling of the existing views, as illustrated in Figure 4–7.

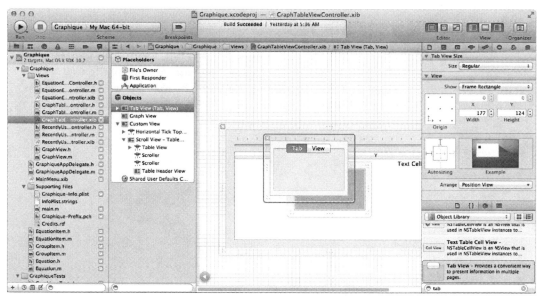

Figure 4–7. *Adding the tab view*

Expand the Tab View item to reveal its structure, as depicted in Figure 4–8. By default, the tab view has two tabs. You can easily add more tabs by going to the Attributes inspector and increasing the number of tabs. For our goal, two tabs works just fine.

Figure 4–8. *The expanded tab view structure*

Adding the Views to the Tabs

We now need to place each of our equation views inside a tab. From the Objects panel, drag and drop the Graph View component onto the View component of the first tab. This will move that component inside the tab. Follow the same procedure with the Custom View component and place it inside the second tab. The resulting structure should look like Figure 4–9.

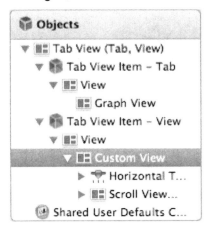

Figure 4–9. *The new tab structure with the components in place*

To make sure everything fits properly, select the Graph View object and go to the Size inspector tab. In the Arrange drop-down, select Fill Container Horizontally and Fill Container Vertically, as Figure 4–10 shows. This properly places the view in the Interface Builder designer so it looks right.

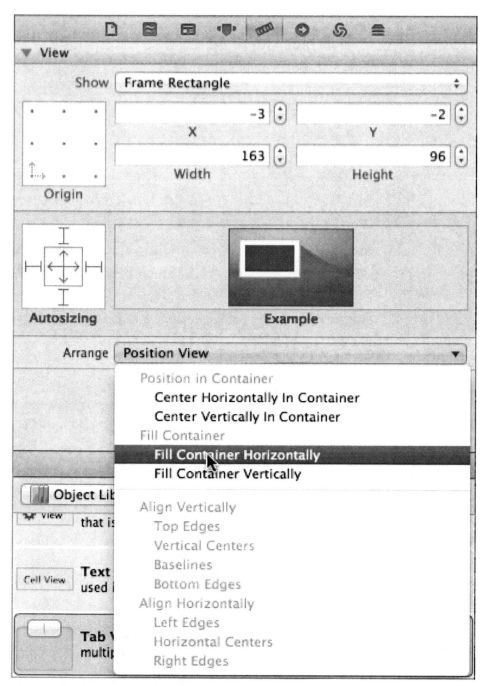

Figure 4–10. *Automatically filling the container*

Because the table view component has several UI components in it, it is faster to adjust them manually in the design panel. Resize the tab view to make it bigger so you see what you are doing and move the slider and table to the right position inside the Custom View. You can also use the Arrange drop-down again and then adjust manually. The resulting view should be similar to Figure 4–11.

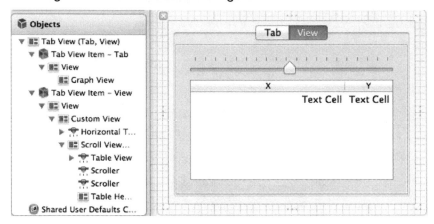

Figure 4–11. *The table view properly set up inside its tab view*

Each tab has a title that helps the user navigate and figure out what to expect from each tab. To change the tab's title, double-click the tab you want to rename and type the new name. We named our tabs **Graph** and **Data**.

Switching the Controller to the Tab View

Now that the individual views are in place, you want to switch the controller's view to the tab view. Select the File's Owner and open the Connections inspector. The view outlet should be attached to the Graph View. Remove that connection by clicking the x next to the connection. Once the connection is cleared, make the connection between the view outlet and the Tab View object by dragging from the empty circle to the Tab View object. The connections should be as shown in Figure 4–12.

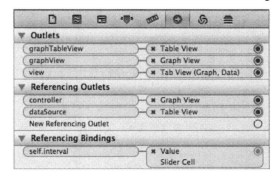

Figure 4–12. *The connection from the File's Owner to the tab panel*

Launch the app, enter **x*x*x** for the equation, and click Graph. Then, select each tab, in turn, to see both the Graph View and the table view. They should match Figure 4–13 and Figure 4–14.

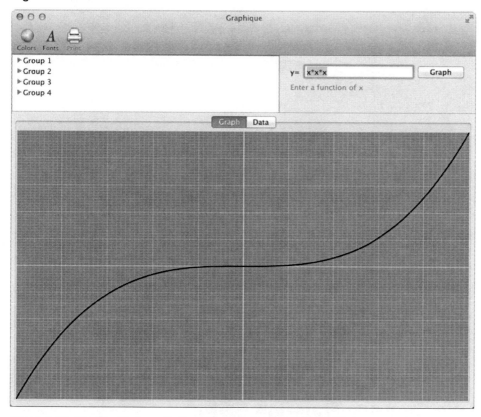

Figure 4–13. *The Graphique application with tabs showing the Graph View*

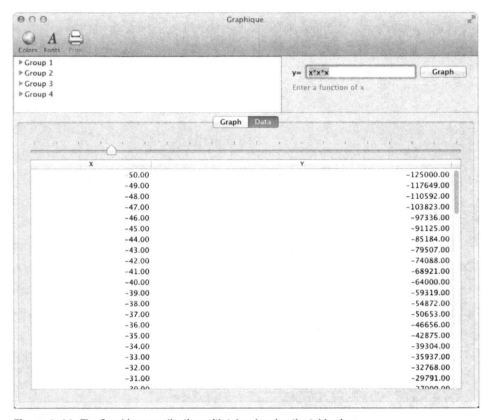

Figure 4–14. *The Graphique application with tabs showing the table view*

Creating a Smarter Equation Editor

We've given users a text field in which to type equations, and that text field works adequately. It's gotten us this far, after all. You wouldn't call it user-friendly or attractive, however. It's all-black text on a white background, for example, requiring users to look closely to differentiate operators from numbers. You can fool its validator by doing things like entering ")x+7(" so that the number of open parentheses match the number of closed ones, but they're out of order. Exponents stand the same height as other numbers rather than displaying in superscript. Implicit multiplication (for example, "2x" vs. "2*x") doesn't work. We can improve this.

Over the rest of this chapter, we improve the equation entry editor by adding the following:

- Syntax coloring

- Parenthesis matching

- Inline error highlighting

- Support for trigonometric functions

- Implicit multiplication
- Superscript exponents
- Implicit exponents
- Symbols (pi and e)

These improvements will touch the equation entry field, the equation validator, and the equation evaluator, and they will require a fair amount of work to complete. Through the rest of this chapter, you'll build these improvements, and at the end of the chapter, you'll be rewarded by a better equation entry editor.

Adding Attributes to the Equation Entry Field

In most widget toolkits, text fields support a single text color, font, and text size. To get the fancy formatting that we want for our equation editor, you'd think you'd have to jettison the `NSTextField` instance and switch to a different widget like `NSTextView`. Don't leap to conclusions and dump the existing text field, however, because the Cocoa `NSTextField` widget supports the rich-text editing that our vision for the equation editor requires. We could certainly switch to a `NSTextView` control, but that control is designed for multiple-line entry. `NSTextField` is for single-line entry and supports all of the colors, fonts, and sizes we need.

The trick to changing colors, fonts, and sizes in the text field revolves around what Cocoa calls an *attributed string*, embodied in the `NSAttributedString` class, which is included in every `NSControl` instance. As its name indicates, an attributed string is a string with attributes—attributes such as color or size across specified ranges of text. To unveil the attributed string in a text field, either you must call `setAllowsEditingTextAttributes:YES` on the `NSTextField` instance or you must turn on Allows Rich Text in Interface Builder, as shown in Figure 4–15. Otherwise, any attributes you specify don't display, contrary to what the documentation for `NSTextField`'s `setAllowsEditingTextAttributes:` suggests.

Turn on attributes for Graphique's equation entry field by selecting `EquationEntryViewController.xib` to open it in Interface Builder, selecting the equation text field, and checking Allows Rich Text in the Attributes inspector. By checking that box, we've transformed the plain and boring text field into a field capable of displaying all the cool attributes we have planned for it.

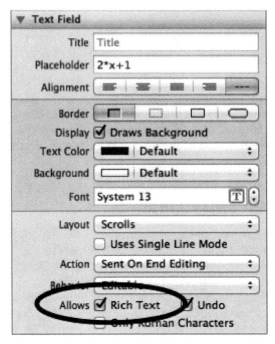

Figure 4-15. *Setting the* NSTextField *to show rich text*

Creating the Tokens

Most of the planned functionality for our improved equation entry editor relies on knowing what the individual pieces of the entered equation are—not just the individual characters but the groups of characters that go together and what they mean. To do this, we must parse or tokenize the equation into its individual tokens and then make decisions about things such as syntax coloring or implicit multiplication using those tokens. The kinds of tokens we support are as follows:

- Numbers
- Variables (only x)
- Operators (for example, + or -)
- Open parentheses
- Close parentheses
- Exponents
- Symbols
- Trigonometric functions (sine and cosine)
- Spaces
- Invalid input

Our strategy is to define an enum with these token types and then a token class that holds the token's type and its value. If, for example, the user enters the number 123, we create an instance of this token class that holds the token's type, which is a number, and the token's value, which is 123. In addition, the token class will hold a boolean field that stores whether this token is valid, since a token can be an valid type yet still be invalid, as in the case of an open parenthesis without a matching close parenthesis.

Create a new Cocoa Objective-C class called `EquationToken` as a subclass of `NSObject`. `EquationToken.h`, shown in Listing 4–8, creates the enum for the token types and declares properties for the token's type, value, and validity, as well as an initializer method that takes a type and value. You can see that the names for the token types unmistakably describe what they represent, which is a good practice that not only makes your code more understandable and maintainable but also lets you shirk documentation in most cases.

Listing 4–8. *EquationToken.h*

```
#import <Foundation/Foundation.h>

typedef enum
{
  EquationTokenTypeInvalid = 0,
  EquationTokenTypeNumber,
  EquationTokenTypeVariable,
  EquationTokenTypcOperator,
  EquationTokenTypeOpenParen,
  EquationTokenTypeCloseParen,
  EquationTokenTypeExponent,
  EquationTokenTypeSymbol,
  EquationTokenTypeTrigFunction,
  EquationTokenTypeWhitespace,
} EquationTokenType;

@interface EquationToken : NSObject

@property (nonatomic) EquationTokenType type;
@property (nonatomic, retain) NSString *value;
@property (nonatomic) BOOL valid;

- (id)initWithType:(EquationTokenType)type andValue:(NSString *)value;

@end
```

`EquationToken.m`, shown in Listing 4–9, handles the getting and setting of these properties. It also initializes each token as valid, except for tokens of type `EquationTokenTypeInvalid`.

Listing 4–9. *EquationToken.m*

```
#import "EquationToken.h"

@implementation EquationToken

@synthesize type;
```

```
@synthesize value;
@synthesize valid;

- (id)initWithType:(EquationTokenType)type_ andValue:(NSString *)value_
{
  self = [super init];
  if (self)
  {
    self.type = type_;
    self.value = value_;
    self.valid = (type_ != EquationTokenTypeInvalid);
  }
  return self;
}

@end
```

Building a class to store tokens is the easier half of the task to tokenize equations. Next, we have to actually parse or tokenize the equation, which we do next.

Parsing the Equation

We could build an EquationTokenizer class to tokenize the equation, but designing with fat models—a term that refers to model classes that also have the smarts to manipulate themselves, rather than rely on controller classes to manipulate them—seems more appropriate. In that vein, we'll build the tokenizing of an equation into the Equation class itself.

Before we start parsing the equation, however, we set up three arrays that hold special strings that we look for when parsing equations. These arrays hold the operators, the trigonometric functions, and the symbols we support, and we use them in our parsing routine to detect operators, trigonometric functions, and symbols. Create them as static arrays inside Equation.m, between the class extension and the start of the implementation, as shown in Listing 4–10.

Listing 4–10. *Declaring the Arrays in* Equation.m

```
...
@interface Equation ()
- (BOOL)produceError:(NSError**)error withCode:(NSInteger)code
andMessage:(NSString*)message;
@end

static NSArray *OPERATORS;
static NSArray *TRIG_FUNCTIONS;
static NSArray *SYMBOLS;

@implementation Equation
...
```

Initialize their contents inside the initialize: method, which is a class method that is called when a class loads. The OPERATORS array contains the operators we support: +, -, *, /, and ^. The TRIG_FUNCTIONS array contains the trigonometric functions we support:

sine (sin) and cosine (cos). Finally, the SYMBOLS array contains the symbols we support: pi (both as the two character "pi" and the single character pi symbol, typed using Option+p) and e. Listing 4–11 shows the implementation of initialize:.

Listing 4–11. *The* initialize: *Method in* Equation.m

```
+ (void)initialize
{
  OPERATORS = [NSArray arrayWithObjects:@"+", @"-", @"*", @"/", @"^", nil];
  TRIG_FUNCTIONS = [NSArray arrayWithObjects:@"sin", @"cos", nil];
  SYMBOLS = [NSArray arrayWithObjects:@"pi", @"e", @"\u03c0", nil];
}
```

You'll see these arrays used later as you develop the method to parse and tokenize equations.

Now, declare a property in the Equation class called tokens that will hold all the parsed tokens. When an Equation object is initialized using the initWithString: method, we'll tokenize the equation's string and store it in the publicly accessible tokens array. Listing 4–12 shows the property in Equation.h.

Listing 4–12. Equation.h *with a* tokens *Property*

```
#import <Foundation/Foundation.h>

@interface Equation : NSObject
{
@private
  NSString *text;
}
@property (nonatomic, strong) NSString *text;
@property (nonatomic, strong) NSMutableArray *tokens;

- (id)initWithString:(NSString*)string;
- (float)evaluateForX:(float)x;
- (BOOL)validate:(NSError **)error;

@end
```

You also must add a synthesize directive in Equation.m, like this:

```
@synthesize tokens;
```

Next, you add a method to do the tokenizing. This method will parse through the current equation, break it into its tokens, create the corresponding EquationToken instances, and put them in the tokens array. The declaration for the tokenizing method, which you put in the class extension in Equation.m, is shown in Listing 4–13.

Listing 4–13. *Declaring the* tokenize: *Method*

```
@interface Equation ()
- (BOOL)produceError:(NSError**)error withCode:(NSInteger)code
andMessage:(NSString*)message;
- (void)tokenize;
@end
```

Edit the `initWithString:` method to create the tokens array, and then call the `tokenize:` method, as shown in Listing 4–14.

Listing 4–14. *Initializing tokens*

```
- (id)initWithString:(NSString *)string
{
  self = [super init];
  if (self)
  {
    self.text = string;
    self.tokens = [NSMutableArray array];
    [self tokenize];
  }
  return self;
}
```

Implementing the Method to Tokenize the Equation

Now, turn your attention to implementing the `tokenize:` method. We have some serious work to do. We must walk through the equations that users enter and turn them into tokens of one or more characters. Some of this gets a little messy, so we build the method for tokenizing the string in several steps through the next several sections, adding more parsing capabilities as we go.

At its core, tokenizing the equation means going through its characters, one by one, and creating tokens that represent the characters' types and values. Because some tokens can comprise multiple characters, however, we can't just walk through the string of characters one by one. Numbers, for example, can have multiple digits, and we should create a single token to represent the number 100, rather than three tokens (one for "1" and one for each "0"). Instead, we must read ahead into the string to create multicharacter tokens as appropriate. With that in mind, first import the `EquationToken.h` header into `Equation.m`:

```
#import "EquationToken.h"
```

Then, start creating the `tokenize:` method with the code in Listing 4–15.

Listing 4–15. *The Initial* `tokenize:` *Method*

```
- (void)tokenize
{
  [tokens removeAllObjects];
  NSString *temp = @"";
  EquationToken *token = nil;
  for (NSUInteger i = 0, n = text.length; i < n; i++)
  {
    unichar c = [text characterAtIndex:i];
    temp = [temp stringByAppendingFormat:@"%C", c];

    // Something goes here

    [tokens addObject:token];
    temp = @"";
```

```
    }
}
```

This code creates an array to store all the tokens it will create and creates a temporary string variable to hold the one or more characters that represent the token. It creates a pointer variable to a token that it will use to temporarily hold the current token, before adding it to the array. Then, the code loops through the input string, stored in the member variable `text`, a character at a time, appending each character to the temp string. It clears the temp string before looping. This code is clean and straightforward, but it doesn't yet accomplish anything useful. See the comment "Something goes here"? We still must add code to recognize the characters being parsed and create the appropriate token.

Converting a String to a Token

To create the token, create a new method called `newTokenFromString:` that accepts a string and returns a corresponding token, with the corresponding token type and value. Since this method shouldn't belong to the public interface (no other code should create tokens), add the declaration to the class extension, as shown in Listing 4–16.

Listing 4–16. *Declaring* `newTokenFromString:`

```
@interface Equation ()
- (BOOL)produceError:(NSError**)error withCode:(NSInteger)code
andMessage:(NSString*)message;
- (void)tokenize;
- (EquationToken *)newTokenFromString:(NSString *)string;
@end
```

The implementation of `newTokenFromString:` creates a lowercase version of the string and then compares it with various known token values to determine what type of token to create. Remember, for example, the arrays we created for the operators, trigonometric functions, and symbols we support? We compare the specified string to the contents of these arrays to determine whether to create a token of one of those types. We also check for parentheses, variables (the letter "x"), numbers, or spaces. If the passed value matches none of these, we recognize it as an invalid token. Listing 4–17 shows the implementation for `newTokenFromString:`.

Listing 4–17. *newTokenFromString:*

```
- (EquationToken *)newTokenFromString:(NSString *)string
{
  EquationTokenType type;
  string = [string lowercaseString];
  if ([OPERATORS containsObject:string])
  {
    type = EquationTokenTypeOperator;
  }
  else if ([TRIG_FUNCTIONS containsObject:string])
  {
    type = EquationTokenTypeTrigFunction;
  }
```

```objc
  else if ([SYMBOLS containsObject:string])
  {
    type = EquationTokenTypeSymbol;
  }
  else if ([string isEqualToString:@"("])
  {
    type = EquationTokenTypeOpenParen;
  }
  else if ([string isEqualToString:@")"])
  {
    type = EquationTokenTypeCloseParen;
  }
  else if ([string isEqualToString:@"x"])
  {
    type = EquationTokenTypeVariable;
  }
  // Digits are all grouped together in the tokenize: method, so just check the first
character
  else if (isdigit([string characterAtIndex:0]) || [string characterAtIndex:0] == '.')
  {
    type = EquationTokenTypeNumber;
  }
  // Spaces are all grouped together in the tokenize: method, so just check the first
character
  else if ([string characterAtIndex:0] == ' ')
  {
    type = EquationTokenTypeWhitespace;
  }
  else
  {
    type = EquationTokenTypeInvalid;
  }
  return [[EquationToken alloc] initWithType:type andValue:string];
}
```

Having a method to create the appropriate token from a string allows us to update the "Something goes here" comment in the tokenize: method to actually create the token, so remove the comment and add a call to newTokenFromString:, as in Listing 4–18.

Listing 4–18. *Calling* newTokenFromString: *from the* tokenize: *Method*

```objc
- (void)tokenize
{
  [tokens removeAllObjects];
  NSString *temp = @"";
  EquationToken *token = nil;
  for (NSUInteger i = 0, n = text.length; i < n; i++)
  {
    unichar c = [text characterAtIndex:i];
    temp = [temp stringByAppendingFormat:@"%C", c];

    token = [self newTokenFromString:temp];

    [tokens addObject:token];
    temp = @"";
```

```
  }
}
```

This is a good start; this implementation of `tokenize:` recognizes single-character tokens accurately: parentheses, variables, e, the single-character version of pi, operators, and numbers that happen to be a single digit. We're not ready, however, to release this version, or even test it, until we add support for multiple-character tokens. Although recognizing each kind of multiple-character token shares similar approaches, each requires some special handling that requires different code. We tackle each of these scenarios in turn, sacrificing some code optimization opportunities for the purpose of maintaining clarity.

Recognizing Numbers

As we walk through the characters of the input string, when we come across a digit character we want to continue to read characters and tack them onto our `temp` string until we come to the first nondigit character (or the end of the string). This way, we contain a valid, multidigit number in a single token. We also want to support decimals, so we treat a period like a digit. Our code for recognizing multidigit numbers is shown in Listing 4–19.

Listing 4–19. *Recognizing Multidigit Numbers*

```objc
- (void)tokenize
{
  [tokens removeAllObjects];
  NSString *temp = @"";
  EquationToken *token = nil;
  for (NSUInteger i = 0, n = text.length; i < n; i++)
  {
    unichar c = [text characterAtIndex:i];
    temp = [temp stringByAppendingFormat:@"%C", c];

    // Keep all digits of a number as one token
    if (isdigit(c) || c == '.')
    {
      // Keep reading characters until we hit the end of the string
      while (i < (n - 1))
      {
        // Increment our loop variable
        ++i;
        // Get the next character
        c = [text characterAtIndex:i];
        // Test to see whether to continue
        if (isdigit(c) || c == '.')
        {
          // Append the character to the temp string
          temp = [temp stringByAppendingFormat:@"%C", c];
        }
        else
        {
          // Character didn't match, so back the loop counter up and exit
          --i;
```

```
            break;
        }
      }
    }

    token = [self newTokenFromString:temp];

    [tokens addObject:token];
    temp = @"";
  }
}
```

Notice that if we get to a nondigit or nonperiod character, we back up the loop counter by one so that the character we read isn't lost but rather is read the next time through the loop as we start reading a new token.

You might also notice that this code allows a number to have more than one decimal point, which shouldn't be valid. Rather than complicate this code with decimal point counting, however, we'll catch multiple decimal points later.

Grouping Spaces

Although some people can comfortably squash their equations together, with numbers, operators, parentheses, and any other characters mashed together without any spaces, others like their equations to breathe a little, inserting spaces between numbers and operators to increase readability. We shouldn't care about spaces and should treat these three equations identically:

```
x^2+2*x+7
x^2 + 2*x + 7
x ^ 2   +   2 * x   + 7
```

We should also lump multiple consecutive spaces into a single token with the type `EquationTokenTypeWhitespace`. To combine consecutive spaces, we can employ an algorithm that's nearly identical to our digit detection code. Listing 4–20 shows the addition of code to detect multiple spaces.

Listing 4–20. *Code to Recognize Multiple Spaces*

```
- (void)tokenize
{
  [tokens removeAllObjects];
  NSString *temp = @"";
  EquationToken *token = nil;
  for (NSUInteger i = 0, n = text.length; i < n; i++)
  {
    unichar c = [text characterAtIndex:i];
    temp = [temp stringByAppendingFormat:@"%C", c];

    // Keep all digits of a number as one token
    if (isdigit(c) || c == '.')
    {
      // Keep reading characters until we hit the end of the string
      while (i < (n - 1))
      {
```

```objc
      // Increment our loop variable
      ++i;
      // Get the next character
      c = [text characterAtIndex:i];
      // Test to see whether to continue
      if (isdigit(c) || c == '.')
      {
        // Append the character to the temp string
        temp = [temp stringByAppendingFormat:@"%C", c];
      }
      else
      {
        // Character didn't match, so back the loop counter up and exit
        --i;
        break;
      }
    }
  }

  // Keep all spaces together
  else if (c == ' ')
  {
    // Keep reading characters until we hit the end of the string
    while (i < (n - 1))
    {
      // Increment our loop variable
      ++i;
      // Get the next character
      c = [text characterAtIndex:i];
      // Test to see whether to continue
      if (c == ' ')
      {
        // Append the character to the temp string
        temp = [temp stringByAppendingFormat:@"%C", c];
      }
      else
      {
        // Character didn't match, so back the loop counter up and exit
        --i;
        break;
      }
    }
  }

  token = [self newTokenFromString:temp];

  [tokens addObject:token];
  temp = @"";
  }
}
```

Read through this code and note the similarities to the digit detection code. We could try to do something clever to reduce the code duplication—Objective-C's relatively new support for blocks comes to mind—but we'll leave the code as is to keep things relatively simple.

We've now written code to recognize multicharacter digits and multiple consecutive spaces. We have two other multiple character token possibilities, however: trigonometric functions and symbols. We knock out those two token types in the next section.

Recognizing Trigonometric Functions and Symbols

Remember the arrays we created, called TRIG_FUNCTIONS and SYMBOLS, to hold the trigonometric functions and symbols we support? We're ready to use them now to detect whether the current token belongs to one of these groups. The approach for both these arrays is the same:

1. Loop through the elements in the array.

2. For each element, determine whether its length could fit in what remains of the input string.

3. If the length fits, compare the element to the input string to see whether they match.

4. If they match, move the index counter to the end of the matching string.

To compare the element to a piece of the input string, we use NSString's substringWithRange: method, which grabs a piece from the string using the specified range. Ranges specify a starting index and a length. To create the range, we use the NSMakeRange function, which takes an index and a length and returns an NSRange struct. The index we use is the current index, i, and the length is the length of the element we're comparing the input string to. The code to get the substring looks like this:

```
[text substringWithRange:NSMakeRange(i, [element length])];
```

One more thing we want to do when making the comparison: we want to normalize the case of the text so that both sin and SIN, for example, match sin (the sine trigonometric function). We use NSString's lowercaseString: method to convert the input substring to lowercase, which is the case we used for the elements in both TRIG_FUNCTIONS and SYMBOLS.

Listing 4–21 shows the growing tokenize: method with the code added to detect trigonometric functions and symbols.

Listing 4–21. *Detecting Trigonometric Functions and Symbols*

```
- (void)tokenize
{
  [tokens removeAllObjects];
  NSString *temp = @"";
  EquationToken *token = nil;
  for (NSUInteger i = 0, n = text.length; i < n; i++)
  {
    unichar c = [text characterAtIndex:i];
    temp = [temp stringByAppendingFormat:@"%C", c];

    // Keep all digits of a number as one token
    if (isdigit(c) || c == '.')
```

```
  {
    // Keep reading characters until we hit the end of the string
    while (i < (n - 1))
    {
      // Increment our loop variable
      ++i;
      // Get the next character
      c = [text characterAtIndex:i];
      // Test to see whether to continue
      if (isdigit(c) || c == '.')
      {
        // Append the character to the temp string
        temp = [temp stringByAppendingFormat:@"%C", c];
      }
      else
      {
        // Character didn't match, so back the loop counter up and exit
        --i;
        break;
      }
    }
  }

  // Keep all spaces together
  else if (c == ' ')
  {
    // Keep reading characters until we hit the end of the string
    while (i < (n - 1))
    {
      // Increment our loop variable
      ++i;
      // Get the next character
      c = [text characterAtIndex:i];
      // Test to see whether to continue
      if (c == ' ')
      {
        // Append the character to the temp string
        temp = [temp stringByAppendingFormat:@"%C", c];
      }
      else
      {
        // Character didn't match, so back the loop counter up and exit
        --i;
        break;
      }
    }
  }

  // Check for trig functions
  for (NSString *trig in TRIG_FUNCTIONS)
  {
    if (trig.length <= (n - i) && [trig isEqualToString:[[text
substringWithRange:NSMakeRange(i, trig.length)] lowercaseString]])
    {
      temp = trig;
      i += (trig.length] - 1);
      break;
```

```
        }
    }

    // Check for symbols
    for (NSString *symbol in SYMBOLS)
    {
        if (symbol.length <= (n - i) && [symbol isEqualToString:[[text
substringWithRange:NSMakeRange(i, symbol.length)] lowercaseString]])
        {
            temp = symbol;
            i += (symbol.length - 1);
            break;
        }
    }

    token = [self newTokenFromString:temp];

    [tokens addObject:token];
    temp = @"";
    }
}
```

At this point, we've added all the code before the line that calls newTokenFromString:. We're ready to let that line of code run and create an EquationToken object from the input. We still have some cleanup to do after that call, though, which is outlined in the next few sections.

Recognizing Exponents

So far, our tokenizing recognizes all digits as number tokens. It should recognize some of these digits, however, as exponents. We recognize the following tokens as exponents instead of numbers:

- Numbers that immediately follow the ^ symbol (for example, ^2)

- Numbers that immediately follow a variable (for example, x2)

- Numbers that immediately follow a close parenthesis (for example, (x+3)2)

After we've created the current token, then we check to see whether we have a number token and then whether we should change it from a number type to an exponent type. To make the determination, we check whether we have a previous token and, if so, whether it matches any of the three rules listed earlier for exponents. The code to do this follows the line of code that creates the new token and is shown in Listing 4–22.

Listing 4–22. *Finding Exponents*

```
- (void)tokenize
{
    [tokens removeAllObjects];
    NSString *temp = @"";
    EquationToken *token = nil;
    for (NSUInteger i = 0, n = text.length; i < n; i++)
```

```
{
  unichar c = [text characterAtIndex:i];
  temp = [temp stringByAppendingFormat:@"%C", c];

  // Keep all digits of a number as one token
  if (isdigit(c) || c == '.')
  {
    // Keep reading characters until we hit the end of the string
    while (i < (n - 1))
    {
      // Increment our loop variable
      ++i;
      // Get the next character
      c = [text characterAtIndex:i];
      // Test to see whether to continue
      if (isdigit(c) || c == '.')
      {
        // Append the character to the temp string
        temp = [temp stringByAppendingFormat:@"%C", c];
      }
      else
      {
        // Character didn't match, so back the loop counter up and exit
        --i;
        break;
      }
    }
  }

  // Keep all spaces together
  else if (c == ' ')
  {
    // Keep reading characters until we hit the end of the string
    while (i < (n - 1))
    {
      // Increment our loop variable
      ++i;
      // Get the next character
      c = [text characterAtIndex:i];
      // Test to see whether to continue
      if (c == ' ')
      {
        // Append the character to the temp string
        temp = [temp stringByAppendingFormat:@"%C", c];
      }
      else
      {
        // Character didn't match, so back the loop counter up and exit
        --i;
        break;
      }
    }
  }

  // Check for trig functions
  for (NSString *trig in TRIG_FUNCTIONS)
  {
```

```
        if (trig.length <= (n - i) && [trig isEqualToString:[[text
substringWithRange:NSMakeRange(i, trig.length)] lowercaseString]])
        {
          temp = trig;
          i += (trig.length - 1);
          break;
        }
    }

    // Check for symbols
    for (NSString *symbol in SYMBOLS)
    {
        if (symbol.length <= (n - i) && [symbol isEqualToString:[[text
substringWithRange:NSMakeRange(i, symbol.length)] lowercaseString]])
        {
          temp = symbol;
          i += (symbol.length - 1);
          break;
        }
    }

    token = [self newTokenFromString:temp];

    // Determine if this should be an exponent
    // Check that we have a previous token to follow and that this is a number
    if (token.type == EquationTokenTypeNumber && !(tokens.count == 0))
    {
      // Get the previous token
      EquationToken *previousToken = [tokens lastObject];

      // If the previous token is a variable, close parenthesis, or the ^ operator, this
is an exponent
      if (previousToken.type == EquationTokenTypeVariable ||
          previousToken.type == EquationTokenTypeCloseParen ||
          [previousToken.value isEqualToString:@"^"])
      {
        token.type = EquationTokenTypeExponent;
      }
    }

    [tokens addObject:token];
    temp = @"";
  }
}
```

You can see that this code does as we describe, changing the current token from a number type to an exponent type if any of the three exponent rules match. To verify that this code works, create a unit test for it by creating a new Cocoa Objective-C test case class, as shown in Figure 4–16, and click Next. Call the class ExponentTests and set the test type to Logic, as shown in Figure 4–17. Click Next, and save it in the GraphiqueTests folder, the GraphiqueTests group, and the GraphiqueTests target.

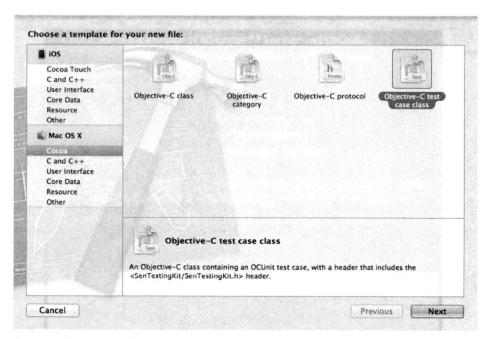

Figure 4–16. *Creating a test case*

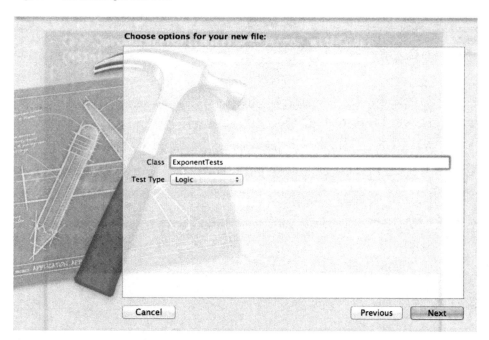

Figure 4–17. *Naming the test class and setting its type*

The header file, shown in Listing 4–23, declares a single method called testExponents:.

Listing 4–23. *ExponentTests.h*

```
#import <SenTestingKit/SenTestingKit.h>

@interface ExponentTests : SenTestCase

- (void)testExponents;

@end
```

In the implementation of testExponents:, create an equation with tokens of various types, including both numbers and exponents, and verify that the numbers stay numbers and the exponents become exponents. Listing 4–24 shows the implementation.

Listing 4–24. *ExponentTests.m*

```
#import "ExponentTests.h"
#import "Equation.h"
#import "EquationToken.h"

@implementation ExponentTests

-(void)testExponents
{
  Equation *equation = [[Equation alloc] initWithString:@"32x2+(x+7)45+3^3"];
  NSArray *tokens = equation.tokens;

  STAssertTrue(tokens.count == 14, NULL);

  EquationToken *token = nil;

  token = [tokens objectAtIndex:0];
  STAssertEquals(EquationTokenTypeNumber, token.type, NULL);
  STAssertEqualObjects(@"32", token.value, NULL);

  token = [tokens objectAtIndex:2];
  STAssertEquals(EquationTokenTypeExponent, token.type, NULL);
  STAssertEqualObjects(@"2", token.value, NULL);

  token = [tokens objectAtIndex:7];
  STAssertEquals(EquationTokenTypeNumber, token.type, NULL);
  STAssertEqualObjects(@"7", token.value, NULL);

  token = [tokens objectAtIndex:9];
  STAssertEquals(EquationTokenTypeExponent, token.type, NULL);
  STAssertEqualObjects(@"45", token.value, NULL);

  token = [tokens objectAtIndex:11];
  STAssertEquals(EquationTokenTypeNumber, token.type, NULL);
  STAssertEqualObjects(@"3", token.value, NULL);

  token = [tokens objectAtIndex:13];
  STAssertEquals(EquationTokenTypeExponent, token.type, NULL);
```

```
    STAssertEqualObjects(@"3", token.value, NULL);
}
```

`@end`

Run your tests using ⌘+U and verify that they all pass. Assuming they do, you have successfully implemented exponent recognition.

Creating a Stack for Parenthesis Matching

Effectively matching parentheses turns out to be a problem with a straightforward solution, as described in such sites as `www.ccs.neu.edu/home/sbratus/com1101/lab4.html`. To summarize, an approach that works cleanly and simply is as follows:

1. Create a stack.

2. Read through your input, character by character.

3. If the current character is an open parenthesis, push it onto your stack.

4. If the current character is a close parenthesis and you have an open parenthesis at the top of your stack, pop the open parenthesis and match it with this close parenthesis.

5. Any close parentheses without corresponding open parentheses on the stack are unmatched.

6. Any remaining open parentheses on the stack, once you've read all the input, are unmatched.

To implement our parenthesis matching, then, we start by creating a stack. A stack stores and retrieves a collection of data in a last in, first out (LIFO) approach: a "retrieve" operation returns the most recently stored object. Storing an object in a stack is typically called *pushing* the object onto the stack, and retrieving the object from the stock is usually called *popping* it off the stack. Popping an object off the stack both retrieves it from the stack and deletes it from the stack. A typical stack class, then, supports a push and a pop operation. Some stack implementations also support a peek operation that returns the most recently stored object but doesn't delete it from the stack, and some support an operation for determining whether the stack is currently empty (contains no data). Which operations does the Cocoa stack class support? None at all—Cocoa has no stack class!

Luckily, however, writing a stack class is fairly simple, especially because you can leverage Cocoa's `NSMutableArray` class to do all the storage and retrieval. In this section, we create a stack class called `Stack` and incorporate it into the equation editor to do the parenthesis balancing.

Creating the Stack Class

Start creating your stack by creating a new Cocoa Objective-C class called Stack that derives from NSObject. This class will offer three operations:

- push, to push an object onto the stack

- pop, to pop an object off the stack

- hasObjects, to determine whether the stack has any objects

In addition to declaring methods for these three operations in Stack.h, you also must declare the NSMutableArray private member for storing and retrieving data. Listing 4–25 shows the code for Stack.h.

Listing 4–25. *Stack.h*

```
#import <Foundation/Foundation.h>

@interface Stack : NSObject {
@private
  NSMutableArray *stack;
}

- (void)push:(id)anObject;
- (id)pop;
- (BOOL)hasObjects;

@end
```

The implementation file, Stack.m, creates the stack NSMutableArray member in its init: method. The Stack class's push: method adds the passed object to the end of stack. The pop: method retrieves the last object from stack, deletes the object from stack, and then returns the object. Finally, the hasObjects: method returns whether the stack has any objects using NSMutableArray's count: method. Listing 4–26 shows Stack.m.

Listing 4–26. *Stack.m*

```
#import "Stack.h"

@implementation Stack

- (id)init
{
  self = [super init];
  if (self)
  {
    stack = [NSMutableArray array];
  }
  return self;
}

- (void)push:(id)anObject
{
  [stack addObject:anObject];
```

```
}

- (id)pop
{
  id anObject = [stack lastObject];
  [stack removeObject:anObject];
  return anObject;
}

- (BOOL)hasObjects
{
  return [stack count] > 0;
}

@end
```

See how simple that was? The NSMutableArray class takes care of the tricky parts of storage and retrieval.

Before we incorporate Stack into the equation editor, however, we should test it to ensure it works as we expect. Read on to the next section to see how to write automated unit tests for Stack.

Testing the Stack Class

To test the Stack class, create a test case that pushes 1,000 objects onto a stack, makes sure the stack isn't empty, and then pops the objects off the stack, one at a time, and verifies that the 1,000 pushed objects are popped in reverse order. Finally, verify that after all 1,000 objects are popped off the stack, the stack is empty. Create a new Cocoa Objective-C test case class called StackTests, making it a Logic-type test and making sure to add it to the GraphiqueTests folder and the GraphiqueTests target but not the Graphique target. Declare a method called testPushAndPop: in StackTests.h so that it matches Listing 4–27.

Listing 4–27. *StackTests.h*

```
#import <SenTestingKit/SenTestingKit.h>

@interface StackTests : SenTestCase

- (void)testPushAndPop;

@end
```

StackTests.m implements the testPushAndPop: method as outlined earlier, pushing NSString objects that reflect their index number (0–999) in the stack so that we can easily verify that they're popped off in the correct order (999 through 0). See Listing 4–28.

Listing 4–28. *StackTests.m*

```
#import "StackTests.h"
#import "Stack.h"
```

```
@implementation StackTests

- (void)testPushAndPop
{
  Stack *stack = [[Stack alloc] init];
  for (int i = 0; i < 1000; i++)
  {
    [stack push:[NSString stringWithFormat:@"String #%d", i]];
  }
  STAssertTrue([stack hasObjects], @"Stack should not be empty after pushing 1,000
objects");

  for (int i = 999; i >= 0; i--)
  {
    NSString *string = (NSString *)[stack pop];
    NSString *comp = [NSString stringWithFormat:@"String #%d", i];
    STAssertEqualObjects(string, comp, NULL);
  }
  STAssertFalse([stack hasObjects], @"Stack should be empty after popping 1,000
objects");
}

@end
```

Run your tests using ⌘+U and verify that they all pass. Now you can feel confident that Stack is ready to handle its parenthesis-balancing chores.

Balancing Parentheses Using Stack

You're ready to implement the parenthesis-matching algorithm in the tokenize: method. Start by importing the Stack.h header at the top of Equation.m:

`#import "Stack.h"`

In the tokenize: method, create a Stack instance. Then, after the exponent-detection code, include code that uses the Stack instance to perform parenthesis matching. This code should set each new open parenthesis as invalid, because it's not yet matched, and set it to valid only when it's matched to a close parenthesis. Listing 4–29 contains the updated tokenize: method.

Listing 4–29. *Parenthesis Matching*

```
- (void)tokenize
{
  [tokens removeAllObjects];
  Stack *stack = [[Stack alloc] init];

  NSString *temp = @"";
  EquationToken *token = nil;
  for (NSUInteger i = 0, n = text.length; i < n; i++)
  {
    unichar c = [text characterAtIndex:i];
    temp = [temp stringByAppendingFormat:@"%C", c];

    // Keep all digits of a number as one token
```

```objc
if (isdigit(c) || c == '.')
{
  // Keep reading characters until we hit the end of the string
  while (i < (n - 1))
  {
    // Increment our loop variable
    ++i;
    // Get the next character
    c = [text characterAtIndex:i];
    // Test to see whether to continue
    if (isdigit(c) || c == '.')
    {
      // Append the character to the temp string
      temp = [temp stringByAppendingFormat:@"%C", c];
    }
    else
    {
      // Character didn't match, so back the loop counter up and exit
      --i;
      break;
    }
  }
}

// Keep all spaces together
else if (c == ' ')
{
  // Keep reading characters until we hit the end of the string
  while (i < (n - 1))
  {
    // Increment our loop variable
    ++i;
    // Get the next character
    c = [text characterAtIndex:i];
    // Test to see whether to continue
    if (c == ' ')
    {
      // Append the character to the temp string
      temp = [temp stringByAppendingFormat:@"%C", c];
    }
    else
    {
      // Character didn't match, so back the loop counter up and exit
      --i;
      break;
    }
  }
}

// Check for trig functions
for (NSString *trig in TRIG_FUNCTIONS)
{
  if (trig.length <= (n - i) && [trig isEqualToString:[[text
substringWithRange:NSMakeRange(i, trig.length)] lowercaseString]])
  {
    temp = trig;
    i += (trig.length - 1);
```

```
          break;
       }
    }

    // Check for symbols
    for (NSString *symbol in SYMBOLS)
    {
       if (symbol.length <= (n - i) && [symbol isEqualToString:[[text
substringWithRange:NSMakeRange(i, symbol.length)] lowercaseString]])
       {
          temp = symbol;
          i += (symbol.length - 1);
          break;
       }
    }

    token = [self newTokenFromString:temp];

    // Determine if this should be an exponent
    // Check that we have a previous token to follow and that this is a number
    if (token.type == EquationTokenTypeNumber && !(tokens.count == 0))
    {
       // Get the previous token
       EquationToken *previousToken = [tokens lastObject];

       // If the previous token is a variable, close parenthesis, or the ^ operator, this
is an exponent
       if (previousToken.type == EquationTokenTypeVariable ||
           previousToken.type == EquationTokenTypeCloseParen ||
           [previousToken.value isEqualToString:@"^"])
       {
          token.type = EquationTokenTypeExponent;
       }
    }

    // Do parenthesis matching
    if (token.type == EquationTokenTypeOpenParen)
    {
       // Set the new open parenthesis to invalid, as it's not yet matched,
       // and push it onto the stack
       token.valid = NO;
       [stack push:token];
    }
    else if (token.type == EquationTokenTypeCloseParen)
    {
       // See if we have a matching open parenthesis
       if (![stack hasObjects])
       {
          // No open parenthesis to match, so this close parenthesis is invalid
          token.valid = NO;
       }
       else
       {
          // We have a matching open parenthesis, so set it (and this close parenthesis)
          // to valid and pop the open parenthesis off the stack
          EquationToken *match = [stack pop];
```

```
            match.valid = YES;
        }
    }

    [tokens addObject:token];
    temp = @"";
  }
}
```

Detecting Multiple Decimal Points

We said before that you still must catch numbers with multiple decimal points and mark them as invalid. To do this, add code that splits any number tokens into components separated by decimal points. If you have more than two such components (the number before the decimal point and the number after), the token is invalid. Listing 4–30 shows the tokenize: method with this code added.

Listing 4–30. *Detecting Multiple Decimal Points*

```
- (void)tokenize
{
  [tokens removeAllObjects];
  Stack *stack = [[Stack alloc] init];

  NSString *temp = @"";
  EquationToken *token = nil;
  for (NSUInteger i = 0, n = text.length; i < n; i++)
  {
    unichar c = [text characterAtIndex:i];
    temp = [temp stringByAppendingFormat:@"%C", c];

    // Keep all digits of a number as one token
    if (isdigit(c) || c == '.')
    {
      // Keep reading characters until we hit the end of the string
      while (i < (n - 1))
      {
        // Increment our loop variable
        ++i;
        // Get the next character
        c = [text characterAtIndex:i];
        // Test to see whether to continue
        if (isdigit(c) || c == '.')
        {
          // Append the character to the temp string
          temp = [temp stringByAppendingFormat:@"%C", c];
        }
        else
        {
          // Character didn't match, so back the loop counter up and exit
          --i;
          break;
        }
      }
    }
  }
```

```
    // Keep all spaces together
    else if (c == ' ')
    {
      // Keep reading characters until we hit the end of the string
      while (i < (n - 1))
      {
        // Increment our loop variable
        ++i;
        // Get the next character
        c = [text characterAtIndex:i];
        // Test to see whether to continue
        if (c == ' ')
        {
          // Append the character to the temp string
          temp = [temp stringByAppendingFormat:@"%C", c];
        }
        else
        {
          // Character didn't match, so back the loop counter up and exit
          --i;
          break;
        }
      }
    }

    // Check for trig functions
    for (NSString *trig in TRIG_FUNCTIONS)
    {
      if (trig.length <= (n - i) && [trig isEqualToString:[[text
substringWithRange:NSMakeRange(i, trig.length)] lowercaseString]])
      {
        temp = trig;
        i += (trig.length - 1);
        break;
      }
    }

    // Check for symbols
    for (NSString *symbol in SYMBOLS)
    {
      if (symbol.length <= (n - i) && [symbol isEqualToString:[[text
substringWithRange:NSMakeRange(i, symbol.length)] lowercaseString]])
      {
        temp = symbol;
        i += (symbol.length - 1);
        break;
      }
    }

    token = [self newTokenFromString:temp];

    // Determine if this should be an exponent
    // Check that we have a previous token to follow and that this is a number
    if (token.type == EquationTokenTypeNumber && !(tokens.count == 0))
    {
      // Get the previous token
```

```
        EquationToken *previousToken = [tokens lastObject];

        // If the previous token is a variable, close parenthesis, or the ^ operator, this
is an exponent
        if (previousToken.type == EquationTokenTypeVariable ||
            previousToken.type == EquationTokenTypeCloseParen ||
            [previousToken.value isEqualToString:@"^"])
        {
          token.type = EquationTokenTypeExponent;
        }
      }

      // Do parenthesis matching
      if (token.type == EquationTokenTypeOpenParen)
      {
        // Set the new open parenthesis to invalid, as it's not yet matched,
        // and push it onto the stack
        token.valid = NO;
        [stack push:token];
      }
      else if (token.type == EquationTokenTypeCloseParen)
      {
        // See if we have a matching open parenthesis
        if (![stack hasObjects])
        {
          // No open parenthesis to match, so this close parenthesis is invalid
          token.valid = NO;
        }
        else
        {
          // We have a matching open parenthesis, so set it (and this close parenthesis)
          // to valid and pop the open parenthesis off the stack
          EquationToken *match = [stack pop];
          match.valid = YES;
        }
      }

      // Numbers with more than one decimal point are invalid
      if (token.type == EquationTokenTypeNumber && [[token.value
componentsSeparatedByString:@"."] count] > 2)
      {
        token.valid = NO;
      }

      [tokens addObject:token];
      temp = @"";
    }
}
```

The tokenize: method is now complete.

Before congratulating yourself too much, however, you should test it. You've already tested the code for the exponent recognition and the stack. In the next section, you write tests to exercise the rest of the tokenize: method.

Testing the Tokenizer

Create a new Cocoa Objective-C test case class called `EquationTokenizeTests`, with the Logic test type, and put it in the `GraphiqueTests` folder, group, and target. Declare all the test methods in `EquationTokenizeTests.h` that you'll create in this chapter, as well as a helper method that you'll use to test both the type and the value of a specified token. Listing 4–31 shows the code for `EquationTokenizeTests.h`.

Listing 4–31. *EquationTokenizeTests.h*

```
#import <SenTestingKit/SenTestingKit.h>
#import "EquationToken.h"

@interface EquationTokenizeTests : SenTestCase

- (void)testSimple;
- (void)testExponent;
- (void)testExponentWithCaret;
- (void)testExponentWithParens;
- (void)testWhitespace;
- (void)testTrigFunctionsAndSymbols;
- (void)testParenthesisMatching;
- (void)testInvalid;
- (void)helperTestToken:(EquationToken *)token type:(EquationTokenType)type
value:(NSString *)value;

@end
```

In `EquationTokenizeTests.m`, implement the `helperTestToken:type:value` method to test the specified token's type and value against the specified type and value. Listing 4–32 shows the `EquationTokenizeTests.m` file.

Listing 4–32. *EquationTokenizeTests.m*

```
#import "EquationTokenizeTests.h"
#import "Equation.h"

@implementation EquationTokenizeTests

- (void)helperTestToken:(EquationToken *)token type:(EquationTokenType)type
value:(NSString *)value
{
  STAssertEquals(token.type, type, NULL);
  STAssertEqualObjects(token.value, value, NULL);
}

@end
```

Now we're ready to write tests. The next few sections add tests, one at a time. Each of the tests creates an equation, parses it into its tokens, and verifies the number of tokens. It also verifies that each token has the expected type and value.

Testing Simple Equations

Start by testing a simple equation: 22*x-1. This equation should parse into five tokens:

- The number 22
- The multiplication operator
- The variable x
- The subtraction operator
- The number 1

Listing 4–33 shows the method.

Listing 4–33. *Testing a Simple Equation*

```
- (void)testSimple
{
  Equation *equation = [[Equation alloc] initWithString:@"22*x-1"];
  NSArray *tokens = equation.tokens;
  STAssertTrue(tokens.count == 5, NULL);
  [self helperTestToken:[tokens objectAtIndex:0] type:EquationTokenTypeNumber
value:@"22"];
  [self helperTestToken:[tokens objectAtIndex:1] type:EquationTokenTypeOperator
value:@"*"];
  [self helperTestToken:[tokens objectAtIndex:2] type:EquationTokenTypeVariable
value:@"x"];
  [self helperTestToken:[tokens objectAtIndex:3] type:EquationTokenTypeOperator
value:@"-"];
  [self helperTestToken:[tokens objectAtIndex:4] type:EquationTokenTypeNumber
value:@"1"];
}
```

Testing Exponents

The next three methods test exponents. The first, testExponent:, tests the case of an exponent following a variable, x. The next, testExponentWithCaret:, tests the case of an exponent in the more traditional location: after a caret. Finally, testExponentWithParens: tests that an exponent is detected when it follows a close parenthesis. Add the code in Listing 4–34 to EquationTokenizeTests.m.

Listing 4–34. *Testing Exponents*

```
- (void)testExponent
{
  Equation *equation = [[Equation alloc] initWithString:@"x2"];
  NSArray *tokens = equation.tokens;
  STAssertTrue(tokens.count == 2, NULL);
  [self helperTestToken:[tokens objectAtIndex:0] type:EquationTokenTypeVariable
value:@"x"];
  [self helperTestToken:[tokens objectAtIndex:1] type:EquationTokenTypeExponent
value:@"2"];
```

```
}

- (void)testExponentWithCaret
{
  Equation *equation = [[Equation alloc] initWithString:@"x^2"];
  NSArray *tokens = equation.tokens;
  STAssertTrue(tokens.count == 3, NULL);
  [self helperTestToken:[tokens objectAtIndex:0] type:EquationTokenTypeVariable
value:@"x"];
  [self helperTestToken:[tokens objectAtIndex:1] type:EquationTokenTypeOperator
value:@"^"];
  [self helperTestToken:[tokens objectAtIndex:2] type:EquationTokenTypeExponent
value:@"2"];
}

- (void)testExponentWithParens
{
  Equation *equation = [[Equation alloc] initWithString:@"(3x+7)2"];
  NSArray *tokens = equation.tokens;
  STAssertTrue(tokens.count == 7, NULL);
  [self helperTestToken:[tokens objectAtIndex:0] type:EquationTokenTypeOpenParen
value:@"("];
  [self helperTestToken:[tokens objectAtIndex:1] type:EquationTokenTypeNumber
value:@"3"];
  [self helperTestToken:[tokens objectAtIndex:2] type:EquationTokenTypeVariable
value:@"x"];
  [self helperTestToken:[tokens objectAtIndex:3] type:EquationTokenTypeOperator
value:@"+"];
  [self helperTestToken:[tokens objectAtIndex:4] type:EquationTokenTypeNumber
value:@"7"];
  [self helperTestToken:[tokens objectAtIndex:5] type:EquationTokenTypeCloseParen
value:@")"];
  [self helperTestToken:[tokens objectAtIndex:6] type:EquationTokenTypeExponent
value:@"2"];
}
```

Testing Whitespace

We want to verify that spaces are collapsed into a single token, so we write a test that uses an equation that has multiple consecutive spaces. Listing 4–35 contains the whitespace test.

Listing 4–35. *Testing Whitespace*

```
- (void)testWhitespace
{
  Equation *equation = [[Equation alloc] initWithString:@"x   +   7"];
  NSArray *tokens = equation.tokens;
  STAssertTrue(tokens.count == 5, NULL);
  [self helperTestToken:[tokens objectAtIndex:0] type:EquationTokenTypeVariable
value:@"x"];
  [self helperTestToken:[tokens objectAtIndex:1] type:EquationTokenTypeWhitespace
value:@"   "];
```

```
  [self helperTestToken:[tokens objectAtIndex:2] type:EquationTokenTypeOperator
value:@"+"];
  [self helperTestToken:[tokens objectAtIndex:3] type:EquationTokenTypeWhitespace
value:@"    "];
  [self helperTestToken:[tokens objectAtIndex:4] type:EquationTokenTypeNumber
value:@"7"];
}
```

Testing Trigonometric Functions and Symbols

Listing 4–36 contains the `testTrigFunctionsAndSymbols:` method, which tests for sine, cosine, pi (both as "pi" and π), and e.

Listing 4–36. *Testing Trigonometric Functions and Symbols*

```
- (void)testTrigFunctionsAndSymbols
{
  Equation *equation = [[Equation alloc]
initWithString:@"sin(0.3)+cos(3.3)+pi+e+\u03c0"];
  NSArray *tokens = equation.tokens;
  STAssertTrue(tokens.count == 15, NULL);
  [self helperTestToken:[tokens objectAtIndex:0] type:EquationTokenTypeTrigFunction
value:@"sin"];
  [self helperTestToken:[tokens objectAtIndex:1] type:EquationTokenTypeOpenParen
value:@"("];
  [self helperTestToken:[tokens objectAtIndex:2] type:EquationTokenTypeNumber
value:@"0.3"];
  [self helperTestToken:[tokens objectAtIndex:3] type:EquationTokenTypeCloseParen
value:@")"];
  [self helperTestToken:[tokens objectAtIndex:4] type:EquationTokenTypeOperator
value:@"+"];
  [self helperTestToken:[tokens objectAtIndex:5] type:EquationTokenTypeTrigFunction
value:@"cos"];
  [self helperTestToken:[tokens objectAtIndex:6] type:EquationTokenTypeOpenParen
value:@"("];
  [self helperTestToken:[tokens objectAtIndex:7] type:EquationTokenTypeNumber
value:@"3.3"];
  [self helperTestToken:[tokens objectAtIndex:8] type:EquationTokenTypeCloseParen
value:@")"];
  [self helperTestToken:[tokens objectAtIndex:9] type:EquationTokenTypeOperator
value:@"+"];
  [self helperTestToken:[tokens objectAtIndex:10] type:EquationTokenTypeSymbol
value:@"pi"];
  [self helperTestToken:[tokens objectAtIndex:11] type:EquationTokenTypeOperator
value:@"+"];
  [self helperTestToken:[tokens objectAtIndex:12] type:EquationTokenTypeSymbol
value:@"e"];
  [self helperTestToken:[tokens objectAtIndex:13] type:EquationTokenTypeOperator
value:@"+"];
  [self helperTestToken:[tokens objectAtIndex:14] type:EquationTokenTypeSymbol
value:@"\u03c0"];
}
```

Testing Parenthesis Matching

We already wrote code to test our stack implementation that the parenthesis matching uses, but you also should test the parenthesis matching directly. You already know from previous tests that you can detect parentheses as tokens, so this test doesn't use the `helperTestToken:type:value:` method. Instead, it tests the validity of the parenthesis tokens, including tests for both valid and invalid parentheses. It's in Listing 4–37.

Listing 4–37. *Testing Parenthesis Matching*

```
- (void)testParenthesisMatching
{
  {
    Equation *equation = [[Equation alloc] initWithString:@"()"];
    NSArray *tokens = equation.tokens;
    STAssertTrue(tokens.count == 2, NULL);
    STAssertTrue(((EquationToken *)[tokens objectAtIndex:0]).valid, NULL);
    STAssertTrue(((EquationToken *)[tokens objectAtIndex:1]).valid, NULL);
  }
  {
    Equation *equation = [[Equation alloc] initWithString:@"(())"];
    NSArray *tokens = equation.tokens;
    STAssertTrue(tokens.count == 4, NULL);
    STAssertTrue(((EquationToken *)[tokens objectAtIndex:0]).valid, NULL);
    STAssertTrue(((EquationToken *)[tokens objectAtIndex:1]).valid, NULL);
    STAssertTrue(((EquationToken *)[tokens objectAtIndex:2]).valid, NULL);
    STAssertTrue(((EquationToken *)[tokens objectAtIndex:3]).valid, NULL);
  }
  {
    Equation *equation = [[Equation alloc] initWithString:@"()()"];
    NSArray *tokens = equation.tokens;
    STAssertTrue(tokens.count == 4, NULL);
    STAssertTrue(((EquationToken *)[tokens objectAtIndex:0]).valid, NULL);
    STAssertTrue(((EquationToken *)[tokens objectAtIndex:1]).valid, NULL);
    STAssertTrue(((EquationToken *)[tokens objectAtIndex:2]).valid, NULL);
    STAssertTrue(((EquationToken *)[tokens objectAtIndex:3]).valid, NULL);
  }
  {
    Equation *equation = [[Equation alloc] initWithString:@")("];
    NSArray *tokens = equation.tokens;
    STAssertTrue(tokens.count == 2, NULL);
    STAssertFalse(((EquationToken *)[tokens objectAtIndex:0]).valid, NULL);
    STAssertFalse(((EquationToken *)[tokens objectAtIndex:1]).valid, NULL);
  }
  {
    Equation *equation = [[Equation alloc] initWithString:@"())"];
    NSArray *tokens = equation.tokens;
    STAssertTrue(tokens.count == 3, NULL);
    STAssertTrue(((EquationToken *)[tokens objectAtIndex:0]).valid, NULL);
    STAssertTrue(((EquationToken *)[tokens objectAtIndex:1]).valid, NULL);
    STAssertFalse(((EquationToken *)[tokens objectAtIndex:2]).valid, NULL);
  }
  {
```

```
    Equation *equation = [[Equation alloc] initWithString:@"(()))("];
    NSArray *tokens = equation.tokens;
    STAssertTrue(tokens.count == 6, NULL);
    STAssertTrue(((EquationToken *)[tokens objectAtIndex:0]).valid, NULL);
    STAssertTrue(((EquationToken *)[tokens objectAtIndex:1]).valid, NULL);
    STAssertTrue(((EquationToken *)[tokens objectAtIndex:2]).valid, NULL);
    STAssertTrue(((EquationToken *)[tokens objectAtIndex:3]).valid, NULL);
    STAssertFalse(((EquationToken *)[tokens objectAtIndex:4]).valid, NULL);
    STAssertFalse(((EquationToken *)[tokens objectAtIndex:5]).valid, NULL);
  }
}
```

Testing Invalid Cases

You also should test for invalid cases. Listing 4–38 contains a testInvalid: method that tests for an array of invalid tokens and an invalid number (two decimal points).

Listing 4–38. *Testing Invalid Cases*

```
- (void)testInvalid
{
  Equation *equation = [[Equation alloc] initWithString:@"invalid0.3.3"];
  NSArray *tokens = equation.tokens;
  STAssertTrue(tokens.count == 8, NULL);
  [self helperTestToken:[tokens objectAtIndex:0] type:EquationTokenTypeInvalid
value:@"i"];
  [self helperTestToken:[tokens objectAtIndex:1] type:EquationTokenTypeInvalid
value:@"n"];
  [self helperTestToken:[tokens objectAtIndex:2] type:EquationTokenTypeInvalid
value:@"v"];
  [self helperTestToken:[tokens objectAtIndex:3] type:EquationTokenTypeInvalid
value:@"a"];
  [self helperTestToken:[tokens objectAtIndex:4] type:EquationTokenTypeInvalid
value:@"l"];
  [self helperTestToken:[tokens objectAtIndex:5] type:EquationTokenTypeInvalid
value:@"i"];
  [self helperTestToken:[tokens objectAtIndex:6] type:EquationTokenTypeInvalid
value:@"d"];
  [self helperTestToken:[tokens objectAtIndex:7] type:EquationTokenTypeNumber
value:@"0.3.3"];
  STAssertFalse(((EquationToken *)[tokens objectAtIndex:7]).valid, NULL);
}
```

Run all these tests to verify that they all pass. Congratulations—your tokenizing work is complete!

Showing the Equation

You've set the equation entry field to show rich text, and you've tokenized the equations, but you haven't yet integrated the tokenizing into the equation entry field. You also haven't done anything about syntax highlighting or pushing exponents to superscript. In this section, you integrate the `tokenize:` routine into the equation entry controller, adding syntax highlighting and exponent superscripting while you're at it.

Many syntax highlighting applications allow users to configure the colors used for various bits of text, and some even allow users to create and share themes of colors that span all the various token types. We've opted not to be so accommodating, choosing the simpler route of hard-coding the colors. Hard-coding the colors directly into the `EquationToken` instances themselves is tempting, but `EquationTokens` really are model objects, and color is a view attribute, so instead we're going to put color under the control of the `EquationEntryViewController` object. This way, `EquationTokens` don't have any control over how they're displayed, and different views can display them differently with respect to colors or fonts.

Setting the Colors

You want to control both the foreground colors and the background colors for the tokens. For the foreground colors, create a dictionary called `COLORS` that uses the type of the token as the key and an `NSColor` instance as the value. For the background colors, use white for everything except invalid tokens, for which you use red. Start by implementing the foreground colors. Open `EquationEntryViewController.m` and import the `EquationToken.h` header:

```
#import "EquationToken.h"
```

Declare a static `NSDictionary` instance:

```
static NSDictionary *COLORS;
```

Fill the dictionary in the class's `initialize:` method. Because `NSDictionary` requires objects for keys and the type field of an `EquationToken` instance is an enum, which is a primitive `int`, convert the type to an `NSNumber` instance, which is an object, before using it as a key. Listing 4–39 shows the `initialize:` method.

Listing 4–39. *Filling the Colors Dictionary*

```
+ (void)initialize
{
  COLORS = [NSDictionary dictionaryWithObjectsAndKeys:
    [NSColor whiteColor],    [NSNumber numberWithInt:EquationTokenTypeInvalid],
    [NSColor blackColor],    [NSNumber numberWithInt:EquationTokenTypeNumber],
    [NSColor blueColor],     [NSNumber numberWithInt:EquationTokenTypeVariable],
    [NSColor brownColor],    [NSNumber numberWithInt:EquationTokenTypeOperator],
    [NSColor purpleColor],   [NSNumber numberWithInt:EquationTokenTypeOpenParen],
    [NSColor purpleColor],   [NSNumber numberWithInt:EquationTokenTypeCloseParen],
    [NSColor orangeColor],   [NSNumber numberWithInt:EquationTokenTypeExponent],
    [NSColor cyanColor],     [NSNumber numberWithInt:EquationTokenTypeSymbol],
    [NSColor magentaColor],  [NSNumber numberWithInt:EquationTokenTypeTrigFunction],
    [NSColor whiteColor],    [NSNumber numberWithInt:EquationTokenTypeWhitespace],
    nil];
}
```

We're somewhat arbitrary in our color selections, so feel free to change them. Notice, though, that the code uses NSDictionary's dictionaryWithObjectsAndKeys: static method, which takes entries in value, key order. Notice also that the code converts the EquationToken types to objects using NSNumber's numberWithInt: method.

Now it's time to colorize the equation strings.

Colorizing the Equation

Each time the user types in the equation entry field, the controlTextDidChange: method in EquationEntryViewController fires. Graphique currently uses that method to validate the equation. Now, you'll add code to that method to colorize the equation. Earlier in this chapter, we discussed Cocoa's attributed strings. At long last, we're ready to use them to add color attributes to the equation.

The existing controlTextDidChange: method creates an equation instance from the text in the equation text field. Now, it will create a mutable attributed string from the text in the equation text field, add color attributes to the mutable attributed string, and set the mutable attributed string back into the equation text field. When these steps complete, the equation entry will have syntax highlighting colors.

To add the color attributes, loop through all the tokens in the equation, using an index variable, i, to keep track of where the current token is in the attributed string. For each token, create a range (an NSRange instance) that corresponds to the range of characters that the current token occupies in the attributed string. Look up the proper foreground color for the token in the COLORS dictionary and set the foreground color using this code:

```
// Add the foreground color
[attributedString addAttribute:NSForegroundColorAttributeName value:[COLORS
objectForKey:[NSNumber numberWithInt:token.type]] range:range];
```

The addAttribute:value:range adds an attribute to an attributed string. The first parameter specifies the type of attribute to add, which in this case is NSForegroundColorAttributeName, meaning a foreground color attribute. The second parameter, value, specifies the value for the attribute, which in this case is the NSColor value corresponding to the current token's type. Finally, the range parameter specifies the range in the attributed string to which to apply the attribute you're adding.

Make a similar call to set the background color, only this time use NSBackgroundColorAttributeName for the first parameter. Determine the color by checking the valid member of token, passing a white color if the token is valid and a red color if the token is not valid. The call looks like this:

```
// Add the background color
[attributedString addAttribute:NSBackgroundColorAttributeName value:token.valid ?
[NSColor whiteColor] : [NSColor redColor] range:range];
```

Listing 4–40 shows the updated controlTextDidChange: method that colorizes the equation.

Listing 4–40. *Colorizing the Equation*

```
- (void)controlTextDidChange:(NSNotification *)notification
{
  Equation *equation = [[Equation alloc] initWithString: [self.textField stringValue]];

  // Create a mutable attributed string, initialized with the contents of the equation
text field
  NSMutableAttributedString *attributedString = [[NSMutableAttributedString alloc]
initWithString:[self.textField stringValue]];

  // Variable to keep track of where we are in the attributed string
  int i = 0;

  // Loop through the tokens
  for (EquationToken *token in equation.tokens)
  {
    // The range makes any attributes we add apply to the current token only
    NSRange range = NSMakeRange(i, [token.value length]);

    // Add the foreground color
    [attributedString addAttribute:NSForegroundColorAttributeName value:[COLORS
objectForKey:[NSNumber numberWithInt:token.type]] range:range];

    // Add the background color
    [attributedString addAttribute:NSBackgroundColorAttributeName value:token.valid ?
[NSColor whiteColor] : [NSColor redColor] range:range];

    // Advance the index to the next token
    i += [token.value length];
  }
  // Set the attributed string back into the equation entry field
  [self.textField setAttributedStringValue:attributedString];

  NSError *error = nil;
  if(![equation validate:&error])
  {
    // Validation failed, display the error
    [feedback setStringValue:[NSString stringWithFormat:@"Error %d: %@", [error
code],[error localizedDescription]]];
  }
  else
  {
    [feedback setStringValue:@""];
  }
}
```

You haven't run the application in a while, but now is a good time. Build and run Graphique and start typing an equation. Experiment with both valid and invalid equations. You should see your equations in color, which is difficult to show with grayscale screenshots, but Figure 4–18 shows a sample equation with a parenthetical problem. You'll also notice an error message complaining that you've typed an invalid character—the letters in "sin." You'll fix that later this chapter.

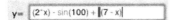

Figure 4–18. *A syntax-colored equation*

Superscripting Exponents

If you type an exponent in the equation entry field, however, whether implicit (follows a variable or a close parenthesis) or explicit (follows a caret), you'll notice that it isn't superscripted at all, as shown in Figure 4–19. All three instances of "2" in that equation are exponents, as evidenced by their orange foreground color. To make them appear in superscript, we must add attributes to our attributed string to superscript them.

Figure 4–19. *Exponents that don't display as superscript*

An attributed string supports an attribute called `NSSuperscriptAttributeName` that sounds tempting but in practice doesn't provide enough display control for our needs. Its documentation says its `value` parameter is an `NSNumber` containing an integer, but it doesn't tell you how far upward that integer will shift your superscripted attribute. Playing with this attribute shows that you want a little better control in how far your superscripted text is offset from the baseline. Fortunately, attributed strings offer an attribute type named `NSBaselineOffsetAttributeName`, whose `value` parameter is documented to take an `NSNumber` containing a floating-point value that represents the points to offset the text from the baseline.

Moving the text upward is insufficient, however; it should also shrink by setting an `NSFontAttributeName` attribute. You could play with absolute values for both the text size and the baseline offset, but you may want to change the size of the equation entry field's font (and in the next chapter, you indeed do). It's better, instead, to make the exponent text a percentage of the current text's size and move it off the baseline some percentage of the size as well. Because you can get the size of the current text, you can easily accomplish this. For exponents, then, make them half the height of the other text and move them halfway up the baseline.

The place to add the code to superscript the exponents is right after setting the background color but before advancing the index to the next token. This code should first determine whether the current token is an exponent and, if it is, perform the following actions in this sequence:

1. Calculate the height of the exponent and baseline shift by multiplying the text height by 0.5.

2. Set the exponent's font to a system font with the size calculated.

3. Shift the exponent's baseline upward by the size calculated.

Listing 4–41 shows the updated `controlTextDidChange:` method with the code to superscript the exponents.

Listing 4–41. *Superscripting the Exponents*

```objc
- (void)controlTextDidChange:(NSNotification *)notification
{
  Equation *equation = [[Equation alloc] initWithString: [self.textField stringValue]];

  // Create a mutable attributed string, initialized with the contents of the equation
  text field
  NSMutableAttributedString *attributedString = [[NSMutableAttributedString alloc]
  initWithString:[self.textField stringValue]];

  // Variable to keep track of where we are in the attributed string
  int i = 0;

  // Loop through the tokens
  for (EquationToken *token in equation.tokens)
  {
    // The range makes any attributes we add apply to the current token only
    NSRange range = NSMakeRange(i, [token.value length]);

    // Add the foreground color
    [attributedString addAttribute:NSForegroundColorAttributeName value:[COLORS
objectForKey:[NSNumber numberWithInt:token.type]] range:range];

    // Add the background color
    [attributedString addAttribute:NSBackgroundColorAttributeName value:token.valid ?
[NSColor whiteColor] : [NSColor redColor] range:range];

    // If token is an exponent, make it superscript
    if (token.type == EquationTokenTypeExponent)
    {
      // Get the height of the rest of the text
      CGFloat height = [[textField font] pointSize] * 0.5;

      // Set the exponent font height
      [attributedString addAttribute:NSFontAttributeName value:[NSFont
systemFontOfSize:height] range:range];

      // Shift the exponent upwards
      [attributedString addAttribute:NSBaselineOffsetAttributeName value:[NSNumber
numberWithInt:height] range:range];
    }

    // Advance the index to the next token
    i += [token.value length];
  }
  // Set the attributed string back into the equation entry field
  [self.textField setAttributedStringValue:attributedString];


  NSError *error = nil;
  if(![equation validate:&error])
  {
    // Validation failed, display the error
    [feedback setStringValue:[NSString stringWithFormat:@"Error %d: %@", [error
code],[error localizedDescription]]];
  }
```

```
  else
  {
    [feedback setStringValue:@""];
  }
}
```

Now run the application and type the same equation. Your exponents should be smaller and should shift upward, as shown in Figure 4–20.

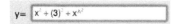

Figure 4–20. *The exponents, smaller and shifted upward*

The equation entry field now stands complete, but you still must integrate it into the validator and tell the graphing evaluation how to interpret things like implicit multiplication. Keep reading to finish integrating the equation entry field into the application.

Updating the Validator

The equation entry field has grown from its humble beginnings, but the validator hasn't kept pace. For example, it flags the trigonometric functions as invalid, shown in Figure 4–21, even though you've explicitly added support for them. It's fooled by invalid parenthesis matching like ")(" as well, shown in Figure 4–22, even though you've built a better parenthesis matcher. It's time for an upgrade.

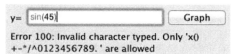

Figure 4–21. *The old validator flagging* `sin()` *as invalid*

Figure 4–22. *The old validator fooled by invalid parentheses*

Happily, you can use the newly tokenized equation to do the validation. Remember that each token stores whether or not it's valid inside its `valid` member? You can loop through the tokens in the equation and test each token's `valid` member to enforce validation.

You've also expanded the list of acceptable characters to include trigonometric functions and the symbols pi and e, so you should update the message for invalid entry. Refer to the comment in the `validate:` method, which is in `Equation.m`, and update the requirements for the first rule:

```
// Validation rules
```

```
// 1. Only digits, operators, variables, parentheses, trigonometric functions, and
symbols allowed
// 2. There should be the same amount of closing and opening parentheses
// 3. no two consecutive operators
```

Gut the rest of the validate: method and add the code to loop through the equation's tokens and test each for validity. If we get an invalid token, test its type to see what error code to return: 102 for an invalid open parenthesis, 103 for an invalid close parenthesis, and 100 for all other invalid tokens.

To enforce rule #3, no two consecutive operators, store a pointer to the previous token in the loop, so you can test for back-to-back operators. Listing 4–42 shows the updated validate: method.

Listing 4–42. *The Updated* `validate:` *Method*

```
- (BOOL)validate:(NSError**)error
{
  // Validation rules
  // 1. Only digits, operators, variables, parentheses, trigonometric functions, and
symbols allowed
  // 2. There should be the same amount of closing and opening parentheses
  // 3. no two consecutive operators

  NSString *allowed = @"x, 0-9, (), operators, trig functions, pi, and e";
  EquationToken *previousToken = nil;
  for (EquationToken *token in self.tokens)
  {
    if (!token.valid)
    {
      if (token.type == EquationTokenTypeOpenParen)
      {
        return [self produceError:error withCode:102 andMessage:@"Too many open
parentheses"];
      }
      else if (token.type == EquationTokenTypeCloseParen)
      {
        return [self produceError:error withCode:103 andMessage:@"Too many closed
parentheses"];
      }
      else
      {
        return [self produceError:error withCode:100 andMessage:[NSString
stringWithFormat:@"Invalid character typed. Only %@ are allowed", allowed]];
      }
    }
    if (token.type == EquationTokenTypeOperator && previousToken.type ==
EquationTokenTypeOperator)
    {
      return [self produceError:error withCode:101 andMessage:@"Consecutive operators
are not allowed"];
    }
    previousToken = token;
  }
  return YES;
```

}

After updating the `validate:` method, run the Graphique tests and verify that they all still pass. They all should, because you've enforced the same rules and returned the same error codes for the same conditions. Now, run Graphique and enter some invalid input. You can see that the rules are all applied as you'd expect. See, for example, Figure 4–23, which shows some invalid input.

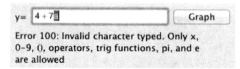

Figure 4–23. *Invalid input validated by our new validator*

Updating the Evaluator

You've expanded the range of what's considered valid input in the equation entry field. You've added implicit multiplication, implicit exponents, and the symbols pi and e. The graphing function still works as long as equations don't use these additions, but any equation that uses the additional functionality doesn't graph properly. Compare, for example, the graph for x^2 in Figure 4–24 with the graph for x^2 in Figure 4–25. They should be identical, but they obviously differ.

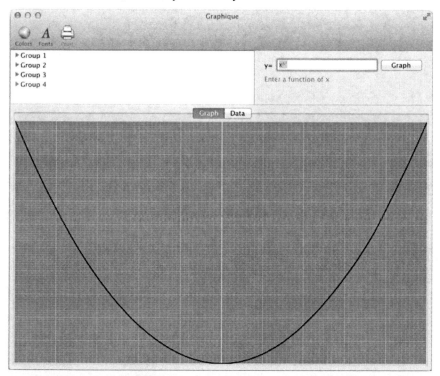

Figure 4–24. *The graph for x^2*

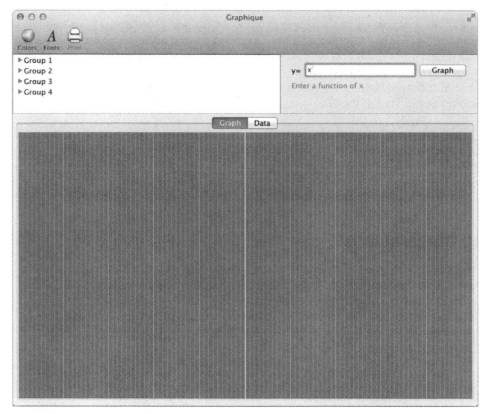

Figure 4–25. *The graph for x^2*

The graph for x^2 shows a nice parabola. The graph for x^2 remains starkly blank. Although both the parser and the validator recognize the 2 as an exponent, the evaluator doesn't.

As you'll recall, the evaluator uses awk to evaluate the equation, passing the text of the equation entry field to awk as the equation. To add support for implicit multiplication, implicit exponents, and symbols, you must alter the equation that we send to awk. Do that in a method called expand:. Declare this method in the class extension at the top of Equation.m, as shown in Listing 4–43.

Listing 4–43. *Declaring the expand: Method*

```
@interface Equation ()
- (BOOL)produceError:(NSError**)error withCode:(NSInteger)code
andMessage:(NSString*)message;
- (void)tokenize;
- (EquationToken *)newTokenFromString:(NSString *)string;
- (NSString *)expand;
@end
```

In the implementation of expand:, build an equation string by iterating through the equation's tokens. When you detect that a particular token requires special handling, inject any special handling into the expanded string. When you're done iterating through the equation's tokens, return the expanded string.

The following are the special cases you must adjust for:

- For implicit exponents, if the current token is an exponent and the previous token isn't already a ^ operator, insert a ^ operator before appending the exponent.

- For implicit multiplication, if the current token is an open parenthesis and the previous token is a variable or a number, insert a * operator before appending the open parenthesis.

- Also for implicit multiplication, if the current token is a variable or a symbol and the previous token is a number, insert a * operator before appending the variable or symbol.

- For pi (whether "pi" or "π"), put in the value M_PI from math.h instead.

- For e, put in the value M_E from math.h instead.

See Listing 4–44 for the implementation of the expand: method.

Listing 4–44. *The* expand: *Method*

```
- (NSString *)expand
{
  NSMutableString *expanded = [NSMutableString string];

  EquationToken *previousToken = nil;
  for (EquationToken *token in self.tokens)
  {
    // Get the value of the current token
    NSString *value = token.value;

    if (previousToken != nil)
    {
      // Do implicit exponents
      if (token.type == EquationTokenTypeExponent && ![previousToken.value
isEqualToString:@"^"])
      {
        [expanded appendString:@"^"];
      }

      // Do implicit multiplication when token is an open parenthesis
      if (token.type == EquationTokenTypeOpenParen && (previousToken.type ==
EquationTokenTypeVariable || previousToken.type == EquationTokenTypeNumber))
      {
        [expanded appendString:@"*"];
      }

      // Do implicit multiplication when token is a variable or symbol
      if ((token.type == EquationTokenTypeVariable || token.type ==
EquationTokenTypeSymbol) && previousToken.type == EquationTokenTypeNumber)
      {
```

```
        [expanded appendString:@"*"];
      }
    }

    // Convert pi
    if ([value isEqualToString:@"pi"] || [value isEqualToString:@"\u03c0"])
    {
      value = [NSString stringWithFormat:@"%f", M_PI];
    }

    // Convert e
    if ([value isEqualToString:@"e"])
    {
      value = [NSString stringWithFormat:@"%f", M_E];
    }

    // Append the current token's value, which we may have adjusted
    [expanded appendString:value];

    // Keep a pointer to the previous token
    previousToken = token;
  }
  return expanded;
}
```

You now must change your code in two places in Equation.m to call the expand: method:

- In evaluateForX:, where it builds the equation string to pass to awk

- In description:, where it returns the equation string it's graphing

Listing 4–45 shows the updated methods.

Listing 4–45. *The Updated* evaluateForX: *and* description: *Methods*

```
- (float)evaluateForX:(float)x
{
  NSTask *task = [[NSTask alloc] init];
  [task setLaunchPath: @"/usr/bin/awk"];

  NSArray *arguments = [NSArray arrayWithObjects: [NSString stringWithFormat:@"BEGIN {
x=%f ; print %@ ; }", x, [self expand]], nil];
  [task setArguments:arguments];

  NSPipe *pipe = [NSPipe pipe];
  [task setStandardOutput:pipe];

  NSFileHandle *file = [pipe fileHandleForReading];
  [task launch];

  NSData *data = [file readDataToEndOfFile];

  NSString *string = [[NSString alloc] initWithData:data encoding:
NSUTF8StringEncoding];
  float value = [string floatValue];
```

```
  return value;
}

- (NSString *)description
{
  return [NSString stringWithFormat:@"Equation [%@]", [self expand]];
}
```

Now, run Graphique again, and try some equations with pi, e, implicit multiplication, and implicit exponents. Figure 4–26 shows the graph for the equation "$2x^2 + 3(x + pi)^3$."

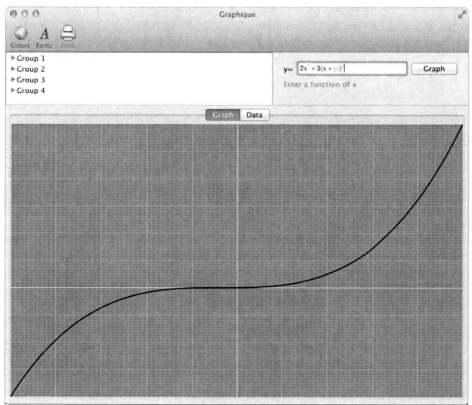

Figure 4–26. *The updated equation validator with implicit exponents, implicit multiplication, and pi*

Put a breakpoint on the first line of the evaluateForX: method and click the Graph button. Execution will stop at that line of code, and in the debugger window, type the following:

```
po self
```

and hit Enter. You'll see the expanded equation, as shown here:

```
(gdb) po self
Equation [2*x^2 + 3*(x + 3.141593)^3]
```

Summary

Programmers often speak disdainfully about improved user interfaces, calling them "eye candy" and haughtily referring to themselves as "back-end programmers." You can ride disdain for UI to obscurity, or you can focus on improving the UI for your programs so that they're easier to use and they provide more value. They say a picture is worth 1,000 words, and we can see that a graph is worth more than 101 values in a table. You gain much more understanding about an equation from a graph than from a textual list of values.

Graphique's improved equation editor makes equations easier to enter and understand as well. By colorizing the equations and matching their syntax to how people normally phrase equations, we minimize barriers for end users and invite them to use and experiment with Graphique.

Chapter 5

User Preferences and the File System

Every time you launch Graphique, it starts over. Any equations you've entered disappear. Any graphs you've created, however clever or stunning, vanish. Graphique has no permanence. This might be fine for utility or one-shot applications, but users expect more out of applications like Graphique. They expect to be able to recall recent work or preserve output. They also expect to be able to set some preferences to customize behavior. In this chapter, we add some permanence to Graphique.

One of the things we do in this chapter is finally use the Fonts and Colors toolbar items to allow users to set the font used to enter equations and the color used to draw the line of the graph. We also implement the Preferences menu item so that users can decide whether the Graph view or the Data view appears first when Graphique launches.

We introduce you to writing data to the file system by allowing users to export their graphs as image files, so they can keep their graphs, post them to Flickr, or tweet them.

At the end of this chapter, Graphique will look like Figure 5–1. What's more, it will have permanence.

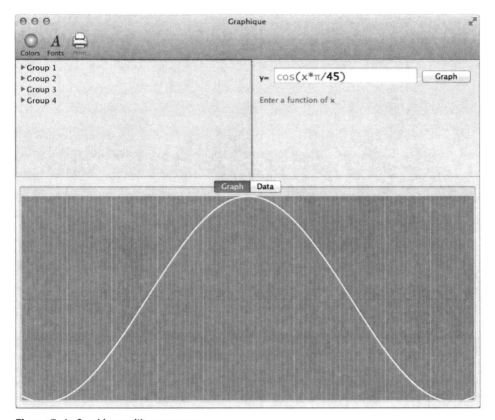

Figure 5–1. *Graphique with permanence*

Managing User Preferences

Major operating systems provide ways for applications to store user preferences, or settings, so that users can configure applications to look or behave a certain way and have them continue to look and behave that way any time they're launched. Microsoft Windows, for example, provides the system registry and an API on top of it to store user preferences. Linux and the various Unix flavors traditionally use dot files, which are hidden files whose names start with a dot (for example, .vimrc) that are stored in a user's home directory and contain the user preferences. Despite being a Unix-based operating system, OS X provides yet another way to store user preferences: user defaults, also known as *user preferences*, that are stored in property lists, which are binary XML files with a .plist extension and are often called *plist files*. They're usually found in a user's home directory, under the Library/Preferences directory, and use the applications' bundle identifiers and names in their file names. You can find one for Xcode, for example, called com.apple.Xcode.plist. Depending on whether you've clicked any toolbar buttons in Graphique, you may find that one for Graphique already exists. If it does, it's called book.macdev.Graphique.plist. You'll recognize book.macdev.Graphique as the bundle identifier you entered when you first created the project in Chapter 1.

Opening a property list file in most text editors reveals some recognizable strings like NSObject splattered among a load of gibberish, forcing you to admit that these files do indeed use a binary format. Apple provides an editor for these files as part of the Developer Tools called Property List Editor. Like Interface Builder, it was a stand-alone tool before Xcode 4's release but now comes integrated with Xcode. It displays a property list's values inside a two-column table. Other options for editing plist files exist as well: BBEdit and TextWrangler, two text editors offered by Bare Bones Software (http://barebones.com), decode the binary data from the file and display the file as if it were normal XML. Fat Cat Software offers a specialized property list editor called PlistEdit Pro (www.fatcatsoftware.com/plisteditpro/) that offers both a structured editor and a text editor. You can use Xcode's Property List Editor or one of the third-party offerings to edit these files. Take care when editing these files, however, because messing them up can cause some applications not to launch and can even cause problems with the operating system. It's no coincidence that Apple doesn't provide tools for nondevelopers to edit these files.

What Apple does provide to all users, however, is a command-line tool called defaults. This tool allows you to both read and write user defaults. To see the defaults tool work, go to a terminal prompt and type the following:

```
defaults read com.apple.dock
```

You'll see some output that reflects your preferences for the Dock that comes with OS X. The output on one of our machines, for example, starts like this:

```
{
    autohide = 1;
    "checked-for-launchpad" = 1;
    "mod-count" = 55;
    orientation = left;
    "persistent-apps" =     (
    );
```

We can change preferences settings in the property list files by passing write instead of read as the first argument to defaults and specifying what we want to change. We could, for example, turn off autohide for our Dock by typing the following:

```
defaults write com.apple.dock autohide -boolean NO
```

This will change the value in the property list file, and to make it take effect, you must restart the Dock by typing this:

```
killall Dock
```

Preferences in OS X applications can be set through the defaults tool, but most applications offer GUI screens as well to read and write user preferences. In this chapter, we let users set their preferences for the font used for the equation entry editor. We use the toolbar button that Graphique already sports, Fonts, to control this setting. We use the Colors toolbar button to allow users to change the color for the line drawn in the graph. We also create a custom preference panel that will appear when users select Graphique ➤ Preferences... from the application menu that lets users set the initial tab (Graph or data) to display when Graphique is launched.

Understanding NSUserDefaults

Apple provides the `defaults` tool for command-line preference interaction and the `NSUserDefaults` class for programmatically interacting with user preferences. The `NSUserDefaults` class allows you to get and set user preferences much as you get and set values in a dictionary object, and it reduces the property list file to an implementation detail. You as a programmer don't have to know anything about property list files to use `NSUserDefaults` (although understanding them comes in handy when debugging issues with your code).

To use `NSUserDefaults`, you call the `standardUserDefaults:` class method, which returns the current user's `NSUserDefaults` instance, which represents that user's defaults database. You then call type-specific getter and setter methods on the `NSUserDefaults` instance to get and set preference values as you need them. For example, the following code sets the default (for some fictional application) for the key `TwitterName` to the string `@hoop33`, the default for the key `MaxTweets` to the number 75, and the default for the key `CheckAutomatically` to the boolean `YES`:

```
NSUserDefaults *userDefaults = [NSUserDefaults standardUserDefaults];
[userDefaults setObject:@"@hoop33" forKey:@"TwitterName"];
[userDefaults setInteger:75 forKey:@"MaxTweets"];
[userDefaults setBool:YES forKey:@"CheckAutomatically"];
```

You can read the defaults back using this code:

```
NSUserDefaults *userDefaults = [NSUserDefaults standardUserDefaults];
NSString *twitterName = [userDefaults stringForKey:@"TwitterName"];
NSInteger maxTweets = [userDefaults integerForKey:@"MaxTweets"];
BOOL checkAutomatically = [userDefaults boolForKey:@"CheckAutomatically"];
```

Persisting Default Values

`NSUserDefaults` uses a caching mechanism to reduce disk access, so you can read and write user preference values in your applications without worrying about impacting I/O performance. `NSUserDefaults` takes care of periodically flushing the cache to disk. We'll verify this later in this chapter when we set a user default and then use the `defaults` tool from the command line to read Graphique's property list file from disk to see a delay before the value appears. If you want to flush the cache yourself, call `NSUserDefaults`'s `synchronize:` method directly, like this:

```
NSUserDefaults *userDefaults = [NSUserDefaults standardUserDefaults];
[userDefaults synchronize];
```

Understanding Search Domains

Up to now, we've used the words *preferences* and *defaults* interchangeably without justifying ourselves. In the real world, *preferences* means settings that the user has specifically indicated that he or she wants, while *defaults* means sensible settings that the programmer has set up beforehand to be used in lieu of any user-set preferences. In

Apple-world, however, *preferences* and *defaults* mean the same thing, and indeed the class is called NSUserDefaults, not NSUserPreferences. To understand this, you must understand what Apple calls *search domains*.

When you set up a user defaults object using code like this:

```
NSUserDefaults *userDefaults = [NSUserDefaults standardUserDefaults];
```

Cocoa sets up a search list in a specific order for accessing default values. Each item in the search list is called a *domain*, and when applications access preference values through the userDefaults object, Cocoa starts at the top of the search list, looking for a value that matches the key specified. When it finds a match, it returns the value. If it doesn't find a match, it returns nil. The domain order in the search list is as follows:

1. Command-line arguments, which are passed in the format -key value

2. The application's property list file

3. Global defaults

4. Language-specific defaults for any of the user's preferred language settings

5. Registered defaults, which are temporary defaults registered by the application

You'll rarely use command-line arguments for anything other than occasional debugging, because users launch their apps through LaunchPad, the Dock, the Finder, or a quick-launcher like Alfred, QuickSilver, or LaunchBar, so they don't as a rule pass any command-line arguments. We've covered the second search domain, the application's property list file, and will continue to do so in the chapter. Your application may use some global settings, and we're not going to go into language-specific settings. Registered defaults, however, are worth exploring a little deeper.

If the search has arrived at registered defaults, it means that no command-line default has been set, the user hasn't specified anything in the application property list, no global default has been set, and no language-specific setting has been specified. We're at the end of the line, but before the search drops off the cliff into nil, registered defaults allow us as programmers to apply sensible defaults for any properties we read. So, instead of writing code like this:

```
NSUserDefaults *userDefaults = [NSUserDefaults standardUserDefaults];
NSString *importantSetting = [userDefaults stringForKey:@"Important"];
if (importantSetting == nil)
{
  // Whoa -- nothing has been set for this important value!
  // Set it to a reasonable default so our application doesn't crash
  importantSetting = @"ReasonableDefault";
}
```

we can instead register a default and be guaranteed that we'll get that value returned if no other value trumps it earlier in the search chain, so that the code to get the value is simply this:

```
NSUserDefaults *userDefaults = [NSUserDefaults standardUserDefaults];
NSString *importantSetting = [userDefaults stringForKey:@"Important"];
```

To register defaults, you call the `registerDefaults:` method on your `NSUserDefaults` instance, passing a dictionary of keys and values. You normally do this in your application delegate's class method `initialize:`, which is called when your application delegate's class loads. This is an example of registering defaults:

```
+ (void)initialize
{
  NSUserDefaults *userDefaults = [NSUserDefaults standardUserDefaults];
  NSDictionary *appDefaults = [NSDictionary dictionaryWithObject:@"ReasonableDefault"
forKey:@"Important"];
  [userDefaults registerDefaults:appDefaults];
}
```

Note that any defaults you register aren't persisted to disk, in the application's property list file or elsewhere. They're a volatile fallback mechanism to provide sensible defaults, so should stay in your code, in your application delegate's `initialize:` method, as long as your application relies on sensible default values.

Resetting Defaults to Reasonable Values

`NSUserDefaults` provides a static method called `resetStandardUserDefaults:` that is often mistaken as a method to rid the application's property list file of any defaults the user has set. That's not at all what this method does. Instead, it flushes the defaults cache and unloads it so that a subsequent call to `standardUserDefaults:` reloads the cache with the default search order. This can be useful if you alter the domain search order for any reason and need to reset it, but since you probably won't, we don't cover that in this book.

What you really are aiming for when you want to reset any user settings to reasonable defaults is to delete any defaults they've set in the application's property list and allow searches to fall through to your registered defaults. To delete a default, call the `removeObjectForKey:` method on your `NSUserDefaults` instance, passing the name of the key you want to remove. To reset the "Important" default to use our registered default, for example, you'd use this code:

```
NSUserDefaults *userDefaults = [NSUserDefaults standardUserDefaults];
[userDefaults removeObjectForKey:@"Important"];
```

Now, searches for the Important key won't find a match in the application's property list domain and will fall through to the registered default.

Setting the Font for the Equation Entry Field

Armed with an understanding of `NSUserDefaults`, we're ready to allow users to set the font used in the equation entry field and have that setting persist through subsequent launches of Graphique. When we built the user interface for Graphique, we added a toolbar at the top of the Graphique window that includes a Fonts toolbar button. You may have tried clicking that button; if you haven't, click it now. When you click the Fonts toolbar button, the Font panel displays, as shown in Figure 5–2. The fonts listed on your machine will differ, depending on what fonts you've installed, but the panel itself should match.

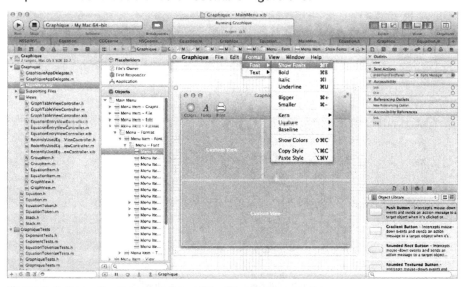

Figure 5–2. *The Fonts panel*

The menu for Graphique also includes a way to open the Fonts panel: **Format ➤ Font ➤ Show Fonts**. If you select that menu item, you should see the same Fonts panel you saw when you clicked the Fonts toolbar button. To understand how Graphique knows to display the Fonts panel, let's start by dissecting the **Show Fonts** menu item. Select MainMenu.xib in Xcode to open it in Interface Builder, and then drill down into the **Format ➤ Font ➤ Show Fonts** menu item. Once you've selected that, open the Connections inspector. Your Xcode should resemble Figure 5–3.

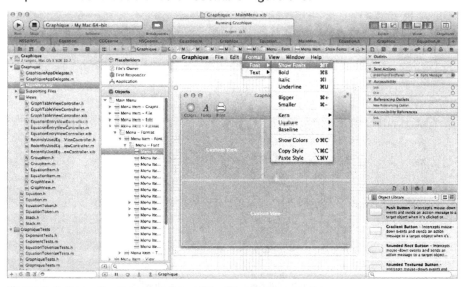

Figure 5–3. *Inspecting the connections of the Show Fonts menu item*

In the Sent Actions section, you see that the `orderFrontFontPanel:` selector is connected to Font Manager. Font Manager is an object that Xcode created for us when we created the Graphique project, and you can find it in the object hierarchy in `MainMenu.xib` (shown as the last item in Figure 5–4). It's of type `NSFontManager`, which you can verify in the Identity inspector, and it's connected to five menu items, as the Connections inspector (shown in Figure 5–5) shows: the Show Fonts menu item that we already looked at and the menu items for Bold, Italic, Smaller, and Bigger.

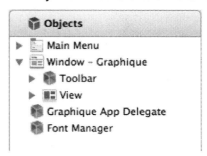

Figure 5–4. *The Font Manager object*

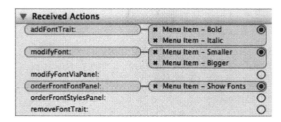

Figure 5–5. *The Font Manager's connections*

As you'd expect, the `orderFrontFontPanel:` selector is a method on `NSFontManager` that opens the Fonts panel, if it's not already open, and brings it to the front. You'd expect the Fonts toolbar item to be wired the same way, but if you select the Fonts toolbar item in the object hierarchy in Interface Builder and open the Connections inspector, you'll find no connections. Open the Attributes inspector instead, and you'll see that it lists its identifier as `NSToolbarShowFontsItem`, as shown in Figure 5–6.

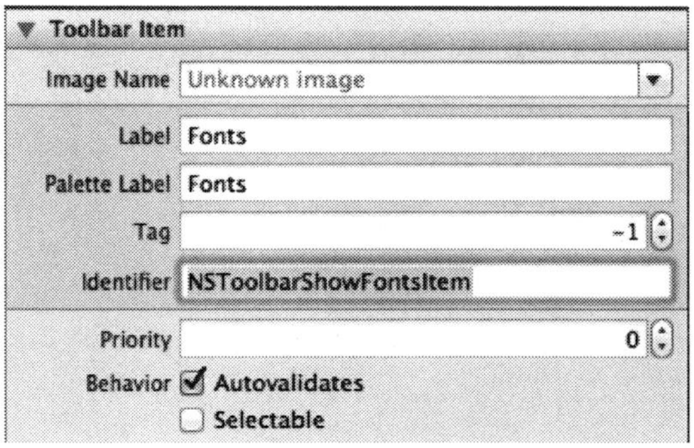

Figure 5–6. *The attributes for the Fonts toolbar item, including the* `NSToolbarShowFontsItem` *identifier*

When the toolbar detects that an item with this identifier is clicked, it knows to tell the Font Manager to open the Fonts panel. This is a standard toolbar item that comes with Cocoa.

Responding to Font Changes

After users display the Fonts panel, they can change the selected font. We must detect that change and update two things: the user preferences and the font used in the equation entry field. By updating the user preferences, we ensure that the user's selected font persists through application launches. By updating the font used in the equation entry field, we let the user see the chosen font.

When the selected font in the Fonts panel changes, the application's shared NSFontManager instance sends a message called changeFont: up what's called the responder chain. Think of the various objects that comprise your application as a line of eager customer service representatives ready to respond to your needs. When messages are sent to this line, each representative, or object, has the opportunity either to respond to the message or to ignore it and let the next object in line have the opportunity to respond. The message then continues to travel down the line until either someone responds or it passes the last object in line, typically your application delegate. This is a fairly typical pattern in event-oriented programming.

The entire responder chain doesn't always get the opportunity to respond to each message, because the message doesn't always start at the "front" of the line. Where the message starts depends on what currently has the focus in the application. The selected object is called the First Responder (which, like an unruly customer service representative, it can refuse to become, but let's not get too carried away with the metaphor), and the message starts there and works its way up the hierarchy. Understanding this is crucial to implementing our font-changing code. If, for example, we put our code to handle the font change in the equation entry controller, our code would get the changeFont: message only if the equation entry controller, or one of the objects it contains (such as the equation entry text field), has the focus. If the focus is currently anywhere else in the application, users could change the font in the Fonts panel and nothing would happen, which would lead to frustration and bug reports. Instead, we want the equation font to change in response to Fonts panel selection changes, no matter where the focus is in the application. We'll put our code, then, in our application delegate, so we'll always get the message.

We have one more hurdle to jump, though. As we said before, when the user changes the selected font in the Fonts panel, the changeFont: message is sent. We can put code to handle that message in our application delegate, and it would look something like this:

```
- (void)changeFont:(id)sender
{
  // Handle the font change
}
```

This works as long as the equation entry field doesn't have the focus. If the user is typing in the equation entry field, however, and then changes the font in the Fonts panel, nothing happens. Our changeFont: selector doesn't get called, and the font in the equation entry field remains the same. When the equation entry field has the focus, you see, it becomes the First Responder, and it swallows the changeFont: message and doesn't pass it on for our application delegate's implementation to handle. It's a little confusing why this happens, because it's an instance of NSTextField, as you'll recall, which has no changeFont: selector in its object hierarchy. When the equation entry field has the focus, however, Cocoa automatically overlays it with what it calls a *field editor* to handle the text entry and editing chores. This field editor is an NSTextView instance, which inherits from NSText, which implements changeFont: and swallows the message.

To help us avoid this pitfall, NSFontManager allows us to change the selector it calls when the font changes to anything of our choosing, so we can prevent the field editor from stealing our font change messages and can handle all font changes in our application delegate. We'll take advantage of this ability in the initialize: method of our application delegate after we set up the user defaults. Add this code in Listing 5–1 to GraphiqueAppDelegate.m to get the user defaults, register a reasonable font, and change the selector called when the font selection changes to changeEquationFont:.

Listing 5–1. *Registering a Font in the User Defaults and Changing the Font Change Selector*

```
+ (void)initialize
{
    // Get the user defaults
    NSUserDefaults *userDefaults = [NSUserDefaults standardUserDefaults];

    // Set the font to a reasonable choice and convert to an NSData object
    NSFont *equationFont = [NSFont systemFontOfSize:18.0];
    NSData *fontData = [NSArchiver archivedDataWithRootObject:equationFont];

    // Set the font in the defaults
    NSDictionary *appDefaults = [NSDictionary dictionaryWithObject:fontData
forKey:@"equationFont"];
    [userDefaults registerDefaults:appDefaults];

    // Change the action for the Font Panel so that the text field doesn't swallow the
changes
    [[NSFontManager sharedFontManager] setAction:@selector(changeEquationFont:)];
}
```

You'll notice that we had to convert the NSFont to an NSData object, because NSUserDefaults doesn't support NSFont instances, but it does support NSData instances.

Implementing changeEquationFont:

The next step is to implement the changeEquationFont: method to get the user defaults, pull out its existing equation entry font, and ask the NSFontManager (stored in the sender object passed to changeEquationFont:) to convert it to the new selected font. Then, the implementation should store the new font in the user defaults and tell the equation entry controller to update itself to use the new font. You'll find this code in Listing 5–2.

Listing 5–2. *Responding to Font Selection Changes*

```
- (void)changeEquationFont:(id)sender
{
  // Get the user defaults
  NSUserDefaults *userDefaults = [NSUserDefaults standardUserDefaults];

  // Get the user's font selection and convert from NSData to NSFont
  NSData *fontData = [userDefaults dataForKey:@"equationFont"];
  NSFont *equationFont = (NSFont *)[NSUnarchiver unarchiveObjectWithData:fontData];

  // Convert the font to the new selection
  NSFont *newFont = [sender convertFont:equationFont];

  // Convert the new font into an NSData object and set it back into the user defaults
  fontData = [NSArchiver archivedDataWithRootObject:newFont];
  [userDefaults setObject:fontData forKey:@"equationFont"];

  // Tell the equation entry field to update to the new font
  [self.equationEntryViewController controlTextDidChange:nil];
}
```

Applying the New Font

The final step for responding to font changes is to actually use the new font in the equation entry field. In the `controlTextDidChange:` method in `EquationEntryViewController.m`, we already decorate the text with colors and exponent sizing. We'll augment this method to get the selected font from the user defaults and add a font attribute with the new font to the entire string. We also use the font manager's `setSelectedFont:isMultiple:` method to make sure that the font selected in the Fonts panel is the same font we're using in the equation entry field. That code looks like this:

```
// Get the user defaults
NSUserDefaults *userDefaults = [NSUserDefaults standardUserDefaults];

// Get the selected font
NSData *fontData = [userDefaults dataForKey:@"equationFont"];
NSFont *equationFont = (NSFont *)[NSUnarchiver unarchiveObjectWithData:fontData];

// Set the selected font in the font panel
[[NSFontManager sharedFontManager] setSelectedFont:equationFont isMultiple:NO];

// Set the font for the equation to the selected font
[attributedString addAttribute:NSFontAttributeName value:equationFont
range:NSMakeRange(0, [attributedString length])];
```

We also change the code for the exponents to use the selected font. It looks like this:

```
// Calculate the height of the exponent as half the height of the selected font
CGFloat height = [equationFont pointSize] * 0.5;

// Set the exponent font height
[attributedString addAttribute:NSFontAttributeName value:[NSFont
fontWithName:equationFont.fontName size:height] range:range];
```

Finally, we adjust the height of the text field to fit the selected font, like this:

```
// Adjust the height of the equation entry text field to fit the new font size
NSSize size = [textField frame].size;
size.height = ceilf([equationFont ascender]) - floorf([equationFont descender]) + 4.0;
[textField setFrameSize:size];
```

The method now looks like Listing 5–3.

Listing 5–3. *The* controlTextDidChange: *Method*

```
-(void)controlTextDidChange:(NSNotification *)notification
{
  Equation *equation = [[Equation alloc] initWithString: [self.textField stringValue]];

  // Create a mutable attributed string, initialized with the contents of the equation
text field
  NSMutableAttributedString *attributedString = [[NSMutableAttributedString alloc]
initWithString:[self.textField stringValue]];

  // Get the user defaults
  NSUserDefaults *userDefaults = [NSUserDefaults standardUserDefaults];

  // Get the selected font
  NSData *fontData = [userDefaults dataForKey:@"equationFont"];
  NSFont *equationFont = (NSFont *)[NSUnarchiver unarchiveObjectWithData:fontData];

  // Set the selected font in the font panel
  [[NSFontManager sharedFontManager] setSelectedFont:equationFont isMultiple:NO];

  // Set the font for the equation to the selected font
  [attributedString addAttribute:NSFontAttributeName value:equationFont
range:NSMakeRange(0, [attributedString length])];

  // Variable to keep track of where we are in the attributed string
  int i = 0;

  // Loop through the tokens
  for (EquationToken *token in equation.tokens)
  {
    // The range makes any attributes we add apply to the current token only
    NSRange range = NSMakeRange(i, [token.value length]);

    // Add the foreground color
    [attributedString addAttribute:NSForegroundColorAttributeName value:[COLORS
objectForKey:[NSNumber numberWithInt:token.type]] range:range];

    // Add the background color
    [attributedString addAttribute:NSBackgroundColorAttributeName value:token.valid ?
[NSColor whiteColor] : [NSColor redColor] range:range];

    // If token is an exponent, make it superscript
    if (token.type == EquationTokenTypeExponent)
    {
      // Calculate the height of the exponent as half the height of the selected font
      CGFloat height = [equationFont pointSize] * 0.5;
```

```
    // Set the exponent font height
    [attributedString addAttribute:NSFontAttributeName value:[NSFont
fontWithName:equationFont.fontName size:height] range:range];

    // Shift the exponent upwards
    [attributedString addAttribute:NSBaselineOffsetAttributeName value:[NSNumber
numberWithInt:height] range:range];
  }

  // Advance the index to the next token
  i += [token.value length];
}

// Adjust the height of the equation entry text field to fit the new font size
NSSize size = [textField frame].size;
size.height = ceilf([equationFont ascender]) - floorf([equationFont descender]) + 4.0;
[textField setFrameSize:size];

// Set the attributed string back into the equation entry field
[self.textField setAttributedStringValue:attributedString];

// Clean up
[attributedString release];

NSError *error = nil;
if(![equation validate:&error])
{
  // Validation failed, display the error
  [feedback setStringValue:[NSString stringWithFormat:@"Error %d: %@", [error
code],[error localizedDescription]]];
}
else
{
  [feedback setStringValue:@""];
}
[equation release];
}
```

Build and run Graphique, bring up the Fonts panel, and change the font. You can see that, wherever your focus, you can change the selected font and see the new font in the equation entry panel. Figure 5–7, for example, shows the equation entry field using the Marker Felt font.

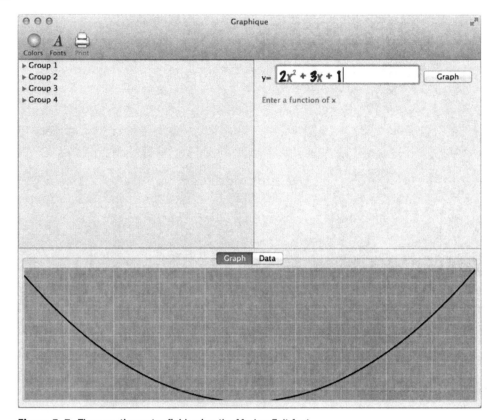

Figure 5–7. *The equation entry field using the Marker Felt font*

Setting the Line Color

Clicking the Colors button in Graphique's toolbar displays the color selection panel, as shown in Figure 5–8. Programming the color selection panel resembles programming the font selection panel, so you'll be able to transfer many of the concepts you just learned to selecting colors.

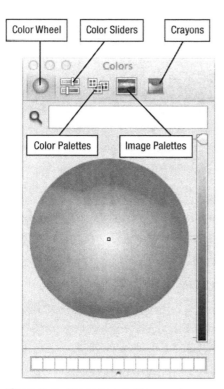

Figure 5–8. *The color selection panel*

Understanding Color Selection Modes

You'll notice in Figure 5–8 the five icons across the top of the color selection panel. Each of those icons represents a different color selection mode. The standard modes are as follows:

- Color Wheel
- Color Sliders
- Color Palettes
- Image Palettes
- Crayons

Each mode represents a different interface to select the same thing: a color. Although all five modes are available by default, you can restrict the Colors panel to display only some of these, and you can also create your own custom color selection modes. In Graphique, we demonstrate mode restriction by restricting the color selection to Crayons mode. To restrict the mode, you call NSColorPanel's static setPickerMask: method, passing one or more mode masks bitwise OR'ed together. To restrict the Colors panel to Color Wheel and Color Palettes modes, for example, you'd code the following:

```
[NSColorPanel setPickerMask:
         (NSColorPanelWheelModeMask | NSColorPanelColorListModeMask)];
```

Note that you must make this call before any Colors panel instances have been created. If you display a Colors panel after calling the preceding code, it looks like Figure 5–9.

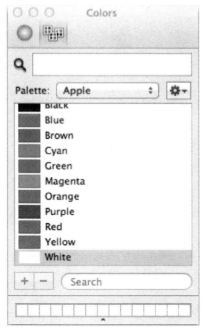

Figure 5–9. *A Colors panel with only two modes*

Displaying the Color Selection Panel

Clicking the Colors toolbar item passes the identifier NSToolbarShowColorsItem to the toolbar, which you can see in the Attributes inspector. This is similar to how the Fonts toolbar item passes the NSToolbarShowFontsItem identifier. When this identifier is passed, Cocoa knows to display the color selection panel.

For our implementation, we start by registering a reasonable user default for the line color: black. We also set the Colors panel to Crayons-only mode. Update the initialize: method in GraphiqueAppDelegate.m accordingly, as shown in Listing 5–4.

Listing 5–4. *The updated* initialize: *Method*

```
+ (void)initialize
{
  // Get the user defaults
  NSUserDefaults *userDefaults = [NSUserDefaults standardUserDefaults];

  // Set the font to a reasonable choice and convert to an NSData object
  NSFont *equationFont = [NSFont systemFontOfSize:18.0];
  NSData *fontData = [NSArchiver archivedDataWithRootObject:equationFont];
```

```
    // Set the color to a reasonable choice and convert to an NSData object
    NSColor *lineColor = [NSColor blackColor];
    NSData *colorData = [NSArchiver archivedDataWithRootObject:lineColor];

    // Set the font and color in the defaults
    NSDictionary *appDefaults = [NSDictionary dictionaryWithObjectsAndKeys:fontData,
@"equationFont", colorData, @"lineColor", nil];
    [userDefaults registerDefaults:appDefaults];

    // Change the action for the Font Panel so that the text field doesn't swallow the
changes
    [[NSFontManager sharedFontManager] setAction:@selector(changeEquationFont:)];

    // Set the Colors panel to show only Crayons mode
    [NSColorPanel setPickerMask:NSColorPanelCrayonModeMask];
}
```

You'll notice that, as with the font, we had to convert the NSColor object to an NSData object before storing in the user defaults. You'll also notice that the key we use for the color is lineColor.

Responding to Color Changes

When users click a new color in the color selection panel, a changeColor: message is sent up the responder chain, similar to how the font selection panel sends a changeFont: message. As with the changeFont: message, however, the equation entry field swallows the changeColor: message when it has focus. Since we want to have the color selection always refer to the graph's line, we must change the message sent when the color changes so we can always catch it in our application delegate.

We must deal with one more twist, however—we must call NSColorPanel's setTarget: method to set the target for our color change messages to be the application delegate. This means that, unlike with changing the font change messages, we can't make this change in the initialize: method. The initialize: method is a class method, called before our GraphiqueAppDelegate instance is created. We want our GraphiqueAppDelegate instance to be the target for our color change messages, because we have to tell the graph instance to redraw itself to the new color. Update the applicationDidFinishLaunching: method, adding code to set the target for color changes to the application delegate instance, and to set the action for when the color selection changes to changeGraphLineColor:. Stick these two lines of code at the end of that method:

```
[[NSColorPanel sharedColorPanel] setTarget:self];
[[NSColorPanel sharedColorPanel] setAction:@selector(changeGraphLineColor:)];
```

Add a declaration for the changeGraphLineColor: method to GraphiqueAppDelegate.h:

```
- (void)changeGraphLineColor:(id)sender;
```

We'll catch this message in our application delegate, store the new color in the user defaults, and then tell the graph view to redraw itself. Add a changeGraphLineColor: method to GraphiqueAppDelegate.m that matches Listing 5–5.

Listing 5–5. *The changeGraphLineColor: Method*

```
- (void)changeGraphLineColor:(id)sender
{
  // Set the selected color in the user defaults
  NSData *colorData = [NSArchiver archivedDataWithRootObject:[(NSColorPanel *)sender
color]];
  [[NSUserDefaults standardUserDefaults] setObject:colorData forKey:@"lineColor"];

  // Tell the graph to redraw itself
  [self.graphTableViewController.graphView setNeedsDisplay:YES];
}
```

> **NOTE:** As of Mac OS X Lion and the use of Automatic Reference Counting (ARC), you can no longer have forward declarations in your code. Be sure to import `GraphView.h` at the top of `GraphiqueAppDelegate.m` so the compiler knows what class we are talking about.

The last thing we must do is update the drawRect: method in GraphView.m to use the selected color. The existing code, which looks like this, sets the line color (stored in the variable curveColor) to black:

```
// Set the color scheme
NSColor *background  = [NSColor colorWithDeviceRed:0.30 green:0.58 blue:1.0 alpha:1.0];
NSColor *axisColor = [NSColor colorWithDeviceRed:1.0 green:1.0 blue:0.0 alpha:1.0];
NSColor *gridColorLight = [NSColor colorWithDeviceRed:1.0 green:1.0 blue:1.0 alpha:0.5];
NSColor *gridColorLighter = [NSColor colorWithDeviceRed:1.0 green:1.0 blue:1.0
alpha:0.25];
NSColor *curveColor = [NSColor colorWithDeviceRed:.0 green:0.0 blue:0 alpha:1.0];
```

Change the code to instead read the color from the user defaults, like this:

```
// Set the color scheme
NSColor *background  = [NSColor colorWithDeviceRed:0.30 green:0.58 blue:1.0 alpha:1.0];
NSColor *axisColor = [NSColor colorWithDeviceRed:1.0 green:1.0 blue:0.0 alpha:1.0];
NSColor *gridColorLight = [NSColor colorWithDeviceRed:1.0 green:1.0 blue:1.0 alpha:0.5];
NSColor *gridColorLighter = [NSColor colorWithDeviceRed:1.0 green:1.0 blue:1.0
alpha:0.25];

// Get the line color from the user defaults
NSData *colorData = [[NSUserDefaults standardUserDefaults] dataForKey:@"lineColor"];
NSColor *curveColor = (NSColor *)[NSUnarchiver unarchiveObjectWithData:colorData];
```

Now you can build and run Graphique and, with a graph showing, open the color selection panel and select a new color. You'll see the line color immediately update to the new selection. Figure 5–10 shows the graph with the Snow crayon selected.

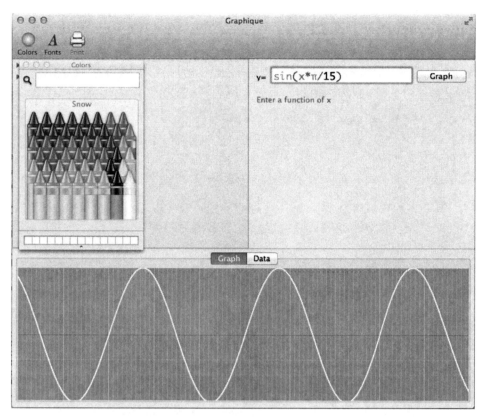

Figure 5–10. *The graph with the Snow crayon selected*

Creating a Custom Preferences Panel

Most OS X applications provide a menu item called Preferences that, when selected, shows a panel that allows users to set custom preferences. Graphique has a menu item called Preferences, but it's grayed out since we've provided no such preferences panel. In this section, we create a preference panel that displays when users select the Preferences menu item. It contains a single check box to determine whether the initial view for a rendered equation is the table view or the Graph view, and it looks like Figure 5–11.

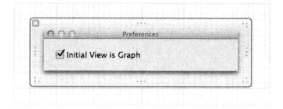

Figure 5–11. *The Preferences panel*

Creating the Preferences View

We'll start by creating the code to control the preferences view. Create a new Objective-C class in your Views group, make it a subclass of `NSWindowController`, and call it `PreferencesController`. In this class, we want to create an outlet for a check box that determines whether the initial view is the graph and create an action that responds when the user checks or unchecks that check box. The header file, `PreferencesController.h`, is shown in Listing 5–6.

Listing 5–6. *PreferencesController.h*

```
#import <Cocoa/Cocoa.h>

@interface PreferencesController : NSWindowController
{
  NSButton *initialViewIsGraph;
}

@property (nonatomic, retain) IBOutlet NSButton *initialViewIsGraph;

-(IBAction)changeInitialView:(id)sender;

@end
```

The implementation file for the `PreferencesController` does three things:

1. In the init: method, it loads `PreferencesController.xib`.

2. When the Preferences panel appears, it retrieves the value for the initial view from the user defaults and updates the check box accordingly.

3. When the user checks or unchecks the check box, it determines the state of the check box and updates the user defaults.

The code for `PreferencesController.m`, shown in Listing 5–7, implements the behavior for step 2 in the `windowDidLoad:` method, which is called when the Preferences window loads. The action method `changeInitialView:` implements the behavior for step 3.

Listing 5–7. *PreferencesController.m*

```
#import "PreferencesController.h"

@implementation PreferencesController

@synthesize initialViewIsGraph;

- (id)init
{
  self = [super initWithWindowNibName:@"PreferencesController"];
  return self;
}

- (void)windowDidLoad
{
  [super windowDidLoad];
```

```
// Get the user defaults
NSUserDefaults *userDefaults = [NSUserDefaults standardUserDefaults];

// Set the checkbox to reflect the user defaults
[initialViewIsGraph setState:[userDefaults boolForKey:@"InitialViewIsGraph"]];
}

- (IBAction)changeInitialView:(id)sender
{
  // Get the user defaults
  NSUserDefaults *userDefaults = [NSUserDefaults standardUserDefaults];

  // Set the user defaults value for the initial view
  [userDefaults setBool:[initialViewIsGraph state] forKey:@"InitialViewIsGraph"];
}

@end
```

Now we're ready to create the actual user interface with the check box.

Create a new Empty Interface Builder document, as shown in Figure 5–12, and call it
`PreferencesController.xib`. Open `PreferencesController.xib` in Xcode and drag a
Panel object onto the blank canvas. Next, drag a Check Box object onto the Panel
object and change its text to "Initial View is Graph." Resize the Panel object to get rid of
most of the empty space. Open the Attributes inspector and change the Window Title to
Preferences and uncheck the Resize box. Your view should look like Figure 5–13.

Figure 5–12. *Selecting an Empty Interface Builder document*

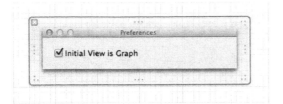

Figure 5–13. *The view for* PreferencesController

With PreferencesController.xib still open, select File's Owner, open the Identity inspector, and select PreferencesController as the class, as shown in Figure 5–14.

Figure 5–14. *File's Owner set to* PreferencesController

Now you can Ctrl+drag from the check box to File's Owner, select the changeIntialView: action, and then Ctrl+drag from File's Owner to the check box and select the initialViewIsGraph outlet. Finally, Ctrl+drag from File's Owner to the panel itself and select the window outlet. If you forget this step, the Preferences panel will display the first time you select the Preferences menu item (when we get that far), but once you've closed it, it won't display anymore, no matter how often you select the Preferences menu item.

We've now wired our user interface to the PreferencesController class, but we haven't yet done anything to make the PreferencesController user interface display. Read on to close that loop.

Displaying the Preferences Panel

To display the preferences panel we've created, we must tell our application delegate about it and wire it to the Preferences menu item in MainMenu.xib. Open GraphiqueAppDelegate.h and add a forward declaration for the PreferencesController class, a PreferencesController member to the interface, and a PreferencesController property. Also, add an action method to display the preferences panel. See Listing 5–8.

Listing 5–8. *Updating* GraphiqueAppDelegate.h *for* PreferencesController

```
#import <Cocoa/Cocoa.h>
#import <CoreData/CoreData.h>

@class EquationEntryViewController;
@class GraphTableViewController;
@class RecentlyUsedEquationsViewController;
@class PreferencesController;

@interface GraphiqueAppDelegate : NSObject <NSApplicationDelegate>
```

```
@property (strong) IBOutlet NSWindow *window;
@property (weak) IBOutlet NSSplitView *horizontalSplitView;
@property (weak) IBOutlet NSSplitView *verticalSplitView;
@property (strong) EquationEntryViewController *equationEntryViewController;
@property (strong) GraphTableViewController *graphTableViewController;
@property (strong) RecentlyUsedEquationsViewController
*recentlyUsedEquationsViewController;
@property (strong) PreferencesController *preferencesController;

- (void)changeGraphLineColor:(id)sender;
-(IBAction)showPreferencesPanel:(id)sender;

@end
```

In GraphiqueAppDelegate.m, import PreferencesController.h, add a @synthesize line for the preferencesController instance, and then implement the showPreferencesPanel: method. This method should instantiate the preferencesController instance, if it hasn't already been instantiated, and then display the preferences panel. See the code in Listing 5–9.

Listing 5–9. *The Method to Show the Preferences Panel*

```
- (IBAction)showPreferencesPanel:(id)sender
{
  // Create the preferences panel if we haven't already
  if (preferencesController == nil)
  {
    preferencesController = [[PreferencesController alloc] init];
  }

  // Show the panel
  [preferencesController showWindow:self];
}
```

All that's left to display the preferences panel is to wire it to the Preferences menu item. Open MainMenu.xib, select the Preferences menu item, Ctrl+drag to the Graphique App Delegate instance, and select showPreferencesPanel:, as shown in Figure 5–15.

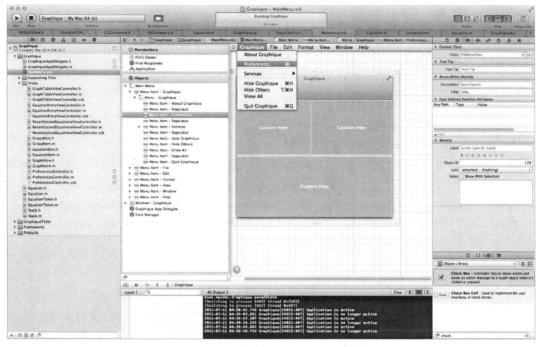

Figure 5–15. *Wiring* `showPreferencesPanel:` *to the Preferences menu item*

Build and run Graphique, and then select **Preferences...** from the menu. The Preferences window displays, as shown in Figure 5–16.

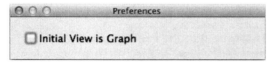

Figure 5–16. *The Preferences panel*

Check the box, and quit the application to flush the cache. Then, open a Terminal instance and type the following:

```
defaults read book.macdev.Graphique
```

Among the output, you should see a line like this:

```
InitialViewIsGraph = 1;
```

The Preferences panel is working and is writing the preferences to the user defaults. The last step in implementing the custom preference is to actually heed its setting in the application.

Using the Custom Preference

To use the custom preference, we must tell Graphique to check the value for the InitialViewIsGraph setting in the user defaults and select the appropriate tab. Note that this happens only on user startup; once a user starts interacting with the application, entering equations and selecting tabs, we leave automatic tab setting alone.

To programmatically select a tab, we need a handle to the tab view in the Graph view. Open GraphTableViewController.h and add an NSTabView property called tabView. Listing 5–10 shows the updated code file.

Listing 5–10. *GraphTableViewController.h*

```
#import <Cocoa/Cocoa.h>

#import "Equation.h"

@class GraphView;

@interface GraphTableViewController : NSViewController <NSTableViewDataSource>

@property (nonatomic, retain) NSMutableArray *values;
@property (weak) IBOutlet NSTableView *graphTableView;
@property (nonatomic, assign) CGFloat interval;
@property (weak) IBOutlet GraphView *graphView;
@property (weak) IBOutlet NSTabView *tabView;

- (void)draw:(Equation *)equation;

@end
```

In GraphTableViewController.m, add a @synthesize line for tabView, and then create an implementation of awakeFromNib: that will automatically be called when the user interface loads. In this method, you get a handle to the user defaults, you read the value for InitialViewIsGraph, and you select the appropriate tab using tabView's selectTabViewItem AtIndex: method. Listing 5–11 shows the code for the awakeFromNib: method.

Listing 5–11. *The awakeFromNib: Method That Selects the Proper Tab*

```
- (void)awakeFromNib
{
  // Get the user defaults
  NSUserDefaults *userDefaults = [NSUserDefaults standardUserDefaults];

  // Determine which tab to select based on the user defaults
  NSInteger selectedTab = [userDefaults boolForKey:@"InitialViewIsGraph"] ? 0 : 1;

  // Select the proper tab
  [tabView selectTabViewItemAtIndex:selectedTab];
}
```

Finally, connect the Tab View object in Interface Builder to the tabView property by selecting GraphTableViewController.xib in Xcode, Ctrl+dragging from File's Owner to the Tab view, and selecting tabView from the pop-up. Your custom preference should now function as expected. Launch Graphique, open the Preferences panel, and deselect the check box. Close Graphique and then relaunch it. The Data tab should be selected, as shown in Figure 5–17. You can reselect the check box in the Preferences panel and relaunch Graphique to see the Graph tab selected.

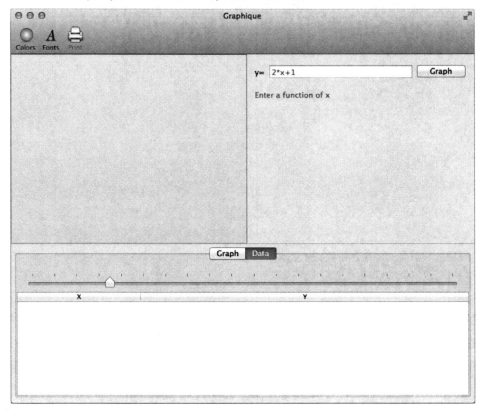

Figure 5–17. *Graphique with the Data tab initially selected*

Using the Local File System

One of the major advantages of running a desktop application is access to local resources. Some common local resources are CPU, memory, and also the file system. The file system used to be synonymous with access to the hard drive. Nowadays, file systems are much more than that. Yes, you can access the local hard drive. But you can also access any mounted remote drives such as Dropbox or WebDAV accounts. All of the access protocols are unified under one file manager API that we review in this section. We then utilize the newly acquired knowledge in Graphique to export graphs as images.

Browsing the File System

In Objective-C, the overt interface to the file system is the NSFileManager class. This is the class that gives access to the usual file manipulations. The NSFileManager class makes no assumption about what it finds on the file system, so it calls everything (folders, files, symbolic links, and so on) items.

Enumerating Through the Mounted Volumes

To browse the file system, you first need to know what volumes are mounted, and that is done through a simple NSFileManager call:

```
NSFileManager *fm = [NSFileManager defaultManager];

NSArray *mountedDisks = [fm mountedVolumeURLsIncludingResourceValuesForKeys:nil
options:NSVolumeEnumerationSkipHiddenVolumes];
NSLog(@"Found %lu volumes", mountedDisks.count);
for(NSURL *path in mountedDisks)
{
  NSLog(@"\t%@", path);
}
```

Running the previous code will provide you with a list of URLs representing the mounted volumes on your system:

```
FileSystem[32607:903] Found 6 volumes
FileSystem[32607:903]    file://localhost/
FileSystem[32607:903]    file://localhost/Volumes/Backup/
FileSystem[32607:903]    file://localhost/Volumes/jdoe/
FileSystem[32607:903]    file://localhost/Volumes/Media/
FileSystem[32607:903]    file://localhost/Volumes/Data/
FileSystem[32607:903]    file://localhost/Volumes/jdoe_HomeDir/
```

Each URL can be used as the starting point for further exploration.

Enumerating Through a Folder

Let's pretend you created a folder called MyData directly in your home directory using Finder and copied a few files in there, as shown in Figure 5–18.

Figure 5–18. *A directory with sample files*

You would list its contents and whether each item is a file or directory using the following code:

```
NSFileManager *fm = [NSFileManager defaultManager];

NSString* path = [NSHomeDirectory() stringByAppendingPathComponent: @"MyData"];
NSArray *list = [fm contentsOfDirectoryAtURL:[NSURL URLWithString:path]
includingPropertiesForKeys:nil options:NSDirectoryEnumerationSkipsHiddenFiles
error:nil];

NSLog(@"Found %lu items", list.count);
for(NSURL *itemURL in list) {
  BOOL isDirectory;
  [fm fileExistsAtPath:[itemURL path] isDirectory:&isDirectory];

  NSLog(@"\t%@, directory? %@", [itemURL path], (isDirectory ? @"Yes" : @"No"));
}
```

> **NOTE:** We've used the NSHomeDirectory function to find the current user's home directory. There are other similar predefined functions such as NSHomeDirectoryForUser or NSTemporaryDirectory.

If you've created the content as previously illustrated, then the output would be similar to the output shown here:

```
FileSystem[34747:903] Found 3 items
FileSystem[34747:903]    /Users/michael/MyData/Image0001.TIF, directory? No
FileSystem[34747:903]    /Users/michael/MyData/Image0002.TIF, directory? No
FileSystem[34747:903]    /Users/michael/MyData/Others, directory? Yes
```

Notice how only two out of the four image files are listed. This is because the two others are inside the Others directory, and if you wanted to list them, you'd have to recurse through the subdirectories.

Writing to the File System

Writing a file to the file system is just as simple. Both NSString and NSData have methods for writing content to the file system. To write a text file to the file system, the code would look as shown here:

```
NSString *myText = @"This is sample text I would like to store in a file.";
NSString* path = [NSHomeDirectory() stringByAppendingPathComponent: @"MyData"];
NSString *filePath = [path stringByAppendingPathComponent:@"sample.txt"];
[myText writeToFile:filePath atomically:YES
encoding:NSStringEncodingConversionAllowLossy error:nil];
```

This works fine when the data to write is a string. If the data is binary, however, you must use the NSData class. In this case, the code is very similar:

```
NSData *myData = ... // Obtain some data
NSString* path = [NSHomeDirectory() stringByAppendingPathComponent: @"MyData"];
NSString *filePath = [path stringByAppendingPathComponent:@"sample.data"];
[myData writeToFile:filePath atomically:YES];
```

> **NOTE:** Both writeToFile: methods have an atomically parameter. When that parameter is set to YES, the file content is first written to a temporary location. When the writing is complete, the temporary file is then moved to the new location. This preserves the integrity of the file in case of system interruption during the write operation. If that parameter is set to NO, then the content is written directly to the final location. In the event of an interruption, the file is left in an incomplete state.

Reading from the File System

Reading from the file system is obviously equally as important as writing. This is such a common task that Apple has, once again, added convenience methods to the NSString and NSData classes.

To read the sample.txt file back into a string, use the following code:

```
NSString* path = [NSHomeDirectory() stringByAppendingPathComponent: @"MyData"];
NSString *filePath = [path stringByAppendingPathComponent:@"sample.txt"];
NSString *myText = [NSString stringWithContentsOfFile:filePath
encoding:NSStringEncodingConversionAllowLossy error:nil];
NSLog(@"Result: %@", myText);
```

Similarly, the data file can be read using the following:

```
NSString* path = [NSHomeDirectory() stringByAppendingPathComponent: @"MyData"];
NSString *filePath = [path stringByAppendingPathComponent:@"sample.data"];
NSData *myData = [NSData dataWithContentsOfFile:filePath];
```

Exporting Graphs as Images

Now that we know how to interact with the file system, we put our newly acquired knowledge to the test. We add a new item in the menu that allows us to export a graph as a PNG image. Upon selecting the menu item, a save dialog will open so that the user can select the export location.

Creating an Image from a View

Before doing anything else, we need to make sure the GraphTableViewController is able to produce an image representation of its current graph. Open GraphTableViewController.h and declare a new method:

```
-(NSBitmapImageRep*)export;
```

Now open GraphTableViewController.m so we can implement the new method we just declared. This is done by painting the image into a bitmap cache and returning that cache.

```
-(NSBitmapImageRep*)export
{
```

```
    NSSize mySize = graphView.bounds.size;

    NSBitmapImageRep *bir = [graphView
bitmapImageRepForCachingDisplayInRect:graphView.bounds];
    [bir setSize:mySize];
    [graphView cacheDisplayInRect:graphView.bounds toBitmapImageRep:bir];

    return bir;
}
```

Next, open GraphiqueAppDelegate.h and declare a new selector to receive the menu
item action:

```
-(IBAction)exportAs:(id)sender;
```

Then edit GraphiqueAppDelegate.m to implement the new method:

```
-(IBAction)exportAs:(id)sender
{
  // Obtain the image representation
  NSBitmapImageRep* imageRep = [graphTableViewController export];

  // Create the PNG representation
  NSData *data = [imageRep representationUsingType: NSPNGFileType properties: nil];

  // Create the Save As... dialog
  NSSavePanel *saveDlg = [NSSavePanel savePanel];
  [saveDlg setAllowedFileTypes:[NSArray arrayWithObject:@"png"]];

  // Open the dialog and save if the user selected OK
  NSInteger result = [saveDlg runModal];
  if (result == NSOKButton)
  {
    [data writeToURL:saveDlg.URL atomically:YES];
  }
}
```

Calling the setAllowedFileTypes: method allows you to specify the file extension for the
files you are saving. In this case, we chose png. If the users provide a different extension,
they are automatically prompted to clarify whether they really want to use a different
extension, as Figure 5–19 shows.

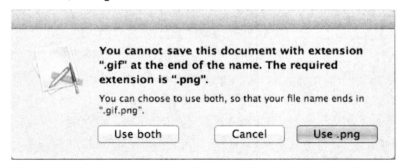

Figure 5–19. *An alert generated when the wrong file extension is selected*

Adding the Export Graph Menu Item

Our next task is to add the new menu item. Open MainMenu.xib and expand the File menu, as shown in Figure 5–20.

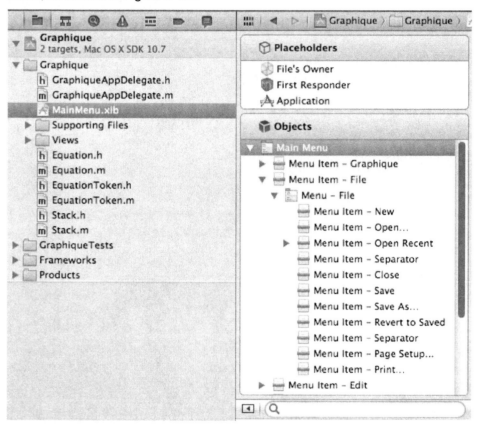

Figure 5–20. *The File menu item expanded*

Find Separator Menu Item in the Object Library and drag it inside the expanded File menu. Then find Menu Item and drag it into the File menu as well, as illustrated in Figure 5–21.

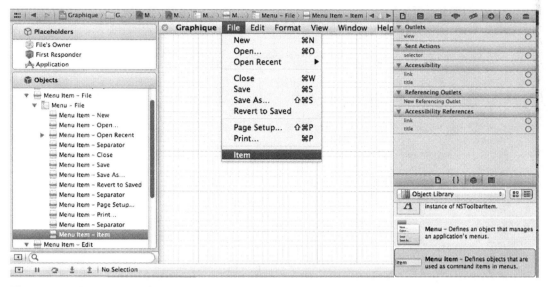

Figure 5–21. *The new menu item*

Open the Attributes inspector and change the menu item title to Export As..., as shown in Figure 5–22.

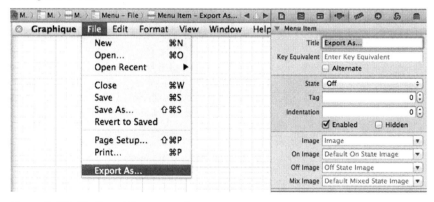

Figure 5–22. *The Export As... menu item*

In the Objects pane, you should already have the Graphique App Delegate object. Ctrl+drag from the Export As... menu item to the Graphique App Delegate object to link the action to the `exportAs:` method. The connection should be visible in the Connections Inspector, as shown in Figure 5–23.

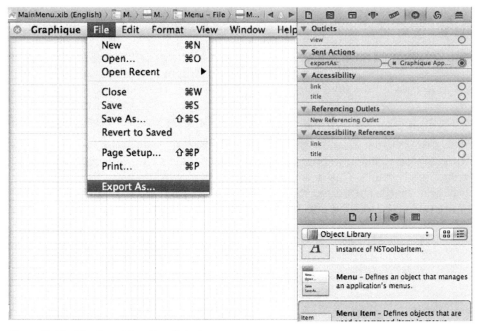

Figure 5–23. *The Export As... item linked*

Run the application to test all you've done. Once the application starts, enter an equation and plot it. Then select **File ➤ Export As...** to see the Save As dialog, as shown in Figure 5–24.

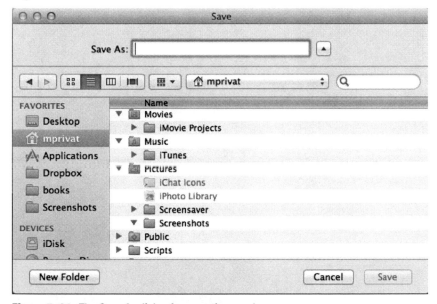

Figure 5–24. *The Save As dialog for exporting graphs*

Summary

In this chapter, you learned how to take the application to the next level by adding some level of persistence. You should have a good understanding of managing user preferences and accessing the file system. Graphique now remembers the user's preference by using NSUserDefaults, and we've used these preferences with colors and fonts. It also export graphs as an image to the file system using the NSFileManager API.

Using the file system is great for storing unstructured data, such as an image. But it gets a bit more complicated to manage efficiently when the data is structured and has to be editable and even searchable. This is where you need to step up to a persistence framework that can handle structured data. In the next chapter, we expand our persistence capabilities by looking into the Core Data framework.

Chapter 6

Using Core Data

Picking up where we left off in Chapter 5, we now get a glimpse of Cocoa's powerful object storage framework, Core Data, which we use to store recently entered equations so that users can retrieve and redisplay them.

At the end of this chapter, Graphique will look like Figure 6–1. It will store the recently entered equations into Core Data storage so that the equations users enter will still be present across launches of Graphique, so that users will be able to retrieve their interesting equations even after they close and reopen Graphique.

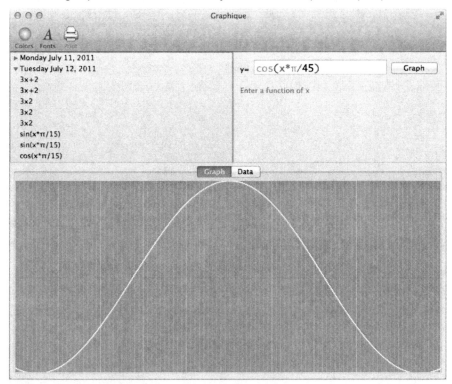

Figure 6–1. *Graphique with equations in Core Data*

Stepping Up to Core Data

Core Data is the persistence framework that comes with Mac OS X. Core Data is not a database, and it's not a file system either. Instead, it's an abstraction layer that stands between your code and the actual storage mechanism (database, file system, and so on) you use. There are many benefits to using Core Data instead of directly welding your code onto your chosen storage mechanism. These are some of them:

- Unified API for storing, retrieving, and searching
- Ability to change storage without changing much of your code
- Automatic bidirectional object to storage mapping
- Ability to use the built-in Xcode tools

In this section, we first go through the steps required to add Core Data to the existing Graphique project. We then create a data model for storing recently used equations. We then hook all this up into the user interface to tie everything together.

Adding Core Data to the Graphique Application

If you've done enough planning and you already know you will use Core Data for your application, you can attach it to your application directly from the New Project wizard when you go through it. In many cases, however, you won't realize until later that you want to use Core Data for your project. In this section, we show you how to add Core Data to an existing project.

Enabling an application to leverage Core Data is a three-step process:

1. Add the Core Data framework.
2. Create a data model.
3. Initialize the managed object context.

We walk you through these three steps so you can add Core Data support to any existing Mac OS X application.

Adding the Core Data Framework

In the Objective-C world, libraries are bundled into frameworks, and an application refers to a framework to gain access to those libraries. To see which frameworks are linked to your application, navigate to the project's build phases with the following steps:

1. Select the Graphique project at the top of the Project navigator.
2. Once the project information is displayed, select the Graphique target.

3. Click the Build Phases tab.

4. Expand the item called Link Binary With Libraries.

Figure 6–2 shows the resulting screen.

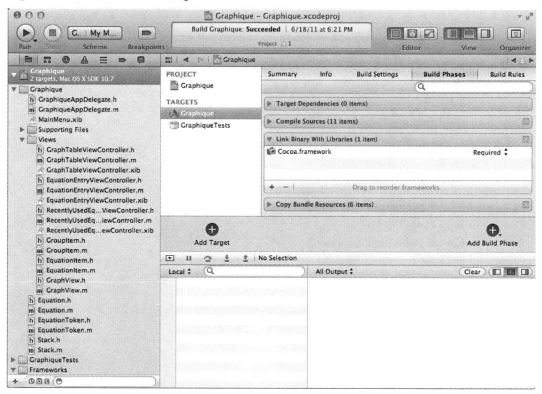

Figure 6–2. *The frameworks linked to the application*

The application should be linked to the Cocoa framework, which is the library that we've been using all along and that provides all the windows, buttons, and so on.

Click the + button right below the linked frameworks to add a new framework. When the framework browser opens, look for CoreData.framework and add it to the application, as shown in Figure 6–3.

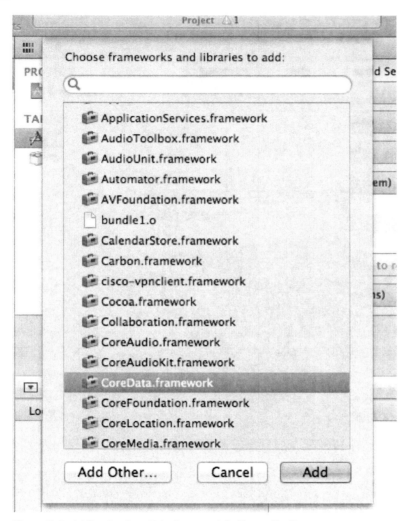

Figure 6–3. *Adding the Core Data framework to the application*

Once added, CoreData.framework is listed in the linked frameworks, as illustrated in Figure 6–4.

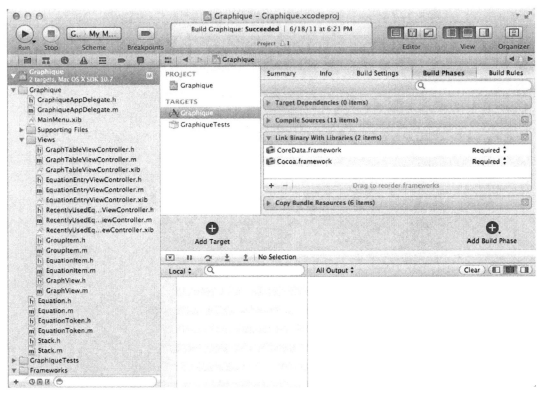

Figure 6–4. *The Core Data framework added to the application*

After these simple steps, your application is now ready to start tapping into the power of Core Data.

Creating a Data Model

Core Data is a persistence framework. It is a unified bridge between your objects (including the relationships among them) and a data persistence mechanism such as a database or an XML file, for example. When using Core Data, you rarely have to worry about the actual persistence mechanism. Everything rotates around an object model that defines how your data is laid out. Core Data converts that model into a data model if your back end is a database or an XML schema if your back end is an XML file. Regardless of the actual storage mechanism we use, we have to create an object model.

> **NOTE:** Note that we use the term *object model* and not *data model*. *Data model* is a term commonly used in the relational database world to represent the physical layout of the data in a database. This task is left to Core Data. Instead, we define an object model, which serves to define how we want our data objects to relate to one another.

For the Graphique application, we want to use Core Data to store the recently used equations. To keep everything neatly organized, we want to also create groups of equations. Our object model should therefore contain two kinds of objects: Equations and Groups.

Designing the Data Model

Since we added Core Data after the project was already created, we need to create the new object model. Right-click Supporting Files in the Project navigator and select New File, as shown in Figure 6–5.

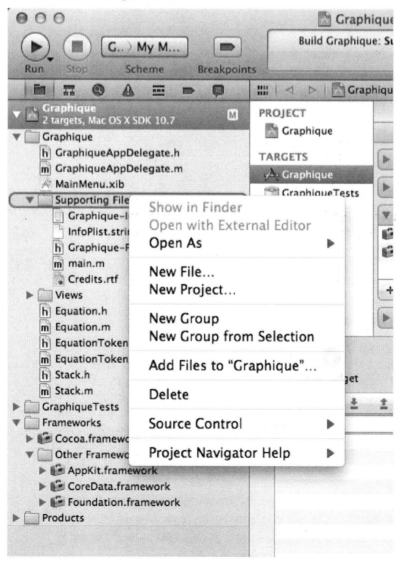

Figure 6–5. *Adding a new object model file*

From the list of templates, select Data Model from the Mac OS X Core Data category, as illustrated in Figure 6–6.

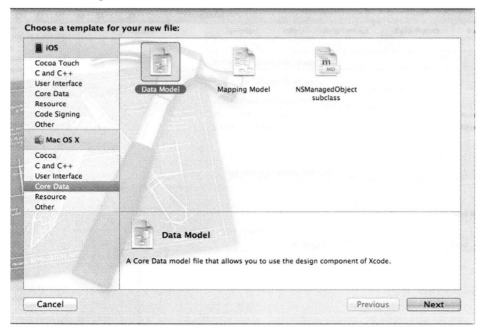

Figure 6–6. *Adding a new data model*

Save the new file as GraphiqueModel, as shown in Figure 6–7, and select the newly created file to see the model editor.

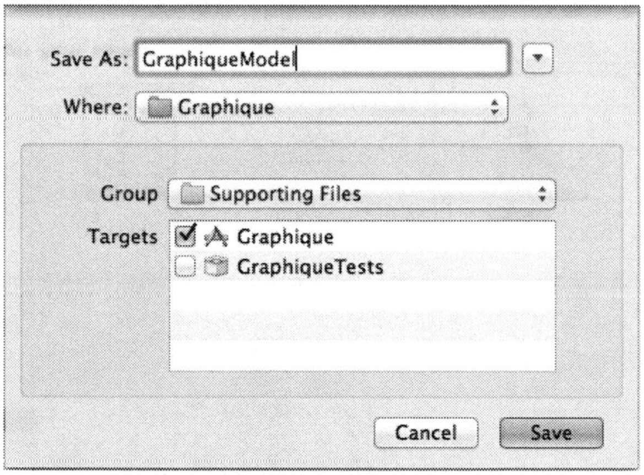

Figure 6–7. *Saving the new data model*

The most important feature of a data model is the list of entities. Entities represent data objects, in other words, the objects that that contain the data and that we want to persist in the data store. Since we just created the model, there is no entity in it. Click the Add Entity button in the model editor and name the new entity Equation, as illustrated in Figure 6–8.

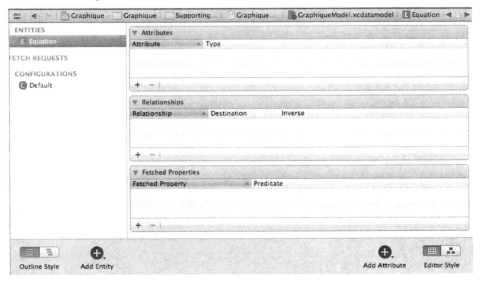

Figure 6–8. *Adding a new entity*

The list of entities should now contain only an entry for Equation. Much like objects, entities have attributes. Attributes contain the data and can use one of several predefined data types. Table 6–1 lists all the Core Data data types and what Objective-C type they map to.

Table 6–1. *The Predefined Core Data Attribute Types*

Core Data Attribute Type	Objective-C Data Type	Description
Integer 16	NSNumber	A 16–bit integer
Integer 32	NSNumber	A 32-bit integer
Integer 64	NSNumber	A 64-bit integer
Decimal	NSDecimalNumber	A base-10 subclass of NSNumber
Double	NSNumber	An object wrapper for double
Float	NSNumber	An object wrapper for float
String	NSString	A character string
Boolean	NSNumber	An object wrapper for a boolean value

Core Data Attribute Type	Objective-C Data Type	Description
Date	NSDate	A date object
Binary Data	NSData	Unstructured binary data
Transformable	Any nonstandard type	Any type transformed into a supported type

> **NOTE:** Transformable attributes are a way to tell Core Data that you would like to use a nonsupported data type in your managed object and that you will help Core Data by providing code to transform the attribute data at persist time into a supported type. We don't expand on this more advanced subject in this book.

A recently used equation is defined only by its string representation and a timestamp, so the equation entity will have two attributes: a representation attribute of type String and a timestamp attribute of type Date.

In the Core Data model editor, make sure the Equation entity is selected, and in the Attributes section, click the + button to add a new attribute. Call the attribute representation and set its type to String. Repeat the procedure to add the timestamp attribute, using the Date type this time. The Equation entity should be defined as illustrated in Figure 6–9.

Figure 6–9. *The Equation entity*

Since we want to use arbitrary groups to create groups of equations, we have to define the Group entity in the same fashion. We define our groups only by a name. In a more evolved application, you may want to include other attributes such as creation time or a description. For now, and to keep things simpler, a group has only a name.

Create the Group entity and add a name attribute of type String, as shown in Figure 6–10.

Figure 6–10. *The Group entity*

Near the bottom right of the Core Data model editor, there is an Editor Style button. Use it to toggle from Table view to Graph view. The graph illustrates the relationships between entities. As you can see in Figure 6–11, no relationship currently exists between groups and equations.

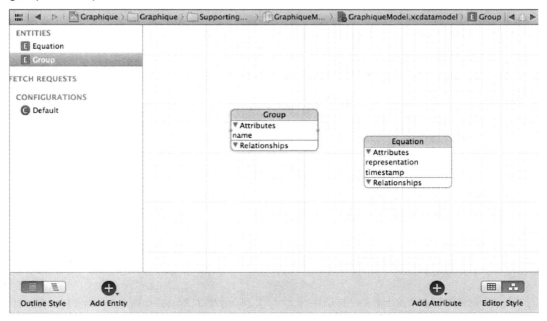

Figure 6–11. *Core Data entities in the graph view*

Since groups contain equations (or equations belong to groups), we need to create the relationship between the two. Switch the editor back to table style. Select the Equation entity and click the + button in the Relationships section. Name the new relationship group and set the destination to Group. This will tell Core Data that an equation might belong to a group. To make sure that Core Data enforces that all equations belong to a group, you must expand the Utilities panel, make sure the newly created relationship is selected, and uncheck the Optional check box, as shown in Figure 6–12.

Figure 6–12. *Relationship from Equation to Group*

To help Core Data manage the object graph, Apple strongly recommends that each relationship have an inverse relationship. For each relationship from entity A to entity B, we must create an inverse relationship from B to A. Select the Group entity and add a new relationship called equations, set its destination to Equation, and its inverse to group. Since a group may contain more than one equation, select To-Many Relationship in the Utilities panel. This tells Core Data that this relationship may lead to multiple equation entities. Since a group may be empty (in other words, does not contain any equations), we leave this relationship as optional. Figure 6–13 shows the resulting relationship configuration.

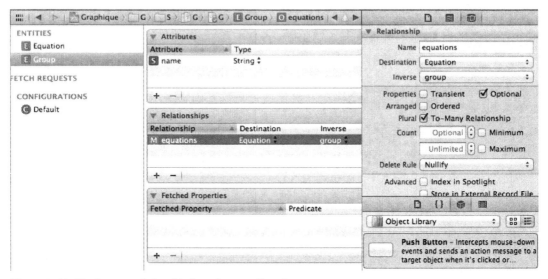

Figure 6–13. *The inverse relationship from Group to Equation*

This completes our data model for now. If you switch the editor to graph view, as shown in Figure 6–14, you can see that now the two entities are related. Note how the relationship from Group to Equation has a double arrowhead. This is to symbolize the To-many nature of the relationship.

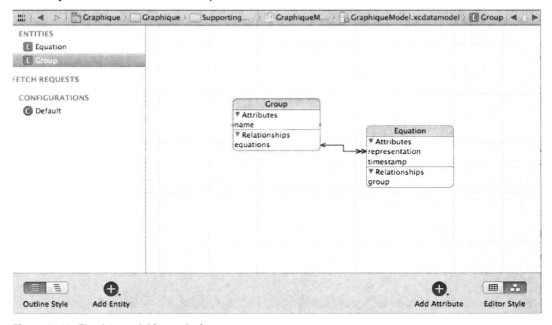

Figure 6–14. *The data model in graph view*

Initialize the Managed Object Context

Now back to our code. So far, we've made our project aware of Core Data by linking the Core Data framework, and we've defined our data model by creating entities and relationships. When data are pulled out of the persistent store, they are materialized as subclasses of NSManagedObject and offer methods to access their data. Any application using Core Data, however, must first initialize the framework before any operation can be performed. The framework uses the NSManagedObjectContext class as an interface between your code and the persistent store. The initialization process consists of properly setting up the managed object context and the other classes it relies upon, as shown in Figure 6–15.

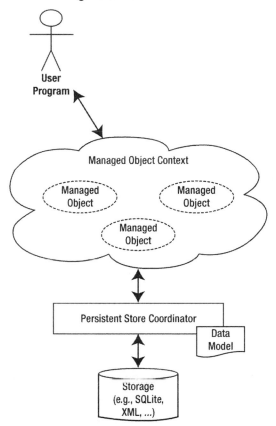

Figure 6–15. *The high-level Core Data framework layout*

The managed object context relies on a persistent store coordinator (NSPersistentStoreCoordinator) that serves to reconcile the physical persistent store (database, XML file, and so on) with the object model we created and that gets loaded into the framework as an NSManagedObjectModel instance.

The initialization process consists of setting up the NSManagedObjectModel, the NSPersistentStoreCoordinator, and finally the NSManagedObjectContext. For the most part, these steps are identical from project to project, and we give them to you in the following text. Open `GraphiqueAppDelegate.h` and add an import statement near the top:

```
#import <CoreData/CoreData.h>
```

Define three properties for the three main Core Data components, as illustrated in Listing 6–1: `managedObjectContext`, `managedObjectModel`, and `persistentStoreCoordinator`.

Listing 6–1. *GraphiqueAppDelegate.h with Core Data*

```
#import <Cocoa/Cocoa.h>
#import <CoreData/CoreData.h>

@class EquationEntryViewController;
@class GraphTableViewController;
@class RecentlyUsedEquationsViewController;
@class PreferencesController;

@interface GraphiqueAppDelegate : NSObject <NSApplicationDelegate> {
  @private
  NSManagedObjectContext *managedObjectContext_;
  NSManagedObjectModel *managedObjectModel_;
  NSPersistentStoreCoordinator *persistentStoreCoordinator_;
}

@property (strong) IBOutlet NSWindow *window;
@property (weak) IBOutlet NSSplitView *horizontalSplitView;
@property (weak) IBOutlet NSSplitView *verticalSplitView;
@property (strong) EquationEntryViewController *equationEntryViewController;
@property (strong) GraphTableViewController *graphTableViewController;
@property (strong) RecentlyUsedEquationsViewController
*recentlyUsedEquationsViewController;
@property (strong) PreferencesController *preferencesController;

@property (nonatomic, readonly) NSManagedObjectContext *managedObjectContext;
@property (nonatomic, readonly) NSManagedObjectModel *managedObjectModel;
@property (nonatomic, readonly) NSPersistentStoreCoordinator
*persistentStoreCoordinator;

- (void)changeGraphLineColor:(id)sender;
- (IBAction)showPreferencesPanel:(id)sender;

@end
```

Open `GraphiqueAppDelegate.m` to implement the getter methods for these properties. We start with `managedObjectModel`:

```
- (NSManagedObjectModel *)managedObjectModel {
  if (managedObjectModel_ != nil) {
    return managedObjectModel_;
  }
  managedObjectModel_ = [NSManagedObjectModel mergedModelFromBundles:nil];
  return managedObjectModel_;

}
```

Note that we don't specify the model we created specifically; `mergedModelFromBundles:` will find and load all appropriate model files in the project. Now that we've loaded the object model, we can leverage it in order to create the persistent store handler. This example uses NSSQLiteStoreType in order to indicate that the storage mechanism should rely on a SQLite database, as shown here:

```
- (NSPersistentStoreCoordinator *)persistentStoreCoordinator {
  if (persistentStoreCoordinator_ != nil) {
    return persistentStoreCoordinator_;
  }

  NSString* dir = [NSSearchPathForDirectoriesInDomains(NSDocumentDirectory,
NSUserDomainMask, YES) lastObject];
  NSURL *storeURL = [NSURL fileURLWithPath: [dir stringByAppendingPathComponent:
@"Graphique.sqlite"]];

  NSError *error = nil;
  persistentStoreCoordinator_ = [[NSPersistentStoreCoordinator alloc]
initWithManagedObjectModel:[self managedObjectModel]];
  if (![persistentStoreCoordinator_ addPersistentStoreWithType:NSSQLiteStoreType
configuration:nil URL:storeURL options:nil error:&error]) {
    NSLog(@"Unresolved error %@, %@", error, [error userInfo]);
    abort();
  }

  return persistentStoreCoordinator_;
}
```

> **NOTE:** We are telling Core Data to use a SQLite database called Graphique.sqlite and store it in the user's Documents folder. You may change this to store the file anywhere you'd like.

Finally, we initialize the context from the persistent store that we just defined:

```
- (NSManagedObjectContext *)managedObjectContext {
  if (managedObjectContext_ != nil) {
    return managedObjectContext_;
  }

  NSPersistentStoreCoordinator *coordinator = [self persistentStoreCoordinator];
  if (coordinator != nil) {
    managedObjectContext_ = [[NSManagedObjectContext alloc] init];
    [managedObjectContext_ setPersistentStoreCoordinator:coordinator];
  }
  return managedObjectContext_;
}
```

The application can now use the managed object context to store and retrieve entities.

Storing Recently Used Equations

In the Graphique application, the `RecentlyUsedEquationsViewController` class is the user interface controller responsible for dealing with recently used equations. Since it will need to interact with the persisted data, the first step is to give it access to the `NSManagedObjectContext` object that represents the interface to the persistent store. Open `RecentlyUsedEquationsViewController.h` and add the following:

1. An `#import <CoreData/CoreData.h>` statement at the top.

2. A new property for holding the managed object context.

Listing 6–2 shows the resulting `RecentlyUsedEquationsViewController.h` file.

Listing 6–2. *RecentlyUsedEquationsViewController.h*

```
#import <Cocoa/Cocoa.h>
#import <CoreData/CoreData.h>

#import "GroupItem.h"

@interface RecentlyUsedEquationsViewController : NSViewController
<NSOutlineViewDataSource, NSSplitViewDelegate> {
@private
  GroupItem *rootItem;
  NSManagedObjectContext *managedObjectContext;
}
@property (nonatomic, strong) NSManagedObjectContext *managedObjectContext;

@end
```

Don't forget to open `RecentlyUsedEquationsViewController.m` and add a `@synthesize` statement for the new property right after the `@implementation` statement:

```
@synthesize managedObjectContext;
```

Finally, we have to make sure the app delegate passes the context along when it initializes the controller. Open `GraphiqueAppDelegate.m` and edit the `applicationDidFinishLaunching:` method to match this code:

```
- (void)applicationDidFinishLaunching:(NSNotification *)aNotification
{
  equationEntryViewController = [[EquationEntryViewController alloc]
initWithNibName:@"EquationEntryViewController" bundle:nil];
  [self.verticalSplitView replaceSubview:[[self.verticalSplitView subviews]
objectAtIndex:1] with:equationEntryViewController.view];

  graphTableViewController = [[GraphTableViewController alloc]
initWithNibName:@"GraphTableViewController" bundle:nil];
  [self.horizontalSplitView replaceSubview:[[self.horizontalSplitView subviews]
objectAtIndex:1] with:[graphTableViewController view]];
```

```
  recentlyUsedEquationsViewController = [[RecentlyUsedEquationsViewController alloc]
initWithNibName:@"RecentlyUsedEquationsViewController" bundle:nil];
  recentlyUsedEquationsViewController.managedObjectContext = self.managedObjectContext;
  [self.verticalSplitView replaceSubview:[[self.verticalSplitView subviews]
objectAtIndex:0] with:[recentlyUsedEquationsViewController view]];
  self.verticalSplitView.delegate = recentlyUsedEquationsViewController;

  [[NSColorPanel sharedColorPanel] setTarget:self];
  [[NSColorPanel sharedColorPanel] setAction:@selector(changeGraphLineColor:)];
}
```

Now, let's go back to RecentlyUsedEquationsViewController.h and define a new
method that other controllers can use to tell it to remember an equation:

```
-(void)remember:(Equation*)equation;
```

With the new method, RecentlyUsedEquationsViewController.h should look like Listing
6–3.

Listing 6–3. *RecentlyUsedEquationsViewController.h with a New Method for Remembering Equations*

```
#import <Cocoa/Cocoa.h>
#import <CoreData/CoreData.h>

@class GroupItem;
@class Equation;

@interface RecentlyUsedEquationsViewController : NSViewController
<NSOutlineViewDataSource, NSSplitViewDelegate> {
@private
  GroupItem *rootItem;
  NSManagedObjectContext *managedObjectContext;
}
@property (nonatomic, strong) NSManagedObjectContext *managedObjectContext;

- (void)remember:(Equation*)equation;

@end
```

> **NOTE:** Do not confuse the Equation object with the Equation entity we created earlier in the model. Right now, while they represent the same thing semantically, they aren't related in code. Right now, data in the `Equation` entity is represented as an object of type `NSManagedObject` and not an object of type `Equation`. It is possible to make Core Data use a custom class (in other words, other than `NSManagedObject`) to represent data entities as objects, but it falls out of the scope of this book and encourage you to get a book dedicated to Core Data for more information.

Open `RecentlyUsedEquationsViewController.m` to implement the `remember:` method. The algorithm for the method is as follows:

1. Create a group name based on the current date (month/day/year).

2. Query Core Data to find out whether the group already exists.

3. If it does exist, then use it; otherwise, create a new one, save it, and use it.

4. Create a new equation entity as an `NSManagedObject` and attach it to the appropriate group.

5. Commit to the persistent store.

The next few sections walk you through the implementation for the `remember:` method.

Querying the Persistent Store to Get the Group Entity

Creating the group name is trivial using the `NSDateFormatter` object:

```
NSDate *today = [NSDate date];
NSDateFormatter *dateFormat = [[NSDateFormatter alloc] init];
[dateFormat setDateFormat:@"EEEE MMMM d, YYYY"];
NSString *groupName = [dateFormat stringFromDate:today];
```

We then query the persistent store to see whether the group exists already. Retrieving objects from the persistent store is done using the `NSFetchRequest` object, which defines what to retrieve:

```
// Create the fetch request
NSFetchRequest *fetchRequest = [[NSFetchRequest alloc] init];
// Define the kind of entity to look for
NSEntityDescription *entity = [NSEntityDescription entityForName:@"Group"
inManagedObjectContext:self.managedObjectContext];
[fetchRequest setEntity:entity];
// Add a predicate to further specify what we are looking for
NSPredicate *predicate = [NSPredicate predicateWithFormat:@"name=%@", groupName];
[fetchRequest setPredicate:predicate];

NSArray *groups = [self.managedObjectContext executeFetchRequest:fetchRequest
error:nil];
```

```
NSManagedObject *groupMO = nil;

if(groups.count > 0) {
  // We found one, use it
  groupMO = [groups objectAtIndex:0];
}
else {
  // We need to create a new group because it did not exist
  groupMO = [NSEntityDescription insertNewObjectForEntityForName:@"Group"
inManagedObjectContext:self.managedObjectContext];

  // set the name
  [groupMO setValue:groupName forKey:@"name"];
}
```

> **NOTE:** We use the key/value pair generic accessor methods to interact with the data contained in the NSManagedObject. [object valueForKey:@"myAttribute"] will retrieve the value of myAttribute, while [object setValue:@"theValue" forKey:@"myAttribute"] will set the value of myAttribute.

At this point, we have a managed object representing the right group. If the group did not exist before, we added it using the insertNewObjectForEntityForName:inManagedObjectContext: method.

Creating the Equation Managed Object and Adding It to the Persistent Store

Now that we have a valid group managed object, we simply create a new equation managed object and link it to the group:

```
NSManagedObject *equationMO = [NSEntityDescription
insertNewObjectForEntityForName:@"Equation"
inManagedObjectContext:self.managedObjectContext];

// set the timestamp and the representation
[equationMO setValue:equation.text forKey:@"representation"];
[equationMO setValue:[NSDate date] forKey:@"timestamp"];
[equationMO setValue:groupMO forKey:@"group"];
```

Committing

In Core Data, nothing is permanent until you tell it to commit. Upon committing, the managed object context will flush all of its content to the persistent store, making it permanent. The commit operation is triggered by calling the save: method:

```
NSError *error = nil;
if (![self.managedObjectContext save:&error]) {
  NSLog(@"Unresolved error %@, %@", error, [error userInfo]);
  abort();
}
```

Putting Everything Together into the Final Method

Listing 6–4 documents the entire remember: method. Be sure to import Equation.h at the top of RecentlyUsedEquationsViewController.m.

Listing 6–4. *The remember: Method in RecentlyUsedEquationsViewController.m*

```
-(void)remember:(Equation*)equation
{
  NSDate *today = [NSDate date];
  NSDateFormatter *dateFormat = [[NSDateFormatter alloc] init];
  [dateFormat setDateFormat:@"EEEE MMMM d, YYYY"];
  NSString *groupName = [dateFormat stringFromDate:today];

  // Create the fetch request
  NSFetchRequest *fetchRequest = [[NSFetchRequest alloc] init];
  // Define the kind of entity to look for
  NSEntityDescription *entity = [NSEntityDescription entityForName:@"Group"
inManagedObjectContext:self.managedObjectContext];
  [fetchRequest setEntity:entity];
  // Add a predicate to further specify what we are looking for
  NSPredicate *predicate = [NSPredicate predicateWithFormat:@"name=%@", groupName];
  [fetchRequest setPredicate:predicate];

  NSArray *groups = [self.managedObjectContext executeFetchRequest:fetchRequest
error:nil];
  NSManagedObject *groupMO = nil;

  if(groups.count > 0) {
    // We found one, use it
    groupMO = [groups objectAtIndex:0];
  }
  else {
    // We need to create a new group because it did not exist
    groupMO = [NSEntityDescription insertNewObjectForEntityForName:@"Group"
inManagedObjectContext:self.managedObjectContext];

    // set the name
    [groupMO setValue:groupName forKey:@"name"];
  }

  NSManagedObject *equationMO = [NSEntityDescription
insertNewObjectForEntityForName:@"Equation"
inManagedObjectContext:self.managedObjectContext];

  // set the timestamp and the representation
  [equationMO setValue:equation.text forKey:@"representation"];
  [equationMO setValue:[NSDate date] forKey:@"timestamp"];
  [equationMO setValue:groupMO forKey:@"group"];

  NSError *error = nil;
  if (![self.managedObjectContext save:&error]) {
    NSLog(@"Unresolved error %@, %@", error, [error userInfo]);
    abort();
  }
}
```

Finally, we must call this method. We want to remember an equation when it is entered. Open EquationEntryViewController.m and add an import statement at the top:

```
#import "RecentlyUsedEquationsViewController.h"
```

Then, edit the equationEntered: method to match Listing 6–5.

Listing 6–5. *The updated equationEntered: Method*

```
- (IBAction)equationEntered:(id)sender
{
  NSLog(@"Equation entered");
  GraphiqueAppDelegate *delegate = [NSApplication sharedApplication].delegate;

  Equation *equation = [[Equation alloc] initWithString: [self.textField stringValue]];

  NSError *error = nil;
  if(![equation validate:&error])
  {
    // Validation failed, display the error
    NSAlert *alert = [[[NSAlert alloc] init] autorelease];
    [alert addButtonWithTitle:@"OK"];
    [alert setMessageText:@"Something went wrong. "];
    [alert setInformativeText:[NSString stringWithFormat:@"Error %d: %@", [error
code],[error localizedDescription]]];
    [alert setAlertStyle:NSInformationalAlertStyle];

    [alert beginSheetModalForWindow:delegate.window modalDelegate:self
didEndSelector:@selector(alertDidEnd:returnCode:contextInfo:) contextInfo:nil];
  }
  else
  {
    [delegate.recentlyUsedEquationsViewController remember: equation];
    [delegate.graphTableViewController draw: equation];
  }
}
```

Reloading Recently Used Equations

We have everything in place to store equations as they are entered. Of course, we haven't wired the outline view with the data, so the application won't appear to be doing anything different. You can launch the application nonetheless to check that everything is hooked up correctly.

Once the application is started, try typing an equation like x2 (in other words, "x squared") for example and graph it. Everything should behave like before. But open the Terminal.app application and go into the Documents folder to open the data store:

```
sqlite3 ~/Documents/Graphique.sqlite
SQLite version 3.7.5
Enter ".help" for instructions
Enter SQL statements terminated with a ";"
sqlite> .schema
CREATE TABLE ZEQUATION ( Z_PK INTEGER PRIMARY KEY, Z_ENT INTEGER, Z_OPT INTEGER, ZGROUP
INTEGER, ZTIMESTAMP TIMESTAMP, ZREPRESENTATION VARCHAR );
```

```
CREATE TABLE ZGROUP ( Z_PK INTEGER PRIMARY KEY, Z_ENT INTEGER, Z_OPT INTEGER, ZNAME
VARCHAR );
CREATE TABLE Z_METADATA (Z_VERSION INTEGER PRIMARY KEY, Z_UUID VARCHAR(255), Z_PLIST
BLOB);
CREATE TABLE Z_PRIMARYKEY (Z_ENT INTEGER PRIMARY KEY, Z_NAME VARCHAR, Z_SUPER INTEGER,
Z_MAX INTEGER);
CREATE INDEX ZEQUATION_ZGROUP_INDEX ON ZEQUATION (ZGROUP);
sqlite> select * from ZGROUP;
1|2|1|Wednesday July 6, 2011
sqlite> select * from ZEQUATION;
1|1|1|1|331670216.49823|x2
```

Use the `.schema` command to display the schema. You can see that Core Data created two tables to hold the equations and group. By querying each table, you can see that a new group was created and that it contains the equation you just typed. The data is getting stored, and now we just have to pull it back out and display it properly.

Before we hook everything to the user interface, we need to edit the GroupItem and EquationItem objects. These objects are used as the data structure of the outline view we want to populate. First, we edit EquationItem to make text a property instead of a method that returns dummy data. Edit EquationItem.h and EquationItem.m to look like Listing 6–6 and Listing 6–7, respectively.

Listing 6–6. *EquationItem.h*

```
#import <Foundation/Foundation.h>

@interface EquationItem : NSObject {
@private
  NSString *text;
}
@property (nonatomic, strong) NSString *text;

@end
```

Listing 6–7. *EquationItem.m*

```
#import "EquationItem.h"

@implementation EquationItem

@synthesize text;

- (NSInteger)numberOfChildren {
  return 0;
}

@end
```

Next we want to make sure we can reload the data in a group item without having to throw away the object each time, so we add a reset: method that will remove its children and a boolean flag to help us keep track of whether the members of the group have been loaded. Edit GroupItem.h and GroupItem.m to match Listing 6–8 and Listing 6–9, respectively.

Listing 6–8. *GroupItem.h*

```
#import <Foundation/Foundation.h>

@interface GroupItem : NSObject {
@private
  NSString *name;
  NSMutableArray *children;
  BOOL loaded;
}

@property (nonatomic, strong) NSString *name;
@property BOOL loaded;

- (NSInteger)numberOfChildren;
- (id)childAtIndex:(NSUInteger)n;
- (NSString*)text;

- (void)addChild:(id)childNode;
- (void)reset;

@end
```

Listing 6–9. *GroupItem.m*

```
#import "GroupItem.h"

@implementation GroupItem

@synthesize name, loaded;

- (id)init
{
  self = [super init];
  if (self) {
    children = [[NSMutableArray alloc] init];
    loaded = NO;
  }
  return self;
}

- (void)addChild:(id)childNode
{
  [children addObject:childNode];
}

- (NSInteger)numberOfChildren
{
  return children.count;
}

- (id)childAtIndex:(NSUInteger)n
{
  return [children objectAtIndex:n];
}

- (void)reset
{
```

```
  [children removeAllObjects];
  loaded = NO;
}

- (NSString*)text
{
  return name;
}

- (void)dealloc
{
  [children release];
  [super dealloc];
}

@end
```

We now turn our interest toward the RecentlyUsedEquationsViewController class. To help read the data from the persistent store, we add a method that will take an item, either a GroupItem or an EquationItem, and populate its children if it's a group. If the item is an equation, nothing is done since equations are leaves in our outline tree. Open RecentlyUsedEquationsViewController.h and declare the following method:

```
-(void)loadChildrenForItem:(id)item;
```

Then edit RecentlyUsedEquationsViewController.m to provide the method implementation, as shown in Listing 6–10.

Listing 6–10. *The loadChildrenForItem: Method*

```
-(void)loadChildrenForItem:(id)item
{
  // If the item isn't a group, there's nothing to load
  if(![item isKindOfClass:GroupItem.class]) return;
  GroupItem *group = (GroupItem*)item;

  // No point reloading if it's already been loaded
  if(group.loaded) return;

  // Wipe out the nodes children since we're about to reload them
  [group reset];

  // If the group is the rootItem, then we need to load all the available groups. If
not, then we only load the
  // equations for that group based on its name

  if(group == rootItem) {
    NSFetchRequest *fetchRequest = [[NSFetchRequest alloc] init];
    NSEntityDescription *entity = [NSEntityDescription entityForName:@"Group"
inManagedObjectContext:self.managedObjectContext];
    [fetchRequest setEntity:entity];

    NSArray *groups = [self.managedObjectContext executeFetchRequest:fetchRequest
error:nil];
    for(NSManagedObject *obj in groups) {
      GroupItem *groupItem = [[GroupItem alloc] init];
      groupItem.name = [obj valueForKey:@"name"];
```

```
      [group addChild:groupItem];
    }

  }
  else {
    NSFetchRequest *fetchRequest = [[NSFetchRequest alloc] init];
    NSEntityDescription *entity = [NSEntityDescription entityForName:@"Equation"
inManagedObjectContext:self.managedObjectContext];
    [fetchRequest setEntity:entity];
    // Add a predicate to further specify what we are looking for
    NSPredicate *predicate = [NSPredicate predicateWithFormat:@"group.name=%@",
group.name];
    [fetchRequest setPredicate:predicate];

    NSArray *equations = [self.managedObjectContext executeFetchRequest:fetchRequest
error:nil];

    for(NSManagedObject *obj in equations) {
      EquationItem *equationItem = [[EquationItem alloc] init];
      equationItem.text = [obj valueForKey:@"representation"];
      [group addChild:equationItem];
    }

  }

  // Mark the group as properly loaded
  group.loaded = YES;
}
```

The previous method loads only the data for a given node. It does not recurse down the children to load their data as well. This is commonly referred to as *lazy loading*. Lazy loading is a technique that consists in loading only the data necessary to display the user interface. We make sure to call the previous method only when the user interface needs the information. The information is needed when the outline view wants to determine whether a node can be expanded (in other words, a group with equations) or to find out how many children a node has (in other words, how many equations in a given group). While still in `RecentlyUsedEquationsViewController.m`, edit the `outlineView:numberOfChildrenOfItem:` and `outlineView:isItemExpandable:` methods to match Listing 6–11 and Listing 6–12.

Listing 6–11. *Loading a Group When the Number of Children Is Needed*

```
- (NSInteger)outlineView:(NSOutlineView *)outlineView numberOfChildrenOfItem:(id)item
{
  [self loadChildrenForItem:(item == nil ? rootItem : item)];
  return (item == nil) ? [rootItem numberOfChildren] : [item numberOfChildren];
}
```

Listing 6–12. *Loading a Group to Find Out If the Group Is Expandable*

```
- (BOOL)outlineView:(NSOutlineView *)_outlineView isItemExpandable:(id)item
{
  return [self outlineView:_outlineView numberOfChildrenOfItem:item] > 0;
}
```

Of course, we need to make sure we remove any dummy data we had created in a prior chapter. Clean up `initWithNibName:bundle:` to make it look like Listing 6–13.

Listing 6–13. *The initWithNibName:bundle: Method*

```
- (id)initWithNibName:(NSString *)nibNameOrNil bundle:(NSBundle *)nibBundleOrNil
{
  self = [super initWithNibName:nibNameOrNil bundle:nibBundleOrNil];
  if (self) {
    rootItem = [[GroupItem alloc] init];
  }
  return self;
}
```

If you launch the application now, the outline view should load the equation you had recorded in the previous run, but if you graph another equation, despite that it is recorded, the table does not refresh itself. To address this issue, we need to make the controller aware of the outline view so it can tell it to refresh. To do this, we add a new property of type NSOutlineView and tag it with IBOutlet so Interface Builder can see it. RecentlyUsedEquationsViewController.h should match Listing 6–14.

Listing 6–14. *RecentlyUsedEquationsViewController.h*

```
#import <Cocoa/Cocoa.h>
#import <CoreData/CoreData.h>

#import "Equation.h"
#import "GroupItem.h"

@interface RecentlyUsedEquationsViewController : NSViewController
<NSOutlineViewDataSource, NSSplitViewDelegate>
{
@private
  GroupItem *rootItem;
  NSManagedObjectContext *managedObjectContext;
  NSOutlineView *outlineView;
}
@property (nonatomic, strong) NSManagedObjectContext *managedObjectContext;
@property (nonatomic, strong) IBOutlet NSOutlineView *outlineView;

-(void)remember:(Equation*)equation;
-(void)loadChildrenForItem:(id)item;

@end
```

Make sure you open RecentlyUsedEquationsViewController.m to add the @synthesize directive after @implementation:

```
@synthesize outlineView;
```

Finally, open RecentlyUsedEquationsViewController.xib and link the new outlineView property from the File's Owner to the Outline View object. Select the File's Owner, open the Connections inspector, and drag the circle next to the outlineView outlet to the Outline View object. The result should look like Figure 6–16.

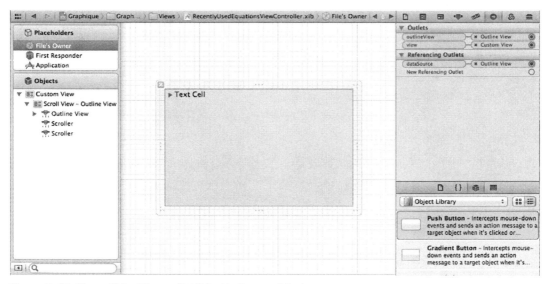

Figure 6–16. *The outlineView outlet linked to the user interface*

All we have to do now is tell the outline view to reload itself when we are told to remember an equation. In RecentlyUsedEquationsViewController.m, add the following couple of lines of code at the end of the remember: method:

```
// Reload outline
[rootItem reset];
[outlineView reloadData];
```

Launch the app and see how it now remembers equations as you graph them.

Tightening the Control over the Outline View

So far, we have loaded our data into the outline view. Now we need to deal with the user interacting with the view. Much like most other Cocoa components, outline views use a delegate to handle interactions. We now set our controller as the delegate for the outline view and implement the necessary methods to catch the events we care about.

Using NSOutlineViewDelegate

If you've followed this book page by page and notice the naming patterns, you most likely already guessed that the outline view delegates must conform to the NSOutlineViewDelegate protocol. This protocol has no required methods. Edit the interface definition of RecentlyUsedEquationsViewController.h to add NSOutlineViewDelegate in the list of protocols it conforms to:

```
@interface RecentlyUsedEquationsViewController : NSViewController
<NSOutlineViewDataSource, NSSplitViewDelegate, NSOutlineViewDelegate>
```

All that is left to do is to edit RecentlyUsedEquationsViewController.xib, select the Outline View object, and connect its delegate to the controller (that is, the File's Owner). The resulting connection should look like Figure 6–17.

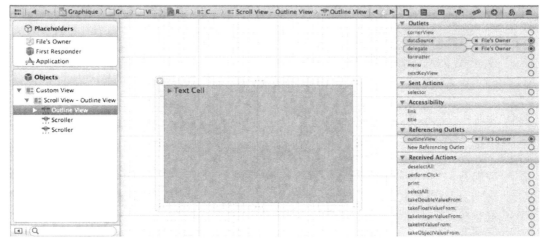

Figure 6–17. *The NSOutlineView delegate properly connected*

At this point, the outline view is told to send all events to its delegate, the RecentlyUsedEquationsViewController controller. We can now intercept the events we care about and do what we need to do.

Handling Equations Selection

The most obvious use of the recently used equations is to retrace them by selecting them from the outline view. In addition to the methods it declares, the delegate protocol is automatically registered to receive messages corresponding to NSOutlineView notifications. These inform the delegate when the selection changes or is about to change, when a column is moved or resized, and when an item is expanded or collapsed. See Table 5-2 for the delegate messages and the corresponding notification types.

Table 5-2. *NSOutlineView Delegate Messages and Notifications*

Delegate Message	Notification
outlineViewColumnDidMove:	NSOutlineViewColumnDidMoveNotification
outlineViewColumnDidResize:	NSOutlineViewColumnDidResizeNotification
outlineViewSelectionDidChange:	NSOutlineViewSelectionDidChangeNotification
outlineViewSelectionIsChanging:	NSOutlineViewSelectionIsChangingNotification
outlineViewItemDidExpand:	NSOutlineViewItemDidExpandNotification
outlineViewItemDidCollapse:	NSOutlineViewItemDidCollapseNotification

To catch the selection change, we provide an implementation of the outlineViewSelectionDidChange: method in RecentlyUsedEquationsViewController.m, as shown in Listing 6–15.

Listing 6–15. *Handling Selection Change in an Outline View*

```
- (void)outlineViewSelectionDidChange:(NSNotification *)notification
{
  NSOutlineView *outlineView_ = [notification object];
  NSInteger row = [outlineView_ selectedRow];

  id item = [outlineView_ itemAtRow:row];

  // If an equation was selected, deal with it
  if([item isKindOfClass:EquationItem.class]) {
    EquationItem *equationItem = item;

    Equation *equation = [[Equation alloc] initWithString:equationItem.text];

    GraphiqueAppDelegate *delegate = [NSApplication sharedApplication].delegate;

    [delegate.equationEntryViewController.textField setStringValue: equation.text];
    [delegate.graphTableViewController draw:equation];

    [delegate.equationEntryViewController controlTextDidChange: nil];
  }
}
```

Make sure you add the proper import statements at the top of RecentlyUsedEquationsViewController.m:

```
#import "GraphiqueAppDelegate.h"
#import "EquationEntryViewController.h"
#import "GraphTableViewController.h"
```

Preventing Double-Clicks from Editing

Our outline view is populated from the database, so we don't want users to be able to edit its nodes by double-clicking them. An outline view always asks its delegate before allowing a cell to be edited. All we have to do is make sure we always say no. Add an implementation for the appropriate method to RecentlyUsedEquationsViewController.m, as shown here:

```
- (BOOL)outlineView:(NSOutlineView *)outlineView shouldEditTableColumn:(NSTableColumn
*)tableColumn item:(id)item
{
  return NO;
}
```

Launch the app and try selecting an equation from the recently used equations. It populates the entry field and draws the equation as expected.

Summary

In this chapter, you learned about Cocoa's powerful object storage mechanism, Core Data, and got a taste for how to use it. Feel free to experiment with Core Data and read further on the topic to add power to your applications. Don't be fooled by the simplicity of the API; Core Data has much more to offer and should be on your mind any time you think about storing structured application data. We strongly encourage you to pick up a book dedicated to the subject.

In the next chapter, we integrate Graphique more fully with the Mac OS X Lion desktop so that it takes advantage of what the Lion environment offers.

Chapter 7

Integrating Graphique into the Mac OS X Desktop

Right now, Graphique is an application island in the sea of the Mac OS X desktop. You can launch it, run it, use it fruitfully, and close it, and it's all self-contained. There's nothing wrong with that, but Mac users have grown to expect more from an application: they want it to work with the rest of the Mac OS X ecosystem. In this chapter, you integrate Graphique into that ecosystem, expanding its borders beyond the current shoreline into Finder and the menu bar. At the end of this chapter, you'll be able to save your equations to files, and then double-click them in Finder to launch Graphique and display their graphs. You'll also be able to use Quick Look to see your graphs from within Finder. Finally, you'll be able to display an icon in the menu bar and launch the most recent ten equations from it.

Dealing with Graphique XML Files

Most applications produce data that they store in files. For example, Microsoft Word produces .doc files that we commonly refer to as *Word files*. The expectation is that when you click to open a Word file, the operating system will know to open Microsoft Word. The same thing happens to Photoshop files, Pages files, and countless other types of files. This section illustrates how to create "Graphique files." It then registers the newly created file type with the OS and the file preview capability built in Mac OS Finder.

Producing a Graphique File

At any time, Graphique should be able to save an equation to a Graphique file, which is a file with a .graphique extension. Rather than defining a new file format for Graphique files, though, you'll leverage Mac OS X's support for property list files and store Graphique files as property lists. The first step toward saving a Graphique file is to create a method to respond to user requests to save an equation.

From a design perspective, typically an application has both Save and Save As menu items. Before a document has ever been saved, the application has no idea where to save it and enables only the Save As menu item. When users select this menu item, they must specify a location to save the file. At this point, the application enables the Save menu item, which, when selected, saves the open document to the location already specified.

With Graphique, an equation is a short snippet of text. If a user changes the text, are they modifying the original equation as another version of itself, in which case subsequent Save operations should overwrite the original equation? Or are they typing in a new equation, in which case the application should prompt for a new location to save the file each time? We've opted for the latter, since equations are so short that we think people are more likely to type in new equations rather than fine-tune existing equations, so we implement only the Save As method.

Creating a Save As Method

Open MainMenu.xib and expand the File menu. You can see that Xcode generated only a Save menu item and not a Save As menu item. You're going to change the Save to Save As. Select the Save menu item, open the Attributes inspector, and change the title to Save As.... Select the Key Equivalent field and press ⌘+Shift+S, the standard keyboard shortcut for Save As. See Figure 7–1.

Figure 7–1. *The Save... menu item changed to Save As...*

The text now says Save As…, but if you open the Connections inspector, you see that the menu is linked to the `saveDocument:` method, not the `saveDocumentAs:` method. Delete the existing connection to `saveDocument:` by clicking the X next to First Responder (next to `saveDocument:`). Then, drag from the circle next to selector, under Sent Actions, to the First Responder object on the left. In the ensuing pop-up menu, select `saveDocumentAs:`, as shown in Figure 7–2.

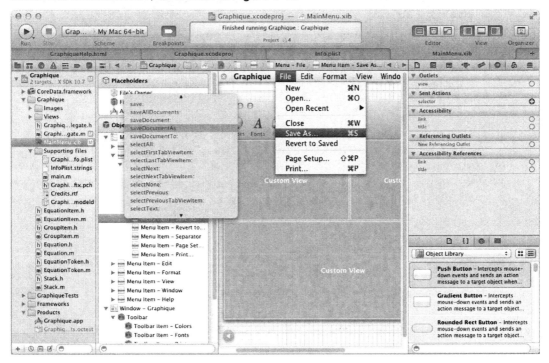

Figure 7–2. *Connecting the Save As… menu item to the* `saveDocumentAs:` *method*

When users select the Save As… menu item, the `saveDocumentAs:` action method will be sent up the responder chain. To respond, implement the `saveDocumentAs:` method in the first responder: the `GraphiqueAppDelegate` class. The implementation will perform the following steps:

1. Grab the current equation.

2. Prompt the user to select a location to save the new file.

3. Produce the property list file.

4. Save the file to the selected location.

Grabbing the Current Equation

Grabbing the current equation is as simple as querying the equation entry view controller for the current text in the text field, like this:

```
NSString *text = [self.equationEntryViewController.textField stringValue];
```

This line of code puts the text of the equation into the text variable. Since you don't actually need an Equation object, you leave it as a string.

Prompting the User to Select a Destination File

The NSSavePanel class prompts the user for a file location for saving the data. Listing 7–1 shows how this is done.

Listing 7–1. *Opening an NSSavePanel*

```
NSSavePanel *saveDlg = [NSSavePanel savePanel];
[saveDlg setAllowedFileTypes:[NSArray arrayWithObject:@"graphique"]];
NSInteger result = [saveDlg runModal];
if (result == NSOKButton) {
}
```

This code creates an NSSavePanel instance, constrains the allowed file types to .graphique files only (the standard Graphique file extension) and then calls the runModal: method to display the NSSavePanel instance as a modal window. It then tests the return value of the runModal: method to see whether the user clicked OK to see whether to actually save the file or cancel the operation.

Producing the Graphique File

As mentioned, Graphique files are simply property list files. To save the file, create an NSDictionary object with a single entry: equation as the key and the text in the text variable as the value. NSDictionary objects can conveniently be serialized into a property list file and can also be reread back into the object. Listing 7–2 shows the completed saveDocumentAs: method, which you should place in GraphiqueAppDelegate.m.

Listing 7–2. *The saveDocumentAs Method*

```
- (void)saveDocumentAs:(id)sender
{
  // 1. Grab the current equation
  NSString *text = [self.equationEntryViewController.textField stringValue];

  // 2. Open the NSSavePanel
  NSSavePanel *saveDlg = [NSSavePanel savePanel];
  [saveDlg setAllowedFileTypes:[NSArray arrayWithObject:@"graphique"]];

  // Open the dialog and save if the user selected OK
  NSInteger result = [saveDlg runModal];
  if (result == NSOKButton){
    // 3. Producing the Graphique file
    NSMutableDictionary *data = [[NSMutableDictionary alloc] init];
    [data setObject:text forKey:@"equation"];
    [data writeToURL:saveDlg.URL atomically:YES];
  }
}
```

Launch the application and type an equation, as you normally would, in the equation entry field. Click the Graph button to view the graph so that you know it's something worth saving. Then, select File ➤ Save As… from the menu. This will open the NSSavePanel, as shown in Figure 7–3.

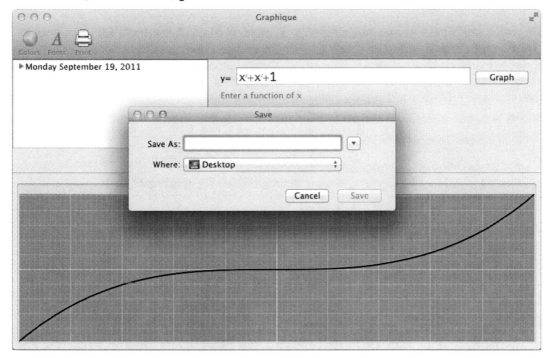

Figure 7–3. *Prompting the user for a file location*

Enter a file name and click the Save button. Finally, check the content of the newly created file using your favorite text editor. It should look something like the following example:

```
<?xml version="1.0" encoding="UTF-8"?>
<!DOCTYPE plist PUBLIC "-//Apple//DTD PLIST 1.0//EN"
"http://www.apple.com/DTDs/PropertyList-1.0.dtd">
<plist version="1.0">
<dict>
    <key>equation</key>
    <string>x3+x2+1</string>
</dict>
</plist>
```

As you can see, the dictionary object was serialized directly into the property list file. In fact, the Mac OS X property list files are backed by the NSDictionary class, which is why this file uses Apple's PropertyList DTD. Notice that the file is automatically given the .graphique extension because this is how you've configured the NSSavePanel. Graphique can now save equations to a file.

Loading a Graphique File into the Application

Now that Graphique can save equation files, it's only natural to provide a way to reopen the files at any time to view the equations again.

As we've shown in the previous section, you can use the MainMenu.xib file to find out what actions menu items are linked to. The Open menu item is automatically linked to a message called openDocument:. In GraphiqueAppDelegate.m, provide an implementation for this method, as shown in Listing 7–3. This implementation calls a new method that you haven't implemented yet, so initially it won't compile.

Listing 7–3. *The* openDocument *Method*

```
- (void)openDocument:(id)sender
{
  NSOpenPanel *openDlg = [NSOpenPanel openPanel];
  [openDlg setAllowedFileTypes:[NSArray arrayWithObject:@"graphique"]];

  NSInteger result = [openDlg runModal];
  if (result == NSOKButton)
  {
    NSMutableDictionary *data = [[NSMutableDictionary alloc]
initWithContentsOfURL:openDlg.URL];
    [self loadData:data];
  }
}
```

The method uses the counterpart to NSSavePanel, a class called NSOpenPanel, which allows users to open files. The code configures the panel to use Graphique files and lets the user choose the file to open. It then delegates the loading of the data to a loadData method that we still need to implement. We delegate to that method to have a central place where to input data into the application, regardless of how the data got into the application. In this case, the NSOpenPanel is the way in. Later, we learn how to load files by double-clicking them. At the end of GraphiqueAppDelegate.h, add a declaration for the loadData method:

```
- (void)loadData:(NSDictionary*)data;
```

Then implement the method in GraphiqueAppDelegate.m as shown in Listing 7–4.

Listing 7–4. *Loading the Graphique File*

```
- (void)loadData:(NSDictionary*)data
{
  NSString *equationText = [data objectForKey:@"equation"];
  Equation *equation = [[Equation alloc] initWithString:equationText];

  [self.equationEntryViewController.textField setStringValue:equation.text];
  [self.graphTableViewController draw:equation];

  [self.equationEntryViewController controlTextDidChange:nil];
}
```

The loadData: method uses a dictionary with the same format as the one we exported earlier, so all we need to do is produce a dictionary from the file and then extract the equation from it. NSDictionary provides a very convenient way to get to the data.

Start Graphique and select **File ➤ Open**. Choose the file you stored earlier. It loads the equation and plots it.

Graphique can now save and open Graphique files. Users expect to be able to double-click files in Mac OS X Finder to open them in the proper application, however. The next few sections show you how to launch Graphique when users double-click Graphique files from Finder, load the selected files, and display their equations.

Registering File Types with Lion

Any self-respecting operating system lets you register new file types so that users can double-click them and let the OS handle them. Some do it more elegantly than others. In Mac OS X, you have to reuse an existing or declare a new Uniform Type Identifier (UTI) to make the OS aware of file type associations. Apple defines a fairly large set of UTIs for common file formats such as PNG images or PDF documents. In our case, we need to create a new one for the .graphique extension.

> **NOTE:** The list of default system-declared Uniform Type Identifiers is available from Apple at http://developer.apple.com/library/mac/#documentation/Miscellaneous/Refe rence/UTIRef/Articles/System-DeclaredUniformTypeIdentifiers.html.

You must perform three steps to properly handle the .graphique file type:

1. Define the new UTI for the .graphique extension.
2. Register the application as an editor for .graphique files.
3. Implement a method for handling the file.

The next sections walk through each of these steps in detail.

Defining the New UTI for the .graphique Extension

UTIs are declared in the application's *-Info.plist file under the UTExportedTypeDeclarations key. Xcode, however, gives us a simple interface for defining UTIs on the Info tab of the Targets view. To view it, select the root Graphique project in the Project navigator, make sure the Graphique target is selected in the middle of Xcode, and select the Info tab, as shown in Figure 7–4.

Figure 7–4. *Viewing Info for the Graphique target*

In there, we set some basic metadata, we set the file extensions we want to associate with the new UTI, and we give our type a unique identifier. Three fields are required:

- Identifier
- Conforms To
- Extensions

To these, we add a fourth, Description, just to make this UTI simpler to identify. Enter **Graphique Equation** in the Description field.

The Identifier field is what other components will use to when they want to refer to the new UTI. To ensure uniqueness, organizations typically use their inverted Internet domain identifier as a prefix for the type, usually matching the bundle identifier of the application. Often, they follow that with some basic name for the document type. For example, the UTI for PDF documents is com.adobe.pdf. The UTI for Excel spreadsheets in XLS format is com.microsoft.excel.xls. We'll stick with the same identifier as the bundle identifier; enter **book.macdev.graphique** in the Identifier field.

The Conforms To field declares what other UTIs the Exported Type UTIs being defined conform to, in a hierarchy similar to an object hierarchy. The Graphique file UTI should conform to two Apple-provided system UTIs: public.content, which is the base type for all document content, and `public.data`, which provides the basis for byte stream data such as flat files and data on the clipboard. Enter **public.content, public.data** in the Conforms To field.

Finally, the Extensions field holds the valid file extensions for the UTI. Enter **graphique**, the only valid file extension for Graphique, in the Extensions field. The Exported UTIs section should now match Figure 7–5.

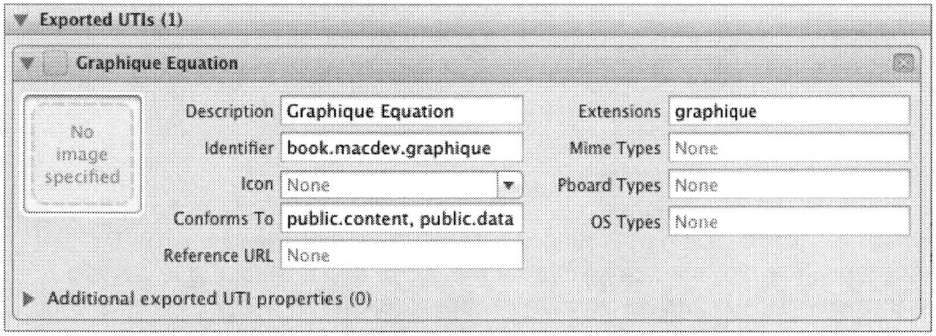

Figure 7–5. *The Exported UTIs configuration screen*

The Graphique application is now configured to export its UTI but solves only half the puzzle. You must also register Graphique as an editor for Graphique files. Read on to understand how to do that.

Registering Graphique as an Editor for Graphique Files

All we've done at this point is tell the operating system that `.graphique` files are "Graphique Equation" files. The next step is to advertise that Graphique is an application that can open Graphique Equation files. We configure this information on the same screen we configured the Exported UTIs section, in the Document Types section. Open that section to see what's shown in Figure 7–6.

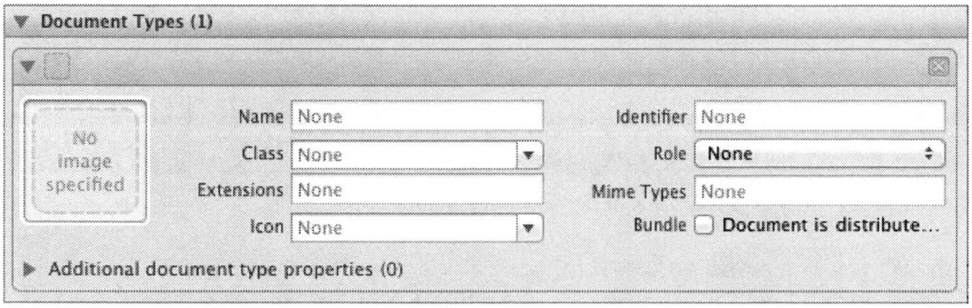

Figure 7–6. *The Document Types configuration screen*

Give this document type a human-readable name by typing **Graphique Equation** in the Name field. Enter the extension, **graphique**, in the Extensions field. Tie the document type to the exported UTI by entering **book.macdev.graphique** in the Identifier field.

Finally, select Editor in the Role field, indicating that Graphique can edit Graphique Equation files. The screen should match Figure 7–7.

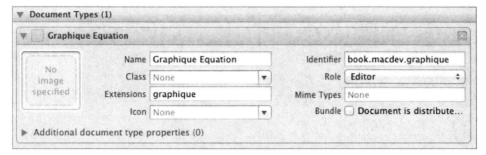

Figure 7–7. *The Graphique Equation document type*

Launch Graphique once to let the operating system know about the new exported UTI and document type. You can then close Graphique. Now, find a .graphique file you generated with the application earlier and Ctrl+click it. Select Open With, and see that Graphique is listed as an editor for it, as shown in Figure 7–8.

Figure 7–8. *The Graphique file type registered with the operating system*

Since you haven't yet implemented any method for opening files from Finder, trying to open the file fails. When users try to open a Graphique Equation file from Finder, you have two scenarios to handle: opening the file if Graphique isn't already running and opening the file if Graphique is already running. The next section implements code to handle both scenarios.

Handling Graphique Equation Files

When users open a file from Finder, the appropriate application is notified. More specifically, the application:openFile: method is called, passing in the name of the file that was opened. If Graphique is already running, it can just load the contents of the file and display the equation. If not, it can store the name of the file and then, when the applicationDidFinishLaunching: method is called after the application is ready to display its window, Graphique can load the contents of the file and display the equation. To store the name of the file, add a private attribute called fileName to the GraphiqueAppDelegate.h file, as shown in Listing 7–5.

Listing 7–5. *GraphiqueAppDelegate.h with a fileName Attribute*

```objc
#import <Cocoa/Cocoa.h>
#import <CoreData/CoreData.h>

@class EquationEntryViewController;
@class GraphTableViewController;
@class RecentlyUsedEquationsViewController;
@class PreferencesController;

@interface GraphiqueAppDelegate : NSObject <NSApplicationDelegate> {
  @private
  NSManagedObjectContext *managedObjectContext_;
  NSManagedObjectModel *managedObjectModel_;
  NSPersistentStoreCoordinator *persistentStoreCoordinator_;
  NSString *fileName;
}

@property (strong) IBOutlet NSWindow *window;
@property (weak) IBOutlet NSSplitView *horizontalSplitView;
@property (weak) IBOutlet NSSplitView *verticalSplitView;
@property (strong) EquationEntryViewController *equationEntryViewController;
@property (strong) GraphTableViewController *graphTableViewController;
@property (strong) RecentlyUsedEquationsViewController
*recentlyUsedEquationsViewController;
@property (strong) PreferencesController *preferencesController;

@property (nonatomic, readonly) NSManagedObjectContext *managedObjectContext;
@property (nonatomic, readonly) NSManagedObjectModel *managedObjectModel;
@property (nonatomic, readonly) NSPersistentStoreCoordinator
*persistentStoreCoordinator;

- (void)changeGraphLineColor:(id)sender;
- (IBAction)showPreferencesPanel:(id)sender;
- (void)loadData:(NSDictionary*)data;

@end
```

The application:openFile: method, implemented in GraphiqueAppDelegate.m, stores the name of the file in the fileName attribute. Then, if the application is already running, it loads the file using the loadData: method we've already implemented to load and display the equation. See Listing 7–6.

Listing 7–6. *Implementing* application:openFile:

```
- (BOOL)application:(NSApplication *)theApplication openFile:(NSString *)fileName_
{
  fileName = fileName_;

  if ([theApplication isRunning])
  {
    NSMutableDictionary *data = [[NSMutableDictionary alloc]
initWithContentsOfFile:fileName];
    [self loadData:data];
  }

  return YES;
}
```

We can then alter applicationDidFinishLaunching: in GraphiqueAppDelegate.m to add handling for opening the file, as shown in Listing 7–7.

Listing 7–7. applicationDidFinishLaunching: *with Handling for Opening a File Automatically*

```
- (void)applicationDidFinishLaunching:(NSNotification *)aNotification
{
  self.equationEntryViewController = [[EquationEntryViewController alloc]
initWithNibName:@"EquationEntryViewController" bundle:nil];
  [self.verticalSplitView replaceSubview:[[self.verticalSplitView subviews]
objectAtIndex:1] with:equationEntryViewController.view];

  self.graphTableViewController = [[GraphTableViewController alloc]
initWithNibName:@"GraphTableViewController" bundle:nil];
  [self.horizontalSplitView replaceSubview:[[self.horizontalSplitView subviews]
objectAtIndex:1] with:graphTableViewController.view];

  self.recentlyUsedEquationsViewController = [[RecentlyUsedEquationsViewController
alloc] initWithNibName:@"RecentlyUsedEquationsViewController" bundle:nil];
  recentlyUsedEquationsViewController.managedObjectContext = self.managedObjectContext;
  [self.verticalSplitView replaceSubview:[[self.verticalSplitView subviews]
objectAtIndex:0] with:recentlyUsedEquationsViewController.view];
  self.verticalSplitView.delegate = recentlyUsedEquationsViewController;

  [[NSColorPanel sharedColorPanel] setTarget:self];
  [[NSColorPanel sharedColorPanel] setAction:@selector(changeGraphLineColor:)];

  if (fileName != nil)
  {
    NSMutableDictionary *data = [[NSMutableDictionary alloc]
initWithContentsOfFile:fileName];
    [self loadData:data];
  }
}
```

Launch Graphique once to make sure the updates are sent to the operating system. Quit it immediately. Now you can double-click a .graphique file in Finder and watch the operating system launch Graphique and open the file. You can also double-click a .graphique file in Finder while Graphique is already running to display its equation.

Graphique can now respond when a user double-clicks a Graphique Equation file in Finder. Within Finder, however, Graphique Equation files look homely, with a bland, default icon. Read on to see how to improve the look of Graphique Equation files within Finder.

Using Quick Look to Generate Previews and Thumbnails

Mac OS X Leopard introduced the notion of file previews and thumbnails. When users select a file in Finder and press the spacebar, they see a preview of that file. If you do that with an image file, for example, you get a preview of the image. This technology is often referred to as "Quick Look"—you get a quick look at the file without actually opening an application to display it.

Also, Finder can display a thumbnail representing the contents of a file in place of a generic or an application-configured icon. Open a Finder window to your Pictures folder, for example, and look at the files Finder shows. For pictures or movies, it shows a thumbnail of the file, as shown in Figure 7–9.

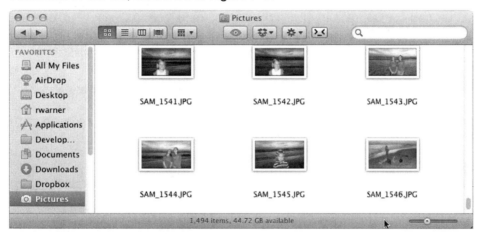

Figure 7–9. *Pictures shown as thumbnails*

In this section, you implement both previews and thumbnails for Graphique Equation files.

If you try to see a preview of a .graphique file by hitting the spacebar with it selected in Finder, all you get is an embarrassing reminder that we haven't yet told the operating system how to handle previews for Graphique Equation files, as illustrated in Figure 7–10.

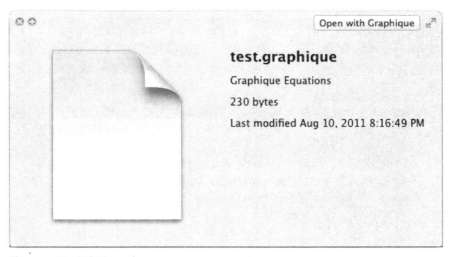

Figure 7–10. *Default preview*

Clearly, the blank document is not very professional and literally not portraying the right image of the application. Mac OS X uses a feature called Quick Look to produce previews that we can display instead of this blank document icon. A Quick Look plug-in is a binary that is deployed in the operating system that helps Finder generate previews using your own code. Ideally, we'd want the preview for an equation file to display a graph of the equation.

The same holds true for thumbnails. Thumbails are smaller representations of the content of a file. They are used in the various Finder views. Once again, since the operating system doesn't know how to depict a Graphique file, it simply presents a blank generic document icon, as shown in Figure 7–11.

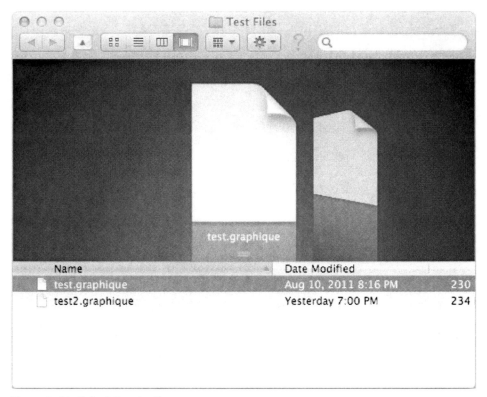

Figure 7–11. *Default thumbnail*

In this section, we show you how to implement a Quick Look preview and a thumbnail for .graphique files.

Creating the Quick Look Plug-in

A Quick Look plug-in produces an executable that is copied to /Library/QuickLook (or ~/Library/QuickLook for current user only installations). To create the plug-in, you create a new target within the Graphique project. Select the Graphique project node in the Graphique Xcode project, and choose File ➤ New ➤ New Target from the menu. In the list of targets, choose System Plug-In on the left and Quick Look Plug-In on the right, as shown in Figure 7–12, and click Next.

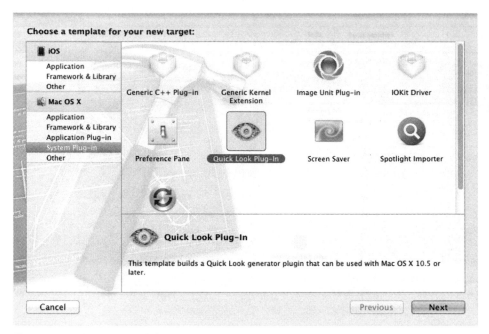

Figure 7–12. *Selecting the Quick Look Plug-In target*

The next screen prompts you for a product name. Enter **GraphiqueQL** for Product Name, enter **book.macdev** for Company Identifier, check the Use Automatic Reference Counting box, and make sure Graphique is selected for Project. Your screen should match Figure 7–13. Click Finish to generate the plug-in.

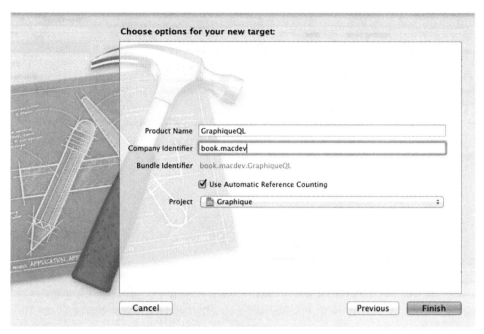

Figure 7–13. *The options for the Graphique Quick Look plug-in*

Xcode has generated the new plug-in with its related files in a group called GraphiqueQL, as illustrated in Figure 7–14.

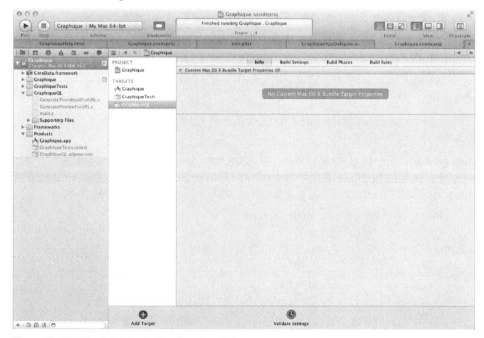

Figure 7–14. *The Quick Look plug-in generated*

The first thing to note is that the plug-in source code GenerateThumbnailForURL and GeneratePreviewForURL comes in .c files. Simply rename them with a .m extension so that you can use Objective-C syntax. Leave main.c with the .c extension.

You must tell the plug-in the type of file it supports, so select the GraphiqueQL target and the Info tab to see the associated property list. Note that you may have to select some other target and then reselect the GraphiqueQL target to coax it to display its contents. Expand the Document types section until you see the string SUPPORTED_UTI_TYPE. Change SUPPORTED_UTI_TYPE to **book.macdev.graphique**, as shown in Figure 7–15.

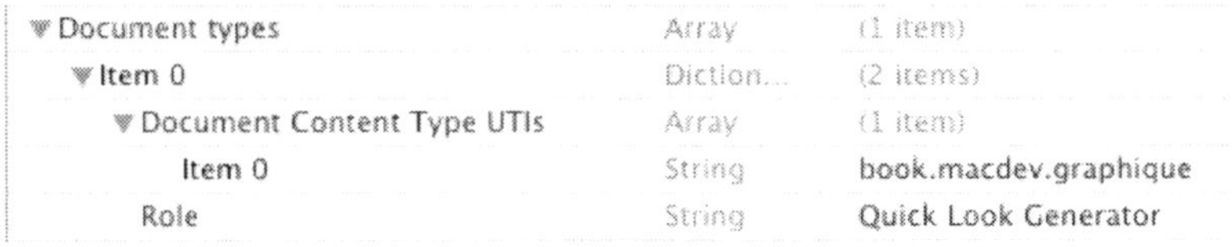

▼ Document types	Array	(1 item)
▼ Item 0	Diction…	(2 items)
▼ Document Content Type UTIs	Array	(1 item)
Item 0	String	book.macdev.graphique
Role	String	Quick Look Generator

Figure 7–15. *Changing the Document Content Type UTIs*

You've created the plug-in and told it what kind of file it supports, but your plug-in doesn't actually generate previews or thumbnails yet. The next sections explain how to do that.

Implementing the Preview

As you might have guessed already, the code for generating the preview should be placed in GeneratePreviewForURL.m. This class bridges the Quick Look preview generator with your code.

You can follow one of two strategies for generating Quick Look previews:

- Save an image to use for the preview when you save the file from Graphique.

- Invoke the image generation code in the Quick Look preview each time a file is previewed.

Since we have an easy way to generate images from the view while Graphique is running, we opt for the first option. First, open GraphTableViewController.h and add the already-existing export: method to the public interface, as shown in Listing 7–8.

Listing 7–8. *Adding the* export: *Method to the Public Interface*

```
#import <Cocoa/Cocoa.h>
#import "Equation.h"

@class GraphView;

@interface GraphTableViewController : NSViewController <NSTableViewDataSource>

@property (nonatomic, retain) NSMutableArray *values;
@property (weak) IBOutlet NSTableView *graphTableView;
@property (nonatomic, assign) CGFloat interval;
```

```
@property (weak) IBOutlet GraphView *graphView;
@property (weak) IBOutlet NSTabView *tabView;

- (void)draw:(Equation *)equation;
- (NSBitmapImageRep *)export;

@end
```

Next, open GraphiqueAppDelegate.m and edit the saveDocumentAs: method, as shown in Listing 7–9, to create a bitmap image, in the PNG format, and store the image inside the Graphique Equation file.

Listing 7–9. *The* saveDocumentAs: *Method Stores a Preview in the File*

```
- (void)saveDocumentAs:(id)sender
{
  // 1. Grab the current equation
  NSString *text = [self.equationEntryViewController.textField stringValue];

  // 2. Open the NSSavePanel
  NSSavePanel *saveDlg = [NSSavePanel savePanel];
  [saveDlg setAllowedFileTypes:[NSArray arrayWithObject:@"graphique"]];

  // Open the dialog and save if the user selected OK
  NSInteger result = [saveDlg runModal];
  if (result == NSOKButton){
    // 3. Producing the Graphique file
    NSMutableDictionary *data = [[NSMutableDictionary alloc] init];
    [data setObject:text forKey:@"equation"];

    // Create the preview image
    NSBitmapImageRep *imageRep = [graphTableViewController export];
    NSData *img = [imageRep representationUsingType:NSPNGFileType properties:nil];
    [data setObject:img forKey:@"image"];

    [data writeToURL:saveDlg.URL atomically:YES];
  }
}
```

Open Graphique, type an equation, and save it into a .graphique file. If you open that file with a text editor, you will see that in addition to storing the equation, the file contains an image tag with the image data built in:

```
...
<dict>
    <key>equation</key>
    <string>x2+x3</string>
    <key>image</key>
    <data>
    iVBORw0KGgoAAAIHCAYAAAAl7UvFAAAKkmlDQ1BJQOMgUHJvZmls
    ...
    </data>
</dict>
...
```

Generating the preview is now simply a matter of extracting this image data and painting it in the Quick Look graphics context. Open GeneratePreviewForURL.m and edit the GeneratePreviewForURL function to match Listing 7–10.

Listing 7–10. *The GeneratePreviewForURL Function*

```
OSStatus GeneratePreviewForURL(void *thisInterface, QLPreviewRequestRef preview,
CFURLRef url, CFStringRef contentTypeUTI, CFDictionaryRef options)
{
  NSRect canvas = {0, 0, 100, 100};

  CGContextRef cgContext = QLPreviewRequestCreateContext(preview, *(CGSize
*)&(canvas.size), false, NULL);
  if(cgContext) {
    NSGraphicsContext* context = [NSGraphicsContext
graphicsContextWithGraphicsPort:(void *)cgContext flipped:YES];
    if(context) {
      [NSGraphicsContext saveGraphicsState];
      [NSGraphicsContext setCurrentContext:context];

      NSDictionary *data = [[NSDictionary alloc] initWithContentsOfURL:(__bridge
NSURL*)url];
      NSData *imgData = [data objectForKey:@"image"];
      NSImage *image = [[NSImage alloc] initWithData:imgData];
      [image drawInRect:canvas fromRect:NSZeroRect operation:NSCompositeSourceOver
fraction:1.0];

      [NSGraphicsContext restoreGraphicsState];
    }
    QLPreviewRequestFlushContext(preview, cgContext);
    CFRelease(cgContext);
  }

  return noErr;
}
```

You will need to make sure to import the Cocoa library at the top of the file:

```
#import <Cocoa/Cocoa.h>
```

Add Cocoa.framework to the list of frameworks that GraphiqueQL plug-in links to by selecting the Graphique project, the GraphiqueQL target, and the Build Phases tab. Expand the Link Binary With Libraries section, click the + button below it, and select Cocoa.framework. Xcode should look like Figure 7–16.

Figure 7–16. *Adding Cocoa.framework to the libraries*

Testing the Plug-in

Testing the plug-in requires a bit more setup. Quick Look comes with an executable called qlmanage located in /usr/bin. The steps required to set up Xcode 4 to run your Quick Look plug-in are detailed here.

Open a Terminal window and type the following:

```
cd ~ ; ln -s /usr/bin/qlmanage
```

You can then close the Terminal window. Go back to Xcode and do the following:

1. From the menu, choose **Product ➤ Manage Schemes** to list the current schemes.

2. Select GraphiqueQL and click the button labeled Edit....

3. Select the Run scheme on the left.

4. Select the Info tab.

5. From the Executable drop-down, select Other....

6. Select your home directory from the sidebar (Note: if your home directory isn't currently displayed in the sidebar, go into the Finder preferences, select the Sidebar tab, and check the box next to your home directory.)

7. Select the `qlmanage` link you created from the Terminal

The window should resemble Figure 7–17.

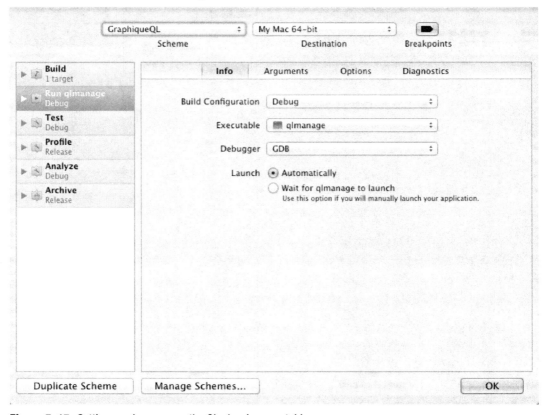

Figure 7–17. *Setting up qlmanage as the QL plug-in executable*

Next, go to the Arguments tab and, in the Arguments Passed on Launch section, add a -p argument with the path to your .graphique file (any such file you've created will work). For example, if the full path to your `.graphique` file were /Users/michael/Desktop/Test Files/test.graphique, you'd click the + button below the Arguments Passed On Launch section and type the following:

```
-p "/Users/michael/Desktop/Test Files/test.graphique"
```

See Figure 7–18.

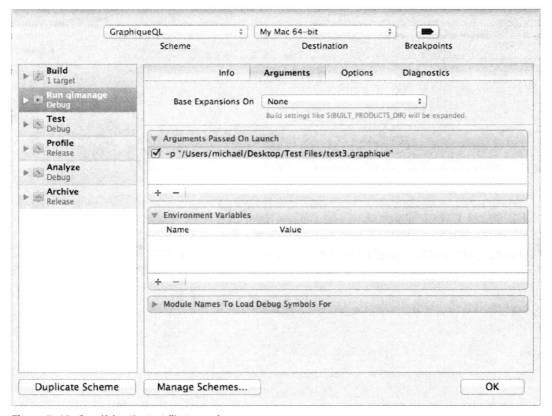

Figure 7–18. *Specifying the test file to preview*

Click OK to validate the run scheme and dismiss the dialog.

The last step of the setup process is to put the plug-in in a place where the operating system will find it. Follow these steps:

1. Select the Graphique project and select the GraphiqueQL target.

2. Go to the Build Phases tab and add a Copy Files build phase by clicking the Add Build Phase button in the bottom-right corner of Xcode and selecting Add Copy Files.

3. Expand the Copy Files sections it adds to the Build Phases.

4. For Destination, select Absolute Path.

5. For Subpath, enter **~/Library/QuickLook/**.

6. Click the + button at the bottom left of the selection.

7. Scroll to the bottom of the file list and select GraphiqueQL.qlgenerator, which you'll find beneath Products.

Your Xcode should match Figure 7–19.

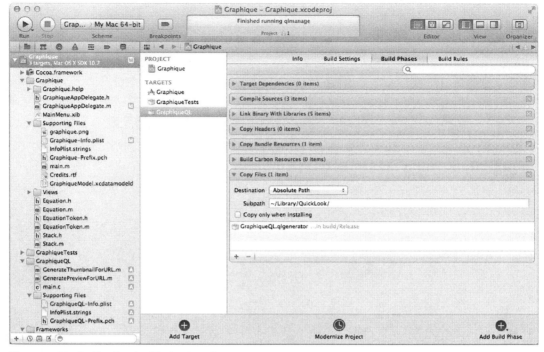

Figure 7–19. *Configuring the QL plug-in build phases*

Select the GraphiqueQL scheme, as illustrated in Figure 7–20, and hit the Run button to run the preview.

Figure 7–20. *Selecting the GraphiqueQL scheme*

If everything was configured properly, you should get a preview window like the one shown in Figure 7–21. Make sure the test file you are using was generated after amending the `saveDocumentAs:` method to save the preview in the file. If you don't have a test file that contains the preview image data, launch Graphique, create a test file, and return to this step.

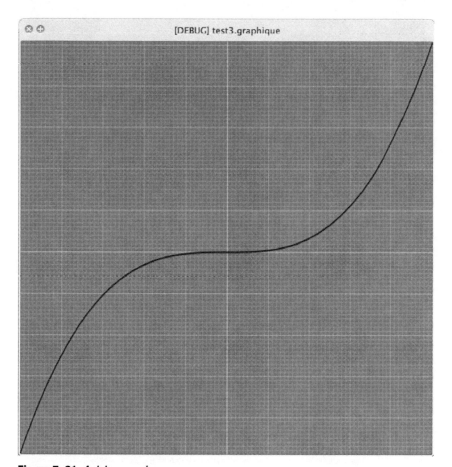

Figure 7–21. *A debug preview*

> **NOTE:** You should now be able to see previews of your .graphique file from Finder. Quick Look
> uses a cache of known plug-ins. If it hasn't yet discovered your new plug-in and is still showing a
> generic preview, open a Terminal window and run the command qlmanage -r to make it
> reload its plug-ins.

Implementing the Thumbnail

Generating thumbnails is almost identical to generating previews. This time, we edit
GenerateThumbnailForURL.m by adding an import for <Cocoa/Cocoa.h> at the top and
implementing the GenerateThumbnailForURL function, as shown in Listing 7–11.

Listing 7–11. *Generating a Quick Look Thumbnail*

```
OSStatus GenerateThumbnailForURL(void *thisInterface, QLThumbnailRequestRef thumbnail,
CFURLRef url, CFStringRef contentTypeUTI, CFDictionaryRef options, CGSize maxSize)
{
  NSRect canvas = {0, 0, 100, 100};
  CGContextRef cgContext = QLThumbnailRequestCreateContext(thumbnail, *(CGSize
*)&(canvas.size), false, NULL);
  if(cgContext) {
    NSGraphicsContext* context = [NSGraphicsContext
graphicsContextWithGraphicsPort:(void *)cgContext flipped:YES];
    if(context) {
      [NSGraphicsContext saveGraphicsState];
      [NSGraphicsContext setCurrentContext:context];

      NSDictionary *data = [[NSDictionary alloc] initWithContentsOfURL:(__bridge
NSURL*)url];
      NSData *imgData = [data objectForKey:@"image"];
      NSImage *image = [[NSImage alloc] initWithData:imgData];
      [image drawInRect:canvas fromRect:NSZeroRect operation:NSCompositeSourceOver
fraction:1.0];

      [NSGraphicsContext restoreGraphicsState];
    }
    QLThumbnailRequestFlushContext(thumbnail, cgContext);
    CFRelease(cgContext);
  }

  return noErr;
}
```

You can test it in Xcode by editing the GraphiqueQL run schema, replacing the qlmanage argument from -p to -t, as shown in Figure 7–22.

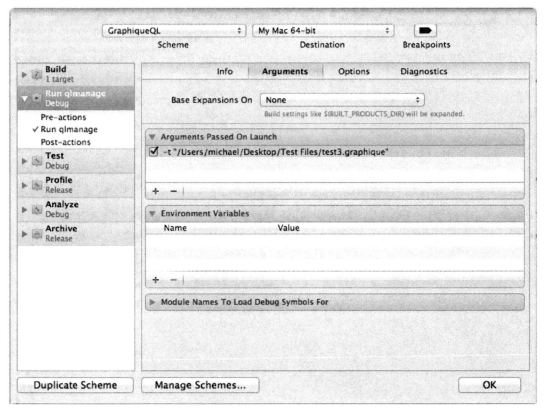

Figure 7–22. *Changing the QL plug-in configuration to show thumbnails*

Run GraphiqueQL in Xcode, and you should get a thumbnail image of your file, as illustrated in Figure 7–23.

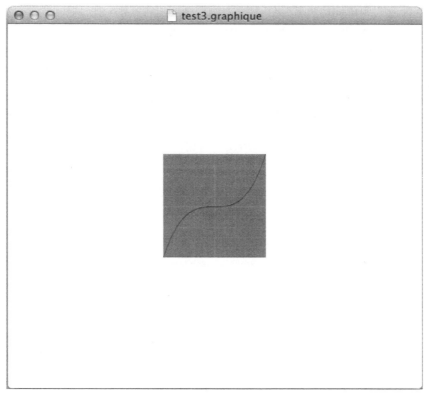

Figure 7–23. *Testing the Quick Look thumbnail*

Open a Terminal window and run `qlmanage -r` to reload the plug-ins. Then go to Finder and view your files to see the thumbnail and previews work. The Finder window should look like Figure 7–24.

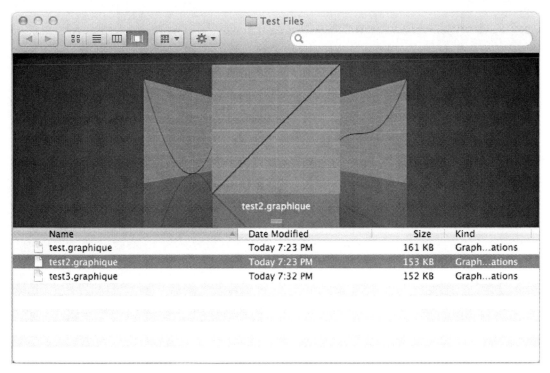

Figure 7–24. *Quick Look in action*

Distributing the Quick Look Plug-in with the Graphique Application

To finish your work on the Quick Look plug-in, you must set up the plug-in to be distributed with the Graphique application. First, dismantle the Copy Files Build Phase you created for testing the Quick Look plug-in by selecting the GraphiqueQL target and clicking the X in the upper-right corner of the Copy Files Build Phase you created.

Then, go to the Graphique target and, in the Target Dependencies section, add GraphiqueQL to the dependencies list, as shown in Figure 7–25. This will ensure that the Quick Look plug-in is built whenever Graphique is built.

Figure 7–25. *Adding GraphiqueQL as a dependency of Graphique*

Quick Look plug-ins are stored in one of three locations:

- `/Library/QuickLook`

- `~/Library/QuickLook`

- `(Your application bundle)/Contents/Library/QuickLook`

Since the ultimate goal is to distribute Graphique from the Mac App Store, we want to put the Quick Look plug-in inside the Graphique application bundle. To accomplish this, we must copy the Quick Look plug-in into that directory.

Copying the Plug-in

To copy the Quick Look plug-in to the Graphique application bundle, click the Add Build Phase button and select Add Copy Files. Expand the Copy Files section that Xcode adds, select Wrapper in the Destination drop-down, enter **Contents/Library/QuickLook** in the Subpath field, and drag `GraphiqueQL.qlgenerator` from the list of files on the far left, under Products, and drop it into the Copy Files section.

The added Build Phase should match Figure 7–26.

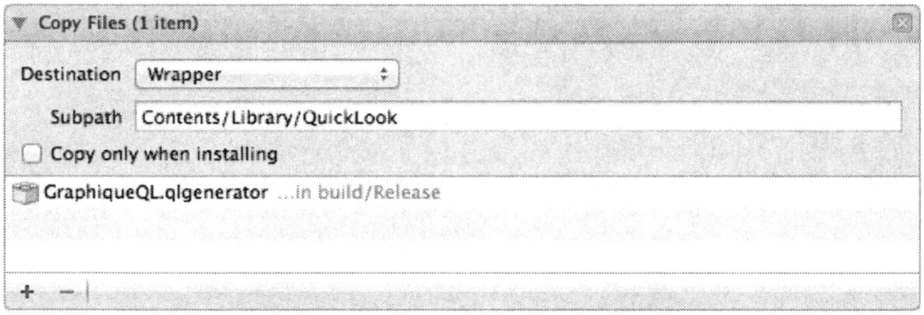

▼ Copy Files (1 item)

Destination Wrapper ⬩

Subpath Contents/Library/QuickLook

☐ Copy only when installing

🗐 GraphiqueQL.qlgenerator ...in build/Release

+ −

Figure 7–26. *Setting up the Quick Look plug-in to copy into the application bundle*

Now, when you build Graphique, the Quick Look plug-in will automatically be copied to the appropriate location within the application bundle.

Adding an Item to the Menu Bar

Across the top of screen, starting from the right corner and working left, Mac OS X displays icons in what it calls the *menu bar*. Some of these icons come standard with OS X, such as the ones for Spotlight or Volume Control. Others get put there by various third-party applications like Alfred or Twitter for Mac. Figure 7–27 displays a sample menu bar showing icons from both Mac OS X and from third-party applications.

Figure 7–27. *Menu bar icons*

These icons do various things, defined by the application that put them there. Some, like FaceTab or Blast, display the application's only window hanging below the icon. Others, like Caffeine, incorporate the application's entire user interface within the icon. Most, however, act like Twitter for Mac: they display a menu of actions so that you can quickly access application functions without having to switch to the application's window. We'll take that road for Graphique, creating a menu bar icon that, when clicked, displays the last ten recently used equations in a menu. Users will be able to click the Graphique menu bar item and then select an equation, and the application will display that equation and its corresponding graph or table.

Understanding NSStatusBar and NSStatusItem

Cocoa uses the NSStatusBar class to represent the menu bar and the NSStatusItem class to represent menu bar icons. The menu bar is a single, systemwide instance, which you can retrieve by calling NSStatusBar's systemStatusBar: class method, like this:

```
NSStatusBar *statusBar = [NSStatusBar systemStatusBar];
```

You add icons to the system status bar using its statusItemWithLength: method, which not only creates the NSStatusItem instance but also returns it. The parameter you pass to the `statusItemWithLength:` method is the desired width for the icon, in pixels. To create a status item that's 30 pixels wide, for example, you'd use code like this:

```
NSStatusBar *statusBar = [NSStatusBar systemStatusBar];
NSStatusItem *statusItem = [statusBar statusItemWithLength:30.0];
```

Cocoa provides two constants that you can pass in place of the pixel width: `NSSquareStatusItemLength`, to make the width of the status item the same as its height, and `NSVariableStatusItemLength`, to tell the status bar to determine the width to fit its contents.

We've been saying "icon" each time we talk about status items, but you can also make status items display text (as the menu bar's clock does). To set a status item's text, call its `setTitle:` method. You can also create your own custom view for your status item and call `setView:` to use it. We'll stick with the traditional icon setup for Graphique, however, and call `setImage:`.

You control what happens when the user clicks your status item by either calling `setAction:`, passing a selector to be called any time the user clicks the status item, or creating a menu and setting the menu on the item using `setMenu:`. The menu then controls the action that's called when users click and navigate through it, just as any menu item does.

Since we now understand enough about status bars and status items, let's add the status item to Graphique.

Adding a Status Item to Graphique

Prepare for adding the status item by securing an icon for its use, either by creating one, downloading one, or using the one we've supplied with the source code. It should be a PNG file about 18 pixels square to fit with the other status bar icons. The one we've created is shown, zoomed in, in Figure 7–28.

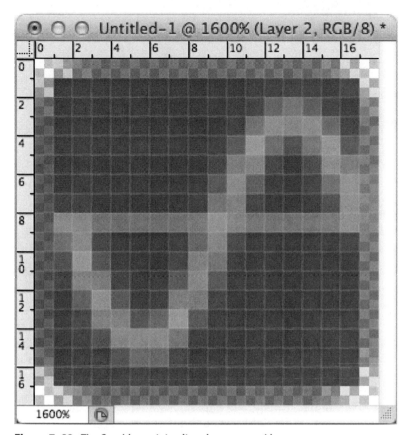

Figure 7-28. *The Graphique status item icon, zoomed in*

Name your icon graphique18.png, create a directory inside your Graphique project called Images, and save the icon file in that Images directory. Then, add the icon file to your project in Xcode, inside a new group called Images.

Building the Status Item Menu

Cocoa defines a protocol called NSMenuDelegate that offers methods for building menus. In this section, we create a class to implement this protocol so that we can use it from GraphiqueAppDelegate to handle menu chores. Create a new Cocoa class, derived from NSObject, called GraphiqueStatusItemMenuDelegate. This is the class that will build the menu and respond to selections on the status item's menu, so we make it conform to the NSMenuDelegate protocol. Listing 7-12 shows the code for GraphiqueStatusItemMenuDelegate.h.

Listing 7–12. *GraphiqueStatusItemMenuDelegate.h*

```
#import <Foundation/Foundation.h>

@class GroupItem;

@interface GraphiqueStatusItemMenuDelegate : NSObject <NSMenuDelegate>

@property (weak) GroupItem *rootItem;

- (id)initWithRootItem:(GroupItem *)rootItem;
- (void)statusMenuItemSelected:(id)sender;

@end
```

This class is initialized from a GroupItem instance, which you'll recognize from the Recently Used Equations view as representing a node in the tree. For our menu, we'll pass in the root node, so that we can access all equations in the tree.

This class also contains an action method, statusMenuItemSelected:, that will be called any time a menu item from the status item menu is selected.

You can create menus for status items in Interface Builder, just as you would with any other menu. If we were creating a static menu, with all the menu's items and actions known at build time, we'd most likely create our menu this way. We want to populate the menu in Graphique with the ten most recent equations, however, so we must build the menu dynamically. In fact, we really should build the menu each time the user clicks it, because the contents of the menu change any time the user graphs an equation. To have the opportunity to build the menu each time the user clicks it, we implement the menuNeedsUpdate: method, which gets called right before the menu is displayed.

To build the menu with the recent equations, we must work backward, first by date and then by the equations for each date, until we get to our limit of ten items. For each equation, we add a menu item with the equation as the text of the item. We use the same action for each menu item (statusMenuItemSelected:), and we pass an empty string for the shortcut key (passing nil for this parameter will crash the application). Listing 7–13 shows the implementation.

Listing 7–13. *GraphiqueStatusItemMenuDelegate.m*

```
#import "GraphiqueStatusItemMenuDelegate.h"
#import "GroupItem.h"
#import "Equation.h"
#import "GraphiqueAppDelegate.h"

#define MAX_ITEMS 10

@implementation GraphiqueStatusItemMenuDelegate

@synthesize rootItem;

- (id)initWithRootItem:(GroupItem *)rootItem_
{
  self = [super init];
```

```objc
    if (self != nil)
    {
      self.rootItem = rootItem_;
    }
    return self;
}

- (void)menuNeedsUpdate:(NSMenu *)menu
{
  // Remove all the menu items to rebuild from scratch
  [menu removeAllItems];

  // Keep track of how many menu items we've added so we know when we've reached the
limit
  int numItems = 0;

  // Loop backwards through the date items
  for (NSInteger i = [rootItem numberOfChildren] - 1; i >= 0 && numItems < MAX_ITEMS; i-
-)
  {
    // For each date item, loop backward through the equations
    GroupItem *dateItem = [rootItem childAtIndex:i];
    for (NSInteger j = [dateItem numberOfChildren] - 1; j >= 0 && numItems < MAX_ITEMS;
j--)
    {
      // For each equation, add a menu item with the equation as the menu title
      GroupItem *equationItem = [dateItem childAtIndex:j];
      [[menu addItemWithTitle:[equationItem text]
action:@selector(statusMenuItemSelected:) keyEquivalent:@""] setTarget:self];

      // Increment the counter
      ++numItems;
    }
  }
}


- (void)statusMenuItemSelected:(id)sender
{
  // Get the selected menu item
  NSMenuItem *item = (NSMenuItem *)sender;

  // Graph the equation
  GraphiqueAppDelegate *delegate = NSApplication.sharedApplication.delegate;
  [delegate showEquationFromString:item.title];

  // Bring Graphique to the front
  [NSApp activateIgnoringOtherApps:YES];
}


@end
```

This code will not yet compile, because it expects a method called showEquationFromString: to exist in GraphiqueAppDelegate. The next section implements that method and performs the other steps necessary to integrate the status item menu.

Integrating the Status Item

To integrate the status item into the Graphique application, open GraphiqueAppDelegate.h and add members for the status item, the status item's menu, and the menu delegate. Also, add a method to set up the status item and to show an equation from a specified string. See Listing 7–14 for the updated GraphiqueAppDelegate.h.

Listing 7–14. *GraphiqueAppDelegate.h*

```
#import <Cocoa/Cocoa.h>
#import <CoreData/CoreData.h>

@class EquationEntryViewController;
@class GraphTableViewController;
@class RecentlyUsedEquationsViewController;
@class PreferencesController;
@class GraphiqueStatusItemMenuDelegate;

@interface GraphiqueAppDelegate : NSObject <NSApplicationDelegate> {
  @private
  NSManagedObjectContext *managedObjectContext_;
  NSManagedObjectModel *managedObjectModel_;
  NSPersistentStoreCoordinator *persistentStoreCoordinator_;
  NSString *fileName;

  NSStatusItem *statusItem;
  NSMenu *statusItemMenu;
  GraphiqueStatusItemMenuDelegate *statusItemMenuDelegate;
}

@property (strong) IBOutlet NSWindow *window;
@property (weak) IBOutlet NSSplitView *horizontalSplitView;
@property (weak) IBOutlet NSSplitView *verticalSplitView;
@property (strong) EquationEntryViewController *equationEntryViewController;
@property (strong) GraphTableViewController *graphTableViewController;
@property (strong) RecentlyUsedEquationsViewController
*recentlyUsedEquationsViewController;
@property (strong) PreferencesController *preferencesController;

@property (nonatomic, retain, readonly) NSManagedObjectContext *managedObjectContext;
@property (nonatomic, retain, readonly) NSManagedObjectModel *managedObjectModel;
@property (nonatomic, retain, readonly) NSPersistentStoreCoordinator
*persistentStoreCoordinator;

@property (strong) NSStatusItem *statusItem;
@property (strong) NSMenu *statusItemMenu;
@property (strong) GraphiqueStatusItemMenuDelegate *statusItemMenuDelegate;
```

```
- (void)changeGraphLineColor:(id)sender;
- (IBAction)showPreferencesPanel:(id)sender;
- (void)loadData:(NSDictionary*)data;
- (void)configureStatusItem;
- (void)showEquationFromString:(NSString *)text;
```

@end

Move on to GraphiqueAppDelegate.m. Add an import for the new delegate's header file:

```
#import "GraphiqueStatusItemMenuDelegate.h"
```

Add a @synthesize line for statusItem, statusItemMenu, and statusMenuItemDelegate:

```
@synthesize statusItem, statusItemMenu, statusMenuItemDelegate;
```

As the last line of the applicationDidFinishLaunching: method, add a call to the configureStatusItem: method that we're going to implement, like this:

```
[self configureStatusItem];
```

Listing 7–15 shows the implementation of configureStatusItem:. In that method, you create the status item, set its icon, and set it to highlight when selected. Then, you create the menu, leave it blank, and add it to the status item.

Listing 7–15. *The configureStatusItem: Method*

```
- (void)configureStatusItem
{
  // Create the status item
  self.statusItem = [[NSStatusBar systemStatusBar]
statusItemWithLength:NSVariableStatusItemLength];

  // Set the icon
  [statusItem setImage:[NSImage imageNamed:@"graphique18.png"]];

  // Set the item to highlight when clicked
  [statusItem setHighlightMode:YES];

  // Create the menu and delegate
  statusItemMenu = [[NSMenu alloc] init];
  self.statusItemMenuDelegate = [[GraphiqueStatusItemMenuDelegate alloc]
initWithRootItem:self.recentlyUsedEquationsViewController.rootItem];
  [statusItemMenu setDelegate:self];
  [statusItem setMenu:statusItemMenu];
}
```

Whoa—another compiler error. The rootItem member of RecentlyUsedEquationsViewController isn't available as a property, so add it in RecentlyUsedEquationsViewController.h:

```
@property (nonatomic, readonly) GroupItem *rootItem;
```

And in RecentlyUsedEquationsViewController.m, add this:

```
@synthesize rootItem;
```

Finally, you must implement the showEquationFromString: method in GraphiqueAppDelegate.m. This method should accept an equation as a string, create an equation from it, set its text into the equation entry field, and graph the equation. This sounds an awful lot like the existing loadData: method, except that it doesn't have to pull the equation string out of a dictionary. To leverage the existing code, refactor loadData: to pull the equation out of the specified dictionary, and then call the new showEquationFromString: method that now contains the rest of the code that was in loadData:. Listing 7–16 shows the refactored methods.

Listing 7–16. *The* loadData: *and* showEquationFromString: *Methods*

```objc
- (void)loadData:(NSDictionary*)data
{
  NSString *equationText = [data objectForKey:@"equation"];
  [self showEquationFromString:equationText];
}

- (void)showEquationFromString:(NSString *)text
{
  Equation *equation = [[Equation alloc] initWithString:text];

  [self.equationEntryViewController.textField setStringValue:equation.text];
  [self.graphTableViewController draw:equation];

  [self.equationEntryViewController controlTextDidChange:nil];
}
```

You can build and run Graphique now (make sure to switch the scheme back to Graphique if it's still set to GraphiqueQL) to see the status item added to the menu bar. You may need to graph a few equations to build your recently used pool, but then click the Graphique icon in the system menu. You should see a list of equations similar to Figure 7–29. Select one, and Graphique should graph it, coming to the front of your display if it wasn't already.

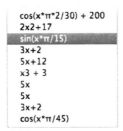

Figure 7–29. *The equations in the status menu*

Heeding Apple's Advice Regarding Menu Bar Icons

Apple's documentation for NSStatusBar warns against overuse of menu bar items, pointing out that space is limited and to create them only if other alternatives aren't appropriate. It highlights that the operating system doesn't guarantee that the menu bar icons will always be available (it might not have sufficient space to display them all) and states that applications should always allow users to hide their menu bar icons. For Graphique, we add a user preference to hide the icon.

Adding the Preference to the Interface

To add this preference, we follow the pattern we established in Chapter 5 with the preference for which tab to display on Graphique's launch. We won't spend time explaining the steps, so if you have questions, refer to Chapter 5.

Start by opening PreferencesController.h, add a check box member for the preference, and add an action method for when the check box changes state. Listing 7–17 shows the updated PreferencesController.h file.

Listing 7–17. *PreferencesController.h*

```
#import <Cocoa/Cocoa.h>

@interface PreferencesController : NSWindowController
{
  NSButton *initialViewIsGraph;
  NSButton *showStatusItem;
}

@property (nonatomic, retain) IBOutlet NSButton *initialViewIsGraph;
@property (nonatomic, retain) IBOutlet NSButton *showStatusItem;

- (IBAction)changeInitialView:(id)sender;
- (IBAction)changeStatusItem:(id)sender;

@end
```

In PreferencesController.m, set the new check box in windowDidLoad: and add the implementation for the changeStatusItem: method to update the user defaults. In that method, we also must notify the application delegate that the check box changed so that it can either show or remove the status item. The compiler will complain after you add this code, because the updateStatusItemState: method doesn't yet exist on GraphiqueAppDelegate, but we'll soon rectify that. Listing 7–18 shows the updated PreferencesController.m file.

Listing 7–18. *PreferencesController.m*

```
#import "PreferencesController.h"
#import "GraphiqueAppDelegate.h"

@implementation PreferencesController

@synthesize initialViewIsGraph;
@synthesize showStatusItem;

- (id)init
{
  self = [super initWithWindowNibName:@"PreferencesController"];
  return self;
}
```

```
- (void)windowDidLoad
{
  [super windowDidLoad];

  // Get the user defaults
  NSUserDefaults *userDefaults = [NSUserDefaults standardUserDefaults];

  // Set the checkbox to reflect the user defaults
  [initialViewIsGraph setState:[userDefaults boolForKey:@"InitialViewIsGraph"]];

  // Set the status item checkbox
  [showStatusItem setState:[userDefaults boolForKey:@"ShowStatusItem"]];
}

- (IBAction)changeInitialView:(id)sender
{
  // Get the user defaults
  NSUserDefaults *userDefaults = [NSUserDefaults standardUserDefaults];

  // Set the user defaults value for the initial view
  [userDefaults setBool:[initialViewIsGraph state] forKey:@"InitialViewIsGraph"];
}

- (IBAction)changeStatusItem:(id)sender
{
  // Get the user defaults
  NSUserDefaults *userDefaults = [NSUserDefaults standardUserDefaults];

  // Set the user defaults for the status item
  [userDefaults setBool:[showStatusItem state] forKey:@"ShowStatusItem"];

  // Notify the application delegate that the preference for the status item changed
  [(GraphiqueAppDelegate *)[[NSApplication sharedApplication] delegate]
updateStatusItemState];
}

@end
```

Open PreferencesController.xib, make the window bigger to accommodate another check box, and add the check box for setting the preference. Figure 7–30 shows the updated preferences window. Then, wire up the showStatusItem outlet and the changeStatusItem: action to the new check box.

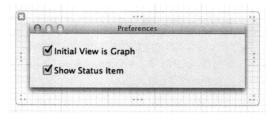

Figure 7–30. *The preferences window with the status item preference*

Now, switch to the GraphiqueAppDelegate class. In the header file
(GraphiqueAppDelegate.h), declare the updateStatusItemState: method:

- (void)updateStatusItemState;

In GraphiqueAppDelegate.m, register the user default in the initialize: method to
display the status item. Listing 7–19 shows the updated initialize: method.

Listing 7–19. *The intialize: Method*

```
+ (void)initialize
{
  // Get the user defaults
  NSUserDefaults *userDefaults = [NSUserDefaults standardUserDefaults];

  // Set the font to a reasonable choice and convert to an NSData object
  NSFont *equationFont = [NSFont systemFontOfSize:18.0];
  NSData *fontData = [NSArchiver archivedDataWithRootObject:equationFont];

  // Set the color to a reasonable choice and convert to an NSData object
  NSColor *lineColor = [NSColor blackColor];
  NSData *colorData = [NSArchiver archivedDataWithRootObject:lineColor];

  // Set the font, color, and status item in the defaults
  NSDictionary *appDefaults = [NSDictionary dictionaryWithObjectsAndKeys:fontData,
@"equationFont", colorData, @"lineColor", [NSNumber numberWithBool:YES],
@"ShowStatusItem", nil];
  [userDefaults registerDefaults:appDefaults];

  // Change the action for the Font Panel so that the text field doesn't swallow the
changes
  [[NSFontManager sharedFontManager] setAction:@selector(changeEquationFont:)];

  // Set the color panel to show only Crayons mode
  [NSColorPanel setPickerMask:NSColorPanelCrayonModeMask];
}
```

The updateStatusItemState: method should look up whether to show the status item in
the user defaults. If it should show the status item, it calls configureStatusItem:. If not,
it removes the status item, releases the status item and menu, and sets them to nil.
Listing 7–20 shows the updateStatusItemState: method.

Listing 7–20. *The updateStatusItemState: Method*

```
- (void)updateStatusItemState
{
  BOOL showStatusItem = [[NSUserDefaults standardUserDefaults]
boolForKey:@"ShowStatusItem"];
  if (showStatusItem && statusItem == nil)
  {
    [self configureStatusItem];
  }
  else if (!showStatusItem && statusItem != nil)
  {
    [[NSStatusBar systemStatusBar] removeStatusItem:statusItem];
    statusItemMenu = nil;
    statusItem = nil;
```

```
    }
}
```

Finally, change the call in `applicationDidFinishLaunching` from `configureStatusItem:` to `updateStatusItemState:` so it looks like this:

```
[self updateStatusItemState];
```

Now you can build and run Graphique, open the preferences window, and check and uncheck the Show Status Item check box to hide or display the Graphique status item.

Summary

John Donne said no man is an island, and we say no application should be one either. Successful applications integrate into the Mac OS X desktop, availing themselves of the services that Mac OS X offers. By integrating Graphique with the Finder's launcher, with Quick Look, and with the menu bar, you've increased Graphique's appeal and utility.

In a general sense, you should always seek ways to make your applications more integrated into the Mac OS X desktop. Users learn patterns of how applications work, and as they move from application to application, they expect their knowledge to transfer. By making your applications behave in ways that users expect, you help users get more use from your applications.

Chapter 8

Creating Help

You've made your application as easy to use as possible. You've thought through the various workflows in your application and tweaked the user interface to make those flows intuitive and simple to understand. You've considered novices and experts and everyone in between, and you've crafted a UI masterpiece that should be eminently straightforward, discoverable, and useful.

And yet people don't always get it.

As much as you focus on improving your user interface (and, incidentally, that is indeed time well spent), your users likely will still need help navigating your screens and buttons and menus to accomplish the tasks they're using your application to fulfill. Help files can provide the handholding your users need to familiarize them with your application, discover new features, and perform tasks the way you've designed for them to be performed.

Although the trend established by iOS apps is to make your applications intuitive and discoverable to reduce the need for help, Mac OS X applications can still improve users' experiences by offering some guidance through help. If you run Graphique and select the **Help ➤ Graphique Help** menu item, however, you'll see the dialog shown in Figure 8–1. It's true: Graphique currently offers no help. In this chapter, we build help for Graphique.

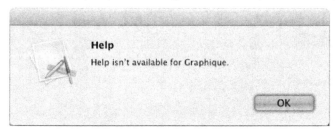

Figure 8–1. *Graphique offers no help.*

A Word on Help

Apple's documentation on help files can be confusing and outdated, admonishing you to include data that in fact isn't required, directing you to review complex examples as models for your help files (examples that break some of the rules in Apple's own documentation), and making you feel that the help on help is not at all helpful. Its documentation hasn't kept pace with the changes in new versions of the operating system, for whatever reason. Some apps have opted to ditch the confusion altogether and simply launch a browser and display their help from the Web, which is fine if your users are always connected to the Internet, have a fast connection, and don't have bandwidth cap concerns. Distributing help with your application is usually the better approach. This chapter clears up the mystery of help files, opting for a straightforward approach to crafting help that works.

Understanding Help Books

The collection of files that constitute the help that an application offers is called a *help book* and consists of HTML and XHTML files, a property list, graphics, QuickTime movies, and even AppleScript scripts. Apple recommends, for speed purposes, that the main file you create, which stands as the entry point to your help book, should conform to the XHTML 1.0 specification, while the rest of the help page files should conform to the HTML 4.01 specification. For the Graphique help book, we'll start by creating the main help file and then add a linked help page for one of the features. Within the text of the book, we won't reproduce the entire text of all the files in the completed help book to save space. You can peruse the finished product in the downloaded source. Instead, we'll focus on the essentials of help book creation so you can understand how to become a help author.

Like a Quick Look plug-in, your help book is a resource bundle that lives inside your application's resource bundle. When you're done adding your help book to Graphique, the resource bundle's directory structure will look like this:

```
|-Graphique.app
|---Contents
|-----MacOS
|-----Resources
|-------Graphique.help
|---------Contents
|-----------Resources
|-------------English.lproj
|-------------shared
|-------GraphiqueModel.momd
|-------en.lproj
|-----Library
|-------QuickLook
|---------GraphiqueQL.qlgenerator
|-----------Contents
|-------------MacOS
|-------------Resources
|---------------en.lproj
```

Creating Your Help Book

You might be tempted to search for a Help Book template in Xcode's "new file" templates, but such a search would end fruitlessly. Although help books have certain key elements and structures, you're on your own for creating all the necessary files. Luckily, however, the files and structure are straightforward enough that you can re-create them. These are the steps to follow for creating a help book:

1. Create the directory structure for your resource bundle.

2. Create your main help file.

3. Create the rest of your help files, graphics, movies, and so on.

4. Create your help index.

5. Set up your plist file describing your help book.

6. Import your help book into your Xcode project.

7. Update your application's plist file to point to the help book.

8. Set up Graphique's build phases.

The order in which you perform these tasks generally doesn't matter. As long as you do them all correctly, when you're done, you can launch Graphique, select Help ➤ Graphique Help from the menu, and view help on Graphique.

Creating the Directory Structure

On your file system, inside the Graphique project directory, create a directory called Graphique.help. Your project directory should now have five subdirectories:

- Graphique
- Graphique.help
- Graphique.xcodeproj
- GraphiqueQL
- GraphiqueTests

If you view this directory in Finder, you'll see that Finder, as with your application bundles with the .app extension, handles this directory differently from normal directories. It gives it a different icon—a life preserver, instead of a folder—and double-clicking it doesn't open the folder in Finder but instead launches the help viewer and tries to display any help files in that bundle. This is good for launching help books but bad for navigating the directory structure while you're creating the help book. To get around this, you can either launch a Terminal window and perform these tasks from the command line, or you can right-click the Graphique.help directory and select Show Package Contents to drill into the directory through Finder.

Inside the `Graphique.help` directory, create this directory structure:

```
|-Contents
|---Resources
|-----English.lproj
|-----shared
```

Apple's documentation suggests more directories than we show here, and indeed you can make the directory hierarchy as simple or as complex as you'd like. Smaller help books probably don't merit complex directory structures, though, so we keep Graphique's help book directory structure simple. As your project grows, however, you may find your help book easier to manage with more structure. Most of the directory names don't matter. The ones that do are `Contents`, `Resources`, and `English.lproj`. See Table 8–1 for an explanation of each directory.

Table 8–1. *The Help Book Directories*

Directory Name	Purpose
Contents	Part of the bundle structure
Resources	Part of the bundle structure
English.lproj	The localized version of the help book for English. Each language you support will have its own localization directory
shared	Files that are the same across all localizations (typically graphics and style sheets)

Creating the Main Help File

In the `English.lproj` directory, create a file called `GraphiqueHelp.html`. When users select **Help ➤ Graphique Help** from the Graphique menu, this is the first help page they see. Typically, this file gives a brief description of the app and links to specific topics about the application. Follow suit by using the code shown in Listing 8–1.

Listing 8–1. *GraphiqueHelp.html*

```
<?xml version="1.0" encoding="utf-8"?>
<!DOCTYPE html PUBLIC "-//W3C//DTD XHTML 1.0//EN"
"http://www.w3.org/TR/xhtml1/DTD/xhtml1-strict.dtd">
<html xmlns="http://www.w3.org/1999/xhtml">
  <head>
    <meta http-equiv="Content-Type" content="text/html; charset=utf-8" />
    <title>Graphique Help</title>
    <link rel="stylesheet" href="../shared/graphique.css" type="text/css"
media="screen">
  </head>
  <body>
    <h1>Graphique Help</h1>
    <p>Graphique is a graphing calculator that draws the equations you enter, both in
graphical and in tabular format.</p>
    <ul>
```

```
        <li><a href="equations.html">Entering equations</a></li>
        <li><a href="results.html">Seeing results</a></li>
        <li><a href="recent.html">Reviewing recent graphs</a></li>
        <li><a href="font.html">Changing the font</a></li>
        <li><a href="color.html">Changing the graph's color</a></li>
        <li><a href="status.html">Using the status item</a></li>
        <li><a href="save.html">Saving a graph</a></li>
        <li><a href="quicklook.html">Using QuickLook</a></li>
      </ul>
  </body>
</html>
```

You can see that this file has an XHTML 1.0 doctype and that the markup is simple. Open a browser and view this file, which you can easily do from the terminal by navigating to its directory and typing this:

```
open GraphiqueHelp.html
```

You should see a browser window that looks like Figure 8–2.

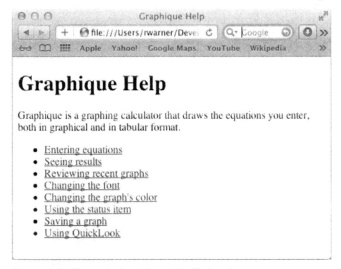

Figure 8–2. *The main Graphique help file in a browser*

This page references a style sheet called graphique.css in the shared directory. Create that style sheet, shared/graphique.css, to change the fonts used. See Listing 8–2 for the style sheet code.

Listing 8–2. *graphique.css*

```
body {
  background-color: #fff;
  font-family: "Lucida Grande", Helvetica, Arial, sans-serif;
  font-size: 14px;
  padding: 20px;
  margin: 0;
}
```

```
h1 {
  font-size: 1.2em;
  padding-left: 42px;
  background: url(../shared/graphique32.png) no-repeat top left;
  line-height: 32px;
}
```

You can see that the h1 style puts a 32x32 pixel icon to the left of its text. Create a 32x32 pixel icon, or copy it from the downloaded source, called graphique32.png, and place it in the shared directory alongside graphique.css. Refresh your browser window to see the effect of your styles. Figure 8–3 shows the updated help page.

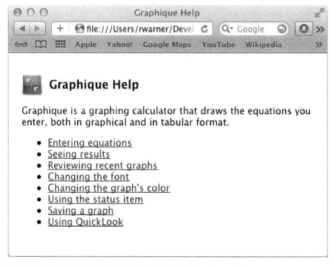

Figure 8–3. *The main Graphique help file after styling*

Creating the Rest of Your Help Files

This book walks you through creating one more help file—one that includes graphics. The additional help files follow the same pattern and are available in the downloaded source code for this book at www.apress.com/9781430237204. The file you'll create is the one for the first link on the main help page: Entering Equations. This means that none of the other links in your help book will work until you either create those pages or copy them in from source.

In the English.lproj directory, create a file called equations.html and edit it to match Listing 8–3.

Listing 8–3. *equations.html*

```
<!DOCTYPE HTML PUBLIC "-//W3C//DTD HTML 4.01 Transitional//EN"
"http://www.w3.org/TR/html4/loose.dtd">
<html>
  <head>
    <meta http-equiv="Content-type" content="text/html; charset=utf-8">
```

```
    <link rel="stylesheet" href="../shared/graphique.css" type="text/css"
media="screen">
    <title>Entering Equations</title>
    <meta name="description" content="How to enter equations that Graphique can graph.">
    <meta name="KEYWORDS" content="eqaution,trig">
  </head>
  <body>
    <h1>Entering Equations</h1>
    <p>You enter equations into Graphique's equation editor as a function of x. When no
equation is present, Graphique shows an example equation: 2*x+1.</p>
    <img width="274" height="77" src="../shared/equation_editor.png">
    <p>Graphique supports addition, subtraction, multiplication, division, exponents,
and the trigonometric functions sin (sine) and cos (cosine).</p>
    <p>You can depict exponents using the caret (^). Graphique also interprets as
exponents any numbers that follow x or a closed parenthesis.</p>
    <p>Example:</p>
    <img width="332" height="77" src="../shared/equation_editor_example.png">
  </body>
</html>
```

Two pieces of metadata merit explanation: `description` and `KEYWORDS`. The content for the `description` tag shows in search results below the name of the page. The values in `KEYWORDS`, separated by commas, offer additional items that will provide hits for this page in a search. You shouldn't include words that already appear in the page, because the search engine will already find those. You can see that we've included two keyword terms: a misspelling of *equation*, so that if the user mistypes the term in a search, this page will still be found. The other keyword that will find a hit on this page is *trig*.

This page references two graphics, shown in Figure 8–4 and Figure 8–5. Create these graphics from screenshots, or copy them from the downloaded source code, and put them in the `shared` directory.

Figure 8–4. *equation_editor.png*

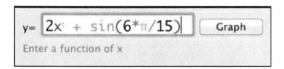

Figure 8–5. *equation_editor_example.png*

Go back to your browser window and click the Entering Equations link. Your browser window should now match Figure 8–6.

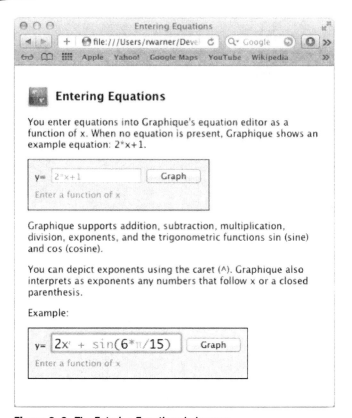

Figure 8–6. *The Entering Equations help page*

Before moving on, you need two more files: one, a 16x16 pixel icon that the help viewer uses for bookmarks, and the other, a file called InfoPlist.strings, which is used for localizing strings. Place the icon, called graphique16.png, in the shared directory. The InfoPlist.strings file goes in the English.lproj directory and has the content shown in Listing 8–4.

Listing 8–4. *The Entering Equations Help Page*

```
/* Localized versions of Info.plist keys */
HPDBookTitle = "Graphique Help";
```

You can set this string to whatever you want to display in the help viewer's breadcrumb and search results.

Creating the Help Index

The help index allows users to search your help book and is a file you create and store in the localization folder of your help book (for example, English.lproj). You use a command-line utility called hiutil to create the index file. You can get more information on hiutil by viewing its man page. Any time you change the contents of your help book, you should re-create that file. You can also use a GUI app called Help Indexer.app, found in /Developer/Applications/Utilities, but its interface has quirks and serves simply as a front end for hiutil anyway.

Open a terminal and navigate to the English.lproj directory. Type the following command to create the help index:

```
hiutil -Cgf Graphique.helpindex .
```

When this command completes, verify that this command worked by using hiutil to list the files that your help index includes. At the prompt, type the following:

```
hiutil -Fvf Graphique.helpindex
```

You should see output like this:

```
/GraphiqueHelp.html
    Title: Graphique Help
    Descr: Graphique is a graphing calculator that draws the equations you enter, both
in graphical and in tabular format.

/equations.html
    Title: Entering Equations
    Descr: How to enter equations that Graphique can graph.
```

You see that both pages you've created are included in the index. You also see that the -g flag used when you created the help index generated a description for GraphiqueHelp.html, which you didn't explicitly specify in its HTML file. The Entering Equations page uses the description you explicitly specified.

Setting Up Your Plist File

Your Graphique.help bundle must contain a plist file, called Info.plist, inside its Contents directory. This file contains keys that allow the Mac OS X help viewer to understand your help book and display it properly. Create the Info.plist file using Xcode, BBEdit, or some other plist-aware editor. If you're using Xcode, you create a new Property List file and then either you can open it as source and paste in the XML content or you can go through the Property List editor's interface and add the rows and values. If you're using BBEdit, you can just create a file called Info.plist and paste in the XML content. Listing 8–5 shows the XML content of Info.plist, and Figure 8–7 shows Info.plist in the Xcode editor.

Listing 8–5. *Info.plist*

```xml
<?xml version="1.0" encoding="UTF-8"?>
<!DOCTYPE plist PUBLIC "-//Apple Computer//DTD PLIST 1.0//EN"
"http://www.apple.com/DTDs/PropertyList-1.0.dtd">
<plist version="1.0">
    <dict>
        <key>CFBundleDevelopmentRegion</key>
        <string>en</string>
        <key>CFBundleIdentifier</key>
        <string>book.macdev.graphique.help</string>
        <key>CFBundleInfoDictionaryVersion</key>
        <string>6.0</string>
        <key>CFBundleName</key>
        <string>GraphiqueHelp</string>
        <key>CFBundlePackageType</key>
        <string>BNDL</string>
        <key>CFBundleShortVersionString</key>
        <string>1</string>
        <key>CFBundleSignature</key>
        <string>hbwr</string>
        <key>CFBundleVersion</key>
        <string>1</string>
        <key>HPDBookAccessPath</key>
        <string>GraphiqueHelp.html</string>
        <key>HPDBookIconPath</key>
        <string>shared/graphique16.png</string>
        <key>HPDBookIndexPath</key>
        <string>Graphique.helpindex</string>
        <key>HPDBookKBProduct</key>
        <string>Graphique</string>
        <key>HPDBookKBURL</key>
        <string>http://example.com/kb.html?q='query'</string>
        <key>HPDBookTopicListCSSPath</key>
        <string>../shared/graphique.css</string>
        <key>HPDBookTitle</key>
        <string>Graphique Help</string>
        <key>HPDBookType</key>
        <string>3</string>
    </dict>
</plist>
```

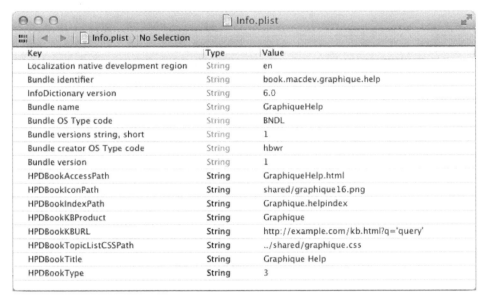

Figure 8–7. *Info.plist in Xcode's plist editor*

See Table 8–2 for an explanation of each of the keys in Info.plist.

Table 8–2. *The Keys in Info.plist for Your Help Book*

Key	Value	Description
CFBundleDevelopmentRegion	en	Apple-supplied value
CFBundleIdentifier	book.macdev.graphique.help	The identifier for your help book; matches the value you'll put in your application bundle's plist file so your application can find your help book
CFBundleInfoDictionaryVersion	6.0	Apple-supplied value
CFBundleName	Name	Name for your help book bundle
CFBundlePackageType	BNDL	Apple-supplied value
CFBundleShortVersionString	1	Short version of your help book bundle
CFBundleSignature	hbwr	Apple-supplied value
CFBundleVersion	1	Version of your help book bundle

Key	Value	Description
HPDBookAccessPath	GraphiqueHelp.html	Your help book's title page
HPDBookIconPath	shared/graphique16.png	The icon to use for bookmarks
HPDBookIndexPath	Graphique.helpindex	The index file used for searches
HPDBookKBProduct	Graphique	Knowledge Base code to identify your application
HPDBookKBURL	http://example.com/kb.html?q='query'	URL to your support site
HPDBookTopicListCSSPath	../shared/graphique.css	Style sheet for topics
HPDBookTitle	Graphique Help	Title for help book
HPDBookType	3	Apple-supplied value

Importing Your Help Book into Your Xcode Project

In Xcode, Ctrl+click the Graphique folder and select **Add Files to "Graphique"**... to see the Open dialog for adding files. Select the Graphique.help directory, deselect the check box for "Copy items into destination group's folder (if needed)," select the radio button for "Create folder references for any added folders," and select the Graphique target. Click Add. Your Graphique.help directory should now appear in your project, as shown in Figure 8–8.

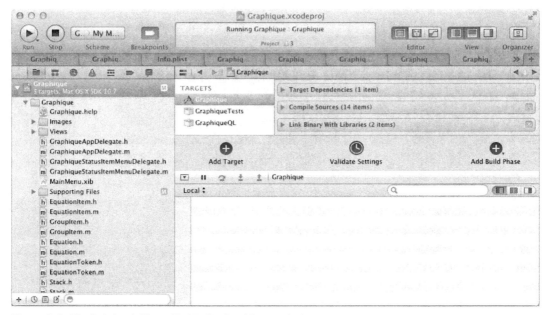

Figure 8–8. *The help book files added to the Graphique project*

Updating Your Application's Plist File

Your application must know a little more about your help book so that the help viewer can find it. To tie your help book to your application, add two keys to your application's plist file, Graphique-Info.plist. Listing 8–6 shows the code for the two keys, and Figure 8–9 shows the keys in the Xcode Property List editor.

Listing 8–6. *Tying Your Help Book to Your Application*

```
<key>CFBundleHelpBookFolder</key>
<string>Graphique.help</string>
<key>CFBundleHelpBookName</key>
<string>book.macdev.graphique.help</string>
```

| Help Book directory name | String | Graphique.help |
| Help Book identifier | String | book.macdev.graphique.help |

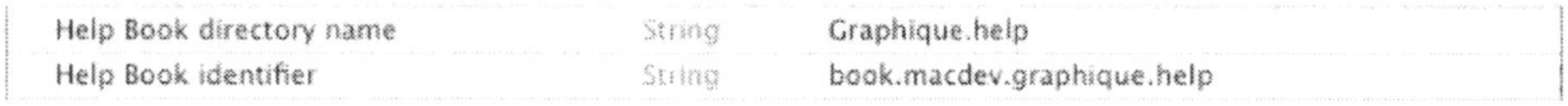

Figure 8–9. *The Help Book Files Added to the Graphique project*

Viewing the Help

Building and running Graphique registers your help book with the Mac OS X help viewer.
You can now select Help ➤ Graphique Help to see your help book, as shown in Figure 8–10.

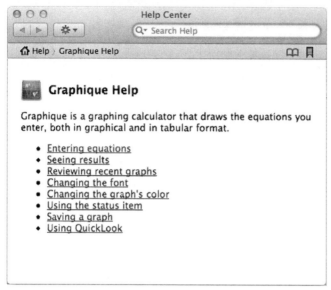

Figure 8–10. *The Graphique help book*

Click the Entering Equations link to verify that your subtopic help displays, as shown in
Figure 8–11.

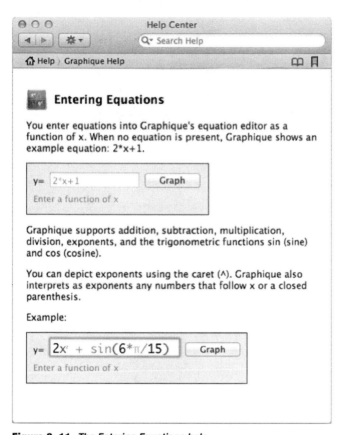

Figure 8–11. *The Entering Equations help*

Bookmarking a Page

With the Entering Equations page displayed, click the bookmark icon in the upper right of the help viewer window. This turns the icon red and, if it's your first bookmark, adds a book icon next to the bookmark. If you already had bookmarks, the book was already present. You can now click the bookmark icon to access all your bookmarks, as shown in Figure 8–12.

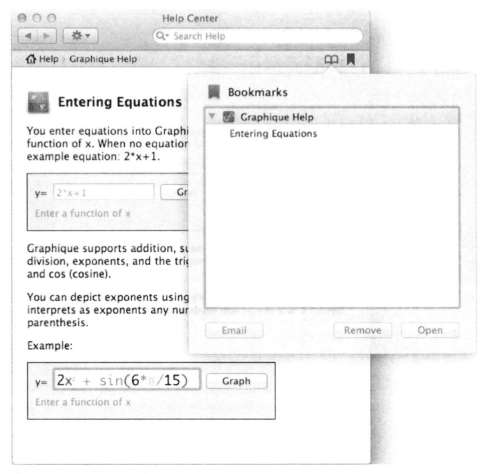

Figure 8–12. *Your bookmarks*

The icon displayed by the Graphique Help title is the 16x16 pixel icon you specified for the HPDBookIconPath key in Info.plist, graphique16.png. Selecting that bookmark will take you right to that help page, no matter where you are in the help viewer.

Performing a Search

The help viewer allows you to enter search terms in the search field, and it searches the current help book and all other help books on your system using their help index files. With the Graphique help showing, enter **equation** in the search field and press Enter. You should see both Graphique help pages listed, because they both contain the word *equation*. You also see the page descriptions listed below the page titles. Figure 8–13 shows the search results.

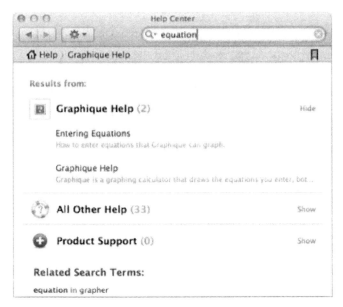

Figure 8–13. *The search results for equation*

Wait, the Graphique icon is missing! Actually, that's expected. The icon used for the search results comes from the application bundle, not the help book bundle. Because you haven't yet created an icon for Graphique, the help viewer has nothing to display. Revisit this screen in Chapter 10, after you've created the Graphique application icon.

Remember that you also included the misspelled *eqaution* as a keyword for the Entering Equations page. Try entering **eqaution** in the search field now, and you'll see that the help viewer does indeed find your Entering Equations page, as Figure 8–14 shows.

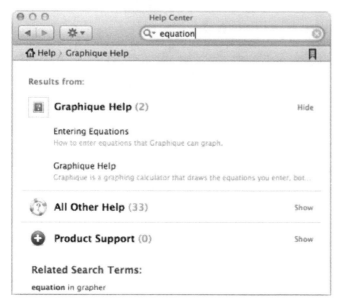

Figure 8–14. *The search results for the misspelled eqaution*

Summary

Software engineers often claim that well-written and intuitive software does not need any documentation. Although this may be true in the eyes of a technically savvy individual, there are legions of users out there who don't adhere to this pernicious philosophy and are silently internalizing their frustration while trying to figure out how to use an app. The App Store gives them an outlet to voice their accumulated frustration and take a shot at your rankings and profits. In a marketplace environment like the App Store, the ratings you get are paramount to your success. Anything you do to keep the users from getting frustrated with the app and leaving a bad review in the App Store will translate into higher rankings.

Chapter 9

Printing

Although we live in the digital age, most applications that produce data offer support for printing that data. Word processors obviously allow users to print their documents, but even the Mac OS X Calculator has an option for printing its virtual paper tape. Users expect to preserve the words they type, the numbers they enter, and the graphics they create onto paper and ink. In this chapter, we explore some of the printing capabilities of Mac OS X and how to add printing support to Graphique. We start with a naïve printing implementation of the graph view that would use enough ink to put Hewlett-Packard back in the black. Next, we optimize the graph view for printing so that we can feel good about actually printing it. Finally, we build a print view that spans three pages and includes both the graph view and the table view.

Printing the Graph View

With Cocoa, Apple offers a printing framework that is simple to understand and execute. The NSView class exposes a print: method that requests that the view draw itself and its subviews onto a printer device. We use this method in our very first, simplistic approach to printing the GraphView.

Printing the Graph

As usual, we continue with the Graphique project. Run Graphique, type an equation, and hit the Graph button. Your equation will be graphed as usual. Leave the focus on the equation entry field. If you then choose File ➤ Print from the Graphique menu, the print preview window opens, and the preview shows the equation you typed, in rather small type, as shown in Figure 9–1.

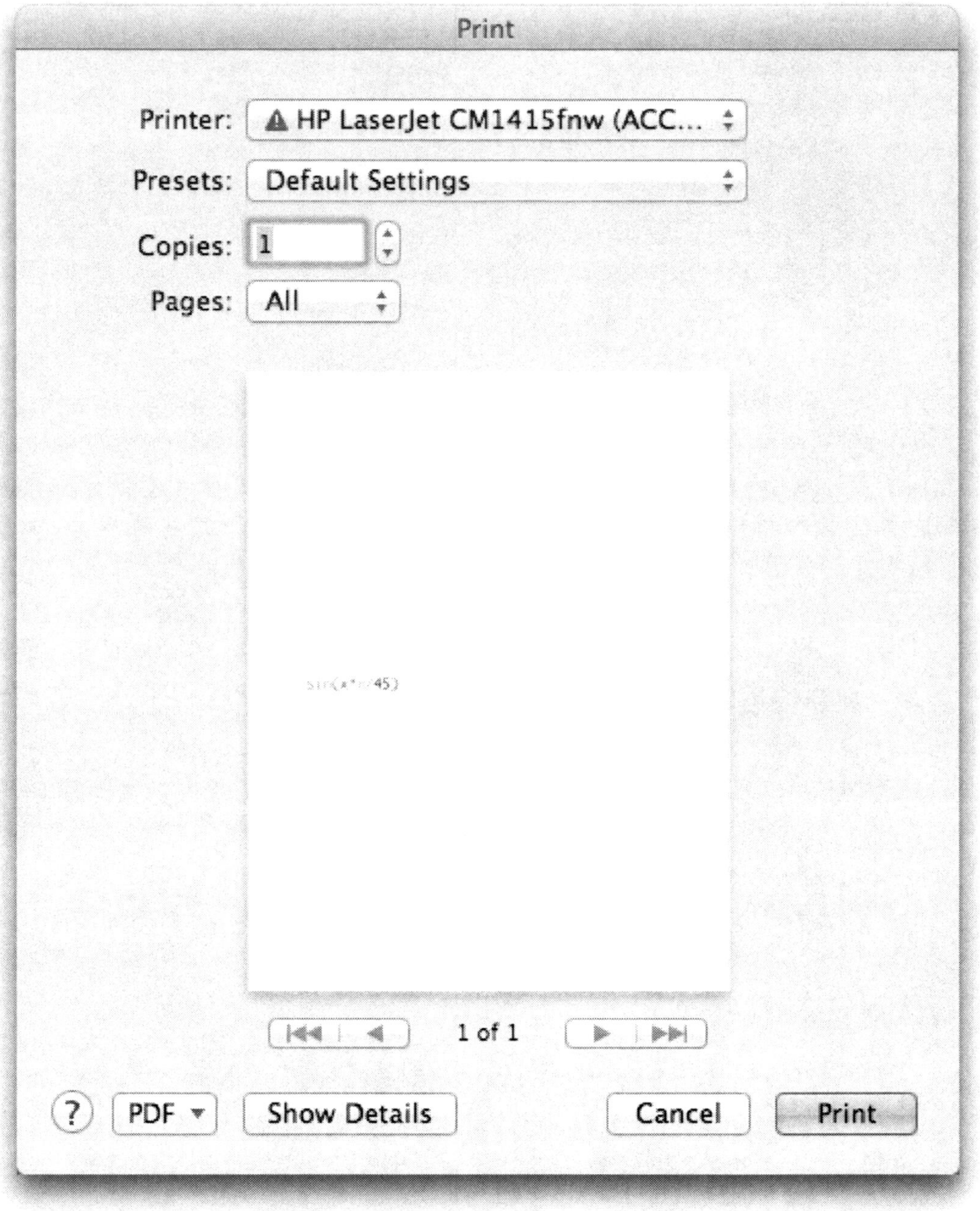

Figure 9–1. *The print preview window showing the equation*

You are witnessing the default print behavior of printing the first responder view, which is the equation entry field since it has the focus. If you click the Recently Used Equations view, however, and then select **File ➤ Print** from the menu, you instead see the tree view of recent equations in the print preview window, as shown in Figure 9–2.

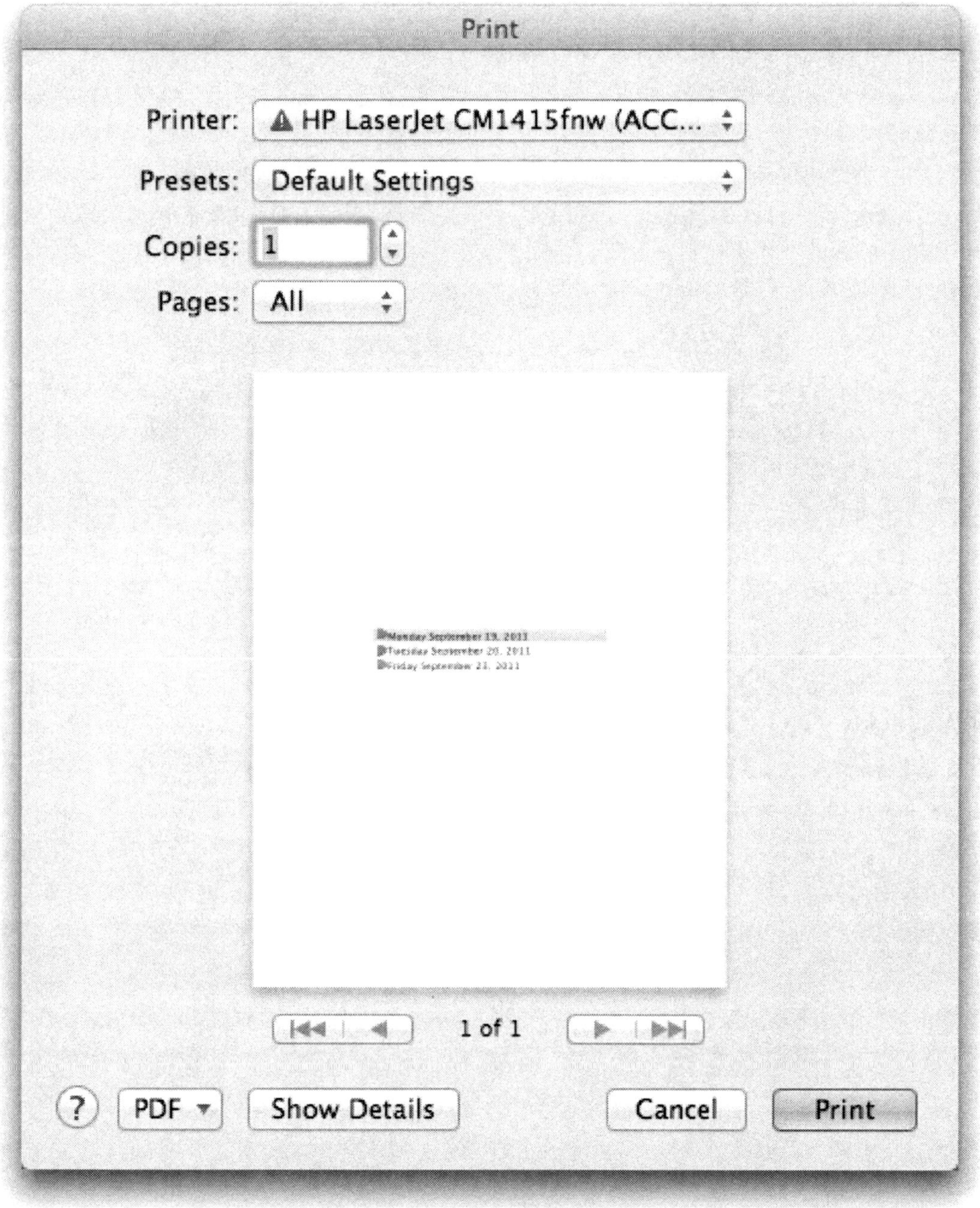

Figure 9–2. *The print preview window showing the recently used equations*

Graphique should take a clearer approach to printing: it shouldn't depend on where the focus lies for deciding what to print. Further, simply printing the equation that the user typed is probably not what the user would want. Users want to see the graphs of their equations.

Implementing the Method to Print

To print the graph, we print the existing graph view. Open GraphiqueAppDelegate.h and declare a printEquation: method:

- (IBAction)printEquation:(id)sender;

Then, open GraphiqueAppDelegate.m, import GraphView.h, and implement the printEquation: method, as shown in Listing 9–1.

Listing 9–1. *printEquation: in GraphiqueAppDelegate.m*

```
- (IBAction)printEquation:(id)sender
{
  GraphView *printView = [[GraphView alloc] initWithFrame:NSZeroRect];
  printView.controller = self.graphTableViewController;
  [printView print:sender];
}
```

This method creates a new GraphView object and attaches it to the same controller that the GraphView used in the user interface uses. By reusing the controller, we can have access to the plot data. Note, however, that the new GraphView instance isn't added to any subview. This is because we intend to use it off-screen only. Instead of invoking the draw: method, we call its print: method to indicate that it needs to paint itself on the printer's graphics context.

Wiring the Method to the Menu

The next step is to rewire the Print menu item to the printEquation: method. Select MainMenu.xib and expand the Main Menu to find the Print action, as shown in Figure 9–3.

Figure 9–3. *Expanding the menu to find the Print item*

In the Connections inspector you can see that the action is linked to the print: method of the First Responder. This is why when you tried to print before, it printed the equation entry text field (that is, the first responder) when the equation entry field had the focus and printed the recently used equation tree (again the current first responder) when it had the focus. Remove this link by pressing the x next to First Responder in the Connections inspector. It should now look as illustrated in Figure 9–4.

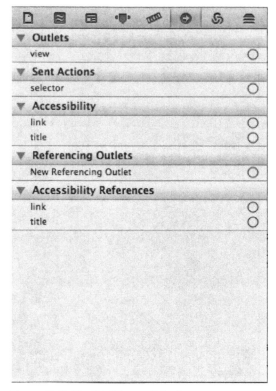

Figure 9–4. *The Print item unlinked*

To attach the print action to the printEquation: method, drag from the circle next to selector in the Connections inspector to the Graphique App Delegate object, and then select printEquation:, as shown in Figure 9–5 and Figure 9–6.

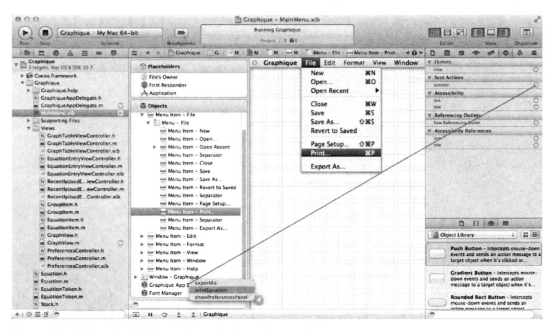

Figure 9–5. *Linking the Print item to the* `printEquation:` *method*

Figure 9–6. *The Print item linked to the* `printEquation:` *method*

We also want to enable the Print item on the toolbar. When it is clicked, it sends a
`printDocument:` message up the responder chain. To enable the Print item, implement a

printDocument: method in GraphiqueAppDelegate.m that simply calls the printEquation: method, as shown in Listing 9–2.

Listing 9–2. *printDocument:*

```
- (void)printDocument:(id)sender
{
  [self printEquation:sender];
}
```

Sizing the Printed View

If you launch Graphique at this time and select the Print menu item, the print preview shows you that you are about to print a blank page. This is because we sized the offscreen view with NSZeroRect, which, like it sounds, is a rectangle with a width and height of zero. At the time of creating the view, we did not know the printer paper settings yet.

Before the view is asked to print itself, users are presented with print options in which they can choose the destination printer and set up the paper layout. The operating system asks our view how many pages it should print by calling knowsPageRange: and what their sizes should be by invoking rectForPage:. Both of these methods are defined in NSView and should be overridden by our custom view.

As users change options, the current print options are put in the current context, and the view receives a drawRect: message in order to generate the preview in the print options panel. This allows the print preview to respond to changes in print options.

To add support for printing graphs, open GraphView.m and add a method to help the print system know how many pages to print. In our case, we want our graph to fill only one page, so we return a range of [1; 1], as shown in Listing 9–3. At the time when this method is invoked, we know we're about to print the view, so we size it accordingly.

Listing 9–3. *Returning the Number of Pages to Print*

```
- (BOOL)knowsPageRange:(NSRangePointer)range
{
  NSPrintOperation *op = [NSPrintOperation currentOperation];
  NSPrintInfo *pInfo = op.printInfo;
  NSRect bounds = pInfo.imageablePageBounds;

  [self setFrame:NSMakeRect(0, 0, bounds.size.width, bounds.size.height)];

  range->location = 1;
  range->length = 1;
  return YES;
}
```

We then override rectForPage: in order to specify the size of the page (full page). Keep in mind that the GraphView instance isn't the same one that is displayed in the user interface. This one is purely offscreen, and its sole purpose is printing. Listing 9–4 shows the implementation of rectForPage: in GraphView.m.

Listing 9–4. *Sizing the View for Printing*

```
- (NSRect)rectForPage:(int)page
{
  NSPrintOperation *op = [NSPrintOperation currentOperation];
  NSPrintInfo *pInfo = op.printInfo;
  NSRect bounds = pInfo.imageablePageBounds;

  return NSMakeRect(0, 0, bounds.size.width, bounds.size.height);
}
```

Now start Graphique, graph an equation, and select File ➤ Print from the menu. In the print preview window, you see a full-screen graph similar to Figure 9–7.

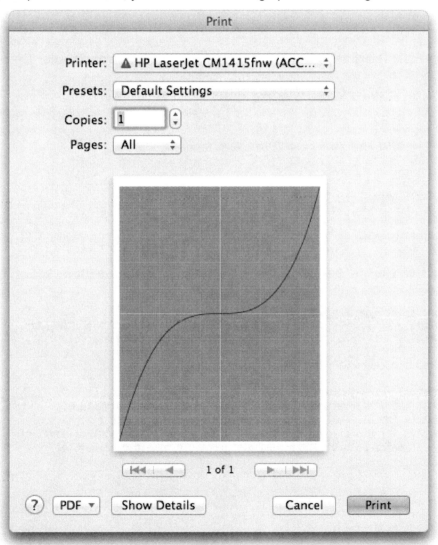

Figure 9–7. *Printing the graph*

Before clicking that Print button, however, read on so you can save yourself some ink.

Drawing for the Printer

Printing the view is nice, but if you want to save some ink, you might want to consider lightening up the print view. For example, we should remove the blue background because it will really suck the ink out of your printer. To remove the blue, customize the view's drawRect: method to take different actions based on whether we are drawing to the printer or to the screen.

To determine whether we're printing, look to see whether there is a print operation in the current context:

```
BOOL isPrinting = [NSPrintOperation currentOperation] != nil;
```

We use this flag in the GraphView's drawRect: method to adjust the color schemes for printing. Listing 9–5 shows the resulting drawRect: method.

Listing 9–5. *The drawRect: Method Adjusted for Printing*

```
- (void)drawRect:(NSRect)dirtyRect
{
  ... // code removed to keep book clearer and save some ink

  // Step 2. Paint the background

  // Set the color scheme
  NSColor *background  = [NSColor colorWithDeviceRed:0.30 green:0.58 blue:1.0
alpha:1.0];
  NSColor *axisColor = [NSColor colorWithDeviceRed:1.0 green:1.0 blue:0.0 alpha:1.0];
  NSColor *gridColorLight = [NSColor colorWithDeviceRed:1.0 green:1.0 blue:1.0
alpha:0.5];
  NSColor *gridColorLighter = [NSColor colorWithDeviceRed:1.0 green:1.0 blue:1.0
alpha:0.25];

  // Get the line color from the user defaults
  NSData *colorData = [[NSUserDefaults standardUserDefaults] dataForKey:@"lineColor"];
  NSColor *curveColor = (NSColor *)[NSUnarchiver unarchiveObjectWithData:colorData];

  if ([NSPrintOperation currentOperation] != nil)
  {
    // Adjust the color scheme to more greys
    axisColor = [NSColor colorWithDeviceRed:0.2 green:0.2 blue:0.2 alpha:1.0];
    gridColorLight = [NSColor colorWithDeviceRed:0.4 green:0.4 blue:0.4 alpha:1.0];
    gridColorLighter = [NSColor colorWithDeviceRed:0.6 green:0.6 blue:0.6 alpha:1.0];
    curveColor = [NSColor colorWithDeviceRed:0.0 green:0.0 blue:0.0 alpha:1.0];
  }
  else
  {
    // Paint the background
    [background set];
    NSRectFill(dirtyRect);
  }

  // Step 3. Plot the graph
```

```
    if(controller.values.count == 0) return;
```

... // code removed to keep book clearer and save some ink

}

Figure 9–8 shows the printer-optimized result of drawing the view.

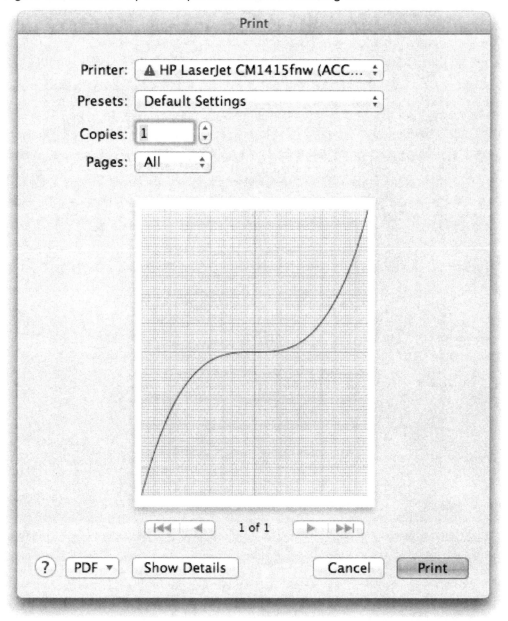

Figure 9–8. *The printer-optimized result of drawing the view*

Feel free to go ahead and print this one. You should get exactly one page, with your graph filling all but the margins.

Spanning to Multiple Pages

Until now, we've used the same view, GraphView, for both screen and print views. Often, though, you must use completely different views for printing from those used in the user interface to produce a good printout—especially when the printed version of the data is significantly different from the user interface data. In this section, we want to print the graph view but also the data table that goes along with it. We create a new view to accommodate this need.

So far, we've seen how to print a view to a page, but what happens when the view is so big that multiple pages are required? This is where pagination comes into play. When a view is about to be printed, the print system queries it by calling its knowsPageRange: method to find out how many pages ought to be printed. In our previous example, we returned a range of [1; 1]. For each page to be printed, the view is asked via the rectForPage: method to indicate where the page rectangle is located on the view. In our paginated version, we create a view that is large enough to contain all the pages to print. Each page is a copy of a rectangular area of the view, as shown in Figure 9–9.

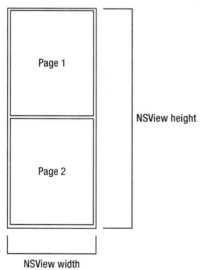

Figure 9–9. *The pages layout on the* PrintView

In Xcode, create a new class called PrintView that's a subclass of NSView. Change the printEquation: method in GraphiqueAppDelegate.m to utilize the new class, as shown in Listing 9–6. Add an import for PrintView.h to the top of GraphiqueAppDelegate.m, but leave the import for GraphView.h there as well. Note that, until we flesh out the PrintView class, GraphiqueAppDelegate.m won't compile.

Listing 9–6. *The* `printEquation:` *Method Adjusted to Use the Specialized View*

```
- (IBAction) printEquation:(id)sender
{
  PrintView *printView = [[PrintView alloc] initWithFrame:NSZeroRect];
  printView.controller = self.graphTableViewController;
  [printView print:sender];
}
```

Edit `PrintView.h`, as shown in Listing 9–7.

Listing 9–7. `PrintView.h`

```
#import <Cocoa/Cocoa.h>
#import "GraphTableViewController.h"

@interface PrintView : NSView
{
  GraphTableViewController *controller;
  NSFont *font;
  CGFloat heightPerLine;
}

@property (nonatomic, strong) GraphTableViewController *controller;

@end
```

We keep track of the font to use and the height of each line of text in pixels so that we can properly compute the formatting of the pages and the page count.

Calculating the Number of Pages

Then comes the real meat of the print view. Open `PrintView.h`, add a `@synthesize` directive for the `controller` property, and edit the `initWithFrame:` method to properly initialize the class attributes, as shown in Listing 9–8.

Listing 9–8. *Initializing the* `PrintView`

```
- (id)initWithFrame:(NSRect)frame
{
    self = [super initWithFrame:frame];
    if (self) {
      // Set up the font
      font = [NSFont fontWithName:@"Helvetica" size:12.0];

      // The height of a line is the height of the font
      // plus some proportional spacing so the lines
      // are not stuck together.
      heightPerLine = [font capHeight] * 1.5;
    }
    return self;
}
```

To manage the pagination, we have to compute the number of pages by calculating how many lines of data we can fit on a page. We also reserve the first page for the graph. We then resize the view to encompass all the pages. As in the implementation of GraphView, the knowsPageRange: method is responsible for all this computation. Listing 9–9 shows PrintView's knowsPageRange: implementation.

Listing 9–9. *Computing the Number of Pages*

```
- (BOOL)knowsPageRange:(NSRangePointer)range
{
  NSPrintOperation *op = [NSPrintOperation currentOperation];
  NSPrintInfo *pInfo = op.printInfo;
  NSRect bounds = pInfo.imageablePageBounds;

  NSUInteger linesPerPage = bounds.size.height / heightPerLine;
  NSUInteger totalPages = 1 + controller.values.count / linesPerPage;

  totalPages++; // Count a page for the graph itself

  [self setFrame:NSMakeRect(0, 0, bounds.size.width, bounds.size.height * totalPages)];

  range->location = 1;
  range->length = totalPages;
  return YES;
}
```

Determining the Page Size

Now that the number of pages has been computed, we need to be able to specify the rectangular area that each page will cover on the view. We use the schema from Figure 9–9 to lay out the pages. The view's height is big enough to include all the pages so that computing the page area is simpler, as Listing 9–10 demonstrates. We simply move the rectangle down based on the current page being queried. Remember that the page parameter is one-based (in other words, the first page is page=1, not zero).

Listing 9–10. *Computing the Page*

```
- (NSRect)rectForPage:(int)page
{
  NSPrintOperation *op = [NSPrintOperation currentOperation];
  NSPrintInfo *pInfo = op.printInfo;
  NSRect bounds = pInfo.imageablePageBounds;

  return NSMakeRect(0, bounds.size.height * (page-1), bounds.size.width,
bounds.size.height);
}
```

Drawing the Page

Lastly, we implement the drawRect: method, which is smart enough to figure out which data to display based on the current page. If the current page is page one, then we simply make a new GraphView instance and make it draw itself on the current graphics context. Otherwise, we just paint data on the page. Listing 9–11 shows the entire drawRect: method. Be sure to import GraphView.h at the top of PrintView.m since we are delegating some work to that class.

Listing 9–11. *Printing Each Page*

```
- (void)drawRect:(NSRect)dirtyRect
{
  NSPrintOperation *op = [NSPrintOperation currentOperation];
  NSRect pageBounds = op.printInfo.imageablePageBounds;

  if (op.currentPage == 1)
  {
    // First page, print the graph
    GraphView *graph = [[GraphView alloc] initWithFrame:pageBounds];
    graph.controller = self.controller;
    [graph drawRect: dirtyRect];
  }
  else
  {
    NSUInteger linesPerPage = pageBounds.size.height / heightPerLine;

    // The print operation pages are 1-based. So we remove one to make it
    // zero-based and remove one to make room for the first page (the graph)
    long dataPage = op.currentPage - 2;

    NSDictionary *attributes = [NSDictionary dictionaryWithObject:font
forKey:NSFontAttributeName];

    for (int i = 0; i < linesPerPage; i++)
    {
      NSUInteger index = dataPage * linesPerPage + i;
      if (index >= controller.values.count) break;

      NSValue *value = [controller.values objectAtIndex:index];
      NSPoint point = value.pointValue;

      NSRect xRect = NSMakeRect(pageBounds.origin.x, op.currentPage *
pageBounds.size.height - (i+1) * heightPerLine, 100, heightPerLine);
      [[NSString stringWithFormat:@"%.2f", point.x] drawInRect:xRect
withAttributes:attributes];

      NSRect yRect = NSMakeRect(pageBounds.origin.x + 100, op.currentPage *
pageBounds.size.height - (i+1) * heightPerLine, 100, heightPerLine);
      [[NSString stringWithFormat: @"%.2f", point.y] drawInRect:yRect
withAttributes:attributes];
    }
  }
}
```

Launch Graphique, enter an equation, and click the Graph button to plot it. Then, select to print it. The print options open up with a preview. You can navigate through the pages of the preview to see how the data is laid out. Figure 9–10 shows the print preview window. We've set it to print four pages per sheet so you can see all the data on one preview window. Go ahead and print this one, as well, to get three pages' worth of your equation as both graph and tabular data.

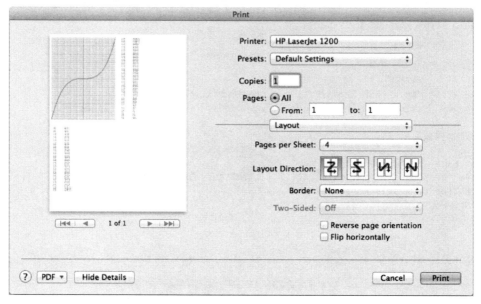

Figure 9–10. *The print preview with pagination*

Summary

Printing can be a difficult task to manage in many languages and platform. Ask any Java programmer, for example, to show you how much work is involved in producing a reasonable-looking printout. Most often, it requires some third-party libraries. In contrast, Mac OS X and Cocoa make this task easy. Printing is second nature to the framework and is supported by default by all views. For some less trivial needs such as pagination, only a little bit more work is required to achieve great results and control how pages are laid out.

This chapter purposely kept the example lean and simple so that you can best adapt it to your needs. Some possible enhancements would be to add a frame to the data table along with column headers. All this would be done with the usual drawing methods, just as if we were drawing them on a regular user interface view.

Chapter **10**

Submitting to the Mac App Store

With the hard work of development, debugging, and a little more debugging complete, you're ready to apply the final polish to Graphique and submit it to the Mac App Store. This moment is both exhilarating and terrifying. It's exhilarating to be done, to distribute your work, and to perhaps earn some money from your labors. It's terrifying because your work now comes under the scrutiny of millions of Mac users. Will they like it? Will they pan it? How will the reviews turn out? Will they even notice your app amidst the thousands of other apps available on the Mac App Store?

In this chapter, we complete Graphique, applying an icon and sandboxing it, and then we walk you through the Mac App Store submission process. After that, the reviews are up to you and your customers.

Reviewing the Guidelines

Apple maintains a list of guidelines for Mac App Store apps at
`https://developer.apple.com/appstore/mac/resources/approval/guidelines.html`.
This list can change over time, so be sure to review that list regularly to stay within Apple's guidelines. Apple can and will reject apps that don't adhere faithfully to them.

The list isn't onerously long but is still too long to include here. Despite some of the controversy these guidelines have sparked, nothing on the list should be too surprising. Useful apps that follow the practices in this book, don't do anything out of the ordinary (such as install kernel extensions), don't crash, and don't fake flatulence should sail through the process. Just remember to review the list often.

Finishing the App

Although Graphique is nearly complete, the gap between "nearly" and "absolutely" can cost you sales, and even bar your entry to the Mac App Store. Users don't want nearly done software; they want software that's complete. Even though useful software rarely stops growing and changing as you add features, improve workflows, and fix bugs, each release of your software should feel finished.

Terminating Graphique When Its Window Closes

Because Graphique is a single window application, it should terminate if the user closes the window. To add this feature, add the code in Listing 10-1 to GraphiqueAppDelegate.m.

Listing 10-1. *Telling Graphique to Terminate If Its Window Closes*

```
- (BOOL)applicationShouldTerminateAfterLastWindowClosed:(NSApplication *)sender
{
  return YES;
}
```

This method will be called when Graphique's last window, which is its only window, closes. By returning YES, we tell Graphique to terminate.

Adding the Icon

Your application's icon parades across the Mac App Store, on web sites, in users' Docks, and in the Mac OS X Finder. The application's icon offers both a first and a repeated impression on both users and prospective users, and users believe the quality of the icon reflects the quality of the application. Your app's icon should convey that professionalism and should also indicate the application's function. Use care when creating or selecting the application's icon, because a gross misstep could sabotage all your efforts.

If you're facile enough with graphic design, feel free to create your icon yourself. If not, turn to one of your graphic artist friends, hire a graphic artist, or turn to one of the many crowdsourcing design sites on the Web. However you arrive at your final product, you should have images in the following sizes, measured in pixels:

- 512x512
- 256x256
- 128x128
- 32x32
- 18x18 (not in the .icns file—used for the status item)
- 16x16

Generally, the icons should depict the same image but at different resolutions and likely different levels of detail (especially for the smaller icons). The Graphique icon, for example, uses the same image at different sizes, except for the smallest icons; the 18x18 icon and the 16x16 icon ditch the grid, x, and y labels.

Apple publishes guidelines for your icons at `http://developer.apple.com/library/mac/#documentation/UserExperience/Conceptual/AppleHIGuidelines/IconsImages/IconsImages.html` that demonstrate Apple's legendary attention to detail. This document provides invaluable information; we recommend you read it periodically to make sure your icons fit the Mac ethos.

Once you have your images assembled, you use the Icon Composer application to combine them into a single icon file with an `.icns` extension. Launch Icon Composer, found in `/Developer/Application/Utilities`. You should see a screen with some empty squares, ready to accept your image files, as shown in Figure 10-1.

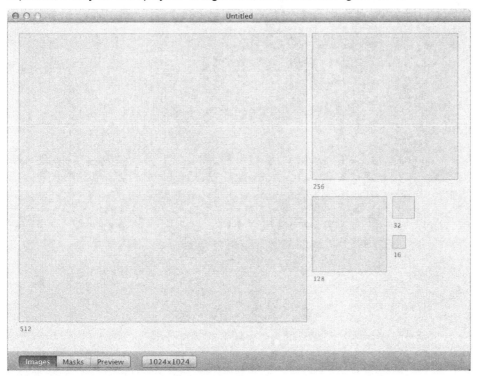

Figure 10-1. *Icon Composer with a blank window*

Drag each of your images to the appropriate rectangles, one at a time, until all the rectangles are filled, as shown in Figure 10-2. Notice that the images for 512, 256, 128, and 32 are all resizings of the same image, while the image for 16 has the details reduced and is the image we used for bookmarks for the Graphique help book, built in Chapter 8.

Figure 10-2. *Icon Composer with images added*

Save this file as Graphique.icns somewhere on your local drive. Then, in Xcode, select your project in the Project navigator, select the Graphique target under Targets, and select the Summary tab. You should see an empty image well labeled App Icon, as shown in Figure 10-3. Drag and drop Graphique.icns from the Finder to the App Icon image well to copy the icon to the project and set it for the application, as shown in Figure 10-4.

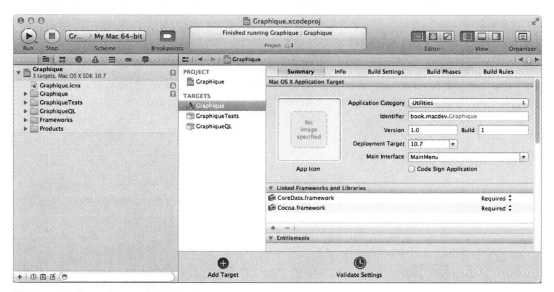

Figure 10-3. *Preparing to set the App Icon*

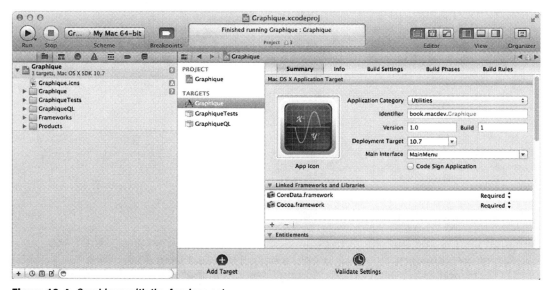

Figure 10-4. *Graphique with the App Icon set*

Reviewing the Property List File

With the project and target still selected, click the Info tab to display Graphique's property list file. This file is mostly correct at this point, but the copyright string it contains is the one Xcode generated at the outset of the project, which may or may not be correct. Check the text of the copyright string, in the key "Copyright (human-readable)," and update as appropriate. Do the same for the GraphiqueQL target.

Cleaning Up the Menu

When we first generated the code for Graphique, Xcode generated a menu for us. As we've grown Graphique, we've made some changes to that menu. Some unused or incomplete vestiges remain, however, so in this section we square the menu from what it is to what it should be.

Finishing the About Box

If you run Graphique and select **Graphique ➤ About Graphique** from the menu, you see its About Box, as shown in Figure 10-5. You can see the effects of the changes you've made in this chapter: it displays the icon and copyright you just configured.

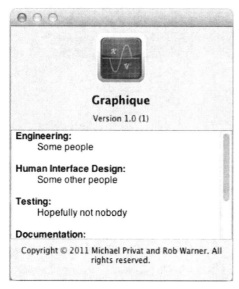

Figure 10-5. *Graphique's About box*

Although the top and bottom parts of the About Box show correct information, the middle remains clearly unfinished. Graphique pulls that text from a file called Credits.rtf, found in the group Supporting Files. Open that file in Xcode and modify it appropriately. You can preserve the Xcode-generated headings and put appropriate information in those sections, or you can change the file entirely. See Figure 10-6 for an example.

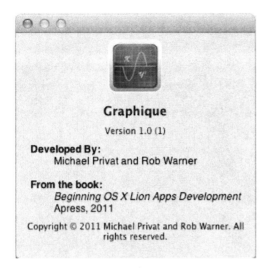

Figure 10-6. *The updated About box*

If the text you enter fits in the allotted space, its background will be gray, and no scroll bar will be present. Longer text, however, will have a white background with a scroll bar.

Centering the Preferences Panel

When users select **Graphique ➤ Preferences** from the menu, the preferences panel displays in the lower left of the screen, which is kind of odd. Let's change it to display in the center of the screen. Open `PreferencesController.xib` in Xcode, select Panel – Preferences under Objects, and select the Size inspector. In the Initial Position section, select Center Horizontally and Center Vertically in the two drop-downs, as shown in Figure 10-7.

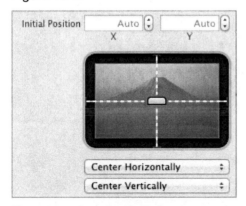

Figure 10-7. *Centering the preferences panel*

Build and run Graphique, and then select to display the preferences panel to confirm that it appears centered on the screen.

Removing Unused Menu Items

Not every menu item generated by Xcode has meaning for Graphique, and so several remain unimplemented. Rather than leave them in the menu, as if they did something, remove them. To remove them, select `MainMenu.xib` in Xcode, select the item menu to remove, and press the Delete key on your keyboard. The items to remove are as follows:

- File ➤ New
- File ➤ Open Recent
- File ➤ Close
- File ➤ Page Setup…
- Edit ➤ Undo
- Edit ➤ Redo
- The separator that was below File ➤ Redo
- Format ➤ Text

Cleaning up the menu to include only implemented items is always a good practice. If future versions of your application add features that require those menu items, you can always add them back.

Adding a Menu Item for Full-Screen

Graphique supports OS X Lion's full-screen mode, offering users the standard full-screen button in the upper-right corner of its window. To conform with Apple's interface guidelines, however, it should also offer a menu item and key equivalent for entering full-screen mode. This item should be called Enter Full Screen and have the keyboard equivalent Ctrl+⌘+F. The Enter Full Screen menu item should be under the View menu (note: applications that don't have a View menu should put this item under the Window menu).

To create the Enter Full Screen menu item, expand the View menu in Interface Builder, and drag a Menu Item instance from the Object Library beneath it. In the Attributes inspector, type **Enter Full Screen** for Title and press the keys Ctrl+⌘+F for Key Equivalent. See Figure 10-8 for guidance.

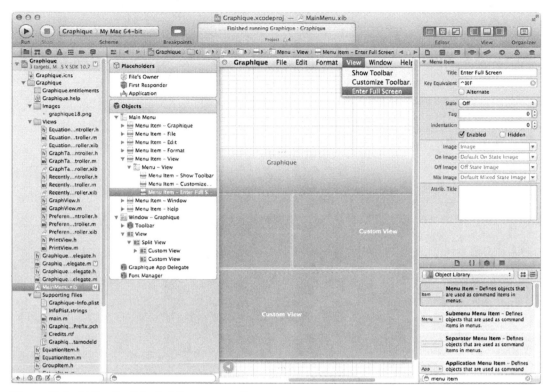

Figure 10-8. *Adding the Enter Full Screen menu item*

The action that the Enter Full Screen menu item should trigger is `toggleFullScreen:`. To connect the menu item to the action, Ctrl+drag from the menu item to the First Responder item and select `toggleFullScreen:` from the menu. If you build and run Graphique, you can enter full-screen mode by selecting **View ➤ Enter Full Screen** or by pressing Ctrl+⌘+F. To exit full-screen mode, press Esc or Ctrl+⌘+F.

Setting the Initial Window Size and Location

When users first launch Graphique, the initial size of the window is too narrow to adequately display the equation field, as shown in Figure 10-9. Sure, they can resize the window, but the equation entry field is the most important part of the window, at least until a graph displays, so we should make it more visible.

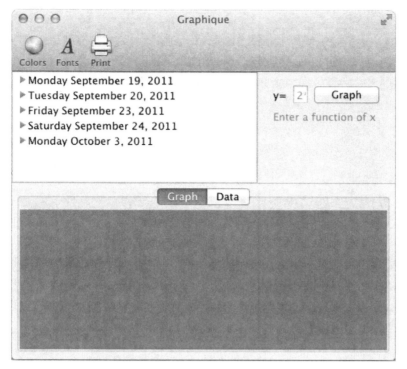

Figure 10-9. *The initial Graphique window*

To set the initial size and position of the Graphique window, open `MainMenu.xib` in Xcode, select Window – Graphique, and open the Size inspector. The Initial Position option, set to Proportional Horizontal and Proportional Vertical, is fine. Depending on where the window shows on the screen, though, you can drag it to a better location— perhaps toward the upper-left corner. In the Size section, though, change the width field from 480 to 800, as shown in Figure 10-10. Build and run Graphique to see your changes, as shown in Figure 10-11.

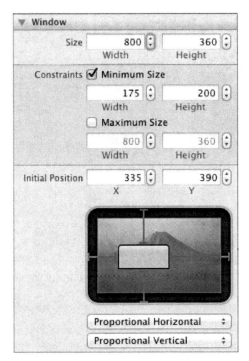

Figure 10-10. *Setting the width to 800*

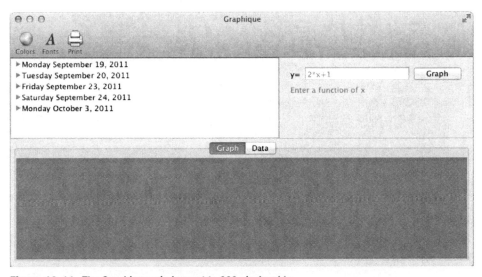

Figure 10-11. *The Graphique window set to 800 pixels wide*

However you initially size and position the window, however, you should respect that your users might have their own ideas for sizing and positioning. To embrace their preferences, use OS X's Autosave feature to remember how the user sizes and positions Graphique's window so you can restore it on launch. To use this feature, select

MainMenu.xib in Xcode, select the Window – Graphique item, and open the Attributes inspector. In the Autosave field, enter **MainWindow**. Graphique will now store the window's size and position in its user defaults and will automatically restore the window to that size and position when Graphique launches.

Signing the Code

When you grab a pen and scrawl your signature on a check, your mortgage document, or an 8x10 glossy of yourself, you attest approval of the intent of the thing you signed. Signing code plays a similar role, allowing you to digitally attest that you authored the code. The operating system can detect if digitally signed code has been altered after its creation, whether by hackers, viruses, or file corruption. This provides users an additional layer of safety when using your application.

Signed code establishes that it hasn't been altered, that it comes from a specific source, and that it can be trusted for a specific purpose, such as accessing keychain data from a previous version of the same application. Submissions to the Mac App Store must all be digitally signed.

Using the Developer Certificate Utility

To begin the code-signing process, go to http://developer.apple.com and sign in to your account. If you have not yet joined the Mac Developer Program, you can do so at http://developer.apple.com/programs/mac/. As of this writing, it costs $99 per year and is required to distribute your apps through the Mac App Store.

Once logged in, go to the Developer Certificate Utility page at http://developer.apple.com/certificates/index.action, as shown in Figure 10-12. From this page, you create App IDs for the apps you develop, create and download certificates for establishing your identity, register systems for ad hoc distributions of your apps, and create provisioning profiles to marry App IDs, certificates, and optionally systems together to distribute your applications.

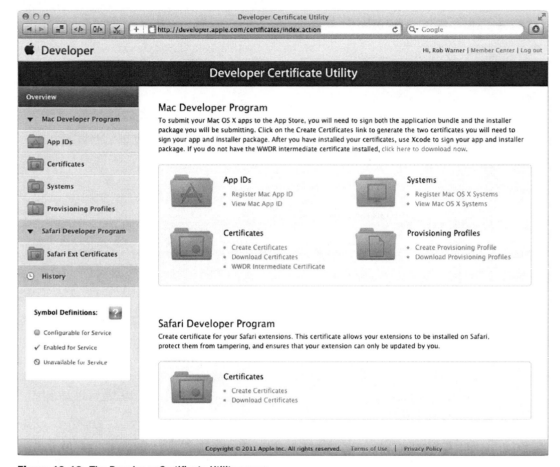

Figure 10-12. *The Developer Certificate Utility screen*

Registering Your App IDs

Each app you create carries a globally unique App ID that matches the bundle identifier specified in your app's property list file. Remember that this is usually your domain name, in reverse order, followed by the name of your app in lowercase.

Click the Register Mac App ID link to see the form for registering your App ID. The first field, Name or Description, is for your benefit, to identify this App ID in a friendly way so you remember which app you've tied the App ID to. For Graphique, we've entered Graphique for the Name or Description field, and book.macdev.Graphique in the Bundle Identifier field, as shown in Figure 10-13. If you're following along, note that you can't register that same App ID because we already did.

Figure 10-13. *Registering Graphique's App ID*

When you click Continue, you see a confirmation screen that allows you to review the App ID you're registering. Review it carefully, because you can't edit a registered App ID; you can only view it and delete it. If satisfied, click Submit. Apple will register your App ID, which you can review at any time by clicking the App IDs link on the left of the Developer Certificate Utility screen, as shown in Figure 10-14.

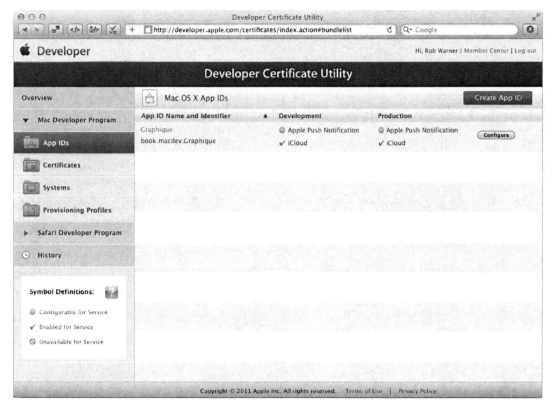

Figure 10-14. *The registered Graphique App ID*

Since Graphique doesn't support iCloud services, you must verify that the App ID isn't configured for iCloud. To do that, click the Configure button, and if the box titled Enable for iCloud is checked, uncheck it and click Done.

Installing Apple's Certificate

Apple provides a certificate it calls the World Wide Developer Relations (WWDR) certificate that ties the certificate you will create back to Apple. Apple is the root certificate authority that vouches for your certificate. To install this certificate, return to the main Developer Certificate Utility screen by clicking the Overview link on the left. Underneath the Certificates section you see a link that says WWDR Intermediate Certificate. Click the link to download the certificate in a file called AppleWWDRCA.cer, and then double-click it in Finder to install it. Open the Keychain Access app on your computer, found in the Utilities folder under the Applications folder, and look in the login certificates to find the certificate called Apple Worldwide Developer Relations Certification Authority you just installed.

Creating Certificates

You can click the Overview link on the left to return to the main Developer Certificate Utility screen shown in Figure 10-11 to reveal the Create Certificates link, or you can click the Certificates link in the left menu to reveal the Create Certificate button. However you get there, click to create a certificate. You'll see the screen shown in Figure 10-15.

Figure 10-15. *Creating certificates*

You can either create a development certificate, useful for distributing code-signed apps to a limited audience for testing, or create distribution certificates. Each Mac App Store app requires two certificates: one for the application and one for its installer. Since we're creating certificates to submit to the Mac App Store, select the radio button next to Distribution, make sure both check boxes are checked, and click Create.

The next screen, shown in Figure 10-16, instructs you open the Keychain Access app on your computer to generate a certificate-signing request. Follow the steps it gives you:

1. Within the Keychain Access drop-down menu, select **Keychain Access ➤ Certificate Assistant ➤ Request a Certificate from a Certificate Authority**.

2. In the Certificate Information window, enter the following information:

- In the User Email Address field, enter your e-mail address.

- In the Common Name field, create a name for your private key (e.g., John Doe Dev Key).

- In the Request is group, select the "Saved to disk" option.

3. Click Continue within Keychain Access to complete the CSR-generating process.

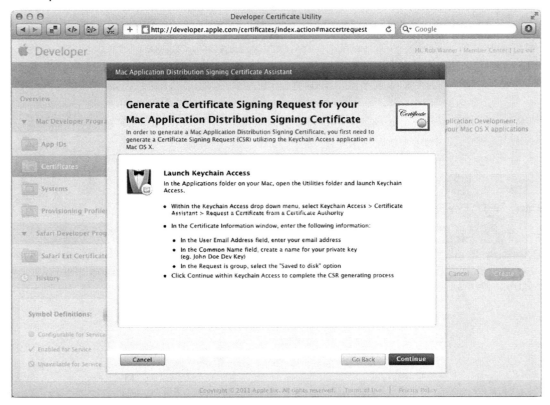

Figure 10-16. *Generating a certificate-signing request*

When you select the menu item **Keychain Access ➤ Certificate Assistant ➤ Request a Certificate from a Certificate Authority** from the Keychain Access app, you see the screen shown in Figure 10-17.

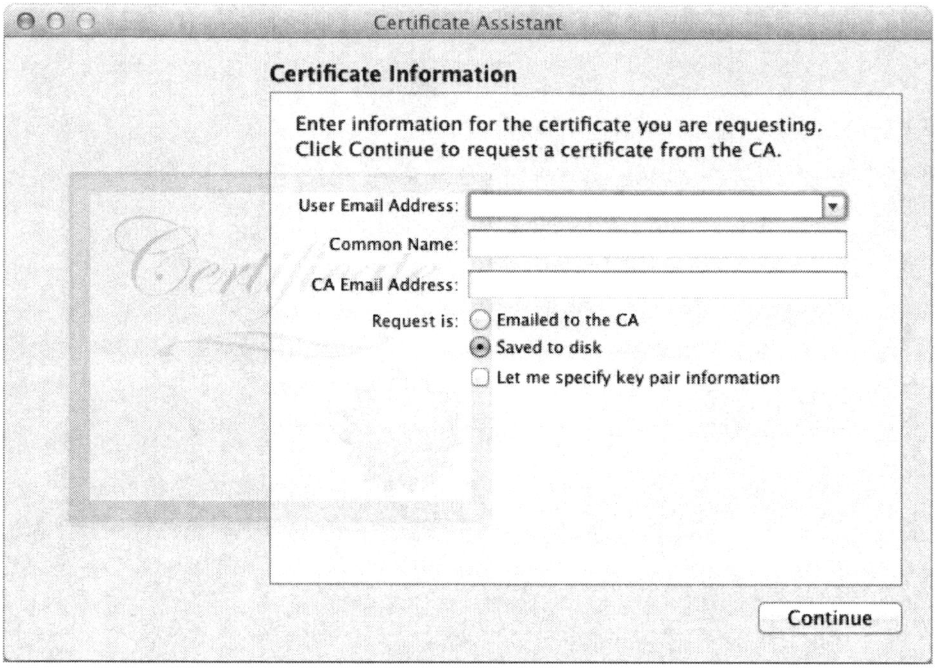

Figure 10-17. *Entering certificate information for requesting a certificate*

Enter your information, making sure to select the "Saved to disk" option, and click Continue. It will prompt you to save the file, a shown in Figure 10-18. Click Save to save it to your desktop, and you'll see the dialog shown in Figure 10-19 affirming that your request was saved. Click Done to dismiss it.

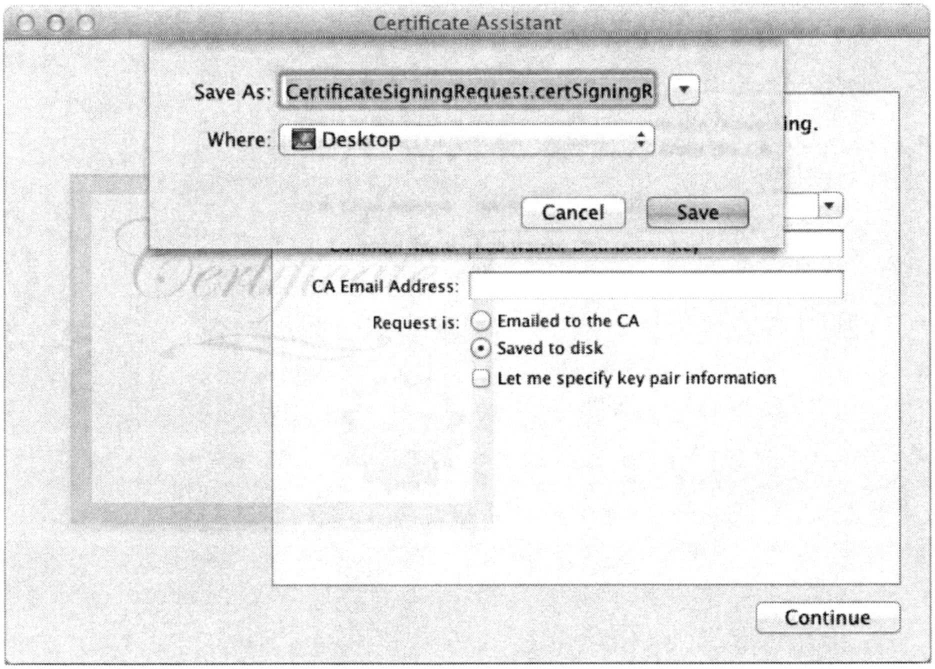

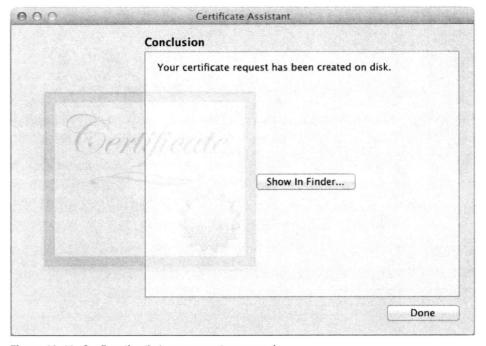

Figure 10-18. *Saving your certificate-signing request*

Figure 10-19. *Confirmation that your request was saved*

Return to the Developer Certificate Utility in your web browser, and click Continue. You'll see the screen shown in Figure 10-20 requesting you to upload the certificate-signing request file you just created. Click the Choose File button, select the file you created, and then click the Generate button to upload your request and generate the certificate. After a few moments, you'll see the screen shown in Figure 10-21 telling you that your certificate was generated.

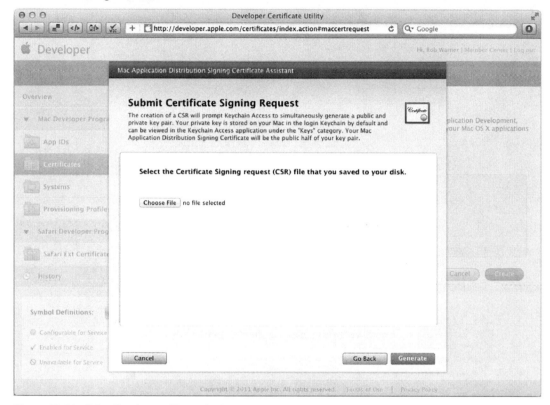

Figure 10-20. *Uploading the certificate signing request file*

Figure 10-21. *Seeing that your certificate was generated*

Click Continue to see the screen shown in Figure 10-22, which allows you to click the Download button to download your certificate. Download your certificate and then double-click the certificate file in Finder to install the certificate. Then, click Continue.

Figure 10-22. *The certificate download screen*

The Developer Certificate Utility takes you through the same steps again, only this time for your Mac Installer Package certificate. Go through the same steps again to generate the certificate signing request, upload it, download the certificate, and install the certificate. When you've completed these steps, verify that both certificates were installed by opening the Keychain Access app, selecting login under Keychains and My Certificates under Category. You should see your newly installed certificates, as shown in Figure 10-23.

Figure 10-23. *The certificates installed*

Creating the Provisioning Profile

A provisioning profile ties an App ID and certificates together. You can also tie the profile to specific systems by first creating the systems using the Systems section in the Developer Certificate Utility. This is useful for creating profiles to distribute your applications on an ad hoc basis to certain users, usually for testing purposes. Since we're uploading Graphique to the Mac App Store, though, and want it available to all systems, we don't include specific systems in the provisioning profile.

Click the Provisioning Profiles link on the left to see any existing profiles you have, as shown in Figure 10-24. Click the Create Profile link on that screen to begin creating your profile.

Figure 10-24. *The Provisioning Profiles screen*

The next screen, shown in Figure 10-25, asks for some information for the provisioning profile. For Kind, select Production Provisioning Profile. This adds a section to the screen for which certificate to use, as shown in Figure 10-26. Since we have only one production certificate, that one is listed. If we had selected Development Provisioning Profile, our development certificates would have been listed.

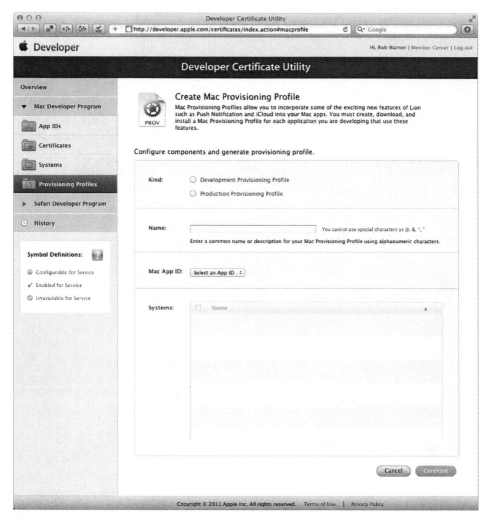

Figure 10-25. *Creating a provisioning profile*

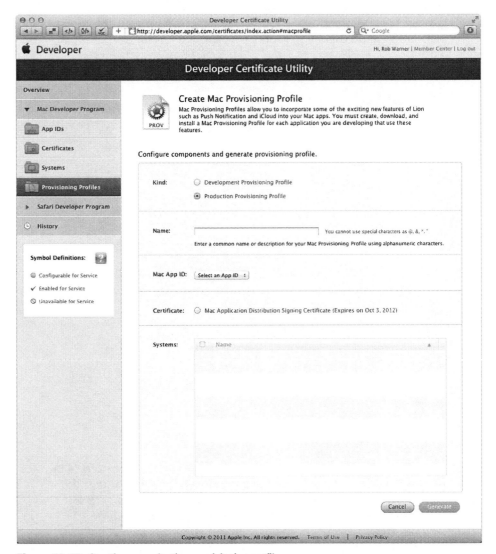

Figure 10-26. *Creating a production provisioning profile*

Continue to fill out the screen. For Name, enter a friendly name for the profile. For Graphique, we entered **Graphique Production Distribution**. Select the App ID for your app, select the proper certificate, and click Generate. Your provisioning profile is generated, and then you're prompted to download and install the provisioning profile. Click the Download button. The provisioning profile downloads, and then the Profiles preference pane automatically launches and asks you if you want to install the provisioning profile, as shown in Figure 10-27. Click Cancel, because you can't install this profile on your system: this profile doesn't have any system IDs in it. It's the profile for the production distribution, remember? You must install it in Xcode, however, so that you can use it to sign your build. You can do this by dragging the file onto the Xcode Organizer window, onto the Provisioning Profiles section, or clicking the Import button on the Xcode Organizer window and following the instructions to import the provisioning profile. You can also drag the provisioning profile file from the Finder and dropping it on the Xcode icon in the Dock.

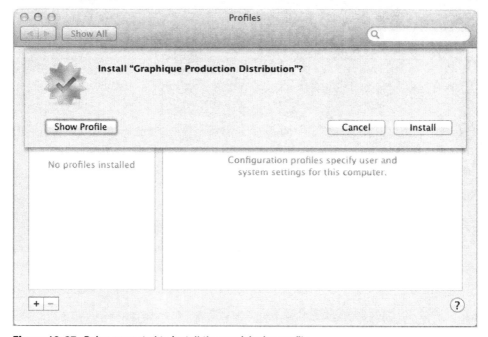

Figure 10-27. *Being prompted to install the provisioning profile*

Configuring the Build to Sign the Code

Finally, you must configure the build to sign the code using the provisioning profile you just created. Go to Xcode and select your project in the Project navigator and the Graphique target under Targets. Select the Summary tab, and in the Mac OS X Application Target section, you should see a check box that says Code Sign Application. Check it, as shown in Figure 10-28. This will automatically select the provisioning profile and configure your builds to use it.

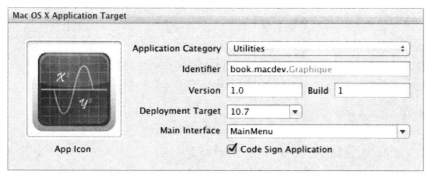

Figure 10-28. *Configuring the build to code sign the application*

For most of your applications, checking this box is all that's required for configuring code signing. Because of the Graphique QuickLook plug-in that Graphique contains, however, you must do a little extra work to get the proper code-signing configuration. With the Graphique target still selected, click the Build Settings tab and find the Code Signing section. For the Other Code Signing Flags, enter the following:

```
-i book.macdev.Graphique
```

This tells Xcode to ignore specific App IDs and use Graphique's App ID when code signing all bundles within the Graphique target, which includes the Graphique QuickLook plug-in.

You must also configure the QuickLook plug-in to sign the code as part of its build. Xcode doesn't provide a nice Code Sign Application check box for a QuickLook plug-in, so instead you must configure the code signing in the build settings. Select the GraphiqueQL target and the Build Settings tab. Find the section called Code Signing and, for the Code Signing Identity field, select 3rd Party Mac Application under Automatic Profile Selector (Recommended). The Code Signing section should match Figure 10-29.

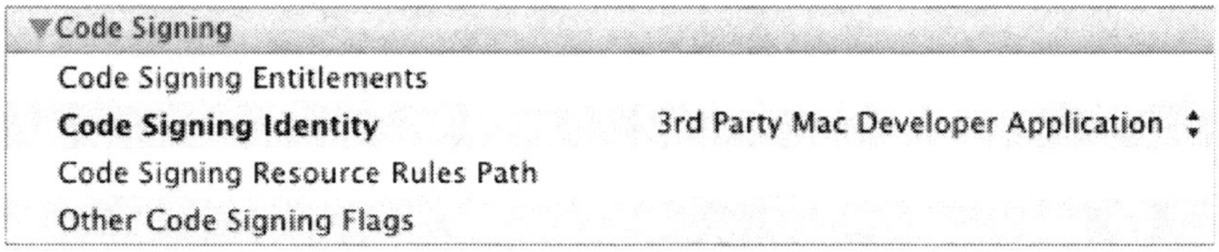

Figure 10-29. *Signing the Graphique QuickLook plug-in code*

You must do one more thing for the Graphique QuickLook plug-in. With the GraphiqueQL target still selected, find the section called Deployment and the entry that says Skip Install and set it to Yes.

> **NOTE:** Don't forget to set Skip Install to Yes for the Graphique QuickLook plug-in.

Sandboxing the App

Apple has introduced sandboxing to OS X application development as an additional security measure to curb applications from malicious behavior and is requiring that all submissions to the Mac App Store, as of November 2011, implement sandboxing. This section explains sandboxing and its companion concept, *entitlements*, and sets up Graphique's sandbox and entitlements.

What Is Sandboxing?

By default, OS X applications run with all the rights and privileges of the user account under which they run. This means that anything you can do on your Mac without entering your system password, any running app can do: silently, clandestinely, without any notice or plea for permission. Can you delete songs in your iTunes library? So can an app. Can you send an e-mail to your boss? So can an app. Can you, in a moment of delirium, zip up your documents containing private information like bank account numbers and medical history and post them on a web site for identity thieves to peruse? So can an app, and it doesn't even require the delirium.

We rely on the honor of developers not to do any of these things, and the vast majority don't—at least not intentionally. Whether wrongdoing happens by intent or coding error, however, the effects of bad application behavior can range from annoying to devastating. Sandboxing reins in bad behavior by limiting what an application can do. It provides the app a metaphorical sandbox, isolated from the rest of the operating system, and prevents it from the following activities:

- Reading and writing files
- Accessing the network, whether incoming or outgoing
- Accessing connected hardware devices:
  - Camera
  - USB drives
  - Printers
  - Microphones
- Reading or writing user data from the address book, calendars, or location information

Many applications can perform in such an environment, although the list of restrictions is onerous and is designed for security, not utility. Many more applications, however, can't abide all the restrictions that a sandbox imposes. Imagine, for example, a word processor that can't save, open, or print documents, or a web browser that can't open web sites.

To escape the restrictions of sandboxes in a controlled way, Apple provides what it calls entitlements.

What Are Entitlements?

Entitlements grant specific permissions to applications that sandboxing prevents. As a developer, you build in the entitlements your applications receive. Sandboxing takes all privileges away, and entitlements give specific privileges back. Using entitlements, you can restore an application's ability to read and/or write files (even to specific folders, like the Download or Music folder), access the network (incoming, outgoing, or both), print, see the world through the camera, and a handful of other privileges. See Apple's documentation on Entitlement Keys at http://developer.apple.com/library/mac/ #documentation/Miscellaneous/Reference/EntitlementKeyReference/EnablingAppSandb ox/EnablingAppSandbox.html for more specific information on what privileges you can grant your application.

By sandboxing an application from the rest of the computing environment and then entitling it to access specific computing resources, you establish a trust between developer and user that establishes what the application can and cannot do.

As we set up Graphique's sandbox, we must grant it privileges to do the following:

- Read and write files
- Print documents

Graphique should have no other entitlements.

Establishing the Sandbox

To establish a sandbox, you create what's called an entitlements file that contains information about what your application is entitled to do. The entitlements file is a property list file for which Xcode provides a point-and-click interface. Select the project in the Project navigator, the Graphique target under Targets, and the Summary tab. Expand the Entitlements section, which looks like Figure 10-30.

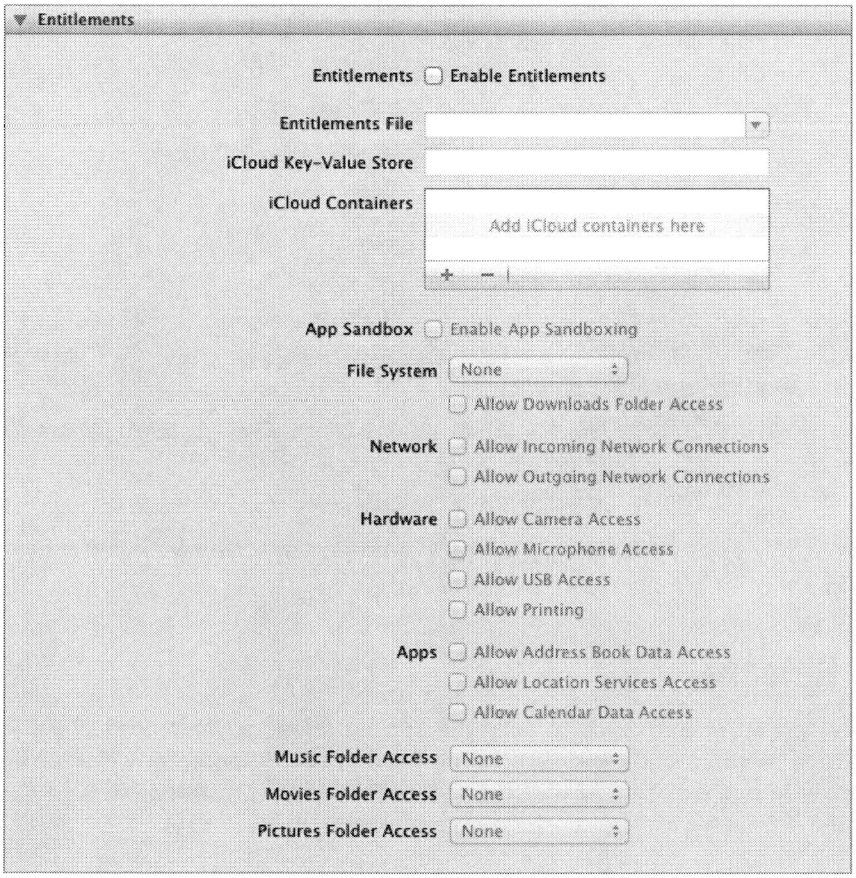

Figure 10-30. *The Entitlements settings before configuration*

Check the Enable Entitlements check box, and Xcode fills out a few values for you. Leave the Entitlements File set to Graphique, but erase the iCloud Key-Value Store entry. Select book.macdev.Graphique in the iCloud Containers section and click the minus button to delete it. Change the File System setting to Read/Write Access and check the Allow Printing check box. Your settings should match Figure 10-31.

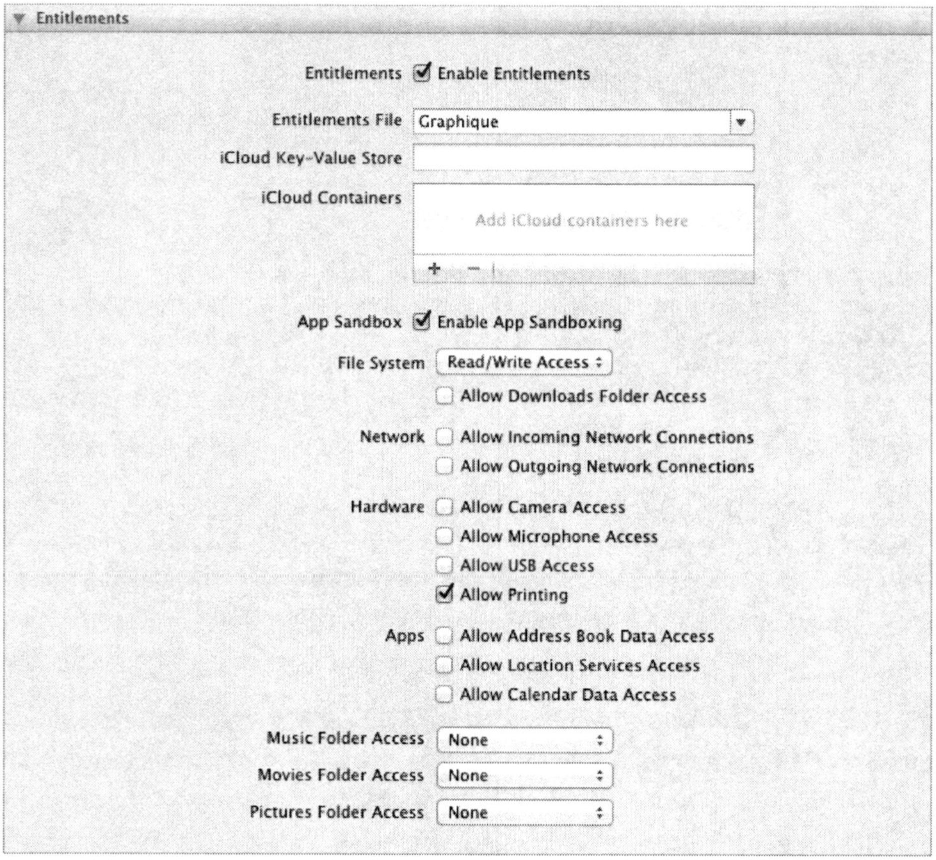

Figure 10-31. *The configured entitlements for Graphique*

You'll notice that Xcode added a file called Graphique.entitlements to the project that contains this configuration information as a property list.

Building for Release

With everything configured, you're ready to build the app for release. Select **Product ➤ Archive** from the Xcode menu to build and archive the release. Your computer will churn a bit and then display Xcode's Organizer window with the Archives tab selected, as shown in Figure 10-32.

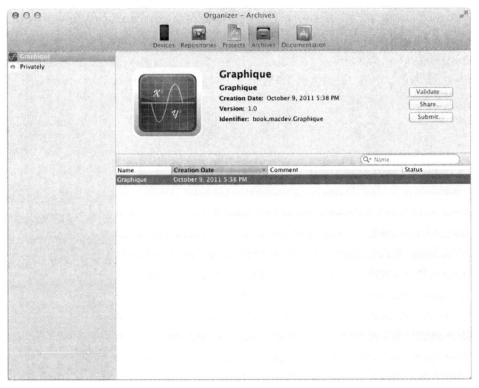

Figure 10-32. *Archive for Graphique*

We'll come back to this archive later when we're ready to submit Graphique to the Mac App Store.

Setting Up Your Web Site

Each app in the Mac App Store provides a link to the app's web site so that users can learn more about the app and the company or developers behind it and get support for the app. The web site can be as simple or as complex as you want, using whatever technologies you want. This is your web site running on your servers; Apple just links to it from the Mac App Store.

Apple does provides some artwork for you to use on your web site and guidelines for the usage of that artwork, though. The artwork is available at `http://developer.apple.com/appstore/mac/resources/marketing/`, and the guidelines are found at `http://developer.apple.com/appstore/mac/MacAppStoreMarketingGuidelines.pdf`. You should read and understand those guidelines before setting up your web site. Read those guidelines carefully to make sure you understand and follow them.

Using the Artwork

Apple provides an "Available on the Mac App Store" logo, in Photoshop format, for you to use on your web site. The image helps you follow the spacing guidelines set forward by Apple by providing the appropriate margin around the logo. Open the image, resize it to fit your web site (minimum: 40 pixels high for the visible logo, not including the margin), hide the Background and Notes layers, and export it as a PNG (or whatever format you want to use).

Apple also provides images of computers so you can display screenshots of your application as if it were running on a computer. The images come in two versions: one for showing screenshots as windows and one for showing screenshots in full-screen mode. You can use the full-screen ones only for apps that are designed to run in full-screen mode.

Whichever set of images you use, follow the instructions in the "Placing Your Application Screen on the Apple Product Image" section in the guidelines document referenced earlier.

Creating the Web Site

Your app's web site is an opportunity to sell your app, so focus on what your app does and why users should go download it from the Mac App Store. This isn't a marketing book, so that's all we'll say about that.

You should link the "Available on the Mac App Store" logo to your app in the Mac App Store. To get the URL, after your app is configured in iTunes Connect (which you'll do later in this chapter), you can get a link to your app on its summary screen—it's the link behind View in App Store, under Links, as shown in Figure 10-33.

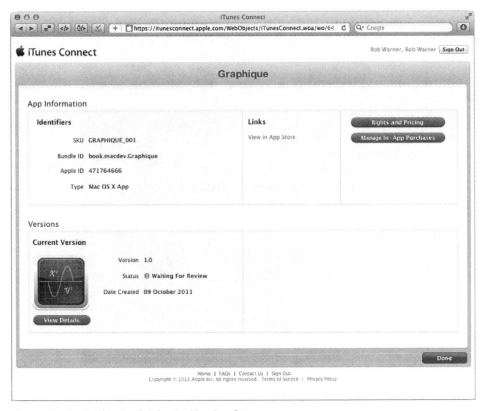

Figure 10-33. *Getting the link for the Mac App Store*

Figure 10-34 shows Graphique's web site, available at http://grailbox.com/graphique.

Figure 10-34. *Graphique's web site*

Submitting the App

You still have a fair amount of work to do to submit your app, so plan your schedule for more than just a few minutes to get this done. The next sections walk you through the app submission process.

Setting Up Your iTunes Connect Account

Your iTunes Connect account allows you to manage the apps you have in the Mac App Store. In it, you specify information about your apps, such as the Mac App Store category to display them in, and you specify details that allow you to get paid, such as your bank account information. You can then use your iTunes Connect account to get download and sales information, among other things, for your apps.

To set up your iTunes Connect Account, point your web browser to
http://itunesconnect.apple.com/, and enter your Apple ID and password when
prompted. Follow the instructions to set up a contract for Mac OS X Paid Applications,
including contact information and associated bank account information.

Uploading Your Application

After all the work of developing and testing your application, you're finally ready to
upload it. Click the Manage Your Applications link to see a list of all your existing apps in
both the Mac App Store and the iOS App Store. To upload a new app, click the Add
New App button and select Mac OS X App to begin creating your new app.

Setting the App Name

If this is your first app in an Apple App Store, you'll next be asked for your primary
language and the developer name to display for all your apps on Apple's App Stores.
Since you can't change these values once set, choose these items with care.

On the next screen, enter an app name and an SKU number, and select the Bundle ID of
your app (which you should have already configured using the Developer Certificate
Utility). For App Name, enter the name of your app (Graphique, in our case). For SKU
Number, enter some string that will be unique to your app. Large companies have more
need for this field than small ones, and this can be whatever you want. We enter
GRAPHIQUE_001, imagining that if we ever release a Pro version of Graphique we can
use SKU **GRAPHIQUE_002** for that. For Bundle ID, select your previously configured
Bundle ID. You can also click the link to register a new Bundle ID, which will throw you
back to the Developer Certificate Utility.

Selecting Availability and Pricing

The next screen has you select your availability and pricing for your app. The availability
defaults to the current date, which you should leave unless you have some reason to
launch your app on a specific date. For pricing, click the link to view the pricing matrix to
understand the pricing tiers. The tier you select establishes the price for the app in the
many countries iTunes does business in. For Graphique, we select Tier 1, which means
it costs 99 cents in the United States and 85 yen in Japan, for example. Click Continue
to proceed to the next screen.

Entering Additional Information

The next screen requests loads of information, so you'll be happier if you've prepared
some of this before you get here. Some of this information should match information in
your app's property list. Fill out the fields appropriate to your app. Read the discussion
of each of the sections to understand what the fields mean and how we filled them out
for Graphique.

Metadata

The Metadata section contains information about your app, some of which should match your app's property list. The fields and their explanations are as follows:

- *Version Number*: This should match the Version field from your app's property list. For Graphique, we entered **1.0**.

- *Description*: This is your opportunity to sell your app, explaining to prospective customers what your app does and why they should download it. You have 4,000 bytes, so make them count. Feel free to review the descriptions for other apps on the Mac App Store to give you ideas for what to write. For Graphique, we entered this:

    > Graphique is a graphing calculator for OS X Lion that was developed in conjunction with the book Beginning OS X Lion Apps Development (Apress 2011). It features a smart, syntax-highlighting editor, results in both graph and table format, a QuickLook plugin, and printing capabilities. Complete source code is available at the Apress site.

    > Buy the app so you can visualize your equations. Buy the book so you can understand how to build OS X Lion applications!

- *Primary Category*: This should match your app's property list. Category refers to the Mac App Store category to list your app under. For Graphique, we selected Utilities.

- *Secondary Category*: This is an optional field that you can use to specify an additional category. For Graphique, we selected Graphs & Design because of Graphique's ability to display graphs.

- *Keywords*: When users search for apps on the Mac App Store, you want your app to pop up if they're looking for something that your app can do. Be accurate with your keywords so your app appears for all the searches it should, but for none of the searches it shouldn't. For Graphique, we entered **graph, graphing, equation, calculator, sine, cosine, trig**.

- *Copyright*: This should match your app's property list. For Graphique, we entered **Copyright © 2011 Michael Privat and Rob Warner. All rights reserved.**

- *Contact Email Address*: When users have problems with or questions about your app, they e-mail you at this address. For Graphique we entered `graphique@grailbox.com`.

- *Support URL*: The Mac App Store links to this site so users can quickly get help and support for your app. This URL could point to your main web site, or it could point to a specific help forum or documentation site for your app. For Graphique, we entered `http://grailbox.com/graphique`.

- *App URL*: This is an optional URL that points to your app's web site. For Graphique, we entered `http://grailbox.com/graphique`.

- *Privacy Policy URL*: This is an optional URL that points to your privacy policy. For Graphique, we left it blank.

- *Review Notes*: This is an optional field that allows you to communicate information about your app to Apple's app reviewers. The site suggests that, for sandboxed apps, you explain why your app needs the entitlements it's requesting. For Graphique, we entered the following:

  > Graphique is sandboxed and requests entitlements for reading and saving files and for printing. In the app, you enter equations and see them graphed. You can save the equations to files and later read them back in to Graphique. You can also print your graphs. Graphique also includes a QuickLook plugin so you can see your graphs in Finder.

Rating

Apple will reject apps that it deems objectionable or offensive. The Ratings section gives you an opportunity to disclose how much of any potentially objectionable material appears in your apps, on a scale of None – Infrequent/Mild – Frequent/Intense. Be honest in your assessment. Apple uses this information to help potential customers know the appropriate audience for your apps. For Graphique, we selected None for all categories.

EULA

The EULA section lets you specify your own End User License Agreement (EULA) you want to attach to your app. You can also use the standard EULA for your app by not changing anything in this section. For Graphique, we left this section alone.

Uploads

You must specify at least one screenshot for your app for the Mac App Store entry to display. You can specify multiple screenshots as well. The first screenshot you specify is the one users will see first, although you can change the order of the screenshots after you upload them. Each screenshot should be 1280x800 pixels. For Graphique, we uploaded four screenshots.

When you click Save, you're taken to a screen that identifies your app, as shown in Figure 10-35.

Figure 10-35. *The Graphique app in iTunes Connect*

Click the View Details button to view the information you entered, and click the Ready to Upload Binary button. You are asked whether your app uses cryptography so that Apple can make sure it complies with any export regulations. Answer the question appropriately and click Save.

The next screen talks about having the right Application Loader app, which you have with Xcode 4. Click Continue, and you're returned to your app's information screen, only now the status has changed to Waiting For Upload.

Performing the Upload

Go back to Xcode's Organizer window and select the archive you produced earlier. Click the Validate button, which will ask you for your iTunes Connect login credentials. Enter them and click Next. Xcode connects to iTunes Connect and matches the archive to the app you created in iTunes Connect. Assuming it finds a match, it shows a screen that allows you to confirm that it found the right one, as shown in Figure 10-36.

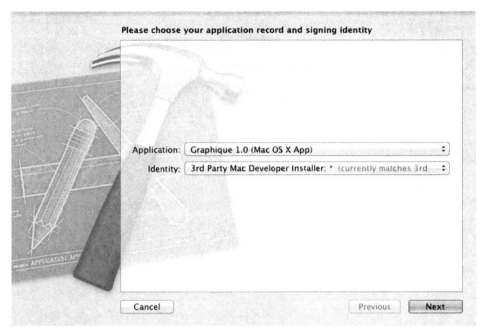

Figure 10-36. *Confirming the application and signing identity*

Click Next, and Xcode will validate the archive. You may get an error saying "Unable to extract package metadata." If you do, you're not alone. Make no changes and simply try again. You should eventually see a screen like Figure 10-37 that says your app is valid.

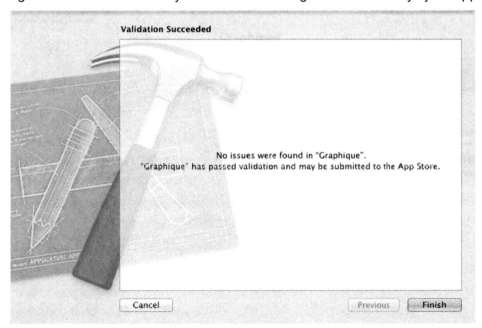

Figure 10-37. *Successful validation*

Click Finish to return to the Organizer window and, with the same archive still selected, click Submit. You'll be asked for your application record and signing identity, as shown in Figure 10-38. When you click Next, your app is uploaded to Apple. On successful completion, you see a screen like Figure 10-39. Congratulations! Your app is waiting for review.

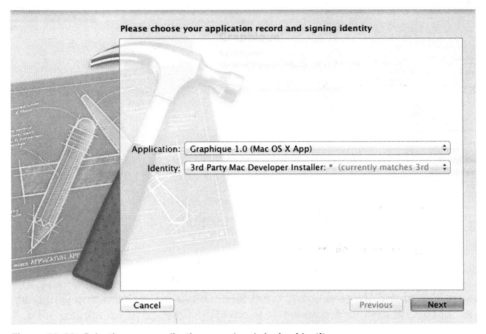

Figure 10-38. *Selecting your application record and signing identity*

Figure 10-39. *Graphique successfully uploaded*

Here we leave you, waiting on the Mac App Store reviewers to approve your app.

Summary

Submitting an app to the Mac App Store can be a daunting experience as you deal with certificates, App IDs, provisioning profiles, SKUs, and the other information you must provide to land an app in the Mac App Store. Once complete, however, you feel a sense of accomplishment as one of your creations enters the marketplace.

For an app to thrive in the Mac App Store, however, you must continue to nurture it from both a technical and a marketing perspective. Technically, you add features, fix bugs, respond to customer issues, and upload new versions. On the marketing side, you've got to do more than simply expect that since you've built it, people will come. Marketing is a never-ending task that requires diligence, time, and insight. But that's a subject for a different book.

We look forward to seeing your apps on the Mac App Store!

Index

CPSIA information can be obtained at www.ICGtesting.com
Printed in the USA
LVOW050731251111

256391LV00011BA/1/P

9 781430 237204

CHERISHED TALES
of the COUNTRYSIDE

CHERISHED TALES
of the COUNTRYSIDE

David & Charles

A DAVID & CHARLES BOOK
David & Charles is a subsidiary of F&W (UK) Ltd.,
an F&W Publications Inc. company

First published in the UK in 2004

A catalogue record for this book is available from the British Library.

ISBN 0 7153 1824 1 hardback

Printed in Singapore by KHL
for David & Charles
Brunel House   Newton Abbot   Devon

Commissioning Editor   Jane Trollope
Art Editor   Ali Myer
Desk Editor   Lewis Birchon
Production Controller   Jennifer Campbell

Visit our website at www.davidandcharles.co.uk

David & Charles books are available from all good bookshops; alternatively you
can contact our Orderline on (0)1626 334555 or write to us at FREEPOST EX2 110,
David & Charles Direct, Newton Abbot, TQ12 4ZZ (no stamp required UK mainland).

CONTENTS

Chapter 1

A BOY AT THE PLOUGH

Tom Quinn

A BOY AT THE PLOUGH

WILLIAM WADE'S FAMILY, ON BOTH HIS MOTHER'S AND FATHER'S SIDE HAVE BEEN FARMERS SINCE AT LEAST THE EARLY PART OF THE 19TH CENTURY. WILLIAM, WHO IS 87, WAS BORN AT PLASWORTH NEAR CHESTER-LE-STREET IN COUNTY DURHAM WHERE HIS GRANDFATHER HAD SETTLED IN THE MIDDLE DECADES OF THE 19TH CENTURY AFTER LEAVING FAMINE-STRICKEN IRELAND.

'I started working on the farm before I left school, which is what most farmer's sons did. School was alright, but you only needed so much of it if you knew you were going on the land. I was already driving a pair of horses at the plough when I was 11. As a ploughboy to an older, more experienced man you just picked it up; you'd walk by his side, up and down the field or lead the horses now and then, just watching and waiting your turn. And your turn would come when the ploughman thought you were ready. He'd start by letting you get the feel of the handles, gradually increasing the length of time you were in charge of the team. If you started to go off the line he was there to set you straight.

'I can remember mowing hay for the army in the first war. We used a horse for that, too, gradually walking it round the field with the blades off to the side of the mower, which was towed behind; a simple gearing system meant that the cutting blades were turned by the motion of the wheels as the mower was pulled by the horse. I also drove the horses on the wagon that went round to pick up the hay. We were working with soldiers then, who'd been sent to help us; they pitched the hay up to us, while we made sure it was piled nicely on the wagon.'

William Wade has a rich store of memories of farming during the Great War. Illness has now virtually confined him to the house, but his mind is as quick as ever – although he says himself, this is not necessarily a good thing. 'I find it sad, looking back all those years, very sad. The idea that it is all over for me now, even though I had a good life, I find it sad even thinking about all those horses I worked with; the fact that they have all gone, too, and everything has changed.'

One of William's six sons now runs the family farm, and like so many farmers he employs no labour at all today. 'We just can't afford to, and we don't need to, with modern tractors and equipment,' says William. But things were very different 70 years ago: 'Well, the Great War made the biggest difference because suddenly we found that the army was commandeering just about everything – suddenly we farmers were central to the national effort, and the army was commandeering every haystack round about. When they helped themselves to a stack they used to put a pole in it, with WD – for War Department – written on it in big letters, and no one would dare touch it then.

'The soldiers who were sent to work with us were mostly pretty good, although some had no experience of working on the land. But others were real countrymen, and

Taking a breather together: Horses were marvellous to work with because they remembered how to do things

there were some first-class horsemen among them. On this farm at that time we would have between 12 and 14 horses at any one time. We used to breed from them, and when the youngsters were old enough they were sold, and went to work either in the towns or down the mines. Nowadays this may seem cruel, but horses were essential because there was no mechanical means to get the coal back from the face to the shafts, and we all needed coal; everyone did, for fires, heating and industry. Apart from wood, if you were in the country, there was nothing else.

'The small ponies went to the coal mines, and the slightly bigger ones to the ironstone mines at Cleveland. Countryside without horses was inconceivable then; even when the new tractors were being talked about – and you could get one from about 1920, although the early ones were unreliable – no one believed they would ever take over from the horse. Horses were

everywhere and used for just about everything: moving people and goods, carting farm produce, drilling, ploughing, harrowing, haymaking – everything.'

William's farm is only a dozen or so miles from what used to be one of Britain's greatest shipbuilding and industrial centres: Teeside. With much of the 1914-18 war effort centred on increasing industrial production, the urban population had to be organized in a way that was previously unheard of. Yet in spite of this, food distribution then, and for many years after, was still locally organized. 'Yes, for many years after we first came here we used to deliver all our produce locally. I remember we used to cart our wheat to a mill at Stockton about eight miles away. We sold 20 tons once, and delivered it in what was called a Rolley, a great heavy four-wheeled wagon that took two tons at a time and needed two horses to pull it. For this work the horses were harnessed one in front of the other, not abreast. Ordinary carts normally carried about a ton, and we would put the corn in sacks which were filled differently for different crops: a sack of wheat always weighed 16 stone, barley 18 stone, beans 22 stone, and so on.'

William has particularly fond memories of farm horses and although, as he admits himself, there is an element of sentiment in this, it has a practical side, too: 'Horses were marvellous to work with because they remembered how to do things – you try teaching a tractor anything! If you took your horses the same way each day, or through the same routine, eventually they would virtually work on their own. I enjoyed riding too, and learned when I was four.

'With working horses on a mixed farm like this we generally got them out to the fields by seven in the morning. But we'd have been up at 5.30am doing other work before having breakfast at 6.30am. We came

back in at midday for our lunch, then back out again till 5pm when we fed the horses and came in for our tea. After tea we'd go and groom the horses, and then it was time for bed.' Work with horses was more time-consuming than directly arduous, although invariably it involved a great deal of walking: 'You always led, drove or walked your horses; they never went at the trot' says William. And the work got slower and harder on heavier soils.

'This is strong clay land; in fact, to be honest, there's too much clay here. It's good land for wheat and grass, but pretty hopeless for crops like potatoes which we've never bothered with much as a result, except during the war when we had to grow them. With a horse we ploughed about an acre a day; with a tractor it's about 20 because you have five furrows on a machine as against one, or at best two, on a horse plough. Mind you, horses and ponies were tough too, and it was nothing to drive a pony 25 miles out and 25 back in a day.'

Though he has always been a working farmer, William was shrewd enough to buy land whenever he could, and today he has some 840 acres, with 250 sheep and 400 cattle. 'We've amalgamated three small farms: Foxhill, Larberry and ours which is the oldest, Long Newton Grange; three of my sons now farm the whole lot in partnership.'

A major problem for William until well into the 1940s was the lack of water. There was a well, but in summer it would dry up, and like many farmers, William had to rely on regular rainfall. 'We just had to hope it would rain when the well started to get difficult. A water pipe was laid nearby in the early 1940s, but the people who were responsible for it were worried that I'd use too much water so they wouldn't connect me at first, which I thought was a bit unfair.'

The last few Long Newton horses were

used for general carting until about 1960, which was long after most farmers had got rid of them. 'I liked working with horses because they'd nearly always go without being driven, and knew exactly what they were doing and what you wanted them to do – they only had to do a task a few times to pick it up. Here they used to walk between the stooks of corn, and they'd stop at just the right place without being told so we could lift the hay on to the wagon. A few people round about still use horses even now, but it's rare. Vaux, the brewery in Sunderland, they still use horses for local deliveries; horses are cheaper and just as efficient as motors for local deliveries.'

The great staple in Durham, as in so many northern counties, was always wool; and if there happened to be a glut of wool at any time, the Durham farmers of old didn't rely on modern ideas like intervention buying, they had a far more novel solution: 'Farmers would shear their sheep and if the wool price was too low they'd bury the wool for a year or more! It's hard to believe, I know, and you'd think it would rot, but it never did. Wool is amazing stuff. I'll tell you something else which will show you just how remarkable it is: when the Victorian

engineers had to build the main north-south, east coast railway over the Cleveland bog, it was always said that they first packed tons of wool into the bog and then ran the rails over that; they knew that wool would make it just as stable as drainage and filling in. It's a true story, and the rail has never been taken up so it still runs over the wool. And in medieval times they used to put wool into a riverbed first, before laying bridge foundations – oh, yes, it's marvellous stuff!'

On this traditionally mixed farm, sheep and corn were the mainstay, but William decided many years ago that there was also money in milk. 'I started our milk herd: father didn't like the idea much because he'd never done it, and it was a bit of a step into unknown territory. I remember the first cow we bought cost just £13!'

It wasn't until he was well into his teens that William heard his first wireless, but he can still remember the sense of disbelief as the weak sound crackled over the crystal set. 'It was like magic, you just couldn't believe it. At that time we'd only heard talk of radios, and, of course, television wasn't even an idea. That set I first heard wasn't even ours, it belonged to one of our farm

Lambing time:
'If the wool price
was too low they'd
bury the wool for
a year or more'

workers – the sound was a bit crackly, but it was very exciting. The only other entertainment the modern world had brought us was the cinema, and every now and then we'd traipse off to the pictures in Stockton or Darlington to see the silent films; people would travel miles to see them in those days.'

But farm work being what it was, there was little time for excursions. Every day brought a series of almost endless tasks, for as well as growing crops and rearing animals, farmers had to sell their own produce, as well as buy and sell from each other. 'We used to buy some of our horses from other farmers, perhaps if they had a foal to sell, or we'd go to the regular horses sales at Yarm or at Newcastle. Although we bred our own horses, they were in short supply during the Great War because so many were needed at the front. All we could ever buy in then were horses branded with a "C" on the shoulder, meaning "cast" – in other words they had been rejected by the army, perhaps because they were gun shy, or just unsuitable for war.

'The four or five foals we bred each year were sometimes sent to Scotland, to Glasgow where they pulled trams, coal carts and just about everything else. However, horses used to the farm were often terrified by the traffic in the towns and it might take them a while to settle to the work. On at least two occasions I remember horses bolted with me in Stockton – I think they thought they were being chased by a tram!

'Horses can be very funny, too. I had a strange mare, for example, who wouldn't budge for anyone except me and even then I had to feed her a bit of chocolate first! For years I rode an old pony to school. The road at the end of the farm track was just a tiny, overgrown, unmetalled lane then, and in fact stayed like that until just before the second war. I used to trot the pony through the snowdrifts in winter unless we were really snowed in, which did happen occasionally. When my sister started going to school we drove together in the pony and trap. It was lovely to trot along the snowy lanes, and when we got to school, which was in the village about two miles away, we'd leave the pony and trap in the pub stables.

'Driving a horse and cart could be very exciting; I remember the first time I took the milk into Stockton it was in a blinding snowstorm, we could hardly see where we were going and there wasn't a soul about – talk about the bleak mid-winter! That would have been about 1925. We got 6d a gallon for the milk then, and you couldn't just take it to one dairy; there were several small ones round about, and I'd have to take different amounts to each one. Sometimes they wouldn't want any, and if there was a glut of milk, of course the price would get lower and lower. The dairies could really dictate terms, too – we asked 8d a gallon from one dairy owner, and he said he'd only

pay for it if the milk reached him every day by 7am. To get it there by then we had to start milking at about 4am; friends said that only two fools like my dad and me would have done it! We stuck it out for a year. All the milking was by hand, then; there was no real skill to it, but some milkers were very fast. We had 12 cows, and it wasn't until about 1942 that we reached 40.

'We had a milking machine by the end of the last war, but still had oil lamps in the farmhouse. I thought I'd be clever and try to light the house using old bus batteries; we were already using them to drive the milk machine, but actually they turned out to be useless for the house so we stuck with the oil lamps until the mid-1950s when the electricity finally came. Even then they didn't want us to have it, but they needed to lay the cable over my land so I told them if they didn't connect me, they couldn't lay the cable. That soon sorted it out, although the contractor still had to squeeze something extra out of me – he said he'd connect us if I gave him a goose, but then I thought that was a pretty good bargain!'

'All the milking was by hand ...'

course, the greater the difference, which is why we could tell if a passing cart wasn't a local one. For example, Scottish carts were very different from the English ones: the Scottish cart had a lot of iron in it, where the English cart was almost entirely of wood. Irish carts had shafts back and front. The Irish also had special, long, high-sided carts for hay and I remember going to Ireland with my father to buy cattle before the war and seeing 15 or maybe 20 long Irish hay-carts moving slowly along the road towards Dublin; high up on the hay on every single wagon sat groups of men drinking and playing nap. That was a glorious sight!'

William often went to Ireland in those early days, to buy livestock and to see relatives who were still living there. Though railways and steamers made the longer journeys much easier than they had once been, local transport hadn't advanced much since medieval times. 'Up here in the north-east the roads were all unmade until after the second war, and even then a lot of the minor ones were left as tracks. No one really had responsibility for the upkeep of the roads, it was just as it had been centuries before. We used to try to keep the roads near us as well surfaced as we could by going to collect cinders from a works on Teeside. We'd cart the cinders and then spread them over the potholes and ruts, and this gave the cartwheels something to bite into.

'A fellow who worked for us used to take the horse and cart and go for the cinders regularly. After he'd been going for quite some time I decided I'd do it instead. First time out I'd got halfway to the place where we used to collect the cinders when the horse turned into a pub yard. Horses remember these things, you see, so I knew what the previous fellow had been doing!

'Every pub in the land had stables then,

'Every village and hamlet would also have had a cartwright ...'

One constant revealed through William's memories is the fact that until the 1960s, rural Durham had changed little in centuries. Away from industrial areas, life continued much as it always had done, with little time for entertainment and pleasure in a farming year that demanded almost all the energy a man had. 'It's hard to imagine, now, what it was like round here up to the early 1960s. Just take certain individual things which have vanished, like the local blacksmith. Today the blacksmith is a rarity, but until about 30 years ago he was one of the most important men around; every village, however tiny, had a blacksmith and he would make anything and everything – hinges, bolts, and metal bits of wagons, hooks and so on.

'Every village and hamlet would also have had a cartwright, or wagon-maker, and styles of wagon would vary between district and even between individual makers. The further afield you went, of

because everyone arrived by cart or on horseback. On market days in the town you often couldn't find a stall for a horse, the place was so packed with carts and ponies, horses and dogs and other livestock. It's a sight few can remember now, and it will never be seen again.

'Quite a few working horses were still helping on the farms well into the 1950s and 1960s in this area; you'd see them along the roads, although they became rarer almost by the day. And even farmers who loved to have them about, found that when the old ones died there was really no point in replacing them; and in many cases you couldn't even if you wanted to, because the farm-horse sales had gone.

'The horse fairs were great fun. I remember once going to Yarm Horse Fair, which was always held in September, to get a pony to run the milk. I found one I liked, and asked the man holding it what he wanted for it; £40 he said, so I offered £30 and we settled on £35. That horse ran the milk every day for seven years; it also worked the horse-driven binder for us at haymaking time, along with two other horses. They were harnessed three abreast, and we always put the weakest horse on the outside; the first or inside horse was called master because he controlled the turn.

'I must have trained hundreds of horses in my time. The best policy was to let them be until they were two years old, or perhaps three; they were allowed to run at grass all that time. We usually started to train a young horse sometime around Christmas, I don't know why then, exactly, but it was usually the time. You got the horse used to being handled, and then put a bridle on it. When it was used to that, you harnessed it in the middle of three horses harnessed abreast, putting it between two old, quiet, experienced horses. At first a young horse was kept in harness for only half a day at a time because it would get sore shoulders if you didn't take things slowly and gradually. It was also important to make sure you had a good, well-fitting collar, and there was a real skill to making a good collar that

'You got the horse used to being handled, and then you put a bridle on it ...'

and "gee back" if we wanted it to turn left. Horses were harnessed abreast for ploughing in many areas, but here I often ploughed with a team of three in a line; the quickest was always put at the front and the strongest at the back or in the heel position, because turning at the headlands relied on the back horse and it was hard work for her.

'A horse-drawn plough is difficult to control at first because it must cut in a straight line and to an even depth; this isn't easy, since while you concentrate on these things you also have to concentrate on three great horses. We used a wheeled plough, which is easier, but my father, who was a champion ploughman in his time, used a most difficult plough which had no wheels at all. He once took the wheels off my plough and I got in a right mess! The wheels made it easier because with the big wheel in the furrow and the small wheel on the land, the top of the furrow, the whole thing naturally tended to stay on an even keel. Without wheels the plough slipped up and down and from side to side unless you really knew what you were doing.

'Ransome, Simms and Geoffrey were famous plough-makers, and they used to employ my father to plough with their equipment; he did it so well that it was a good advertisement for their tackle. In return, when the ploughshare wore out, or any other part, the company always gave my father a new part for nothing. All the metal parts of the plough were of locally made iron and very strong, cast by Teesdale Bros who had a foundry nearby. They made everything – ploughshares, drills, scufflers, everything.

'All the time I was growing up we kept the cattle chained in their stalls and every cow was fed individually. Leaving the cattle in the fields is a recent thing. You had to feed individually because different cows needed different amounts if you were to get

wouldn't rub. We went to the local saddler for that: he made just about everything and anything to do with leather, and he would always make a one-off, for example, if you had a horse with an odd-shaped neck. He'd also make you a pair of boots if you asked him. One saddler from the old days remains round here, Mr Sample from Great Smeaton; he adapted his business and now makes saddles and bridles for riding ponies and horses.

'In the old days, farm horses were fed on a mixture of hay, oats, flaked maize and crushed beans, and if a horse was well treated it might work for up to 20 years. Here in the north, when a mare foaled we'd leave the foal in a farm building during the day and put the mare to grass till lunchtime. She'd then be put with the foal for a while, then put out again till evening. That's the way we did it, though I know that in the south the foal went to the fields with the mare.

'For ploughing we had only two instructions for the horses: we'd shout "haa" if we wanted the horse to turn right,

'I started with shorthorns ...'

the maximum yield of milk from them. I started with Shorthorns – they were red, white or a mix of the two colours, or sometimes roan. Then in 1932 we went over to Ayrshires because they'd been tested for tuberculosis. These days my sons have half Ayrshires and half Friesians. I started with 135 acres in father's time. He added 214 acres to that, and since then we've added bits and pieces and we're now ring-fenced, as it were, by roads.'

Amid the tales of increasing prosperity, William acknowledged that, like most farmers, he's had his ups and downs; 'inevitably the 1930s, which is probably why the government and the Europeans don't want to go back to the sort of free market for farm produce we had then. At that time the free market meant thousands of farmers going out of business. During those days the only way we could make a living was by buying Irish cattle, fattening them, and selling them on, and even that didn't always work. I remember one year we bought 30 Galloway bullocks and fed them all winter. We'd paid £14 per head for them,

and after feeding them for months we got only £20 each for them. It just wasn't worth doing.

'The second war really got farming out of the doldrums because suddenly everyone needed us and all the food we could produce; and that might also explain why, after the war, there was another slump.'

The economics of farming have always been difficult or controversial, but whether their standard of living was high or low there seems to be a lasting commitment to the land among farmers that overrides temporary economic realities. This attachment to the land undoubtedly contains an element of sentiment, which is presumably why so many farmers refuse to pack up and do something else during difficult periods; but it is tempered with the notion that farmers are born to that way of life, however hard it may be. Most of William Wade's memories are of difficult times, but it is impossible to imagine him doing anything else; it is almost as if the harshness of life on the land is a part of what makes it so compelling.

skulls. It was terrible, but we knew no better then. If you left their horns to grow they could do a lot of damage to each other and to you. We had one lovely old cow called Ghandi, and she was such a nice old thing we couldn't bring ourselves to cut her horns off; but being among a lot of cattle without horns she quickly realized that she could dominate them all, and became a terrible bully.

'I think the funniest thing I remember from my long farming years was the time I drove a flock of sheep into Stockton town centre. Driving sheep through big towns was an everyday occurrence at that time because there were no lorries and no other way to move them. Usually it went all right and the sheep stayed close together, but on this occasion for some unaccountable reason one of my sheep jumped straight through the plate-glass window of a shop. The sheep was alright, but the shopkeeper wasn't amused!'

'I remember bringing about 30 cattle from the railway station 20 miles away. We'd bought them in Ireland and I had the dog to help me, but 20 miles along rough roads is a long way to drive that many cattle in a day. By the time we'd got halfway back to the farm the dog's pads were worn away and its feet were bleeding, so I had to put it over my shoulders and carry it.

'Farming could be a cruel business in those days too, and particularly, I think, in Ireland. For example, I remember de-horning hundreds of cattle without using an anaesthetic as you would have to now. There was blood absolutely everywhere and the cows were obviously in pain; we just sawed the horns off, and if you looked down the stump you could see into their

Chapter 2
A FAMILY AFFAIR

Valerie Porter

A FAMILY AFFAIR

TUCKED AWAY IN THE COTSWOLDS AND APPROACHED BY VERY NARROW LANES WITH LITTLE IN THE WAY OF SIGNPOSTS, GUITING POWER IS A DELIGHT. WITH ITS STONE COTTAGES, CHURCH AND TWO SMALL VILLAGE GREENS (ONE WITH A WAR MEMORIAL AND THE OTHER WITH A HUGE CHESTNUT TREE) IT HAS THE LOOK OF AN OLD ESTATE VILLAGE, ALTHOUGH IT IS NOT TRULY ONE. IN 1958 WHAT WAS LEFT OF THE ORIGINAL MANOR WAS BOUGHT PRIVATELY, INCLUDING ABOUT HALF THE HOMES IN THE VILLAGE AND SOME 1,200 ACRES OF SURROUNDING LAND. THE NEW LORD OF THE MANOR, DEVOTED TO THE COTSWOLDS AND TO ARCHITECTURE (INCLUDING THE VERNACULAR), MODERNIZED AND RESTORED THE DWELLINGS, SET UP A CHARITABLE TRUST AND DECIDED TO CONSERVE THE COMMUNITY BY GIVING PREFERENCE TO YOUNG LOCALS WHEN THE HOUSES WERE LET.

This visionary is a friend and client of Kenneth and Evelyn Day, veterinary surgeons. Evelyn has been one of the trustees since 1976, while Kenneth is a director and adviser of the company that farms the trust's land and in which the trust is a majority shareholder.

The Days moved to their low but spacious stone house in Guiting Power in 1978, their younger son Christopher having taken on the family home and practice in Stanford-in-the-Vale. Evelyn went on working in the Stanford practice for two days a week and every other weekend, while Kenneth had a coronary and reduced his work to five half-days a week: 'I didn't like that because half the time I wasn't there to follow up my cases, and I don't like to "let go". I was always taught: "Either bury or cure your cases" – but fortunately my son Christopher was able to take over the management of the practice.'

Evelyn retired completely from the practice in 1988 because of the effects of spinal and neck arthritis, an occupational hazard; Kenneth retired two years later after a triple bypass heart operation. These two constantly active people, always accustomed to being busy, are now in their seventies. They had been in practice together for most of their married life and it was obviously a good partnership, both professionally and personally. They celebrated their golden wedding anniversary in February 1994.

Kenneth's childhood was in suburban London. 'I used to disappear on my bike and go to work for stables in Blackheath and Bexley Heath and Shooter's Hill. I would do anything for money then! They used to have a clearing house for these hacks, bring them in from fairs, all rogues and bandits. They'd put me up on these ponies to see what they'd do, and first they'd try and bite your leg and kick you as you got on, then they'd buck and roll with you. And what I learned from that was never to be afraid to admit that you've fallen off! Most people pretend that they've been thrown; I'd just say I'd fallen off. I was absolutely potty about horses. And I did a lot on farms as a boy in the school holidays, learned to milk cows and so on.'

At the age of 11 he decided that he was going to be a vet. Why?

'Well, we had lots of animals when I was a child – birds and rats and rabbits. I bred budgies, and did experiments with colours and so on. I was fascinated with animals. And living in suburbia, I was quite determined that I wanted an outdoor life, a country life, which meant forestry, farming, vetting, something like that. Vetting was my first choice.

'I went to a marvellous school, St Olave's and St Xavier's Grammar School at Tower Bridge. My subject was classics, and my headmaster told me I was too clever to be a vet and that I should be a doctor. But I wanted to be a vet. It was obstinacy, really. So eventually he agreed. I said that I'd better do science. He disagreed, maintaining I could do that sort of nonsense at college and that I should stick to my classics; and that is what I did. He assured me they would teach me how to learn, and they did. And how lucky I was. I have met so many vets who have never read a book for pleasure, and I'm sure that I was a much better vet for my wider interests. Anyway, then I went straight into veterinary college and did all the science side of it there. You couldn't do that now!'

He entered the Royal Veterinary College in London in September 1938. 'Going to London was wonderful. The new Beaumont hospital at the Royal Veterinary College in Camden had not long been built, and I was

thrilled with it all. I'd always enjoyed my education, and continued to do so while I was there.'

It was at college that he met Evelyn. She, too, had had a 'total fascination' with animals all her life and she, too, decided to be a vet when she was 11 years old. Her father was in the army and she was born in India (Poona). But she had typhoid when she was four and a half years old and her mother suffered from repeated bouts of malaria, so they came back to England and Evelyn went to school at Talbot Heath in Bournemouth.

'We had dogs and cats at home, and I was just so interested in them. It was not so much a conscious love of animals as an interest in them. When I decided to be a vet, they were all rather horrified; every year at my school, each new form mistress tried to persuade me not to do this. But I was determined…'

'We were both obstinate,' Kenneth interjects.

'Finally my sixth-form mistress said that she would come up to the college with me to find out what it was all about. We went to the Royal Veterinary College and saw the bursar, whom she grilled thoroughly, wanting to know whether I would have any chance in the profession.'

Evelyn won her battle and went straight into the second year in January 1940, as the autumn term was fully taken up by the evacuation of the college after the outbreak of World War II. 'Because of the war, in the first year students were evacuated to Reading University; the second year was partly in Reading and partly at Sonning; the third was all at Sonning; and the fourth and fifth years were at Goring, or rather Streatly. And with makeshift facilities at that: at Sonning the dissection rooms were in the stables.'

They variously saw practice while they were at college; for Kenneth, it was largely horse work. As a student he worked with laconic Irish vet, Mr TAR Filgate of Faringdon, who was excellent with horses. He was a well-bred man from a county family.

'Of course,' says Evelyn, 'we saw practice in wartime, when the push was for food production. We were a reserved occupation and were told that we were needed and should not go into the forces or any other war work; our whole motivation was to help the farmers achieve maximum production. That was when these great disease control and eradication schemes got going, because they were vital – in our own lifetime, TB, swine fever and brucellosis have been eradicated. It was quite a challenge.

'This sort of disease control cost the country the most enormous amount of money. When we were testing herds for TB we had to visit on three days: do a double intradermal in each animal's neck, the same again the next day, and then read it on the third day. At that stage it was optional, for farmers who wanted it. Then it was decided that enough herds were clear to make testing imperative (to protect the ones that were clear). It became two-

monthly testing and single intradermal. All the animals had to be handled, with all the labour that was available; then there was all the paperwork to be sent in, and isolating the doubtfuls and slaughtering the reactors – it cost the country millions.

'Under the old scheme we went round every three months "udder-punching", early in the morning immediately after milking. The maximum we could get from the Ministry was £4 a day. We'd visit four or five herds, leaving home at 5.30 in the morning. We'd feel each udder, take samples if they were suspicious. TB produced hard, non-painful udders with a thin, clear watery discharge. There could be pulmonary TB cases as well; we would hear their coughing, and we had to take sputum samples from the backs of their throats while they coughed in our faces.'

'It was essentially large animal work – farm animals and horses,' says Kenneth, 'with just a little small animal work for the gentry and also for farm workers, but we didn't charge the latter much, if anything at all. Evelyn would do her small animal work in the evenings. I used to calve a cow for a pound, and if it was difficult I'd charge a guinea. They were still blowing up udders in cases of milk fever then; people used to think milk fever was a form of mastitis and so they pumped the udder with acriflavine – and yes, it did cure some of them. Then in the days shortly before we qualified, there was a Danish vet who had no acriflavine when asked to treat a milk fever case; the cow was in extremis, so he pumped plain air into the udder and found that this worked just as well! What actually happened was that the back-pressure halted milk secretion and the drain on blood calcium which occurs very markedly after parturition.

'The farmers had a lot of faith in the blowing-up of udders. When we first went into practice, we used calcium solutions injected into the veins for treatment; but they always wanted us to pump up the udders as well. They didn't trust us, especially when we were fresh out of college; although later they accepted us, because we knew our job.'

'I always felt that I was in no position to tell people who had been farming all their lives what to do,' Evelyn remarks. 'One of our farmers said to me that he didn't get on with the young vets. So I told him that we were all young once, and that he must remember that the vets are helped in their developments by the farmers: it's up to the farmers to make their vets!'

Kenneth had planned to go to South America in a cattle boat after leaving college, but in fact it was straight into work, and straight into the Faringdon practice in which he would spend the rest of his career.

He had been asked to join Filgate at Faringdon when he was still a student seeing practice there, and he was only 27 when he took over the entire practice. 'We always say he asked me because I was the only one who cleaned up the kennels properly!' About three years after he came to the practice, Filgate offered him a one-third partnership. 'I didn't have any capital, but we took a loan from my father-in-law and agreed to pay off the rest of the purchase price out of my salary; this was seven guineas a week for a man with a wife and child!'

It was not long before Filgate decided to move to Ireland and the Days took over the whole practice, though they still had no money. 'We didn't take over his house because we liked our own house in Stanford-in-the-Vale, and anyway couldn't afford the move.' They had moved into the large stone house in Stanford-in-the-Vale in 1946. It was very much a family home and one for animal lovers; the house and paddock, over the years, would contain about five dogs, assorted goats, sheep, horses and two or three Jersey house-cows. 'We had moved into what was one of the densest cattle areas in the country at the time,' Evelyn remarks. By contrast, she had previously spent six months in a Wimbledon practice with Colonel Perry and Charles Perry.

'I clocked 80 hours a week working in the Wimbledon practice. They decided to let me have Charles's Austin 16, but the Perrys were both about 6ft 4in tall and they'd had the seat pushed back for such a long time that it wouldn't fasten forward – it just slid all over the place. So I went down Wimbledon Hill with my bosom in the steering wheel, and up it clinging on for dear life because the seat kept sliding backwards.

'When I was seeing practice in Derbyshire, the vet wanted to send me out in his car without any driving lessons. I then had six lessons through the middle of Leicester (where my parents were at the time) in the days when they were using horse-drawn drays among the trams. Most of the short-haul work was being done by horses, right through the war, and there were some terrible accidental injuries to them: when those ash shafts broke, they were as sharp as spears.'

'Horses seemed to lose their importance and their relevance when the war came,' says Kenneth. 'We were moving into mechanical transport. I loved the heavy horses, I loved the vanners, but they were going out and the leisure horses didn't appeal to me – the hunters and so on. So I went into cows, I went milking cows before I qualified, and I milked our house-cows twice a day for most of my professional life.'

Evelyn continues her narrative: 'The

Wimbledon practice gave me four guineas a week and my room in Wimbledon, and I put some money aside so that I had something to spend when we got married. Kenneth was in the countryside at the time and kept sending me presents of eggs and honey, but I wasn't getting them. I'd thought something was odd when I had to go to the Ministry of Employment one day and they asked my name, and then if I was born in Highgate, and if I was 40 years old. "No, I was not born in Highgate," I said, "and I'm only 23 this November!" Some time after I had realized that I wasn't getting the eggs and honey, I had a letter from a complete stranger; she said "I have been eating your food and I feel terribly guilty – come and have supper!" It was signed by my namesake, Evelyn Ingram, and she also lived in Wimbledon High Street, like me. Mystery solved! But I still had eggs: my mother used to send them to me in newspaper inside a tin.

'When I was seeing practice as a student in Derbyshire during the war, farmers would say to the vet, "Would you like a drop of milk, or an egg?" And they would not expect him to pay – unless they were big farmers!'

Kenneth, meanwhile was finding life was fun, as always; he has a great capacity for enjoying life, getting the most out of it, and being grateful for it. 'One of the things I found when I was seeing practice as a student, and later in practice as a veterinary surgeon, was that it was the most enormous privilege to be accepted and welcomed in everybody's house in a completely classless fashion. Remember that the country at that stage was very much in layers still: the gentry, the owner-farmers, the tenant farmers, the workers and so on, all very separate. But I was acceptable to all of them, and this was such a privilege, that they all treated me as an equal, whoever they were.

'And I would also emphasize the respect that the professional man had, before and after the war. We were trusted. The police trusted us; nobody queried our word; we could carry morphine, strychnine, arsenic and things – I had a little pochette in the car with all these. And we had humane killers, guns, in the car. We were trusted completely, and the great majority of us responded to that and behaved very reasonably. Your word was never queried…'

Evelyn interjects: 'They queried me when I applied for petrol – they sent me only a quarter of what I needed for my autocycle to Lechlade.'

'They didn't believe a vet would ride an autocycle!'

But she wrote back and demanded what

she needed, and did eventually receive the requisite coupons. That was when she was helping in the neighbouring practice, and her autocycle was recalcitrant and frequently broke down.

'We did drive an Austin 7 round the practice,' says Kenneth. 'After the war, the first new car we had was in 1952, though it had been ordered early in the war. We'd started in the Faringdon practice in January 1944, and we had second-hand cars for eight years – some of them even had to be hand-cranked, and none of them had heaters. I can remember often going out in the middle of the night and being unable to open the frozen boot to get our tackle out. And in bad weather nobody had any hot water, and you would wash in cold water and dry your hands on a piece of sack, if the farm had some.'

'Our assistants would weep if they didn't have heaters in the cars,' says the ever-practical Evelyn. In truth, some of their assistants did not impress them: they seemed to be lacking any feeling of vocation. 'There was a little Pekinese in the practice,' says Evelyn, 'named Tojo, after the Japanese wartime prime minister, because he was a little swine. I came back home after a holiday and this assistant had cut Tojo's toenails so badly that he had made every toe bleed. I said to my husband: "If it is beneath that man's dignity to cut a dog's toenails properly, he is no good and we don't want him." Some of them were going into the profession because they thought they would make a lot of money.'

They talk about matters of principle and integrity, and the importance of always honouring the trust of their clients: 'I was at Faringdon for such a long time,' says Kenneth, 'that eventually I was vet to some of my original clients' grandsons: I'd worked for their grandfathers, the whole family over the generations. And although

we had very few social friends, because we were working all the time, all our clients were our friends. I could always pop into a farm to make a phone call and have a cup of tea. I absolutely loved the old farm kitchen with the bacon hanging in the smoke, the big kitchen table covered with everything so that it all had to be pushed aside for you to sit. It was the welcome that was so wonderful; they didn't worry about the

house being tidy, and if you were dirty from your work it didn't matter. We were in our practice there for a very long time, so we were trusted. There were never any arguments about our bills…'

'We never ran up bills that they would not accept…'

'Always did things as cheaply as I could…'

Evelyn takes up that point: 'We had a very poor lady with a cat. We had sulphur drugs and antibiotics, but in fact the cat had a virus and we were only treating secondaries. Then this enthusiastic young assistant produced the latest high-falutin' drug. I asked him what he was going to charge for it. He said, "Well, there's my time and the medicine and…" "Do you know," I said, "how much money that old lady hasn't got? You could have used this, which costs far less, with equally good results." It's so important that newly qualified vets should have some idea of the cost of drugs. Even now, when average earnings are so much higher for everybody, it is quite possible to incur too much expense for owners and to cause them terrible anxiety.

'Present-day methods and equipment are marvellously improved, but we should also remember what nature herself will do. A golden retriever came in with a broken hind leg, a bad spinal fracture; I took a series of x-rays and then told the owner that the dog could go away for an extremely expensive operation, or it could be confined in a large barrel to heal itself, with proper attention to pain control and nursing. I wanted her back at six weeks, and also at six months so I could take x-ray pictures and then show the evidence to students and assistants who had never had spontaneous healing described to them. The leg would be a little short but it would probably be as good a job as internal fixation, because of the nature of the fracture.

'I once took a student with me to visit an Alsatian belonging to a groom who had three or four children and was not a well-paid man. The dog was very dodgy, very nervous, and it had a broken leg. I asked my companion what we should do about it. He said that it would have to go away and have its leg pinned, and then be in a veterinary hospital for two or three weeks. And I asked what the dog would be like when it came back to a home with small children in it, and how much all this would cost. He didn't know. So I said, "Right, I shall give the dog something now to ease the pain. We'll put a mattress on the floor in the corner there and put a fence across so that it can't run all over the house and to keep the children out of that corner; we'll see

that it has food and water there and is properly looked after, and we'll come back in 48 hours." We did so, and the dog was out of immediate pain; its leg swung about if it walked, but without hurting. I said we would come back again in another six weeks. That was all we needed to do, and it cost very little. The lad said he never knew that such healing would happen; they'd never taught him that. He was of the generation who would only use super-technology, because it's there and because that's what he had been taught.'

'Money was never the motivation for our work,' says Kenneth. 'If a farmer was in serious trouble, there was no point in bankrupting him – you charged him as little as possible until he got on his feet again.'

In 1945 their first child was born. Evelyn continued to help with the practice by taking samples, filling in forms and so on. Then her second son, Christopher, came along, and when he was about six weeks old she started doing three hours a morning for the practice, which she loved.

'Mind you, it was all jolly hard work. The cows in the early years still had horns and were as wild as anything – the sucklers and heifers weren't used to being handled and people were frightened of them when they came in, so they would be very rough with them. I've been gored and kicked at the same time by cattle. We didn't use crushes then; the cows were tied up but they could still swing their heads and kick. You'd have youngstock in a loosebox and you had to mix in with them. Some of those heifers had never been handled before, and in those days they might be up to three years old. I went into a box to test some heifers one day and had to earmark them – give them a tattoo in the ear with those big calipers, and sometimes I had to put in more than one mark. They got very cross!

One of them landed on my knee and kicked it right through — everybody heard it go crack! And I've been heaved up into a hayrack when marking an ear: a very big man had been holding the cow, and we both ended up in the hayrack!'

Kenneth interjects: 'Lyn did one of the first rumenotomies in the neighbourhood, and a Caesarean on a cow long before anyone else.'

Evelyn seems to relish her large animal surgery, and remembers a particularly challenging case. 'There was this farmer, and he could be quite a demanding man, with a good herd of Friesians being graded up, some of them very heavy milkers. This was the time when all dairy cows had horns and bullied each other, and one of his most precious ones had her hip knocked down when she was struggling through a doorway. This was an all-too-common injury: it meant that a corner of the ileum (the large and prominent hip bone) was broken off, and the attached muscles would pull it right down towards the stifle as the cow walked. In many cases the fractured edge would ride up and down on the shaft of the bone and there would be necrosis and pus formation; the pus would discharge to the outside and attract flies in the summer. I saw this cow in the spring and was asked what I could do, or she would have to be put down.

'I supposed that I would have to remove the sequestrum of bone and drain the site. I'd never done such a thing before, never heard of its being done and never worked out how to go

about it. However, Mr E asked me to go ahead, so there was no way out.

'I gave the cow chloral hydrate as a sedative and painkiller, an epidural anaesthetic and some local anaesthetic; then I scrubbed everything up and went in with a scalpel. It was a fairly hair-raising experience: I was working in what became an ever-deeper cavity, and blindly dissecting out this piece of bone — a triangle with sides five or six inches long.

'Mr E was most encouraging. "You go on, Mrs Day," he kept saying, "you're doing fine." It was a case of trying to observe first principles and keeping going. And then I heard that awful "thrr thrr thrr" — I had hit an artery and it was pumping, it was a big one. I quickly put on some artery forceps, deep in the cavity. I had also snicked a bit of the oblique tendon, so I had to tie off the artery and repair the tendon. When we got the bone out, the muscle all retracted and left a hole as big as your head. What on earth do I do with this, I wondered. I pulled the skin across it to help it heal, I packed it with a good sulphonamide, and left the artery forceps in place for six days. And the whole thing healed up a treat: she just had a little three-corner scar.

'We used to have only ourselves to depend on. My husband would not be there to help me, except for some of the calving cases. We had to be self-sufficient.' Evelyn pauses to hand round some very good home-made cake, and Kenneth points out that the training was very different in their day.

'We were of the early, five-year course, and had a reasonable scientific education at college, but the point is that we had no rules that were specific; we had no real specific cures for anything. The only specific before penicillin was in general use – and sulphonamides were still extremely expensive – were sodium iodide for wooden tongue and calcium for milk fever. Basically you were treating symptoms and nursing the animals and relying on nature to cure the condition while you kept the animal alive and as comfortable as possible. There was no question of giving it a shot of penicillin: you would sit up all night with a case of mastitis, stripping out the udder; you'd put mustard plasters on chests in case of pneumonia. The nursing of the animal was so much more important than the expensive drugs. Your role was to keep the animal alive so that nature could cure it.'

This theme leads neatly into the subject of homeopathy, which seems to run in the family. Kenneth uses it, but 'I don't like being restricted in any way! I just use it when it seems to be the most appropriate approach in a particular case.'

Evelyn is much more positive about it: 'We were on holiday in Germany in 1958, staying with one of Kenneth's cousins who is a homeopath, a consultant physician. His wife is a homeopath, too, but a surgeon by training. One day I had some terrible horsefly bites, really awful; I felt ill and quite delirious. The cousin gave me a homeopathic remedy and I was so impressed! So I read a few books, because I'd found so many conditions that would not clear up with other treatments. And I started using it for both small and large animals, and often my clients would come back and ask for "more of your little pills" because they were excellent.

'Christopher was only 11 in 1958, so he grew up with homeopathy through his school days and became more and more interested. He has gone much further with it than I have done – he's international now. I'd have liked to have gone as far, but there was no time for me to travel about, as I had a home and a family to look after as well as the practice.

'An older generation like ours feels more at home with homeopathy perhaps than the present generation because we all started with the old Pharmacopoeia; we knew more about plants and chemicals and poisons and their actions and uses. The modern vets know very little about those. You have to study your remedies and gradually, over many years, you begin to see the picture of each remedy and recognize the picture in the symptoms that you encounter. You learn from your cases; and you don't start off by saying: "This is penicillin, which treats Gram-positive bacteria." It's the other way round. Each remedy is linked with a complete picture of symptoms or one disease.'

Kenneth says gently: 'The success of my life was a wife who was extraordinarily competent, who worked with me and backed me up, always a guide, comforter and friend, someone I could discuss cases with, who contributed together with me, and who was so interested in it all. What more could one ask?'

The Days have worked extremely hard all their lives, and even after retirement from practice they continue to work hard and be busy – the secret recipe for not getting old. They describe themselves unfairly as 'garrulous old fools', but one thing is for sure: they do not need an oxometer. A what? Their son Christopher had told me to ask his father what an oxometer was.

'He did, did he? Well, easy really. An oxometer is an instrument for measuring bullshit…'

Chapter 3
JACK STRANGE, BLACKSMITH

Euan Corrie

JACK STRANGE, BLACKSMITH

Ellesmere in Shropshire was one of the principal maintenance centres of the Shropshire Union Canal system. What is now Ellesmere Yard was first established during the construction of the canal by Thomas Telford and his engineering team, under the supervision of William Jessop. With expansion and amalgamation of the region's canal system, this yard came to have responsibilities extending far beyond the original Ellesmere Canal.

Not far up the road at Welsh Frankton, Jack Strange now joins with his brother Alf in demonstrating blacksmithing and guiding visitors around their fascinating collection of rural bygones. It was in this shady and low-roofed workshop that Jack and I sat and talked. All around were the tools and products of a blacksmith's trade. The only item out of place among the ironwork was the old church pew we used, which usually

The blacksmith's shop

accommodates a row of visitors who can watch in comfort just out of range of any sparks from hearth or anvil.

Jack, very dark haired and perhaps shorter and less solidly built than one expects to find a blacksmith, talked quietly with the gentle accent of the Welsh border country: 'I left school in 1935. I was going to be a blacksmith because my dad was a blacksmith; he had a shop just down the road here, at Welsh Frankton. The time came and I went to work for him but, well, you don't always get on, do you? So I was just turned 14 when I went to work for another blacksmith who wanted an apprentice at a little place called Alberbury, by Shrewsbury. I worked for him for two-and-a-half years or so, and I got 5s a week. Hours didn't matter, though – I used to have to milk his cows in a morning and then I'd have to be in the shop for eight. I finished in the shop for five and milked the cows, and then I'd finished for the day. But if there was shoeing to be done at night, then we were shoeing! There was no worry about overtime because I got none! Back then, a half-day on Saturday was four o'clock!

'So, I'd been there about two-and-a-half years and there come a job on the canal for an apprentice blacksmith. I started about the beginning of 1939. It was the LMS railway then, that owned the canal. It was 16s a week! Quite a rise from 5s, wasn't it? After I'd been there six months they gave me another 6s because I was 17 then! The inspector down there was a Mr Boyne, and the first morning he took me up in the shop to introduce me to the blacksmiths. Of course, he didn't come to work before nine so I'd to wait from half-past seven to nine. Then he took me in the shop and introduced me and told me that this was where I was going to spend me time; and he said, "Just remember tomorrow morning, lad, it's in the shop at half-past seven, not standing down by the clock!" So that's what I'd to do; though really, you'd to be in before that because you were supposed to have the fires going at half-past seven, ready to start work on the dot. So I went there as a "temporary improver blacksmith" and I worked there until I retired, near enough 49 years, and nobody ever told me any different! So I was a temporary improver blacksmith right through!

'We did all the ironwork for the boats, and the lock gates, and everything; and all the lift-up bridges, they had handrails going off them. There were handrails through the tunnels as well, to stop people falling in in the dark, and we'd to repair them, as well – they wore out in time with the ropes, you see, the towing ropes used to cut through them.

'I'd been at the yard probably about three days, and the head blacksmith sent me down to the paintshop; I don't remember what for, now. But as soon as I went through the paintshop door it was shut and locked. Well, I was only a lad and there was three big fellows in there as well as the painter, they just lifted up my shirt and painted SUC [Shropshire Union Canal]

across my belly – in red lead paint. They said, "You'll never leave, now!" It wouldn't be possible now, it'd go to court, abuse, but then you daren't complain like. If you went down to the boss he'd just tell you to get back in the shop. But they were right, I never did leave, not till I retired!

'There was no such thing as a pleasure boat when I started. There were trade boats to Peates, who had the mill at Maesbury on the Montgomery Canal, as they call it now. They had a burst down Perry Moor, where they're building the new aqueduct at present; it burst there about 1936. Well, the LMS railway that owned the canal then did repair that because there were boats trapped up this canal [the Llangollen Canal] that were taking grain to Maesbury Mill. At that time Peates were gradually changing over to steam, they'd got quite a few steam waggons on the road. So I think the LMS must have had the idea that they wouldn't use the canal for long, and once Peates'd got their boats through they ran the water out again. You see, they filled it up to get all the boats past, and then let it all out again! It was never reopened again, until 1996.

'I know that because I lost my first job through that. I'd started work with Dad at 14 but I had a paper round – I used to go up to the village shop early in the morning and do a paper round. I had to take a paper to the house by the hump-backed bridge, Lockgate Bridge as they call it, and when I got down there, there was all this activity going on and no water in the canal – so I walked off down the towpath to see what had happened, and I didn't get back to the paper shop till two o'clock! So I was given my notice at the weekend.

'Then all this canal was legally closed about 1944, wasn't it, by act of parliament. It was a secure job when I came to Ellesmere because we worked for other sections, you see; so although the Montgomery was closed, we still made the lock gates and all that for the other sections, so they kept this canal open. But it closed in the war. I got called up, like, and I wasn't here, I went in February 1941, when I was 19, and I didn't come back until 1947. All they were really keeping it open for was to feed down to that reservoir at Hurleston.

'When I started at Ellesmere we could make pretty well everything in that yard. You see, when the canal was being built, Telford's idea was to plant trees on any banks and spare land, and by the time the lock gates wore out, the trees would be mature enough to renew the lock gates with them.

'The sawyers used to go out, you see, and they would fell the mature trees, ash, or whatever they wanted, and fetch them into the yard. We had a timber boat to fetch them: it was like an ordinary narrowboat, but it had quite a big hand-winch on it. They would cut the trunk into the lengths which they wanted for the heels of gates or whatever and fetch them into the yard. Well, there was a big gantry crane at the yard which went right out over the canal. It used to take five of you in the little box where the winch was for the grab, and you'd two fellows at each end on the chains; that was nine of you to work it. That's how we used to unload the trees, you see. Then the sawyer would number them and the yard foreman had a little book with all the details in. Then they were left to season for so many years. We made lock gates for the Trent & Mersey, Staffs & Worcs and so on, not just the Shropshire Union or even the Ellesmere and the Montgomery Canal. We made the gates for everywhere, all round the North West. We'd send them out, when they were made, on a boat, load them with that same gantry crane. If they were going to the Trent & Mersey, for instance, they'd send their own boatman

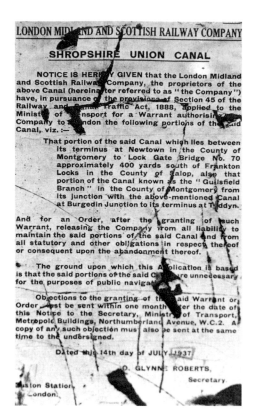

The LMS railway gives notice of its intention to apply for powers to close the canal below Frankton (Author's collection)

for them. With a horse boat, of course.

'They'd all got carpenters on their own sections, but mostly it was Whitsun time that the gates were put in, and our lock-gate makers would go out there then. Often our blacksmiths would have to go too: we had a little portable forge. You used to have to renew the paddle-rod ends, where they were fitted onto the board that covered the hole to shut the water off, you know. You'd have made a selection of paddle-rod ends in our yard, and they'd be sent on the boat – but they were all different lengths. Whilst you were putting a pair of gates in you might stay there for a week or ten days. You could weld the rod ends when they were wanted to the right length, fire-weld them. We went out like that at every Whit and there were good sports on that weekend at Ellesmere but I never got to them because I was always out at a stoppage somewhere! You got a shilling a night for lodging. You might be out ten

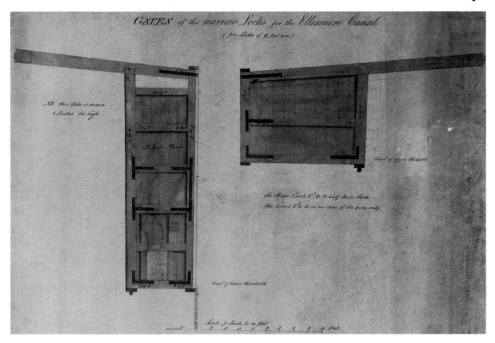

William Jessop's drawing of lock gates for the Ellesmere Canal (BW Archives, Gloucester)

days, especially with those big gates down the Chester Canal where the locks are wide. The company would find you a lodging and you got a shilling a night, but you took your own food. Mostly the lady of the house where you were staying, she would cook it for you if you took bacon or eggs and things like that.'

Nowadays, of course, British Waterways carry staff to and from remote work sites day by day in minibuses. Much time that was worked in Jack's earlier days is now spent in travelling. Materials too come by road transport from centralized workshops at Northwich, as Jack was later to explain: 'In those days, you see, we had two sawyers; there was two blacksmiths and two strikers in the shop; a fitter who worked the steam engine as well; a boilerman; also three boatbuilders, four painters, four in the lock-gate shop, two carpenters upstairs who made the patterns (they were the top notch), then of course six in the bricklaying gang (three bricklayers and three mates) and three in the dredging gang. They were all classed as tradesmen. Then of course

you'd a man on every three-mile length of the canal. You'd got your water control man on at Llangollen. There was 35 to 40 fellows on this section, that's from Llangollen to Nantwich.

'Our power was from an old railway engine because we were run by the LMS; they put it in, and set it up vertically so instead of it being on its wheels it was upright. There was a big boiler and the boilerman used to start an hour before everybody else, at half-past six in the morning to get steam up for when we got there. The fitter always started the engine up. Now, that drove one big belt, which went to a set of bevel gears. The one of those cogs was made out of cast iron, and the other had wooden teeth, because if you had two cast-iron ones running together there would have been a hell of a noise. The teeth were made out of a wood, which used to come from America, called hornbeam. It's very hard-wearing, as hard as the cast iron.

A portable blacksmith's hearth the first used at lock stoppages

The actual wheel was made out of cast iron and the wooden teeth were fitted to it and wedged.

'The engine drove all the shaft which went through the length of the blacksmith's shop and the carpenters' shop – there were belts going off it in all directions. One went upstairs and drove the planing and thicknessing machine, a lathe and the bandsaw in the carpenters' shop. In our shop it drove two lathes, a planing machine, a screwing machine, the fan that provided the wind for the fires and the guillotine. Oh, what didn't it drive? There were the saws as well for the sawyers. But there was no electric light, we had gas, in the first instance. When the electricity come we thought we'd gone to Blackpool illuminations!

The Ellesmere Canal lift-up bridge at Wrenbury, the ironwork for which, such as handrails, brackets and pivots, was produced by Jack Strange

'Then of course they decided after so many years – it was well after the war – that the old engine had about had it, and so they put motors to every machine. That was all right in the end, but it took a bit of working out because somehow electricity doesn't work like steam. We had problems with getting it to keep going with a load on, or else it would be going too fast and smashing the castings. Eventually they got

it worked out and it was all right then.

'Then, three years after, they took the lock-gate work away from Ellesmere to Northwich – I got an electric welder to help with it! I had only had oxy-acetylene welding till then. That oxy-acetylene welding was slow, you see; the old blacksmith, he wasn't very keen on it at all. He'd do everything on the fire, and of course I was trying to persuade him that the electric welding would be just as good, but he wouldn't have it. The sale irons in a lock gate (which go down the heel of the gate) are the big ones, 4in by ⅝in – you'd got to weld those. We used to slot the one end into the bar, because where you wanted to join them you would get the iron hot in the fire. Then you'd make a chisel point on the end of the bar that was to go into the sale iron, and your mate would get that hot in the other fire; you couldn't get both pieces into the heat of the same fire. Once you'd both got a welding heat on you'd come out together, and bang the chisel end into the slot and give it a tap with the sledge hammer and under the steam hammer, and that would weld it all together flat. But you'd to be pretty quick. Now there's four legs in every sale iron, and the problem was that you might get three in and miss the last one. Well, that would finish that piece of iron because you couldn't get another weld in it, so you've got to start again from square one. Once you've had a welding heat and you've missed it, it won't weld again on the same spot. Well, nobody's perfect, you did miss it occasionally.

'I kept on to this old blacksmith about what he called "glorified soldering!" So I went to Crewe works, with the canal being LMS, on a welding course and started by welding the sale irons. The first one I did, I gave it to the head blacksmith, and he just flattened it and squared it up and then he decided that he would break it. Well, eventually he did break the weld, and said "I told you that it would break." But I said, "Well, we don't hammer our welds like that, those we've done on the fire. Once we've welded them you   leave them go cold, and that's it, like. So why did you hammer that one?" So then he decided that it was all right; he just wanted to see how much it would stand.

'When you fire-welded those irons, as I said, you'd two fires going and two smiths with two strikers – all four of you working together to get the weld done before it cooled off. Well, one day I said to that smith: "Why did you suddenly take to letting me do all those welds?" "I suddenly thought," he said, "that there'd only be you losing any sweat!" But he was quite happy about it, and I used to weld everything after that. Oh, he was all right!

'The other thing we had to do was to shoe the boat horse. They were company horses that pulled the maintenance boats for carrying the lock gates and all the other materials. We had one boat at our yard, but you see, Chester section, for example, they hadn't got a blacksmith, Norbury Section hadn't either, or Welshpool. So they all used to work it so that their horse had to come to our yard to fetch something and it could get shod here. With the towpaths being metalled, as we called it, stoned over, we used to shoe them with the heels thickened up with a caulking and wedges across the toes to take the wear, and these used to last about ten weeks. Of course, as soon as you'd shod a horse with new shoes

you made another set ready for when he'd come again. You always had a set for the Welshpool horse, the Ellesmere, the Chester and the Norbury.

'I shod the last company horse to come up here. She was a lovely horse, that Molly. She was only about ten or 11 year old, nice and quiet, she'd a lovely temper. Of course she was an LMS railway horse, and they used to send their vet every so often to examine her; about every three to six months he would come. Our old boatman at that time was Jack Roberts; he was turned 65 and there were motor boats about at that time, but he wouldn't have a motor boat – he wanted his old horse. Of course, with him turning 65 they wanted to get rid of him, didn't they, and have somebody that would drive a motor boat. Well, the vet came into the yard just as I finished shoeing this horse, Molly, and there was nothing wrong with her. He said, "Run her down the yard" – I could run in those days, too, so I trotted her down the yard and back up again. He got a doctor's stethoscope and he said, "Oh, she's likely to drop dead any time, she's got a weak heart." I said, "You can't tell me that, I'm not daft!"

Loading completed lock gates at Ellesmere Yard using the gantry crane described by Jack Strange

The toothed rack which engages with a pinion wheel to operate lock paddles is attached to a long iron rod extending down through the masonry of the lock structure to an elm board which closes the water culvert when required

He said, "She'll have to go" — but he couldn't even look at me. And I said "Why couldn't you have come an hour sooner?" He said, "Why?" and I said, "Because I've just put four new shoes on her." Well, she went the following day, back to Birmingham, and of course old Jack didn't have a motor boat, and he retired soon after. But there was nothing wrong with that horse. They grieve me, things like that.

'The boat builders in the yard only did repairs in my time. They built new punts for the lengthsmen and maintenance work and put cabins on, and they did a lot of repairs to boats off other sections as well.

'I mentioned before that they decided to transfer the lock-gate making to Northwich — they could weld much quicker than what I could in the fire. So of course I was to be made redundant then, after all that while. There was no room at Northwich to go to, see. But they didn't actually stop me immediately because we did a big repair job then. Ponty [Pontcysyllte] Aqueduct had got into a terrible state — a lot of the railings had gone, the towing path was non-existent — and I

Welding sale irons for lock gates

had the job of repairing all that and putting all the railings back, renewing all the ironwork of the towpath and everything. That was in 1964, and it took nearly nine months to do that.

'I had quite an argument with the personnel officer because I wanted more money to go up there. We hadn't got any scaffolding. Of course, these days you wouldn't think of doing it like that, with all the safety rules. I said, "What happens if I fall off?" "Oh no, you can't have any more money!" Anyway, I refused to go. After about a fortnight this personnel officer came and I took him up there and started to walk over. Well, I'd got about 20 yards across the aqueduct and he hadn't started to walk out on to it. So I shouted to him and said, "Aren't you going to come any further?" He said, "No, will you accept 6d an hour?" Well, 6d an hour was quite a bit then. So I went then, and I was in charge of that job. But as soon as we finished, which was on a Friday night, my 6d an hour stopped, on the Friday night. I didn't get it for that Saturday morning! It just stopped dead.

'Well, then I was for off, and where I was going I didn't know. But then the foreman's job came up at Ellesmere Yard and they gave me that job. Of course they killed two birds with one stone like that, because I was doing the blacksmithing and the foreman's job.

'I don't know why, but they'd let the aqueduct go very badly; they'd suddenly decided they weren't going to do any more repairs to it. Before that we'd had fellows up there in the winter doing nothing but ice-breaking because they didn't want the ice to get solid and bust it. But they suddenly stopped that. It was frightening for one or two winters because we thought it would burst.

'The aqueduct wasn't leaking when we

started to do all those repairs. The horses had gone off the canal so they didn't need the towing path, and the tourists used to go down the bottom and cross the river by the road bridge. A lot of the workers from Monsanto's chemical works lived in The Vron, and they had been able to get a permit to go over the aqueduct because it was the shortest route to work. They paid the company, I think it was about 2s a year. Of course, once the holes started to come in the towing path over the aqueduct they couldn't walk or go on their bikes. I think that was one thing that started them thinking about repairing it.

'The castings were made at a foundry, in Widnes, I think. They were very good castings too; I believe the name of them was Platts. When we come to do the Ponty Aqueduct I found all the patterns in the pattern shop for all the standards and everything, the cross-members of the towing path, everything. The one cross-member was stamped something like 1894, which made me think that it had probably been renewed once before. The canal would be nearly a hundred years old then.

'Every two feet there was a cross-member, like a T-iron from the outside of the trough to standards fixed upright from the trough bottom. Those had an angle bar running along their tops right through from one end of the aqueduct to the other, forming the front edge of the towing path. Then there had been an iron sheet shaped to fit over the top of those angle bars, but we used some old trench sheeting and cut it to size. We filled over the top of that with rubble and tarmaced the towing path surface. When we came to it, we found that each bay, between the flanges of the plates that formed the bottom of the trough, was filled up with ash; I think the reason was to stop mud collecting by giving it a level

A horse-drawn maintenance boat at work near Hurleston on the Ellesmere Canal on 4 September 1957 (Edward Paget-Tomlinson)

bottom – it kept the mud moving out with the movement of the boats. Well, we never refilled it with ash and I think that was a mistake. The most amazing part was that all those big bolts that are through the flanges, the vast majority, if you gave them a tap with the hammer, the nut would spin right off. The original ones couldn't have been made of ordinary iron. It didn't corrode, that's a certainty. We hardly made any new ones, perhaps two or three hundred of all the thousands that are in there. Ours were iron where we couldn't re-use the original ones. We didn't have to do any repairs to the trough: the only thing we did to the trough was to caulk some of the joints with a lead wool. Frank Rowland (he was our painter and plumber) did that with a caulking iron, like you would a boat.

'There was a lot of blisters on the cast plates and we knocked those off, like air bubbles they are. Then we had an epoxy resin which we could mix together and fill the holes in. The only thing was, once you'd put it in the hole you'd to stop with it, or it would just sort of slip out and hang there – so you kept pushing it back. Well, eventually you'd say, "Oh, leave it and we'll push it back in a minute." And then it would go off rock hard and you couldn't do anything with it! You'd got to knock that piece off then and do it again!

'There's two crosses cast in plates on that aqueduct, and nobody knows why. There's no engineering value to them. Whether

there was two fellows killed building it, and somebody in the foundry made two plates with crosses, nobody knows. Otherwise all the plates are the same, and they are wedge-shaped so they wedge themselves in as well as being held with the bolts. Our carpenter, he put a wooden fender all along the edge of the towpath, made from greenheart.

'It's funny, but I don't think anybody was really interested in what we were doing. We worked up there till half-past five, and by the time we got back to the yard the others had all gone. If I wanted anything I'd got to leave a note to Jim Howard, the inspector, and say how many bearers I wanted cast, and so on. We didn't really know how many we wanted until we'd uncovered them, like, and did each section. Then we'd know we wanted another dozen cross-members or whatever. We did a 30ft length at a time so that we never had more than a 10ft gap in the railings at a time. Also, you see, we had to fill the trough every other weekend to feed the water board reservoir at Hurleston. So we couldn't work that weekend. We only had it empty about five or six weeks altogether. During that time we renewed all the standards under the edge of the towing path and put the two angle-iron bars, under the front and back of the path, right the way through. We finished that by Easter. We used to close it at eight o'clock when we got there, and it would be closed till twelve o'clock, and although it had water in it we wouldn't let anybody through. You see, we'd got our own work boat on there, we couldn't keep pulling it off. But dinner time was twelve till one, so we'd pull the boat off and let the pleasure boats go across whilst we had dinner. Then they'd have to stop again for the afternoon, and then we'd open it again when we finished for the night.

'It was a marvellous piece of work, that aqueduct. They must have brought those

Pontcysyllte Aqueduct with a boatman and his donkeys on the towpath (opposite)

Work on the dewatered trough and towpath of Pontcysyllte Aqueduct in 1963–4

plates by horse and cart from the foundry which was where Monsanto is now – but how did they get them across the top of those pillars? They're only seven or eight feet by ten feet at the top, and over 100ft high – hardly room to stand. I can understand them getting them up on the top flat, but how do you hold the next one there while you get the bolts through the flanges? You're talking about 200 years ago, and there'd be no road crane to help you! It's an amazing piece of work. We were there hardly nine months: we started in the January and finished at the end of August or beginning of September, and we were there every day.'

The present re-asserted itself for a few minutes as Alf Strange showed a small party of visitors around the workshop, and talk turned to small items of ornamental ironwork. But soon our thoughts returned to one of the largest iron structures in Britain.

'As I've said, the aqueduct job gave me another nine months' work, and at the end of that time, just as we were finishing off, this foreman's job came up. Fred Thomas had been doing this job, and the engineer at the time was Mr Cotton, Bob Cotton. The first time I met him was after I'd been hanging out for that bit of extra money at the start of the aqueduct job; we got on very well, and after he'd finished work we'd have a couple of cans of beer if ever he was up here.

Puddling clay for leak stopping

'Fred had been doing this foreman's job and everybody thought he would have it. Well, I thought there was no harm in asking, and I'd nothing to go to at the

time. As I've said, Mr Cotton was a friend to me – and he gave me the job. Fred would be 60 odd by then. So I had 22 or 23 years to go, then. I didn't dislike the foreman's job, I knew what I'd got to do, like, but I've always liked working with my hands, you know. But you've got to rely on fellows. It's no good me trying to tell a carpenter what to do. If you're a tradesman you should respect other tradesmen and rely on them. Fred was a good canalman in general, you couldn't beat him on leaks or anything like that, but if he was in charge of a job, the carpenters and so on wouldn't take any notice of him – they'd no respect, because he wasn't a tradesman. If you were a tradesman you could say to them, so-and-so has to be done; and they would say, "How do you want it done?" and I'd say, "Well, you're the carpenter. If you want any blacksmithing doing, I'll do it for you." With Fred they would have played up more.

'On the other hand, if it was night-time or a weekend when you weren't working and you got a leak anywhere, Fred was the first one you called because there was nobody better than him to stop a leak. Brilliant. It was the same with puddling clay. It was only the year after I got the foreman's job that we had a major breach at Bettisfield, and it was up to me to be in charge of it. You have to rely on your canalmen to puddle the clay properly in a situation like that, so you have to have respect for them. They are the fellows that have been puddling clay all their lives. I don't really know why that one went; we didn't know there was any leak there, it just went out

The aftermath of the breach of the newly repaired concrete canal channel near Trevor, demonstrating the scouring power of the escaping water which created this gash in the hillside (Waterways World)

in the night. In those few years we had three or four major breaches in our canal, and every one went on either a Friday night or a Saturday night! It was always when we'd all gone home and you'd to go round knocking people up and that, to turn them out.

'There was one at Bryn Howell, up on the feeder length towards Llangollen. That went about 1946 while I was still abroad, and it washed away the railway which was below the canal. All that along there is an embankment like a terrace along the hillside. The canal is in a clay channel, puddled, and it stands on sand. The sand is all compacted, it's very good for that; you can compact sand very hard. Well, that one went in 1946. There was another one up there in the 1950s, I suppose, and they fixed that the old-fashioned way with compacted sand. You make a wide base and then step it

in a bit to make it narrower, and come up again with more sand, so you are making a base that is a lot wider than the water channel. You keep building it up and making steps in it like that, and then put your clay trough on the top. The sand will stay just moist, and well compacted, and it won't run like that. And it's not long before grass starts to grow on it like that.

'It went again, this breach did, in the early 70s. Well, not in just the same place, but about a quarter mile nearer Trevor. It was in the early morning, and so of course we shot up there and started to clear it all out and put the stop planks in and everything. Well, the engineer was Mr Haskins at the time, and he came up from Northwich, and he said "Do no more – it's going to be put out to contract." I said we'd made a start, but he replied: "I've got my orders – I'm not to get you to do it." Well, these contractors come in, and I used to go up there with Jim Howard and see what they were doing. They were building it up on sand, but I felt they were not doing it right! The base wasn't broad enough. But what can you say if you're not doing the job? They went and put a fellow in charge who was straight out of an office. I used to say to him (and he'd a better job than I'd got), "How on earth can you come out of an office and take charge of a job like this?" He said, "It's just professional jealousy with you!"

'Well, anyhow, they built it. Give Mr Haskins his due, he said, "What do you think of it?" I said, "I wouldn't like to say it'll last, and I wouldn't like to say when it's going to go, but I don't think it'll last long." He said, "What's wrong with it?" and I replied, "Well, they've built it too straight, there's no width to the base, they've come straight up vertically to the concrete channel walls, it isn't going to hold like that." Well, of course, this contractor's bloke out of the office, he said we didn't know what we were talking about. Well, all right, we don't; I was only a blacksmith.

'They had a big notice painted, a terrific thing: "This breach was repaired by such a firm at a total cost of three-quarters of a million pounds, and it was done in such a time" and all this, that and the other. Well, we never had a notice like that when we repaired anything!

'Anyway, the water engineers from Northwich put some piezometers, do you call them, in the bank at this breach, because when they put the water in first it leaked! Straightaway! These things will show them if there's water leaking, and well, they were registering leakage all the while, right from when it was first filled. So I was up there one morning, I forget just what for, and the lads from Northwich were there taking the measurements; and the one shouted to the others to come up on top of the bank and take a look. I went up on the bank too, and the water in the canal was going down like weirs. I said "What's causing that? There's no boats about!" And all of a sudden, whoosh! It was away, right where they had been standing! Concrete and all, down the hillside.

'The first job I had to do was get those notices down! After that they built it all up again, and decided to concrete it near enough all through to Llangollen. I was at Northwich a bit later for a meeting over it, with Jim Howard, and this office fellow from the contractors, and he said, "I don't want you to say anything, either!" And I said, "I shan't say anything, unless I'm asked."

'There's a lot to be said for listening to the old canal people like Fred Thomas who had puddled clay and fixed leaks all his life. When you went out to a leak with chaps like that, they'd find the leak while you were getting out of the van! It was almost like a dog with scent, they seemed to know where to go. You'd find water coming out, and naturally you'd think "It's leaking just over the bank, here." But they'd walk off up the canal and call to you "It's away up here!" They could find it yards away from where you expected it to be. But all that's gone, now.'

Chapter 4
THE BRAKE VAN MAN

Tom Quinn

THE BRAKE VAN MAN

IN THE OLD DAYS, ACCORDING TO JOHN KERLEY, THE DRIVER DROVE THE TRAIN BUT THE GUARD WAS IN CHARGE OF IT. IMMENSELY PROUD OF HIS 40-ODD YEARS ON THE RAILWAYS, JOHN, NOW 73, IS SADDENED BY THE FACT THAT THE GUARD NO LONGER PLAYS SUCH A VITAL ROLE; BUT HE'S ALSO GRATEFUL THAT HE KNEW THE RAILWAY INDUSTRY WHEN THE TRAIN WAS STILL KING OF THE TRANSPORT SYSTEM. HE WAS BORN IN THE STREET WHERE HE STILL LIVES, AND HIS FIRST JOB ON LEAVING SCHOOL AT THE AGE OF 14 WAS AS AN ELECTRICIAN'S MATE. HE WAS IMMEDIATELY THROWN INTO ONE OF THE BUSIEST PERIODS OF HIS LIFE, AS MOST OF LONDON'S HOUSES WERE IN THE PROCESS OF BEING CONVERTED FROM GAS LIGHTING TO ELECTRICITY, A PROCESS THAT CONTINUED THROUGHOUT THE 1930S.

Tiring of the electrician's life, John worked in a dairy, making pats of butter. Then war started and he joined the Navy. It wasn't until he was 25 that he finally found the career that suited him – and this is perhaps rather surprising, given that several members of his family were already employed on the railways: his wife's uncle, her father and his aunt, to name just a few. 'My father-in-law was a loco inspector, and he was sure I'd enjoy working on the railways. He was pretty convincing, too. They were also crying out for staff at the time so it wasn't too difficult to get a job. I was interviewed at King's Cross and my first job was awful – I had to do shifts that started at 1am or 2am or 3am: that was all they gave me because the night trains had to be covered, and the last man to be taken on always started at the bottom in every respect.'

John spent the first three weeks of his career as a porter at Hatfield. He sorted parcels, swept the platforms and helped people with their luggage: 'I did all the basic things. Despite what most people think, carrying people's luggage was not really part of the porter's work; we called it weaselling because you were really trying to ingratiate yourself to get a tip.'

After just three weeks at Hatfield, John left portering behind and was sent to King's Cross as a trainee guard. He spent four weeks working with an experienced guard to get used to the various duties and routines: 'I'd start at 8am by reporting to the guard superintendent who'd tell me which guard to report to. Then I'd be shown the sidings, because guards guarded the train as well as the passengers. We were responsible for backing trains into sidings – they were never driven in, always backed in, with the guard directing operations and signalling to the driver who, of course, couldn't really see where he was going. It could be tricky, too, reversing into the sidings, because you had to know all the signals and setbacks.

'There were no phones either, in those days, which meant that you had to use hand signals and lamps to get the driver to do what you wanted him to do. After four weeks I was put in front of the signals inspector who quizzed me on all the rules and regulations and working practices. I found it all a bit of an ordeal; inspectors in those days always seemed solemn and very important, but I think I passed all right simply because I'd had a really good teacher. The guards in those days really knew their stuff. The other curious thing about this time was that you decided yourself when you were ready to go in front of the inspector. Might sound a funny way to do it, but it actually worked very well because it put the onus on you to learn fast.'

From King's Cross, John went to Barnet and Enfield, where he spent much of his time shunting in the sidings. These were the days before roads and container lorries had begun to eat into the railways' almost total domination of transport. Thus at Barnet and Enfield there were sidings everywhere, and so many coaches that they were kept off the road for as much as six months at a time.

'In these early days,' remembers John, 'I worked mostly on what was called the empty coach link, the shift of men who brought empty coaches into London or took them out from London to Barnet and Enfield and the sidings. When we put the coaches together we had to check all the electrical connections to make sure all the lighting and so on would work, as well as the vacuum and steam pipes. We'd also check that windows were closed and handbrakes off. As guards working in the shunting yards we were so busy we hardly had time to breathe; it was mucky work,

too, but we were never given overalls, and this always struck me as odd – firemen, cleaners and drivers all got overalls, but not us. Just one of the peculiarities of the old railway, I suppose.'

But John is keen to emphasize that drivers relied heavily on the skill and experience of the guard. And if the mainline guard knew which guard had checked the train and put it together, he'd know whether or not to make his own checks. These days, on the other hand, as John himself points out, the guard is a sort of glorified ticket collector.

'In my day the guard was an important man, vital to the safe operation of the train. There were three links among the guards: the lowest, where we all started, was the empty coach link when you were simply getting coaches ready and bringing them to where they needed to be. Then, strictly according to seniority, you moved up to the local link, which meant you worked on trains doing local runs; and finally the top link meant you were on mainline trains. There were also two volunteer links, for the Newcastle and Edinburgh run – they were volunteer because you had to lodge away from home, but they paid extra.

'Trains were machine-washed every day if they were going to the sidings at Hornsey; but if they were destined for Holloway they weren't washed by machine, they were all washed by hand, simply because there were enough people to do the work!'

Like drivers, guards had to know the road before they were allowed out. John learned the road to various places from King's Cross – places like Peterborough – and then had to sign a legally binding document to confirm it. Placing the responsibility on the individual in this way was important as lives depended on it, in a very real sense. John and his fellow guards used to make their own 'road books', notebooks in which they drew the various routes and lines, and the positions of signals and crossings on them.

'There were always moments of drama, too – I remember trains occasionally lost steam on a steep incline north of Wood Green in North London where what we called a jack catch was installed. This was a device designed to derail a train that lost all steam and began to slip back. We used N2 steam engines for local work, and on another incline, this time towards Finsbury Park, they'd get stuck occasionally if they hadn't had a run at the hill or if the sand was poor and the line wet.

'If the train stopped here we used to leap out and put detonators on the track, the idea being that when a relief train approached to give us a hand, it would know how close it was to the stalled engine

The King's Cross guards' rest room in 1951, with John on the far left

as it backed into position. The rescue engine driver would then blow what we called a cock crow on his whistle before he got going with the stalled train behind him. I'd usually be out there with a lamp helping when this sort of thing happened – and I remember, too, it was awful if you had to do all this in a tunnel, because the noise of the detonators used to bring down great falls of soot from the tunnel roof; by the

time you got out you were covered in the stuff. The drivers hated the noise of the detonators going off in tunnels, too, and they'd try to get you to put down fewer than you were supposed to.'

As time went by John found that he could spot problems long before they arose, although that didn't always mean he was able to do anything about them. For instance: 'At Wood Green I could always tell when a train was about to get stuck – we'd have a run at the hill, and if the engine and first carriage got over the top of the hill I knew we were all right; but if only the engine got over, we were in trouble.' In a situation like this the train stopping would mean delay and serious disruption to the timetable. Drivers, guards and firemen always hated unpunctuality – but despite the best efforts of all concerned, things still, occasionally, went wrong. It was the price that had to be paid for a railway system that relied heavily on the skills of train crews and on what by today's standards were remarkably primitive, if magnificent, engines.

'Drivers, and everyone else for that matter, were very proud of their good time-keeping, which is probably why we didn't get stuck that often. When it did happen, I'd walk back to the nearest signalbox so the signalman knew we'd blocked the line up ahead. The guard always had a vacuum brake in his van and that went down, too, if the train was stuck. When you think that the old Pullman train might weigh 440 tons you can see that they took some pulling, and that there were bound to be problems now and then; certainly the sand would always be running as we approached a hill. Certain things were not such a problem in the steam days as they are now: wet leaves, for example, because the old engines would crush through the leaves. Diesels are lighter and don't crush through, so they are more likely to slip. Snow was always more of a problem with diesel electrics, too, because it used to make their motors short out, something that obviously could never happen with steam trains. The only problem with snow in the steam era was that it mucked up the mechanical signalling.

'I remember on the 7.45am to Leeds once there was so much snow that we didn't get back till three o'clock the following morning. That was caused by two feet of snow, and with that much, all the signals broke down and you had to crawl along. You had to stop at every light and go back and protect your train with detonators under what was called time interval service; and of course as a result of all this, journeys would be badly delayed.'

With electronic signalling unaffected by weather, the responsibilities of all railway workers, but especially guards and porters, have been greatly reduced – and that, of course, means that the jobs are more mundane, and so less satisfying than they were.

John also points out that guards and drivers were often quite close in their relationship because they relied on each other: 'They trusted each other because they had to. I remember some marvellous drivers. There was Tiddler Wilson, for example, a wonderful man, who was so short he had the regulator bent in order to reach it. The other reason you tended to work closely with the drivers was that you worked regularly with the same small group of men, and a lot of people knew each other or were even related to each other. On the local link, I worked mostly with ten drivers, and my wife's uncle was one of them.'

When the present Duke of Kent got married, John was the guard on the VIP train that took Winston Churchill and

Clement Atlee to York where the wedding took place; it was packed with dignitaries and MPs, most of whom John remembers as friendly and courteous. At one time or another he has also met Lord Home, Harold Wilson, Ted Heath and numerous football teams!

'In those days almost everyone went by train,' he says wistfully. 'Prince Philip was a frequent rail traveller, and he always seemed to be in a hurry when I saw him, striding along and oblivious to everything. Famous people could be surprisingly forthcoming, too; I remember being astonished early one Sunday morning to find Douglas Home – he was then foreign secretary, so it must have been late 1950s or early 1960s – waiting for his car. We started chatting, and he told me what he was

June 1961: John was proud to take his place as one of the guards on the Royal Train on the occasion of the Duke and Duchess of Kent's wedding

'... a side rod had come away from the engine ...'

planning to do as foreign minister. I suppose he was really just thinking aloud, but I was terrified for a minute that he might ask my advice!'

Despite the early years of unsocial shift work and low pay, John stuck at the job and began to move slowly up the links. He also began to enjoy himself, although the level of responsibility never diminished: 'Bowling along in the guard's van was enjoyable once you were on a good link, but I had six big journals to keep up to date – all the stations we passed and the times at which we passed them had to be filled in, and even in the dark you always had to know where you were. Twenty minutes were allowed for the King's Cross to Hatfield journey, and if we were late I was held to account for it; a couple of yellow signals followed by a red would all be logged in one of my books as evidence for delays. I might even attribute delay to the driver if I felt he wasn't driving particularly well. The book, or journal, was seen by every area you passed through so that all information could, if necessary, be corroborated.'

British Railways had standardized brake vans by the mid-1950s, and they were fitted with a periscope so the guard could see over the top. Earlier guards' vans had a sort of bulge at the top fitted with windows; but despite greater visibility and improved equipment, mishaps still occurred, though they were rare; for instance: 'I can remember approaching Arlsey in Hertfordshire when part of the motionwork came off the train – a side rod had come away from the engine. One end was still attached and the other was smashing into the gravel ballast at the side of the rail and throwing huge amounts of it up and over the carriages; I could hear it raining down on the roof. That was a nasty incident, because if the rod had come off completely the train would probably have been derailed. Luckily it stayed on long enough for us to be able to stop.'

One interesting little trick remembered by John was the use of scent bottles to give advance warning of bearings overheating, often the cause of serious failure. These small bottles of scent were fitted next to the motions under the boiler – if the motionwork got too hot, the bottle broke, and the driver smelled the evaporating scent and knew he had a problem. John was always fascinated by the ancient heating systems on the old steam trains, but he is adamant that, in most cases, they did their job. In fact, these trains were heated directly by steam from the engine itself.

'On a very cold winter's day,' explains John, 'you had to watch it because if you lost power you lost heat, too, for the passengers. The steam went through thick pipes under the seats. I knew when we were in trouble because at the back of the train I needed 20lb pressure at least, and if it got below that I knew it was time to start worrying. In my time I worked on N1s, N2s, J50s and J52s, A1s, A2s, A3s and A4s – just about everything. The best was the A3, I think; the drivers loved them too, because they provided a good ride.

'Guards' vans were always freezing, though; until British standard vans came in you had a little cubby hole in the corner of the van with a tiny heater and a little coal fire that would get white hot sometimes, with the draught created by our speed. In the guard's van in the early days you also had a little cooker where you cooked your breakfast. I'd always managed a very nice fry-up by the time we got to Peterborough!'

By 1957 John was working in the top guards' link at King's Cross, with the mainline passenger trains: 'It's a curious thing, and I'm by no means saying it was a good thing, but in those days everyone – train drivers, guards, porters and engineers – went to the pub at lunchtime and had a beer or two, and there were never, or very rarely, any accidents. But then railways were not just a way to make a living, they were a way of life. That's why when it snowed you would often find guards, supervisors, porters and other station staff helping out. I think we had a lot of pride in the job because we always seemed to be doing things we didn't really have to do.

The funniest thing I can remember was being told to get a bunch of yobos out of a first-class compartment; so I went along, but having checked their tickets discovered it was Jimi Hendrix and his entourage!'

But what looked like trouble sometimes really did turn out to be trouble – like the time John came across a particularly rowdy individual on the train to Peterborough. With no telephone or other means to get help he used his wits – and a potato!

'I couldn't think what else to do, so I wrapped a message round a spud and threw it to the next signalman, who telegraphed ahead. The trouble-maker was booted off when we got to Peterborough.'

From his very earliest days John remembers men who would have started work in the early part of the century, such as Old Gore, the stationmaster at King's Cross who always wore a top hat and tails, and always saw the Flying Scotsman off in person at 10am on Fridays. In many ways the railway year was divided up by the seasons and special dates for which special

King's Cross station in 1953, with the Doncaster train about to leave

trains had to be provided; thus there would be excursion trains in summer, and at King's Cross, special trains for the opening of the grouse shooting season: 'August 12 seemed to cause a mass evacuation to the moors of the north by wealthy Londoners,' says John with a grin. 'The trains were packed with sportsmen. They'd turn up with half a ton of stuff – dogs, guns, hampers and countless bags.'

Like many railwaymen, John welcomed the new diesel engines when they began to appear, but he soon realized that in the very process of solving old problems, they created new ones: 'They robbed us of overtime, for a start, because they were quicker – too quick, if you ask me! And

they had no magic about them, just simple efficiency. Even at the time people realized that.'

As the steam trains disappeared and were replaced by diesel, so other changes took place at King's Cross, not least the vast increase in the numbers of railway enthusiasts: 'Train-spotters always struck me as a bit of an oddity,' says John, 'because they knew far more about the engines than any railwayman ever did. Some of those kids were there every day of the week, and they not only knew every engine, but they knew exactly where it had come from!'

John was eventually promoted to cleaning supervisor, which put him in charge, but took him off the trains

NIGHT TRAINS TO SCOTLAND FOR THE TWELFTH

The finest fleet of trains in the world steams North to Scotland every day and is specially augmented for the 12th. Day and night they leave Euston, King's Cross and St. Pancras with their restaurants and sleeping-cars (first and third class) and their excellent staffs of servants. Below is a full list of night trains. Times of day trains will be supplied on request at any L M S or L·N·E·R station or office.

FROM EUSTON (L M S)
WEEKDAYS

P.M.		A.M.	
7.20 AB	"The Royal Highlander"—Perth, Boat of Garten, Inverness, Aberdeen	12.30 DE	Dumfries, Kilmarnock, Glasgow.
7.30 AB	Oban		SUNDAYS
7.40 AB	Stirling, Gleneagles, Dundee	P.M.	
8.0 A	Dumfries, Stranraer Harbour, Turnberry.	7.20 B	"The Royal Highlander"—Perth, Boat of Garten, Inverness.
9.25	Glasgow (On Saturdays, Third Class Sleeping Accommodation only)	7.30 B	Stirling, Oban, Gleneagles, Perth, Dundee, Aberdeen.
		8.30	Dumfries, Stranraer, Turnberry.
10.50	Edinburgh, Stirling, Gleneagles, Perth, Dundee, Aberdeen, Inverness.	9.30	Glasgow (Cent.)
		10.50	Edinburgh, Stirling, Gleneagles, Perth, Dundee, Aberdeen, Oban
11.45	"Night Scot"—Glasgow	11.45	"Night Scot"—Glasgow

NOTES: A Saturdays excepted   B Dining Car Euston to Crewe
D Saturday nights and Sunday mornings excepted   E Sleeping Cars to Kilmarnock.

FROM KING'S CROSS (L·N·E·R)
WEEKDAYS AND SUNDAYS

P.M.		P.M.	
*7.25 R	"The Highlandman"—Edinburgh, Fort William (Breakfast car attached en route) Perth, Inverness	†10.35	Edinburgh, Glasgow (North Berwick. First class only and on Friday nights only.)
*7.40 R	"The Aberdonian"—Edinburgh, Dundee, Aberdeen, Elgin, Lossiemouth	A.M.	
†10.25	"The Night Scotsman"—Glasgow, Dundee, Aberdeen, Perth	§1.5	After-Theatre Sleeping and Breakfast Car Train. Edinburgh, Glasgow, Dundee, Aberdeen, Perth, Inverness.

Nightly (except Saturdays)   † Nightly. § Daily (except Sunday mornings).
R Restaurant Car King's Cross to York.

FROM ST. PANCRAS (L M S)

WEEKDAYS		SUNDAYS	
P.M.		P.M.	
9.15	Edinburgh, Perth, Aberdeen, Inverness.	9.15	Edinburgh, Perth, Aberdeen, Inverness.
9.30	Dumfries, Kilmarnock and Glasgow (St. Enoch).	9.30	Dumfries, Kilmarnock and Glasgow (St. Enoch).

With a return ticket to Scotland, you now have the choice of travelling back by the East Coast, West Coast, or Midland routes, with break of journey at any station. PENNY A MILE SUMMER TICKETS are issued every day (first class only two thirds higher) for return any time within one month—break your journey at any station. Ask at any L·N·E·R or L M S Station or Office for Pocket Timetables and Programme of Circular Tours

IT'S QUICKER BY RAIL

LONDON MIDLAND & SCOTTISH RAILWAY
LONDON & NORTH EASTERN RAILWAY

themselves. Though the job was less interesting, it did, however, bring him into contact with some unusual passengers – such as 20 Miss World entrants – 'I didn't really think much of them, actually,' says John.

By the 1970s John had been promoted to operating assistant at Bounds Green, his last job before retirement in 1989. He had completed 40 years of service, and never really wanted to retire: 'Being a guard meant you became quite well-known, particularly among the drivers. Although it was a serious job, we had a lot of fun and I can tell you that guards were probably the best domino players in the world! I have fond memories of working as a guard.'

John has also achieved a certain immortality through a derailment on the north-east line at a place called Offord: as he was on the train that was derailed, the spot became known as 'Kerley's Corner'. But John's most solemn memory is of the arrival at King's Cross of the funeral train of King George VI. All the pillars in the station had been draped with purple and the station was absolutely silent. 'All you could hear were the quiet commands of the officer in charge,' says John, 'and then the slow march of the pallbearers.'

The old railway was full of anomalies and quirky working practices that by modern standards seem almost bizarre; even John was baffled occasionally. 'I could never understand why guards were issued with a watch, while drivers were not. I've always supposed – but it's a bit of a guess – that it was because once the driver knew the road he would drive almost by instinct, whereas us poor guards had to fill in precise times in our ledgers.'

Chapter 5
COMPETITIVE SPIRIT

Brian P Martin

COMPETITIVE SPIRIT

In 1993, 88-year-old Ivan Birley was given a conservation reward by the BBC's Country File television programme. But it was by no means the first trophy on his bulging Buckinghamshire sideboard. Throughout his long life Ivan has striven to be top of the tree, both at work and play: not only has he shown others the way with prize-winning hedges and cattle, but he has also won many trophies for darts and dominoes. But then, he did gain inspiration from his father, a competitor of equal renown.

Proudly, Ivan told me that his father 'was the first man in England to breed tri-coloured mice: Highfield Sensation, Highfield Fredricka and Highfield Josephia, which were black, white and tan.' To mark the 1905 achievement, the splendidly named National Mouse Club awarded Birley senior a beautiful silver medal, which Ivan still treasures. Rather appropriately, Ivan was also a product of that prize-winning year, being born on 28 November at Long Eaton, in Derbyshire. One of eleven children, of whom he is the sole survivor, he was the son of a lace-maker by trade, but a countryman by instinct. 'Dad was always showing vegetables, and in 1913 he had a bronze medal for kidney beans at Crystal Palace. He also used to judge rabbits, and the cottage I was born in was named "Ancona" after the fowls he used to show.

'In 1913 we went to live at Risley, where my dad took two acres of ploughland and six acres of grass, though he still worked at the factory. He took orders for vegetables, and me and my brother would deliver them with a barrow in the evenings. Also, when I was just eight we went muck-knocking – scattering the cow's heaps about the fields with a fork – for sixpence a day on a nearby farm.'

When he was 12 and a half, Ivan began his long association with cattle, milking half-a-dozen cows at 6am and again after school, on a farm at Long Eaton. At the age of 13 he was taken on full-time. 'You could leave school then if you had put in so many attendances. I also had to pulp mangolds in a machine, put hay through a chaffcutter for cattle feed and help put the bedding straw in the barn when the thresher came round.'

In 1918 Ivan left home for the first time, to live and work on a farm at Chaddesden. 'I worked for a dealer who used to go off and buy about 400 sheep and cattle at a time. Every Tuesday and Friday I walked the three miles with the drover into Derby market, and I'd already done another three fetchin' 'em up from by the river. But the drover walked much further than me. He came all the way from Ilkeston and would gather up various lots of cattle along the way. My pay was ten bob a week, and no "nine-to-five" days.'

Then Ivan moved to a farm at Repton, where he had to feed and muck out the

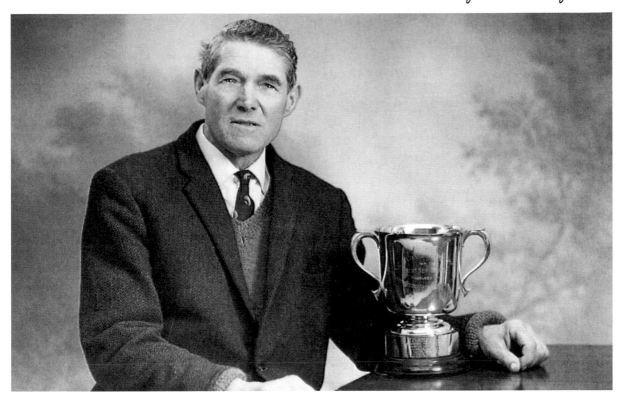

cattle, all shorthorns. He describes the routine: 'In winter they was tied up in sheds in individual stalls and let out into the yard to get water twice a day. In summer they were out in fields and tied up twice a day for milking. In those days there was no proper record of milk yields on most farms, and as long as a bull looked like a bull, that was all right. A shorthorn heifer used to give about one gallon a day and a cow about three gallons, but today it's all scientific and the yields have increased steadily since the war. Now in decent herds a heifer can give five gallons and a cow six or seven gallons.

'After the first war, things were very different. Long Eaton became a ghost town. You used to be able to hear all the clatter-bang of the lace-making machines, but they were all closed down.'

In 1923, at 17 years of age, Ivan joined the army and went to Egypt and India with the Leicesters. His time was up in 1931 'when Ghandi was on the go', but he had to stay on for an extra six months 'for the trooping season: in those days troop ships only came to India from September to March.'

Ivan married in 1931, when he was on a vocational training course to be a chauffeur/gardener at Swindon; but then

Ivan with the Coape-Arnold trophy which he won for the best year's growth in 1966, in competition with 160 hedge-layers

FARMERS WEEKLY

NATIONAL HEDGE-LAYING & DITCHING CONTEST

The Fields, Lowfield Heath, Surrey, 3rd March, 1966.

This is to certify that

IVAN P. BIRLEY

WON COAPE - ARNOLD CHALLENGE TROPHY. PRIZE

IN THE BEST YEARS GROWTH CLASS

DATED THIS DAY 2nd MARCH 1967

Editor

THAME SHOW
1971
HEDGE CUTTING COMPETITION.
CHAMPION

J.B. Hornby.
Secretary.

he was unemployed for 18 months. Eventually he moved back to Long Eaton and worked for a company making artificial silk at Spondon.

Just before World War II he went to work on a farm near Swindon. As he was in a reserved occupation he pretended to be a 'bombed-out shopkeeper' when applying to join the army, but he was still turned down. So he remained in farming for the rest of his working life, mostly in the Midlands and Cotswolds, and the last 30 years on a farm at Oakley, in Buckinghamshire.

It was during the war that Ivan started hedge-laying. 'I was working on a farm near Great Dalby, in Leicestershire, when this old chap of 71 showed me how to go on. As

a cattle-man it was quite a natural thing to learn because a good stockman is a good fencer and hedger; he doesn't want to see his stock get out, so he makes his fences sound.'

Hedge-laying has always been most widely practised in areas where stock farming has predominated. Although it is an ancient craft, it was undertaken on a relatively small scale until many thousands of miles of hedges were planted with the Enclosures Acts and Awards of the 18th and 19th centuries. Throughout most of the second half of the 20th century the craft has rapidly declined, as hedgerows have been ripped out to make way for larger fields and more crops. At the same time mechanization has greatly reduced manpower so that the remaining farm workers are generally far too busy to do any hedge-laying. However, there is now renewed interest in this fascinating craft, as its benefits to conservation and landscape are increasingly recognized.

In the old days, hedging was always a winter activity because most other farm work was slack then and it kept the

Ivan's hedge-laying has been an example to many

labourers busy as well as the hedges manageable and tidy. Also, with most of the herbage down, it was obviously easier to see and get at the job. Over the years Ivan has done most of his hedging between September and May, but he has worked in every month of the year. Let him describe his craft in his own words: 'With the leaves on it's only tricky at first, and there is the advantage that it's better for cutting with the sap up. You must be especially careful in late winter, as then the wood is brittle and comes off easily.'

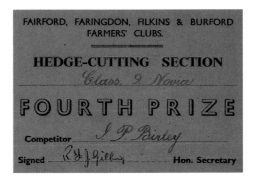

'The first thing to learn is how to sharpen your tools properly. The main tool is the billhook – God knows how many different styles there are.

'Then there's your axe – I've always had a 4lb and a 7lb one; and a long-handled slasher: there's several different shapes of these. I've had my 7lb stake hammer since 1932. Your mittens are always thick leather because the thorn is so sharp, but in my early seventies I started using a chainsaw and you need fingers for that. Unfortunately the modern gloves don't last like the old mittens. But one good new thing is the shredder. Before that we had to burn all the rubbish.

'I lost my hedge tools once, back in the bitter winter of 1962-3. After working on Christmas Eve I put my things under some brushwood, and then the big blizzards came and covered it all up so I didn't know

where the tools were. I couldn't get them back till the March thaw. We had to dig ourselves out of the house several times, and the indoor tank froze so we had to get water from a cattle trough that was surrounded by straw. The snow got so hard the sheep could walk on top.

'There are several different styles of hedge-laying. The Midland style, which *Farmer's Weekly* [the long-standing farmers' magazine] called the Bullock, originates from Leicestershire and has got to be a big, strong hedge to stop a bullock. Then the Welsh have their own style of hedge altogether, only three-feet high on account of the stock being all sheep. The Lancashire and Westmorland style has stakes on both sides, and the Derbyshire is similar to ours, but there are no binders [heathers] on top to keep it all tight. With the South of England style, brush is put both sides to stop sheep and cattle nibbling new shoots. But with ploughland hedging you don't need brush as there's no stock around. Nevertheless it still reduces wind damage to crops.'

Some hedges are centuries old, and regular laying prevents them getting too spindly. Ivan has tackled one not cut for 40 years, but ideally a hedge needs laying every 15 to 20 years; and Ivan has been at it long enough to do some hedges twice. 'After laying you let the hedge grow for about five years, then trim it for about five years, then leave it for about five years before laying it again.'

Ivan admits that hedging can be a lonely job, which is why he takes his old dog Jane along 'for a bit of company. And before her, my Border collie, Jim.' He describes the attraction of the work, and the technique required: 'The job is never monotonous. Every hedge is different. It's like a jigsaw puzzle, and you've got to get into the bones of it before you can solve it. You use your

When the blizzards came, Ivan lost all his hedge tools

billhook, or axe, on the thicker wood, to cut about three-quarters the way through the branch you want to bend over, but you must leave enough wood to let the sap come up. You place your stakes – hazel or other wood, brought with you or cut from the hedge – every 18 inches apart, and weave the pleaches [cut stems] at the same angle around them. As the work progresses, you hammer the stakes home and they are left to rot away or be removed when the hedge is established.

'In competition it is essential to have the stakes at equal distance and in a straight line. If heathers [cut hazel or elm rods] are woven between the stake tops to make the job neat, and to help keep the naturally springy thorn in place, they must be joined together properly. When I'm judging I always give a good shake to test for strength, and I don't like to see stakes left too high. And if the job's done properly there will be plenty of tillering [new shoots] in the hedge bottom come the spring.'

After so many years' practice Ivan can look at a hedge and easily tell where one man left off and another started. And with so many hedge-laying competition wins (notably the Coape-Arnold Cup) to his

credit, he is the ideal judge of others.

Traditionally each competitant is given half a chain (33ft) of hedge to lay in four hours. 'And he's got to do the lot and join the next man properly!' In normal work Ivan reckons on doing about a chain a day. 'You hear 'em talking about two chain a day, but I've never seen it yet. It's a job you can't rush, and should never be spoilt by things like putting string along the top. Once I laid a mile, but that took from November to March, and another time I did a quarter mile from 29 May to 12 August in me spare time. On my 80th birthday I did half a chain from 10pm to 2pm, and still managed an hour playing darts in the Sun!'

Hedges are not generally laid before attaining a height of at least six feet, but the height at which they are maintained thereafter varies considerably. 'If it's too tall, the wind will blow through and the stock won't like that, but if it's just right the wind goes over and by the time it's dropped back on the floor it's over the cattle. And I don't like to see trees in the middle of a hedge, but in the corner if some shade is required.'

The most awkward hedging that Ivan has laid is maple: 'Horrible stuff, brittle as anything. Ash, wych-elm and elder are bad too. Whitethorn [hawthorn] and blackthorn are the best.'

Ivan's Country File – 'Small Green One' – award was given for organizing and helping with the laying of about a mile of hedge which overhung the road adjoining the Berkshire, Buckinghamshire and Oxforshire County Naturalists' trust's Rushbeds Nature Reserve. The trust wanted it tidied in a 'wildlife-friendly way', so Ivan and a team of volunteers worked on it for two winters. Then Ivan decided to speed things up by holding a hedge-laying competition, the 30 entrants coming from as far afield as Lancashire and Devon.

Ivan has also undertaken important work at the Bernwood Meadows Site of Special Scientific Interest, established to protect two flower-rich meadows and ancient hedgerows. There, a long blackthorn hedge is being successively cut over a long period to encourage regrowth. And even at 89 years of age Ivan enthusiastically told me about his plans for further work there.

Unfortunately, health, skill and willingness are not always enough. 'BBONT [the trust] said I couldn't instruct because I hadn't been on a course! After all these years I could only teach others by demonstration. Also, they couldn't get insurance for me to use a chainsaw over the age of 85.'

Ivan had also had problems getting insurance for his scooter. 'I've had one for over 30 years and I was with the Prudential, but they gave up bikes. I looked around, but nobody wanted to know on account of my age, but I've just found a company to take me on again. It's only a low-power scooter, but when I came out of the army I had a Dunelt motorbike and in the 1940s an Enfield side-valve.'

In those days Ivan was on call 24 hours a day as a stockman: 'If someone's dogs was chasin' sheep at 3am you had to get up and deal with it. It was hard work too, and I had many a kick off cows while milking. Before they invented the crush, when we was on TT [tuberculin testing], your milking cows was all chained up in stalls, but your youngstock — about a dozen two-year-old heifers — was in a loosebox and you had to catch 'em and hold 'em while the vet injected 'em. By the time you finished you couldn't see no clothes for muck.

'But I got used to all that activity, which is why I got bored when I went to work for

the Old Berkshire Hunt for a couple of years in the late 1950s. I lived at the kennels at Faringdon and had to open jumps and mend gaps in hedges. I was always careful to pay my respects to the farmer before starting work and enjoyed what I did, but at night I had nothing to do.'

In 1948 Ivan started showing sheep, cattle and beef carcasses at Thame Show, and he is still a steward on sheep there. But there have been years when things went wrong: 'We always showed a lamb carcass, with varying success. One year we had a late lamb and it didn't get a prize as it was too fat. But I thought I'd bid for it when it came to the auction, because it was meat you could really taste before it was even cooked. But to my surprise my boss bid for it, too, and ended up buying his own lamb for £15! The thing is, you weren't allowed to withdraw any animal from sale.

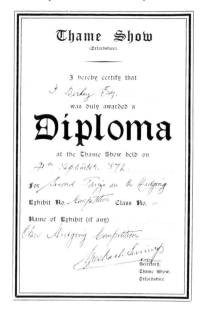

'... you had to catch 'em and hold 'em while the vet injected 'em ...'

Ivan with his prize-winning heifer at Thame Fatstock Christmas Show in about 1970

'Another time at auction my boss's nephew accidentally bought his uncle's heifer for 150 guineas. They'd seen this wool millionaire mark £150 next to it in his catalogue, and arranged that the nephew should stop bidding when uncle took his cigar out of his mouth. But it all went wrong, and there was the boss's wife moaning at having to pay the auctioneer's £10 fee on top. But I pointed out that it was money well spent, as people would now know what good cattle we had.'

Ivan's father only lived to the age of 68, but Ivan himself remains remarkably fit and active for his age, having already survived his wife Peggy by 14 years. Apart from his hedge-laying (including frequent instruction of others), he still keeps an allotment, and he has been a regular beater, with his dog Jane, on the local Boarstall shoot for over 30 years. He was dominoes champion at the local Red Lion, and individual darts champion at the Royal Oak at the age of 73, and he still enjoys a game of 'arrows'!

However, this accomplished father of four has some regrets. He says: 'Brill is more of a dormitory village now, with only about 25 per cent of the original villagers left. Most of the rest are incomers, either retired businessmen or people who work right away in London and other places. Also, today's farms are such miserable, quiet places, unlike the old days when everyone helped out with the harvest and there was always a horse and cart taking a load of kids out for lots of fun.' But whatever farms generally have become, there is no doubt that at least some have been considerably enriched through the vitality and competitive spirit of Ivan Birley.

Chapter 6
HIGH DAYS AND HOLIDAYS

Tom Quinn

HIGH DAYS AND HOLIDAYS

AMID THE CROWDED TOWNS AND CITIES OF THE ENGLISH MIDLANDS THERE ARE OCCASIONAL GREEN

OASES, AND TUCKED AWAY IN ON OF THESE AND JUST A FEW MILES FROM THE BUSY TOWN OF RUGBY IS

REG DOBSON'S HOME FARM. IT HAS CHANGED LITTLE SINCE IT WAS BUILT 300 OR MORE YEARS AGO

AND IT HAS A CURIOUS MEANDERING FEEL TO IT, WITH STAIRCASES HIDDEN BEHIND DOORWAYS AND

BEDROOMS TUCKED AWAY IN ODD CORNERS HERE AND THERE, AND IN UNDER THE EAVES.

Reg is now in his late eighties, but he still helps his son to run their farm; and like so many traditional farmers he looks back with great fondness to the days when farming was a way of life rather than a means simply to make money. Reg has an unusual memory for the mass of incident and detail from long ago, and he is a fund of marvellous stories about the characters he knew as a boy and as a young man.

Though Reg has farmed in Warwickshire since the 1950s, he started life on a farm further west in deeper Shropshire, as he explained when I met him in his massive kitchen with its beamed ceiling and roaring fire: 'I was brought up at a place called Cheswardine Park at Market Drayton. I had one brother and four sisters, and I was the eldest. We had a big old house, and it always seemed to be crowded with people; I think all farmhouses were well filled in those days because so many people worked on the land, and by tradition they lived in with the farmer and his family. So as well as us children and my parents we had a nursemaid, a kitchenmaid, my aunt Katy and her son George.

'My mother was a very kindly woman, and although she died when I was only nine, I remember her well. One thing that was particularly unusual about her was that she would not tolerate any cruelty to the farm animals – that may not sound so special now, but in those days people cared a lot less about animal welfare.

'On Saturday nights we were always bathed in a tin bath in front of a massive log fire. I remember I once refused to get undressed, so the nursemaid undressed me; but when she turned her back I bolted through the back door and out into the pitch-dark garden – after a long chase I was caught, however, and carried back to the house.

Reg takes great delight in talking about the past, and he has a genuine ability to bring it alive: 'I can't remember ever really falling out with my brother and sisters, though I do remember once making my sister eat coal, which we used to feed to the pigs for the minerals! We used to walk across the fields to school unless it was very wet, and then mother or one of the girls in the house took us in the pony and trap. We loved that.

'Horses were a big part of my life because Dad made a lot of money during the Great War by selling horses. We were quite well dressed and shod, unlike a lot of children and adults at that time. Mother used to give

the poor our old clothes and shoes. We also had hens, and in those days, of course, every hen in the country was free range – they just wandered about the yard and we fed them on wheat and maize. However, the grain used to attract hundreds of sparrows and this annoyed us, so we used to catch them by tying a long piece of string to a coal riddle and propping it up on a stick. We'd then put a pile of corn under the riddle and when a sparrow landed we'd pull the string, down would come the riddle and we'd catch it! We used to give them to Mother who made them into pies.

'We were terrible then for using catapults – all country boys were – and we'd fire at anything and everything, I'm afraid. Mostly, though, we'd fire at empty glass bottles; in those days they used to have a marble inside, so when we'd broken the bottle with the catapult we'd collect the marbles. We became experts at marbles, my brother and I.

'After my mother died, father was away virtually all the time dealing in horses, land or one thing or another. One of my best childhood memories was of visits to my maternal grandparents. Grandma always made a big fuss of me, and for some reason she always insisted on buying my boots for me, I think perhaps because she'd worn shoes that were too tight when she was a girl. As a result she had to have a toe amputated when she was 80 – and without anaesthetic! I remember she just lay there

and I held her hand while they cut off her toe: she never made a sound.

'Just before she died she lay in bed and pointed to a drawer in an old cupboard and said to me, "When I die, all the money in that drawer is for you." Alas, I never got a penny of it, because as soon as she died the housekeeper rifled the drawer and disappeared forever with all the money!'

Reg's family have been farmers on both his mother's and his father's side for generations. His maternal grandfather was also a trained blacksmith and shod all his own horses on the farm. He had a great fondness for beer, too; every Wednesday he'd set off for Market Drayton, as Reg recalls: 'He'd always take the horse and wagon – or a float as we used to call it – and he'd invariably take his neighbour, who was an old friend, with him. They'd put the horse up at the pub – every pub had stables then – and proceed to get gloriously drunk. At chucking out time the publican would help them out of the door and into the wagon, then he'd lead the horse into the middle of the street and away they would go. They would soon fall fast asleep and the horse would slowly make his way home five miles away; he would walk into the yard where he would stop, then my grandma would come out to wake the two men up and give them a good telling-off. The telling-off never did any good, though, because the following week they'd be off again.'

Market Drayton seemed to be alive with characters like Uncle Arthur: 'He was one of the first in our area to get a car, though it was such an old banger that a horse had to pull it

'We were terrible then for using catapults . . .'

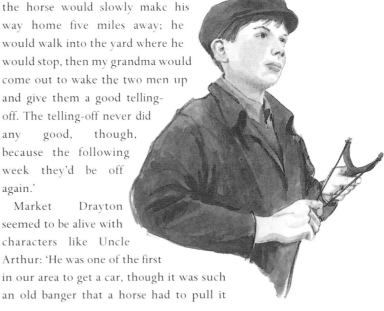

before it would start. He once drove all the way to Bishop's Castle on the wrong side of the road; if he met a wagon or another car (very rare) he would simply curse and yell at the other driver as if it was his fault that we were on the wrong side of the road!'

But apart from odd moments of hilarity, life in Shropshire in the early part of this century tended to be hard and unremitting, and this produced a tough independence of character, typified by Reg's father. 'Dad was a very fierce man; he had only to look at us and say "That will do", and we were terrified into silence. He'd taken over Cheswardine Park from his mother when she died, leaving him ten young brothers and sisters to look after. At the time, Cheswardine was in a very poor state, as were most farms in the 1920s; but when he sold it years later it was one of the best farms in Shropshire – he was a tough, determined man.'

Inevitably horses were an important part of young Reg's life, and to this day he retains a keen interest in horse racing; for his father, however, horses were everything. 'He was horse mad: he just loved them, whether riding, driving or buying and selling them. I remember he bought two really good ponies for me – they were a bit wild, but that's what people wanted in those days; they only wanted quiet ones for the trap or cart, but lively ones to carry them around the place.

'I remember one filly we had which was kept in a loose box between two cowsheds. Every night and morning we gave her about a gallon of milk straight from the cow. At about 18 months, father took her to a racing trainer because she was such a like-looking horse; just three months later she was dead from TB. She was rotten with it through and through. TB was rife in those days; we always lost two or three cows each year from TB, but people just accepted that it was a part of life then. It was called John's disease. Why we didn't get it I'll never know, particularly as my father would never get rid of a sick cow – he'd always assume it would get better if you left it long enough.

'Dad was into livestock of all kinds. He used to breed greyhounds now and then, for example, and one of them won several races so my father sold it for a good price; it never won again! Animals were right at the heart of our lives, and we associated them with work as well as with good fun. For instance, when we were very young we used to love to ride in the heavy carts when the men were bringing in the roots or mangels, though farms could be just as dangerous then as they are now; my sister fell out of a cart once and the great heavy wheel ran over her hand and completely crushed it. And then father had a hell of a game getting the teachers at the school to let Dorothy learn to write with her left hand – in those days you had to write with your right hand even if it didn't work!'

Soon it was time for Reg to go to boarding school, which he hated. 'I went from the village school to Adams Grammar School in Newport. The masters were very strict, and I was caned regularly; one master, Tubby Gill, used to beat us till we couldn't sit down! I left after four years, which was the best thing that ever happened to me. I was 16 and started work full-time on the farm, which I loved.'

Escape from school might seem every schoolboy's dream come true, but for Reg it meant long hours and hard work – he was expected to work seven days a week, from

six in the morning till six at night. There were 125 cows to milk by hand every day: 'Unless you've actually done that yourself you can have no idea of the work involved' he says now. 'There were 12 of us did the milking, and we did it according to a numbering system so that each person had his or her fair share of difficult cows – you know, cows that held their milk up or that kicked like hell. If they thought they could get away with it, people would deliberately take a long time at an easy cow until they could see that another easy one was next in line to be milked. We used to put a special leather strap on the kickers to keep their legs still, though some started to kick before you even got near them.

'An old man called Punch used to carry off the pails of milk as they were filled. He wore a great wooden yoke, like you'd put on a pair of oxen, with a pail hung on each side.

'In my first year I had to do the sheep, too, mostly Cheviots, and the devil to catch because we had no proper pens. I used to get the dog to hold them in a corner of the field and then run in and catch the one I wanted. Half the time it was a question of

run in and dive at a fleeing sheep, a bit like a rugby tackle. An old local poacher called Jim Carne used to come at shearing time. I used to turn the handle of the wheel that drove the shears – we'd come on a bit from simple hand-shears – and he did the clipping. He was very good at it, but it was hard work for a 16-year-old turning that thing all day.

'If you had any hope of surviving on a Shropshire farm early this century you had to be a shrewd dealer. Selling your produce in the days before intervention buying by the EC was the severest test of a farmer's ability in the market place. Dad was a sharp one for selling sheep. He'd buy them and get us to trim them and clean them till they looked really smart and he'd take them straight back to market and usually get a pound or two more for each one than he'd paid for them.'

Self-sufficiency was important at a time when many farms were part of isolated communities, and much of the 300 gallons of milk a day the Dobsons' cows produced went to make cheese. The cheese was made on site by a cheesemaker who lived in with the family; nothing was ever wasted, and the large quantities of whey, a by-product of the cheesemaking process, were stored and then fed to the pigs. 'It was kept in a big brick tank and I used to take it by bucketful to feed the pigs. I had a yoke on my shoulders which made it a bit easier, but it was incredibly hard work, particularly on your legs. In those days we had what would now be considered very unbalanced rations for the animals – we'd prepare a great barrow full of maize-germ

Learning from the mole-catcher: a land girl at work in the Usk Valley early in the 1940s

meal and tip it in the pigs' trough, and then we'd pour the whey on top; there was an awful lot got trodden in and slopped about. These days animal feeding is a very scientific business.

'Most of the feed we were able to buy came on the train to Drayton which was three miles away, and it was a full day's work to take a cart there to collect the feed and get it back to the farm.

'Father always used to buy the biggest pigs he could find; they'd weigh seven or

eight stone when he brought them home, and then we'd feed them till they weighed 17 or 18 stone apiece. When we took them to market they were really big, in fact one was so fat that it dropped dead as it walked up the ramp into the cart! I went with father once to Welshpool and he bought every single pig in the market. One lot in a pen had great long snouts and I didn't think they'd do any good. "They're the best of the bunch," he said, and he was right.'

The pig was the great saving of many farmers and smallholders. It was a hardy animal that grew quickly and could be relied upon to hoover up any and every kind of vegetable waste with enthusiasm and turn it into delicious bacon.

'We loved it when we killed a pig,' remembers Reg, 'which may sound terrible, but you have to remember that a lot of people went hungry in those days and there was no time for sentimentality. When we killed a pig we ate every last bit of it. We had the liver and kidneys, and sausages and pork pies were made from some bits, pork scratchings from the skin. We even used the bladder, as with a bit of effort you could turn it into a really good football. You just blew it up and tied a knot in it and it lasted for ages!'

Reg Dobson has a positive, no-nonsense outlook, and is dismissive of what he sees as fads and fancies among townsfolk. 'Today, all the talk is about animal fat killing you. Well, let me tell you, we lived on it. For

breakfast we'd have two eggs, six rashers of bacon and fried bread with masses of dripping, and this would be after porridge with huge dollops of cream all over it. Mind you, we had to work like blazes so I suppose we worked it off; and we've all lived to a pretty ripe old age, too, except my brother Lionel who was only 43 when he died.'

Standards of hygiene on those Shropshire farms would shock many people today, but with water available only from a well, and no mains gas or electricity, a big family had to take a far more practical view of these matters. 'After a day's work in the farmyard we'd be covered in muck of one sort or another, but we only rarely had a change of trousers. Trousers were just trousers and we wore them all the time whatever their state

– and there were no wellies or overalls. When you came in you just sat by the fire and the muck dried and steamed away. No one thought anything of it, it was just the way things were.'

There is no doubt, too, that you had to be very ill indeed to be excused a day's work, even if you were the farmer's son. 'I had serious problems with my left hip when I was a young man; it was displaced, and eventually the doctor told my father I should not carry anything heavy. But I still had to work, and had to help old Jack with the cows. Jack was an old soldier who had a bad right leg, and I often thought we must have looked a lovely couple walking across the farmyard, him limping one way and me the other!'

'After a day's work in the farmyard we'd be covered in muck of one sort or another'

A typical day for Reg would start at 5.30am: he would put hay in the racks at the head of each cow's stall, and then the milking would begin. 'No one under the age of 60 or 70 will remember what it is like to feed and muck out 125 cows every day,' he says with a wry smile. Women and men would start work together in the mornings; after breakfast they would let the cattle out to water, as none was piped to the farm in those days, and then roots and mangolds would be mixed together with corn and mash as feed.

'There was no cattle cake in those days, I'm afraid,' says Reg. 'Then we'd muck out. That was a perilous job, I can tell you, because we always seemed to have so little straw and the muck was almost liquid. We used to load it into a barrow and then push

the barrow on to the top of the midden, where we tipped it. After a few years the midden might be 12ft high, and at that height, with a slippery muck-covered plank, there were bound to be accidents. I've slipped off that plank many times and ended up waist-deep in cow muck!

'After cleaning out, we fed the cows individually, and you had to be smart while you were at it or greedy ones ate up first and then started knocking the others around. There was also the risk of being kicked; if you were, in those days you'd belt the cow with a stick or with the milking stool, though I eventually realized that this made them worse, and that if you were kind and gentle they responded in the same way. Nowadays we never put a stick on our animals.'

Reg's memories of Cheswardine Park are characterized by his sense of camaraderie and good fun, the spirit of enjoyment that seems to have survived in spite of the long hours of hard work in all weathers. Many of the men and women Reg worked with became friends for life, and one or two, like Reg Boffey, married into the family.

'Reg eventually married one of my sisters; he used to cut the hay while I forked it in to the animals, and we had great fun together, but he was a devil for cutting the wads bigger and bigger. They'd start at about a yard square and soon be two yards square, and the more he could get on the pikel the better he liked it. One day I just managed to stagger out of the barn with a massive load he'd put on my fork, then collapsed in the yard with all the hay on top of me. I didn't think much of it, but he fell about laughing.

'We were always playing good-natured jokes on each other and on the others. I remember Frank Chidlow who used to cart for us — we used to fill his cart so full of muck at muck-spreading time that his horse couldn't budge it an inch. We thought it was hilarious, even though we straightaway had to lessen the load to get the thing moving; either that or Frank would go and get what we called a chainhorse to help pull the cart. And he'd cuss his head off at us while he did it.

'When he was courting a girl at Northwich, Reg used to get back to the farm in the early hours, and he'd shake me and say, "Sam, it's time to get up!" I'd leap out of bed in a panic, and he'd immediately jump into the warm place I'd made in the bed. We were both called Reg, but for some reason we called each other "Sam" all the time. Lord knows why. We used to share the same bed, and the room had two windows which we kept open winter and summer however hard the winter. Some mornings the jerry would be frozen over it got so cold.'

Like many rural areas, Shropshire had its fair share of eccentrics, frequently elderly, often highly superstitious men and women who had spent their lives in tiny out-of-the-way cottages, eking out a living by occasional or seasonal farm-work. 'Pay was very low in the 1920s and 1930s. A man would get just a few shillings a week, his wife less, even if she came to milk night and morning. Apart from Sunday, the farm-workers had only one day a year off – Good Friday, but even then they had to come and milk. However, they'd get a cottage with a big garden so they grew all the vegetables they needed, and they usually kept a pig – and that was all the meat a poor man ever got, except for rabbits.

'Frank Chidlow, our wagoner, had eight children and little money, so when he wanted a beer he'd catch himself a dozen or more rabbits and exchange them for a few pints at the local pub. When he'd had a few pints he'd start to sing, which the other regulars loved, so they'd start buying him

drinks to keep him going. He'd get back to the farm at three in the afternoon, have his dinner and then go to milk; half-an-hour later he'd be fast asleep on the milking stool. Frank's wife, Olive, used to milk, too; when she was pregnant she'd milk until the day she went into labour, and she'd be back at work the day after the child was born.'

The pub was very much the centre of social life in Reg's youth, and men would walk out miles every evening to drink at their favourite local – which might be five or six miles away if they lived in one of the many remote cottages. The pub gave men their only chance to escape the drudgery of everyday life; for the price of a few pints they could enjoy a temporary escape into a world of laughter and good fellowship.

Another pastime Reg recalls was the tug-o-war: 'We used to have horseback tug-o-wars with teams from the various farms and big houses competing. We had one once at the big house where Colonel Donaldson Hudson lived, the local squire; he entered a team, as did the surrounding farms, and we got to the final where we had to pull against the Colonel's team.

'As we got going and took up the strain, one of our horses started misbehaving; so father put his coat over her head to calm her, but that made her worse and she reared. Bubber, a wild boy and a great giant of a man, slipped off her – everyone was riding bareback – but we still held our own. Then seizing his chance, Bubber leapt back on, gave an almighty heave and all the Colonel's men and horses were pulled over. So we'd won; but we were disqualified because you had to let the Colonel's team win. That was the way they thought in those days.

'We used to get our own back on him, though, by laying trails of raisons the day before he was to have a big shoot; the raisins, which pheasants love, led to our wood and of course as a result we had plenty of pheasants!

'Eating competitions were a big thing in my youth in Shropshire, and I believe this was true of many other country districts; I suppose it was good, simple entertainment when we had little else. The wagoner on a farm near us was a phenomenal eater, and people used to come and fetch him to eat for bets. One night a farmer knocked at his door and asked his wife if he would come and eat a whole calf for a bet. She wasn't in the least surprised by the request, but didn't know if he would because he'd already gone out to eat two ducks down at the Fox for a bet. "I'll go down there and ask him," said the man. He found Bill, put the proposition to him and Bill, having eaten his ducks, went off straightaway and ate the calf as well!'

Food was thus a source of great entertainment as well as being one of life's great pleasures, although one or two food sources – most notably rabbit – were not highly thought of at all; perhaps because there were so many and they were considered the staple of the very poorest, few liked the idea of dining regularly on rabbits. But if you found yourself in a tight corner financially you could always catch enough rabbits to earn a few bob: 'It was no trouble in those days to catch a hundred rabbits in a day – they were everywhere, and I think most men on the farm virtually lived on rabbit. A great friend of mine called Cyril used to be mad about cricket, just as I was, and once we went and caught rabbits and sold them until we had enough money to get to Old Trafford on the train to watch England play the Australians.'

Killing rabbits and pigs, and twisting the necks of chickens for the pot, were all part of the less-than-idyllic farming scene which held sway earlier this century; and 'closeness to nature' probably contributed to what Reg still describes as a 'kind of

roughness of character. There's no doubt we were a rough bunch in some ways: I remember one girl used to tease Cyril and me, so we picked her up and dropped her in a barrel of treacle – well, you've never seen such a sight in your life, she could hardly walk; but she never teased us again.

'We were positively medieval in our attitudes to hygiene in those days, too. I don't think it was so much that we didn't care, it was just that without running water, plastic overalls and all the other modern hygiene aids, you just had to accept that things were going to be done as they'd always been done. For example, I've explained how the cows were let out into the fields to water before we had water

piped to the sheds. Well, as they went out through the narrow gateways where all the muck and slurry would accumulate, inevitably they got into a terrible mess. But we used to wipe their udders with just an old piece of sacking, and you can imagine what the milk was like after that! When we stopped making cheese on the farm, we started to sell the milk to the chocolate company Nestlé, and the colour of the milk was like chocolate when we sent it to them! They were always writing to father to complain, so we started washing the cows properly; but I don't think it really made a lot of difference.

'We were only in this position because we didn't have all the modern conveniences. Take haymaking, for example: younger people on the farms today have no idea what a hard job haymaking used to be. Frank Chidlow would go out with the horses at 3am because he needed to work virtually 24 hours a day to get the job done in time; and of course in summer it was cooler working at that time in the morning. Actually Frank loved the horses and he'd often arrive earlier than he needed just to groom them all properly.

'When I moved here in the 1950s, Frank came and sowed a field of oats for me. It ran by Watling Street, and he put a stick at either end to get a straight line and made a hell of a fuss before starting because, as he said, "I'm not having anybody go up the Watling and say, what a mess that field is!"'

At a time when ordinary men and women had few possessions of any note, their greatest pride lay in their work and in what other people thought of their efforts. As Reg observed: 'Oh, yes, when I was young all the men would walk all round different farms on a Sunday, and if any field had been badly ploughed or sown it would be all over the village in no time. Today no one minds what a field looks like, so long as it is all done quickly.'

It is difficult nowadays to conceive the level of poverty at which most agricultural workers once lived. Reg describes how Frank Chidlow and wife and eight children all survived on £2 a week in a tiny cottage. 'How he did it I'll never know, but they all grew up strong and well,' he says.

If the men were indomitable, with rich, idiosyncratic characters, the same was certainly true of many of the farm animals: 'They were real characters. I remember one of our cows had a massive udder, or bag as we used to call it; we used to have to get two people to milk her, one on each side. She was a gentle thing, though; and once when we had four orphaned lambs we put two on each side of this massive udder and she stood quite still and let them feed. She reared them, too, and they used to follow her about everywhere when we turned them out into the spinney.'

The labour-intensive nature of milking and of dealing with pigs and other farm animals was matched by the almost complete absence of technology on the arable fields. 'For our 100 acres of hay, all we had in the way of implements was a turner, a device drawn by a horse that flipped the hay over so that it would dry evenly, and an old horse-rake. After the hay had been dragged up into piles we'd cock it up by hand into small heaps to keep the rain off as much as possible. Next day, or soon after, it had all to be shaken out and turned again by hand. When it was ready to cart, we pitched it on to the wagon by hand, one man on top, one each side of the wagon. Then we had to rope it on because the old cart-tracks were a bit rough and the bumps as we went along might otherwise have thrown the whole lot off. Back in the yard we pitched it into the hayloft by hand, and we'd often be at it until midnight or beyond.

'All the men were real artists when it came to hay, and hated slaphappy methods. Haymaking used to last from about mid-June to about the end of August.'

Rain was an obvious problem at haymaking time, but too much sun could also make it difficult, as Reg recalls: 'I remember Frank Chidlow cut me a 14-acre field of hay one year, and it was so hot that before I could get it in cocks it was already over-made – that is, was so brittle – it started to fall off every time we had half a load on, and I don't think there was much goodness left in it anyway.

'Another time we were in the local pub one Sunday and we decided that after our dinner we would carry Harry Robinson's field – all the men helped each other at harvest time. Anyway, the pub was full, and after we'd had our fill we all trooped out and set to, 11 of us with the horses and wagons. I helped build the rick with the others pelting the sheaves up to us at a terrific rate. We did it very fast, but what a mess we had at the end of it! The rick was leaning towards the road at an angle of about 45 degrees and we had to get every pole from a radius of about a mile to prop it up! It was such a sight that someone sketched it and hung the picture in the pub that night!'

Cheswardine Park was a long way from the nearest town and with four girls and three young men living in close proximity, relationships were bound to develop; pregnancy and scandal were never far away.

'If a girl got pregnant in those days it was a terrible disgrace. I had to pay five shillings a week for 18 years to one young girl I made pregnant. She had the child and I paid the money, but I've never seen either of them since. I was only a lad at the time. I remember, too, that three of our bailiffs married three of our cheesemakers and Dad helped set them up on farms of their own. He was always doing that sort of thing. He lent them £250 apiece, but only one ever paid him back: he sent Father £500 about 20 years after marrying and taking his loan – Dad was highly delighted.

'Another great character was Tom Bennett, the champion hedge-layer of the whole of Shropshire. If he didn't get first prize for the best hedge-laying one year he'd get it for the best-grown hedge the next. Every job he did was perfect. He used to cut our lawn with a scythe as good as any modern lawn-mower could do it. He was a great rick-builder, too, and when he'd finished he'd often come back at night to pull out the loose bits of hay just to make sure it looked perfect.

'All the men were real artists when it came to hay, and hated slaphappy methods.'

'Tom used to chew tobacco twist and he was a deadly accurate spitter – he once hit a cat on the head at about 20 feet! And he had amazing teeth; he used to bite into an iron railing at the bottom of the garden and swing from it. Tom never went anywhere in his whole life, to the best of my knowledge, except one trip after he retired when he got the bus to the Royal Show at Lincoln; but he got lost, missed the bus back, and spent £20 – a small fortune – on a taxi to get home. That was the first and last time he went anywhere!'

One theme that runs throughout Reg's endless series of delightful anecdotes is that in country districts in days gone by, people almost invariably made their own entertainment, and often this meant playing jokes on each other, which was all usually taken in good part. 'I remember two fat butchers used to call at Charlie Denton's place in a pony and trap. They were so fat that when they got in the trap the horse was nearly lifted up in the air. One day Charlie's boys undid the horse's belly strap and as soon as the butchers got in the trap the shafts shot up in the air and they tumbled out into the road. We roared with laughter, but the air was blue with the butchers' curses.

'But country people could be very stick-in-the-mud, too. I remember we had a parish meeting when the council said they would pipe water to the village houses. The older inhabitants didn't want it because they said you could smell the ducks from Stamford Park when you turned the taps on (Stamford Park was the municipal lake where the water would come from). But in spite of all, the water came in the end, and so did electricity.

'After my mother died, Aunt Katy looked after us. She was lovely, and I think she loved my father but he loved somebody else – the local publican's daughter. She got divorced so she could marry Dad, which cost Dad £3,000, an absolute fortune in those days. After they were married they took a hotel in Liverpool for a while, but Dad hated it. In those days you had to be whiter than white to get a publican's licence; and because my stepmother was a divorcee she couldn't get the licence – it had to be in someone else's name. But by 1931 Dad was back on a farm; he just wasn't suited to city life.

'A chap called Walter Thomas used to work for us and he was a wonderful workman. He liked piecework, and he and his wife used to dig our potatoes. They'd dig 11 square roods a day, which is some going, and while they were doing it they used to camp in the field. Walter also used to pull our swedes, and he was so fast there'd be one landing on the heap, one flying through the air and one in his hand. He'd go on like that all day, and when we were all hoeing together he'd leave us standing if he felt like it.

'In winter he cut our hedges. He used a short-handled slasher, and as he was six-feet tall and our hedges were rather small, he could cut both sides as he went along simply by leaning over. As he cut, so his wife gathered the brashings and piled them up and burned them. They were a great team, but all they got for the work was 3d a rood. By working all the hours God sends – milking, hoeing, drilling, sowing and ploughing – they only made about 16d a week.'

It is important to remember that although Reg was officially the boss' son,

there was no significant difference between his daily routine and that of the other farm workers; they simply mucked in together. The only material difference was the fact that the farmer's son didn't get paid at all since his return would come in the long-term when he inherited the farm. This seems to have been pretty universal practice among all except gentlemen farmers with considerable sums of money.

Because his father didn't pay him, Reg had to find other ways to make money. 'I used to go long-netting for rabbits with Walter. One night we got 50 in one go. We also set traps, which I admit was very cruel and I'm glad it's stopped now. Country people did like eating rabbit, although if they had nothing else they got a bit tired of it. We used to go to a local dance sometimes after rabbiting, but we smelled so strong of rabbits that none of the girls would dance with us. Never mind, we used to say, we can still get into the bar!'

Reg's tales of what was obviously a lively and generally happy farming community are not based on a rose-tinted view of the past. As well as the fun and the practical jokes, things could be difficult in a way that many of us find difficult to imagine today. 'In farming it certainly wasn't all good in the old days, and at times it was very difficult indeed to make ends meet. Before the Milk Marketing Board was set up, we had to take our milk to a cheesemaker nearby and got 4½d per gallon for it; after the MMB that went up to 8½d. Selling privately and locally, as we had to do then, had some advantages, but it would mean penury for the small farmer today.

'Farming was difficult and even dangerous in other ways, too – we often used to hear about people being fatally injured by their animals. It nearly happened to me once when we were leading a dangerous bull into a stall. Just as I reached down to put his chain on he whipped round and knocked me to the ground. He then knocked Jim, my stockman, over and started butting the stall. I was lucky and managed to crawl away, but either or both of us could easily have been killed.

'I met the girl I was eventually to marry when I was 11, and even proposed to her one night; but then I went away to school and didn't see her again till I was 19. I used

to cycle about 11 miles every night to see her, along rough roads and narrow, bumpy lanes. She learned to drive, although she never had any lessons; none of us did in those days. Her brothers taught her, just put her in the driving seat and showed her what to do.'

The church seems to have played a lesser part in the life of the countryside in the

early part of the century than one might have imagined, but where it did have a strong influence, individual priests were often heartily disliked. Reg's memories of country parsons perhaps typify the two ends of the spectrum: the parson who was a friend of the community, and the one who let it be known that he felt he was far superior to his flock. 'I was very fond of one parson we had when we were in Shropshire. He used to play in the village cricket team in which I also played, and he used to say that there were only two things he was any good at: cricket and preaching. But another parson I remember was quite different, a real bad lot who treated all the children like dirt, and we hated him. He put me off parsons for life.'

The distinction between town and country was far less defined in 1920s Shropshire than it is now. People who lived in towns were often only one generation away from a farming background, and as a result they tended to cultivate vegetables rather than just flowers in their gardens. Many kept chickens, too, and even pigs. 'Lots of townspeople, although they knew they'd eat the pig eventually, often treated it as a pet while it was with them. I remember some people we knew used to put their pig up on the garden wall so it could see the town band go past!

'But farming always came first in my family – I remember that when I eventually married Gladice we chose 10 September, and my father was most put out because it was also the date of the Ullesthorpe Sheep Fair and he had 100 ewes to sell!

'When we were first married we lived in a way that you just can't imagine: we had a house with no electricity, no gas, no heating other than big old fires, no easy lighting, and no labour-saving devices at all. We had oil lamps for light, and everything had to be scrubbed clean without detergents and washing powders; it was all brute force and elbow grease, really. We had two children, both girls, and Gladice had read somewhere that fresh air was good for babies, so we'd leave them out for a couple of hours every day, even when a gale was blowing! But it didn't seem to do them any harm.

'Eventually we packed up the dairy herd, largely because I was fed up with milking and mucking out 365 days a year, though it's easier today with ready-made feeds. We then went in for suckler cows, fat cattle, sheep and about 140 acres of corn. Weeds were our biggest problem in the early days with corn because there were no chemicals, and although it looked pretty with millions of poppies, it wasn't much good as a crop – when we harvested it the poppies made hell of a stink. But all that is easier now with sprays and chemicals.

'But the minus side to all the modern innovations is that there are fewer people on the land, and a man is stuck in an air-conditioned tractor all day. A lot of the life and fun has gone out of it, and although I had a hard life, it was fun and I enjoyed every minute of it.'

Chapter 7
GAME FOR ANYTHING

Brian P Martin

GAME FOR ANYTHING

As the wife of a professional gamekeeper, Doris Winchester needed to be both tough and very supportive of her spouse in a male-dominated field, coping with everything from lonely nights in isolated cottages to going without holidays, gutting game, feeding ferrets, and even accidentally being peppered by shot. All quite usual for country folk before World War II, but no mean achievement for a gregarious town girl who liked music and dancing. Indeed, friends and family were amazed when dashing Doris declared that she was going to bury herself in the country.

The eldest of three sisters, Doris Phoebe Winchester (née Randall) was born at Horsham in Sussex, on 30 May 1915. Her maternal grandfather had worked as a woodman, earning so little that her granny had to take in washing to feed her nine children. But her parents' work was not concerned with the countryside, her mother being a cook and her father a soldier turned butler. However, Doris always loved the outdoors and from an early age wandered off on long walks, blackberrying or simply enjoying the birds and flowers.

Doris had a happy childhood, but there was plenty of discipline, she recalls: 'We always had to attend church and Sunday school. Dad was a captain and I can just remember him coming back from the Great War with a bulldog he rescued in France. Later he volunteered to serve in the Black-and-Tans in Ireland, helping to track down rebels. And when he became a butler he was meticulous. We hated it when he nailed studs and blakeys on to our shoes, and he made us clean them every night. I

suppose we were poor, with the usual outside loo and a copper boiler fired by wood faggots and chippings, but we seemed to live well. Mum didn't go out to work but she made all our clothes, from flannel vests to knitted socks and jumpers; and she was a great cook, making wonderful suet puddings.'

Doris was not a good scholar, so her dreams of becoming a nurse and dressing up in uniform came to nothing. Instead, she took an opportunity provided by 'this bowler-hatted man who used to come to the school and ask who was leaving. He offered me a job as a trainee window dresser for Timothy Whites. I earned 8s a week and gave it all to Mum, but she gave me two bob back and I'd spend 6d on going to the pictures and 6d on silk stockings.'

After a year working in Horsham, Doris's friend got her a job as a between maid ('half kitchen and half housework'), near Highgate, where she earned £23 a year, paid monthly. Two-and-a-half years later she moved to Warnham, near Horsham, where she was a live-in kitchen maid for Mrs

Gregson, who was a Joint Master of the Crawley and Horsham Foxhounds. From then on she became closely involved with the countryside: 'In my spare time I'd go on lots of walks, and it was at Warnham that I met my first gamekeeper – Traske. He was a real gentleman, always immaculate with shining boots. I assumed all keepers were like this, so it was a real shock when I met Bert, my husband-to-be, who was anything but tidy, except on shoot days.

'Traske used to bring in lots of pheasants, rabbits, pigeons and other game into the kitchen for Mrs Garrett, the cook. She was a real drinker, but a marvellous cook and when sober she taught me so much, including how to skin, pluck and gut game, and saving the blood for jugged hare – the smell from that was absolutely awful. Also I never liked skinning eels as they never

seemed to be dead, their nerves making them thrash about all the time.

'I cycled home, about five miles, on my half day every other Sunday, and was quite happy at Warnham – though butler Simmonds was a dirty old man and you didn't dare be up a ladder when he was around. And you couldn't complain or else you'd be out. Then the cook had an affair with the chauffeur and we were all sacked as the boss thought we were in league.'

Fortunately there was no shortage of domestic jobs in those days, so Doris soon found another position, at Cowfold in Sussex, working for Captain Hodgson, 'a nice old boy and keen shooter.' From there she moved to Herstmonceux Castle, Sussex, as kitchen maid for Sir Paul Latham, MP for Whitby and Scarborough. Under a Belgian chef – 'another boozer' – she started work at 6am each day, lighting the range and scrubbing the floors.

Through Latham, Doris continued to have close links with shooting, even though there was no keepered shoot at the castle, as Doris recalls: 'The boss had a shooting lodge on the moors at Danby, near Scarborough, and I went up there as cook for the parties. I mostly made raised pies and stews and transported them in hay boxes, to serve lunch way out in the wilds [a hay box was an airtight box of hay used to continue the cooking of a dish or dishes already begun]. I also made bread for them, and there were lovely cheeses and lots of drink. Then I'd have to go back to the lodge to prepare dinner for ten or 12 people. We only had silver service up there, but back at the castle we had gold. Also at the lodge I had the servants' hall to cater for, with all the keepers, loaders, valets, and so on; and there was only one girl helping me so I was very busy. But we still had the time and energy to dance at the village hops!'

Unfortunately Doris had to leave

Latham's employ because she developed a badly poisoned hand following a cut, and could not manage the work. For most people there was no sick pay in those days! So Doris returned home to her family until the wound healed. However, this ill fortune was fortuitous, because it led to her marriage: 'I went to the registry office and got a job as kitchen maid at WH Abbey's Sedgwick Park, the perfect estate – sadly now gone – three miles from Horsham. It was a very busy place: in the house there was a butler, two footmen, three housemaids, two nursery maids, a cook, a scullery maid and me. The butler ran everything to the letter, but his wife, the cook, was another drinker, mostly whisky, and he had access to the boss's booze! As a result I did most of the cooking, and the designated cook just shuffled out to hand the food to the footmen. And it was a great deal of work, with several tureens of each vegetable at every dinner.

'Bert, the fifth generation of gamekeepers in the Winchester family, was the second of four keepers at Sedgwick Park, where he

lodged with the headkeeper in winter and the chauffeur in summer. As well as game, he used to bring turkeys and ducks – specially reared on the estate – into our game larder as our boss could eat only white meat.

'When I first saw Bert, I said to the cook: "What a dishy fellow!" But she said, "Get your eyes off him, he's engaged." However, I wasn't put off. I came from a musical family and Bert played the fiddle, so I invited him to a party at my parents' home in Horsham. After that he went over with me quite often and we started cycling back and forth together. Eventually we both played in an old-time dance band, with me on the drums. Everybody liked Bert and I think he took all us girls out in turn.

'We went out together for about a year at Sedgwick, and there was no problem having the same boss. We had a code: in the evening, after the cook and her husband, the butler, had gone up, I'd be left in the kitchen to make sure everything was in apple-pie order. At about 9 or 9.30pm I'd look out the window, and if Bert had left a roll of paper in the drain opposite I knew he was there. So then I'd go out to meet him, under the pretext of going to the dustbin with the rubbish, which I'd deliberately left till last.'

When Doris married Bert in 1937, she gave up her job and thereafter devoted herself to supporting Bert in his various keepering jobs, mainly at Broxmead (Cuckfield, Sussex), Braxted Park (Essex), Peasmarsh Place (near Rye, Sussex), and on the Crown estate at Windsor. Bert also spent some years as a bird trapper and ringer at Abberton Reservoir and in the forestry department at Windsor, in charge of grey-squirrel control. Along the way Bert was unlucky in taking one or two other positions for very selfish and unkind employers, but fortunately, as Doris stresses, 'we were able to throw in the towel without thought of children having a family would have made a very big difference.'

Doris soon settled down to helping Bert with many of his duties. In those days pheasants were mainly reared under broody hens, and at Peasmarsh Doris looked after about a hundred of them at the bottom of their garden. Each morning she lifted them off the nest-boxes and tethered them in fours with a water dish in the middle and corn at each peg. There they stayed for 20 minutes while Doris checked the eggs, damping those near hatching; in those days it was believed that this prevented the egg's inner membrane from becoming so hard that the chick would not be able to peck its way out. As Doris points out, in the wild the eggs are prevented from drying out by the moisture on the mother's underparts when she returns to the nest after feeding.

When the chicks hatched, Doris helped with their feeding, and in the old days this involved a great deal of work in food preparation, pushing boiled eggs through a sieve, mincing onions, chopping boiled rabbits, and so on. 'But today, even a Cockney could do keepering, as everything comes in a paper bag.'

Doris was adept at getting rabbits, although she did go the wrong way once or twice when she first went long-netting at night. And when she first fired a 12-bore she tried to get her head over so that she could use her left eye instead of the right, resulting in 'a bruise as big as a tea-plate.'

Undaunted, Doris went on to become an excellent shot, to a friend's great surprise: 'I was on a rabbit shoot at Braxted with Bert and underkeeper Jack. I stood at the end of a spinney and Jack said: "I'll give you two bob for every rabbit you get," thinking I was useless. Well, I very quickly had four in the bag and Jack soon said: "That's enough!".

'Sometimes I sat in a ditch and Bert would squeak up foxes; he was very good at that, but I always hoped that one wouldn't come along, as to me it would be like shooting a dog. Luckily for me, one never did. I didn't like shooting squirrels, either. Rabbits were my thing.'

For a long time Doris also looked after and worked the ferrets to obtain rabbits, but this came to an abrupt end after an unfortunate incident, as Doris explains: 'One day the ferrets mistakenly thought I had their food for them and they got very excited when I didn't put anything down. One shot up my leg and then the others ran after me, scratching at my legs, and I had to kick them off and climb up out the way. I've never handled them since.'

On shoot days, Doris's kitchen experience was useful when she prepared dinner for

Lord Devonport's guests and she became a first-class cook. At one memorable meal his lordship awarded her the *carte bleu*, 'but it was only one written in blue crayon. He was most annoyed when Bert laughed at his comment: "The wisest thing a man can do is marry a cook."'

When she was not in the kitchen, Doris would often join her husband's team of beaters, 'tramping over that heavy Sussex soil in every weather imaginable, doing our best to put birds over the Guns.' She was not paid for this and was the only lady in the line, but she thoroughly enjoyed 'all the fun and bickering.'

However, there were other times when Doris was very embarrassed. For example: 'One evening Bert and I were out for a walk on the farm next to Peasmarsh estate. I was desperate to spend a penny and went among the trees, but first I had to undo all these buttons down both sides of my brown corduroy breeches. Then I was just enjoying a good pee when this gruff voice called out: "Do you know this here's private?" – it was this horrible old man, farmer Percy Barton, so I had to cut my penny short and dash off. He didn't realize it was me, but when Bert came over he didn't even apologize.'

When Bert was working long days in the rearing field Doris would take his 'dinner' down to him and often stayed to help for the rest of the day. In fine, warm weather, with birdsong and flowers all around, this was quite pleasant work, 'but shutting up the birds in the evening was a real chore: you had to go about in your stockinged feet so that they couldn't hear you coming.'

One aspect of the work that Doris had to accept without question was Bert's unfixed

hours: 'As long as the job required. On some nights – especially in moonlight – he'd be out long after dark watching for poachers, and I was often worried that he'd be attacked. Even now, at the age of 83, he still gets up at 5am.'

During World War II Bert was away in the army, but Doris remained at Peasmarsh. It was a difficult and often unpleasant period, as Doris explains: 'Officially, Lord Devonport had to keep Bert's position open for him, but as far as I was concerned as long as I remained in that cottage Bert had a job to come back to. Although all game rearing was suspended during the war, I had lots to do as I still had to look after the dogs and hens and get rabbits for the ferrets. But when I joined the Women's Land Army I couldn't cope and had to get the underkeeper to take the ferrets away. Luckily Lord Devonport arranged for me to take a WLA job at Peasmarsh.

'It was lonely there on my own, especially as we had no children, though later on two Durham girls came to stay. But then I was told that my cottage had been commandeered by the army and I would have to go. I was really cross, so I cycled up to the big house to see Lord Devonport. "They can't do that," he said: "I'll sort it out, don't worry." Luckily the army agreed, but they insisted that two male officers were billeted with me. They had one bedroom, with me in the second, and their two batmen had to bed down on the stone scullery floor. One poor old boy had no teeth – he'd lost them overboard when coming back from France.

'It wasn't long before I was the veritable scarlet woman in Peasmarsh village, with my house full of soldiers and my husband away in France. But they were only there for six months or so, in 1940, and those officers were real gentlemen. Also, I was in the land of plenty with all the fresh meat and other things the batmen brought back from stores each night.

'Our cottage was deep in the woods, and for some time the area was full of troops massing for D-Day. This was quite intimidating when I was on my own because soldiers frequently passed close by along the lane, on their way back from the pub, and they'd whistle and call out to me.

'The loneliest house we ever lived in was a lovely old place in Swinley Forest, on the Crown estate. There were lots of snakes there. But I was always more concerned about Bert's safety when he went out poacher watching, especially at Windsor. One time it got so bad there the keepers were told not to go out alone at night. But there was always little backing with poaching prosecutions on the Crown estates. I suppose they were worried about any adverse publicity.'

Wherever they lived, Doris and Bert were generally fairly self-sufficient, as Doris recalls: 'We always had a good vegetable and fruit garden and a few chickens. In those days every keeper had 25 or so hens as a perk, so we always had eggs and the occasional boiling fowl. Rabbits and pigeons were plentiful, but we never had a pheasant unless it was given to us. Most keepers did help themselves a bit, but Bert's father always said that every one counts if you want to keep your job, so we carried on in the same way.

'If you were lucky you sometimes had the chance to earn a few extra shillings. For example, Bert once had to prepare a lot of mole skins – at about 9d a time – to line a full-length tweed coat for Lady Devonport. And at Braxted, just after the war, I did well with all the Yanks who came to lunch. They'd stare in amazement at the food I prepared, such as a whole salmon decorated with cucumber slices, and say: "Here's five bob – take yourself off to the movies!"

'The fish man called twice a week at Peasmarsh, and the lake lapped right up to one cottage, so Bert could fish from the dining room with the French windows open, catching perch up to 2lb.

'I sometimes used a bike for shopping, but groceries were often delivered in the old days, even out to lonely cottages like ours. Generally you had to order five bob's worth, and six or seven bob bought a big order. Even as headkeeper Bert earned only 45s a week, and when Lord Devonport gave him a ten bob Christmas box he thought he'd been handed the crown jewels! However, our cottage was rent-free up to the war, and coal was only two bob a hundredweight. The paper man brought the coal, and he shovelled it into the cupboard under the stairs, so the dust went everywhere. Many people kept coal in the bath, but we didn't have one. We also gathered a lot of wood for our fires and kitchen range, and our luxury was a Primus stove.

'Gypsies used to be regular callers, mostly selling pegs, and you always felt obliged to buy. One travelling family, the Wilsons, came round with hardware, and the mother would beg you to buy something. I'd say I couldn't afford it, but she'd say "You have that, my duck, and pay me later!" They loved that, because then they had an excuse to come back.

'There were always a lot of gypsies about, especially in hop-picking time. One man, a pole-puller, always bragged about the number of rabbits he got, and I asked him where his snares were. Then one evening I introduced him to my husband – the headkeeper! – and he didn't know where to put his face!'

Doris and Bert had their first car in 1938, a Baby Austin which cost £60. There was no driving test then, and when Doris was in the Women's Land Army, not only did she drive tractors on the farm but also a van full of produce to market twice a week. She has been driving ever since.

Typical of true countrywomen, Doris was always willing and realistic when it came to the killing of game and livestock, yet she always avoided unnecessary suffering for any animal and was very sensitive when it came to caring for cats and dogs. For example, when she worked for the Women's Land Army she always took Jet, her black cocker spaniel, to work with her. When Jet died aged 15, Doris and Bert put her in their Baby Austin and took her down to Braxted churchyard, where Bert buried her at the dead of night while Doris held the hurricane lamp. They put the turf back neatly over the grave, left no marker, and no one ever knew what they had done. Doris explains: 'We didn't want to put Jet in our garden as we knew we wouldn't be there long and we didn't want someone else to dig her up. I'd had her all through the war years and she was so knowing. She used to sit and look at grandma at a certain time of evening as if to say "When are you going to bed?"

'We also had these two lovely cats, Funf and Woody, which we got as feral kittens. Bert shot their mother with a rifle, as cats can be real killers on a pheasant shoot, and later caught the kittens in a baited trap. He took them up to his cabin, but at first they wouldn't eat and it took ages to tame them. We kept them in a chicken coop and fed them pieces of rabbit, which they snatched off a cane. After a long time they accepted us and came into the house.

'Then there was the time I saw this beautiful cat outside and as it didn't run away I went up to stroke it. As I did so I felt this wire round its body and thought: "Oh, you poor thing: you've been caught in one of Bert's snares." So I carefully loosened the wire and let the cat go. But that evening, when I told Bert about it, he explained that

he'd deliberately set the snare to catch the cat where he'd seen it run up the fence! The animal had taken the heads off a few of Bert's snared rabbits and had quite spoiled them, and it had to go. I don't think I was too popular that day!'

Doris had plenty of other surprises, too. One night at Peasmarsh, when she visited the loo at the end of the garden, the seat was already occupied – by a barn owl! Then there was the time she returned home and, as usual, reached for the candle and matches kept just inside the scullery door. Much to her horror, in the dark she was hit in the face by 'this wet, furry thing': Bert had killed an otter (in the days when they were not protected by law) and hung its skin up to dry. Unfortunately he had omitted to tell Doris about his intention to make a bedroom rug!

There have been more serious surprises too: 'Once, when I was in the Women's Land Army, I was loading hop pokes on to a trailer when the tractor driver suddenly moved off, not realizing I was still up top. I was jerked off the front and fell between the tractor and trailer; however, I had the presence of mind to lie still, so I wasn't injured.

'I was equally lucky when I was peppered by shot at Abberton. A gun took a wild shot at a low partridge but bagged me instead – you could see the pattern of the shot all down my corduroy breeches, but fortunately none penetrated as I was just too far away. Quite rightly, the host really went for that careless gun.'

Looking back over the years, Doris regrets the excessive commercialization of shooting, as she explains: 'The one thing money can't buy is manners. When we were at Braxted all the Plessey guests were tycoons out for a booze-up. They weren't real gentry and had no etiquette, only the ability to make money. It was all show.

In total contrast, there were people like Lord Tavistock who came to Peasmarsh dressed like a tramp, to the extent that one day this chap said, "Morning, mate!" to him, thinking he was a beater. But he was a real gentleman.

'We were always treated with respect by the real aristocracy, who had nothing to prove. They'd come in your kitchen and sit down for a cup of tea with you, but most of these jumped-up businessmen wouldn't dream of doing that.

'At Sedgwick we had these wonderful New Year's parties for all the staff, and we'd also entertain the staff from other estates. Mr and Mrs Abbey would go off to London so that we had the place to ourselves. Then we'd go back to other estates. The owners of Pelsham, Mr and Mrs Scott, even used to join in with us, doing solo songs and so on.'

Having lived on the Crown estate for many years, Doris has met members of the royal family quite a few times. She was particularly excited when first presented to the Queen: 'That year Her Majesty particularly requested that all the keepers and their wives be present at the annual staff Christmas party. So we got all togged up and went up to Windsor Castle, with special badges on us and our cars. We went up the grand staircase and were shown into this room, which was all set out with magnificent food – a sight for sore eyes! We were all given a number where to sit at these round tables, and a band played.

'After the meal we were shown into the ballroom, where an orchestra played. Then it was announced that the royal party was coming and we all had to line up to be introduced by Major Haig, the head ranger. I spoke to Prince Philip and Princess Margaret as well as the Queen. It was lovely – though on shooting days you see them as very ordinary people, with waxproofs and gundogs.

'We always go to the estate's royal chapel, where the hoi polloi have their special entrance, but when they come out we sometimes meet face to face. If the royals want to stop and chat, they will; the Queen Mum in particular never forgot a face and always wanted to talk, saying something like, "Didn't we have some lovely hymns today?" '

For over 50 years Doris has been a very active member of the thriving Windsor Great Park Women's Institute; she plays the piano for 'Jersualem' at the start of every meeting. When the Queen Mother presented Doris with the local WI cup for the third time, it was not surprising that Her Majesty smiled and said: 'I think we've met before.'

Another aristocrat whom Doris and Bert see regularly is the widowed Lady Devonport. However, such meetings are in marked contrast to the old days: 'When we were on her husband's estate she never, ever put foot in our cottage; whereas now, when we go back to Peasmarsh for a few days' holiday each year, we always have to go and have lunch with her. She puts on the full works, with wine, and now she asks us what we would like to eat! She's always asking us about the past "in that awful little concrete cottage" with a stone scullery floor and the living room lino flapping up and down in the draught. "I can't believe you lived like that," she says. So we have to tell her that we had no choice because her husband wouldn't spend any money on the place.

'But we never complained about our lot because we didn't really know any different. Keepering's so different now. With Bert's job it was almost impossible to take proper holidays, so we never bothered apart from a few days busman's holiday here and there. In any case, you still had all the dogs, ferrets and chickens to look after, and if you didn't take your entitlement in March, you'd had it, because you were far too busy for the rest of the year. Also, we were always kept poor by a constant stream of relatives and friends visiting us from the town for their holidays!

'Nowadays there's no comparison, with the keepers all mollycoddled. They mostly work to hours, and on big estates such as Windsor there are even relief keepers so that they can take holidays abroad. Also, they're rarely on their own, and have motorbikes and four-wheel-drives to zip about on, whereas Bert had to walk everywhere. But at least we have this Crown cottage in Sunninghill Park for life –

we've been here 12 years already. Mind you, the good Lord was with us on the night of the 1987 hurricane, when two huge beeches and two great oaks came down just outside. If the wind had been in the other direction we would have been crushed out of sight.'

There is no doubt that Doris has been the perfect partner for Bert. Looking back over their 60 years together, he told me: 'I'm a trying bloke for anyone to live with, and from a woman's point of view the old keepering life was dreadful; but Doris has given me 100 per cent. I've never had a meal set in front of me I couldn't eat, and in my work I certainly couldn't have managed without her. I was extremely lucky to get someone always game for anything.'

Chapter 8

AN ALL-ROUND
HORSEWOMAN

Tom Quinn

AN ALL-ROUND HORSEWOMAN

IF YOU GO TO SHERBERTON FARM TO RIDE AT DIANA COAKER'S TREKKING CENTRE, YOU MAY

BE PUT ON A STARTLINGLY BLUE-EYED HORSE FROM RUSSIA, OR A SOLID-LIMBED PRODUCT

OF FRANCE. HOWEVER, THESE MORE UNUSUAL EQUINES ARE DELIGHTFUL EXCEPTIONS IN A

PLACE WHERE THE TRADITION OF DARTMOOR PONY-KEEPING IS AS SOLID AND ENDURING AS

THE LICHEN-COVERED BOULDERS ON THE SURROUNDING MOORLAND.

I met Diana in her kitchen, hastily grabbing a sandwich having been out with a party of ten 11-year-old children, and she confirmed the long association between the farm and Dartmoor ponies: 'There have been pedigree Dartmoors here for six generations; moreover Anthony, my youngest son, is the sixth generation to farm Sherberton.' The farm is right in the heart of Dartmoor. To get to it you cross several grey stone bridges huddled over clear, tumbling water, the surrounding fields bordered by walls made of rounded boulders.

Diana keeps her riding ponies in an old Devon longhouse. Her Dartmoor ponies are visible from the farmhouse, in fields called 'new-takes' – or 'newtechs' as they are known locally. Dartmoor farmers acquired new-takes through an old tradition whereby every 15 to 20 years they were allowed to take in a new piece of the moor. Usually the new piece was very rough ground and the rocks out of it were used to make the boundary. This is a custom that is no longer permitted; however, existing new-takes have been the subject of a specific project in recent years, something that Diana's late husband, John, initiated with the Duchy of Cornwall and that other farmers have now taken up –

that is, to keep so many Dartmoor ponies in a new-take, liaising with the Duchy in a scheme which helps farmers improve their pony progeny. Diana explains: 'You have a pedigree stallion running with about 15 mares in the area of a new-take. The owner of the mares gets paid so much to run their mare there, and the owner of the new-take also gets money. The idea is to produce registered stock.'

Improving the Dartmoor pony's lot in life is something else that concerns Diana. Under a National Parks scheme, each January Diana, plus another breeder-cum-farmer, a vet and a National Park representative go out to farms all over Dartmoor and inspect ponies; if their condition is good, the farmer will continue to receive a subsidy for them.

Dartmoor ponies are also very much part of the life of Diana's children. Her daughter Susan is the Registration Secretary of the Dartmoor Pony Society; like her mother, she is a well-known judge at shows. She and Anthony are on the Commoners' Council, and one of the rulings it has implemented is to have what is called a 'clear day' for the ponies. This day is in October, and on it, all ponies are taken off the moor and members of the Commons' Council go round and count them. If a farmer has too many, he is told to get rid of the surplus: this prevents overgrazing, and as a consequence, hungry ponies straying in search of forage.

Diana's present personal campaign is to redress the situation whereby Dartmoor has no control over its stallions; it is the only common that she knows of in England that allows any old colt to run around. 'I'm trying to get it that the stallions which run on the moor are inspected and are of a good standard of either Dartmoor or Shetland. At present the problem lies with one- to three-year-old half-bred colts. You see, an older stallion keeps together the more mature mares he likes, and will not have a young mare in his herd. So these young mares then take up with these young colts and they breed awful nondescript things which make two guineas in the market. If stallions were licensed, these colts would have to be cut or taken off the moor.'

It is obvious that Diana becomes deeply concerned about matters when it comes to horses. She confirms this by commenting: 'A few years ago people rode, but they can't ride now – they're taught to ride with their knees stuck out and their hands up in the air, and it doesn't work. I think that's why there are so many accidents. If you watch any of the good riders, they don't ride in this current lackadaisical fashion!'

I ask Diana if she teaches riding to the people who hire her ponies for trekking. She says, 'I teach them as they go along. When I have a party of children they must all learn to shorten their reins before they go on, and they hold on to the front of the saddle until they can rise to the trot.'

Riding at Sherberton goes back a long way. Diana's sister-in-law had riding ponies in 1933, and Diana believes there were probably ponies there before that. She herself came to Sherberton and brought her own ponies when she married in 1951.

'I lived in a house called Kenbury, six miles outside Exeter and which today is under the motorway. My mother hunted, and my father show-jumped and hunted, and also played polo at the army polo club at Exeter. He'd been in the army, and during his army days he'd had a horse called Glad-Eye, which he later wrote a book about.

'Glad-Eye was a short-tailed cob which went right through World War I with father – it even went to Egypt with him, and came back, which a lot of cavalry horses didn't, because the army sold them to Egyptian buyers. I believe they sold over 20,000. In 1930 my Aunt Dorothy, the wife of father's brother who was Major General Brooke, went to Cairo and was shocked at the condition of the surviving cavalry horses. She wrote a letter to the *Morning Post* about them, and it raised over £20,000. She bought the 5,000 horses still working out there; the ones that were very bad were put down, and in 1934 she set up the Brooke Hospital for Animals in Cairo. As many will

tell you, it still exists today and has gone from strength to strength. In fact they have now moved into India too, which I understand is absolutely terrible, with horses still working in mines.

'Anyway, about Glad-Eye – in 1934 or 1936 there was a parade of 24 veterans at Olympia, and my father took Glad-Eye – and Princess Elizabeth (the present Queen) gave him 25 lumps of sugar! Father had met the princess at an officers' garden party, and had talked to her about Glad-Eye and the forthcoming veterans' parade; and she had promised to come to it and give Glad-Eye 25 lumps of sugar. So she kept her word, and afterwards wrote letters to Glad-Eye and sent him sugar.

'I once took a horse by train to a London show; there was another horse on the train, and when we arrived at Paddington it transferred to a really posh horsebox – but I had just my father in his car to meet me. It was early morning and I set off to ride from Paddington to White City, and I shall always remember that when I asked directions of the first two people I met, neither knew the way!'

The phone in Diana's kitchen rings. It is to be the first of several phone calls, all enquiries for puppies she has had advertised for sale. The caller is unlucky, because all of them except one have been sold, and that

one is to stay at Sherberton. Black and white, and called Fly, she is the fifth generation down from a Sherberton collie called Peach. Fly lives in a cardboard box by the kitchen range, and during our talk had crawled out to do some exploring. Diana put the phone down and continued: 'My father used to work his horses on the farm at Kenbury, because when he wasn't playing soldiers he was playing farming! They pulled the mowing machine, the plough and did everything. We had a cowman to help with our herd of 30 cows, and their milk was taken to Exeter by pony and trap; in the winter the hunters took it, and in summer, the polo ponies. At first it went to a little dairy in Alphington Street, and when that closed, Hammet's Dairies took it – but they were the far side of Exeter, so then it had to go by car instead of horse and trap.

'When World War II started we moved from Kenbury to a small house at Lympstone. The milking herd was sold, but we still kept the horses. I was 14 then. I left school at 16 and went to work for our milkman on a farm, and I worked there all through the war and then continued afterwards; it was hand milking in those days, too! My main mode of transport was either horse and cart or my bicycle. Sometimes I'd drive off to some dance in my horse and cart. I remember going to Sidmouth once, which is quite a long drive, to a hunt dance. I left my horse at a hunt-member's stable, then drove it home afterwards, lit by candles on the cart – but of course there wasn't much traffic about in those days! On the occasions I reached home in the early hours I used to leave the cart at the bottom of the drive and walk the horse up the side of the drive so no one heard me come back. Of course, despite coming in so late, I still had to be milking cows at 7.30 in the morning, and sometimes I'd drop off to sleep during afternoon milking – I'll always remember the vet catching me asleep against a cow!'

Diana then explained that at home at this time she looked after her parents' horses, and in the evening used to take children out riding. By degrees the riding stable grew, until in about 1946 she had eight ponies. She also found she was doing a lot for the local Pony Club, so decided to stop working at the farm and concentrate on her horses. Weekends were usually taken up with going to gymkhanas: 'In those days you had open events, and everything was always round a ring. There was no stopping and starting, and it was far more competitive than it is today; you had to have a fast pony and be really quick.'

John Coaker, who was to become Diana's husband, was also a regular competitor at the gymkhanas, and Diana recalled those days: 'He was absolutely unbeatable, really incredible; 'I had two good gymkhana ponies, and as I obviously couldn't ride both, he used to ride one. It was quite usual for us both to go to a gymkhana and win every event. We had this one pony that was very good at musical poles because it could canter on the spot – in fact it was so good we used to take it in turns to ride it.

'However, I think I really got to know John after I'd bought a Dartmoor pony in Exeter

market for four guineas. I took it to Exmouth Show where the Coakers were showing their Dartmoors, and John's father said, "Oh, look! There's my Two Tails!" They recognized it

from its brand, and remembered that it had been reared on a mare which had lost her foal, and they'd skinned the foal and put it on this one and so for a few days it had two tails. That's how it became "Two Tails". Well, you see, Two Tails wanted a husband, so I put her on the train to come here. In those days it was easy to put horses on the train at Exmouth and someone met her at Princetown and led her over. I suppose things grew from there with John.'

In the early 1950s Diana and John were among the first owners and breeders to export their ponies to the Continent: 'In those days there were no roll-on, roll-off ferries, you had to ship them. They went into a little crate which a crane lifted on board, and then they were put in a pen.'

It was also at about this time that they started another venture: 'A chap from the Fells called Jack Williams came to see us. He used to buy ponies and organized pony trekking, and suggested we did this, too. Then an organization which ran recreational holidays asked us if we'd be interested in doing pony trekking and said they'd send five or six people a week. That's how the trekking began. We advertised through horse magazines, and also *Farmer's Weekly* used to bring 50 children every year.

'For a time we had 100 horses each summer, but as it was impossible to keep that number during the winter, we lent some out and sold the rest. We had an annual horse sale on the third Saturday in September. We still hold the sale – we're coming up to our 34th – but now it's collective and other people can enter horses for sale. However, all the horses are sold under very strict warranty and if you've got a pony that's just been broken you have to sell it on a week's trial. A lot of people don't like that.'

In addition to the trekking business Diana used to fit in riding at point-to-

The traditional annual hunt race on Dartmoor, which Diana won several times

points, and often took part in, once fell off in, and won several times, the annual hunt race that took place on Dartmoor. The jumps in this were known as 'banks and flys': the banks were the high-turved field boundaries on the moor, and the flys a ditch dug before a section of stone walling and brushwood laid up against the wall. It is a race that is no longer run: traditionally it was for hunters and was therefore run at a relatively sensible pace, but it became too dangerous when people began riding it on Thoroughbreds and turning somersaults.

Diana's racing career included becoming National Hunt point-to-point champion lady jockey. She cannot remember the exact year of this achievement: 'It was in the days when ladies only rode once at a meeting and in a separate race from the men!'

Sherberton ponies continued to find owners abroad. Diana generally accompanied the horses to their new homes, and Peter, her eldest son, when he became old enough to help out, drove the delivery lorry. It wasn't all plain sailing! In the days before the Common Market they had to contend with various countries' regulations. For example, in Italy, only so many horses were allowed to travel in a horsebox, the rest had to go by Italian rail or lorry. On

numerous occasions Diana has found herself at foreign railway stations organizing gates to act as partitions in trucks to separate herself or a helper from the ponies, and asking for hay and water in a variety of languages. 'It's funny how you could get hay at these border stations,' she recalls.

On one memorable occasion she found herself signing on to a ship's crew list – not for her own business, but to help others: 'A vet and his wife from Tavistock were moving to South Africa, and they'd asked my husband to do the paperwork for them as they were taking twelve ponies and a Thoroughbred with its foal at foot. They also had to have someone to accompany the animals, and so John said, "Take my wife."

'For insurance purposes, on board I had to become able seaman Coaker, and because I was female I had to live in the officers' quarters and abide by set rules. It was very like boarding school!

'As well as looking after the horses I had to look after three bulls and two cows which were being exported for someone else. It was very hot on the equator and I had to wash these cattle down to keep them cool. Despite doing this, one of the bulls became stressed and developed transit fever, which is a lack of calcium. We were on what they call the South African rollers, where it's a bit rough. People refused to give me a hand because they were afraid that the bull would fall on them – in fact the only person who came to help me was the barman. Because of the rolls of fat on the bull I couldn't find his jugular vein, so injected the whole bottle of calcium under his skin. But it didn't do any good, and he died, very quickly actually.'

Diana still makes forays abroad, and the last time we spoke had just returned from a trip which included buying two black Freisian horses in Holland for an undertaker in Ireland.

RESTAURANT & GRILL ROOM

WAITING ROOM
GENTLEMENS TOILET
HAIRDRESSING & BATH ROOMS

GENTLEMEN
HAIRDRESSING SALON
AND BATH ROOMS

Chapter 9
THE PEOPLE'S PORTER

Tom Quinn

THE PEOPLE'S PORTER

Born in 1913 in The Perseverance pub in Islington, North London, Tom Jales started work in 1927. Despite the fact that he has lived in Hertfordshire for many years, he is still a devoted follower of Islington's Arsenal football club: in 75 years he has hardly ever missed a home game. His passion for football is the first thing you notice about him; that, and his passion for the railways.

His first job was as a railway messenger boy in the heart of the old City of London, and he went straight into it from school at the age of 14. He was sent to Bread Street for an interview that had been arranged by a neighbour who worked on the London and North Eastern Railway, as it was then known: 'A Mr Syder – I'll never forget his name – interviewed me. He was what was called the City Manager. We met in a dark old room that by today's standards wouldn't look like an office at all – you have to remember this was before London was bombed, when it was still a city of tiny lanes and old houses.

'Anyway, after my interview Mr Syder said there might be a chance they'd have me; he was completely noncommittal, but it all sounded pretty optimistic to a lad of 14.' A month to the day later, Tom received a letter telling him to report to Farringdon Street station, and so a railway career that was to last more than 50 years began.

'The instant I arrived at Farringdon Street station I was put to work,' he remembers. 'There was no messing about in those days – no induction courses and little chats. I was put straight on to the switchboard, an old mechanical thing with wires coming out like spaghetti. This was relatively early days for the telephone, and for long-distance calls a whole string of operators across the country had to be co-ordinated. I had a national board for these calls, and a board for internal calls – that is, calls within the office.

'I didn't enjoy that job much, but I stuck it for six years until I was 20. It was just that good jobs were hard to come by in those days, and I didn't dare leave. It wasn't the nature of the work I objected to, it was the shifts. At 14 years old I was doing 6am to 2pm, or 2pm to 10pm, or 10pm to 6am, and this meant that, outside work, I had no life at all, no social life that is.

'As well as dealing with calls I had to file all the invoices from the goods yard – there were thousands of them, and sorting out one batch might take from 10pm until 3am. There were few calls at night, however, so you had time for all this then.'

Horses were only beginning to disappear from London's streets at this time. Trams were still to be seen on major roads across the capital, and working people hardly dreamt of owning their own houses. When Tom married in 1938, he and his wife, like most young couples, moved into a small set of rented rooms. Then a month after his 20th birthday he was transferred from the switchboard to Finsbury Park station, still in London, as a grade two porter.

'I stayed there for three happy years,' he remembers, 'and in those days portering was a real job. You had to be diplomatic and deal with people's luggage and with their problems. Effectively you were waiting on the passengers, because that was the tradition; now, most people carry their own cases. In those days they didn't, they expected a porter to be there to do it for them.

'I wouldn't say that most of those I dealt with were toffs, but they were well-to-do, and of course, the porter was just a servant – we were sort of invisible, I suppose. My other jobs were sweeping the platform every day, and unloading the milk – you quickly got the knack of rolling two great churns along the platform to the carts waiting outside. At first it seemed impossible. Rolling one along was difficult enough, and it would sometimes end up falling off the platform on to the line, but after a while you got the hang of it. Normally, in one delivery we'd have about 100 churns to roll – a hell of a back-breaking job, but there were several porters, and we quite enjoyed doing it together.'

At Finsbury Park, as at most stations in those days, there were several porters and an indicator boy who operated the lights on the sign saying where each train was due to stop. If a train stopped at one particular platform a porter was needed on each side of the train because it was a single track and so passengers could get on and off on both sides: 'Once the train was due to depart, the leading or senior porter would shout over the top of the train, "Are you all right there?" If you shouted "Yes!" in reply he'd wave his flag, you'd wave yours and they'd be off.'

Tom always felt that working on the railways gave you a sense that you were doing something important: 'People on trains had somewhere they had to go, and you had to help them get there.' As each train moved off, he and the other porters would check that all the doors were closed; but once one train had gone there was little time to relax before the next one arrived. As Tom explains, porters in the 1930s were kept very busy indeed: 'A lot of people think that there were long gaps between trains and we'd sit around playing cards and drinking tea – well, nothing could be further from the truth. There were trains every few minutes, and we never stopped for a moment, apart from official breaks, of course.'

After three years at Finsbury Park, Tom went to King's Cross; he wanted this move largely because he knew it would give him more work helping passengers with their luggage, and that in turn meant more money because it meant the chance to earn tips. He had been applying for a transfer from Finsbury Park for months, and began to be suspicious about his lack of success:

'Basically I knew I'd get more money if I was moved, but however often I applied for my transfer, nothing happened, so I began to worry that someone was blocking me. Then, quite by chance, I found out what was going on, although I only found out because one of my duties was to empty the waste-paper basket in the stationmaster's office. One morning I picked up the bin and found my latest application for transfer sitting there on the top! I was furious. Everyone was terrified of the stationmaster, but I seemed to have lost all fear that day, I was so angry. I went to see him, and I put the letter I had retrieved from the waste-paper bin in front of him. I told him that if he continued to ignore my applications I'd take the matter up with my union – and by 3pm I'd been told that I was starting at King's Cross the following Monday. That was a good example of how a powerful

Tom hard at work checking the luggage

union could protect the ordinary individual, because without a union I'd have been prevented from transferring, perhaps indefinitely.'

Tom arrived at King's Cross in 1936 and found that rather than dealing with large numbers of people, he was suddenly swamped by parcels. 'It was a shock for me – there were tons of them, and they arrived in a never-ending stream; it took up almost all the porters' time. When I started there I did the 5.15pm–1.15am turn, which was a bit of a nuisance as it meant I had to walk home to the city. It's hard to believe today how many ordinary people lived right in the heart of the City of London then. I lived in Haberdasher Street near Old Street where it's mostly offices now – although funnily enough, one of my relatives still lives in that house today.

'Even in the 1930s I would be passed by quite a bit of horse-drawn traffic, although lorries and cars were very quickly taking over. Opposite my house was a road haulier who had only horses; I remember they had one massive white one that I used to see regularly, and one of their wagons once went over my foot!'

Towards the end of the 1930s, Tom decided to move north a couple of miles from the city back to his home borough, Islington; his first memory of this period in his life is of a landlady who wouldn't let him have his papers delivered! 'Can't remember why now, but landladies could be dragons in those days!' he says with a grin.

Into the swing of things at King's Cross, he discovered the main requirement was for speed, because no sooner had one train been sorted than another was in need of attention. Mailbags were unloaded, not on to the platform side of the train, but down on to the next set of rails: 'Doing it that way meant that we could sort the mail out while the passengers were boarding,' remembers Tom.

When he started work at King's Cross, more than 200 full-time porters were still employed at the station. Many of his fellow porters were elderly men who'd started work at the turn of the century. 'They were always very nice, if a bit old-fashioned,' says Tom, 'but they showed you the ropes, tried to be helpful and so on.'

All the porters wore what Tom thought were terrible uniforms. They were navy, with a cap, but made out of extremely

'We had an inspector who was famous for walking along shouting, 'You know your duty!' – usually when we were sweeping the long platforms

rough, coarse material, and even on the hottest day of the year a porter wouldn't dare be seen without a tie and a hat. The other problem was that they very rarely seemed to fit properly, and the new man would have to go off to The Lotteries in Petticoat Lane where all railway uniforms were made, and where 'they'd sort out a new coat or trousers for you,' says Tom. Then he observed: 'In fact, the real difficulties weren't with uniforms, they were with one or two of the staff. We had an inspector, for example, who was famous for walking along shouting, "You know your duty!" – usually when we were sweeping the long platforms. Then he'd shout, "I don't want to make you do it again," but of course he often did make us do it again.'

Tom remembers that in his early days trains always seemed to be full: 'There were passengers everywhere, and in summer they often had half a ton of luggage, if they were going to Scotland for a few weeks, for example, or grouse shooting.' Streams of porters were always unloading taxis, but if they found themselves with a spare minute they queued with the other porters at the ticket office to help passengers with heavy luggage. Aristocrats were definitely the best tippers, and particularly in August when they were off to the grouse moors. 'That always seemed to put them in a good mood,' remembers Tom.

'I particularly remember the old Duke of Windsor – King Edward who abdicated. He took the royal train often, but he'd always arrive by cab, and at night. He'd get out of the cab, call a porter and walk straight past the booking office. He always seemed to have had a few drinks, and that'd be putting it mildly! I used to take him to a sleeper so no one saw him – he always seemed concerned about that, understandably I suppose. As I helped him out of the cab he'd always say, "You know where I want to go"

– and of course I knew exactly, straight into his carriage. I think I helped him across the station four or five times, but he was never accompanied by Mrs Simpson who, I suppose, preferred to stay in France. He always travelled under an assumed name, too, but we knew who he was.'

In Tom's day the royal train was always kept ready in sidings at Old Oak Common in West London, and when a member of the royal family was expected, it would be brought to King's Cross at night. 'Royal trains were definitely used a great deal more when I first arrived at King's Cross than during my last years; by then I suppose they'd started using the car more often. I can remember George V using the train, we watched him pass in the distance; then, of course, there was the Duke of Windsor, as I've said, then came George VI the present Queen's father. All the sofas in the royal train and the other soft furnishings were a rich green colour, and it was very plush and luxurious, I can tell you.'

Tom's first stint as a porter at King's Cross lasted from 1936 until 1939. After that he worked with the shunters, which meant he helped with coupling the trains, and it was during this period that he nearly lost his life, as he explains: 'I was working at Hornsey in North London at the time and the inspector told me to leave four coaches and release the engine. The carriages each had what was called a buck-eye coupling which weighed about one hundredweight: you'd pull a chain and that would make the knuckle open, and the two carriages would then move together and lock; that was the procedure. Anyway, I was under this train setting the buck-eye when the driver was told by the inspector that it was OK to reverse the train. I only just got out in time. It would have crushed my head like an eggshell.'

When World War II came, most of Tom's friends disappeared into the army, but Tom – in a reserved occupation – had to stay put. He continued with his shunting work through the first years of the war, and remembers endless troop trains: 'We always seemed to be getting them ready to take the men to the troop ships. Normally we'd put 18 coaches behind the engine for a troop train and on one occasion we'd just formed up two trains when I heard a particular noise, one we all knew and dreaded. I looked in the direction from which it was coming, and sure enough saw a doodlebug hurtling towards me straight down the line; I heard its engine cut out, too, and that was the signal that it was about to drop. Luckily, this one just went over our heads and exploded harmlessly on the Alexandra Palace racecourse nearby. It broke every window in the train – you've never seen so much flying glass. My mate Arthur Cove, who had a terrible stutter, was thrown into an awful state by the explosion; I can recall him saying in a very agitated voice, "They've broken every fffff…" and he never got further than that!'

At the end of the war Tom went back to senior portering, but this meant an unfortunate dent in his pay packet: 'A shunter's money in those days was 55s a week, which is why from a financial point of view I wasn't that pleased to be back portering when the war ended – a senior porter was on only 50s a week.'

One of Tom's favourite jobs was winding up the indicator board, which involved cranking a big handle until the right destination appeared. However, his duties changed again in 1946 when he became a summer seat reservation inspector. 'It was a promotion, but only for the summer; a lot of jobs on the railway were done like this. You got a sort of holiday fill-in promotion giving you a chance to move up temporarily to a job that you might or might not like. Likewise the management could see if you were going to be any good at it; if not, then you went back to your normal job at the end of the summer and no hard feelings. Basically, a seat inspector puts the reservation tickets on the seats in the train – not the most fascinating work, but it did mean a pay increase.'

By 1955 Tom was a supervisor foreman in the luggage office. He thinks he was appointed because senior management wanted to avoid a repeat of an earlier incident that had been caused by the fact that two foremen had been put in charge of left luggage, but without a supervisor: 'It used to cost nine old pence, roughly, to leave your suitcase, and you were issued with a ticket. Well, two of the men had apparently been re-using old tickets and pocketing the money. They got caught because the authorities suspected something was going on and set a trap using a policewoman in civilian clothes. The two who were caught were told that they'd be let off if they said who else was involved – it was thought that it had to be more than just two. Anyway, 11 staff went to prison as a result of that little caper. After all the fuss had died down they decided to put in a supervisor, and that was me. I stayed for ten years and started on a wage of £10 8s 2d a week.

'Working in the left luggage at King's Cross was a real education, I can tell you – you wouldn't believe the things people used to leave with us. On two occasions we were left a package that contained a dead baby. I can remember the first time this happened – we'd had this suitcase for a while when my mate noticed the terrible smell coming from it. I went over and it really was appalling, a sort of sweet, decaying smell. We called the police, and by the time they arrived there were flies

everywhere, but we hadn't dared touch the case. Two detectives came and took it away to the Caledonian Road police station. They phoned to tell us they'd found a baby's body inside, but then they came back with the case empty to set a trap for whoever had left it. Eventually a young woman arrived and we kept her waiting while the police were called; she was duly arrested, but later released as the baby had been stillborn.

'Apart from that there used to be thousands of umbrellas, briefcases, wallets, bags, parcels, bits of furniture; it never ceased to amaze me then, and it still does now, that so many items were never collected. Why on earth would a chap who left his briefcase one evening not bother ever to collect it when it was full of his personal effects and papers? Anyway, if the stuff wasn't collected it was eventually sold and the money went to the railway benevolent fund.'

In 1965 – and by this time the old steam trains had vanished – Tom was appointed to a carriage cleaning inspector's job. He was responsible for all the 'turn-around' trains, that is, those that were arriving but had to be got ready to go out again quickly. 'You had to clean them while they were on the platform, just dashing through with a hand broom!'

Tom was also responsible for the red carpet which was ceremoniously retrieved

Tom would have been very familiar with the Great Northern Railway Class C12 4-4-2T tank engines; here one of the last survivors of this once-prolific suburban and branch line types head a farewell special (Milepost)

from a cupboard when a member of the royal family was expected: 'It was kept in a special storeroom at No 11 platform,' says Tom, 'but it wasn't – and isn't – carpet at all, it's a sort of felt material. The point of it is really just to prevent any member of the royal family slipping on the platform, a genuine danger if it happened to be wet. A letter would arrive in the first instance saying that the royal train would be arriving at the station on such and such a date, so myself and two storemen would immediately traipse off to No 11 platform. We'd grab the carpet – and it weighed a fair bit, I can tell you! – load it into an old four-wheeled barrow and wheel it across the station. They used to measure precisely where the door would be when the train stopped; the royal drivers could stop within an inch of the right place, although the inspector at King's Cross would stand there right on the mark to indicate to the driver precisely when he should come to a full halt, and the carpet would always be carefully positioned so it came right opposite the door we knew they'd use.'

Tom's last job, as a divisional inspector, lasted until he retired in 1975 after a total of 51 years' service. He hated retiring after so long, but he still enjoys his memories and his contacts with other retired railwaymen.

He particularly relishes his tales of the Duchess of Kent and certain other aristocrats: 'The duchess was a very friendly woman. Lord Lascelles, however, wasn't quite so friendly – he was always late arriving and he'd be in a tearing rush not to miss the train. He always seemed to be carrying half a ton of records, too. Once he shouted at me because he was in such a panic, and before I realized what I was doing, I shouted back! He used to swear at us too!

'I remember once the Duchess of Kent turned up with her little boy, who was rushing excitedly about all over the place; she was obviously worried about him. "Can I go on the engine?" he kept asking her. She kept telling him no, but he was so insistent that I offered to take him. Bill the driver yanked him up on the footplate, and from then on whenever he was travelling he used to look out for me and then shout: "There's my man!" On another occasion she had both her son and daughter in her compartment. I was talking to her through the window and I could see the kids behind her. I'd obviously started to smile because she suddenly said, "What are they up to now?" Well, they were pinching all the sugar and putting it in their pockets. Kids are the same all over, aren't they?'

Chapter 10

BIRD MAN

Valerie Porter

BIRD MAN

In the beautiful surroundings of the royal estates at Windsor, on the edges of a large swan-bearing lake, there is a cottage protected by a mixed woodland of fine huge trees which are dotted with nestboxes of every shape and size, carefully sited to suit the needs of different species. This is the home of the estate's retired trapper, Bert Winchester. His cheerful wife, Doris, is stirring a seething pan of strawberry jam in the kitchen, and a brew of elderflower wine is quietly fermenting nearby.

Behind the cottage, backing on to a farmyard, the formal flower garden stretches out to an enormous and highly productive vegetable and fruit garden bursting with produce and watched over by a scarecrow slowly turning in the light breeze. This white-faced figure began its career in the pheasant woods, warding off the corvids, and it also scared humans: from a distance it looks exactly like a hanging corpse. Yet it is a favourite perch for a pair of freshly fledged robins that are already almost hand-tame. With so many nestboxes around, the garden is alive with small birds.

Bert was born to be a gamekeeper: he was the fifth generation of keepers in the family. However, his career had some unusual diversions along the way and he has been responsible for helping with the conservation of countless thousands of wild birds – in hugely greater numbers than pheasants reared to be shot. His greatest passion is for waterfowl and even now he continues to be involved in ringing ducks. He loves all birds, web-footed or not.

Bert's family came originally from the tiny village of Pett, set back from the Sussex coast at Fairlight and running right down to the sea marshes. The land was fairly sandy, to the rabbits' delight, but there was a thriving woodland industry based largely on chestnut for hop-poles and especially faggots, which were used locally as sea breakwaters.

They worked on the Earl of Ashburnham's estate. Bert's father Henry Winchester, his grandfather William Winchester and his great granddad Hook

The Earl of Ashburnham's estate

(Top left) William Winchester (died 1934) in about 1925, (top right) Henry Winchester in about 1912; (below) Bert Winchester and Nails (Bert Winchester)

were all keepers in the good old days when the pheasants were wild rather than reared, and were shot over pointers. In those days keepers and their team wore bowler hats and splendid green velvet uniforms with smart brass buttons bearing their employer's crest, while most of the beaters wore smocks.

Bert's grandfather told him that the Ashburnham estate had covered 26 square miles, but that one of the earls started to give away property and money, until the estate was reduced to a few thousand acres. Today it has more or less disintegrated. Bert and his wife made a pilgrimage to the village two or three years ago and could hardly recognize the area. They asked a local man if he knew anything about Bert's ancestors. 'Winchester?' said the old man. 'Last one died two year ago.'

Pett remains 'home' to Bert, though he was actually born at Rowfant, a hamlet near Three Bridges. At the age of 13 he began to work under his father and was soon the proud owner of a crossbred Labrador called Nails, the most intelligent dog he ever knew. Bert loves dogs. 'I had three like that – intelligent. One was an all-liver spaniel. One was a Lakeland terrier. Now, that little terrier, I've never known anything like it: you were into telepathy all the time.'

As a boy at Pett, Bert remembers the old charcoal burners building their clamps. 'They had wood stacked from here to — well, the length of this house. Then they would fire that and keep it damped with sods of earth and turf and that. Because,

you see, the hop kilns were fired with charcoal in those days. That's why there were so many charcoal burners thereabouts. They were characters, these people, black as charcoal themselves. Of course, it was seasonal work mostly, after Christmas usually — well, any time really, but the farmers used to like the charcoal fairly fresh. The burners lived in bivouacs in the woods — oh, they were all characters.

'It's like the woodmen, you see. Down home all the woodland was sold off in cants, which was about an acre, and it was all cut manually by axe and billhook to make up the faggots. And they bound them with those twisted hazel withs. They used to teach me all those sorts of things. "Can you do this, boy?" they'd say. But I could only do it in an amateurish way — you know, if I wanted to take a load of pea-sticks home, then I'd twist a with or two just to show I could do it.'

They taught him the rudiments of hurdle-making and even today he has a few of his home-made miniature ones as plant shelters in the garden, though his wrists are too arthritic now for such work.

'Of course, in those days there was the wood reeve — now, they were quite remarkable people. They knew every cant of wood; they could go and mark up for the wood sales, a piece of bark taken off a tree here or there. We had a most remarkable old man, cunning as a cartload of monkeys but the most interesting of them, and I remember we'd been given a shoot on hundred and hundred of acres. And he said to me one day, "I hear you been given Rufus." "That's right, Albert," I said. He said: "Do you realize you have got the best woodcock bit in the south of England?" "Is that right?" I said. "Yup," said Albert. Well, I thought no more about this at the time. There was so much of this woodland that you would have needed ten thousand pheasants to shoot it. Well, one day I went in and flushed 20 woodcock in about a hundred yards! Choh! That was my first experience of what they call a fall of woodcock — and when you get that intake of them. It was all stunted birch and coarse sedgegrass and heather, and those birds loved it.'

When he was 19, Bert left home and became second keeper at Sedgewick Park, south of Horsham.

'Wonderful place, Sedgewick Park. It was one of those places that spoils you. All clockwork — the butler kept to his pantry, the gardener kept to his garden, the chauffeurs kept to their … everything was in line.' The kitchen maid was Doris. 'It was one of those estate romances,' he grins, and they were married in 1937. 'And here we are, the pair of us, still together even now — we've been about a long time!' Such a long time that the old way of life has now

things but there were the proper travellers, too, in their caravans. And of course every time you passed the caravan, it would be, "What's the time, sir?" And they'd ask if you'd have a cup of tea and if you stopped you were a friend for life. Of course my father always did – and they loved him. He was popular with all of them. The first ones used to come for cherry-picking, then they'd stay right through till potato-picking.

'I knew the gypsies well, but there were things that I never did understand. For instance, when they came into the district you'd see a piece of rag tied on a fence at a crossroads. Now that was a signal they knew but they would never tell me. I suppose it was directions or something. And they were clever – I remember one old man who didn't like them at all; he wouldn't sell them hay or let them have anything, and I remember once they camped near his farm and then away they went. But four days later, four rows of his potato haulms withered – four short rows at the end of the field. They'd sneaked the potatoes out from under the plants! Oh, they were real characters. But I haven't seen a Romany for... oh, more than 50 years now, I should think, a real Romany.

'I'm quite glad to think that I can remember these people. We were only talking about this the other day to a friend and saying we could remember hop-picking, we remembered the charcoal burners, we knew the stone-breakers. Oh yes, and there was a most interesting old man when I was in Essex: he used to come round turning over farmers' dunghills for them – don't know why but they paid him to do it. Dunnels, they called him. One old farmer one day, he said to the old man, "What did you do with that chain you found in that dunnel?" "Chain?" he says, "Never saw a chain." "Well, you go and turn

vanished. The estates have broken up; characters that used to be common in the countryside have disappeared.

'My father was a wonderful person with gypsies,' says Bert. 'We had special names for them. There was Lady Lusted, an old lady who lived in a barn – I don't know why we called her Lady Lusted. And a man called Yorkie, an old lady called Genty – I can't remember her partner's name. Now, my father allowed them into the woods to pick dog violets and primroses up until the first pheasant eggs were laid, you see. He would say to them, "Well, Genty," (or whoever), "I want you to spread the word that my pheasants are laying and I don't want you in the woods." "Right, sir," they'd say, and that would be it. And they were so useful to us: they would let you know if there were any strangers that were doubtful.

'Those old people lived in the barns and

that again – if you'd done it properly you'd have found the chain!"

'Then my father had an operation to remove stones from his bladder. He was a marvellous man, strong as an ox and only 49 years old, but he didn't make good progress after it at all – he had an embolism, you see. And his employer's wife came down to us with a card from the hospital and took us over there. Well, the moment we got in there I knew he'd gone. We came home and I was restless that night; I didn't go to bed and about four o'clock in the morning I heard this clomp, clomp, clomp round the outside of the house and a knock on the door. I opened it and there was old Genty, tears streaming down her face. "Sir," she said, "we heard that Master's gone." (They always called him the Master.) I said: "Yes, Genty, he has." She turned and ran off and, do you know, they sent a most beautiful wreath of primroses and violets. Nobody saw them bring them; they were just there.'

After the keeper's death, the syndicate renting that shoot decided they could not carry on without him and it was taken over by Lord Devonport, Bert's new employer down at Peasmarsh, near Rye, in the south of the country – no distance at all from the family village. It was here that Bert, as head keeper, also became an expert mole-trapper.

'There was a time with Lord Devonport when the whole park in front of the house was so overrun that you could walk across the entire park on mole-casts. "I'll have those bloody things killed!" he said. "Well," I said to him, "it'll take a long time." I bought about six dozen traps and I spent all my time doing it. I cured enough moleskins to make Lady Devonport's daughter a coat – a little coat, she was only small. The agent came along one day and asked me what I was doing out there in the park. "Mole-

trapping," I said. "I know that, you bloody fool. But why you – why not the other chaps?" "Well, they can't do it," I told him. He didn't believe me. "You hang on," he said, and went down the town. He came back with six little sachets of stuff. I read the instructions, put down the sachets – it took three days to go over the whole park with a thistle-spud, lifting up the top of the run, dropping two or three worms in. Three days later I got the tenant farmer to harrow it flat (in Sussex we call that dredging) with a row of faggots, drawn up and down, flattened the whole thing. Not another mole appeared. This was fine; the old man was delighted.

'And then November time I get a note from him: "Must see you at once." I walked straight into his study (I always did that – never bothered the butler). He spun round on his old swivel seat and said: "Winchester, the damn park's flooded! It's never been known in living history before. Why?" "Well," I said, "that's your mole-killing." "Dang and damn it!" he shouted, "I knew you'd know the answer!" "Well, that's it," I said, "they drain the land." And, do you know, it was some years before those moles came back.'

By now World War II was looming and Devonport was keen that Bert should be exempt from the forces. But Bert was determined to do his bit and off he went. He found himself in the desert with the army, and was away from home for four-and-a-half years. Doris joined the Land Army on Devonports's estate: she milked cows, drove the tractor and also drove a little cart laden with garden produce.

After the war, Bert returned to his wife and his old job, but there were problems. He found himself being asked to do all kinds of general estate work, to which he objected. 'Damn it, Winchester! We've all done things during the war that we didn't like doing!' protested Devonport. 'I know my lord, but the war's over now.' He decided to leave. 'And this,' he says, grinning broadly, 'is how I began my inglorious career — my very inglorious career!'

For a while Bert was at Great Braxted Park in Essex. Then came his really lucky break to give him a post where, he claims with glee, he 'never had such a time in my life!'

He had been out on a boat one day as a guest on the Abberton Reservoir, near Colchester, when he was asked: 'Would you like to catch those birds?' There was an experimental floating trap to catch ducks for ringing, though in practice it seemed to catch everything but ducks. But he did well and was offered a job by 'the general', though he could not pay him as much as four pounds a week. Bert looked at Doris and whispered: 'Do you think we could manage?' 'Well, we could try,' she replied. And so they came to Abberton Reservoir, in 1952.

The reservoir was exactly that at the time — a source of water — but the general (CB Wainwright, CBE, an excellent ornithologist) was quietly establishing a ringing station. He decided that the best chance for his plans was to involve Peter Scott, who immediately recognized the site's potential. 'I mean,' says Bert, 'in the four years I was there, I helped the old man to ring 33,000 ducks — a tremendous lot. He was quite right. It was and still is the best place in Europe.'

The traps were purely for ringing and releasing — a strong contrast to Bert's work as a keeper, where sport and killing were the aims of the job. He became a man of the water, spending a great deal of time in a boat, which he loved. The island where the traps were set was a 20-minute row across the water and an excuse for many an adventure — to Doris's increasing dismay. She became quite nervous for him out in the boat.

One winter there was a great freeze. As the thaw began, the island was threatened with submersion by the rapidly rising water level, and the traps were being swept out towards deep water. They dragged out an old tin boat and headed out with grappling hooks to rescue the traps, Bert promising Doris he'd be home by 3.30pm. But it was a pea-souper of a fog and they had to work blind with the aid of a compass. At 6.30pm, in the fog and the dark, they were still out there and a rescue party was sent out, heading for the sound of that tin boat.

Eventually they made it safely to the shore. 'If you don't leave this job,' said Doris, at the end of her tether with worry, 'I shall leave you!'

'And that,' says Bert with a smile, 'was the end of my career as an ornithologist for the Wildfowl Trust.' It had been a wonderful four years and he still retains a great admiration for General Wainwright, a man with imagination and immense skill, who turned Bert into a highly-trained live-trapper and ringer of birds. He still loves to return to Abberton, though on a recent quick visit he was surprised to see how much it had changed. In this time in the 1950s there had been no vegetation other than reedmace and a few willows. 'But over the years people had stuck in pieces of willow for duck hides — and now they are big trees. And they have a colony of nesting cormorants in these willows — it's the only inland nesting colony in the country. And there used to be otters there in the old days — it was lovely for otters, you could see them almost any time if you knew where to look. If I had less than eight there, I was low. Mind you, there was 1,200 acres of water. But they have completely gone now, haven't they?'

His record count at Abberton was 20,000 birds. It was August and the teal came through in huge numbers that year, closely followed by five peregrines. Two of the predators used one of the traps as a viewing post, before launching themselves at the birds. 'To see them going for a teal,' says Bert in admiration, 'was worth seeing!'

He has a particular soft spot for teal. He would go back to Abberton every year to take over when his successor was on holiday, and he remembers trapping a teal one day that he had originally ringed 14 years before. He also recalls a day in 1954: he had ringed 13 teal, when the land agent invited him to join him for an evening shoot. 'I stood in this hide,' says Bert, 'and I shot five teal. Then there was a lull and I let the dogs go to bring them in, and three of those teal were ones I had ringed less than an hour before. I have never shot a teal since.'

He produces a list of numbers ringed over a sample period up to April 1968. It covers a huge range of species, including songbirds. There is an entry for pied wagtails – 3,682 of

them. 'One of my favourite birds – oh, I love all birds,' he says, 'and I used to love the yellow wagtail. I once ringed one as a juvenile and seven years in a row I caught it in the same trap on the same day. It's wonderful to think that it had been to Africa and back in the meanwhile. And you might laugh to see that we were ringing coots – everybody did roar with laughter when we started that, until we began to get recoveries back from as far away as Leningrad.'

Although it was only for four years on a full-time basis, clearly Abberton has been a major part of Bert Winchester's life. But he moved on, and in 1956 he came to Windsor as a keeper on the Flemish Beat running down to the town itself.

Windsor Great Park, with its fertile but heavy clay soil, was originally a hunting forest densely clothed with oaks. In common with other hunting forests like the Dean and Sherwood, however, huge areas were clear-felled during World War I when the country was desperate for timber. Yet one of the few patches of true ancient

'...and I shot five teal...'

Pied wagtail

oak forest remaining in England lies within the boundaries of Windsor Forest. It is very carefully protected – its ecology is far too delicately balanced to withstand intrusion by the general public. It is the centre of a Site of Special Scientific Interest (SSSI) which owes its continued existence to a far-sighted forester who, some 50 years ago, at a time when the government was urging the mass planting of conifers to restock the nation's war-plundered timber resources, held up a barring hand in protection of what others might have seen as a scene of woodland decay, where plenty of huge, stag-headed old trees littered the landscape. The value of these remnants of the old Windsor hunting forest was recognized by this perceptive forester, and today's ecologists bless him for that.

Windsor played its part in commercial forestry: it became part of the Forestry Commission's dedication scheme after the war. Areas that had been clear-felled during World War I were largely restocked with naturally regenerated oak and planted 'intimate' mixtures, though after World War II more conifers were used. There were some 70 different tree species dating from that period.

The altruistic attitude towards conservation has held sway at Windsor ever since and it is often cited by English Nature as a good example to other estates, showing just what can be done to conserve old woodland while at the same time combining the traditional role of producing timber and also allowing ample but judiciously regulated public recreation.

Bert maintained his interest in ringing while he was a keeper at Windsor; indeed, he was now far more interested in ringing than in shooting. While he was at Flemish he ringed an extraordinarily large woodcock one February evening. 'And in April it was shot in Russia: it was the first

ever recovery of a ringed woodcock from Russia. They nest in Windsor Forest quite freely. Funny thing – I was, what, 60 years old before I saw a woodcock carry its young.' He saw the phenomenon 12 times during the summers of 1976 and 1977. Each time the juveniles were fully-grown and capable of flying as strongly as the adults. They were carried to safety when danger threatened and his immediate question was: how? Their legs are short and seem incapable of gripping in the manner of a bird of prey's talons. He noticed that the juvenile was supported by the adult's tail, fully fanned and held vertically, while at the front, support was given by the adult's neck, stretched across and under the juvenile's throat – an uncomfortable looking posture for the carrier. How, then, did the adult load its passenger? In August 1977, a woodcock rose almost vertically from a deep ditch a few paces from him to a height of about 12 feet. Then it folded its wings, plummeted on to the back of a juvenile 'frozen' on the bank of the ditch, and carried it away. But the action was far too swift for him to observe the method of collection – it was even faster than that of a sparrowhawk taking stationary prey from the ground.

During his time at Windsor, Bert took a great interest in the estate's wildlife and observed how the populations varied over the years. Between 1956 and 1987 he carried out his own casual survey of species, which is now lodged in Windsor Castle's private library and which covered Windsor Forest, Bagshot and Swinley Forests, Windsor Great Park, Fort Belvedere, Clock Case and Home Park. He listed 167 species of bird, including a White's thrush and memorably, a golden oriole. 'That was when I was on Flemish. I heard this most beautiful call in the top of some very high beech trees, a lovely mellow sound, in August 1957, and another in August 1958 – probably the same bird. It was the same year that I saw the White's thrush: I saw it several times but didn't know what it was at first. It had an undulating flight, like a woodpecker. Then it settled close to me and I put the glasses on it.' Even today, Bert always carries binoculars wherever he goes.

He noted the decline of many bird species over the period. The harsh winter of 1963 took a heavy toll on the wrens in particular and wiped out a colony of Dartford warblers, a roost of some 4,000 fieldfares and redwings, nearly all the kingfishers and the lesser spotted woodpecker; the little owls and grey herons suffered badly, too, but recovered fairly quickly. But then came a second disaster, and this time Bert pinned the blame fairly and squarely on human use of pesticides: thousands of birds died between 1964 and 1970 from their cumulative effects, particularly the chaffinches and, indirectly, softbills taking insects and worms from sprayed land. Woodpigeons and stock doves littered the floors of the forests with their bodies under their habitual roosts, though they soon built up into large numbers again. Sparrowhawks suffered along the foodchain by taking finches contaminated with pesticides, but they, too, made a spectacular recovery. Grey partridge began to decline rapidly in the mid-1950s and became rare.

Various migrant species use the estate, of course, but these, too, are much lower in numbers than of old – nightingales are now rare and no longer nest on the estate, nor do wood warblers; chiffchaffs, willow

'... a woodcock rose almost vertically from a deep ditch ...'

warblers and skylarks are greatly reduced; wrynecks and nightjars have become rare; and even the cuckoo numbers declined over the two decades of Bert's survey. The enormous starling roost in the Great Park, once a feature that could be traced back for more than 100 years, was abandoned. Barn owls declined sharply with the loss of the old elms and their cavities.

Bert's observations covered mammals, fish, amphibians, reptiles and lepidoptera as well as birds. The estate was rich in butterflies and moths; adders were common in Bagshot and Swinley Forests, but grass snakes in the Great Park declined in recent years, with the only known example of a smooth snake in the park killed by a visitor in 1968. Frogs had become rare but were widespread; toads became very rare from the mid-1960s but were recovering a decade later. Common lizards and slow-worms were quite common.

Hares, like so many other creatures, suffered a huge drop: they had been common up to the mid-1970s but were very low in numbers ten years later. Bat populations, on the other hand, actually increased. Most other mammal populations remained fairly steady, or were controlled by the keepers and trappers.

The whole idea of shooting began to pall while Bert was on the Flemish Beat; he knew he no longer fitted in properly. He grew restless and in 1959 he was delighted to transfer to the estate's Forestry Department, to specialize in squirrel control. Grey squirrels were causing a huge amount of damage at the time and three full-time trapping posts were created.

It was in his role as a trapper that Bert really came to know the forest well. He had access to all the woodlands on the estate, from Broadmoor prison and Sunninghill and Camberley, right through to Datchet. In those early days they were setting up to 18 dozen Fenn traps on the ground; it was a seasonal job, for the squirrels tended to come to ground more often from January to March and again from September to November. They tried cage traps, but unsuccessfully. They also used squirrel poles and attacked some 1,500 dreys.

He was enjoying himself, especially in that freedom to roam the woods. But then in 1966: 'Well, I made my life's one mistake – or one of the biggest mistakes; I knew I had done wrong as soon as I did it. A friend sent me a newspaper advert for a wildfowl curator. Well, I was interested in this because I like to know where all these wildfowl collections are, you see.'

It is a long story but, eventually, Bert took on the job and was fired a month later. Now he had a problem: he had no job and no home. But it was all quickly solved. The head keeper from Windsor came to see him that very day – one of the keepers had suddenly left, without giving any notice at all, and he would be grateful if Bert would take over. So once again Bert became a keeper at Windsor, this time on the 'very boring' Long Walk Beat, and there he stayed until 1972 when, to his joy, his former forestry boss came to ask if he would like to go back into the woods as a trapper. Would he!

Not only was he back in a job he liked, but he was allocated to a home he and Doris remember as their favourite. It had been the laundry to a hunting mansion, which had been dismantled in 1813

'It was a lovely old place, steeped in history, plumb in the middle of the forest. Mind you, most of that forest today has been taken over by the new town of Bracknell. Dear, oh dear!'

Lesser spotted woodpecker

Below the house was a twin row of lime trees stretching over the forest and crossing with another avenue at the site of the mansion, and the trees (according to a book Bert had read) were dated back to '17-something, I think – very, very old.' He and Doris lived in glorious seclusion there.

He began to take more notice of the deer while he was in Swinley Forest. In 1940 the original herd of red deer in the Great Park were removed for the sake of agriculture, but a new herd was introduced in 1979 – wild deer from Scotland, which immediately began to thrive and breed in their new environment. In the 1960s, a pair of sika decided to take up residence in Cranbourne Forest, but unfortunately somebody shot them. Poachers were a frequent problem, especially in the Swinley/Bagshot area, where they used powerful lights to dazzle the animals (a practice known as lamping) and then sent in large dogs to hunt them down. 'I saw one lot of fallow – seven fallow deer, but it was the only time I ever saw fallow there. The red deer would be in clusters of fives or sixes, but Bracknell New Town gradually encroached and the red deer left – they've gone completely now.' They could not adapt to the presence of the public all over

the forests, combined with loss of habitat to Bracknell building and the increased use of noisy equipment by forestry workers. And so the larger deer – red and fallow – gradually disappeared from the Bagshot and Swinley Forests. 'But we still have a lot of roe in Windsor, and a lot of muntjac. One of the chaps who used to be with me, they're training him now for deer.'

Bert looks back with considerable contentment on many parts of his life. Windsor, he feels, suited his lack of ambition after Abberton. 'The main feature of Windsor, I suppose,' he says wryly, 'is a sense of security: you won't get the sack.' The dog curled at his feet looks up with languid brown eyes: it is a Dorgi with very royal connections, a gorgeous soft lapful of Corgi and Dachshund with a most gentle and friendly character. It is temporarily in the care of Bert and Doris, who frequently 'dog-sit' now that they no longer have dogs of their own.

In retirement Bert is gently critical of modern keepers. 'I don't know of many of these young chaps here now, but there were one or two of the older ones that were left when I retired and I said to them, "Well, I shan't come to visit you because there's nothing more boring than an old keeper saying we used to do this, we used to do that." And they took the hint, because they have never been to see me, none of them. I suppose I am a pretty boring sort of bloke!'

That self-deprecating remark is unjustified, and no doubt Bert could teach the new generation of keepers a great deal.

'Well, maybe. There is a lot to learn. We have just got through to the powers that be what an awful slaughter is done by these corvines. The main reason the corvines have increased so rapidly now – well, when I was young, if you didn't control them you didn't have any wild pheasants. So you had to control them. But now it's also artificial

Skylark

– the pheasants aren't wild now, they're all reared, so you just rear a few thousand more rather than controlling the corvines. Three years ago I had 22 nestboxes in use; last year only seven, all through the predation by corvines.'

Bert has a soft spot for badgers. 'Marvellous old thing – I love the badger, always have. We have a lot of them here at Windsor. There are so many established sets, probably centuries old, you see. Many years ago, when Gerald Lascelles was in charge of Belvedere, he came to me one day and said, "What can I do to stop this badger? I don't mind the badgers, but they are making holes in the fence." So I said: "Put a badger gate in." And he did, but he complained that the badgers still continued to come and make a hole in the fence. I went and had a look. There was a gatepost – a straining post – a few feet from where I had told him to put it and he has used the post for the badger gate instead. I told him to move it – they were so used to running in that one set track. And he did, and it worked. They are wonderful animals.'

The big lake by Bert's home had a substantial population of mandarin ducks – he built some 30 nestboxes for them and still helps an ornithologist who monitors the nesting birds annually, weighing and measuring the eggs and so on. As a novice with mandarin boxes, he gave his first one a landing platform – a mistake. 'They don't like that. What they do is fly straight in, absolutely perfect aim every time, straight in the hole.'

Bert was involved in a mandarin project for some time, using his trapping and ringing skills until the project lapsed and he could find no one to support it, as mandarins were not an indigenous species. Yet there are thought to be more of them in this country than in their homeland, China, where they have become rare. At one time there were more than 100 on the lake – the place was not good for mallards, teal and other dabblers as there are no islands for them, but the mandarins are tree ducks and roosted up in the rhododendrons. A few years ago the lake was drained and the mandarin moved elsewhere – there are several attractive private lakes in the area – and they are only now beginning to return, in very small numbers.

By the time that duck-trapping began, he had let his own ringing permit lapse and it was necessary to bring in a group of licensed ringers. 'They hadn't a clue what to do! They were telling me what to do even before they'd been here five minutes.' He could not bear to watch their inexperience and decided to get his own ringing permit again. 'And do you know, I had to fill in this form about how many ducks I had ringed, who'd trained me — och, a whole lot of

Rabbit shoot at Fairlight (Bert Winchester)

bumf, and it didn't make the slightest difference that I'd been trained by one of the best ornithologists in the country and had ringed thousands and thousands of ducks. They gave me a permit, but it was only what they call a B permit, going right down to the level when I very first went into birds for a living. And at that time I remember the old General telling me that I was now in a racket, a big job of one-upmanship – and how right he was!'

It must be hard for Bert not to feel that his huge experience counts for little in the eyes of the bureaucrats, and that his lack of 'paper' qualifications renders that experience void. Yet he has no bitterness in him. 'I've had a lot out of life, but I feel I've been very selfish: I've done what I wanted to do. And what good have I done? None. No good for anybody. Never tried to be what I'm not and never been ambitious.'

Out in the quiet woodland beyond the garden, the nestboxes high up in the trees, the mandarin boxes, owl boxes and countless homes for songbirds bear witness to his love of birds. No good for anybody? Rubbish!

Woodman's cottage

Chapter 11
A HAVEN FOR ALL

Brian P Martin

A HAVEN FOR ALL

WIFE-SWAPPERS, NYMPHOMANIACS, SEX-MAD MEN, DRUNKS, THE POOR AND THE SICK WERE ONLY SOME OF THE MANY EXTROVERTS AND UNFORTUNATES WHO ONCE FOUND A SYMPATHETIC EAR AT THE EIGHT BELLS, IN THE ESSEX VILLAGE OF BELCHAMP WALTER. BUT THEN, IN JOAN GORE THE PUB DID HAVE A PARTICULARLY UNDERSTANDING LANDLADY, WHO DID SO MUCH FOR SO MANY PEOPLE OVER THE TEN YEARS TILL THE DOORS WERE CLOSED TO THE PUBLIC FOR THE LAST TIME, IN 1977. SURPRISINGLY, JOAN WAS FORCED TO LEAVE THROUGH ILL-HEALTH, FOR NOW SHE IS ONE OF THE MOST VIVACIOUS AND YOUTHFUL OAPS I HAVE EVER ENCOUNTERED.

Aided by her daughter Susy, who also used to serve in the pub, Joan told me all about her life and eccentric customers as we sat by the fire in the old Pembrokeshire farmhouse where she has lived for the last 15 years.

'I was born at Wivenhoe and after various jobs, including the Land Army, I married in 1949. My husband John became the actual licensee of the pub when we took over in 1967, but he didn't have much to do with it as he continued with his full-time job as a civil servant.

'We didn't know how long the place had been a pub but the building probably dated back to Queen Anne, and there were hooks in the wall at the front, where horses used to be tethered. We had the odd customer come by horseback even in our time, as we were right out in the wilds there. We learnt quite a lot about the pub's history from some of our older customers.

'There was this dear old boy called George Chatters who bought a farm with the proceeds from running the pub during the war. Through some fiddle he always had lots of beer when rationing was on, so the pub was always full. They say he was so busy he often ran out of mugs so people would bring their own jam jars to drink from.

'Some time after the war they stopped making beer at the pub and the owner, Mr Ward, bought a brewery at Foxearth, about five miles away. The Eight Bells' beer had been made in a very small room which had been sealed off, and we found it when we took the wallpaper off while decorating. There was still a pile of roasted barley in there and buried in the barley was a very old-fashioned gentleman's blue suit, which you could poke your finger through. Everything was covered with rat droppings and it was very spooky.

'Also in the old days a man used to come round with a horse and cart selling kippers once or twice a week. He would go in the pub and all the old boys in the snug would buy the kippers and cook them over the open bar fire. Apparently they used to stink the place out.

'Another thing we learned from old George was that once a year, into the early part of this century, all the men and boys from the village would walk down towards Sudbury and meet up halfway with the men and boys from Ballingdon Hill to fight each other until they were exhausted. He didn't know why this started, but it could have had something to do with the fact that the villages were in different counties, Ballingdon Hill being in Suffolk. Also, even when we were there, the local people, including our customers, were very intermarried and protective of their own patch.

'When we arrived at the pub it needed quite a lot of attention. For a start, our cellar was always getting flooded and we had to put boots on to get the beer, so we often kept customers waiting. Eventually we complained to Mr Ward and he had a slatted floor put in. Also, the brown lino on the floor of the public bar was very dried out and cracked, so we took it up and put carpet down. Unfortunately, our regulars – we only had five at first! – didn't like it so three of them stayed away for weeks. Only Buster and his girlfriend Celia stayed because they had nowhere else to go to do their courting. And they didn't drink that much either. He just had half of bitter while she had a Lucozade.

'One very poor and very dirty old boy used to drink the dregs out of people's glasses, which the landlord before us used to tip into a tray under the beer pump and save for him. Old Albert also used to have all the cigarette stubs out of the ash trays and he'd take them home, break them up and roll his own from them. We didn't continue with either practice, but used to slip Albert the odd pint on the quiet.

'When they had shoots from Belchamp Hall, the ground where the pub car park is now used to be lined out with hundreds of hares, but in our time there were very few hares left. Later on we catered for pheasant and partridge shoots, the beaters having their bread and cheese in one bar while the Guns had something like steak-and-kidney pie in another.

'The local gamekeeper – Olly Barrel – was a wonderful character, only about five-feet high. Whenever he was unwell he always ate a slice of bread which he'd poured boiling water over and put a lot of pepper on. Also, he always wore a celluloid collar because years ago he'd broken his neck when he fell off a haystack, yet he ran everywhere when he was well past 70. When he came in the pub he'd say, "Put a tiger in my tank, Joanie," by which he meant put a glass of ginger wine in his light ale. And when he'd had a lot to drink he'd jump up and down on the spot, then say, "That's jumped it down," meaning his neck!

'Sometimes Olly used to come up and get me to make the soft leather things which they used to put on the reared pheasants' wings so that they couldn't fly. He always said that his fingers were too clumsy for the job, so he sat and watched me do it while he drank his beer along with Major Tuffel, who ran the shoot.

'Olly had a tiny wife – Edie, who couldn't have been more than 4ft 6in. She often used to come in the bar and ask for chips. When I cooked them and brought them out to her, she'd take them all out of the basket, break them in half and lay them in rows along the bar.

'One day Edie got so drunk at another pub that when she got home she fell backwards all the way down the stairs. After that she became very thin and everybody thought that was the end of her. So every morning I used to mix her up an egg with sugar and sherry and a glass of milk, and take it down to her cottage, to try to get her going again. Fortunately she did recover, but it became embarrassing because when she'd had a drink she used to call out to the whole bar: "My landlady's saved my life — she's been down every day with sherry, egg and milk for me." But she was a dear old thing, always making and drinking this ghastly rhubarb wine, which was ever so potent.

'Across the road a little bit further down was a dear little cottage, and living there were Maisie and George Phillips, a tiny man who had ten sons, but they weren't by Maisie. At first they lived in London and George had plenty of money because he was a dentist on Harley Street. After George said goodbye to his wife and set off for work each morning he'd pick up Maisie, who'd be waiting for him round the corner. She'd get in the car and cover herself up on the back seat with a blanket, and when they'd got out of the area she'd uncover herself and climb in the front with George. Unfortunately for George, one day they did this and Maisie said, "Well, we've got shot of the old so-and-so now," but Mrs Phillips was hiding in the boot! Then the Phillipses got divorced.

'George and Maisie then led a very high life, eating at all the smart restaurants, but they drank so heavily they got through all their money and had to give up their London house. They moved down to the cottage near us and George took a part-time job in a dental practice in Sudbury, which was our nearest town. And every day, as soon as George had gone to work Maisie would come into the pub and quaff the beers. In fact she was always first in, both morning and night. But with all the drinking, they neglected themselves and their very old cottage. One day when they were in bed together the whole front wall of the cottage fell out — top and bottom! But they were all right.

'One day Maisie was in the bar when George was very ill, and she had to use our phone to contact the doctor. I asked her if she'd given George his medicine as she'd been told to. She said , "Oh no, that's not for another hour." Then Susy and I had to go shopping, into Sudbury, so I told Maisie that she could stop in the pub to use the phone. Also, I knew she'd be better off there because she wouldn't have a fire alight at home.

'When we came back, about an hour and a half later, Maisie was still there and she was as drunk as a newt because she'd been helping herself to the optics. She said to me: "Oh, Joanie, you've come to see George — how sweet. Come along upstairs and I'll show you." So I told her: "Maisie, you're not in your house but at the Bells!" "Oh, am I?" she said. And when I asked her if she'd phoned the doctor or given George his medicine, she replied: "Oh no, I'll do it later." But poor old George died the next day!

'Maisie never had a fire and hardly ever had any food in the house. After George died we watched her get thinner and thinner, so any time we had a bit of a do in the pub we'd save anything left over — sandwiches or whatever — for her.

'Poor old Maisie. She became so frail and thin and was always so drunk that when the wind blew she had to hold on to the hedge to get home. It was disgraceful that she lived in that way while her daughter was on the council in the next village. In the end I was so cross I phoned this woman and said: "How can you call yourself a caring council worker when you leave your mother to starve and freeze?" Fortunately she listened to me and came over to take Maisie back with her.

'Another thing that shocked us was the wife-swapping among our customers. There was one farmer, who we'd better call Fred to save any embarrassment, and another we'll call John. Now John's wife was a cripple and he used to carry on with our barmaid. But John was also very fond of Fred's wife so he often used to visit her when Fred was away, and whenever he went to bed with her he would leave Fred a bottle of whisky on the sideboard. When they made their arrangements Fred would go with a young lady we'll call Mavis, who was a teacher. What really surprised me was the completely open way they discussed all this in the bar on the very first Sunday we were there, saying things like: "Who are you going to have tonight, then, John?" We watched them pair off and go, and we were dumbfounded because we weren't even used to pubs, let alone that behaviour.

'Susy once had a fanatical admirer and when she chucked him he was very upset. One night he even sat outside her bedroom with a shotgun! Eventually, to get even with her he burgled us while we were out. We knew it was him because both Maisie and Olly saw him go. The police searched his house but it was never pinned on him. Then he joined the army, but when he came back to see us at the pub two years later he was a changed man. The army had turned him into a nice, smart chap, but he brought his girlfriend with him and not only was she called Sue but also she looked like Susy.

'Another odd person was a man we called Sexy. He had a sweet factory in America and came over to promote his goodies. His aged aunt was the honourable somebody or other in Gestingthorpe, and she was supposed to book him into the poshest hotel in the area, the Swan in Sudbury; but by mistake she booked him in with us. When he came I think he was trying to sow all his wild oats in about three days: he was truly shocking.

'The first night this American joined some others dancing to the jukebox in the public bar. He was mauling the girls about, and, of course, our barmaid was there having a lovely time because she liked that sort of thing. Then he asked me to show him where his room was, and when I took him up he politely asked for a glass of water; but when I returned with it he grabbed me by the arm, whisked me into the bedroom and tried to kiss me. So I shoved him away and said, "You've got the wrong one here — you'd better go back down and see if you can find somebody else." After that, when we were cleaning up in the bar while he was having breakfast, or at any other time, I always made sure that my Susy and I were never with him by ourselves.

'Another visitor who surprised us was the man who booked in for six weeks' bed and breakfast and insisted that when he came he did not want "anything to do with the family"; yet he ended up staying for seven years and marrying Buster's girlfriend, Celia!

'We had another strange visitor apparently from the States. One day this well-spoken Yankee turned up and asked if we could put him up for a night or two, so I said yes, and he ended up staying for three weeks. Then two policemen came into the bar and asked if we had a man who said he was a Red Indian, I said yes and they said they were sorry, but they'd have to take him away as he'd been on the run from some institution and had been staying at different places without paying for his keep. "But you can't do that," I said, "he's quiet and well-behaved and he's paid on the dot at the end of every week. And I'm sure he's an Indian because he looks like one and he told us he's the chief of the Iowa tribe. He even showed us his headdress and other regalia." "Oh no he's not," they said, and with that they went upstairs to get this dear little chap and they marched him away.

'After a while we changed the snug into a music room for young people. We put a record player in there and the local boys decorated it themselves, with a black ceiling and lots of posters. It was really nice for them and most of them were well-behaved. Then just before closing one night these three notorious brothers came in and took their drinks into the music room. After about 15 minutes we heard a lot of crashing and banging in there but Susy and I were alone and we wouldn't go in there because we knew of these boys' terrible reputation with girls and drinking. We had to wait for them to go, and when we went in we were horrified to see that they'd broken every glass and all the records and had trodden them into the floor.

'I phoned the local policeman and told him that it must have been these brothers as they were the only people in the room that night. Also I said that one must have a badly cut hand because there was blood over everything. But he did nothing at all about it because he was as frightened of them as everybody else was.

'This policeman came from the next village and he never interfered with us much. He'd always come round about a quarter of an hour before closing time and say: "Everything all right in here?" We'd say, "Yes thanks," and he'd say, "OK — I shan't trouble you again tonight." This was just as well because our customers always wanted to stay to about one o'clock most nights and to three on Sunday. But in the end we knew them so well we'd say: "Right — you can serve yourselves, but here's a pen and pad. Please write your name down and record all the drinks you have and you can pay us on Monday." Then we'd go to bed and we'd hear them clanking about with bottles and things below. It was rather nice

to think that we could trust them like that.

'We had two football teams and the players were more like my sons. When they got tiddly we had great beer mat fights, flicking them at each other, but we had to stop that when someone got cut. The boys often had to stay well after hours because I made them have lots of cups of coffee and something to eat while they sat round the floor in my living room until they were sober enough to go.

'Another lively crowd were the local Irish community of three families. When they came in the pub they'd sing along with Jim Reeves on the jukebox, and then they'd start crying before going back to their homes to play all the old patriotic songs.

'Later on we started to have live music, which became so popular with people from nearby towns the road outside would be blocked with cars. Also, we established a supper room with a late drinks licence to midnight, and this was very successful with people coming from up to 30 miles away; apart from the time I set the kitchen on fire while cooking chips and nearly choked the parrot to death.

'Then the breathalyzer came in and mucked up that supper trade. But soon after, we had to leave the pub anyway as I became ill through doing too much and Susy left to get married. Ward sold out to Bass Charrington, but sadly the place never reopened as a pub. One couple tried to turn it into a glorified restaurant but they went bust while the alterations were going on.

'On reflection, it sounds as though all our customers were either drunks or very immoral, but I must say that the majority were very nice people and I really do miss pub life.'

Chapter 12

THE ROMANY
HORSE DEALERS

Jennifer Davies

THE ROMANY HORSE DEALERS

ACCORDING TO RECENT STATISTICS THERE ARE AROUND 100,000 GYPSIES IN THE UK AND ABOUT HALF
OF THESE ARE NOMADIC. HOWEVER, MANY OF THEIR TRADITIONAL STOPPING PLACES HAVE BEEN LOST
TO DEVELOPMENT, AND THEIR FREEDOM TO LINGER ANYWHERE HAS BEEN LEGALLY CURTAILED AS THE
CRIMINAL JUSTICE ACT OF 1994 GIVES THE POLICE AND LANDOWNERS THE AUTHORITY TO MOVE
NOMADS ON. IT ALSO RELIEVES COUNCILS OF THE RESPONSIBILITY TO PROVIDE SITES FOR VANS.
GYPSIES CANNOT EVEN LIVE IN CARAVANS ON LAND THEY HAVE BOUGHT FOR THEMSELVES.

Gypsy crafts have also suffered over the years. In winter people buy fresh flowers air-freighted in from abroad, not wooden ones hand-made by gypsies. Tumble driers and plastic pegs have spelt the demise of gypsy willow-made pegs, and few people today have their knives and scissors sharpened by gypsy knife-grinders. Collecting and selling scrap metal, trading motors and buying and picking fruit are more likely to be today's gypsy occupations. However, among all these changes one traditional gypsy trade endures: horse dealing.

Gypsies and horses are inseparable – in fact the gypsy language of Romani gave us the word 'jockey', a derivation of 'chookni', meaning a whip. Each year gypsies flock to horse fairs around the country. There's one at Appleby in Cumbria, and another in Barnet, North London; Abergavenny horse sales cater for Welsh custom, and Gloucestershire has Stow-on-the-Wold horse fair each May and October.

Stow received royal permission in the early 12th century to hold a weekly market in the town, and in 1476 Edward IV granted a charter for two fairs to be held there, one in May and one in October. At first these fairs were mainly for sheep, as Stow was a prosperous woollen town, but over the years they became the usual rural servant hiring fairs, which included the selling of produce and animals. The horse-selling side received a boost when local auctioneers concentrated on this aspect, and Stow's fame as a horse fair grew from there. The

Les at Stow Fair, a place to catch up with old friends

auctioneers have now moved their horse sales out of the town, but the gypsies still continue to bring their horses to Stow each spring and autumn. They purchased a field in which to park and conduct their business, but at the time of writing this, they are forbidden by law to use the field and so the selling and buying takes place in the lower part of the town.

Many gypsies arrive a week in advance of sale day and park on the verges and lay-bys in readiness. Some local residents believe they are harmless and consider they add colour to the town's yearly calendar; to others, however, they are clearly a nuisance. On the day of the sale one or two shops display singularly few goods and prop up the following terse message in the window: 'Closed because of the Horse Sales'. Also a few of the town's smart hotels have a bouncer on the door; they let in well-heeled foreign tourists, but anyone considered less desirable would think twice about crossing the threshold. When I turned up in my quest for a gypsy horse dealer, the only place that seemed to be enjoying the custom brought by the sale was a fish-and-chip shop; situated near the hub of the sales, the queue and bustle around it never diminished all day long.

Beyond the shop the clatter of hooves on tarmac frequently sent people scattering. The cause would be either a seller hurtling along in a horse-drawn buggy (with the object of showing off his horse's paces) or a young gypsy buck for the same reason running down the road and leading a smartly trotting pony.

Even in the throng of so many horse copers I found it difficult to pin down a gypsy prepared to talk about horse dealing. A few referred me to a family of brothers, but when I found the eldest, he assured me he only dealt in scrap. Ten minutes later I saw him slapping his hand down on a deal and passing a bundle of notes to a young man who had five donkeys tethered to the car park railings. Eventually someone suggested that I make my way down the road, for somewhere at the bottom, parked in an old-fashioned gypsy caravan was Les Elliott, a renowned and, thankfully, communicative horse dealer.

The journey down the hill wasn't simple, because of the hundreds of people thronging the trade stalls which stood on either side of the road. And threading my way through the crowd it was easy to see what attracted them: there were stalls of every different sort and kind – set with the prettiest Wedgewood and Doulton china, and glistening with cut glass; stalls with piles of frilled linen and pillow cases; stalls selling leather belts, bags and clothes, each piece brightened by brass stars and buckles; stalls of buckets, bowls and bins all decorated with flowers (and a snip for £20 a set of three); stalls hung with pictures of horse-drawn caravans and mugs decorated with horse's heads; useful stalls selling iron kettles and the wherewithal for cooking out of doors, plus the odd bundle of leather ferret collars; and any number of shoe stalls.

Beyond, the crowd thinned, and here I found Les Elliott and his wife Edna. But it was impossible to talk to them. Edna, with the traditional scarf covering her head, was cooking sausages over an open fire on the grass verge, every now and then turning to fetch a bread roll or an extra cup from their old-fashioned flat-bedded dray parked close by. Les stood by the fire. He had dark wavy hair and a moustache, and wore a red spotted handkerchief round his neck, a red-check shirt and was surrounded by people.

Later, I learned that like most Romanies, Les and Edna have a great many relatives, and that the only times they really all meet up nowadays are at fairs, weddings and funerals. And there were friends too, some

already installed by the fire, others passing by and stopping to chat en route.

I made my way to Les and asked if we could talk about horse dealing. We spoke briefly, and I photographed him by the shafts of a neighbour's caravan and also Edna, sat against their own dray, which they towed behind their big wagon. However, it was obviously going to be better if I could see them on another day, which wouldn't be quite so hectic. Les agreed and said that he and Edna had just acquired a house for over-wintering in. His health and the fact that they weren't as young as they had been had prompted this move, although Les really preferred travelling in winter and summer. They would be there until March, then away again.

A few weeks later I arrived at their house. Edna gave me coffee and sandwiches on beautiful china. The house, warm and spotless, was alive with canary song: there were at least a dozen of the birds, some pale lemon yellow, others with flushes of orange to their feathers, each in an individual wooden cage in an annexe by the sitting-room. Apparently they had even more upstairs.

This is Les's story in his own words: 'The Elliotts go back a long way. Someone looked it up once, and it's on record that in 1746 a Mrs Elliott with three children was stopping in Coate's Lane on the borders of Nottinghamshire. She was in a rod tent – benders as they call 'em today – and had three boys. It's also on record that in 1796 an Elliott family was camping four miles further up the road. I say "Elliott", though in fact the family name used to be "Elit"; over the years it's got modern with people writing it and adding an "o" and an extra "l" and "t". I don't know whether I am an Elit or an Elliott because I haven't got a birth certificate.

'Both me grandfathers used to buy horses out of the coal pits. They'd clean them up, and feed 'em and brush 'em down, and soon they could see the ones which was going to survive. They'd say well, that one's all right, but the other two've got to be put down – some would be too old to eat, others'd be too lame, you see. They just fed 'em up and looked after 'em and brushed 'em and watched them over a week or fortnight, and if they could see they was going to alter they knew they'd got one that was going to survive. Then they'd go perhaps into a pub and say: "Oh, I've got three hosses – I'll swop you for that one"; and so they'd swop 'em, and they'd keep on like that and the next man 'ud have 'em.

'Hosses was cheap and everything was horsepower, there were no motors. You could go up a lane and lay in the middle of the road and you'd perhaps see one car a week.

'My father's name was Everett Elliott, and he was a horse dealer too. I was the youngest of 13, and we lived in what they called a "Palace on Wheels" — well, we didn't all live in it because some of my older brothers and sisters had moved out. The caravan's proper name was a "Reading", and it had straight sides, two great big windows and a big mollycroft roof [a small roof on top of the main one; it has windows in it which help to give light and ventilation to the van]. The wood on the van was elaborately carved.

'The caravan I've got today is different. It's a Ledge, Bill Wright, and is named after the man that made them. It hasn't got straight sides, it's got ledges, and it's all mahogany wood inside, and inside the cupboard there's sunflowers carved in the wood. I think mine's the only one of its type that's still travelling today, anyway that I know of; it's about 120 years old, and used to belong to my cousin's great-grandfather. Two horses pull it, and one horse pulls our flat-bedded dray.

'The first time I ever seen a horse was when I was two. We were stopping at Derby on a piece of ground that used to be called Brexall Ground; there was everybody on it, people out of towns what hadn't got no houses. It was like a shanty town, and there were a lot of gypsies on there; in them days there were no money to be had, so they had to do as best they could. I remember me dad fetching up a hoss. I was stood at his side and he give me this halter to hold, and when I looked up all I could see was this big head looking down at me; and me dad said, "Oh, it's a horse, it won't hurt you" — and ever since I've had hosses.

'One day when I was about six or seven my dad said to me: "I want you to take the

horse up to the blacksmith and have it shod." I used to stutter when I was a little boy, and I was leading the horse to the

Les's grandmother, Kazia Booth

blacksmith trying to get the words out, and the blacksmith said to me, I were crying, he said, "What h'ever you crying for?" I said, "Me dad said to take the hoss up to the blacksmith and have it shot."

'Any road, he shoed it — and I've still got a mark in me leg today where a piece of iron flew off the anvil and went into me leg. The blacksmith was making the shoes, cutting and banging, and he did tell me to go back from the forge — but I was so inquisitive I didn't take notice and all of a sudden I felt it like a red-hot bullet, straight into me leg here; I still got the mark. The blacksmith just chucked some water on it and said, "That'll learn you"; and it did!

'Then me dad come and he said: "You're a long time shoeing this horse." "Yes," he said, "I've had to make the shoes special for this one — and you're lad's been crying half the day, thought you said have the hoss shot instead of shod". "Oh, did he," he said, and hit me up the ear-hole.

'Men were all hard in those days; there was no, "I'll buy you this", or "I'll buy you that". Everybody was hard, it was survival, remember.

'When my dad was horse dealing he used to dress up with leggings and a suit, and a cap or bowler hat and smock, and say he was a horse dealer. In them days people wouldn't buy off a gypsy, they used to think we was doing nowt but stealing; that's why we never used to buy coloured horses only blacks and browns, because people wouldn't buy them off him because they'd think he was a gypsy and he'd stolen them. Now it's gone the other way and gypsies favour coloured horses. When he went dealing my dad would leave the wagon and travel in a horse and trap.

'People got to know his name, and would ask him to get them, say, a quiet horse for driving; and he'd ask about until he found one. Then he'd deliver it clean, brushed and respectable, with its mane hogged, teeth cleaned and harness polished, like you'd expect a new car to arrive today.

'If someone was selling, on the other hand, he'd give them a hard luck story, saying, "Well, the horse trade's not very good ma'am" (if it was a lady) and he used to say to me "There's nothing better than to be clean, and polite to people, civility gets you through the world" – and he was right.'

At this point Edna came in from the kitchen with a tray, and held it out to show three fruit cakes. They were not the conventional shape, but flat, traditional gypsy cakes, and they looked and smelt wonderful.

'Come out all right, ain't they, hey? Done on the top, they ain't so good as them done on a fire, but they turned out all right.'

Although Edna likes her electric cooker she maintains that an open fire cooks food better. She can cook roasts, stews, soups, pies and puddings on the grid over her camp fire; in fact, she thinks that there isn't a dish she can't cook on it. She returned to other delicious smells in the kitchen. Les continued his reminiscences.

'The first day I went out with a horse and cart I think I was eight. My dad give me the reins to drive the hoss and the hoss took off, run away with us. Me dad jumped off to grab its 'ead, and it was too fast. I never forget it. dad roly-poly'd in the road, and a policeman come past on a bike and he kept pedalling and trying to grab the back of the dray, but he couldn't make it and we went over a railway bridge. Eventually I pulled the rein on me right-hand side, and hoss and cart went into a fence, and the hoss started kicking and got out of the harness.

'In fact the hoss eventually came to a bad end: it put its head through the fence on the railway siding – in them days it were like iron bars – to get grass, and summat must have frightened it because it tried to jerk its head back through and broke its neck. The knacker man had to come and shoot it in the field. Did you know that the bullet goes straight through an 'oss? They shoot it straight in the centre of the head, but you can't stand behind it because the bullet goes straight through, down its back and out the other end. It's dead as soon as you hear the gun go "click".'

Les breaks off here, and going into the annexe gives each canary some fresh lettuce. He returns and we resume:

'We used to travel all over. When the war was on we was round Derby and Nottingham, but when the war finished we went all over.

'Any horses that we bought at fairs were bought, as they still are today, by the raising and dropping of the buyer's hand on the seller's each time a price is mentioned. You went up in price until a purchase price was agreed – and a man's word was his bond, it was a gentleman's agreement.

'Purchased horses were tied behind the back of the wagon. There was also a pony and cart on the back, for the wives, the women, to drive out in for their business to go selling. They wus as clever as the men at dealing, and would buy any cheap horses. I mean, horses them days weren't a lot of money; you could buy one for 15s, 75 pence nowadays – although even 15s would have taken a long time to earn.

'My wife Edna didn't buy horses, but she did sell a couple of mine. She'd say: "Oh, my husband's got one for sale"; and she'd sell a wagon too if she had a customer. She sold two of mine.

'When I was a lad you weren't allowed to tether horses on the main road, so we travelled on the back lanes which were quiet. I didn't get any schooling because we used to pull the wagon in the end of a lane and they'd say to me "Right, go to the top of the lane and sit there until we send for you and send someone else up." Then they'd loose the horses off the back of the wagon, and they would graze between the wagon and me sat up the end. There was no tethers for them. When they got too far I'd have to send them back.

'I spent hours and hours, all day, like that, and if it rained it was just too bad. I'd make a fire under the hedge. If there was two of you, one would try and catch a rabbit and we'd roast it.

'When the horses had eaten that part of the lane off, they'd put the wagon hoss in and bring it to where we had our fire and then we'd walk down the road another half a mile and that's how they used to do it.

'Sometimes they'd forget to send for you, because there was no set time. Then when they remembered they'd give a certain whistle, and like a sheepdog, you'd be listening for that whistle and come back; or

perhaps they'd send someone up with a pot of tea and some bread and cheese or bread and lard – you got whatever you got. But whatever it was, you were grateful.

'At night-time we used to put the horses in a farmer's field. We used to watch him put his lights out and then we'd put them in the field, and we used to fetch 'em out before he got up, and would go round the field and pick all the droppings up so he never knew. Some of the farmers used to know we'd done it and they used to fetch a policeman and all sorts. We used to have to move, then, when they fetched a policeman.

'There were no friendly farmers in them days, in fact no friendly nobody. People were suspicious of us as soon as we pulled in, and if you had two nights in a place you were fortunate. You see, years ago everyone had horses and living vans and so many

A much-treasured photo of Les's mother and father

used to congregate in one spot — and when one van moved off, another would draw in; and people in the neighbourhood would get fed up seeing 'em, and they'd think it was still the same lot parked.

'But the bitterness against us is dying with the old people. The young generation now if they see me with my horses and my traditional gypsy wagon, they say: "Isn't that beautiful!" [Les pauses and says with a grin:] It's a pleasure for me to be a gypsy now. Years ago you used to be terrified. Although even today I still can't stop somewhere for a week without getting nervous! Yes, we were always on the move, but in a way we liked it. Riding the horses behind the wagon, mares and foals coming on, dogs running at the side, the wagons going on. Nomadic people just going where we wanted.

'Looking back, life wasn't too bad in the summer, but in the winter I'd go to bed when it were dark and get up when it were dark — I used to think I'd never been to bed. And then as I growed up, somebody else would take on the job of minding the horses when they grazed. There'd be two or three families of us together, you see. And they'd say: "Right, you go today and fetch some peg sticks." And I used to get the peg knife and go and fetch a load of peg sticks, cutting them out of the hedge from willa trees. Then the men and the young gals would help to make the pegs.

'I'll show you some; I still make 'em you see. Then we used to make wooden flowers out of elder, they used to look like big white chrysanths.'

To show me what he meant, Les held one hand as if it grasped a knife and the other as if he held a piece of elderwood, and then proceeded to use the 'knife' to peel down the strips of wood. He explained that it was like a petal on top of a petal — it all had to be done quickly until it formed a round ball which curled underneath and looked just like a real chrysanthemum.

'We used to make and sell no end of these. See, in them days there were no silk flowers like there are today, no flowers what you could buy out of season, although you can buy flowers all the year round now. We used to make 'em, dye them different colours with clothes dye, say red and yeller, and people used to buy 'em to put in their winders. The women used to go out with them, and I used to go out with them.

'When you got old enough, to go out to fend for yourself, that's it, you had to do it, and you didn't get no help from nobody. But it wasn't all work. We used to sit round the fire and talk, and make a conversation up. There were no wirelesses, see, and we weren't allowed to go to dances — and we didn't have the money to get nowhere. I mean, our clothes were all old, somebody else's leave-offs. And we always used to have one of these on [indicates his red neckerchief].'

Les unties and reties the neckerchief in the ordinary way, saying at the same time that this wasn't the way his mother used. Untying it again, he showed me her method which involved first putting it round the front of his throat like a vicar's collar, bringing the two ends from behind his neck and tying them in front.

'This way kept me neck warm, and also hid the dirt on the collar of me shirt because there was no time to wash, and anyway, sometimes the clothes we got wasn't fit to wash, there was nowt left to wash.

'I used to wear a man's coat and roll the sleeves up, men's trousers and roll the bottoms up — and to this very day you'll see some gypsy men walk about with their trousers turned up because they're too long. I mean anybody's cast-off clothing was very helpful to us, you know.

'The blankets we had were those old grey and blue army itchy blankets, and they used to make me mad! No soft, warm pillers and soft warm beds, I tell you it was very hard. I mean, every morning you got up you'd got to have a fire outside, you'd got to wash outside, winter and summer.

'I once remember me and me cousin laid under one of these wagons; we used to put a sheet round the wheels, and two bales of straw under it and a couple of pillers, if we'd got 'em. We'd lay under there and then in the morning me dad'd say: "Hey up, boy!" – and if you didn't hear him, that was just too bad for you because he wouldn't shout twice, only the once. One morning I couldn't open me eyes because the sun was shining in them. I woke me cousin up, and we sat up and looked at each other like two mongooses. I said "There's summat missing – where's waggin?" We found out it was about seven o'clock, and my Dad had put the hoss in and pulled the wagon over us, took the sheet down. But the next morning when he shouted, then we said, "Yeah, all right!"

'It was his way of training you. You couldn't afford to lay in bed all day – who's going to feed yer? Oh, they was hard times – and the gals wus brought up just as hard

as the boys, they didn't have a soft, easy life. When they got married they had a child in the sling, a basket on their arm, and perhaps another child dragging behind them.

'I tell you, we used to sell and buy anything, horses, chickens, anything you could make money out of – and that was the way our people was brought up. But I do remember me dad turning down some money once. When the war was on, two lads from the army came to him and asked if he had a horse and cart they could hire. He said we had, and I fetched up the horse and we put the harness on and put it in the cart for 'em; but then they said "Which way do you pull to turn left and right?", and me dad asked if they'd ever driven a horse before. When they replied that they hadn't,

dray, thinking this would help me dad in selling it. Oh, he gave me such a fourpenny 'un, and told me "When you're a man, then you can butt in; until then, shut up!"

'I wasn't allowed out with him when he went horse dealing. In fact mostly I went out with me mam, because the men wouldn't have you with them; in them days children couldn't go in pubs, and a lot of business was done in pubs. When I did go out to buy horses, although I wasn't very old, about 13, I went on my own.

'I might find a horse, but not have enough money for it, so I used to go back to me dad and say "There's a pony down in the village I can buy," and I used to add a little bit on it for myself; I'd perhaps put 3s or 4s on the purchase price, which was a lot of money in them days. It warn't the truth. Then I'd

'Off to the 'oppin'

he said "You're not driving this one, then" – and wouldn't let them have it.

'As it turned out, somebody else come that day and my Dad sold it for £9, the horse, harness and the cart, and that was a lot of money in them days. As it happened I got a good hiding on that occasion, because when gypsy menfolk were dealing you wasn't allowed to speak, you just stood there and looked and listened; but I was going to tell this man that there was a brake on the

bring the horse back and he'd say "Oh, that was all right then." Then he'd say, "How much have I got to give for it?" So you'd add a little bit more on top of what you'd already paid, and by the time you'd finished you had a good bit of profit out of it.

'But some of the old men, they'd say: "Oh, I've got a man as 'ud buy that pony off you, but he can't come and get it, so I'll take it up this afternoon." And they'd put the halter on it, and that would be the end for you. And it were no good saying "Where's me money?" Because they'd just say "Money, money! You don't get fed for nowt, you know!" No, they didn't feed you, you fed yourself.

'The horses' food we used to buy off the local farmers. You'd have say, perhaps, six pennyworth of corn and six pennyworth of hay, and in them days you could buy enough to keep two horses for perhaps a shilling. A truss of hay was as much as a man could pick up. Nearly as big as that sofa [indicating a medium-sized sofa in the sitting room]. Then they'd have a few oats, and you'd feed them like that.

'The winters in them days was a lot harder than they are today. In 1947 Edna was in a caravan on top of that hill, out there in the distance. She, her dad and mam and three brothers were snowed up there for six weeks. They dug themselves out eventually. My family was snowed in at Melton Mowbray.

'By that time I'd left home. I couldn't get on with my dad. He'd keep saying to me "It's time you brought some money in, about time you done this…" you know. I left when I were 14, just walked off. I went to me aunts and uncles who were travelling like us, though I used to see me mam regular. I got me own horse.

'When I married Edna we had a pony, a trap and a tent, and were very fortunate to have these. She come with what she had on her back, her parents were poor as well, and she was the oldest out o' nine of 'em so they didn't have nothing to offer. We got married in a registry office, though some people in those days jumped the broom.

'We used to travel through Derbyshire and Nottinghamshire and up to the North. If we could get a living, and there was plenty of grass for our hosses and somewhere to stop, we'd stop. Just shift round local lanes in the area. If it was hard we'd move on.

Gypsy camp

'Remember our wireless thing we had, Edna?'

Edna comes in from the kitchen. 'It was a good wireless,' she replies. 'Black polished wood. And we had a gramophone with a brass horn … Used to be able to get two records for a penny. They were second-hand, ha'penny a piece … George Formby, Slim Whitman, everybody.' Les and Edna swop record reminiscences. Then we get back to horses; I ask Les if gypsies have a special way with them.

'We're more horse people than a lot. I mean we can tell whether they're going to make good 'uns or bad 'uns. That black and white one on there,' (he points to a photograph on the wall which shows his wagon and horses) 'he's only a yearling on there, but now he's three years old. I broke him in meself and he pulls that wagon, and he's really a good horse, it's very rare I have to use a whip.'

'And,' I ask, 'any secret gypsy remedies if a horse falls ill?' Les thinks, then replies: Well, you'd boil up the mallow plant in a bucket and then strain the water off. It looked a dirty green, and you used to bathe a horse's leg in it if it had a sprain. The liquid was good for human sprains, too. The remedy for colic or a broken leg was a bullet.

'Sometimes a horse would throw a spavin, though I haven't seen one for years. They were usually caused by hard work and the horse would generally go lame on one or both hind legs. In the old days if it was lame on one they used to do summat to the other leg because how could you go lame on two feet?

'Then there's sweet itch, which isn't a pain but rather an irritation. Have you ever had an allergy which makes you scratch your whole body? Well, its similar to that, only it's continuous day and night. It starts in the spring, and lasts from the first of the leaf until the end of the leaf. The horse would rub against anything, a door, a fence, rub and rub until it bled, and you had to be careful where you tethered it. The irritation would start in the top of the tail where the hair is broke and after rubbing it would spread, but only where the harness fits, that is in the mane, on the shoulders, on the back and on the tail. There are powders and treatments today to treat sweet itch, but the only thing we could use to ease it — didn't cure it, but eased it — was waste oil put on with a rag.

'Also sometimes you'd get a horse with a splint and it would go lame. If it had two splints it warn't too bad, it just used to be a bit "pudgy" [pottery] in front. Some horses had a parrot mouth, you know the jaws wouldn't meet properly and it was difficult for them to eat. We believed a lot of that was caused by people putting halters on them and leaving the halter on and their heads grow'd but the 'alters didn't, though I'm told this is not so.'

'Do gypsies use Romani commands to their horses?' I ask.

'No, English,' Les replies. 'Because if you're selling horses to English people you kakka rokker (don't speak) Romani, you've got to say "Whoah, stop". But,' he adds, 'we talk Romani between ourselves. For instance a horse is a "grasni", and a farmer's field is a "puff". In fact it's very rare we talk English, only when out getting us a living, buying and selling.'

Edna is busy preparing food for some afternoon guests. I beg a few more minutes, and ask Les if it isn't a pleasure to have the comforts of a house during the winter (it's their second winter under a tiled roof).

He replies: 'Sometimes, you're right.'

I enquire when they'll be off on their travels again.

'Tomorrer, if she would.'

'But you'd lose your TV and comfortable bed and central heating.' To which Les replied: 'Edna likes the house, it's not so hard for her as on the road — there she has to get a living. Also in the house it's all there for her, light at a switch, and water. But I'm losing me freedom (then quietly so that Edna doesn't hear), and that's more important than all this lot put together.'

He looks through the window. 'We'll go off in the early spring. At present my horses are a distance away, but I've always had 'em where I can see 'em because they know my footsteps, if it's dark at night, they'll whinny, they know it's me. They'll come over and they won't leave me, none of 'em will.'

O, I am not of gentle clan,
I'm sprung from Gypsy tree
And I will be no gentleman,
But an Egyptian free.
George Borrow

Chapter 13
'STONEHENGE' ON POACHING

John Humphreys

'STONEHENGE' ON POACHING

In 1856, the author and countryman 'Stonehenge' wrote a massive and comprehensive work entitled British Rural Sports (Routledge & Co) which included, among others, angling, equestrianism, skating, sailing, shooting and greyhound racing. The tome ran to many hundreds of pages printed in miniscule typeface which even with modern lighting is difficult to read. I wonder if anyone has ever read it from cover to cover. He had advice for keepers troubled with poachers, guidance-based, one suspects, in hearsay, wishful thinking, a modest understanding of the subject and a naïve acceptance that the 'gentleman poacher' was by no means as reprehensible as the 'poaching labourer'. 'Stongehenge' was more at home with greyhounds than mouchers.

His advice to keepers to 'keep the menace at bay' shows a touching and probably ill-founded trust in the willingness of the farm labourer to inform on his mates in return for an extra five bob in his pay packet at Christmas, with or without the moral support of a 'railway whistle' for the more unwelcome visitors from London. However, 'Stonehenge' spoke of the age in which he lived when poaching was seen as a serious rural menace, especially by the squirearchy for whom he wrote, and at a time when the penalties for transgression were almost medieval.

'With regard to the poacher, everything depends on the labourers on the farms. If they like to countenance the poacher or if they are unfortunately poachers themselves, all the efforts of the keeper will be of little avail. The best plan is to make all of the labourers feel an interest in the preservation of the game. Let every man receive at Christmas a certain sum proportionate to the head of game killed during the season and the outlay will be found to be well bestowed, since it will go much further than the same sum laid out on extra watchers. I have known 650 acres of land preserved entirely in the neighbourhood of a large town without any regular keeper and with an outlay in the shape of presents to labourers certainly not exceeding £20 per year.

'On this farm hares were as thick as sheep and partridges sufficient to allow 30 brace to be killed in three or four hours. All parties were in earnest in keeping poachers away and the result was as I have stated. This shows what labourers can do if they like and what they will do if it is made in their interest to do so. They are either a great evil or a great boon to the game preserver and he must make up his mind either to have them as warm friends or bitter enemies.

'The regular and systematic poacher is a

formidable fellow, opposed to all law and making a living the best way he can. After a time nothing comes amiss to him and though at first he has taken to his trade for a love of sport, it has ended in his adhering to it through necessity since he cannot get work when his character is known, for no man going poaching at night can be fit for work in the day also.

'The existence and career of the poacher is the great drawback to the sportsman and it almost justifies the strong desire which so many hold to do away entirely with all game in order to get rid also of the tendency to poach. This is a question upon which I will not enter as it concerns the legislator more than the sportsman. At present the law permits the preservation of game and I believe that the evils attendant upon it are more than counterbalanced by its many advantages. As good subjects, therefore, we have only to avoid encouraging the poacher and the plan I have proposed in making it in the labourer's interest to discourage it is most humane as well as successful.

'Of regular poachers there are four chief varieties, first the systematic London poacher, second the poaching gent, third the regular rural poacher and fourth the poaching labourer.

'The London Poacher ... is almost always one of a gang and they conduct their operations in various ways. Sometimes they scour the country in dog carts drawn by a fast horse by which they are enabled to shoot from the sides of the road, either in covert or by catching pheasants on their feed or by beating the stubbles and turnips adjacent to the road or even invading the moors.

'As soon as a keeper or other person approaches, they take to their heels and on reaching the dog cart are soon out of sight. It is against these men that the regular

labourer may be most useful. Few farms in the shooting season are without a labourer within a field or two of every point likely to be invaded. Let every one of these be provided with a railway whistle and let them blow it loudly as soon as he sees a suspicious person in the vicinity. This may be heard for a mile or more and the keeper may very soon be made aware of what is going on; besides, the whistle itself alarms the poacher as it proves a good system of watching and he prefers moving off to quieter quarters.

'These men generally travel in parties of five of whom one remains with the horse and their other four together surround a small covert and command every side so that a dog put in is sure to drive everything either to one or another of them or else take each side of the road, in the stubble, turnips etc. In this way a heavy load of game is soon bagged by these rascals by selecting a line of road studded with preserves and suited to their purpose. By keeping within the number of five they avoid the penalties of the 32nd section of the Game Laws and only come under the

30th and 31st section if they should be overtaken by a keeper and can only be fined £2 each. They seldom indulge in night poaching but are always ready to deal with the local poachers for the game which they may take in that way.

'The Poaching Gent … is generally a man who is ardently fond of shooting and yet has not the opportunity of indulging his appetite for sport from want of land to shoot over. He therefore is constantly trespassing upon the lands of his neighbours and of course subjects himself to the penalty of £2 on conviction of each offence.

'He is almost always, however, so good a shot that the produce of his gun enables him to pay his sum because he is so wary as to choose his opportunity and often escape detection for a considerable time. He knows where he is least likely to be caught, and the times which will suit him best and acts accordingly.

'There is seldom much difficulty in dealing with these men, and the harm they do in well-preserved districts is very trifling. It is only on half-preserved farms that they are to be dreaded and there they often get the lion's share of the spoil. On the grouse moors an inferior grade of this class is very destructive to the game – he is the sporting miner or blacksmith or perhaps the denizen of some neighbouring small town in which he ought to be standing at the counter of some whisky shop or very often he is a shoemaker or tailor. These men are not regular night poachers but they are infected with a love of sport, to gratify which they are brave all dangers and encounter even the risk of county jail.

'They wait for a day until the keepers are engaged in some particular direction and then by means of keeping on the sides of particular hills or other means suitable to the country, they are enabled to shoot an enormous quantity of grouse.

'The Regular Rural Poacher … is the chief bane to the sport for though the London hand is very successful occasionally, he does not often pay more than one or two visits to the same preserve while the rural one is always on the lookout. It requires nearly as many keepers and watchers as there are poachers to be quite safe against their incursions, and even then if a watch is put upon every known man in the neighbourhood they will outwit you by giving intelligence to some distant friends in the same trade. They pursue their plans partly by day and partly by night.

'If by day their plan is to select a small covert which has just been visited by the keeper for whose round the poacher has long been waiting in concealment, then as soon as he is out of sight the poacher sets his wires and nets in a very few minutes and enters and disturbs the coppice either with or without a dog taught to run mute. In five minutes every hare is caught and quickly disposed of in some secret spot, often a labourer's cottage, until nightfall.

'In this way also a few pheasants are taken but not so easily as the hares as they do not run so easily as the latter and if sufficiently

roused to do this some one or more are sure to give notice to the keepers in the distance by flying off to another covert which is sufficient to arouse suspicion.

'At night the tricks of the regular poacher are most ingenious and are constantly varying in proportion to the discoveries of keepers. In moonlight and on dark windy nights the poacher's harvest is made. He can then see his game without so distinctly being heard as he would on a quiet evening. He shoots the pheasants on their perches either with an airgun or fowling piece, which is made to take to pieces easily for the convenience of putting in the pocket.

'Grouse and partridge are chiefly netted but the former may more easily be shot with an airgun at night since the net is much interfered with in consequence of the heather preventing its acting. The poacher however has no difficulty with either if he can only guess pretty nearly where they are and this he takes care to do by watching them with a glass at the close of the evening. After taking his bearings at that time he is enabled to drop his net over the place without the trouble of using a stalking horse or the wide drag net.

'The only certain prevention against netting is to watch the birds at night and disperse them but this makes them so wild as to spoil subsequent shooting. Bushing the fields interferes with the drag net but not the bag net. It is a very good plan to go round every evening just before the calling of the birds and put a small bush or even with a spade throw a lot of fresh earth on the last night's place of rest which is known by their droppings. This prevents their settling near the same spot, which they would otherwise do, especially grouse. The poacher takes advantage of this fact by noting their droppings by day in order to find their settling place at night.

'Hares are taken by gate nets in the fields or by wires and bag nets in the coverts. It is a very remarkable fact that these cautious animals rarely use a hedge meuse at night preferring the gateways apparently from a fear of being surprised by the stoat or fox while by day the reverse being the case. The poacher cannot take them on the feed with a wire except in going in and out of the covert, but has recourse to the gate net which he fixes to the gate between the feeding field (usually a piece of swedes or clover) and the covert, then sending a mute running dog into the field he waits for the coming of the hare into the net and takes them out as fast as they run in to it.

'There is no certain way of avoiding this mode of poaching excepting by careful watching. The chief guide is the scream of the hare when caught which may be hard on quiet nights but it is a practice very easily pursued by the poacher with little fear of detection if he is a clever and experienced hand.

'A practice has lately been introduced of setting wires in the runs made in the middle of feeding fields. It requires a wire to be set very carefully at a certain height by means of a twig and is very destructive. It is also very difficult to detect but as the poachers cannot find them except in very open moonlit nights, the keeper knows when to have his eyes open.

'The Poaching Labourer ... is a perfect pest to the parish in which he resides. He is constantly committing breaches of trust and does so at little risk and may escape detection for a long time. These men generally have a little terrier, which is capable of being taught to do everything except speak and assists in a woodland degree in the capture of game. They also have an old gun, which takes apart easily and may be concealed under a smock frock. If a covey of birds is seen to collect near the cottage a slight noise is made and up go their heads at which moment the gun goes off and they are all dead at one swoop. The cottage is generally near the road so if a gun is heard some hedge-popping boy is made to bear the blame.

'Again these men generally have small gardens in which are parsley, pinks etc which are a favourite food for the hare. She is almost sure to visit them and in her passage through the garden fence for course makes a meuse or at all events she leaves her mark or prick in the soil. If she goes through the gate this leads to her destruction the next night by wire, gin or net and no one can possibly prevent it with the eyes of Argus.

'Pheasants are also sure to come within the reach occasionally and if they do they may be wired easily enough. A man for instance is put to hedging or draining and is on the ground by six o'clock in the morning, a time when pheasants have not left their feed, and he has only to lay a few horsehair loops along the ditches and by gently driving the pheasants into them, apparently in the course of his work, he captures every now and then the value of a day's work in a few minutes. Of course he conceals the booty until night.

'Such are the most common tricks of poachers, but the most successful are those who invent plans of their own. The keeper has enough to do to outwit them and his grand object should be to find out their plan and circumvent it – then it is diamond cut diamond. A reformed poacher, if really reformed, makes the best keeper but unfortunately for this purpose their exposure to night air and to wet and cold and their habits in intemperance have almost destroyed their constitutions before they think of reforming. It is only when worn out as poachers that they think of turning round and becoming keepers.

'When the head keeper is really up to his business, the poachers stand a very poor chance, especially if the master is ready to support the servant with his influence and protection. In every case, whether on the open moors or in enclosed districts, the first thing to be done is to make a list of all the poachers likely to visit your manor, then discover their habits and haunts and the kind of game they excel in taking. Next get some steady, hardy and useful watchers, if possible strangers to the locality and therefore not likely to be influenced by the ties of affinity or friendship.

'Let these men speedily make themselves conversant with the appearance of all poachers on your manor or your head keeper can initiate them by degrees. They should all have glasses and be made conversant with their use for, even on a comparatively small beat, it often happens that a poacher cannot be approached within many hundred yards and yet it is quite impossible to speak with any certainty of a man's identity at a quarter of a mile.

'When these men know their duties pretty well, each should have one or more poachers allotted to him and should always be able to give an account of his whereabouts. He does this partly by his own powers of watching but chiefly from information gained from other parties. By such a mode of proceeding almost any gang of poachers may be outwitted. They seldom show fight when they find themselves no match in brain, though in personal prowess they may be superior. Intellect and pluck will always be served, even when mere force has totally failed.'

Chapter 14
LIGHTING THE WAY

Brian P Martin

LIGHTING THE WAY

THE SADNESS WHICH SURROUNDS A DISUSED COUNTRY CHURCH OFTEN BEARS FALSE WITNESS TO THE GREAT DEVOTION OF PAST PARISHIONERS. RARELY HAS THIS BEEN MORE TRUE THAN IN THE WEST CORK PARISH WHERE EDWIN TOBIAS WAS RECTOR IN THE EARLY 1950S. HE HAS VIVID RECOLLECTIONS OF THIS.

Edwin with his parents in about 1919

'The main church was in the village of Timoleague, where, during the seasons of Advent and Lent, I had midweek services. One of my outlying churches stood on high ground and served a small number of very devoted people. After service one Sunday during Advent, I was asked if it would be possible to have midweek services there, too. I said: "Yes, of course, but there are no lights in the church"; only to be told: "Leave that to us, sir!"

'A date was fixed, but when I arrived on my bicycle I found the church in darkness. As I waited I began to wonder if I had mistaken the day. Then, looking down over the valley, I saw lights dotted here and there, and somehow they all seemed to be converging on the church. As they drew close my heart warmed as I realized that each member of the congregation was carrying a storm lantern, which they hung up in the church. By the same light by which they milked the cows at home, we worshipped God that evening, as we prepared ourselves for His coming.

'These people were so loyal I arranged for the bishop to visit them. When I took him to the chosen house for tea, we found that the people had painted the whole building, from top to bottom, inside and out, and had even bought new furniture especially for the occasion!

'Afterwards, as we sat in the car, the bishop paused for a minute and said: "It's very humbling." The worst of it is that the church is closed now.'

But just as those lanterns lit the path to peace, Edwin Tobias himself has been among the brightest of guiding lights during over half a century in holy orders, mostly ministering to rural flocks.

One of only two children, 'as is necessary for salvation', Edwin John Rupert Tobias was born in Lisburn, County Antrim, Northern Ireland, in January 1916, and is therefore a British citizen. But his curate father, originally a Methodist, moved the family to Dublin when Edwin was only four months old. He recollects his childhood:

'When I was a boy in Dublin, just 15 minutes on the bicycle would take you to the heart of the country. Our family life revolved around the church, of course, and mother was always a great support to father in his ministry. We had a very busy social life, and always lived in a big rectory with a parlour maid and cook.

'I was always fond of roast beef, which was very cheap then. I loved sausages, too. And when I was a very little fellow my idea of a good tea was plain bread and butter and cups of tea. But one day I disgraced mother when she took me out to tea, turning down all these sweet things offered by our host, and saying: "No thank you, I'll have a good tea when I get home."'

After high school, Edwin took a Bachelor of Arts and then a Master's degree, and also followed a divinity course at Trinity College, Dublin, from 1934 to 1940. He never considered any career outside the church, his father being a great influence on him: 'As the old cock crows, the young one learns.'

In 1940 Edwin was made deacon at St Ann's Cathedral, Dublin, for the curacy of Drumcondra and North Strand. 'It was a grand parish, working with such devoted people near the docks. In those days church would always be full on a Sunday evening and you wouldn't get a seat. The singing was wonderful, it nearly lifted the roof off.'

Edwin moved south in 1944 when he was appointed resident preacher in St Fin Barre's Cathedral, Cork, where he remained for five years. In 1945 he married Miriam Hanna (Merrie) on just £300 per year, 'and I was paid only once every three months. But a house was provided for us in Cathedral Close.' The following year, in 1946, Edwin began a long and close association with the Irish countryside when he was appointed rector of Durrus, a hilly parish in West Cork:

'They were very poor, but beautiful, wonderful people, many of whom came to church on foot every Sunday morning and to vestry on horseback.

'I well remember my first funeral there. These people lived in a little cottage, and on the way we had to pick up the carpenter to take the bedroom window out, as the stairs were too difficult for the coffin. Beforehand the relatives had handed me a paper bag, inside which was a cypress, a white cotton sash about three yards long with a rosette. There was a sash for my hat, too. They liked us to wear that, though hardly any clergy wear hats now. The hearse driver had to wear one, too.

'Like other funerals then, it was a tremendous social occasion, and people from all over came for three days before. All were fed, with roast chicken and ham and so on, and the local women helped with the barm bracks [currant loaves]. The drink was there too, including more than a bit of the hard stuff. At every wake there would be chairs around the bed with the people chatting away to each other. Then after a while they'd get up and go and have tea and cakes. It was very hard on most people to produce so much food. And many people only came for the feed and were not known to anyone. Nowadays they're trying to do away with the wakes, and I've always encouraged people to get the body to the church as soon as possible.'

Even on such serious occasions Edwin could see the lighter side of life. So when one of the mourners said: 'Excuse me sir, I'd like to introduce you to the corpse's brother', Edwin was secretly very amused. He continues: 'We had some well-off people in the parish, but we always had more fun with the poor.

'Later on, when we were in County

The Minister
Solemn and Workmanlike

This prophetic card was sent to four-year-old Edwin from Blackburn on 24 September 1920. On it is written '... a picture of you in years to come. Love to mother. Uncle B'

Meath, there was a man called Movie McCormack, which I thought was very appropriate for an undertaker. And another time someone said to me: "I can't go to the funeral; will a box of chocolates do instead?" But a lot of people couldn't see the humour. It's not something that can be acquired, and some people I've known have had none whatsoever.'

In those days the Durrus district was very isolated. 'One family lived right up on the hill and never saw anybody for weeks on end. A car was essential for my work, and I'd had one since 1945. When the time came to change this old Ford I thought I wouldn't get much for it, as it was all tied up with string. But I managed to sell it to a farmer's wife because she just happened to want a black car. Unfortunately for me, in those days everybody know the cleric's car and when subsequently it was seen outside all the pubs and bars, they thought I still owned it!

'There was a pony and trap to take the children to school, and very few people had cars. But if anyone gave me a lift he would say: "Would you get in the north door?" For some reason everything was east and west then, and not just road directions.

As a rural rector's wife, Miriam, too, had to be very adaptable. 'One day a woman said to me, "Here's a chicken." I said, "Thank you very much," but when I put my hand inside the bag I found the bird was still alive! Fortunately, our cleaner — a great big capable woman — killed it.'

Edwin's predecessor at Durrus had been a great matchmaker. 'Some people there told me they never met their husbands till they got to church door on the day of the wedding, which was more of a business transaction. Once I was asked to help, but I refused to have anything to do with an

'... but when I put my hand inside the bag I found the bird was still alive!'

alliance, because if anything went wrong I'd be for it. There was always a dowry involved. One man refused, simply because the girl's farmer father could only raise £150 rather than the £200 required. A lot of old mothers certainly ruined their sons' lives, and many of the husbands were bullied.'

Superstition, too, could prevent or spoil a marriage. Edwin especially remembers one at Durrus where the groom's parents strongly opposed the union because a weasel had been 'dancing' on the kitchen table. 'When someone was being introduced to the bride, his reaction was: "I'll never shake hands to a weasel". On another occasion our maid was terribly upset when a robin came into our kitchen. She was sure this meant there would be a death.'

A good way for the rector to get to know the people better was through helping with the harvest: 'Farms were so small then; the biggest in Durrus had maybe only three hours thrashing, so we followed the machine all over the district. Sadly, there were some nasty accidents as there was always booze around, and drink and open machinery — especially of the old type — don't mix. But the people were always cute enough not to drink while I was there. At a house we'd have tea, then I'd go out with the pike to help before going back in for more tea.

'At Durrus in 1946 the Roman Catholic priest would pass me on the road and not recognise me; however, that sort of thing wouldn't happen now. Indeed, when I left Kilbixy, in 1977, I even had a present from the catholic community. But thrashing was always an interdenominational effort because at grass roots all the people are great friends. If only the Roman Catholic church would let the Church of Ireland and Church of England people go to the church and take their communion, then there'd be a great change.'

If Edwin ever wanted to find out what was going on at Durras he simply went down to the creamery, 'where everyone brought their milk in between nine and eleven in the morning.' And in the 1940s, with a lot of IRA activity, even a rural rector had to be alert to suspicious circumstances.

'One day I was just off to visit somebody when two men got out of a car and went into the graveyard carrying a spade and a long box. Well, I was responsible for the place, so I thought I'd better make enquiries. But by the time I got over there the box was already in the grave. I said: "Excuse me, but I'm rector of this parish and I think I should ask you what you are doing." One of the men, who was a Roman Catholic — we have mixed graveyards — looked up and declared: "My son's leg is in that box!" I replied: "That's OK, then," and left them to it.

'Another time we found a little dog wrapped in an electric blanket. But there was a name on the blanket, and later we discovered that a chauffeur had been sent 60 miles to bury it! When the Guards [Guarda] went to see the gentle lady who had sent it, she answered the door with a gun!'

In 1949 Edwin became rector of Timoleague, Cork; and in 1955 his father — the Archdeacon of Dublin — appointed him curate for the parish of Holy Trinity, Rathmines, Dublin, a very rare example of father and son working together within the clergy. But the countryside called again, and in 1959 Edwin began 18 years as rector of Kilbixy, curate-in-charge of Killucan Union, also in Meath; he retired from the ministry in 1982.

Of all these parishes, Kilbixy was Edwin's favourite, despite the ghosts. 'When we

went there, the people asked if we would be living in the haunted rectory. We didn't mind, but were still surprised when we heard knocking on the door and there was no one there. However, we never mentioned this if we had visitors stopping!

'We also had a very lucky escape at Kilbixy, when the church roof collapsed just 48 hours after I was taking service. Nobody would have been taken out alive.' Bats, too, bedevilled worshippers at Kilbixy: 'At Almorita church Merrie was playing the organ when a bat was seen on the holy table. An old lady came in and said she didn't mind dealing with it. So she covered it with a scarf, took it outside and shook it out. But when she came back in the bat was still there. She must have thought she had lifted it. Eventually a farmer took it out in his hand.

'I'm terrified of bats, and we've had to have lots of them removed from rectory attics and water tanks. Once at Timoleague there was one hanging on the dining room curtain. Another time there were two in our bedroom when we went home at Killucan, and once there was one behind the hymn board when we took it down at Kilbixy.

Undaunted by ghosts, bats and the roof falling in, Kilbixy's parishioners were extremely devoted. 'One Sunday, Tommy Burnett's car was in dock, and I said: "There won't be many in tonight as Tommy always brings a carful." But later I heard a vehicle on the avenue of the church, and when I looked out, there was Tommy with a tractor and trailer full with people!'

It seems that Kilbixy folk were truly fired up by Edwin's sermons. Indeed, once when he was preaching, lightning was dancing on the wires coming into the church. Afterwards, one of the parishioners said to him: 'That was a very dramatic sermon you gave, lit up in the pulpit, enveloped in fire and brimstone.' But on other occasions lightning was far from welcome, such as when it blew the rectory telephone box off the wall, and in one night killed 30 head of cattle belonging to a local lady farmer.

The boys from a local boarding school only attended church on dry days. 'This was because their building was a bit primitive and they had no facilities for drying coats. So when it rained they used the school chapel. They were certainly very spirited lads, and one day even let an alarm clock off at the back during my service!'

There was plenty of fun with the adult parishioners, too. 'One chap came rushing over to see me at two in the morning, his headlights blazing up through the rectory window. He had more than a few jars on him, but was so pleased at having just left his mother-in-law in hospital that he felt compelled to come and tell me! Unfortunately we were looking after a baby then, and he woke him up, too. He said afterwards, "I knew I was drunk, but not that drunk!"'

Other nocturnal activities in the Westmeath and Longford area included cockfighting. 'They still do it, most at about one or two o'clock in the

morning. Quite a few folk have told me they have woken up and seen a crowd of people in their field. Once we had a lovely cock and one morning we discovered that one of his spurs had been lost overnight.'

It was not really surprising that such ancient sport continued into modern times when some of the participants still lived in relatively primitive conditions. 'Even in my last parish of Killucan, where I was in office from 1977 to 1982, some people still had houses with earthen floors and oil lamps. Some of them had the money to improve things, but simply didn't want to spend it. When one couple on a farm went to retire to a small home they found all their bank notes, which they had put in a drawer, had been shredded by mice.'

It was as well that Edwin had a great sense of humour to sustain him through his long ministry, because there was always a sad side to his work as well. As Merrie said: 'There was always a lot of tragedy. Sometimes I was afraid to answer the phone, which would ring mornings and evenings all the year round. Then Edwin would have to go off and tell the relatives.'

With their only son, Christopher, away in Dublin, Merrie and Edwin now live in the delightful Sue Ryder House at Ballyroan, County Laois, with the church and green fields close by. Although he has lived in cities, there is no doubt that Edwin has been more enlightened by the countryside. 'Once we stayed in a London hotel, and couldn't stand the noise of the lorries. We arrived back home in Ireland in the cool of the evening, and when we went to bed it was so still we could hear the sound of the cows chewing the cud. It was a wonderful peace.'

Chapter 15

THE SILENT DOG

John Humphreys

THE SILENT DOG

A MARK OF THE GENUINE POACHER WAS THAT HE WAS ACCOMPANIED BY A DOG. USUALLY OF UNPREPOSSESSING APPEARANCE, THIS WAS NOT JUST ANY HOUSEHOLD POOCH BUT ONE TRAINED TO A HIGH DEGREE, AND AS GOOD, IF NOT BETTER THAN, THE KEEPER'S OWN SHOOTING DOGS. A POACHER'S DOG COULD START HARES AND RABBITS RUNNING TO GATE-NET OR LONG-NET, BUT STOP SHORT OF PURSUING THEM IN TO IT. IT WAS QUICK ENOUGH TO PICK A HARE FROM A FORM AND BRING IT BACK, WARN OF APPROACHING TROUBLE, BE SILENT AT ALL TIMES, SLIP HOME LIKE A SHADOW WHEN TOLD, MAKE DO WITH VERY LITTLE FOOD AND REMAIN LOYAL TO ITS MASTER UNTO DEATH.

It risked dog spears, poison, steel and shot from the keeper but it slept by day to be fresh for night work, he was companion, foot-warmer, alarm and bag filler. The loss of a good dog was enough to cause the collapse of many a poaching gang.

The Poacher's Dog

A cross between a greyhound and a collie was considered the best, although any sort of mongrel would be pressed into service. Any animal that was capable of snapping up a rabbit where it lay in a hedge bottom couch was deemed good enough, for such was the bread and butter of the wandering moucher's business. However, some poachers' dogs were trained to an astonishing degree. The first cross mentioned combined wisdom with keen sight, speed of foot and excellent scenting powers.

The poacher's dog should never in any circumstances give tongue, no matter how hot the pursuit in which it is engaged. It will search a hedge and start rabbits towards the long net, itself stopping within a yard of the meshes; it should be able to run down a hare and retrieve it to hand, and only to break silence to give a low, warning growl at the approach of an unseen stranger. It is directed by the slightest wave of a hand – the poacher will not need to give away his presence by using verbal commands.

The best dogs seemed to enter the spirit of the game, snatching what sleep they could during the day and ever ready for night work. One old training trick was to teach the dog to go home when the traditional 'come here' whistle or call was sounded. Thus a poacher apprehended and commanded to call up his dog would whistle and shout for all he was worth – but the dog had been trained that at that sound it should immediately slink off safely home. The loss of such a dog was a serious blow to a poacher and sometimes to a whole gang; some were put out of business when the dog was lost for one reason or another.

The keeper was, of course, ordered to destroy all such dogs at every opportunity but with the proviso that on no account should this risk harming a fox, as many

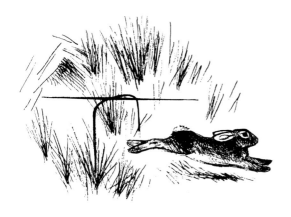

A Bright Lad

Some poachers were out one night with long dogs after hares. One of the dogs came back clearly in distress and to their horror went into convulsions and died on the spot before their eyes. They felt sure that the keeper had left out a carcass baited with strychnine especially for that purpose.

Later in the day the same men came upon the keeper's little lad on his way to school. The burly leader approached the lad and asked in a wheedling voice: 'Sammy, does your father use strike-o-nine to poison folk's dogs with?'

'No', said Sammy, skipping a yard further out of range 'he uses strike-o-ten.' As the old editions of *Punch* used to say, 'Collapse of stout party.'

Night Dog

Then, as now, it was strongly recommended that a keeper should not go on night patrol without the companionship and protection of a suitable dog. A cross between a mastiff and a bulldog was ideal, a creature of natural savagery and tenacity who simply loved nothing more than chasing people and biting them. The dog should be kept muzzled except in cases of extreme emergency – for when loosed without his muzzle he should be a fearsome beast, seeming to wish to make up for all the times he had wanted to bite people in the past but been prevented.

A keeper could train such a dog to chase a poacher and run between his legs, bringing him down. The dog would also warn of miscreants hiding nearby in the bushes, for his keen sense of smell would supplement the sight and hearing of his master; and he could detect the approach of folk in the dark long before a human knew anyone was within a mile of the place.

shooting estates preserved their foxes for hunting. Setting snares always involved such a risk, and there were doubtless many accidents which were kept quiet. A snare should be set where paths intersect, at stream crossings, and in similar well-used places; it should be stout, and a bough bent over and pegged so that when the snare was sprung, the victim was half suspended by the branch springing straight. To avoid foxes the keeper would rub the snare and surrounding vegetation with his hands, the human scent deterring a fox but not a dog.

The Professionals

The keeper went to some lengths to discourage tramps, pedlars and strangers from visiting his house. He had discovered that they rarely had a good reason for the call and their real motive was to spy out the land and discover the disposition of the keeper and their surroundings. What was more, those with transport, the carriers with horse-drawn closed vans, were often used as smugglers for poached game.

A good keeper therefore kept a savage dog at his gate, taught to bark and growl at strangers. Such a dog could be trained by asking genuine visitors to thrust a broom in his face, or even by the keeper himself dressing in rags and acting the part of the vagrant – although I imagine his scent would have given him away.

It did no harm if suitably embroidered tales of the dog's ferocity went round the village. The keeper regularly fuelled this legend with casually dropped 'asides' of the fearful maimings and damage done by his 'little dog' the night before, and of some unfortunate victim languishing in hospital hoping to recover from dreadful wounds; this news would spread swiftly and was further enhanced in the retelling so the reputation for the man-eating dog became well established.

A bitch was to be preferred to a dog for keeper's companion on night work. For one thing, a bitch could be more savage and relentless than any dog – and there was another reason, which the following yarn will explain:

One estate was blessed with a mastiff dog of such unbelievable ferocity that there was little poaching, for none dared risk facing the brute's jaws. In time the keepers grew complacent, and relied too much on their four-legged friend and his reputation to do their work for them. One night in the peak of shooting season they grew so lax that they left but two men on prowl while they attended a servants' ball in a neighbouring mansion.

The two keepers sauntered down the dark rides, taking little care and depending on the dog to be their eyes, ears and protection. Suddenly they were pounced on by a poaching gang who had lain in wait for them in the bushes. They were tied up into neat parcels with rope and tumbled into a dry ditch, where they suffered cold comfort of hearing the poachers knocking down numerous birds from the trees. They could not believe what had happened to the mighty dog; he had dashed off in the right direction sure enough, but then mysteriously had seemed to vanish. Eventually they were rescued, still no sign of the dog, and they concluded that the poachers had poisoned it with baited meat, although no body had been found. The next day, however, they were surprised to see old Titan sleeping in his kennel, none the worse for whatever had happened to him.

It remained a mystery, until later it leaked out that the poachers had come armed with a bitch 'in an interesting condition', and old Titan, preferring love to fighting, had dashed off in pursuit of amour leaving the poachers to carry on undisturbed. Thus, bitches every time, for they do not suffer from pangs of passion.

The Playful Dog

Ian Niall recalls a time when two poachers were saved by the dog who loved a game. 'Two friends of mine who were chased by a keeper ran through the park carrying a gun and a sack containing four birds and accompanied by their lurcher. When a second keeper joined the first and a car began to race ahead of them down an adjoining drive, it seemed certain that they would be caught. One swung off and ran at right angles to the original flight and the other turned to give battle. The two keepers separated. The running poacher who carried the sack and gun became the quarry of one of the keepers. The poacher who stood his ground gave a signal to his dog.

'It ran in quickly and snapped at the heel of the keeper's boot and over he went. The second keeper hesitated and the poacher broke back past him. He turned to give chase and the lurcher somehow ran in between his legs and brought him down as he had the other. The first poacher was by now well into the shelter of a nearby wood. His companion whistled up the dog and ran on and soon he, too, was in cover. It seemed that the dog had been taught the game by the children of one of them and had become a bugbear in the village for the

habit of upending anyone who ran or moved fast. It sobered them both a little when I remarked that it was a good thing the dog had not chosen to turn playful with either of them while the keepers were in chase.'

The Silent Dog

Lynn Doyle writes in *Ballygullion* of Pat Murphy and his friends on a long-netting night on the squire's park. His companions are ill-experienced in the gentle art, and for their purposes they have acquired a 'silent dog' which, in spite of the sternest tests to which they put it, would utter no sound to give away the game.

'Faith' sez I, 'it's well he's some good points about him for be me sowl he's no beauty.' An' nayther he was; a low set, crooked legged baste wi' a dirty brown coat and a wee bunty tail. Wan av his ears was half tore off an' he'd lost two teeth in the front.

'We couldn't have picked a better night,' sez Mr Anthony. 'We'll be able to see what we're doing.' 'Aye, an' the rabbits'll be able to see what we're doing too,' sez I, 'There's no good startin' till it clouds over a bit.' It was rising a bit cloudy behind the wind an' I knowed the moon would soon be covered. 'Maybe you're right,' sez Mr Anthony. 'I'll tell you what I'll do while we're waiting. I'll run back an' get the airgun. It'll make no noise an' I might get a shot at a rabbit.'

'If ye take my advice', sez I, 'ye'll let the gun alone'. But he never listened to me, an' made off up the avenue at a trot, lavin' me an' Mr Barrington standin' there.

After half a mile walk we come to the plantin' below the big house. There's about fifteen acres av it in a sort of half moon, then a big stretch of grass they call the lawn right up to the hall door wi' an odd big tree in it here and there. The upper end av the plantin's fair alive wi' rabbit holes, and av a

fine night the rabbits does be feedin' holes on the lawn in hundreds. Our scheme was to run the nets along in front of the holes, an' thin get round an' let the dog loose to scare the rabbits intil them.

As soon as we got the nets set we slipped round the horn av the plantin' close to the house. Mr Anthony puts the chain he has the dog on in my hand. 'Now Pat', he sez, 'you hould the dog in till we get to the middle av the lawn, and maybe I'll get a shot', sez he, putting a pellet in the airgun.

'Ye auld fool,' thinks I, 'wi' your pop gun; it's as well you don't lame somebody,' for his hands was in such a trimmble wi narvousness that he could hardly snap the breech. Howiver, out we moves, an' just then, as ill luck would have it, out comes the moon. 'Bad cess to ye' sez I, 'ye ould divil ye, weren't ye alright behind there, but ye must come out an spoil sport.'

But Mr Anthony was well plazed. 'Wheesht, Pat,' sez he; 'I see wan.' Wi' that he puts his foot in a rabbit hole, an' down he slaps on his face, an' the gun snaps and pins the dog in the side somewhere. Maybe it was more than the mortial baste could stan', for thim wee pellets is cruel, but anyway the dog sets up the horridest howlin' ye iver heard, an' I was that taken in that I dropped the chain and let him go.

An' thin the fun begins – Mr Anthony rippin' and cusin' an' spitting out bits of grass an' the silent dog runnin' round and round wi' the chain rattlin' behind him like a tinker's cart. 'For a silent dog' sez I, 'he's makin' a brave noise.' 'Shut up ye fool', sez Mr Anthony, as mad as you like, 'an catch the brute. Be the mortial,' sez he 'if I catch him, I'll make a silent dog av him.'

All av a suddin the big front door opens wi' a clatter. 'Come on men,' I hears old Mr

Hastings' voice. 'Scatter across the lawn an' ye can't miss the blackguards. I can hear their dog.' Ye niver saw three men run faster than we did for that plantin'. 'Look out for the nets,' sez I, but wee Mr Anthony was runnin' like a redshank ten yards in front of us and niver heard me. The net took him just on the shin bone, an' he riz about two foot in the air, an lit on belly on the plantin' ditch wi' a sough.

Whin we got up to him, he could hardly spake.

'Up wi you quick'; 'I can't,' sez he wi' a groan; 'me heart's busted,' sez he. 'Not a bit av it' sez Mr Barrington fellin' him, 'it's only your braces.'

(They escape, and hear the pursuing keepers' cries fading into the distance in pursuit of the 'silent dog' which was still making a fearful noise. The fugitives hear two distant shots, then silence. A week later

DEALING WITH THE POACHER'S DOG, 1850 STYLE – ACCORDING TO JOHN WILKINS

Take a rabbit's liver, heart and lights and 'season' them. Put them into a pound canister tin and carry the tin in your breast pocket. You will require four livers, or four 'seasoned' doses and you should lay some blood with each dose. Lay one dose two or three yards away from each gate and, while the poacher is engaged in setting his net, the dog will scent the blood, come up and eat it.

The poacher sets his net and then, not knowing what his dog has been about calls – 'Here Bob, go on, good dog.' Away goes Bob across the field but before he has gone a hundred yards he begins to feel very queer and staggery. He winds a hare and makes a rush for her but, as he is drawing up to her flanks, he pitches head over heels. He tries to rise but only falls over again, his legs going as stiff as iron pokers.

It is all up with poor Bob, he never returns to his master but lays there until next morning. You come to pick up your doses and find one clean gone. Look about you and you will see a great prize. Put him in a bag and bury him with all honours. That gang of poachers is broken up for the season, for it's a hundred to one that they cannot get another dog and if they do, it won't be another 'Bob' but some animal of very little use to them.

I make my own alarm guns and can set them in the field or woods so as to make a dog commit suicide, but the same drawback applies to this as well as the doses – a fox may get killed as well as a poacher's dog.

Mr Barrington and Pat are down by the river, leaning over the bridge and discussing their recent adventure.)

Thin I sees something come floating down the river. 'Be the mortial, Mr Barrington,' sez I, whin I looked at it for a minit, 'it's him.' 'Not a bit av it', sez he; 'it's twice the size.' 'Maybe he's a bit swelled,' sez I; an' whin it floated down the length of the bridge, sure enough, it was himself. Mr Barrington stands lookin' at him till I war near turned, for in troth he was smellin' higher nor a daisy.

'Come on Pat,' sez he at the last turnin' away. 'I'm sorry the poor baste's killed. I'll send someone down to fish him out and give him a dacint burial.'

'It's all ye can do for him, Mr Barrington' sez I. 'Rest his sowl, if he has one, though I did lose two good rabbit nets be him, he's a silent dog now anyway.

Clean Heels

Gil Gaylor, the Gatcombe Park poacher, writes of his experiences. Here he is in a wood at night; he has shot a pheasant in a tree, but has heard a distant dog bark.

It was perhaps the keeper's dog that had barked and for a few minutes I lived in an eternity of suspense. Then, all of a sudden, I heard the heavy tramping of dead leaves some way off. I slipped slowly and quietly from where I stood in a shallow ditch by a hazel thicket.

The keeper passed within 20 yards of me, then paused by an oak tree and stood there, peering into the darkness, listening. Luckily for me he did not have his dog with him. I knew that he heard the crashing of wings and was waiting for the trespasser to betray his presence.

It was a beautiful, moonlit night and from my hiding place I could see him staring to and fro into the darkness of the hazel thickets. The minutes ticked by, then with a further trampling of leaves the keeper moved away in a different direction. I waited several more minutes, then myself moved cautiously away. The night was finished. The keeper might be going for a dog . . .

Chapter 16
CHOCOLATE AND FLOWERS

Jean Stone and Louise Brodie

CHOCOLATE AND FLOWERS

'WELL, IF I CAN GET INTO BOURNVILLE, I'M MADE!' SO SAID JACK BOTTERILL, WHEN HE SAW AN ADVERTISEMENT FOR THE JOB OF GARDENER AT THE CADBURY'S FACTORY OUTSIDE BIRMINGHAM. IT WAS KNOWN THAT THEY WERE VERY GOOD TO THEIR EMPLOYEES, LOOKING AFTER THEM WELL, WITH GOOD SPORTS FACILITIES, SUBSIDISED CANTEEN FOOD, GENEROUS PENSIONS AND OTHER PERKS.

THE JOB PAID £8 A WEEK, WHICH WAS LOWER THAN THE FACTORY WORKERS RECEIVED, BUT JACK THOUGHT IT WAS SUFFICIENT IN 1949 WHEN HE WAS NOT LONG OUT OF THE ARMY. IT WAS ENOUGH FOR HIM TO START BUYING A HOUSE, ANYWAY (TAKE-HOME PAY £6 10S A WEEK, MORTGAGE £8 2S PER MONTH). JACK SAYS OF CADBURY'S: 'THEY WANTED PEOPLE TO FEEL THAT THEY WERE PART OF THE COMPANY FAMILY. I THINK I FELT THAT. THEY WERE HAPPY DAYS.'

DICK CAME TO CADBURY'S A FEW YEARS LATER AFTER JACK; HE HAD BEEN TRAINED AS A GARDENER AT SHIFNAL, NEAR WHERE HE WAS BORN IN SHROPSHIRE, WHERE HIS STARTING WAGE IN 1932 WAS 6S A WEEK.

There was a very strict hierarchy in those days among the 62 gardeners who worked at Bournville in the 1950s; they started at the bottom on the unskilled flat rate, moving through semi-skilled to skilled, with no bonuses. There was a file report on each man, and he would be assessed by the manager and foreman every year to enable him to make a move to the next grade when the time came. Nothing official would be discussed; the employee would simply receive a letter through the post to inform him of his new wages. At the beginning 'You started with a broom and shovel, sweeping the leaves. After a bit, you got rid of your broom and shovel and got a pair of secateurs. When you got a pair of secateurs, that was it, you were then known as a gardener!'

Dick worked in the kitchen garden, where they used to grow espalier trees and fans. He remembers the Blenheim apple trees, which must have been a hundred years old then. These apples have very good keeping qualities, and will keep from one year to the next. 'We've had two ton of apples off those six trees; and the pears, Pitmaston Duchess, we've weighed them at 1lb each.'

The kitchen garden and greenhouse complex used to be part of Bournbrook Hall. The house was demolished when the site was bought for Cadbury's, though these outbuildings remained. Once, part of the

orchard subsided and they discovered the brickwork of the old laundry underground. It had to be filled with rubble and covered over again.

Some produce was grown in the kitchen garden, but Dick remembers mostly flowers. Some of the roses and other blooms they grew were given to photographers to take pictures to adorn the chocolate box lids; then every girl that got married was presented with a carnation and a bible, and another flower was given on leaving the firm. The carnations were grown in the greenhouses, where Dick also worked.

Bouquets of flowers were used regularly to decorate the offices of senior personnel in the works; it was said that in 1932, 4,500 vases of flowers had been used in the factory – for instance 300 indoor chrysanthemum plants had been grown, giving 2,500 blooms. Although by the 1950s the scale was not the same, floral decorations were still ordered every day, and Dick, who had been trained in this work in his previous employment, loved doing them. Special arrangements were called for when there were unusual events or occasions, such as the centenary celebrations in 1979 held to mark the move to Bournville. Then there were official visits to the factory, and garden parties, and events at the Almshouses or College of Education; all these called for extra efforts

Bournville's first motor mower, sold to Cadbury's in 1902, seen here on the Men's Recreation Ground. The driver is Ben Florence, head groundsman until 1920 (Cadbury Ltd)

on the part of the gardeners. The greenhouses would also produce hundreds of bedding plants, either from seed or grown from cuttings. Geraniums and cineraria were popular, cyclamen and carnations, and many others.

Dick used to work on the tomato plants in the greenhouse – hundreds of these, too; some went to the canteen and others would be sold. They used to make all their own leaf mould for the tomato pots. They had five bays to contain the mould, and it would be turned over from one bay to the next every year, so that the one they used was five years old; and then they filled up the first one again. 'It was beautiful stuff.' They put their own soil and John Innes into the mixture, filled the pots and put them in the sterilizer. All the greenhouses would be washed down every winter with soft soap. The greenhouse staff in Dick's early days would not allow the outside staff to go through the houses 'or only when

everything was cleared. You weren't allowed to see or touch, I think it was sacred ground to them. An outside man was a nobody.'

In the 1950s, the gardener's day started at 7.42am and finished at 4.54pm, and the hour was divided into six-minute slots; lunch was an hour's break from 12.18pm. They were allowed a tea-break in the morning, but not in the afternoon; this ruling was ignored, however, and the kettle would be boiled up behind some bushes, or if that was not practicable, a hole would be dug and the stove lit below ground level, out of sight of the prowling foreman. At dinner time in the middle of the day, the men went either to the canteen if they were working in that area, or they would go to their mess room. 'They had a row of bowls to wash in, and that was luxury; the old ones used to tell us that they had had a bucket. They were always saying that we were living in a time of luxury.' A donkey jacket, overalls and clogs were supplied by the company, though Jack could never get on with the clogs, and used to wear his own safety shoes.

One perk was the holiday allowance. Gardeners were allowed a fortnight's holiday after 12 months, and were given £3 for each child and £5 for the wife. The company could also be very generous when it came to helping with the children's education. When Jack's son got into King Edward's School 'He had to have a lot of uniform, and to get a complete outfit all at once, well, on our wages you couldn't do it. I went to the office and they gave me all these forms to fill in, and I am sorry to say that I hate forms – I would do anything to get out of them. But I did it, and gave them back, and a fortnight later I got a cheque which practically paid for all the uniform.'

The grounds, which they had to look after, consisted of all the areas round the factory. The Men's Recreation Ground was overlooked by the canteen, and dominated on the road side by the huge pavilion; the Girls' Grounds were situated on the other side of the road and dated from the time when the sexes were segregated.

The grounds were reached by a tunnel going under the road. Senior staff would chaperone the girls from their place of work, down the corridors, outside and through the tunnel to take the air in their designated place away from the corrupting influence of the men.

There were lawns surrounded by trees and shrubs for seclusion; a pond formed from the cellars of the demolished Bournbrook Hall, and a pergola screening a stage for performances of concerts and plays. There was also a croquet lawn, and many flowerbeds which have long since been turfed over to save costs.

Some distance away, 75 acres of land had been purchased at Rowheath to provide sports fields and other leisure amenities, including nine acres devoted to the gardening club. The club had worked well in the first half of the century; it was held three evenings a week and on Saturdays, with the purpose of helping youngsters to learn to tend a garden. Seeds and tools were bought in bulk with consequent savings, and lecturers were invited to share their expertize. After the war, however, most of those who came were older people, primarily looking for bargains, and interest in the club gradually waned. Rowheath also boasted a lake, lawns and flowerbeds which fronted another pavilion large enough to stage events. (This whole area has now passed out of the hands of Cadbury's; some sporting facilities are left, but they are run by the Bournville Trust, and some of the land has been sold for development.)

Jack Botterill liked to work in the area around the director's offices, feeling that everybody got to know you there. 'The Cadbury's used to take a lot of interest in what was going on in the garden, and I think they used to respect who you were, whoever you were.' By Mr John Cadbury's office there were flowerbeds, window-boxes and a rockery, and there were always masses of spring bulbs. It caused a rumpus when the holly hedge was cut down from about ten foot to a neat three, but after a while it was agreed that it was much better kept that way – they could see out of the windows!

Both Jack and Dick feel that they had happy years at Bournville. They enjoyed themselves at work; they had to work hard and the discipline was strict, but they respected this attitude. Mr Neales, who was the head gardener through the 1950s, might call someone into the office to give them a good dressing down, but then it was finished. For example, Jack's friend, Walter, was always smoking, and they weren't

allowed to smoke on the job. Once Jack saw Mr Neales coming (he always rode a push-bike with a basket on the front) and warned Walter to put his cigarette out; thinking he had gone past, Walter started up again, when a voice came over the hedge, 'Walter, you're smoking!' 'No, I'm not, Mr Neales' said Walter, as he ground his cigarette into the mud. At dinner time there was trouble: 'I caught you this morning, Walter.' 'Yes, and it was a bloody Player and all!' Mr Neales, having made his point, finished the incident: 'Well, you'd better have one of mine then.'

When Neales retired in 1958, the system began to change. The next man had not been trained as a professional gardener; he was easygoing and pleasant, but introduced new ideas such as labelling for the plants: 'He can't remember the names!' and 'It looks like a bloody cemetery!' were typical of the comments. During the 1960s, the manpower had been reduced to about 35 to 40 gardeners, still doing the same jobs as before but aided by better machinery. Then in the 1970s came the merger with Schweppes; a new director came around and said: 'Very nice, but its all gold plate, and the best thing to do is get rid of gold plate.' Eventually the much-reduced gardens and grounds were run by office staff.

'We hardly ever saw them,' said Dick. 'And it's hard work working with somebody who isn't a gardener. You've got to tell them everything, and if you want to buy something, you've got to explain why.' Jack, having started at the bottom as a labourer, got to the top of the department as acting manager. When the head gardener left in 1982, the department was put under the control of Lodges and Security and Jack moved up, but without the dignified title. 'The first Christmas I had to budget for the next year. I'd never done this before and

hadn't got a clue. "Well, how many tools do you want?" I rubbed my hands together with glee, and was asking everyone else. "Oh," they said "you want to get so many spades and so many forks." I gave the list back to the boss and the phone went an hour later. "You've got to cut this by half, Jack, it's far too much – you can't have all this, you know." So the next year I thought I'd double it. "Oh Jack, you can't have all this, you must cut it by half." That's fair enough, I'm going to get what I want then. The next year he didn't wear it at all. "You pulled a fast one last year. You'll sit here and do it with me now."'

When they next asked for a redundancy, Jack, as the oldest man, decided to take it. He had worked for Cadbury's for more than 30 years, but the job had changed radically during the previous decade and as acting manager he was working seven days a week.

Dick Dobson picking Pitmaston Duchess pears at Bournville (Cadbury Ltd)

Jack Botterill outside the director's office in 1955 (Cadbury Ltd)

He has no regrets; it was time for him to go.

A young man of 22, running a single-handed grocery business in Birmingham, started the company. John Cadbury's firm prospered during the 19th century, and it was his son George who, in 1879, moved the company to Bournville. His vision of the future was revolutionary at the time: it included not just the factory on a green field site, but also the provision of housing for all grades of his employees in a healthy environment – his workers should not continue to live in the slums of inner city Birmingham. His vision, successfully put into action, inspired many, and led to other experiments of the same kind.

By 1900, more than 300 houses had been built with educational and leisure facilities to go with them, and George Cadbury transferred the property to an independent body, the Bournville Village Trust, renouncing all financial interest in the property. 'The founder is desirous of alleviating the evils which arise from the unsanitary and insufficient accommodation supplied to large numbers of working classes, and of securing to the workers in factories some of the advantages of outdoor village life, with opportunities for the natural and healthful occupation of cultivating the soil.'

Each house had an ample plot of its own, made ready for the occupant to grow his own vegetables and flowers, and a fruit tree was planted in each. The various trees at the bottom of the garden provided some privacy and looked very pleasant. A lawn was provided for children's play and family relaxation, and hedges were put in place. In the early years, when some of the occupants could be expected to have little experience of gardening, competitions were started to help raise awareness. Gardening associations were formed originally as co-operative groups, buying equipment and

sundries and exchanging ideas and information. The resulting competitions were very popular. To give some scale of the proceedings, in 1906, judging took place among 112 kitchen gardens, 500 flower gardens and 70 boys' and girls' gardens. (This continues today in the form of the Bournville Village Festival. Garden classes are restricted to Bournville residents. They also have children's events unconnected with gardening.)

In the early 1930s, individual gardens were written up in the *Bournville Works Magazine*. Mr G Pickett's garden, for instance, featured a small thatched summer house, three ponds with fountains, – each containing rare lilies – a rockery with choice alpines, mature fruit trees, 350 roses, stone benches, a sundial and a dove-cot with doves. In contrast, at the beginning of the war, an article in the magazine started with an exhortation to 'everyone to make the most of his land', with hints on how to grow a series of vegetables to provide food throughout the year. The company grounds, with the notable exception of the Men's Recreation Ground, were dug up for the same purpose. When life settled down after the war, it can be seen that the tradition of gardening was well established, both on an individual basis, and from the point of view of appreciating the factory gardens and communal playing fields.

Dick Dobson and Jack Botterill continued the tradition, having been trained before the war and starting with the company soon afterwards.

Calvin Green came to Cadbury's in the 1960s, transferring to the greenhouses because of his asthma. As a young man, the complex seemed very large and elaborate to him and he remembers the constant need to stoke the boilers. 'We had to shovel coal in twice a day … and wash pots and generally tidy up. I just got menial tasks because I was not expecting to stay long – chop up old turfs, and line the bottom of the pots with horse manure, by hand. We potted these chrysanths on, grew them up in the ashes, and then bought them in for winter, for the offices as required.' He also had to water the concrete to make a humid atmosphere for the plants. There were six greenhouses and four gardeners working there, doing a great deal of propagation. Unfortunately, the greenhouses were set on fire by vandals in 1993 and the whole set have had to be demolished.

Calvin later went to college to train to be a groundsman. In earlier days, all the gardeners had learnt on the job, the older men showing the youngsters by example. Earlier still, there are records showing that apprentices were sent to events such as the Chelsea Flower Show as part of the learning process; yet in all Jack Botterill's career with Cadbury's, he had only a couple of days away for the company (he went to a show

set up in Ipswich by Ransomes). For Calvin, who is now head gardener, the situation has been rather different: employees must be trained in specialist work such as using sprays and pesticides, and shown the correct way to handle new machinery. In recent years it has been the policy to move the groundsmen around to familiarize them with each and every aspect of the work, rather than giving them one area to look after, as was the case in Dick Dobson's day.

There are now few ornamental areas, and those that there are, are low cost, low maintenance gardens. The emphasis is on sporting facilities, although these too are much reduced in number. What there are, however, are kept in very good condition, so much so that professional teams have played on them: Aston Villa have trained on the football pitches and the Indian team have used a cricket field. Hockey and tennis, and both lawn and crown bowls are among the sports still played today. Previously, if you wanted to play a particular sport, then the company would try to provide it for you.

The young people's welfare was considered to be a matter of legitimate concern to their elders. Ken Sale, one of Calvin's three assistants, went into the gardens as a young man in 1957. He remembers his personal talk with the foreman every six months, when he would be asked what he did in the evenings. He replied that he went to his church youth club, which was a satisfactory answer – he was off the streets. 'We were encouraged to participate. If you were doing nothing, they tended to say, "How about doing this section, what do you like?" In those days we had our own dining room, the youths from 15 to 18. No one else could go in, not girls or older men, about 500 youths, all together.' Earlier still, boys had had to do PT and swimming, and in the men's pool they did not wear costumes. The girls had their own separate

gym and swimming pool and were given uniform swimming costumes on arrival.

For Calvin and Ken, March is the busiest time of year with the changeover from winter to summer sports. Areas of high usage, like the bowling greens or cricket pitches, need top dressing, fertilizing and special cutting. Disease control is important, for this may follow on from the special treatments that these turfed areas receive. Today the groundsmen have a tractor which pulls six different kinds of mower. Other equipment includes a huge stiff brush (which was originally made of whalebone, but now comes in plastic), used to remove the worm casts and to stand the grass up for cutting; and a big cane to disperse heavy dew – a telescopic

aluminium tube 7ft long with a flexible fibreglass end which is 6ft long.

When Calvin came in the 1960s they were still using a Greens motor mower made in the early 1920s. It had been given a new lease of life in 1957 when the Dorman engine and gearbox had been replaced with a Ford engine and gearbox. It was then used as a roller on the Men's Recreation Ground. Cadbury's also had one of the first Land Rovers off the assembly line at this period, for pulling the gang mowers; for the same job at Rowheath, it was two horses with cloths tied around their hooves so as not to damage the turf.

Barry Lyhock took charge of the gardens in 1991, taking over a very different situation from the one that Jack Botterill had known more

Ken Sale (left) and Calvin Green with the Dennis lawn mower

Previously the company had been paternalistic towards its employees, its ethics to develop the whole person, mind and body; looking after them, and guiding them. This was a philanthropic attitude at the beginning of the century, but is wholly unacceptable in today's world. As Barry points out: 'All of a sudden, the youngsters who were born in the 1940s became very affluent in the 1960s, and they were buying first of all scooters, then it was cars. By the time the next generation came along, what we had demanded of our fathers became the norm.

The motor car became easily accessible, public transport became a lot better, so therefore there was no longer the necessity for people who were looking for jobs to look inward in their own little community. They could get out. And once they got married or whatever, they weren't looking for houses where they actually worked.' In addition to this social change, when the company became Cadbury Schweppes in the 1970s, it had to be responsible to the shareholders and the concept of benevolent paternalism had to go.

The gardens at Bournville were designed with a very specific purpose in mind – not to please just one family, but to provide a healthy environment for the work and leisure of the employees. To this end, they were actively encouraged to make full use of the grounds. Today it is a matter of choice whether an individual uses the facilities which, although much reduced, are still a great pleasure and asset.

than 40 years previously. Barry has a budget which covers the salaries of his four groundsmen; they do all they can, and specialist work such as major tree surgery or large spraying jobs will go out to contractors. The sporting facilities have to be self-financing.

Chapter 17

MASTER OF HIS OWN MUCKHEAP

Brian P Martin

MASTER OF HIS OWN MUCKHEAP

FOURTEEN-YEAR-OLD PETER PEARL WAS SOMETIMES REDUCED TO TEARS BY HIS FIRST JOB, BUT PERHAPS IT HELPED TO SHAPE HIS CHARACTER FOR THE MUCH MORE REWARDING WORK THAT WOULD DOMINATE HIS LIFE.

'I'D ONLY EVER THOUGHT ABOUT BEING A FARMER. TO ME THAT WAS EVERYTHING. BUT WHEN I LEFT SCHOOL AT CHRISTMAS IN 1945 TO WORK FOR FATHER I FOUND MYSELF ALL ALONE OUT IN THE MIDDLE OF A 20-ACRE FIELD PICKING STONES WHICH COULD DAMAGE MACHINERY. THERE WERE THOUSANDS OF THEM, AND YOU ONLY NEEDED TWO BIG ONES TO FILL A BUCKET, SO I SOMETIMES SAT DOWN AND CRIED AT THE HOPELESSNESS OF IT ALL. THEN MOTHER GAVE ME A LITTLE CLOCK AND I USED TO LOOK AT IT AND WISH THE TIME WOULD GO QUICKER WHEN I SAT DOWN UNDER THE HEDGE TO EAT MY BREAD AND CHEESE. YOU COULDN'T HAVE HAD A MORE SOUL-DESTROYING JOB. BUT IT DID STAND ME IN GOOD STEAD FOR WORKING ALONE AS A COUNTRY POLICEMAN, WHEN I TRULY WAS MASTER OF MY OWN MUCKHEAP.'

Peter's grandfather was a remarkable man, starting out as a humble road-sweeper for West Suffolk County Council and ending up running a large Hampshire farm. Along the way he found time to father 13 children, including Peter's father, whom he employed first as a haulage contractor carrying stone, later as a farm worker.

An only child, Peter Raymond Charles Pearl was born on 26 October 1931 at Over Wallop, near Andover in Hampshire. In December 1939, Peter's grandfather took a thousand acres of the Marquis of Winchester's estate at Monxton, near Andover; the family moved there because

Peter's father was employed as a farm worker by his grandfather. Overall, Peter enjoyed a happy childhood in the Hampshire countryside, despite some vivid wartime memories.

'Most of all I remember what I looked forward to, especially my *Rainbow* comic and my Friday treat – a free funnel of sweets delivered with the basket of groceries to Nether Wallop by Mr Hawksworth.

'I was always helping dad with his work, walking the horses round the well to draw water, putting corn into the troughs for cattle feed, cutting corn with the binder, making corn ricks, drawing the straw into yelms, (bundles laid straight)

for thatching, and so on. During just one summer in the war father thatched 53 ricks on grandad's 1,000-acre farm.

'We never had a car then as we didn't go anywhere, but once in a while we did go on outings. The first time I saw the sea was in 1937, when I was six, and we had a day trip

content. While we did that we sang songs such as "My bonny lies over the ocean" and "Knees up Mother Brown".

'When I was 11 I went to Andover secondary modern boys' school, daily on a double-decker bus from Wallop. It was a long journey altogether because I also had

to Bournemouth, where we took a steamer to Swanage. I didn't see the sea again for ten years, when I went to Mudeford. I was in a CC41 "utility" suit (with the official mark) and when I saw all these people in bathing suits I knew just how backward I was!

'I went to the village school at Wallop, then Highclere, then back to Wallop. But in 1940 Wallop, school had to be evacuated because it backed on to the airfield, so some of us were sent to Abbotts Ann school while others went to Broughton. At Abbotts Ann school we had two air-raid shelters, and when we were in them during raids we bagged up nettles for the war effort; I think they may have been wanted for their sugar

to walk two miles across the fields from the house to the bus stop. Sometimes I helped Mum walk back with her shopping.

'One day on the school bus we had to stop and take shelter during a raid. Afterwards I saw the RAF men with hessian sacks shovelling up the remains of a German bomber crew in the road ahead. We also used to count the Spitfire squadrons in and out. "Only nine back today," we'd say.

'As well as the 12 full-time staff on his farm, grandad had 14 prisoners of war supplied by the Hampshire War Agricultural Committee. A couple of soldiers remained with their lorry all day,

Posing proudly with their first car: Peter with his father and grandfather

but usually they were well trusted and even drove tractors. The Italians were generally lazy, but most of the Germans and Austrians worked like Trojans. When Grandad got this canvas-topped Austin 12-4, he loaded it up with lemonade and cigarettes for the POWS. They had a razor blade and used to cut each cigarette into three to make it last longer. The POWs couldn't believe how well they were treated and some became good friends. If anything broke down they were the first to help – one even fixed mother's clock.

'We ate quite well on the farm, as Dad was always going out bagging rabbits, pheasants and partridges. Rabbit pie was a great favourite.

'Grandad was a lay preacher and dad was Church of England. Mother was in the choir at St Andrew's Church, Nether Wallop; and so was Bill Purdue, who smoked Churchman's cigarettes and gave me all the cards from the packets – one set was called "In Town Tonight" and had pictures of the stars of the day. During the services I used to sit down on the hassocks

and look with wonder at these cards; I've collected them ever since.

'In those days postman Calloway at Wallop had a blue uniform with red piping; I remember how the top of his flat hat used to be soaked with sweat as it was such hard work delivering all those parcels on a bike. At Monxton the postie had to cycle three miles out to our farm.'

In 1947 the Pearls suddenly decided on a change of direction. 'One day Father told me: "You're not going to work as I did for grandad: we're going to have a farm of our own." Then grandad got to hear of this and sold dad 120 acres of arable at Middle Wallop. Father had no money to spare for the £500 purchase, so he borrowed it from the bank, who then provided a further £1,500 for development, with the farm itself as collateral. He repaid the lot in two years! Using secondhand materials, my uncle built dad a bungalow on the "new" farm, and later on my wife and I moved into it. Meanwhile dad had built another bungalow nearby.'

As well as helping his father with their

excursion was the Tuesday run to Salisbury market, where he enjoyed the company of other young farmers; but he did not usually drink there, 'as Grandad didn't approve.'

Peter's first recollection of a village policeman is of one coming out to the family farm to sign the cattle register. The local bobby was required by law to check records of all cattle movements, as part of his work in preventing and containing livestock disease. Through such contact Peter came to admire the Wallop policeman, whom he regarded as 'very upright, efficient and hardworking, someone who commanded respect.' Sometimes he went to visit him at home, and one day he said to Peter: 'Why don't you join up?' But Peter said: 'No, I don't want to leave dad.'

However, after Peter married Margaret in 1955, he was persuaded to join the Hampshire and Isle of Wight Special Constabulary at Andover. He still lived at Monxton and worked on the farm, as specials were not paid; he was attached to the Wallop policeman whom he had admired so much. However, Peter describes

1950 Fordson Major tractor advert

The Pearls cutting winter oats in 1950

chickens and herd of dry (beef) cattle, Peter did a lot of ploughing for cereal production. As a result, he became very proficient with his Fordson Major and in 1951, at the age of 17, won first prize with his trailer plough in the Wallop Growmore Club competition. He was also a member of the Wallop Growmore quiz team and remembers what an adventure it was when they went 'all the way to Binstead, near Alton, in the dark!' The only other regular what happened next, a tragedy which changed his life completely:

'For a couple of years I used to float around and fly the flag when it was officer Jim Dolan's rest day. We had what were called "duty scales", where we'd register a route with the station so that they knew which telephone box to ring when they wanted you. However, expected arrival times were not too reliable when you were out on your bike wearing the cape in a headwind, with punctures to contend with. But generally you managed to make your patrol points, noting anything suspicious along the way. Sometimes I did odd things such as attend the local flower show. Once I even went to a house to help with a big two-day furniture sale. I also did a bit of traffic control, for which you needed eyes in the back of your head.

'Suddenly Jim Dolan was posted to Weyhill, near Andover, and I thought: "Oh my God, my friend's gone." Then one night Jim was called out to check vehicles for a stolen car. Unfortunately, as he stood in a main road in his dark uniform he was hit in the back by a car whose driver hadn't seen him, and was thrown into the path of the vehicle he was attempting to stop. Even more sadly, he was killed by a person he knew.

'In some strange way this spurred me on to join the police full-time. At the time we had our first child and I was only on poor wages. Farming had been good during the war with home production at a premium, but with the decline that followed the only alternative to expansion was going under. So one day I went over to Andover police station and asked to join. When I did so the sergeant nearly fell out of his seat, because only rarely did people who had been specials want to be regulars.

'However, after I had taken the exam I was turned down on account of my height,

being only 5ft 9in when Hampshire then wanted men of 5ft 10in. So I tried Dad's old county, West Suffolk, where they usually took men as short as 5ft 8in – but then it is flat country! To my surprise, I had a letter back saying they'd already accepted too many at my height and had temporarily pushed the height up to 5ft 9½in. So I was bitterly disappointed again.

'But I was determined to get in, so I went to Andover to see the local inspector whom I knew quite well, as I had supplied manure for his garden. He suggested that I tried Essex police as he knew the force there and they only wanted 5ft 8in. So after passing a written examination, I went off to Chelmsford for interview with Captain Peel, who had been chief constable since 1933; he was a direct descendant of Sir Robert Peel, who reorganized the London police force and gave rise to the terms "bobby" and "peeler" for a policeman. When Captain Peel found out I was from Wallop he was most impressed, and when I told the panel I delivered manure to the inspector they laughed their heads off. That afternoon I passed the medical, and I was officially accepted the very next day.

'I trained at Eynsham Hall, Oxfordshire, then the centre for several police forces. But whereas marching to music was easily managed by most of the other recruits because they'd been in the forces, it was very strange for me. The training sergeant used to say to me: "Come on Pearl, you haven't got a pitchfork in your hand now." Altogether I found the 13 weeks training very hard going as I'd had a very sheltered existence back on the farm.

'My first posting was to South Ockendon, near Grays, which was a village with industry and a London-overspill area, but a good place to start a career as I was thrown in at the deep end and given bags of experience. However, I still stood out like a sore thumb with my broad Hampshire accent.'

One major change for Peter was a considerable rise in income. Back on the farm he had only been getting about £5 a week, and as a volunteer special all he received was a boot allowance. But as a full-time, fully trained policeman he earned a weekly wage of £13 8s 4d gross, £9 13s 5d net, and he still has that first payslip – for 31 May 1958 – to prove it. After two postings, Peter had two ambitions: to be a village policeman and to earn the long-service and good conduct medal. At 29 he was very young to take on a village alone, yet he was posted to Kelvedon Hatch, near Brentwood. There he spent the two hardest years of his life, but it was also an interesting and rewarding time.

'I was based in the first countryside you get to on the way out of London so I had no end of work with poachers, and the duty periods were very tiring, especially the one from 5am to 8am. One morning I saw a dairyman walking to work along a country lane, and that evening the chief superintendent paid me a surprise visit and asked me what I'd seen that day. I said,

"Only a dairyman on his way to work, sir." But he said: "Ah, that's good: he'll go into the pub tonight and tell people he saw the policeman. There's nothing like showing the flag." And I must agree.

'One morning in early 1963 a farmer said he had poachers and picked me up in his Land Rover. When we got to his farm we saw three figures in the distance, sunlight glinting on gun barrels, and a black dog. "There they are," the farmer said, "and they've no right to be there." So he dropped me off to apprehend them while he went for further assistance. As I walked up this lane I heard voices and looked up to see them coming through the spring wheat, about 200 yards away. Nearby was a motor car. I noted its detail and also a cartridge belt in the back window. These chaps were well dressed in brogues and suits, and said they had permission from the farm nearby, but they were not aware of the boundaries. So I took their guns and bandoliers and reported them for poaching offences.

'The men were duly convicted of poaching, but as they did not have game in their possession they got their guns back. Little did I realize that two of them were to become household names in connection with the Great Train Robbery that August; their conviction for poaching was their last before the famous event took place. As a result I helped the detectives on the big case and we revisited the scene of the poaching, though nothing was found. It seemed that the men had simply been poaching when I accosted them, and quite honestly, I couldn't see what harm they'd done that day. They were most impressed when they got their guns back in good condition as they obviously valued them quite highly.

'We also used to get a great many horse-drawn gypsy caravans in the area, and were inundated with complaints from the parish council. One day when I went to their camp

PC Pearl in Kelvedon in 1963

there was this lady with a string of washing out and making artificial flowers. When I confronted her, she said: "We don't need permission to camp here, we're gypsies." And she added: "I can't go, sir, as I've a child in hospital," which was always a favourite excuse. But Britannia Smith was clearly in the wrong, and was taken to court for parking along the highway.

'Another time a local landowner complained that the gypsies had been stoning his cows, so I went and seized these two boys' catapults. Their father was another one who pleaded: "We can't go, sir, as we've a child in hospital."

'A while later I was at the landowner's house and there was a relative of his there, a well-known politician, who said: "You British policemen do an exceptionally fine job; I'm going to bring this up in the house." He'd obviously been told that we managed to move the gypsies on again — but what he didn't know was how we did it.

My sergeant had shown them a piece of blue paper which they took to be a form for their arrest as they couldn't read. But we said: "If you go within the hour we haven't seen you." You haven't seen anybody move so fast in your life, and as they went one of them – Leafy Low – said: "You're gentlemen policemens, sir, you really are."

'Generally I always had a good relationship with the gypsies; they always treated me with respect and called me sir or constable, and I was always happy to sit round their fire drinking a mug of cocoa – yet next day, by way of total contrast I'd be talking to some gentleman by the fireside in some great house. The only really serious incident I remember involving gypsies was when I had to help out at Ongar show and a lot of them were drinking there. In the evening some of them were driving like mad around the pub car park back in my village and I had to jump on the running board and pull the keys out of the ignition to make them stop. Then half a dozen of them set on my special and me. And later on a man from one gypsy faction nearly severed the arm of a rival when he pushed it through a car window. They came to the house and Margaret had to rip up a sheet to make a tourniquet.'

At Kelvedon Hatch, Peter had a list of livestock owners and he was required to sign their registers every three months, to make sure that all animal movements had been recorded. It was also a good way for him to get to know people, though not everybody kept to the letter of the law. Peter recalls one man in particular:

'I went to see a livestock keeper of Church Lane, but was very surprised by what I found. There was this small, dirty bungalow surrounded by high nettles, and nearby a little galvanized building with a wooden cross, all badly needing repair. When I knocked on the door it was answered by a lady in her nineties, wearing a black hat with a big pin through. I said: "I'm the new policeman." "Oh," she said, "have we done anything wrong? I'll get my son." Then out came this man wearing a green pork-pie trilby hat, a jumper with a hole where the belt had frayed through, and an old grey jacket. He was just like a character from Dickens.

'This gentleman said to me: "I knew your predecessor. He was a very good man and gave me a lift when I wanted it." "What, in his car?" I asked. "No," he said, "with a coffin. Would you be able to help me if I need it? Also, I wonder if you would recommend me to people who need my services."

'Then I asked him to get his cattle register, and it was in a terrible mess, not having been completed for two years. After that I asked if he had a chapel of rest for his undertaking business. "Yes," he said, pointing to the dilapidated corrugated iron building engulfed by undergrowth. "Could I have a look?" I said, "I've never been in a chapel of rest before." "I'm afraid it's inconvenient," he replied, "as I'm rearing some turkeys in it for Christmas!"

'So I told him to get his register made up and then I left; and my wife went to Brentford and bought the official movement book, which I gave him. It turned out that he was a single man who lived there with his mother and sister. At a later date I saw him "in action", when he wore a black frock coat which appeared green with age. But he was a most agreeable, sincere man and I had a lot of time for him.

'When I went to my first sudden death on that beat he was the only undertaker I knew, so I recommended him to the relatives. But he rolled up in a pale-blue, ex-Frigidaire Dormobile to collect the body and I had to help him get it on board! Then he said: "Put your bike in with the coffin

and I'll give you a lift!" But I really couldn't do that, as the relatives were looking out of the window. "OK," he said, "You follow me round the corner and load up when we're out of sight," which we did.

'On another occasion I cut my finger badly when carving the Sunday joint, but Margaret couldn't take me to the local doctor to have it stitched up because she didn't drive at that time. The only person we knew who could get me there was the undertaker, so we phoned him and he took me over in his blue undertaker's van! When the doctor asked how I had got to him, I had to reply: "The undertaker brought me."

One day the rector of Kelvedon Hatch asked Peter to serve on the parochial church council. Peter readily agreed, but he had to be confirmed first. Peter particularly remembers one Christmas Eve when he was on point outside the church.

'It was snowing like hell and this car drew up. Out came my inspector, Payne from Chipping Ongar, and he said, "I've just come out to wish you a happy Christmas and sign your pocket book." Then he asked: "What's going on over there?" and I replied "Midnight service, sir." Then he said: "Well, let's go over and join them," so we did. That was a time I will never forget. So was my last day in Essex, when Chief Constable John Nightingale bothered to pay me a surprise visit in the village, to say goodbye. He wished me well, and told me always to remember that Essex had trained me.'

In 1963 Peter was accepted for transfer to his native Hampshire. After two years at Romsey, Peter was posted some ten miles away, to the village of Broughton, where he would remain for 22 years and become the longest-serving rural beat officer in the Hampshire and Isle of Wight Constabulary. This was all the more remarkable because Peter's birth certificate was registered at Broughton, and it was unusual for someone to be posted near to his birthplace.

Immediately Peter noticed how very different the villagers were from people in the areas where he had been working; he

An agricultural accident

found them a very introverted community, and began to realize how much he had changed. The Pearls also found that the 1931 house – one of the three oldest police houses in Hampshire – was small compared to the one they had left behind in Romsey. Furthermore, because there was no proper office, the children had to leave the sitting room whenever there was a knock at the door and Peter needed to take a statement, or help a road accident victim with cuts and bruises, or issue a pig licence to a farmer in muddy boots, and so on. And if Peter was out on duty his superiors knew they could always get hold of Margaret to initiate things, unlike today when many of the police officers' wives are out at work. Yet Broughton was a place the Pearls soon came to love: the children went to the local school, and the whole family gradually became very involved in many village activities, not least the drama group.

During Peter's time there, Broughton had a very stable population of about a thousand, mainly farming folk; however, the number of shops fell from six to one. His beat also included the village of Houghton and the smaller parishes of Bossington and Buckholt. Unfortunately the area had two fast main roads through it, bringing many accidents, as Peter recalls:

'Two of the worst places were on the A30, at Leonard's Grave and Nine Mile Water, described by one local solicitor as "a crossroads for the quick or the dead." But at first I wasn't always that prompt to get on the scene because all I had was the pushbike, a Raleigh three-speed of my own but which I had an allowance for. Therefore I often had to rush out, stop the first vehicle passing and ask the driver to take me to the scene. Fortunately I generally had good co-operation.

'From 1968 I could get to accidents much quicker because I was given a grey Velocette motorbike with a water-cooled engine. It was known as a "Noddy bike" and I had to share it with the Wallop policeman. Neither of us had driven motorbikes before and we were just told to get a provisional licence and to practise up and down the road outside the police house. I finished up with a Honda, which was much more powerful. Unfortunately, having a motorbike and radio meant that I was easily called upon by Winchester HQ and despatched to incidents over a much wider area.'

There were plenty of other sudden deaths to deal with too, through natural causes, accidents and suicides. Here Peter describes how he had to deal with this sort of thing: 'A retired gardener in the village, old Charlie, was missing from his wardened flat for over a week and I walked everywhere looking for him, even along the River Test.

'Then two lads offered to help look for him – and it wasn't long before one of them came running back with his face white as a sheet. He'd found Charlie in a 22,000-gallon water tank up on stanchions. It appeared that he'd climbed the ladder, kicked it away, climbed in, closed the lid with a wire and drowned himself. When I looked in, the first thing I saw was his grey cap, which I knew well. He was floating but I just couldn't get him out so I went back home for my daughter's skipping rope, and this did the trick when the sergeant arrived and gave me a hand. Inside Charlie's jacket was a tin containing his pocket watch and it had stopped at two o'clock, just ten minutes after he had last been seen.

'One young man had taken his life with a shot in the stomach simply because he was worried about his car insurance following an accident.

'One of the saddest things I remember dealing with was when I had to tell a wife and mother I knew that her husband had passed away in hospital after a massive coronary. She asked me to say a prayer there and then, which I readily did, and that was the most poignant moment in my career: it was then I realized that you had to be deeply understanding to be a good policeman.'

Animals, too, sometimes needed Peter's assistance. In 1967 he rescued a dog which had fallen down a dry well at Dunbridge. To find out the depth, Peter dangled a rope down, pulled it up and measured it on the ground: it was over 30ft. The only way he could get down was to strap two ladders together, which he did, and the dog was returned safely to the surface. Later he was awarded the RSPCA's bronze medal 'for courage and humanity' – but he got into trouble with his boss for not calling out the fire brigade!

Every year, when Peter was on parade, Lord Louis Mountbatten asked him why he was wearing that RSPCA medal on the right and not the left. Each time Peter told him: 'Because it's a civilian award, my lord.' Nonetheless, he had great respect for the Queen's uncle: 'He was a wonderful man. Sometimes I was one of the police officers who went to his Broadlands home when there was a security alert, and then he always made us feel at ease, often inviting us inside.'

Among the more unusual people Peter had to deal with was a man who did a lot of walking; he was always handing in pound notes he found along the way, for which Peter would give him receipts, and after a month or so the man would be given any unclaimed money.

Much more eccentric was a lady who imagined she had rats in the roof. 'She kept on asking me what I was going to do about it so I went round just to keep her happy. She'd put rat poison everywhere, even over the furniture. "Can you hear them?" she asked. "No," I replied, but I did say that I would ask the council to check. When I did so they said: "Oh, we know all about that lady."

'After a while she complained to my boss that I hadn't done anything about the rats, and eventually she came in with a letter from Harold Wilson at Number 10, demanding action. So I telephoned the environmental officer. When they heard that I'd called about this lady I was told that he was out; but when I said I had a letter from the prime minister he was suddenly in.

'As a result, a man was sent out with a bag of ordinary flour, a spoon and a stick to make her think something was being done. But then the woman accused the poor pest controller of trying to poison her, so he came scurrying back to my wife with the flour saying that he was going to keep it as evidence in his defence! She never stopped complaining about the rats until eventually she was moved to a flat.'

At Broughton, Peter only used his truncheon once, to break a window to get into a house whose elderly lady owner had not been seen for a while. But he did use his handcuffs a few times, once quite unnecessarily. He describes what happened:

'A local man had entered into an agreement with a family to buy a typewriter, and they accused him of stealing it when he went away. So Strathclyde police arrested him and I was sent in plain clothes, on the plane, all the way up to Scotland to collect him. There was the most tremendous fuss. I even had to bring the typewriter back and accompany the man to the toilet on our journey. It was the only time I've ever been to Scotland and I was only there for half an hour – in the dark! Then, after all that trouble and expense, when the man appeared in court next day he was acquitted after the magistrate said he had a legal right to the typewriter. And we'd only bought a single air fare for him!'

Sometimes Peter had to deal with hardened criminals who showed no compunction in stealing from the church. He recalls two cases involving remarkable audacity: 'After a spate of thefts from country churches, we were circulated with

a description of a suspect and I took the details down to the rector at Broughton.

'A few months later the rector came to see me and said that he'd just passed a man walking along the road and he fitted the description. Also, the ladies cleaning the brass had recently reported a strange man in the church. So I rang Stockbridge station and asked for a car, and we got over to the remote church of Bossington as quickly as possible.

'We parked the car and crept out, and as we were walking down towards the church a rotund man with a rolling gait came along the path. "Good morning," we said. And he replied "Good morning officers: what a lovely morning." We asked him what he was up to, and he said that he'd wanted to visit the church but it was locked, so he was going to get the key. He added that he was a Methodist minister from Farnham and was very interested in old churches; but we were suspicious, because the time of day he was there didn't

tie up with the bus timetable. Then he asked if he could see the church, and we said he could. As we walked along we enquired about his rolling gait and he said he had been a padré in the first war. But that didn't seem right, either, because he was too young and we thought he was carrying some considerable weight.

'After that we said we were not satisfied with his explanations and told him that we were going to search him. "How dare you insult a minister of the cloth," he said. Then we undid his jacket, and under his jumper was a rope with the most amazing conglomeration of antique church keys all round it. "OK, the game's up," he said. Then we asked him what he had done that day, and he admitted that he had been to King's Somborne church and drunk the communion wine.

'Later we discovered that the man was actually wanted for stealing petrol; he was even drawing on someone else's pension book, and had a string of convictions going back to 1921. In short, it was a good "nick", and it showed excellent co-operation between the village bobby and the rector, as well as how crucial the alertness of the cleaning women had been.

'But sometimes people are too trusting. One day the vicar of Houghton found a man asleep in the church porch, felt sorry for him and let him in. After the morning service it was found that the offertory box attached to a pew had been rifled. The vicar called me out, and I discovered that at the service there'd been only three people, all of whom were known. I asked what was likely to have been in the box and the vicar said that one of the regular worshippers usually rolled up a ten-shilling note and put it in. So I rang her and asked if there was any way her note could be identified. "Yes," she said: it was one of a sequence of

ten she had from her bank, and so we were able to trace the number.

'Next I phoned Romsey police, gave them the vicar's description of the suspect, and said that the vagrant was probably walking along the road from Houghton to Mottisfont with the stolen money in his pocket. So off they dashed – and picked him up. He even had the ten-shilling note still rolled up in the fashion it was put in the box. Subsequently, not only was he charged with theft, but also sacrilege, breaking and entering a divine place of worship. He got three months.'

Other villagers had a surprisingly indifferent attitude to crime prevention, not least the late landlord of The Greyhound at Broughton. When Peter was carrying out a survey he asked the licensee what his security system was. He replied: 'Oh, I got a good one. I have a loaded shotgun and if I heard anyone I'd rush upstairs and I'd fire it out the window. The man from the garage would hear it and he would phone the police.' This was because the inn had no telephone.

When Peter first arrived in the village he went into the pub just after drinking-up time, at about 11.15pm, to encourage a little respect for the law, as 'last orders' were being called too late. Not surprisingly, for a time he was regarded as a 'hot copper'. Nevertheless, there were many occasions when Peter had a good laugh with the villagers, not least through his involvement with television. Here he explains how this came about. 'Southern Television filmed a large part of the Wurzel Gummidge series at Broughton, and I was required to be on hand to control the traffic and so on. I had permission to do this, the TV company paid for my services, and when I helped out my normal police work was covered by someone else. The local children were always allowed out of school to watch, and in the afternoon the TV crew would give them tea and buns.

'One day the crews adapted the local post office to their liking and I was standing there with my bike, cycle clips and helmet, talking to Wurzel, who was played by the actor Jon Pertwee. Suddenly, into the village came a van with "Bowyer's Wiltshire Sausages" painted on the side, on its way to deliver to the village shop. I approached the driver and said, "Shhh, switch the engine off, please." At that, the driver said, "What the …'s going on?" Then over came Jon Pertwee and said, "It's all right matey, we's only doin' a bit of wangling" (angling). That was enough for the driver! "Bloody hell," he said: then reversed, and I didn't see him again that day. He must have thought we were a right lot, me with my bike and all, looking like a character from the set!'

There were even a few lighter moments resulting from road accidents, as Peter recalls: 'Once, when a car was travelling too fast and hit a tractor, one of my witnesses was the comedian Cyril Fletcher. In court the magistrate asked the tractor driver how long he'd been driving. "I've been drivin' tractor all my life, sir," he replied. And Cyril whispered to me, "That'll make a good line; I must remember that."

'Another time, after an accident on the A30, the people with injuries were taken off by ambulance. But when I was clearing up on the road I found a budgie in a cage, which one couple had been taking on holiday. So I put it between my knees on the motorbike and took it home. Later I phoned the people at Winchester hospital and told them I'd look after their bird till they were discharged. When they came to collect it they were really pleased, and even resumed their holiday.'

A poaching incident, too, seemed funny at first, but had a surprising link with a more serious crime. Peter describes what happened: 'One night when we were out after poachers at Horsebridge, near Houghton, I heard this "pad pad" of someone running along the road. When the figure approached, I jumped out and

shone my torch in the face of this gypsy. "And what are you up to?" I enquired. "I missed the bus, sir," he said. But when I challenged that he changed his mind and said he was " took short". So I searched him and found a catapult plus lovely round pebbles for ammunition. Unfortunately he wasn't carrying any game so nothing could be proved, but I took his catapult and pebbles and gave him a receipt.

'Nine months later Southampton police were investigating a burglary and found a jacket at the scene; inside it was my receipt for one catapult and six pebbles. They asked me if I could identify the person. "Yes," I said, and took them to the place where the man worked. As soon as he saw me he said: "Hullo, Mr Pearl," and he was arrested on the strength of that little bit of paper which he'd kept all that time.'

Another of Peter's stories illustrates the importance of the village bobby's role as mediator when people become incensed by relatively trivial things: 'A man who lived near the goal at the local playing field kept getting the football in his garden, and would keep it. Despite pleas from the players, he would only ever return it to PC Pearl, so they were always having to stop the match and send for me. Eventually the man got really fed up with all this because he had a lovely garden and he didn't want it threatened by anybody or anything. So he put a garden prong through the ball, and I had no choice but to apply the full rigour of the law.

'Even after that it looked as if the antipathy would continue, so I suggested a meeting, as a result of which a high net was put up. Fortunately this solved the problem. Diplomacy, as in so many aspects of life, was the name of the game.'

There were quite a few retired service officers in and around Broughton, and some insisted on calling Peter by his surname. Such formality was by then unusual among the villagers, but it reflected much earlier times, when policemen generally were lower down the social scale. As an example of this: during the late 19th century a party was held by the staff at a large village house, to which the Broughton policeman was invited. But when the owner found out he took umbrage and complained to the chief constable; the bobby was fined about 15s, then a week's wages, and dismissed from the service.

Such a tough regime continued well into this century. Indeed, between the two wars, when Broughton was part of the New Forest police division, the constable still had to cycle the 23 miles each way to collect his weekly pay!

During the great storm of October 1987 a tree fell on the Pearls' police house, just a couple of days before Peter was due to retire. Nobody was injured, but the family certainly regarded it as an omen: it was the end of an era.

Not surprisingly, Peter was made a freeman of the village he had served so well. The man who had spent over two decades doing everything from seeing children safely through the streets on their way to harvest festival, to putting up cyclists with nowhere to stay, was retiring to nearby Romsey. He is justly proud of his record; as he stressed: 'In a village you're not just a man in uniform. The people see you in "civvies", too, and both you and your family have to set an example.'

Chapter 18
ROUGH AND READY

Brian P Martin

ROUGH AND READY

BEING ONE OF NINE CHILDREN IN A STRUGGLING WORKING-CLASS FAMILY JUST AFTER WORLD WAR I, FREDERICK ERNEST LADHAMS HAD NO EASY UPBRINGING. 'IT WAS CERTAINLY ROUGH AND READY AND THE WEAK 'UNS WENT TO THE WALL.' BUT AT LEAST HIS TOUGH CHILDHOOD NEAR LONDON GAVE HIM THE MENTAL ARMOUR TO COPE WITH THE ROGUES HE WOULD MEET LATER IN LIFE.

THE SON OF A FOUNDRY WORKER AND GRANDSON OF A BUILDING LABOURER, FRED WAS BORN IN A RENTED HOUSE ON 31 JANUARY 1913, AT EPPING IN ESSEX. 'THERE WERE NO BATHROOMS THEN AND FATHER USED TO COME HOME FILTHY, STRIP OFF TO HIS WAIST AND WASH OUTSIDE WITH WATER BOILED OVER AN OPEN FIRE. I CAN STILL SMELL THE CARBOLIC SOAP.

'NOW AN INSURANCE COMPANY'S OFFICE STANDS ON THE SITE OF OUR OLD HOUSE, BUT THEN IT WAS ALL FIELDS ROUND ABOUT AND I WAS ALWAYS INTERESTED IN THE COUNTRY.'

'Our old headmaster at Epping Boys School used to let keeper Robin Taylor take about 12 to 20 of us beating at Copped Hall on a school day. There was no fixed age – all you had be was big and strong enough. We got half a crown, a bottle of pop and two sandwiches – one saltbeef, the other cheese – which you could hardly get in your mouth.'

But although he allowed the boys to go off beating, the headmaster was, like most of his contemporaries, 'a real disciplinarian. You were caned for fighting and even if you was heard cheekin' someone in the town. Also, whenever the infants messed themselves, because they wasn't properly house-trained, us older ones had to take 'em out and clean 'em up. But the head and two masters lived at the school, where there was good garden and we learned how to grow things and prune trees.'

Fred had several ways of earning pocket money. 'In those days there were lots of horses in London and I used to help uncle take hay and bedding down to them. When I was a bit older I was allowed to drive a second horse and cart down behind him. And on a Sunday I sometimes used to go down the local golf course to carry the clubs and get a bob or two.

'Also there used to be lots of wildflowers about Epping then. There was white and purple violets, peggles [cowslips], primroses and bluebells and we used to go and get 'em without the keeper seeing us. Then on a Sunday we used to sit out on the green and sell them to the cyclists for 3d a bunch. There were lots of cycling clubs came out of London then.'

In addition, Fred had the customary schoolboy's paper round for which he earned 1/6d a week. 'You 'ad to be 13 and me and another lad 'ad to be down the station with a trolley to meet the half-six train. There were loads of other boys there and we all used to race downhill on our trolleys. My patch 'ad mostly the *Mirror*, the *Daily Herald* and the local rag, but in the higher up, posher districts there was papers like *The Times*.'

But there was also plenty of wildlife to interest a budding young countryman in Epping between the wars. 'Lots of fallow deer, of course, and always plenty of badgers and birds' nests to find. And all of us boys and girls used to bathe together in a local pond. We took down a bar of soap and 'ad great fun. In them days you had to make your own entertainment.'

On leaving school at the age of 14, Fred replaced his older brother as boy keeper at Copped Hall, then owned by the 'very autocratic Mr Whyse and recently bought by pop star Rod Stewart. There was a massive staff then, including two chauffeurs for two Rolls Royces, three

Teenager Fred Ladhams (right, with sack over shoulder) at Copped Hall, his first estate

people in the laundry alone, and an old lady who made butter.

'The butter lady was given one cock pheasant each year. When I took it up to her she always put a shilling on the table in front of me, along with half a glass of port — good stuff that was. Each farmworker had an annual brace of rabbits, but tenants, farmers and local police had a brace of pheasants each.

'I was allowed to pick myself out two each week and at Christmas I always got a ticket from the squire for so much beef. The last one I 'ad was worth about 7/6d. Then I got a couple of dozen eggs a week and we used to collect blackberries for the squire at 6d a pound. Altogether I got about £4 for the berries and a woman used to come down from the squire's London home in

We used to collect blackberries for the squire

Nightingale Square to collect them for jam, etc. She also took back chickens, cream and other fresh produce.

'My wage was ten shillings to start and after seven years I was on 25 shillings. I always gave money to mum. I didn't get a suit of clothes till I'd been there three years.

'The headkeeper lived down in the Warren – a wood of big, old chestnut trees. I used to look after half his garden as well as the ferrets, chickens and dogs, including those Sealyham terriers for huntin' the wood out for rabbits. I even 'ad to clean the headkeeper's wife's brass.

'Two or three days before a shoot I'd get a big bit of beef and cook it in a big, black pot in the copper house. This was for the beaters' sandwiches, each lot being wrapped in greaseproof paper. There was also coffee provided, and five-gallon casks of Whitbread's beer. The Guns always went to the shooting box and the butler and maid brought out their lunch from the hall.'

The estate pheasants were fed in the traditional way. 'Armitages of Nottingham was just startin' to fetch out that half-cooked feed then – all oily stuff. Most of it we cooked over an open fire and mixed it with chopped rabbit. When the birds went to wood they was gradually weaned on to boiled corn cooked in the copper.'

The shoot had just over 100 coops, each holding about 15 birds, 'but I don't know the exact amount raised – the headkeeper never told you that! Anyway, the Guns killed about 200 a day then.'

Poaching was a considerable problem on London's doorstep. 'They was mostly after rabbits with snares, but we never stood for any nonsense. Even if we walked on someone pickin' blackberries we tipped their basket upside down. You 'ad to be tough then and nip things in the bud. I even used to go down to some ivy trees, where birds was vulnerable, to drive pheasants out from roost so nobody could creep in and shoot them.'

Fortunately, natural predation was not a huge problem, 'though there was always plenty of foxes. There was just the odd crow and sparrowhawk, and that's where the grey squirrels first started to get about the country.'

In those days partridges were still common around Epping. 'One time in

September, Mr Dashwood, the agent, and three Guns, with us four keepers and the gardener beatin', shot 50 brace of partridges. It was mostly English birds then and they were all wild. The cropping just suited 'em perfectly. You got your roots and you got your arable, with plenty of stubble left too. We generally walked the stubbles into a root field and the head blew a whistle to warn the Guns when birds got up.

'We 'ad some good shots there. One of them was the local vicar, who later on married Iris and me. Her father worked in the foundry too.'

Another of Fred's sidelines at Copped Hall was, 'rearing about six litters of ferrets in the summer. We used to advertise them at ten bob each in *The Exchange and Mart* and I got a shilling for each one sold. We got enquiries from all over and often sent 'em to southern Ireland. The Irish stamps always came upside down on the envelopes. People used to say it was a deliberate insult to the Crown.'

At the age of 21, in the spring of 1935, Fred left home for the first time, to become one of three underkeepers at Sir Fred Jones's Irnham Hall, near Bourne in Lincolnshire. 'I only earned 35 shillings a week and paid 31 for lodging with the cowman, but meals was included. Iris joined me in 1936, when we were married; the gate lodge where we stayed was like a little castle.'

However, Fred was able to add significantly to his income through

Tea-break for 21-year-old Fred on the Irnham estate, Lincolnshire, where the hours were very long

rabbiting, being paid 6d a couple for those caught. 'From September we started catchin' around the woods. We ran about 100 snares and it was much easier then because the stubble was left about 2ft high. It worked in well with your other jobs too, because when we started the pheasants was just beginnin' to get off your hands. The butcher collected the rabbits and paid the estate and we were paid every four weeks. It often used to amount to a week's wages too.

'It was there I first learnt long-netting. We took out one 100yd net and two of 50yds, plus a bagful of hazel pegs. And your coat 'ad no buttons on so as not to snag the nets. You just had a thin cord round your waist. There was one man at each end of the net and you held the top line with your fingers so you knew when the rabbits hit. They were proper nets too – not like this modern rubbish which throw rabbits as soon as they get in.

'I always remember one night we set the three nets in a corner and later one of the smaller ones was missin'. Turned out there was so many rabbits hit it they carried the whole thing into the wood. There was only one setting a night, from about 10pm to midnight, and it was all carry then – very hard work. The rabbits was all gutted straightaway and we took a short spade to bury all the rubbish.'

There were some 150 coops of pheasants plus wild partridges in Irnham. 'They killed about 200-300 pheasants a day and in my first year they had a record 50 brace partridges on my beat. Sir Fred was 80 then and his chauffeur actually had to hold him under the arms while he shot. A year later he died and his son Walter took over.

'On a Saturday I used to pick up as many as 200 pheasant and partridge eggs along the roadsides. It was all arable there and they had tractors when everyone else was still using horses.

'Once the miners came out to plant a wood. The government fetched 'em down in camps. When they came they was as thin and pale as that heater in the corner, but when they went back they was a tanned and healthy as anythin'.

'It was at Bulby Wood, which was supposed to be haunted, that I had the first instance of foxes being turned in on me [brought from another area and released] – for the hunt. There were three let go, but I shot 'em easily the next morning as they were very tame. I'd seen their tracks in a sandbar along the beck. Later on they did the same to me in Oxfordshire, with a lot of big 'uns, but I nailed 'em all right. No way

were we going to have foxes on the beat, hunt or no hunt!'

In 1937, at the age of 23, Fred became underkeeper for Colonel Clifton at Clifton Hall, just south of Nottingham. 'We had to go to Beeston to be measured up for our suits – real Robin Hood jobs in Lincoln green.

'I got the job through the Gamekeepers' Association, but it was an awful place for poachers. They even used to creep round our bungalow at night to see if we were there talking.

'One night on roost watch, this motorbike and sidecar went by us and later on, after we'd been home, we looked up and saw three fellows stickin' out like turkeys in the moonlight. We went up to the wood to head them off, but there was not a twig crackin' or bird twitterin', so we went round the other end and then ran straight into 'em.

'The old one kept comin' in and comin' in. then I left off to set after the others. When I caught them we 'ad a good set to and they threatened to shoot me, so I went back to help the head with the old boy. He still kept comin', but eventually the head 'it 'im with a stick and cut his face right open. Then we spun 'im round and got the cuffs on.

'Then we went back and got the car and chauffeur to take 'im down to Shire Hall at Nottingham. When we got him in the light there was blood all over the place and the sergeant said: "What the hell you been doin' with 'im?" He was a real poacher. His case came up just before Christmas and he got three months. We found out 'e was 59 and he 'ad convictions goin' back to when he was a boy in 1890 – for everything from fowl stealing to pheasant poaching. His mates were in the court watchin', but unfortunately we couldn't prove anything and they got away with it.'

Occasionally it was the keepers who came off worse. 'Once Johnny was cut right down the face by a long-netter's stick with a spike on the end. It really was a bad place and you 'ad to be watchin' all the time. As far as the birds was concerned, we always used to say that if you don't sleep with 'em you don't get 'em!

'Another time we were out in the moonlight when we heard 36 shots on nearby Thrumpton, the small place which Lord Byron used to own. Next day we went to see the keeper there and he said he'd been out and never got 'em. He claimed 'e challenged 'em and they dropped a bag with 36 pheasants in. But I said to Johnny Thomas, the headkeeper, "I reckon he stood off a bit because 'e was too scared."'

But at least the endless hours of nightwatching sometimes brought Fred light relief. 'Once I was walkin' home in the bright moonlight and spotted this ol' bull-nosed Morris just turned off the road.

There was a couple inside havin' a right old go – at 2am!'

While courting couples have entertained many a keeper, few have had such a surprise as that which lay in store for Fred when blanking-in Clifton Wood one day. 'We were goin' along nicely when one of the chaps called out, "'ey up Fred, there's a lass lays 'ere." So I went over and there she was, half under a bush. Her hair was perfect, but when we turned her over her face was half gone with maggots.

'The lads said, "What's to do Fred," so I said we'd carry on and beat the wood out as she wasn't goin' anywhere. Then after the drive I 'ad a conflab with the boss and he said we'd finish the shoot. When we got back we told the police, but it was 10pm that night before the sergeant and a constable came knockin' on the door. Then we got the tractor and took 'em down. The sergeant poked about under 'er and found some bottles and a note. "Oh, it's a suicide," he said, "we don't bother much about those." Anyway, we got her on a hurdle to carry her to the tractor. But what a stink! I made sure I was upwind when we took her up. A few weeks later I discovered that her fiancé had died suddenly – very sad.'

Fred had another encounter with tragedy at Clifton. 'We were goin' along the road lookin' for eggs when we came upon this old woman wringing her hands. She told us that her husband was missing and asked if we would help look around for him.

'Nearby was a stackyard with a well in the middle and I noticed a stick was on it. I said, "I bet he's in there," and sure enough 'e was – floatin' face down! He'd drowned himself and we found out later that they were going to put 'im in the infirmary, but he didn't want to go.'

Not surprisingly, Fred was keen to move on to pastures new, to gain valuable experience, and he was offered two positions

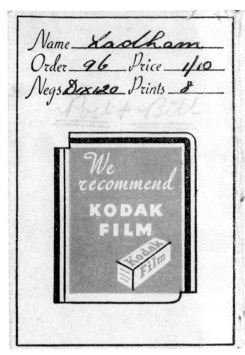

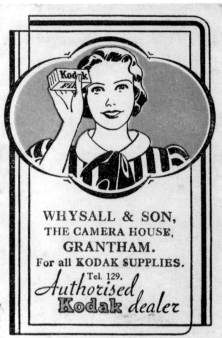

when Clifton's headkeeper advertised on his behalf. So in the spring of 1939 he accepted a post at Blenheim, the Duke of Marlborough's estate in Oxfordshire. 'I took a partridge beat on the old Euston system and that really suited me.

'I had 200-300 dummy eggs and replaced the wild ones every second or third day. I put about 20 under a bantam and about 30 under a broody. Them as was in the most dangerous places was chipped off first. Before going to a nest I used to watch for the partridge to go off for her first feed at five or six o'clock in the morning, so as not to disturb her. This was very important. And at the same time I used to put Keating's flea powder in under the clutch, especially if you saw any blood spots on the eggs, which showed you the birds were lousy. You could always tell when the chicks were about to hatch because the cock would go and sit by the hen.

(below left) The Cotswold rearing system was welcomed by Fred just after the war. (below right) Fox control on the fells. Fred is assisted by his son

'Headkeeper Mr Grey was no worker, more of a gentleman who just rode around on a BSA 250 motorbike makin' sure everythin' was all right. And there was another chap who did nothing but fetch the feed for us keepers with his pony and trap.

'We might put out as many as 21 to 22 eggs in a nest – always as many as we could because the birds could always rear 'em better than you. Any Euston system eggs we couldn't get back out we used to rear ourselves, and we also bought about 100 Hungarian partridge eggs and put about two in each nest to change the blood. Our egg chipping bank was well suited to partridge production, providing plenty of natural food. 'We used to fetch the eggs for 'em from the ant 'eaps in the fields. When the sun was out the ants brought the eggs to the surface and then we took a spade to 'em and popped 'em in a bucket – just like slicing off a molehill. Baby partridges thrive on ant eggs, but you mustn't give 'em too many as they like 'em so much they might refuse anything else. Blenheim was the only place I've been where we could do this. The 'eaps were on the rough grazing and Iris used to help me with them.

'Nowadays people just moan about the disappearance of the partridge, but if you want them back you've got to strip every pheasant egg of a partridge beat as the pheasant is just like a cuckoo and will lay in every nest.

'Our house was pretty primitive at Blenheim, with all oil lamps and water from the well. The track down to it was a rough old thing and Iris used to say it shook all the nuts off the pram.

'I earned two guineas a week at Blenheim and was given the feed for 30 hens, which kept us in eggs. My leggings was brown leather, whereas they were boxcloth back in Lincolnshire. And I had a black bowler which I was supposed to wear all the time, but whenever I could I only wore it on shoot days because you looked a real case in it.

'They was very strict and you only spoke to the duke when you was spoken to. Your hat 'ad to come off pretty smart and you didn't 'ave to 'ave a fag on your lip. Nowadays they get away with murder. But at the same time a keeper was really somethin' in the community then.'

Notwithstanding the strictness of the regime, Fred soon settled in and produced the required results. 'When they shot my beat in September 1939 they got 100 brace and 90 per cent were young. Actually the Guns killed 95 brace, but the headkeeper told me to take some cartridges and go out in the morning to get another ten birds so that it would look better in the gamebook. Nobody knew any different.'

There was some superb shooting at Blenheim during Fred's time. 'With two lines of beaters there was never any hanging about. There were only four big-bang drives – two in the morning and two in the afternoon. Combe Bottom was fantastic – no bang-bang and then a space like at most places. The birds came out like clouds of starlings and in 1939 they shot 400 on just that one drive when there was 1,500 pheasants for the day. I think it must have been some sort of record at the time because I remember there was a fair bit of jealousy with Lord Derby's Knowsley Hall. But there were some crack Shots to get the bags. The then duchess was one of the best I've seen. It was all double guns.'

The duke, too, was a keen Shot. 'Even if anyone missed on his family day, when they went round in an old bus, he used to shout at 'em; "If you can't hit them you might as well go home." He was a great big feller who used to march straight through the irrigation channels followed by his very short loader carrying his gun over his head.

It was very comical. And there was a model railway at the palace which was supposed to be for the young marquis, but the duke spent most of his time on it.'

One of the Guns stands out in Fred's memory for his political associations rather than sporting prowess. 'It was Duff Cooper, the ambassador to France. I stood behind him all morning, but at lunchtime he 'ad to go back to France with all the carry on.

'Later on they tried to get us Blenheim keepers to form a special brigade of territorials, but in the end, with the war, all rearing stopped and in spring 1940 everyone of service age had to leave. So then Iris and me went back to Essex and I had just odd jobs – mostly building tank traps – before I was called up.'

In due course, Fred was summoned to Walthamstow for a medical and was 'pronounced A1, but they always gave you the opposite of what you wanted to do. Three weeks later I was called to Exeter and then posted to Blandford, Dorset, as part of the Royal Artillery Searchlight Regiment – 546 Battery. There were about 11 men on a small site and 33 on a big one. The big one picked up the planes and the small one zoomed in on it.'

In 1941 Fred was posted to Northern Ireland, 'to Dunoon in the Antrim Hills around Belfast, where there were miles of heather and I saw my first grouse as well as lots of brown trout in the tarns. We stayed there till the summer of 1943, but there was not much doin'. I never saw a single keeper when I was goin' around the woods and most of the lads with me there came out of London and had never seen a tree let alone a pheasant. But one good thing over there was that they would give you anything as long as you 'ad the money to pay for it. There was never any worry about coupons.

'After that we went to Hull, Bath, Bristol and York, before the regiment broke up and we joined the 68th Searchlight Regiment, billeted on Bath reacecourse. Then we were sent to Lord Mostyn's place at St Asaph in North Wales, where we went down to the woods and at last met a keeper. He spoke real broad Welsh and we got on well.

'After that we were in Palestine, Syria, Turkey, Lebanon and Egypt, where I saw the Frankie Howerd show in Cairo. In those days you could go to the Forces Club there and they'd make up a £1 parcel to send home for you, though it took six weeks. It was mostly sweets such as sugared almonds and Turkish delight, but someone popped a banana in mine. When it arrived the banana was still green so Iris hung it up in her mum's sittin' room, but it never did ripen. Our son had never seen a banana before.'

Although he was only 31, Fred decided that he was too old for the infantry and, 'wangled it to go in the cookhouse,' eventually leaving the army as a private in 1946, without any regrets. 'I tell you what – England's the place to be. When we were on the boat comin' home there was an announcement saying, "Anyone want to see the white cliffs of Dover?" Well, it's a wonder the boat didn't turn turtle there was such a rush to one side.'

The war years had been far from pleasant for Iris too. To begin with, when the Ladhams moved from Blemheim to London the pipes in their house froze, eventually bursting and causing such a damp that their first son died of pneumonia at only two years old. And when Fred was abroad,

Iris had a telegram to say he was missing. 'But it turned out he had a touch of malaria and was in hospital, where they mixed him up with another chap. And they never paid me any pension while he was missing!'

When Fred left the army he had accrued ten weeks' paid leave. 'I was free as a bird and I took every day of it. But I always intended to go back to keepering. I wrote to Blenheim and Nottingham, but it was dead there so I asked keeper Johnny Thomas to advertise for me. I ended up going to Lowther, near Penrith, in July 1946, under headkeeper William Semple, and remained there till I retired.

'Viscount Lowther was a bit autocratic – just like it was before the war. He used to ride around on a big, white horse and every Sunday for a few weeks before the season opened he'd get the keepers out and walk in line with us just to see what the grouse was like. He was a very keen Shot and hated shooting any gamebird up the arse. He died of cancer at 59.

'There were some real characters about then. One old farmer – Isaac Cookson from Sceough Fell – used to cut the bracken for cattle bedding using a long-handled corn scythe and bring it down with a sledge drawn by a Galloway pony. He also took the ling for his fire. His long beard tucked into his belt, and when he took his home-made butter to Penrith market, people were scared to sit beside him on the bus.'

Fred's first beat at Lowther was Buck Holme Woods, but later he had others. 'And the 6,000 to 7,000-acre Helton beat, between Ullswater and Haweswater, had it all, with red deer, roe deer, blackgame and partridges, as well as grouse and pheasants.

'The whole estate was about 70,000 acres and some 50,000 was shot. One season we 'ad 40 shoot days on grouse and pheasants and none was reared. Also only cock pheasants was shot because the Viscount said it was best to leave the hens. When I had Buck Holme we shot 119 cocks. Well, it was 120 with one hen – a very dark bird, bagged by Chief Constable Brown of Cumbria, but he did apologize for his mistake.'

When Fred arrived at Lowther he joined an ageing team. 'I was one of the first new blood. We were paid on the first Monday of the month and when I went up for it I was like a baby compared to the others. Before that I'd been paid fortnightly. My wages were £3 5s plus 2s a day shoot lunch money, 1s a week each for keeping two ferrets, 3/6d a week each for two retrievers and 1/6d a week for a terrier. The dog and lunch money was paid every six months and they made you sign in a book for it. The secretary was old John Peel – a descendat of the real one.

'Viscount Lowther ran the estate for the sixth Earl – Lance, and when he died the grandson James took over very young as the seventh Earl. So then I worked for the Hon Captain Lowther. It stayed entirely a private shoot till 1949 and we used to shoot for six days solid from the 12th. The third year I was there we killed 168 brace on Shap.

'I used to load for Viscount Lowther and 'e was a strict ol' boy in the butt. One day 'e asked me whether it was 13 or 14 grouse he 'ad down and I said I wasn't quite sure. He said: "You should bloody well know that's why you're here." But next time round he asked for me again, so I couldn't have done that badly.

'It was nothin' to get 14 to 20 birds round a butt in them days, but you 'ad the Guns then! The best grouse Shot I saw was Sir John Jardine, who used to fetch 'is headkeeper with 'im for a week. But they all used to have their own valet/loaders with 'em.'

During Fred's time at Lowther the estate held coursing meetings. 'We used to go

Fred and Iris Ladhams with their son Trevor on Askham Fell in 1946

round to the other estates and net hares to bring in. There was never too much trouble with poachers as once a year Captain Lowther used to give the gypsies – about 40 to 50 of 'em – a Sunday runnin' greyhounds at hares on Askham Fell. Shocker Bowman used to get 'em all together and they would bet against each other. That kept 'em all happy for a 12 month. The seventh Earl stopped all that.

'But there used to be quite a bit of trouble with salmon poachers on the river. So one day in my second year we were joined by three water board fellers and I got another young chap to help. We saw a light comin' down to the swing bridge and there were some men either side of the river. We were in a hollow and you could 'ave 'eard 'em comin' at Penrith they made so much noise.

'Then suddenly they were there, looking huge on the skyline above. One chap 'ad a gaff and two salmon over his shoulder, so I went for 'im and grabbed him round the waist. But my mate Brodie jumped on top of me and the others didn't come in, so we only got one. It cost 'im 16 guineas, but 'e said: "Will you take a cheque?" The fine was nothin' to 'im. He made hundreds out of salmon during the war, and they were great big fish then. Still, it was hell of a shock to 'em as they'd been gettin' away with it for years, and things quietened down a bit after that.'

Sometimes Fred also had to take people stalking. 'One chap was so excited at shooting a royal 'e left 'is glasses on the spot. But he told me it was too dark to do anythin' about it. So next morning I took a couple of others up there to search for 'em. Well, we were just walking up the moor in line when I saw the glasses glinting in the sunlight. He were a lucky chap.

'We also used to take the occasional two-year-old pricket stag in and fatten it up for the castle – just like raisin' a steer.'

Like so many keepers, Fred first had a motorbike for transport. 'It was a BSA 125 which ran on Petriol and you could take it anywhere.' Then he had a Bond three-wheeler car, 'which you 'ad to kick-start on a cold morning because the battery was hopeless.'

Later on, Captain Lowther's Whitbystead syndicate bought Fred a new, M-registration Robin Reliant, the three-wheeler being popular because it could be driven with only a motorcycle licence. 'I had that for four years and then they bought me another new one for £900, and 14 years ago a third for £3,000. I still had the Robin when I retired and did not give it up until 1990. I even used to take it out on the grouse moor, but the only trouble was in snow, when you couldn't follow the tracks of the other vehicles.'

The worst winter that Fred could remember was that of 1946-7. 'It was the July before all the snow went at Haweswater; our house was completely cut off for three weeks. You could only just see the tops of some of the telegraph poles and our only fuel was some dead oak trees which we cut down.

'We were down to our last cup of flour before they dug us out. Then just after I managed to get out for some supplies the wind got up and blew the snow back in again. It was no good shootin' a rabbit as they was all skin and bone. And thousands of sheep were wiped out on the fells, but it was a good year for carrion crows with all the dead meat to feed off.'

But despite all the hardships, Fred Ladhams 'would do it all again. After all, there were plenty of good times. And I've been all over with the bosses loadin' – it was just like bein' on holiday with your keep found.'

Fred retired in 1978, but did a further two years part-time for the Lowther estate. He and Iris are still close to the Cumbrian countryside, in a block of retirement flats in the small market town of Kirkby Stephen, not too far from their two sons – a head gardener and a police sergeant – and grandchildren. But the days of stripping off to wash outside are long past.

Chapter 19
CUT ABOVE THE OTHERS

Brian P Marlin

CUT ABOVE THE OTHERS

'I DON'T AGREE WITH ALL THIS FACTORY FARMING,' DECLARED RETIRED BUTCHER LEWIS BLENCOWE WHEN WE MET AT HIS SILVERSTONE HOME, ABOVE AND BEHIND THE SHOP HE NOW LETS. 'THE PORK MAY LOOK BETTER NOW THAN IT EVER DID, BUT WHERE'S THE TASTE? NO BEAST IS GOOD THAT'S NEVER SEEN THE EARTH. IN THE OLD DAYS EVERY PIG WAS DIFFERENT, WITH DISTINCTIVE FLAVOUR AND COLOUR. AND I'D NEVER KILL A BEAST [BULLOCK] UNTIL IT HAD TWO BROAD TEETH, COMIN' UP TO TWO YEAR OLD, SO THAT IT HAD THE RIGHT FLAVOUR AND MATURITY.'

'The other day an old friend said to me: "Wouldn't it be nice if we had consistently good beef every week, like you used to supply?" I always wanted all my customers to have the best of everything. It's nice to think you've pleased people as well as made money.' With such commitment, it's no wonder that Lewis remained a cut above most other butchers throughout a long lifetime in a business has changed dramatically.

Not content to rest on his laurels and cleaver, during his retirement years Lewis has channelled his endless enthusiasm and energy into growing prize vegetables. The result has been a perennial harvest of cups won at shows throughout the region, and like his meat, his veg have always been as good as they look. And with near-perfect food to fuel him, it's no wonder that Lewis is one of the most youthful octogenarians I have ever encountered.

One of two children, Lewis Mervyn Blencowe was born in the village of Whitfield, near Brackley, on 18 May 1908. In those days this was an area dependent on farming, but it was chiefly his father's success in other fields that inspired Lewis to work hard and achieve so much. Lewis remembers those days: 'Father never stopped. For example, in April, just before I was born there was this terrific deep snow, which Father said took the shape of everything. He told me he had never put up so many spoutings [iron gutterings], as they all came down with the weight of the snow.

'Grandad went to America to try his hand at farming, but came back within a year. Dad was just a village lad who, with my uncle, was apprenticed as a carpenter and joiner. I can take you now to houses that they built, a tribute to their great craft. Anyway, they did so well they took a bit of land and uncle had the mill farm, where I spent all my time. I had a marvellous childhood there and soon became very fond of horses.

'We always used to hear the nightingales, any time. And after the dawn chorus you always heard old Tom Chambers, the wagoner who lived opposite, open the field gate and call the horses, at around 5.30am in the summer. There were 15 of 'em shod, and they'd come clip-clopping into his stone causeway, along the street and into the horse yard and stable. They were all loose, and some were a bit bossy, so Tom would shout at them. Altogether it was a lovely

sound in the quiet of the early morning, the shoes on the stones and just this one voice in total command of all that power.

'We had 50 working farm horses in Whitfield then, as well as all the driving horses and float horses and so on. Even the builders' carts were pulled by horses. Now on the land you just get in one of those massive machines and press the button. No generation has seen changes like mine. In our village there used to be two men who could never read or write.

'It was wonderful as a boy to take a horse to Jimmy Baldwin the blacksmith and get it shod, with one man holding the red-hot iron and striking it. One day there, John Thomas, who had one of the first two cars in the village, didn't put his handbrake on properly so his vehicle ran down the hill and smashed some railings. Amazingly, the car wasn't damaged, but John had to pay the smith to repair the railings.

'I always looked forward to school holidays as I enjoyed the farm work so much. The forest binder was pulled by three horses, two on one pole and a third in the front ridden by me or another boy. Harvest used to be so lovely and seemed to go on so long then. Now, unless you actually work on a farm, you hardly know when harvest has started and when it is over.

'The earliest thing I can remember was when I was going along with a wagonload of sheaves, and one fell off on to the mare's back and she bolted. The men called out to me: "Let her go, boy!" After a good run, during which the wagon had hit the gate-post, she calmed down. I got a good ticking-off.

'Another time, when I was 14, I had a strong cob which I decided was ready for harness. So I put him in an old trap and went to Brackley, where I was so proud, parading up and down. But just as I was going over the railway bridge a train let off steam and the cob bolted. He ran for two-and-a-half miles, but luckily the only thing we met on the way was a man on a bike who jumped off and hopped over a gate to save himself. Eventually I managed to pull the cob in at Whitfield. We went off for a few miles and he was perfectly all right.'

Lewis attended Whitfield school to the age of 12, after which he went to Brackley Church of England school; he made an excellent drawing of the school, which he still has. He remembers: 'Father always wanted to push me on to be an architect, as he built houses an' everything. The family firm made almost everythin' in that workshop — windows, stairs, the lot. The men even did the brickwork and plastering. Father also built wheel and wagons, and did some undertaking besides.

'We were lucky to have a very nice house, which dad built himself on the site of two old thatched cottages, which he knocked down. We were one of the first in the area to have an indoor tap, the water running by gravity after a windmill pumped it up to a reservoir on the hill.

'The men called out to me: 'Let her go, boy!'

'Mum was able to keep working as a schoolteacher as we had a wonderful gran and granddad. He was a chief horseman and at first wouldn't let me have a saddle, so that my feet wouldn't get caught up in the stirrups if I came off.'

Even as a schoolboy Lewis was exceptionally independent and had very green fingers: 'In that very dry year of 1921, father bought this small field, and it became my little "farm" where I reared poultry and goats. Dad was secretary of the allotment association, too, and I was allowed a chain square of my own. I used to go down after school and at weekends to shut in the hens, do the sowing and weeding and suchlike, as well as a bit of work on the farm. The ol' chaps could see I was really keen and used to come along and say: "'ere you are boy, 'ere's a few seed potatoes." One year I put a

ton of potatoes in a clamp and one ol' boy used to take a hundredweight a week off me. He was always saying, "Well done boy, they're really nice!" But later on, when I was courtin', those old boys were worried I was "goin' the wrong way," as my allotment grew the best crop of poppies you've ever seen!'

Helping hands were always needed at his uncle's watermill, which Lewis often used to operate with his cousin.

'Flour hadn't been ground there since dad was a boy, but we used to grind grist for cattle feed all winter. We booked the farmers in and they brought the grain on floats. Farmers never bought much of anythin' in those days. They really lived off the land.

'Us boys had great fun working at the mill. We used to grab the chain, pull a cord and go up through the trap with leather hinges where the sacks used to go. It was a risky business with so much machinery about, and we were often told off. We had a big ol' grease tin and spatula to keep the wooden cogs turning nice.

'In April, after the end of grinding corn, we cleared the mill and tidied up ready for sheep washing. In early May we used to do up to about two thousand. All booked in. And we could deal with three flocks at once – one coming down the lane, one holding in Miller's Close (a field), and one in the wash. This was about six-feet deep, created by damming the brook, and each sheep was put under a strong spout. In those days lots of sheep fed on the ploughland and got very dirty, so they had to be washed just before shearing to get a better price for the wool; there was great shame on the farmer who didn't bother. Most of them were very generous and would send us boys up to the pub to fetch beer in a can while their sheep were being washed. Our millstream was a tributary of the Ouse, and there were other mills working at Turweston and Brackley, all within a few miles.'

But there was at least one day when the sheep in Lewis' care were far from co-operative: 'On a Saturday when I was about 14, I was taking about 150 wild Cheviots on the road with my cousin. We had a good sheepdog, but it was a very humid day and this made the sheep restless.

'As we passed a row of alms-houses on a bend a couple of sheep shot through a pale-gate which wasn't fastened properly, and it closed behind them. Our ol' dog knew they were missin' all right but didn't know where they'd gone. It turned out that the front door of the house was open too, and the sheep had charged right in where this ol' gal, who had no taps or sink, had a big bucket of water on the table – the sheep had upset everything. Well, this ol' dear was standin' there shakin' and I wanted to console her, but I had all those sheep there in the road and couldn't stop.

'When we got back to the farm we were very thirsty and given all this rough ol' cider, so by the time we went out to get on our bikes everythin' was goin' round and round. After a bit our front wheels touched and I went one way, my cousin the other, and I just lay there on the bank for a while, very hot and confused. Then there was a terrific thunderstorm and we took shelter at Brackley station.

'Other times it was nothing to be sent out with a big drove of bullocks. But you always had to send someone ahead to close all the gates. It wasn't so much them getting' in the gardens, it was getting' them out again that was the problem!'

As a boy, Lewis never had much time for sport. 'I was always workin'; but we did take a wire occasionally and noose the odd eel.'

Typical of the time, the village was a close-knit community, where everyone

knew and trusted each other. 'No one locked up then. The butcher and baker would let themselves in, and if anyone did lock a door you generally knew where to find the key.

'Aunt kept a wonderful little grocer's shop, and our farm supplied milk to the village at 9am and 5pm. She had this stand with a snow-white tablecloth on for the pails of milk, and there was another table next to it where the people left their pans and cans. Aunt always knew whose they all were.

'Everybody had good food, all home-grown. Most people killed a bacon pig, and you cooked with suet then to get the flavour. The butcher always came midweek and Saturday with his big horse van and opened up the side. Eight shillings would buy plenty for a week for a whole family.

'Local bread was baked almost every day. Dad always said you couldn't beat Gramp [Harry] Humphrey's cottage loaves, which he brought round on a cart pulled by his horse Ginger. To heat his bread oven he used thorn-shank faggots tied up by the hedge-layers. After the faggots were burnt inside the brick oven, the ashes were raked out, and Gramp would look at the glow of this pebble set in the back – a kind of early thermostat – to see if the temperature was right for the bread to go in.

'There were two bakehouses, one for each end of the village. As well as for bread, they were used for cooking people's dinners. At the weekend, families used to set in at 11 o'clock, then draw their Yorkshire puddings at half-past midday.

'There was none of this convenience stuff. The only ice-cream you had was at a fete, though much later on the Walls man used to pedal out into the hayfield with his "Stop me and buy one".'

When Lewis was a teenager there was still no telephone in Whitfield, so there could be considerable delay in summoning help after an accident. 'When I was 14, word came that Andrew Ayres – one of the workers who set the fires in the baker's oven – had chopped his thumb clean off. This lady went to assist and did the best she could, but there was no car, and the fastest transport was my uncle's trap. I can still picture them racing past with Andrew Ayres holding his bandaged hand up n the air, on their way to Brackley cottage hospital.'

On another day it was a very distinguished visitor in need of a telephone at Whitfield: 'I saw this chap comin' up through the village on horseback late on a winter's afternoon. He was all in red and had been huntin' with the Grafton. He stopped and said: "Hello. Is there a telephone here?" I said: "It's the Prince of Wales, isn't it?" and he said, "Yes." It was the future King Edward VIII.

'I knew the first phone in the area had come into a nearby farm, so I pointed him in the right direction. He went up there and tapped on the door, and poor Elsie the maid was so surprised. The prince gave her half-a-crown, and when I last saw her she still had that actual coin.

'I can still picture them, Andrew Ayres holding his hand up in the air ...'

'An ol' farmer, Freddie Smith, over at Slapton also saw Prince Edward out hunting. Freddie was a real character, with a smock and a bag tied with string round his waist, and he'd always say what he wanted. So when this other ol' chap told him "That's the Prince of Wales, over there," Freddie scratched his head in his usual way and just called out: "Ay up. How are you?" but the prince was very good and came over to shake hands.

'I remember very well, too, the girl Alice who came to work at our farm just after the first war. We were all down in the fields busy with the harvest and I was sent back to fetch some tools or something. At the time there was this sow and a litter of pigs – all sandy and black, with no white – and I passed the barn where Alice always hung her dinner. This ol' sow came trotting out holding a pudding basin in her mouth by the cloth wrapped around it. As she ran off I hit her with these sheaves until she dropped the basin. It seemed all right, so I put it back on the hook and said nothing. Later on, when we all sat together at dinner, Alice asked us boys what we were tittering about; but she never knew the truth!'

At the age of 18 Lewis stopped working for his family and became apprentice to Peredge-Salmon. 'This was the leading butcher in Brackley. I was bound over until I was 21, and got £1 a week, 15s of which went to mother.

'In those days all the animals came into town live and we did our own killing. Imagine bringing cows and pigs into the centre of Brackley now, with all that traffic.

'For deliveries we had this wonderful Welsh cob and a London butcher's car, all covered in – not even a fly could enter. We also had shop bikes with carriers and I used to go all over the place to surrounding villages. One of these was Turweston, which was a place of gentry then. There were five or six big houses there, and in the winter there would be 50 hunters in the village, following the Grafton hounds.

'Sometimes I went to Turweston and back six times in a day, but some of those ol' cooks would always have a cup of tea and a big cake for you. The big houses were often let for the hunting season, and then almost every butcher in the district would be on the doorstep fighting for the trade. One day I saw this furniture van going in, so I thought I'd beat the competition, stop off and get a big order. But I had to wait some time to see the housekeeper, and when I got back the boss's wife told me off for being late. But you just had to get the trade then, and my boss knew that, so that Saturday night, when I got my wages, he said, "Well done, boy" and gave me an extra half-a-crown for looking after the business.'

When Lewis started courting his future wife, Bella (Frances Isabel), a Yorkshire farmer's daughter, his parents were very wary as she was from 'far away'. '"How do you know who she is?" they asked. I said: "I know exactly who she is, and what's more I know who she's going to be!" After that they said nothing else!' Lewis recollects those times clearly:

'. . . this ol' sow came trotting out holding a pudding basin'

'There was one night when I was comin' back from courting that I'll always remember. I was goin' along on my three-and-a-half horsepower BSA motorbike that I'd bought for £12, when I saw this bright light comin' and goin' through the trees. So I followed round to it, and there was Cottesford manor house on fire.

'The three maids were in night attire and trapped on top by the parapet, and the ol' gent of the house was runnin' about in his dressing gown with a few books under his arm. There were only one or two other people there and we got a long ladder to fetch the girls down.

'After a while the Bicester fire brigade came; they had their first motorized engine, which they couldn't handle. And then came the old Amos horse-drawn vehicle from Brackley. By this time it was towed by a lorry, but I can still remember the two old greys, pensioners from World War I – one with an ear shot off – which used to pull it. These horses were also used by the people who owned the pub for carting stones and other jobs, but if they heard the fire alarm bell they'd go mad and tip up their load because they wanted to get moving. They knew where they'd got to go all right!

'Anyway, this night I knew all the Brackley chaps, who wondered what on earth I was doing there, and they damned soon pumped the pond dry, while the Bicester crew, struggling with their new vehicle, got nowhere. But it was all in vain, and nothing could be salvaged. I looked through the French windows, and there was this lovely grand piano which suddenly came alive with flame; then it went bang and collapsed, and all the keys went everywhere. The owners had an old bloodhound, too, but he was never seen again. When we left at 3am, the house was just a shell, with the water-tanks hanging in the roof. It took me ages to find my motorbike then, too, because I'd just thrown it down behind a wall in a rush and couldn't remember where.'

On completing his apprenticeship, Lewis started work straight away: 'I went to a top man in Brackley. But when he retired he didn't let me have the business as he'd promised. So I got very itchy feet, as I wanted to work on my own, especially as I'd already married in 1931, when we'd bought a little cottage for £150; besides which, wages were only £2 10s for a top man working 70 or 80 hours a week.

'So I looked at this ol' broken-down business, Jarvis's, just up the road at Syresham, and got it reserved till the Tuesday. I asked father what he thought, and he took me into Barclays to see the manager, in about 1934. I needed £100 just to go into the rented premises, and then we hadn't even finished paying for our house. The shop had no fridge, only a deep cellar, and a lot of the tackle was useless. But the price did include an ol' Morris van and we was always prepared to have a go. Anyway, the bank man let me have £200 to get started, and he said: "Don't be mean, but look after the ha'pennies!"

'Among the first things I did was pay a friend to put in electricity, and get a fridge. Uncle had left the rented mill farm, so we let our house to him at 5s 6d a week, and he lived there till a great age.'

One of the reasons why Lewis got off to a good start at Syresham was that he had 'a few good ol' pals' to help him. 'One of them said: "Should you want some pigs any time you can 'ave 'em off me at only so much a score dead weight."

'The first time I took ol' man Payne up on this I scrubbed out the delivery van and put in some straw to collect the animals. You can imagine what the hygiene people would think about that now. Anyway, when I went to get the first few pigs he helped me load and then went over to open the gate; he obviously didn't want his sons to hear him speak to me as I drove through. He said: "Boy, if you've got anyone else to pay before me, don't you worry, I knows what it's like setting up in business." Ain't that a wonderful thing for him to say. You'd be lucky to get help like that nowadays.'

Things went well, and Lewis soon built up a marvellous business: 'Each week I killed two bullocks, ten lambs and about four pigs. I never minded the slaughtering side of it and was always as kind as possible to the animals. It's a job you haven't to push yourself at — if a chap worked up a sweat you knew he'd be no good at it. When I first started I just pole-axed the bullocks. For the pigs I had a wonderful mallet which I made myself, and they'd roll over beautiful before I slit 'em. But it was a skilful job and you'd have to be accurate with the knife as it was only narrow where the main artery was, next to the food passage.

'Humane killers came in just before the war, but the "bell" one was dangerous to the operator as you had these hard blue bricks and the bullet could ricochet anywhere. In any case, slaughtering was always very hard work, with pulley blocks and so on, but I've done hundreds by myself. Fortunately, in all my years butchering and farming I've never broken a bone, even though I've been lain on, kicked and thrown many a time.

'In 1938 everythin' was comin' wonderful. It was the best period I ever had, with good, steady family business. In the thirties rump and fillet was only about 1s 4d a pound, brisket 8d and stewing steak 10d to 1s. For most people chicken and turkey was only ever a treat at Christmas, but you got proper birds then, which were kept longer and fed better.'

But the good times were soon to change with the outbreak of war. Lewis sold his old business and bought half of the old Manor

Lewis in July 1928, aged 20

Farm at Syresham, a hundred acres; but as hostilities continued, he was increasingly bogged down by bureaucracy.

'It would have been a lot easier if I'd gone to war. With rationing we were formed into butchers' groups, 17 of us in Brackley and Rural District, and we were allocated meat according to permit through the only stock buyer, which involved a lot of extra work, such as going to Brackley at 5am several days a week to allocate meat. It was a hell of a job as the butchers' permits varied every week. And you had to report in all weathers. With no antifreeze, sometimes you had to boil a kettle to get the vehicle goin', and very often go out with Jerry flyin' over the top.

(Far right) Farm auction details from when Lewis sold up in 1948

'I was also a cattle grader, and for all this I only ever got expenses. At first we used to assess many animals by hand as there was no weighing for sheep, but cattle could be weighed at the gasworks. But us practical chaps were happy to weigh by hand; it wasn't much trouble. I could work day and night then and never get tired. I reckoned I could do it sleepwalkin'.'

One of Lewis' most vivid wartime memories is of the time when Coventry was bombed: 'You could hear these ol' planes droning over with their heavy loads on, then bmmm-bmmm-bmmm as they dropped their bombs, followed by the singing noise of the lightened aircraft

'...rationing was kept on far too long...'

veering away. We had some terrible dos then when the planes thought they were somewhere else. One night they killed all these cattle and I had to go out and put the wounded ones out of their misery.

'After the war, things got even worse for butchers. Quite apart from the bitter winter of 1946-7 — when it was so bad getting about you had to buy slatted headlamp covers for your vehicle to throw the light down on the snow — rationing was kept on far too long. But I was determined to rebuild everything. They'd already confiscated our best field with a compulsory purchase for housing, so I sold up all the land and buildings at Syresham in 1948, and in the year of the first grand prix, came here to Silverstone where I bought this shop and ten acres down the road.

'With that 8d meat ration, it was the worst ol' driest time you ever 'ad; but when rationing ended, I was prepared. I got the ol' slaughterhouse ready out the back here, and I declared I was one going back to how I'd left off in 1938. By then the wholesalers had come in, but I said "No, I'm not havin' meat brought here by nobody. I'll kill my own, as we used to." And that's what I did with another butcher nearby. We'd slaughter three beasts [cattle] a week, one for him and two for me. I had my ring of farmers, and I knew exactly where the cattle could be fed and where they couldn't.'

Eventually Lewis was helped by Siverstone's development and growing fame as a top motor-racing venue, although he was increasingly called out to destroy animals injured in road accidents. But during his first years there it was more traditional work that made his business thrive. 'Much of the land around here is not good for cultivation, but it is good for forestry, so Silverstone was a big timber village with a great many big-eating people wanting good food. Everything had to be

Particulars.

SYRESHAM

NORTHANTS

OSBORNE & SON, F.A.I.

Are favoured with instuctions from Mr. L. M. Blencowe (having sold the farm) to Sell by Auction on the premises known as "BELL LANE" on

MONDAY, 27th SEPTEMBER, 1948

at 2 p.m. prompt

The whole of the

Live & Dead Farming Stock

comprising

17 Head of CATTLE

7 D.C. Cows & Heifers; 2 Barreners; 7 Heifer Calves (6-8 months) LINCOLN RED Pedigree Bull (3 yrs.) Good Stock getter & bred by Messrs Reid & Sigrist, Leicester.

2 HORSES

br. gelding (9 yrs.) Good worker all gears; Rn. Cob (aged) (Well known in the district).

12 Head of POULTRY

Sussex Cks. (Messrs. Turney strain)

together with

IMPLEMENTS & MACHINERY

FORDSON TRACTOR rubbers on rear (excellent condition); 2-furr. Ransome Plough; Cambride Tractor Roll; Flat roll (1 h) Massey Harris Disc. drill (for tractor); 1 h. Hay Sweep; Set Adkinhead Harrows; Seed & drag Harrows; Massey Harris Binder; Albion Mower for Tractor (equal to new); Hay Loader; Horse Rake; Blackstone Swath Turner; Ladders (34 & 20 rds); 4-wh. Trolley (for horse or tractor) with side boards; Hay holders; Rick Sheet 24 ft. × 18 ft.; Wagon Sheet; Farm tip Cart on rubbers (with raves); 4 h.p. Lister Engine on Trolley; Root Pulper (unchokeable); Milk Float; 120 Gal. Paraffin Tank; Sheep troughs, Hay Knives; etc. etc.

HARNESS. Set thiller; Set Cob; G.O. Tackle etc. etc.

DAIRY UTENSILS : Cooler & hopper; Buckets, strainer. etc.

No Catalogues.   On view morning of Sale

Further particulars apply : The Auctioneers; Land Agency Offices, Buckingham (phone 2120).

quality. However, it wasn't the increasing number of visitors I relied on, but providing a reliable product for local families. If you hadn't wanted meat one week I'd want to know why. At first the disruption caused by the building of the racetrack, and then on race days themselves was terrible, but we did get to supply some contractors. Now my shop tenant welcomes visitors.'

Consistent quality was vital. 'If you made a real country sausage, the secret was always keepin' 'em right. You don't alter 'em if they sell well because people will only ever have one bad sausage and they won't have any more. It's what people say about you that counts.' But there was also a right approach in handling customers. In Lewis' opinion: 'To serve, you haven't got to be a wooden man, but you must adapt. If our most gracious Queen came in I could serve her just as I could deal with an ol' diehard from the village. People must have faith in you. But you can also tempt them. I'd cut a steak in front of them in such a way that it fell down right, and they couldn't resist a second one.

'Today a lot of butchers wouldn't know how to cut things like a proper saddle of lamb and a wing rib of beef. They couldn't cure a ham or prepare an ox tongue. I used to sell two pickled tongues a week. For that you must be very clean and accurate with your mix of salts, else they won't last. I could never get enough of 'em, but few are sold now. People are more interested in all this barbecue business, which never used to come into it.

'We sold a few pheasants and hares, but never used to push 'em as it was mainly a good, traditional family business. Rabbits were never a big seller as so many people caught their own, and they mostly went out with myxomatosis. There wasn't much call for geese, either. People always wanted good farm turkeys and chickens at Christmas, and I daren't face the festive season without 40 pickled ox tongues, so then I had to buy a few from a wholesaler.

'Another thing today is that meat's handled too much. If you haven't got to touch it, then don't. Always stick a hook in it and hang it up. Also there's all these stupid rules now, with Europe insisting in things like a plastic block. It's a wonder they don't want plastic knives. But there's been no improvement in hygiene. In the old days a butcher's pride and joy was his block and his benches all scrubbed clean. You were judged on that. You can give one chap everythin' there is for modern cleanliness, and another one a good old-fashioned place, and it won't make any difference – if a chap's goin' to wipe his nose on the back of his hand, he'll do so when you're not there. You can't be too clean. No, your food today is definitely handled too much, and the individual craftsman has died out.'

With the ending of rationing, Lewis was in great demand as a stock judge all over the country. Unfortunately, most of the main shows came just before Christmas, when Lewis was already very busy with special orders. But with his great experience in butchery and farming he was the ideal man to judge an animal's conformation. They used to call him 'the bloke that looked through 'em'. 'But as well as looking, it's in these,' said Lewis, holding his hands up. 'People used to rely on my fingers.'

One fatstock show at Winslow provided a good illustration of why Lewis was also known as 'the man with x-ray eyes'. Lewis relates this occasion: 'My fellow judge was a British beef buyer and I thought, "I've got a bright spark here!" As soon as we started I could tell he was hopeless, always letting me decide and then agreeing all the time.

'Eventually all the prizewinners were called out to decide the championships. I was working on this beast and putting it down to reserve champion when all of a sudden, for the first time, this chap didn't agree. So I pressed him and told him to handle the pair, which he did, and then he agreed with me. After that he was a bit niggly for the rest of the day. He'd obviously let himself be influenced by the crowd.

'As it turned out, the same butcher bought both champion and reserve, so I was happy about that. And both owners were at the abattoir to see how their beasts came out. When they saw the carcasses they immediately shook hands in agreement that the best animal had won, confirming that I had been right all along.'

Lewis, too, would sometimes buy a champion animal, 'so that you got into the local paper, and this boosted your business. And it's nice for the public to see that the judge has the strength of his own convictions. I would pay up to about £600 for a beast over 20 years ago, so sometimes your pal would say you were a fool. I still buy a few beasts for my tenant. The odd

thing is that they're now auctioned by the kilo, but still sold in the shop by the pound. Luckily I have no trouble converting!'

Good horses, too, were irresistible to Lewis: 'Country butchers always used to have a good cob, and I've done a lot of driving; for years I had the fastest cob around here. There used to be some challenges between us, but nine times out of ten someone would call it off if they saw you go beforehand. In the old days I could never see any danger, but then you don't when you're younger. Eventually, as I was going off to a show, my wife said, "Don't bring another horse back today."

'One day a friend said to me: "How can you stand all that hard work slaughtering?" So for the last few years I was persuaded to use a good abattoir run by friends at Northampton. I retired from butchery at the age of 64.'

Since then Lewis has remained exceptionally active. Even in his late eighties he has continued his lifelong interest in hunting, often following the

Lewis was in great demand as a stock judge

Stowe School Beagles for six or seven miles on foot. He describes his sport: 'I've been a member since it was formed, and I shall go with my terrier as long as I can. I also follow the Grafton and have ridden with them on the odd occasion. I've always loved it, since we first sang 'John Peel'.

'The Stowe is one of the best beagle packs in the country. Us older boys can't keep up quite like we used to, so we find a good vantage point and just watch. Some places are still OK for hares, but it's very variable from day to day. I always say to people: "You can come if you pay the cap, but don't expect anythin' marvellous: it doesn't always happen!" Also, it's all becoming more difficult for hunting as there's always another road comin' through and cuttin' the country up. With most big estates becoming split up there's a lot more landowners, and if just one refuses us permission to cross his land it can cut off a big area of countryside.

'Like everyone else, we've had our share of trouble with the anti-fieldsports brigade, such as in 1993, when we met at Lower Boddington. The antis had been to upset the Bicester and met us along the way, and we couldn't get the hounds out of the trailer. But overall it's not so bad now, as they're being made to tow the line more. I've never been attacked, but I've been abused a lot. They generally breathe somethin' awful as they go past, such as: "You ought to have been dead a long time ago," and if you answer 'em they start on. Unfortunately for me I'm apt to get in the middle of it, so when one girl went to take my photograph I very soon told her what I'd do. I don't see why anyone else should interfere with our great traditions.'

Throughout the spring and summer Lewis spends most of his time in his half-acre garden nurturing huge vegetables such as leeks, onions and celery. Every year he spends hundreds of hours, sometimes working till late at night, lovingly preparing the best and biggest of his produce for some eight to ten shows within about a 25-mile radius. It's not surprising that some of the cups for individual vegetables and collections have returned to his trophy cupboard year after year.

With such strong interests to keep him at home, Lewis has 'never been a holiday man. I've always enjoyed the calendar of the year, from sowing and showing to harvest and hunting. And I've never been to a Grand Prix, even though the circuit is on my doorstep. Nowadays there's enough of a racetrack outside my front door, and you have to say a prayer before crossing the road. But if I get knocked down tomorrow I couldn't complain because I've had a grand life. A man's greatest blessing is to have a good wife and partner by his side, as I did for 55½ years, and a good family. Now I'm well looked after with all three daughters still living in the parish, and I have four grandsons and three great grandchildren.'

Chapter 20
ENCHANTED BY THE RIVER

Tom Quinn

ENCHANTED BY THE RIVER

JIM 'THE FISH' SMITH WORKS ON THE 20-ODD MILES OF THE SUSSEX OUSE OWNED BY THE OUSE

ANGLING PRESERVATION SOCIETY, WHICH WAS FOUNDED IN 1875. JIM IS IN A UNIQUE POSITION AMONG

RIVERKEEPERS BECAUSE HE LOOKS AFTER A RIVER THAT IS BOTH AN IMPORTANT COARSE FISHERY AND A

GAME FISHERY. FAMED FOR ITS GIANT CHUB AND ROACH, THE SUSSEX OUSE IS ALSO ONE OF THE VERY

FEW RIVERS OF ANY IMPORTANCE FOR BIG SEA TROUT IN THE SOUTH EAST.

JIM IS A MARVELLOUSLY AVUNCULAR MAN WITH A DELIGHTFUL SUSSEX DRAWL AND WITH THE IDEAL

TEMPERAMENT — TOLERANT, FRIENDLY AND HELPFUL — FOR A MOST DIFFICULT JOB.

Jim was born just a few miles from where he now lives in the tiny village of Isfield. Now 45, he has worked on the river for more than 25 years. His father was a carter in the days before the coming of the motor car and when Jim left school he started work as a cottage gardener for Lord Rupert Neville. The estate was sold soon after Jim started work and the land is now — as he ruefully told me — a massive housing estate.

Already a keen fisherman, he was approached by the secretary of the Ouse Angling Preservation Society and asked if he would like to take over as riverkeeper. I wondered if the offer had come as a surprise. 'Good heavens no. I'd fished since I was a little boy and I fished here on the Ouse from the time I was six. The job is ideal and since I started I've never thought of doing anything else. The job is particularly interesting for me because it involves a lot of conservation, which is a real enthusiasm of mine, particularly now that we get so much hassle from farm pollution and the like.'

Unusually for a riverkeeper, Jim works in an area of the country that is both densely populated and close to London. This causes problems in a multitude of different ways, as he explained.

'Pollution is the really big problem for us because the local sewage works' consent conditions – that's how much sewage they can legally pump into the river – have been relaxed. There's nothing we can do about it, but at least when things go wrong and we do get a big pollution we can keep the pressure on them for compensation.

'Flow levels are much reduced these days too. With so many big towns nearby they take an awful lot of water through abstraction. But my great fear is that one massive pollution is going to come along one day and wipe out all our fish. It's like being on a knife's edge. We're a sort of disaster waiting to happen.

'The other big problem on the Sussex Ouse I suppose is that coarse and other game fishermen are so different. Don't let anyone tell you they're all brothers of the angle. That's nonsense. They couldn't be more different. I don't know why it is but the game fishermen are nearly always clean and tidy while the coarse fishermen are not so good; in fact some of them are bloody awful. I don't know why they have to chuck their rubbish all over the place.

'Then, of course, with so many new housing developments round and about we get a fair bit of poaching. I spend a lot of time just sitting and waiting to catch them, but we've got a good relationship with the police and the local grapevine helps. We know a lot of poachers and where they are.'

Jim laughs about these poaching problems and makes light of them, but the potential seriousness of the problem in his area can be judged by the fact that, several years ago, he was badly injured in a poaching attack.

'Oh yes, that was a bit of a do. I'd seen a fellow with a net in the river and a sea trout. I challenged him; I know that sounds a bit threatening, but what I mean is I just asked him if he had permission to fish. Next thing I knew I was covered in mud and blood. I had to be taken to hospital and I had nine stitches in my lip. They caught the man who thumped me and he was fined £50 for the assault. The thing that got me most about the incident was the surprise. I just didn't expect him to hit me.

'Over the years I've been threatened many times, even though I'm always careful when I approach people who shouldn't be fishing. I don't mind so much when it's a youngster fishing where he shouldn't be – some of the younger ones turn out to be good fishermen in the end.'

Jim exudes good cheer even while he is speaking about matters that would depress an ordinary mortal, but after 25 years he is still enchanted by the river's unique reputation for giant sea trout.

'I think the main reason the society was set up all those years ago was that, even then, they realized the value of the river. The society was actually started by a group of farmers who wanted to preserve the Ouse and its fishing. And in those days the river really was worth preserving. It used to produce some really massive fishing trout. The record is held, I believe, by the late John French. He landed a sea trout of 16¾lb, but those early fish – for which, unfortunately, we don't have exact records – undoubtedly often weighted over 20lb. The river was always renowned for its big fish. It never produced large numbers. It's odd, but that's what makes it so unique.

'In some ways the river's future is more serious now than it was 20 or 30 years ago, although, after serious floods in 1960, the water authority dredged the river in a very insensitive way. They pulled out far too many trees, threw up great banks and generally altered the character of the river for the worse and, in fact, the fishing suffered. These days I think they would be a bit more careful with their dredgers.

'The saddest thing I remember wasn't the dredging, it was the time we had a serious outbreak of disease among the fish. I remember walking the banks one day in the early 1960s and every few yards I pulled another 14 or 15lb sea trout. It was terrible, but there was nothing we could do except let the disease take its course. Then, to top

it all, we had that other terrible disease, UDN, in the 1970s. We found hundreds of fish running into side streams and dying.'

What makes Jim so continually surprised by his stretch of the Ouse and the quality of its fishing is the fact that, superficially at least, it looks so unprepossessing: 'Oh yes, it's a funny old river, and when you look at it you'd never think any decent fish would ever bother to come into it, but come they do. Most people who fish for sea trout here use a Mepps. The Sussex Ouse is not really a fly river, although a friend of mine – he's the local expert really – had one on a fly. I landed a sea trout of 15lb myself, but that was in 1967 when there were a lot more fish than there are now. Mind you they seem to come and go in cycles. We'll have a bad period followed by an upturn and then things get bad again. I would say that in an average year we'll get about 150 fish, but they will all be big.'

The Ouse Angling Preservation Society has some 400 members, most of whom concentrate on the river's excellent coarse fishing. There are numerous 5lb chub, roach to over 2lb and vast shoals of good-sized bream. Some of the members come from London and beyond, but most still live locally. The Ouse is not a chalkstream; it relies on rainfall for its flow and there is little weed-cutting to be done. 'We've never really had to cut the weed, but with more and more fertilizer getting washed into the river from surrounding farms we might have to start. Fertilizer really gets the weed going.'

Apart from worries about weed growth and pollution, Jim spends a lot of time worrying about the next oddity he'll find on the river: 'Oh we've had some hilarious

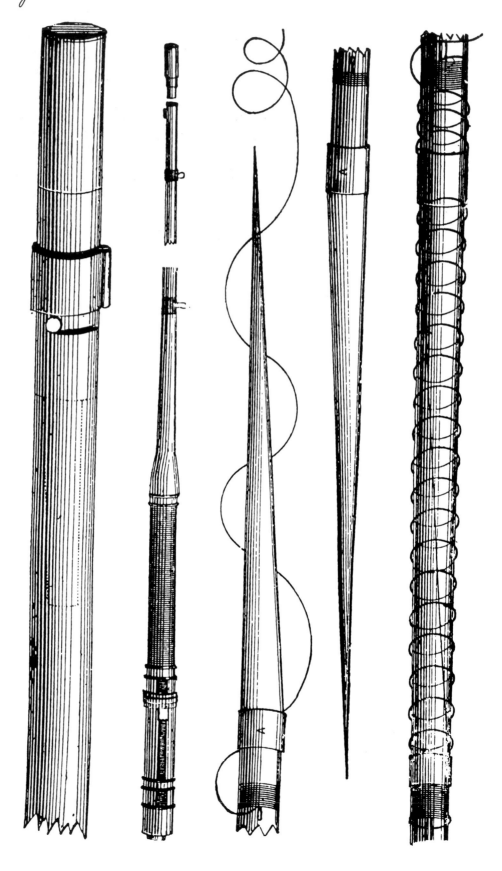

hunts for all kinds of things down here. I remember many years ago our local MP, who was a keen fisherman, mentioned a constituent who kept a crocodile as a pet and when the crocodile grew too big for its tank, the owner put it in the bath. Then, of course, it grew too big for the bath and he put it in the river. We electro-fished to try and catch it – I'm sure the story was true – but we never found it. We've also had terrapins in the river. A mate of mine once caught one on a great piece of mackerel. Mind you, come to think of it, I wonder why he was fishing with mackerel bait in the first place!'

Jim smiled gleefully at this point and invited me to go down to the river and walk the banks with him. I saw exactly what he meant when he had earlier described the river as unlikely looking. The stretch I walked looked pretty much like a drainage ditch. Jim was generous when he said the water authority had dredged it insensitively. That was putting it mildly. But in spite of everything, we soon spotted several chub that looked well over 4lb and in an old mill pool Jim pointed out an enormous shoal of big bream sunning themselves. Jim clearly enjoys talking about his river. Indeed, he almost takes a fatherly interest in it and he has many stories of strange goings on up and down the banks.

'I know this sounds ridiculous, but one thing we get a lot of is safes – you know bank safes. People seem to make a habit of chucking them into the river down here. We usually find them under the bridges.

'One of the strangest incidents in my time happened late one night. I was just going home when a chap came up to me and told me he'd been fishing with his wife and they'd seen a ghost. I was a bit sceptical, but he really seemed genuinely frightened. He was absolutely convinced he'd seen something. I thought no more of it, but

then I remembered someone else had contacted our local radio station about ghosts down by the river. The chap who'd phoned the radio station said the ghost he'd seen looked like a Roman soldier and I think it was significant because it just happened that the ghost had been spotted at a point on the river where the Romans are known to have had a crossing place. But if the Roman soldier story was true that meant we had two ghosts because the fisherman who'd come up to me said he'd seen a fully dressed woman throw herself into the river from a bridge. He was so convinced we decided to check all the local missing persons lists. He said she'd been wearing a white shawl and a veil and I really think he must have seen something because he never fished there again.

'But perhaps the funniest thing that ever happened to me was when I rescued someone who'd fallen in. I just happened to pass a couple who were both fishing. They weren't fishing very close together and just as I passed the woman she slipped and fell in. I heard her scream so I ran across to help. I grabbed her to pull her out and the next thing I knew her dress had come right off in my hands.'

Gales of laughter from Jim. Like most riverkeepers he takes things as they come, although he doesn't have an easy life. He has some assistance from a few part-time helpers, but is still very much a one-man operation in the main and there is a lot of river to look after. Jim's day usually starts at about eight in the morning and often doesn't end till 11 o'clock at night.

'A typical day for me starts with an early walk along the different sections of the river and I might just drop in and take a look at our reservoir. I look at the footpaths, tidy the banks, check regularly for pollution and, of course, keep my eyes peeled for poachers. I also issue water authority licences. I suppose I'm a bit like a bobby on his beat. It's a good life, though, because I get to meet the members and I know many of them very well. Our oldest member is 95 years old and we've got several in their 80s, one of whom insists on fishing with a fly the whole time. We've got several Members of Parliament on the membership list and entertainers like Frankie Vaughn come down to fish now and then.'

Apart from human poachers, Jim also has to put up with predations of mink and cormorants: 'Those damned cormorants are a nuisance. They fly up the valley and take a lot of our fish, particularly if the smoults are running. The mink problem really only started in the 1960s when there was a sudden craze for mink farms. There were a lot of escapees and, of course, they played havoc with our fish.

In spite of being attacked by a poacher, Jim's favourite story is a poaching one. 'The Ouse runs through Lord Callagahan's land and on one occasion we heard there was some poaching going on down his place. What started as a small poaching warning ended up as a full-scale security alert. Someone, somewhere, obviously hit the button and suddenly there were hundreds of police everywhere. That poacher must have got the fright of his life when the helicopters came circling round him. I only hope it was the bugger who hit me!'

Chapter 21
BEWARE OLD VELVETEENS

John Humphreys

BEWARE OLD VELVETEENS

THE GAMEKEEPER WAS THERE TO PROTECT HIS MASTER'S GAME FROM ENEMIES OF THE TWO- AND FOUR-LEGGED SORT. IN OLDEN TIMES HE SPRANG AWAY FROM THE SAME VILLAGE STOCK AS HIS ARCH-ENEMY THE POACHER. THE LOCAL MOUCHER WHO USED THE ANCIENT ARTS TO TAKE GAME WAS A MAN THE KEEPER COULD UNDERSTAND AND HE SEEMED AT TIMES ALMOST TO ENJOY THE CUT-AND-THRUST, THE DIAMOND-CUT-DIAMOND OF THE AGE-OLD BATTLE.

A good poacher was less easy to poach than was an idler, but sometimes he met his match; now and then fisticuffs were resorted to while cudgels swung and clunked on pates in the moonlit aisles of the woods. The keeper kept himself to himself and his real friends were few; his velveteen suit proclaimed his calling, and he was a feared and respected man in the community. He enjoyed the patronage and protection of his powerful employer and the retributive engine of the Game Laws. The odds in the poaching war were in his favour.

The Victorian Poacher

Gilbertson and Page used to make gamekeeping aids for the royal estates, one of the first firms to do so. Their products included all manner of game-rearing equipment, cures for gapes ('The Certain and Complete Cure'), a patent warm-water box for transferring young pheasants from hatching box to coop, game food, duck meal, dog biscuits and so on. Today they concentrate on the manufacture of dog food, their Valumix brand name being well known among dog owners and trainers. In the heady days of the 1890s, when vanloads of keeping equipment left the firm each day and reared pheasants were in their heyday, they published a handy little manual for keepers warning them of telltale signs of poachers at work and how to combat them.

It was entitled *Poachers versus Keepers*, an amusing and instructive treatise concerning poachers and their artifices — dealing with the many phases of poaching directed against game both fur and feathered (they went in for wordy titles in those times) and priced at 6d (or about 2p modern equivalent). This is a very rare book in its original form, and it contains jewels of wisdom and wit.

The Keeper As A Detective

Unlike the policeman, the keeper cannot rely on the evidence of an aggrieved party but must use his eyes and ears to detect poaching. He is on his own. He must use all the fieldcraft of a plains Indian and be sharp-eyed to notice torn-up earth, a barked twig, tracks in the morning dew, or black footmarks on frosted herbage, all of which indicate that an intruder has been visiting at night. In those days the keepers were oft abroad and not confined to the rearing shed or seat of the Land-Rover as many are today.

Like the observant Sherlock Holmes, a keeper can tell much from a few bent twigs and a fragment of wood, which would be hidden to the eye of an amateur. Such signs tell him that a hare has been snared in that run — the fresh-bitten bark is a giveaway; and the twig is a pricker dropped by the poacher — it is new and fresh-cut, otherwise it would have been polished from the friction of a pocket lining. This is therefore not the work of a practised old hand but of a less-experienced chap, probably a local, a loafing labourer engaged on farm work or road mending.

A search down the hedge reveals an ash tree where the stick was cut, and even the

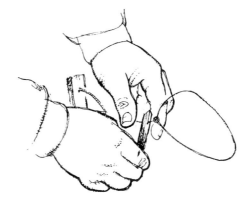

whittlings in the ground, fresh and dry, which show it was the work of last night. But see, there is another stub, white and fresh-cut, so another snare has been set. The good keeper hunts the fence and finds the place of the second snare, but this one has drawn a blank and what is more, the string holding the snare in place has been cut, so the poacher was disturbed and left in a hurry.

A further search of the ground reveals footprints. In the days of nail-shod boots this was as good as a fingerprint, for invariably there is a nail or two missing; the keeper notes this carefully and observes that the man tends to stand with his right foot pointing outwards. He takes the string home and compares it with the others he has found and matches them. The new one is not tied with the practised skill of the ones from the hand of a noted local poacher whom he has yet to catch red-handed, so the newcomer is a young chap with a crude notion of how to set a

associates with a young chap known to history as 'Artful'. The keeper seeks him out and engages him in conversation; he notices that his right foot has a tendency to turn outwards, and by the simple subterfuge of leading him over a muddy track, he can confirm that the boot has the same nails missing from its sole. Thus 'Artful' identified, and it will be but a matter of time before he is nabbed.

Observation

The keeper will have his eyes peeled all the time, looking in the muddy gateways for signs of footprints and disturbed grass on the edge of the cornfield. Tobacco smoke is detectable a long way off and a keeper would not be averse to leaving a lump of smouldering baccy near a spot where he suspected intruders. The poacher would catch a whiff of tobacco on the breeze and make good his escape, laughing at the keeper for his clumsiness.

wire but with access to an expert who supplies him with proper snares.

So much from a little broken ground and some scuffed bark, which anyone else would pass by without a second glance. It so happens that our observant keeper recalls that the old hand well known to him

The keeper would be alert for bird movements, the harsh rattle of a jay warning of intruders, the clatter of pigeons leaving a distant stand of ash; something was disturbing those birds and he would not rest until he knew what it was. Blackbirds are also good guardians of woods and will always shriek their alarm at an intruder. Guinea fowl or geese could be kept in pens – these are probably the best guards of all.

A good keeper had a telescope or pair of binoculars always to hand, not only to spy on the intruders from a distance but to note the resting place of the coveys at night, the movement of hares on the short stubbles and all manner of things useful to his job.

The Keeper and the Locals

A good keeper appeared to be friends with one and all, but such was only his deviousness. In fact he trusted nobody and had few if any friends outside his own profession.

A wise keeper showed friendliness to the locals, and so got to recognize the characters and hoped by his manner to lull them into a false sense of security. He might establish a 'mole' who would keep him informed of nefarious goings-on: this man would be rewarded with small cash sums and all meetings with him would be secret in case he blew his cover.

Such a keeper would be near the roads late at night, watching who came home from work late, who slipped out of the pub before closing time for no apparent reason, and what itinerant labourers were working in the area. In this way he knew who was there at what time, and was better able to spot someone acting suspiciously.

When approaching someone working in the fields the keeper never took a direct route but retreated and approached from an unlikely direction, the better to catch folk off their guard and maybe overhear some careless conversation before they knew he was there. In addition, his habit of popping up out of the blue at unexpected times made folk feel uneasy, never quite sure where he would appear next; this was all to the keeper's advantage.

In conversation, the keeper would sham tiredness, as a man who was abroad at all hours. He might remark at how light it was still at midnight last night, and mention in passing the sharp rainstorm which fell at 2am. In this way word would spread like wildfire of what a vigilant man he was, how he never slept and was constantly out on watch. This did his reputation no harm.

Keeper In Drag

Many a criminal has escaped arrest due to no more than the shiny buttons on a

THE SHEPHERD BAGGED

A shepherd lived in a cottage adjoining a barn on the outskirts of the village. His kitchen garden held a splendid array of greenstuffs which stood well into winter and which never seemed to be cut for cooking. The alert keeper suspected that the greens were left solely to attract game which the shepherd was culling at his convenience.

Calling by the cottage, the keeper saw two small boys playing in the garden. 'Ever see any bunnies in the garden, Tommy?'

'Yes sir; they be here often; my daddy ties 'em up in the hedge.' Fools, drunkards and children usually speak the truth, so he examined the hedge and saw a well-worn hare run which had been disguised with thorns. He decided on a night watch, and creeping back later with one of the other keepers, saw that the thorns had been removed and a snare left in the gap.

They hid in a wood nearby, hoping to catch the shepherd red-handed removing a hare from the snare. After some hours the squeal of a hare broke the silence, for one had run into the wire. The keepers were confident that the poacher would appear to remove his catch – but not so. 'I wonder why he doesn't fetch her,' shivered one.

After a while they made a cautious survey and found

that the hare had vanished along with the snare; and yet no man had been seen, that they would swear to. Exactly the same occurred two nights later, at which point the head keeper himself made a closer examination of the wire. He discovered a hidden cord which ran from the snare straight up to the shepherd's bedroom window; the old rascal hauled the hare up to his window — which explained the sudden squealing followed by the inexplicable silence.

The head keeper sent his man home to fetch a hare from the game larder; they put it into the snare and gave a passable imitation of the hare's squeal of distress. Sure enough, the cord tightened, but this time met an unexpected resistance. There came a muffled voice from above: 'The old bugger's caught up on the fence; I shall have to go an fetch her!'

The shepherd emerged in his nightgown with no slippers and crept down his garden where he was duly collared. The keepers would not allow him to go back inside and get dressed, but frog-marched him as he was — all but naked — over four large fields to the keeper's house. There he was given a worn suit of velveteens and locked up on the charge of night-poaching.

The shepherd had not rigged up the string retrieval system to avoid capture, but only to avoid having to leave his warm bedroom in the chill of a winter's night.

policeman's tunic; they betray his presence as a ray of light catches them. For this reason some keepers were averse to the showy livery which became customary on some great shoots at the turn of the century. Such garb stood out a mile away and acted as a flag of warning to potential wrongdoers and watchful poachers. A wise keeper persuaded his employer to allow him to wear fustian about his daily duties and keep his smart livery for the shooting day only.

Sometimes a keeper would go to much more extreme lengths and assume a disguise to throw the poacher off the scent. One especially inventive man disguised himself variously as a peasant in a smock, a priest in a felt hat and frock coat, a soldier in uniform, and once as a woman selling apples, complete with a wicker basket and feminine attire. He even went to the lengths of shaving off his luxuriant beard, the better to throw suspicious folk off the scent — even in those days bearded lady apple-sellers could not have been that thick on the ground.

Night-Poaching

Night-poaching was the most difficult of all to eradicate. The only remedy was constant watching, changing places, acting on information received, and the keeper doing his best to anticipate the poacher's next move. Night-watching was described as the curse of the keeper's life, but it was an essential task, and he also had to be on parade on his usual rounds in the day-time, so in the winter he could get very little sleep. Even when he assured himself that all was well and that he might safely go home and snatch a few hours well-deserved sleep, the illusive gang would be out with their nets sweeping his stubbles; for their information was usually more reliable than his, they being many had the advantage over a solitary keeper.

The Alarm Gun

This was one recommended answer. The gun was set by a footpath and the wire stretched across it at a distance from the ground high enough to be avoided by a passing hare or fox. The sudden explosion had the double effect of startling the poacher and sending him running off and also of alerting game in the area that danger was afoot. At the sound of the shot

THE TAR BABY

A certain keeper was suffering great annoyance from a solitary poacher. Often he would hear the sound of shots in his woods but no matter how quickly he was at the spot, the poacher had made good his escape. The keeper was single-handed and had no-one to help him watch, and a man has to sleep sometime. However, the shooting season was approaching and at last he hit on a likely way of catching his tormentor.

On every latch on every gate in his woods he set a small stone, so that anyone going through must dislodge them — that way he would at least know the route used by his adversary. Again, that night there was the sound of shots but the keeper stayed safe in bed, secure in the knowledge that the mystery poacher was as good as caught. But, to his surprise, the next day he found that not one of his stones had been dislodged; obviously the poacher's route cleverly kept clear of potential danger points.

Next the keeper marked all the gaps and stiles, placing a tuft of grass on the top of each stile so that anyone crossing could not avoid knocking them down, and he drew a thin briar across every gap in the fences and hedges. The next morning a dislodged tuft showed the track the poacher used to enter the wood. The keeper needed no more information, but set about the digging of a huge pit some six-feet across and nine deep. It was a whole day of heavy labour but he felt the effort to be worth it. The going was easy enough, being for the most part sand. The spoil he wheeled away on a barrow and hid.

The pit looked a formidable obstacle when complete, but the keeper's feeling was that it would not be enough simply to send the poacher crashing down to the bottom, possibly firing his gun as he did so. His instinct was to cover the bottom of his trap with pointed stakes, though in the end his Christian feelings caused him to abandon this drastic punishment. Instead he filled the bottom of the pit with tar. He had a good supply at home in readiness for fuming out rabbits, and he supplemented this with a fresh barrel bought from the local gas works.

The hole he lovingly covered with rotten twigs, bark, moss and dry grass, and in the end he would have defied the sharpest eye to have spotted its presence; and he was further comforted by the reflection that the poacher would be walking the track under the cover of darkness. He took pleasure from the picture of the man wandering along gazing upwards for roosting pheasants and then plunging to his doom.

The trap worked with spectacular success. Eagerly the keeper hurried down next day, to see that the unlucky victim had fallen his length into the pit, firing his gun as he crashed down, but presumably without injuring himself, for the man had climbed out, although the path and plentiful tracks of black footprints and finger marks on every gate and stile as he made his way home.

Suddenly it was noted by all in the village that a

certain individual had retired from circulation and was not to be found in his usual haunts. At the same time the demand for soap in that particular house became enormous, special preference being for the especially strong Monkey brand. This utterly astonished the village shopkeeper, for the family hitherto had not expressed much interest in cleanliness, as the grimy faces of the children made all too clear. The reason for this sudden desire for soap was a mystery to all save the keeper.

Often afterwards he would be sitting in his cottage and would break into a chuckle at the remembrance of his own particular piece of cleverness. 'What be you a-larfin' at?' queried the missus. 'Do you ever hear any shots in the woods now a' nights?' 'No,' says the missus. 'Well, that's what I'm a-larfin' at.'

rabbits would scuttle to their buries and hares sneak into the next field.

The experienced poacher would feel his way cautiously along a ride, groping like a blind man with a twig or reed for any wire set across the path. When he came across one he would snip it and thus disarm the gun. A cool customer would not dash away in a panic at the sound of the gun going off, but lie in wait to make sure someone was coming. If the gun had not done its job and given the alarm, he would continue on his way.

The keeper would fox a counterweight on the gun and set the trigger very fine so that even with the wire cut the gun would still detonate. Alternatively he would set the wire at chest height, or he would vary it, so that the probing cane of the poacher would miss it. A more sophisticated response was the double alarm gun. On

hearin the first shot – all unexpected – the watchers often had a job to pinpoint the exact location of the sound, especially on an estate where a great number of guns were set. The double gun was designed to go off some 15 seconds after the trip wire was broken; the first shot aroused the keeper and set him alert, the second allowed him to calculate precisely whence the sound had come.

The Whistle

The old-fashioned police whistle was a favourite communication system of keepers. Today they are armed with two-way radios, but in Victorian times there was no such thing. The shrill sound carried great distances and by a series of different calls the keepers could pass messages to each other. Also, a number of whistles blown from different places made it quite

THE FARM LABOURER

The hardest poacher to bring to book was the farm worker. He had a legitimate reason to be on and about the land, and even the most vigilant keeper could not keep watch on him all day. It is an easy matter for a man in the fields to set a snare and keep half an eye on it as he works with a scythe or pitchfork. A tell-tale sign was the man who spent his lunch-hour wandering about 'just to keep myself warm,' when anyone with any sense would have been resting under the hedge, having been on his feet for six hours. The wanderer was looking at the dyke edges and hedge bottoms for signs of rabbit and hare runs.

Another chap to watch was the one who left his work after his mates had departed. Leaving early one could understand, but the man who lingered after everyone else had gone whistling and talking down the lane had a reason for doing so, and it was not a pure love of hard work. It was more likely that he would be checking snares and traps set earlier in the day, things he would not dare to do with onlookers.

A poaching labourer would not be averse to stealing a vermin trap set by the keeper. A wise keeper marked his traps by filing a small notch on each one, insignificant to all eyes but his own, so that he could identify it should he miss it, and find it craftily set in another place by the person who had stolen it.

Even the innocent bird-scarer at a penny a day was worth keeping a beady eye on, especially one to whom the farmer had loaned an old muzzle-loader to help him with his work. Only a very foolish farmer indeed would allow shot to be taken on to the field, but should issue only powder. Shot would be pointless as the lad would be such an execrable marksman that he could never hit a flying rook or, indeed, a flying anything, while sitting rooks were, and are, far too cunning to allow him to creep into range. However, a cunning lad could use substitutes – a handful of iron-hard wheat, home-made shot, tin-tacks or even small stones were more than sufficient to rake a covey at close quarters, shoot a pheasant in a tree or a hare in a form.

A good keeper would be able to differentiate between the distant sound of a shot from a gun fully charged and one loaded with powder only. If in doubt, the keeper had only to engage the lad in conversation, ask to look at his gun, duly admire it and then 'accidentally' discharge it into the ground. He would know instantly by the recoil and by the hole blown into the stubble if the gun was loaded with shot, in which case he knew just what to do with the unlucky lad. If the gun was innocently loaded with powder only, he would curse his clumsiness and apologize for wasting the charge.

clear to the poachers that the keeper was not alone, and might make them think twice before they launched a cowardly attack on what they would have preferred to have been one man alone.

Psychologically, the police whistle had a great advantage, just as a siren has today.

In the Bag

Some nights poachers were more desperate, and would come armed to the teeth with the sole intention of raiding a keeper's coverts, making no pretence at secrecy and more than ready to show fight

if approached. The lone keeper was warned on no account to approach such a fearful gang, and only to face up to them if his numbers equalled or exceeded theirs. The only good advice was to stay clear, possibly bag small groups of the gang as they made their way home separately by different paths, or to get them after they had sobered up; poaching gangs were usually the worse for drink and all the more dangerous for it.

One ingenious keeper managed to defeat a large gang. When on night-watch he heard the sound of many footfalls crunching on the fallen leaves. From his hiding place he counted 13 poachers, well armed and purposeful, walking in Indian file long the ride. None of them was known to him and he realized that it would be madness for him to tackle them alone; but he was a determined man, and was keen to save his master's game.

He raised his voice in a loud alarm call, then again in a lower tone, cheered at several pitches of his voice and interspersed it with view halloos, crashing about in the bushes the while in an attempt to represent a veritable army of keepers and police. The echoes of the woods aided his deception and to his delight the poachers broke up in disarray and made off in panic in all directions. One of them actually stumbled on the keeper's prostrate form as he hid in the bushes and he gave the man a good thrashing before arresting him. The general confusion caused by the poachers' flight added to the illusion that an army was come upon them.

Gypsies

The Victorian keeper had little time for gypsies, with their packs of lurcher dogs and cunning ways. They were as versed in the ways of the countryside as was he. Their womanfolk would call at his house with some paltry excuse such as selling clothes pegs, but really to establish whether he was at home. The men would set wires close to

THE POACHING FAMILY

Then, as now, poaching tended to run in the blood of certain families, from the youngest to the oldest and stretching back many generations. Hearing nothing but poaching yarns and tricks from their mother's knee, it is not surprising they were more than willing to join in at the earliest opportunity what was represented to them as exciting adventures and hairbreadth escapes. They were taught the underlying principle that game was the rightful spoil of anyone who could take it.

Such children were not long waiting for an apprenticeship. The traditional first employment as bird-starver at a penny a day gave legitimate access to the fields and preserved ground. Their sharp eyes could spot a sitting bird and a hare track more quickly than most. They could hide their small persons in the tiniest nook, and whistle and sing a warning of approaching officialdom as well as an adult and with less chance of arousing suspicion.

The Victorian moralist was at pains to point out the hardships of poaching. As well as being damned to eternal fires, the poacher was likely to be often unwell as a result of exposure to all weathers, irregular meals, lack of sleep and excessive drinking, usually of 'ardent liquors.' He was regarded by respectable folk as an outlaw and generally mistrusted and shunned; although admired by a very few who envied his disrespect for the law but dared not follow his example.

The poacher's wife was a subject of sympathy, for the only time she saw her husband he was likely to be drunk, and of course he was out at night about his business. She found what money she could by going through his pockets when he was incapable, and more often than not was buffeted for her pains when the good man discovered his loss. When he failed to return home it was not for the common reason of being with another woman but because the keepers had bagged him and marched him off to gaol. At least the wife had the comfort of knowing where he was and that he could do no harm, and rather preferred life with her man in gaol than out of it.

She dreaded his return, for not only would he be as surly as before, but he would now be a man with a grudge – and she could but guess and fear at how he would seek redress for his punishment.

their caravans and snatch them up quickly when the keepers appeared. Their rough dogs would range the countryside not only snapping up hares and rabbits, but causing great disturbance to the game covers.

Even the allotment holder was one to be watched. A cunning gardener was not averse to allowing some winter greens to grow thickly near his boundary, knowing well that hares would be attracted to them in the winter when the snow lay thick. Rabbits would burrow into his carrot clamp, and the gardener who tended to work his ground early in the morning and late at night was worth watching. A wise keeper would chat to the man on some pretext or other and allow his dogs to run through the vegetable plot so that any game sheltering there would be disturbed.

THE CONTRIBUTORS

JOHN BAILEY studied history at university and then taught the subject for several years before concentrating on a life of travel, writing and photography. He specialised in the 18th and 19th centuries, notably the social history of the countryside. he is the author of several books, is co-presenter of BBC2's *Countryside Hour*, and now lives on the 18th-century Gunton Estate in Norfolk.

LOUISE BRODIE lived abroad for many years before returning to England to bring up her children. After completing an Open University degree she worked for the Museum of London, where one of her responsibilities was to conduct over two hundred interviews with people who worked on the River Thames and in Docklands. She has also worked on a television series on this subject.

EUAN CORRIE was brought up in southern Manchester, and on leaving school worked for a ship's agent, dealing mostly with Soviet cargo ships. He was then skipper of a pair of hotel narrowboats on the canals, before joining the editorial staff of the leading inland waterway magazine *Waterways World* in 1986. Since 1997 he has been Books & Guides Editor for Waterways World Ltd, also contributing a wide variety of articles to *Waterways World*, particularly of a historical and photographic nature. Euan bought his own narrowboat in 1979 and has travelled the English inland waterway system widely.

JENNIFER DAVIES' father was a Herefordshire farmer of the old kind, who used horses until tractors became prevalent. She has worked as a television researcher and associate producer, and has written a series of books concerning the Victorian garden and kitchen. She has also written books on Gypsies and the progress of the flower shop in Britain. She lives near Ledbury and combines writing with looking after poultry, old hayfields, bees and trees.

JOHN HUMPHREYS was born and brought up in a Fenland village where the land was worked by Shire horse power and the people were close to the land. The eldest son of a parson, early exposure to the countryside and its pastimes were to shape his life. He has written the popular 'country Gun' column in *Shooting Times* for many years, and twenty books on fieldsports and country ways, including *Poachers' Tales* for David & Charles. He trains gun dogs, runs a lowlands shoot, chases grouse in Yorkshire and geese in Scotland, and fishes for trout and carp on his own little reserve in Cambridgeshire, Hunter's Fen, which won a Laurent-Perrier conservation award in 1991.

BRIAN P. MARTIN has written numerous books on country life and natural history, including seven in David & Charles 'Tales from the Countryside' series, as well as the award-winning *Sporting Birds of Britain and Ireland*. After many years as a commissioning editor for *Shooting Times* and *Country Magazine*, he has been a full-time author since 1991. He has contributed to many magazines and newspapers, and is well-known for his 'Rusticus' column in both *Shooting Times* and *The Countrymen*. When not writing, he may be found propping up the bar in his local village pub, the Dog & Pheasant, where he has been a regular for over twenty years.

TOM QUINN has worked on everything from *The Times* to *Trout and Salmon* magazine and is a former editor of *The Countryman*. He has written three books for David & Charles in the 'Tales of the Countryside' series and has also written books about sporting art, World War One, antique collecting, and a biography of the artist and writer Denys Watkins Pitchford.

VALERIE PORTER lives in a Sussex cottage next door to a vet. She edits numerous agricultural veterinary and biology books, as well as writing her own books about wildlife, livestock, pets and rural life in general, three of which have been published by David & Charles. She is also the author of the highly successful title, *Yesterday's Countryside*, also published by David & Charles.

JEAN STONE is an historic garden consultant and garden designer who has lectured for horticultural societies, garden schools and the Architectural Association. Once winner of the *Sunday Times* 'Design a Period Garden' competition, her entry a 'Victorian Rustic Garden', was built at the RHS Chelsea Flower Show, where it won a silver medal. This was followed by her book, *The Rustic Garden*. Another of her books, *Voices from the Waterways*, is an invaluable record of an almost vanished way of life as once lived on British Waterways.

PHOTOGRAPHS FOR THE JACKET AND FOR THE FOLLOWING PAGES WERE SUPPLIED BY THE HULTON ARCHIVE:- 3, 7, 19, 29, 43, 61, 77, 87, 93, 103, 117, 123, 135, 141, 147, 167, 183, 197, 211, 219

INDEX